Let's keep in touch!

Stella

Un gran abrazo Ma

Ronald

GW01425201

HANDBOOK ON DEVELOPMENT AND SOCIAL CHANGE

Handbook on Development and Social Change

Edited by

G. Honor Fagan

Professor of Sociology, Maynooth University, Ireland

Ronaldo Munck

Head of Civic Engagement, Dublin City University, Ireland

EE Edward **Elgar**
PUBLISHING

Cheltenham, UK • Northampton, MA, USA

Published by
Edward Elgar Publishing Limited
The Lypiatts
15 Lansdown Road
Cheltenham
Glos GL50 2JA
UK

Edward Elgar Publishing, Inc.
William Pratt House
9 Dewey Court
Northampton
Massachusetts 01060
USA

A catalogue record for this book
is available from the British Library

Library of Congress Control Number: 2017959422

This book is available electronically in the **Elgar**online
Social and Political Science subject collection
DOI 10.4337/9781786431554

MIX
Paper from
responsible sources
FSC
www.fsc.org   FSC® C013056

ISBN 978 1 78643 154 7 (cased)
ISBN 978 1 78643 155 4 (eBook)

Typeset by Servis Filmsetting Ltd, Stockport, Cheshire
Printed and bound in Great Britain by TJ International Ltd, Padstow

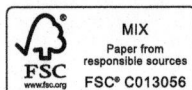

Contents

PART II POLITICAL ASPECTS

PART III SOCIAL ASPECTS

Figures and tables

FIGURES

TABLES

Contributors

Alberto Acosta is an Ecuadorian economist. He is a university professor, ex-Minister for Mines and Energy, ex-President of the Constituent Assembly 2007–2008 and ex-candidate for the Presidency of the Republic of Ecuador. Author of many books and articles in magazines. Companion of struggle of social movements.

A. Haroon Akram-Lodhi teaches agrarian political economy. He is Professor of Economics and International Development Studies in the Department of International Development Studies at Trent University in Peterborough, Canada. Haroon Akram-Lodhi is also the Editor-in-Chief of the *Canadian Journal of Development Studies* and an associate editor of *Feminist Economics*.

Cecilia Allami is an economist and PhD candidate in social sciences at the University of Buenos Aires, and a researcher and Professor of Political Economy at the Universidad Nacional de General Sarmiento in Buenos Aires, Argentina. Her research interests include theories of economic development, financial systems, agribusiness and Argentina's economic history. Her research has resulted in numerous publications in national and international venues.

James Van Alstine is Associate Professor in Environmental Policy and Co-Director of the Sustainability Research Institute at the University of Leeds. His research focuses on the governance of natural resources in the global North and South, with a particular focus on the politics of climate compatible development and the extractives-led growth strategies. James seeks to bridge the academic-practitioner divide by pursuing action-oriented research that aims to maximize policy and pro-poor development impacts. James has conducted research on resource politics in Brazil, Ghana, Ireland, South Africa, Uganda, the United Kingdom, the United States and Zambia.

Tanja Bastia is Senior Lecturer at the Global Development Institute at the University of Manchester. Her research focuses on transnational migration for work, particularly on the relationship between power relations, mobility and space. She has conducted multi-sited ethnographic research with Bolivian migrants in Bolivia, Argentina and Spain since the year 2000. Her most recent research articles have been published in *Geoforum*,

Urban Studies, Cities and *Environment and Planning A.* She is currently co-editing (with Ronald Skeldon) the *Routledge Handbook of Migration and Development* and has previously edited *Migration and Inequality* (2013, also Routledge).

Milford Bateman is a freelance consultant on local economic development policy, since 2005 Visiting Professor of Economics at Juraj Dobrila University of Pula, Croatia, and since 2014 Adjunct Professor of Development Studies at St Mary's University, Halifax, Canada. He is the author of '*Why Doesn't Microfinance Work? The Destructive Rise of Local Neoliberalism*' published by Zed Books in 2010, and is co-editor, with Kate Maclean, of '*Seduced and Betrayed: Exposing the Contemporary Microfinance Phenomenon*' published in 2017 by the University of New Mexico Press and the School for Advanced Research Press.

Matthew Louis Bishop is Senior Lecturer in International Politics at the University of Sheffield, UK. Previously, he worked at the University of the West Indies, and was the founding managing editor of the *Caribbean Journal of International Relations & Diplomacy*. He researches the political economy of development, with a particular focus on small states in general, and the Caribbean specifically. He also works on trade politics, democratization, rising powers and drug policy. Matt's books include: *The Political Economy of Caribbean Development*; *Democratization: A Critical Introduction* (with Jean Grugel); and *Post-Colonial Trajectories in the Caribbean: The Three Guianas* (with Peter Clegg and Rosemarijn Hoefte).

Patrick Bond is a Professor of Political Economy, and combines political economy and political ecology in his research and applied work. He is a Professor of Political Economy at the Wits School of Governance, and Honorary Professor at the University of KwaZulu-Natal School of Built Environment and Development Studies where from 2004 until 2016 he directed the Centre for Civil Society. Prior to that he was a professor at the WSG from 1997 until 2004, an assistant professor at the Johns Hopkins University Bloomberg School of Public Health, and also held visiting professorships at York University and the University of California/ Berkeley on sabbaticals. During the 1990s he served at the Johannesburg NGOs Planact and the National Institute for Economic Policy, and from 1994 until 2000 drafted more than a dozen government policy documents, including the White Paper on Reconstruction and Development. Patrick has also written several books.

Alan Cibils holds a PhD in economics and is Professor and Chair of the Political Economy Department at the Universidad Nacional de General Sarmiento in Buenos Aires, Argentina. His research interests include monetary theory and policy, financial systems and economic development, Latin American critical theories of development and Argentina's economic history. He is the author of numerous publications on those topics.

Alberto D. Cimadamore is the Director of the Comparative Research Programme on Poverty (CROP) of the International Social Sciences Council (ISSC), located at the University of Bergen (UiB), Norway. He is Professor of Theory of International Relations at the School of Social Sciences, University of Buenos Aires (UBA) and Researcher of the National Council of Scientific and Technological Research (CONICET) of Argentina (currently on leave). He is also Honorary Professor at the University of KwaZulu-Natal, South Africa. He is a lawyer (UCSF, Argentina) and a political scientist (UNR, Argentina) and obtained his MA in Social Sciences (FLACSO, Buenos Aires) and PhD in International Relations at the University of Southern California (USC), Los Angeles. His most recent research and publications are focused on the political economy of poverty, the international relations of poverty and development, and on global social justice.

Gareth Dale teaches politics at Brunel University. He has published on the 'growth paradigm', Karl Polanyi, East Germany, migration, and social movement theory.

Philippe De Lombaerde is Associate Professor of Economics at NEOMA Business School in Rouen (France) and Associate Senior Research Fellow at the United Nations University Institute on Comparative Regional Integration Studies (UNU-CRIS) in Bruges (Belgium). Previously he has been Associate Director at UNU-CRIS and Associate Professor of International Economics at the Universidad Nacional de Colombia, among other appointments. Philippe (PhD RWTH) has worked and published on: international trade and investment, comparative regionalism, globalization and regionalization indicators, Latin America and Southeast Asia.

Raúl Delgado Wise is author/editor of 26 books and more than 200 book chapters and refereed articles. He has been a guest lecturer in over 40 countries, and is president and founder of the International Network on Migration and Development, co-director of the Critical Development Studies Network, and professor and director of the Doctoral Program in Development Studies at the Autonomous University of Zacatecas. He is also Editor of the journal *Migración y Desarrollo* and UNESCO Chair on Migration, Development and Human Rights.

G. Honor Fagan is Professor of Sociology at Maynooth University and a member of the Steering Committee of Development Studies Association

Ireland. Her theoretical project and publishing have focused on the development of a social sustainability paradigm from a sociological perspective. She has previously lectured in sociology departments in Northern Ireland, South Africa and the UK. Her research interests focus on human security and international development, social sustainability, and gender and governance. She is currently leading the social science component of WaterSPOUTT (http://www.waterspoutt.eu/), an EU-H2020-funded project, in Ethiopia, Malawi, Uganda and South Africa.

Ben Fine is Professor of Economics at the School of Oriental and African Studies and Visiting Professor, Institute of Social and Economic Research, Rhodes University. He has contributed 20–30 books and 200–300 articles covering many issues across economic theory, political economy, history of economic thought, economic methodology, and applied economics and policy, all often in the context of development. He is contributing editor with Jyoti Saraswati and Daniela Tavasci, to *Beyond the Developmental State: Industrial Policy into the 21st Century*. He is Chair of the International Initiative for Promoting Political Economy (iippe.org), and a Fellow of the Royal Society of Arts.

Su-ming Khoo is a lecturer in the School of Political Science and Sociology at the National University of Ireland, Galway. Her research interests include human rights, public goods, human development and capabilities, alternative development, public advocacy and activism, higher education, internationalization, global learning, public scholarship, and inter- and transdisciplinary methods. Her recent publications explore the role of solidarity in health and human rights; the meaning and measurement of sustainable development; new approaches to public goods and democracy; health governance; global health and social justice; ethical internationalization of higher education and the role of research in global learning.

Ray Kiely is Professor of Politics, Queen Mary University of London. His books include *Rethinking Imperialism* (Palgrave, 2010), *The BRICs, US 'Decline' and Global Transformations* (Palgrave, 2015) and *The Neoliberal Paradox* (Edward Elgar Publishing, 2018).

Stephen Kingah obtained his degrees from the University of Yaoundé II (Bachelor in Law), the University of Oxford (Masters in Law) and the Free University of Brussels (PhD in International Law). Since completing his doctoral studies he has worked for the European Union Commission, first as an intern and later as an administrator for relations with international financial institutions. He has also worked at the UN University's Institute on Comparative Regional Integration Studies (UNU-CRIS), where among others he was involved in the EU NETRIS,

CRIFT, GR:EEN and ELCSID Projects. He is a visiting professor at the University of Maastricht and also at the Pan African University's Institute for Governance at the University of Yaoundé II in Cameroon.

Rowan Lubbock holds a PhD in International Relations from Birkbeck, University of London. His doctoral project focused on the contested implementation of a 'food sovereignty' regime within the Latin American regional institution of ALBA (Bolivarian Alliance for the Peoples of our America). His research focuses broadly on the political implications of global development, with a particular interest in regionalism, global governance, agrarian development and critical IR/IPE theory. He has published on the topics of neoliberalism, imperialism, development, and Latin American history.

Philip McMichael is Professor of Development Sociology at Cornell. He has authored *Food Regimes and Agrarian Questions* (Fernwood, 2013), *Development and Social Change: A Global Perspective* (Sage, 2016), and the award-winning *Settlers and the Agrarian Question* (Cambridge, 1984). He has also edited *Contesting Development: Critical Struggles for Social Change* (Routledge, 2010), and co-edited *Biofuels, Land and Agrarian Change* with Jun Borras and Ian Scoones (Routledge, 2011). He is a member of the Civil Society Mechanism in the FAO's Committee on World Food Security, and worked with UNRISD, the FAO, Vía Campesina and the IPC for Food Sovereignty.

Christopher A. McNally is Professor of Political Economy at Chaminade University and Adjunct Senior Fellow at the East-West Center in Honolulu, USA. His research focuses on comparative capitalisms, especially the nature and logic of Sino-capitalism and the implications of China's international re-emergence in the global order. He has edited four volumes, including an examination of China's political economy – *China's Emergent Political Economy: Capitalism in the Dragon's Lair* (Routledge, 2008) – and authored numerous book chapters, policy analyses, editorials and articles in journals such as *Business and Politics, Comparative Social Research, International Politics, World Politics,* and *Review of International Political Economy.*

Ronaldo Munck is Head of Civic Engagement at Dublin City University and Visiting Professor of Development Studies Association at the universities of Liverpool and Buenos Aires. He was the founding chair of the Development Studies of Ireland and has written widely on globalization, labour and development from a southern perspective. His recent work includes *Rethinking Latin America: Development, Hegemony and Social Transformation.* Professor Munck is a lead author for the International

Panel on Social Progress chaired by Amartya Sen due to report in 2018 on alternative futures for global democratic development.

Stefano Palestini is Postdoctoral Fellow at the Freie Universität Berlin (Germany). He holds a PhD in Political and Social Sciences from the European University Institute, Florence (Italy), and a *Licenciatura* in Sociology from the Alberto Hurtado University in Santiago de Chile. He has been a consultant at the United Nations Development Programme (UNDP) and visiting researcher and lecturer at universities in Brazil, Chile and the United States.

Gabriel Pollen is a PhD candidate in economics at SOAS, University of London. He is an economics lecturer at the University of Zambia. He has also recently taught at the University of Huddersfield, UK. He has previously served as researcher and consultant for institutions such as the World Bank. His recent research interests are in applied research in development economics, with a strong focus on structural change and the role of the state in development.

Fenella Porter with an academic background primarily in gender and international development, she has taught in international development and international labour studies. She has supervised research on using a variety of research methods, including feminist research, critical analysis and engaged participatory research. She is a member of several professional and activist networks and associations, and is currently a Trustee of Womankind Worldwide. She has published widely, as well as presented at conferences and workshops both in the UK and internationally. Her publications cover both academic and practitioner spaces, and she continues to pursue opportunities to bridge the gap between these two worlds, with a concentration on praxis and on embedded and engaged research.

Liliana Lizarazo Rodríguez is a lecturer and researcher at the Faculty of Law of the University of Antwerp (Belgium) and is also an Attorney at Law in Belgium, Spain and Colombia. She has been working and publishing on: constitutional law, judicial activism, international economic law, law and development, business and human rights, among other topics. She studied law at the Universidad del Rosario (Colombia), pursued postgraduate studies in law and public administration in Colombia, Spain and Belgium, and obtained her PhD in Law from the University of Ghent (Belgium).

Susanne Schech teaches international development studies at Flinders University in South Australia. She co-authored, with Jane Haggis, *Culture and Development: A Critical Introduction* (Wiley, 2000), edited *Development*

Perspectives from the Antipodes (2014), and publishes on a range of policy issues including participation, gender justice, poverty reduction and international development volunteering. She also works on geographies of race and whiteness in Australia in the context of humanitarian migration.

Laura Smith is a PhD candidate and part-time teaching fellow at the University of Leeds, in the Sustainability Research Institute and in the School of Politics and International Studies. Her PhD research explores Uganda's emerging oil assemblage and the micropolitics of international oil company CSR activities. She holds an MA in Peace Studies from the University of Bradford and a BA in International Business Studies from the University of Northumbria. She is administrator for the Centre for Global Development at Leeds University.

Anne Tallontire is Senior Lecturer in Business, Environment and Corporate Responsibility at the Sustainability Research Institute at the University of Leeds. Her research focuses on how the private sector affects development, e.g. through supply chain relationships and sustainability standards. Anne has extensive research and consultancy experience, undertaking projects for the UK Department for International Development, the Department for Food and Rural Affairs, Fairtrade Labelling Organizations International, and the Ethical Trading Initiative and field work in African countries including Tanzania, Kenya, Uganda, Zambia, Sudan and South Africa. Currently she is a member of the Steering Group for the Fair Trade International Symposium.

Henry Veltmeyer is Research Professor at Universidad Autónoma de Zacatecas (Mexico) and Professor Emeritus of International Development Studies (IDS) at Saint Mary's University (Canada), with a specialized interest in Latin American development. He is also co-Chair of the Critical Development Studies (CDS) network, and a co-editor of a Routledge series of books on CDS. He has authored and edited over 40 books on the political economy and sociology of development in the Latin American context. Recent publications include *The Class Struggle in Latin America: Making History Today* (Routledge, 2017), *Power and Resistance* (Haymarket, 2017) and *Agrarian Change, Migration and Development* (Practical Action, 2016).

Preface
G. Honor Fagan and Ronaldo Munck

Development and social change is a broad optic from which to view human history. While contested in many ways, it is an inescapable problematic to evaluate the prospects for humanity. We now live in an era which can provide for the well-being of all. The forces of production are at the very peak of possibilities and they are only constrained by relations of production which prevent a consistent move towards greater equality for all and a continuous deepening of democracy. Social progress is only possible if these constraints are addressed and the unprecedented concentration of wealth and power since around 1990 is reversed. The second crisis looming is that of the environment, where climate change and the depletion of national resources lead to enrichment of a fear in the short term at the cost of the longer-term sustainability of humanity as a whole.

By many criteria, the period from 1990 to the present has been one of spectacular development and social change. The Human Development Index has increased steadily, for example in terms of longevity, and at least some of the Millennium Development Goals (MDGs) have been met. Long-standing inequalities and hierarchies in terms of gender, race and even sexual orientation have been reduced (overall) and made illegal. Global connectivity increased dramatically and no one should minimize the potential impact of Information and Communication Technologies (ICTs) in terms of development and social change. Yet, over the same period, the proportion of people affected by climate change and global warming has increased dramatically. In terms of air pollution, the recurring smog of Mexico City, Beijing and Delhi point towards a bleak future, as do the inundations in Bangladesh and Jakarta. When the first great transformation of the industrial era elevated the market above society and nature, it posed the now urgent need to re-embed the market in society and its placing under social control.

The main impediment to development and socially beneficial social change today is undoubtedly global inequality. For all the hope around the folk tale that 'a rising tide lifts all boats' and the dramatic market expansion in China in particular, global inequality has not decreased with globalization even though absolute poverty levels have been reduced. Industrialization of what was called the Third World from the 1970s onwards did not lead to convergence with the afferent or 'developed' countries, but simply recast the North-South divide through a new international division of labour. Economic globalization from the 1990s onwards did lead to the incorporation into the global market of what was once called the Second World, and created the conditions for the rise of the semi-peripheral BRICS (bringing together the five major emerging economies of Brazil, Russia, India, China and South Africa) to become industrial powers. But, after many attempts to show a reduction of global poverty and inequality (only plausible at all due to the inclusion of China), the latest data on global income distribution, based on household surveys, contradicts this optimistic scenario. The period from 1998 to 2008, from the collapse of the Berlin Wall to the Great Crash, was one of accelerated globalization and an optimistic outlook that the market would deliver greater equality. But Branko Milanovic and colleagues at the World Bank now find categorically that 'the level of global inequality' (combining between country and within country in dimension) and the Gini Index which measures it 'might not have gone down at all' due to an under-estimation of the top of national income distributions in previous studies (Lakner and Milanovic, 2015, pp. 47–8).

The introductory chapter of this volume by Ronaldo Munck seeks to develop a genealogy of the various theories of development and social change. It addresses the contradictory nature of capitalist development within which it situates current debates around development and social change. It is an approach to these epistemological terrains which acknowledges global complexity and is open to ruptures and a move beyond the status quo.

Part I then addresses some of the main 'economic' aspects of development and social change, though the label is more one of convenience and is not intended to indicate an autonomous and self-continued domain. Philip McMichael (Chapter 2) addresses the urgent need for an ecology of development on the basis that the modern development paradigm is essentially 'bankrupt'. The notion of 'sustainable development' is also questioned, given that it does not address the need to rehabilitate the world's degraded ecosystems and sustain them with ecological development. In Chapter 3 Rowan Lubbock addresses a fundamental issue, namely the historical relationship between development and imperialism. There are key issues here – such as whether imperialism hinders or promotes development, which is highly relevant to the era of globalization. Furthermore, is imperialism still an organizing principle for the geographical distribution of poverty and plenty?

These opening chapters are followed by a set of interlocking treatments of development and the private sector (Laura Smith, Anne Tallontire and James Van Alstine), financialization (Cecilia Allami and Alan Cibils), regionalism (Philippe De Lombaerde, Stephen Kingah, Liliana Lizarazo Rodríguez and Stefano Palestini) and the role of microcredit (Milford Bateman).

In the last decade, many international development organizations have promoted the need for greater involvement by the private sector, especially from the Northern side. This fits with the critique of development as a national state-led process. As Chapter 4 shows, there is a big gap between the rhetoric and the practice of business engagement with development and a case study of the oil industry in Uganda shows the limitations of the Corporate Social Responsibility (CSR) frame. The 1990s were also characterized by 'financialization', as finance capital assumed dominance over industrial capital in what seemed to augur a new phase of international development. Chapter 5 takes this broad concept and seeks to apply it in the global South (too often ignored in the relevant literature), and shows how it now plays a dominant role in development and underdevelopment today.

Regionalism, which has been a constant, if somewhat neglected, aspect of development is addressed in a systematic way in Chapter 6. It focuses on the role of regions and Regional Organizations (ROs) in the design and implementation of social development policies, broadly defined, including: regional redistributive policies, regional promotion and protection of democracy, and regional protection of human rights. Chapter 7, for its part, takes up the issue of microcredit as a development policy tool, and situates it critically as part of the dominant neoliberal development paradigm. Rather than ushering in new bottom-up forms of development, it is seen to reproduce neoliberalism at the local level.

The final chapter in this section by Gareth Dale (Chapter 8) tackles the widespread view that 'a rising tide lifts all boats' in terms of economic growth and inequality. Dale questions whether we should think of 'the economy' as an identifiable social sphere with an inherent propensity to grow, as both mainstream and critical development theories seem to believe. This reprise of classical themes is useful in reminding us about the genealogy of development.

Part II turns to some of the main 'political' aspects of development and social change, again understood in a political economy sense. Chapter 9 by Matthew Louis Bishop examines the troubled relationship between development and democracy from a global perspective. Does development lead to democracy? Does democracy require development to prosper? These are key questions as we enter another era of global turbulence. Su-ming Khoo in Chapter 10 offers a wide-ranging consideration of the international non-governmental organizations (NGOs) and their levering political role. Are the development NGOs part of the dominant system or allies of the poor and oppressed? In Chapter 11, Ben Fine and Gabriel Pollen turn to the origins of, and current debates around, the developmental state. Can, or should, the state be a driver of development and if so, how might it achieve its objectives? If not the market and not the state, what will drive development and social change now?

We then follow with three chapters on development issues in particular regions of the world: Latin America (Chapter 12 by Raúl Delgado Wise and Henry Veltmeyer); sub-Saharan Africa (Chapter 13 by Patrick Bond); and China (Chapter 14 by Christopher A. McNally). They ask what development and social change means in the current era. They trace the development of capitalism and its contradictions in each region. They also show how social movements can construct another development, and how society always finds ways to contest the naked rule of the market. The global South has changed with globalization but it still sparks social transformation in different ways, insofar as development generates new social contradictions.

The final chapter of this section, Chapter 15 by Susanne Schech, takes up the complex and contested relationship between culture and development, effectively taking us into the terrain of cultural political economy. An appeal to culture by development practitioners can take a very ethnocentric direction, as in generalizing certain cultural requirements for development, but it also takes us into the radical perspective of post-colonialism.

Finally, in Part III of the volume we turn to the 'social' dimension of development, tackling some of the key issues of the day that will determine the direction of social change in the years to come. Chapter 16 by Tanja Bastia takes up the critical and topical issue of migration and development. The movement of people, nationally and transnationally, has been as crucial to the development of capitalism as the movement of goods and capital. What are its prospects in the decades to come? A. Haroon Akram-Lodhi in Chapter 17 critically evaluates the 'sustainable livelihoods' approach to development which, for a long time, prevailed as an action-oriented rural development paradigm. This chapter provides an account of why this approach has gone into decline over the last decade, providing us with valuable lessons for the future.

In Chapter 18 Ray Kiely tackles the absolutely central relationship between development and inequality. The proponents of free market globalization argued that this new model of development would reduce inequality between nations but that is not how it turned out. G. Honor Fagan, in Chapter 19, turns to the vital question of water and development from a critical perspective. Water is clearly a key component of social sustainability, as much as of economic development. It has also featured prominently in the debate between those who consider it a human right and the advocates of water privatization. In Chapter 20, Fenella Porter returns to the topic of the international NGOs, but specifically their role in regard to gender equality. Deploying a discourse analysis approach, she shows the very real limitations of the NGO engagement with advancing gender equity within development. Alberto D. Cimadamore, in Chapter 21, turns our attention to what was, for a long time, the *raison d'être* of development, namely poverty eradication. He argues that the persistence of extreme poverty, after decades of high economic growth, undermines the legitimacy of current governance structures and makes urgent the search for an alternative.

As a fitting theme for a concluding chapter, we turn in Chapter 22 by Alberto Acosta to the post-development concept of Buen Vivir (living well) that has emerged out of a period of turbulent change in Latin America. Picking up on a pre-conquest philosophy of a nature-centred and harmonious form of existence, it may yet provide a viable utopia for our times. To imagine a better future for development and social change is a difficult task, and one that is somewhat neglected in the dominant literature, but one that is essential today.

The social sciences are loath to get into the prediction game, for good reasons, but should we not seek to develop methods to anticipate and shape the future of development and social change? We can certainly extrapolate from current tendencies to obtain the basic parameters of where development and social change are heading if those trends persist. Climate change science is, of course, based on just such extrapolations and these are taken seriously by the climate change deliverers, who can, of course, have the power to prevent the necessary measures being taken. Likewise, if we seek to address the likely future impact of gross inequality – such as 1 per cent of people holding 40 per cent of the global wealth – here again power concentration can prevent the necessary corrective measures being taken. Nevertheless, in a complex, interdependent and rapidly developing world we have no option but to explore alternative futures of social change if we are to be progressive and not regressive, which is always, of course, a possibility.

Many of the contributions to this volume show that, in many ways, the status quo is failing. The unregulated market will simply not deliver progressive development and social change. However, 'the old is dying but the new has not yet been born' (Gramsci) in terms of offering a viable and sustainable alternative future. In that context all sorts of morbid, backward looking, reactionary and isolationist tendencies will emerge. While aspects of the future are already with us – 'smart cities', 3D printing, the internet of things, and so on – futures thinking in the social sciences is lagging behind. For the fear of being dubbed utopian – and thus not realistic – complex systems thinking has not been deployed sufficiently to democratize a future which is clearly being colonized by the big corporations. The next great transformation is about to commence and, if society is to benefit, the thinking reflected in this volume needs to be pushed forward to rethink, and thus impact, the future.

REFERENCE

Lakner, C. and B. Milanovic (2015), 'Global income distribution: from the fall of the Berlin Wall to the Great Recession', World Bank Economic Review, published 12 August 2015.

1. Development and social change: a genealogy for an era of complexity
Ronaldo Munck

INTRODUCTION

Theories of development and social change most often seek to trace a continuity to the era of Antiquity, presumably to show its centrality to the 'human condition' and its universal relevance. It is often submerged within an overarching teleological concept of 'progress' that colours all aspects of the theory and its application. For us, following Foucault, the pursuit of origins is necessarily essentialist 'because it is an attempt to capture the exact, and pure [trans-historical, immanent] essence of things' (Foucault, 1984, p. 78). But, as for Foucault, 'what is found at the historical beginning of things is not the inviolable identity of their origin, it is the dissension of other things. It is disparity' (ibid., p. 80). For a genealogy which rejects the pursuit of origins, this means a refusal of faith in metaphysics, a careful listening to history and a search for the details and accidents that accompany every beginning. As Foucault argues for 'liberty' so we might argue for 'development': 'genealogical analysis shows that the concept of liberty is an "invention of the ruling classes" and not fundamental to man's nature or at the root of his attachment to being and truth' (ibid., p. 81).

The critical discourse, or genealogical, approach we adopt needs to be set in the context of complexity, too often elided in both mainstream and oppositional development theory. With the social world becoming more complex and elusive, our research approach has to itself become more nuanced and not be reduced to the study of discrete hierarchical entities. Our approach to development needs to be adequate for 'a world that enacts itself to produce unpredictable and non-linear flows and more mobile subjectivities' (Law and Urry, 2004, p. 399). Development cannot be understood in a mechanical way through a linear analysis of structure and agency. Pre-complexity disciplines and models of research are ill-equipped to engage with the far-from-equilibrium structures and practices of actually existing development. We thus follow Law and Urry in moving beyond development theories which 'deal poorly with the non-causal, the chaotic, the complex' (ibid., p. 403). Our approach needs to be fit for purpose in an era of global complexity and open to ruptures and a move beyond the status quo.

CAPITALIST DEVELOPMENT

Development theory and practice has been marked by the power-knowledge relations within which it emerged and which set its various phases. 'Development' tends to stand in for the Western development model, a vague Enlightenment notion of progress and even, for some, civilization itself. As to 'social change', it is more or less impossible to define and it sometimes becomes 'development' through a naturalist operation in which history becomes organic and naturalized. This form of Western universalism – based on the notions of Enlightenment and a one-way rationalization process – can also be seen as a form of secular utopianism. Robert Nisbet, in his classic *Social Change and History* (Nisbet, 1969), saw developmentalism through Christian redemptorist eyes 'throughout its history the idea [of progress] has been closely linked with, has depended upon, religion or upon intellectual constructs derived from religion' (ibid., p. 352). This convergence of discourses gave developmentalism a resistance to change but also inserted a basic contradiction at its very core.

The origins of development theory are usually traced in the dominant discourse back to Antiquity, but these links are quite tenuous. Even the supposed lineage through to the Scottish Enlightenment and the work of Adam Smith is not quite convincing. These eighteenth-century thinkers did indeed postulate a series of stages of human activity which led to the early liberal doctrine of progress 'to resolve the Hobbesian problem of how social and thus political order might be attained' (Cowen and Shenton, 1996, p. 11). However, it was the Saint Simonians who, much later in the 1820s, broke with the early liberal doctrine of progress as national progress, to advance a theory of development characterized by purposive design. It was then Auguste Comte, in breaking with the Saint Simonians, who proposed a 'science of society' with the objective of discovering the 'law of human social evolution' (Comte, 2009). Comte's positivism was driven to control the effects of industrialism and secularism and impose order on social transformation. Knowledge would, henceforth, guide action rather than accept 'laissez-faire' as the source of disorder.

Development, as we understand it, is inseparable from the British Industrial Revolution and the French democratic Revolution, which ushered in a great transformation of society. The upheavals caused by these twin earthquakes created the need to deal with the social, economic and cultural problems emerging with the new capitalist order. Development, in a way, can be seen as the new philosophy and practice, seeking to impose a moral order on the chaos of progress. This was not only a discourse, but was grounded in the state practices of the mid-nineteenth century. It emerged in Europe to deal with the European transition to capitalism so it is hardly relevant to categorize these ideas and practices as Eurocentric. In the work of John Stuart Mill who developed the ideas of the Saint Simonians and Comte it also had an impact in India where Mill was an employee of the East India Company. As to Comte himself, he inspired a whole phase of development policy in nineteenth-century Latin America, and Brazil's flag still carries his logo *Ordem e Progresso* (Order and Progress). Development is an empty signifier we would argue, and to have any critical purchase we need to articulate a more specific theory of capitalist development. That way we can ground the concept in the mode of production and reproduction which is coterminous with modernity as we know it. For Marx and Engels, development and capitalism were almost synonymous as the vision presented in *The Communist Manifesto* made clear: 'The bourgeoisie cannot exist without constantly revolutionizing the instruments of production, and thereby the relations of production and with them the whole relations of society' (Marx and Engels, 1973, p. 71). This exhilarating roller-coaster of modernization is the essence of Marx's conception of development. Nature is subjected to humankind, chemistry is applied to industry and agriculture, the railway and the telegraph revolutionize communications. The insatiable drive of capitalist development tears up all obstacles in its way. Crisis and chaos are but springboards for further development. This system will inevitably take to the world stage; sweep away all the old social orders and revolutionize the modes of production.

Where there is considerable debate around the emergence of this new mode of production as development model is whether its inevitable corollary was 'underdevelopment' at the periphery. For one school of thought (Frank, Wallerstein), the capitalist 'development of underdevelopment' in the colonized world was a result of incorporation into the world market. Producing for this market for profit was what determined capitalist economic development beyond the European origins. However, this approach has been roundly criticized as 'neo-Smithian', insofar as the rise of the market is seen as sufficient to explain capitalist development. Instead Robert Brenner, along with other theorists of the transition to capitalism, argues that the rise of trade cannot determine the transformation of class relations of production. Thus, for Brenner, 'the historical problem of the origins of capitalist economic development in Europe comes down to that of the process of "self-transformation" of class relations from serfdom to free wage labour – that is, of course, the class struggle by which this transformation takes place' (Brenner, 1977, p. 81). This perspective has great relevance for the contemporary study of development and underdevelopment as it stresses 'internal' social change.

The vital conundrum about capitalist development, we would argue, is whether it tends towards global development or whether development has, as its necessary counterpart, underdevelopment. This question can be framed by two ultimately contradictory statements made by Karl Marx in the mid-nineteenth century. In the 1867 preface to the first edition of *Capital*, Marx argued that 'The country that is more developed industrially only shows, to the less developed, the image of its own future' (Marx, 1976, p. 91). This mechanical view was and is shared by all stageist, unilineal and teleological views of development. Yet Marx himself, in engaging with the emerging Russian revolutionary forces late in life, began to argue a less necessitarian case which underpins future theories of uneven development. Thus in 1881, in a letter to a Russian follower, Marx was saying that 'to metamorphose my historical sketch of the genesis of capitalism into Western Europe into a historico-philosophic theory of the general path every people is fated to tread, whatever the historical circumstances it finds itself . . . is honouring and shaming me too much' (cited in Shanin, 1983, p. 59).

COLONIAL DEVELOPMENT

To answer the question posed above we need to introduce the category of colonial development, insofar as colonialism and imperialism were integral elements in the making of development. First, however, we need to qualify the concept of capitalist development by explaining how it has always been uneven development in practice (see Smith, 1984; Van der Linden, 2007). Uneven development is characterized by differential growth rates by economic sector, and unequal socio-spatial processes and class formations at local, sub-national, national, regional and global levels. Development patterns are not only quantitatively unequal (for example different GDP per capita rates) but qualitatively different, due to different histories of class formation. Yet this basic characteristic of uneven development is always 'combined' since the rise of the global economy. As Rudolf Hilferding (early theorist of finance capital) put it in 1910, 'Capitalist development did not take place independently in each individual country, but instead capitalist relations of production and exploitation were imported along with capital from abroad' (Hilferding, 1981, p. 322).

We have already mentioned one approach to development which sees 'underdevelopment' as its necessary counterpart. From that vantage point there has been much emphasis on the role of colonial pillage and the practice of slavery in the early development of capitalism. In reality, though, the profits from slavery were quite low and its casual influence on the Industrial Revolution was quite tenuous. As to the trade with the New World, O'Brien concludes that commerce between core and periphery in the three centuries after 1450 'proceeded on a small scale, was not a uniquely profitable field of enterprise, and while it generated some externalities, they could in no way be classified as decisive to the economic growth of Britain' (O'Brien, 1982, p. 3). It was not until the mid-nineteenth century that this early mercantile imperialism was to give way to the 'free trade imperialism' of the liberal era. This was also the period in which liberal ideologies constructed the case for empire in terms of a civilizing mission with regard to the 'backward' peoples of the world.

The era of 'free trade imperialism' (Gallagher and Robinson, 1953) is particularly interesting, given its parallels with contemporary globalization theory if not practice. The basic idea is that mid-nineteenth-century British imperialism (for example in relation to India) was not consciously planned but resulted simply from the strength and exuberance of British industrial capitalism which needed ever-expanding markets. International trade was driven by British (and European) technology, capital and shipping. In the inevitable clash with the moral economy of the rest of the world, European military superiority inevitably prevailed. But what is particularly relevant today about this phase of colonial development is that it shows how economic relations can be grossly exploitative and that the market and empire are complementary. In Latin America during this period we saw the consolidation of a British 'informal empire' in the newly independent republics which, interestingly, Lenin classified as suffering from 'dependence' in his treatise on imperialism.

Classical imperialism (1880–1945) was dubbed by Lenin the 'highest stage' of capitalism, insofar as its contradictions now came to the fore. In fact colonial capitalism proved remarkably sturdy and its impacts are still felt today through neo-colonialism and dependency. The late nineteenth-century 'scramble for Africa' is emblematic of this formal colonial phase of imperialism. A conscious ideology of Empire was developed, the effects of which are still felt today. The economic drive to seek new markets, new opportunities for profits and cheap natural, and labour, resources seemed insatiable. This period (up until 1914 anyway) has been deemed the first phase of globalization. The impact on the non-European world was, however, almost uniformly negative and there was a conscious policy to prevent industrialization and thus modern development in the colonial world. When the collapse of formal empire eventually came after the Second World War it was remarkably rapid, with the independence of India and Pakistan in 1947 being the watershed event.

The age of imperialism led to some important theorizing which is still relevant to a contemporary understanding of capitalist development on a global scale. Perhaps the most interesting, and of contemporary relevance, is the approach by Rosa Luxemburg, first articulated in 1913 (Luxemburg, 1951). Against the then prevalent focus on the nature of advanced capitalism and the inter-imperialist rivalries it was generating, Luxemburg focused on the broader expanded reproduction of capitalism across the globe. Capital needs to 'realize' surplus value, that is to say, the goods produced need to be bought. Capitalist expansion into non-capitalist societies necessarily transforms them into petty commodity producers which paves the way for capitalist industrialization. This focus on the social relations of the non-European world was novel at the time and opens up a decisively non-Eurocentric perspective. Her emphasis on the continued need of capitalism to engage in 'primitive accumulation' in the South prefigures David Harvey's influential contemporary theory of 'accumulation by dispossession' (Harvey, 2003). For Rosa Luxemburg, 'Capitalism must . . . always and everywhere fight a battle of annihilation against every historical form of natural economy that it encounters . . . The principal methods in this struggle are political force (revolution, war), oppressive taxation by the state, and cheap goods' (Luxemburg, 1951, pp. 368–9).

Finally, we note that the colonial experience qualified the concept of capitalist development by introducing the phenomenon of the development 'latecomer', which lies behind the contemporary development project. It would seem that the more industrially developed countries did not show the less developed what their future held as Marx opined. Building on the notion of uneven but also combined development, Alexander Gerschenkron (in the 1950s) analysed the comparative advantages of late industrialization where backwardness could allow leaping over the 'stages' of development (1962). In relation to Russian industrialization in the 1890s, he saw the role of the state as an essential element for development, as was the emancipation of the serfs. This strand of analysis leads us from the colonial to the postcolonial period of capitalist development. It argues against all linear theories of the essential role of the state in the development process, outside original industrializing countries like England. Whether the state could, in fact, subordinate the capitalist market to human needs was, of course, another question.

THE DEVELOPMENT PROJECT

Following the decline of British imperialism and the rise of decolonization in the 1950s, a new development project emerged in a US-driven discourse.

In the post-war decolonization era we saw the emergence of the 'Third World' between the capitalist and communist antagonists of the Cold War. The low level of economic development in decolonizing Africa in particular was contrasted to the booming economy of the United States, rapidly becoming the hegemonic global power. Decolonization would lead to development in the American vision of the brave new world which was emerging after the retreat of the old colonial powers. In 1949, US President Truman declared that 'We must embark on a bold new programme for making the benefits of our scientific advances and industrial progress available for the improvement and growth of the underdeveloped areas' (cited in Esteva, 1992, p. 6). For post-development theorists like Gustavo Esteva: 'Under-development began, then, on January 20, 1949 on that day, two billion people became underdeveloped' (ibid., p. 7). There is no doubt that uneven development – or development/underdevelopment – did not begin in 1949, but there was a new discourse and political project then emerging.

To credit US President Truman with the 'invention of development' (Sachs, 1992) as the discourse-focused, post-development writers (see next section) do, is clearly an invention itself, but there is a sense in which development theory and practice took a new turn in the 1950s. Development and social change was no longer something that just happened but a process that could be actively promoted. Development became something that one party could do to another. The divide between the colonizer and the colonized of the imperial period now became the development-underdevelopment divide which characterized the postcolonial period. This paradigm suited the economic and political interests of the now rising hegemonic power, the US. Taking credit for decolonization and promoting the equality between nations, the United States moved seamlessly into constructing a neo-colonial order where formal political independence was matched by strong, economic dependence for the 'developing' nations.

Walt Rostow's *The Stages of Economic Growth* (1960) with its subtitle 'A Non-Communist Manifesto' was emblematic of this new development paradigm, with its optimistic and teleological vision of the inexorable advance of modernization under US tutelage. The 1950s were also, however, a period of import substitution industrialization in many parts of the Third World, with inward-looking development, guided by the state, being a dominant feature. The developmental state promoted industrialization but also, and crucially, accelerated the social division of labour. The economic structures and social relations of production were transformed utterly by this strategy, which took on the previously dominant oligarchy and landed interests. Of course this process was more advanced in Latin America and later in East Asia than it was in sub-Saharan Africa. The point of signalling diverse national development strategies is that Walt Rostow's vision of development following some preordained path was not the only option, and that the countries of the South had agency and an 'internal' development process determined by social and political forces and struggles.

The 'development project' began to run out of steam in the 1970s and 1980s across some regions while, paradoxically, the period also saw the rise of the Newly Industrializing Countries (NICs) in East Asia. In Latin America we saw the exhaustion of the 'easy' phase of import substitution industrialization and the growing contradictions between a state-led development process and the needs of the transnational corporations. During the 'easy' phase of industrialization, there was a developmentalist alliance forged between the state, private and foreign sectors. International capital was seeking new investment possibilities and the consolidation of the internal market was in everybody's interest. Protectionist barriers provided benefits for all, including the foreign investors. When the process slowed down, the contradictions between the various partners came to the fore and foreign capital began to pressurize for a more clearly leading role. The consumers, who were also workers, were now beginning to demand a share of the gains made by the developmentalist alliance which the capitalist sectors were not prepared to divide.

Latin America was also the paradigmatic case in terms of the emergence of an 'internal' critique of the development project from the so-called dependency school. Reflecting the contradictions in the developmental model, these theorists began to articulate an alternative model, based on a clear reflection of foreign 'dependency'. In some way it was the binary opposite of Rostow's modernization theory: where one saw the diffusion of capital into underdeveloped areas as the key to development, the other saw it as simply developing underdevelopment. Furthermore, dependency theory, as much as the dominant modernization theory, took for granted, and saw as natural, the nation-state as the self-sufficient framework for development. The two perspectives also shared a strong economic bias that led them to downplay the political process and basically ignore the cultural dimension. They were also equally teleological, insofar as modernization had an end point at US-style 'modernity', and dependency had its as Cuban-style 'socialism'.

The dominant development project represented a global discourse, but also a coherent strategy, for the pursuit of nationally managed economic growth. The United States – with its perceived anticolonial heritage, commitment to liberalism and rapidly rising standards of living – was the undisputed role model and discourse leader. Third Worldism – of which Latin American dependency theory was a variant– came to mean as McMichael puts it, 'correcting the distortions, or imbalances of the colonial division of labour' (McMichael, 1996, p. 74). Operating within the same logic of economic growth and industrialization, development became a singular enterprise even from a critical development perspective. The international aid framework consolidated this new regime. For the critics, such as dependency theorists, the emphasis on integration into the global economy as a source of underdevelopment meant that their only plausible alternative was some form of delinking, or withdrawal, from the emerging global system which was hardly a viable or progressive option.

POST-DEVELOPMENT

In terms of critical development discourses, the overarching concept now is that of 'post-development', which began to emerge in the 1980s. Whereas the dependency paradigm was still set firmly in a modernist frame, post-development springs from the postmodernist world view. Undermining the universalist pretensions of the Enlightenment is a key element in the postmodern critique of modernist social theory. The notion that the whole world could be analysed according to universal criteria of justice, truth and reason looks particularly hollow from a Third World perspective. A key theme is Lyotard's call for 'an incredibility towards metanarrative' (1984, p. xxiv), and there is no clearer metanarrative than the discourse of development. Notions of truth and objectivity are seen to mask underlying power relations or, put simply, a claim to truth is also a claim to power. Searching for the master key to development and the expertise of the development expert to solve development problems must be viewed with considerable scepticism from this perspective.

The critical discourse of post-development takes many different forms as might be expected from such a radical perspective (see Crush, 1995; Ferguson, 2006). One of the most significant theoretical influences was the work of Michel Foucault and, in particular, his analysis of power, knowledge and discourse. Development discourse from a Foucaultian perspective is about disciplining difference, that is establishing what the norm is and what deviation from it is. Clearly the development-underdevelopment couplet can be analysed in such terms; with the latter being portrayed as the other of the West's development. Western forms of rationality and the imbrication of power and knowledge in the development discourse/industry/practices have thus sought to normalize the Third World and its peoples. The focus on language, knowledge and power has also helped understand local knowledge as sites of power and also resistance. We now accept much more readily that there are multiple, unstable and permanently reconstructing identities involved in the development and social change processes.

Since its emergence the post-development perspective has been criticized, largely for homogenizing development discourse and for not articulating an alternative development perspective. One of its original proponents, Arturo Escobar, does accept some of this counter-critique but still holds to 'the need to decenter development as a social descriptor, the questioning of development's knowledge practices, and post-development's embedded critique of the ideas of growth, progress and modernity' (Escobar, 1995, p. xviii). This vision does not entail the anti-politics of some post-development theorists and its propositions are now quite widely accepted. We are also much more prone, in general, to accepting that social change is not a linear, cumulative process (if it ever was) and that it is characterized by discontinuity and fragmentation. Social movements in the Third World or developing world have clearly laid to rest the myth of totality, and reinforce the notion that society has no centre. The very meaning of development, democracy and community is being reconstructed before our eyes in the old and new movements of contestation.

Post-development has clear links to the 'new' social movements of the 1960s which broke with the class focus of the modernist paradigm. The shift from the modernist national and labour movements to the more 'postmodern' women's, environmental and indigenous movements was both a paradigm and political shift. As McEwan writes, the latter 'although they are often characterized as a form of resistance to development, they are effective in using identity-based forms of participatory politics to extend the boundaries of citizenship to marginal groups' (McEwan, 2009, p. 235). Progressive social movements can perhaps be seen as realizing the values of post-development. Subaltern social movements articulate subaltern forms of knowledge and a political practice that goes beyond economic growth. They are often place-based strategies where issues of environmental degradation, gender oppression and the marginalization of indigenous peoples come together around struggles over the privatization of water, destructive open-cast mining, big dams and the destruction of traditional livelihoods.

It is not easy to offer a simple conclusion on the success or otherwise of post-development in terms of development theory and practice. The anti-development approach that simply rejects all development modalities has limited appeal and, at best, has led to localized development efforts. The fate of the Zapatistas in Mexico – although not really anti-development in an explicit way – is perhaps indicative of how a critical perspective can end up being inward-looking and unable to expand to provide a rounded political alternative. From a more pragmatic perspective, we might consider the verdict of Knippenberg and Schuurman for whom 'models of alternative or "another" development, which do not include solving the problem of material scarcity, are theoretical exercises with no practical value' (Knippenberg and Schuurman, 1994, p. 105). Be that as it may, there are oppositional and liberatory strands of post-development – especially when expressed within a broader postcolonial frame – which articulate a healthy scepticism toward metanarratives which is where postmodernism began (see Kapoor, 2008; Wainwright, 2008).

In terms of impact on the mainstream development perspective it is perhaps the less radical 'alternative development' school which has had the most significant role. From the 1970s onwards, there was an increasing shift in mainstream discourse, away from the simplistic ethnocentric modernization perspective of the 1950s. A vast literature emerged around 'gender and development' and 'sustainable development' was widely accepted as a desirable. We had 'bottom-up' development, participatory development and popular development (see Brohman, 1996). Indicative of the new mood, was the 1975 report of the Dag Hammarskjöld Foundation, which argued that development should be geared towards the satisfaction of human needs and that it should be in harmony with the environment. Continuously promoted by critical thinking, the 'alternative development' model gradually became mainstreamed. Jan Nederveen Pieterse can thus argue persuasively that the main divide in development theory 'now runs between human and alternative development on the one hand, and . . . the positivism of growth on the other' (2010, p. 96). Expressed institutionally, it is the UN agencies versus the IMF with the World Bank somewhere in the middle.

THE GLOBALIZATION PROJECT

What the development project was for the 1950s, so the globalization project became for the 1990s, an uncontested new development paradigm. Since the mid-1970s, the internationalization of production, finance and trade had been accelerating and a new regime of capital accumulation emerged by the late 1980s. As Philip McMichael notes 'although the globalization project replaces the development project, "development" has not lost its currency. Its frame of reference has simply shifted' (McMichael, 1996, p. 150). The new frame of reference was set by the emergent dominant paradigm of economic liberalization, somewhat abusively dubbed 'neoliberalism' when, in fact, what we witnessed from the 1980s onwards was a process of neoliberalization (Venugopal, 2015). Neoliberalism was never a static and unified theoretical or policy statement and its application in different parts of the world took different forms. Neoliberal globalization did, however, mark a new phase of capitalist development, insofar as it was truly global and marked a decisive break with the paradigm of national development led by the state.

For the liberal globalizers, the essence of the new regime was the freeing of market forces to allow the 'magic of the market' to ensure the rational distribution of resources. The liberal globalizer world view goes beyond economics, to offer an alternative to all collective, or social, views of the world. The free, or unregulated, market is not only seen as the source of material wealth, but also of freedom and democracy. Globalization would, according to this view, lead to a decline of poverty and inequality worldwide. Globalization follows the earlier 1950s modernization theory in positing development as an inevitable process leading teleologically towards a predefined end. While globalization led to the increasing elimination of spatial barriers and the compression of time, it did not spell a homogeneous spatial development which continues to be uneven. If anything, the changing spatiality of global capitalism was more heterogeneous, differential and fragmented than in the past. Above all, globalization has led to an increased interconnectedness of the social fates of households, communities and peoples across the world.

The impact of the new neoliberal economic model was uneven across countries, economic sectors and social classes. While it did not restrict absolutely the choices open to developing countries, it did set clear parameters on what was possible and what was not. Fernando Henrique Cardoso, one-time dependency theorist, more recently President of Brazil, argued that globalization was 'more like a fragmenting force than a levelling force which would make the world more homogeneous. It disconnects and reconnects segments of countries locally and internationally as economic growth produces more inequality' (2009, p. 302). Just as with the earlier moves towards industrialization in the postcolonial era, the adaptation to the new era of globalization in the 1990s depended on the prior level of economic diversification. The larger, more diversified, developing countries (Brazil, Russia, India and China (BRIC)) were able to achieve integration – albeit subordinate – into the new world order, while smaller, less diversified countries were more likely to continue within a more traditional agro-export development model.

From a critical development perspective, a key issue in terms of assessing the globalization project has been its impact on inequality within and between nations. The promise of the globalization project was that income inequality and poverty would steadily reduce under the new free market global order. For optimists like Stuart Corbridge, we need 'to acknowledge that the Age of Development (1950–2000) saw improvements in global life expectancy the likes of which had never been seen before . . . The average person in China and India living more than twenty years longer in 2000 than in 1950' (2007, p. 190). But then, of course, China and India had embarked on an endogenous modernization and development programme, driven by the state in a national development mode. The East Asian 'tigers' (Korea, Taiwan, Japan), used to 'disprove' dependency theory in the 1980s, were also state-driven protectionist models, which hardly go to show the merits of an unregulated global market.

The debate around global poverty and inequality is both highly technical in terms of measurement, and highly political in terms of the conditions to be drawn from results. The global 'catch-up' story is simply not borne out by the facts. If we compare regions, measuring income in terms of Purchasing Power Parity (PPP) between 1950 and 2000, 'the broad trend towards divergence [between North and South] is clear' according to Robert Wade (2010, p. 149) with Asia being the exception. If China is excluded there is no evidence for catch-up whatsoever. When we examine global incomes in terms of Market Exchange Rates (MERS) between 1960 and 2007 'we see no catch-up growth after the onset of trade and financial liberalization in the 1980s' (ibid., p. 56), whether China is included or not. The simple fact is that between country income distribution has become more unequal since 1980, with a small reversal in the 2000s, due to the global commodity boom and not liberalization. The much-vaunted fall of 'extreme poverty' (less than US$1 per day) in terms of PPP is also a mirage, if we take China's rather questionable statistics out of the equation.

The Millennium Development Goals (MDGs), which dominated the official development industry and the radical discourse of civil society since 2000, need to be understood in terms of the underlying dynamics of the globalization project. Despite their discursive dominance across the 'development industry' and NGO practice, they were never actually a development strategy. The blatant, though not often remarked on, absence of an industrial strategy in the MDGs, goes to show that. As Samir Amin puts it 'the MDGs are part of a series of discourses that are intended to legitimize the policies and practices implemented by dominant capital and those who support it' (Amin, 2006, p. 35). Effectively the MDGs (now known as the Sustainable Development Goals (SDGs)) are the 'human face' of neoliberal globalization, and represent a way of co-opting the UN family which, as we saw above, has had some ideal of the need to maintain a degree of social cohesion in a development model that prioritizes financialization, privatization and an export-oriented model. This, however, is an unstable marriage and the post-Washington Consensus has not achieved the coherence and stability of its predecessor.

POST-GLOBALIZATION

Post-globalization, like post-development before it, marks the rupture of a dominant paradigm, although not necessarily the emergence of a new one. Many of the early proponents of globalization thought that the 2008–9 crisis showed that globalization 'had gone too far' (Rodrik, 1997). The consensus on what was seen as a virtuous circle of economic integration, political demoralization and social inclusion seemed shattered. Even Martin Wolf, author of a glowing globalization manifesto in 2004 which argued that 'The failure of our world is not that there is too much globalization, but that there is too little' (Wolf, 2004, p. 4) was, after 2009, taking a much more critical stance (see Wolf, 2010). Global Keynesianism was back on the agenda and the role of the state (so central in attenuating the effects of the financial crisis of 2008–9) was clear to all. However, globalization – in the sense of increasingly transnationalized social, economic and cultural relations – continues to be a dominant feature of our era, so it is hard to sustain a strong post-globalization thesis.

For many analysts, the effects of the 2008–9 global crisis were also to mark the start of a post-neoliberal era. Keynesian reflation policies, bank nationalizations and strong industrial policies seemed to mark the end of neoliberalism. However, we can only refer to post-neoliberalism if we take the latter to be a unified, static and totalizing strategy. Conversely, if we accept like Peck et al. that neoliberalization was defined by 'a prevailing pattern of regulatory restructuring, driven by a family of open-ended social processes and associated with polymorphic forms and outcomes' (2010, p. 101), then our verdict would be far less simplistic. Certainly, in terms of a development theory, neoliberalism has suffered a severe blow. But no paradigmatic shift has occurred, insofar as a new dominant alternative paradigm has not emerged beyond the somewhat nebulous conceptions of 'sustainable development'. In keeping with the uneven development of capitalism that we have highlighted above, we can expect to see an uneven development of neoliberalism, partly reinventing itself and partly deepening some tendencies as it is implemented differentially across the globe.

The post-globalization and post-neoliberalism paradigms tend to miss the element of continuity with the previous era. As has always been the case with capitalist development, a crisis is an opportunity for recomposition at a higher level. The immediate post-crisis calls for re-regulation of the financial sector to prevent a recurrence soon gave way to 'business as usual' with the bankers bonuses reinstated and so on. However, if we take a more long-term Polanyian view of the 2008–9 crisis we might conclude that society began to create a social counter-movement to protect itself from further commodification and the disembedding of the economy from social relations (see Fraser, 2014). No model of development and social change based on assumptions of stability and equilibrium will be adequate to the task of understanding the crisis or creating alternative development strategies. Arguably, we need to foreground instability and complexity more, and understand that the Polanyian 'double movement' (market deregulation and social protectionist counter-movements) is always with us.

If we are to take a broad view of capitalist worldwide development today, unconstrained by premature labels, one of the first tendencies to come to mind would be the rise of the BRICs. Whatever the limitations of the 'emerging' economies, they have clearly helped supersede the traditional paternalist development discourse that portrays the North as 'developing' the South. In Brazil, Russia, India and China (and to some extent South Africa) we have seen the return of the developmental state, a strong public sector and a refusal to go along with all of the North's anti-developmental state proposals (see Kalinowski, 2015). In the aftermath of the 2008–9 crisis there was, certainly, an undue optimism placed in this group of countries' ability to buck the trend of the global downturn. Nevertheless, growth rates in the global South are much higher than those in the global North, which has still not emerged fully from the 2008–9 crisis. Whether this will lead to a new Bandung Consensus – referring to the rise of the non-aligned or 'Third' World in the 1950s – remains to be seen but we can be sure that the old development models – radical as well as conservative – need to be revisited.

The other major distinguishing mark of development in the twenty-first century would be the return of the state to a central role. The dominant neo-developmentalism in Latin America is a good example of a contemporary strategy which returns to 1950s-style state-led development, but is now tempered by the pro-market and anti-protectionism of 1990s-style neoliberalism. Overall, the pendulum has swung from the market to the state, with few illusions left in the self-regulating capacity of the former. That does not mean that the state holds the answers to development. State capacity has been severely weakened by several decades of pro-market development policies, and through its capture by power elites, of course. Uneven development has led, in turn, to uneven state capabilities to engage proactively with development. Stateness itself is also unevenly developed and the capacity of the BRICs is not matched across the broader developing world. All we can say is that there is no development without the state, a statement that takes us back to Gerschenkron and the debates around the late industrializers.

Taking a broad retrospective view of capitalist development, we might posit complexity as the third analytical priority. Complexity, as John Urry outlines, 'repudiates the dichotomies of determinism and chance, as well as nature and society being and becoming, stasis and change' (2003, p. 22). What this means, in terms of development and social change, is that we must be wary of binary oppositions between, say, modernization and post-dependency theory. We have seen already how there is no clear dividing line between neoliberalism and post-neoliberalism. Complexity points us towards the end of certainty and, of course, the inherent teleology in many development theories. There is always order and disorder in all development and social change processes. What the crisis in the dominant global development model since 2008 allows us to do is reimagine post-globalization (as we knew it) by developing future scenarios for change which will, of course, be multiple.

FURTHER READING

Escobar, A. (2012), *Encountering Development. The Making and Unmaking of the Third World*. Princeton: Princeton University Press.
The 'classic' statement of the post-development school, quite influenced by Michel Foucault and, in its turn, influential in social movement analysis.
Kiely, R. (2010), *Rethinking Imperialism*. Houndmills: Palgrave.
An accessible overview of classical theories of imperialism through to the contemporary issues around Americanization and Empire.
McEwan, C. (2009), *Postcolonialism and Development*. London: Routledge.
An interesting and accessible text bridging the gap between postcolonial and development theories thus pointing towards a postcolonial development agenda.
McMichael, P. (2012), *Development and Social Change. A Global Perspective*. Los Angeles: Sage.
A broad overview of the 'development project' (1950s–1970s), its crisis and its succession by the 'globalization project' (1980s onwards), now itself in crisis.
Nederveen Pieterse, J. (2010), *Development Theory. Deconstructions/Reconstructions*. London: Sage.
A theoretically-oriented overview of development theory dealing critically with issues such as Eurocentrism, critical globalism and delinking/alternative development approaches.

REFERENCES

Amin, S. (2006), 'The Millennium Development Goals: A Critique from the South', *Monthly Review* Vol. 57, No. 10, pp. 1–15.
Brenner, R. (1977), 'The Origins of Capitalist Development: A Critique of Neo-Smithian Marxism', *New Left Review* I/104.
Brohman, J. (1996), *Popular Development. Rethinking the Theory and Practice of Development*. Oxford: Blackwell.
Cardoso, F. H. (2009), 'New Pathways: Globalization in Historical Perspective', *Studies in Comparative International Development* Vol. 44, pp. 450–56.
Comte, A. (2009), *A General View of Positivism*. Cambridge: Cambridge University Press.
Corbridge, S. (2007), 'The (Im)Possibility of Development Studies', *Economy and Society* Vol. 36, No. 2, pp. 179–211.

Cowen, M. P. and Shenton, R. W. (1996), *Doctrines of Development*. London: Routledge.

Crush, J. (ed.) (1995), *Power of Development*. London: Routledge.

Escobar, A. (1995), *Encountering Development. The Making and Unmaking of the Third World*. Princeton: Princeton University Press.

Esteva, G. (1992), 'Development', in G. Sachs (ed.) *The Development Dictionary*. London: Zed Books, pp. 6–25.

Ferguson, J. (2006), *Global Shadow. Africa in the Neoliberal World Order*. Durham, NC: Duke University Press.

Foucault, M. (1984), 'Nietzsche, Genealogy, History', in P. Rabinow (ed.) *The Foucault Reader*. New York: Pantheon Books, pp. 76–100.

Fraser, N. (2014), 'Can Society be Commodities all the Way Down? Post-Polanyian Reflections on Capitalist Crisis', *Economy and Society* Vol. 43, No. 4, pp. 541–58.

Gallagher, J. and Robinson, R. (1953), 'The Imperialism of Free Trade', *Economic History Review* Vol. I (I), pp. 1–15.

Gerschenkron, A. (1962), *Economic Backwardness in Historical Perspective*. Boston, MA: Harvard University Press.

Harvey, D. (2003), *The New Imperialism*. Oxford: Oxford University Press.

Hilferding, R. (1981), *Finance Capitalism*. London: Routledge.

Kalinowski, T. (2015), 'Crisis Management and the Diversity of Capitalism: Fiscal Stimulus Packages and the East Asian (Neo-)Developmental State', *Economy and Society* Vol. 44, No. 2, pp. 244–70.

Kapoor, J. (2008), *The Postcolonial Politics of Development*. London: Routledge.

Kiely, R. (2010), *Rethinking Imperialism*. Houndmills: Palgrave.

Knippenberg, L. and Schuurman, F. (1994), 'Blinded by Rainbows: Anti-modernist and Modernist Deconstructions of Development', in F. Schuurman (ed.) *Current Issues in Development Studies*. Saarbrücken: Verlag Breitenbach.

Law, J. and Urry, J. (2004), 'Enacting the Social', *Economy and Society* Vol. 33, No. 3, pp. 390–410.

Luxemburg, R. (1951), *The Accumulation of Capital*. New York: Monthly Review Press.

Lyotard, F. (1984), *The Postmodern Condition*. Manchester: Manchester University Press.

McEwan, C. (2009), *Postcolonialism and Development*. Abingdon: Routledge.

McMichael, P. (1996), *Development and Social Change. A Global Perspective*. Thousand Oaks, CA: Pine Forge Press.

Marx, K. (1976), *Capital*, Vol. I. Harmondsworth: Penguin.

Marx, K. and Engels, F. (1973), *The Communist Manifesto*. London: Penguin.

Nederveen Pieterse, J. (2010), *Development Theory. Deconstructions/Reconstructions*. London: Sage.

Nisbet, R. (1969), *Social Change and History. Aspects of the Western Theory of Development*. Oxford: Oxford University Press.

O'Brien, P. (1982), 'European Economic Development: The Contribution of the Periphery', *The Economic History Review* Vol. 35(1), pp. 1–18.

Peck, J., Theodore, N. and Brenner, N. (2010), 'Postneoliberalism and its Malcontents', in N. Castree, P. Chatterton, N. Heynen, W. Larner and M. Wright (eds) *The Point Is to Change It. Geographies of Hope and Survival in an Age of Crisis*. Oxford: Blackwell.

Rodrik, D. (1997), *Has Globalization Gone Too Far?* New York: Institute for International Economics.

Rostow, W. (1960), *The Stages of Economic Growth: A Non-Communist Manifesto*. Cambridge: Cambridge University Press.

Sachs, G. (ed.) (1992), *The Development Dictionary*. London: Zed Books.

Shanin, T. (ed.) (1983), *Late Marx and the Russian Road*. London: Routledge.

Smith, N. (1984), *Uneven Development, Nature, Capital and the Production of Space*. Oxford: Blackwell.

Urry, J. (2003), *Global Complexity*. Cambridge: Polity Press.

Van der Linden, M. (2007), 'The "Law" of Uneven and Combined Development: Some Undeveloped Thoughts', *Historical Materialism*, Vol. 15, pp. 145–65.

Venugopal, R. (2015), 'Neoliberalism as Concept', *Economy and Society* Vol. 44, No. 2, pp. 165–87.
Wade, R. (2010), 'Is the Globalization Consensus Dead?', in N. Castree, P. Chatterton, N. Heynen, W. Larner and M. Wright (eds) *The Point Is to Change It: Geographies of Hope and Survival in an Age of Crisis*. Oxford: Blackwell.
Wainwright, J. (2008), *Decolonizing Development. Colonial Power and the Maya*. Oxford: Blackwell.
Wolf, M. (2004), *Why Globalisation Works*. New Haven: Yale University Press.
Wolf, M. (2010), *Fixing Global Finance*. Baltimore: John Hopkins University Press.

PART I

ECONOMIC ASPECTS

2. Towards an ecology of development
Philip McMichael

INTRODUCTION[1]

In a world increasingly challenged by structural unemployment, environmental degradation and climate emergency, the modern development paradigm appears increasingly bankrupt. 'Development', as we know it, privileges a global consumer class, but at the expense of the world's majority peoples and planetary health. While development agencies and policy-makers recognize the threats of declining biodiversity and rising greenhouse gas (GHG) emissions, they are beholden to the idea of 'sustainable development', as if there now remains sufficient natural world to sustain. 'Sustainable development' focuses on sustaining 'development' in a compromised environment, rather than on how to actually *rehabilitate* degraded ecosystems, and sustain them with ecological development.

The so-called 'green economy' does not necessarily reduce material throughput,[2] nor is it able to respect ecological integrity, as it 'stands for a new relation to nature, and new types of intervention in nature. Nature is increasingly considered as a specific type of capital, which needs to be measured, conserved, produced and even accumulated [revealing] an increasing "economization" of environmental discourse' (Kenis and Lievens, 2015, p. 8). It is also unlikely to bridge the gap between 'economic time' and the temporality of self-organizing natural cycles.[3] In order to sustain natural cycles, development itself needs a fundamental reformulation as an ecological, rather than an economic, paradigm. This chapter addresses this issue via a critique of *extant* visions of development as 'ecologically challenged', that is, as devaluing socio-ecological relationships. In particular, it focuses on the development narrative's disregard for the integrity of agrarian culture which remains important to sustaining ecosystems and secure and inclusive food provisioning.

A CRISIS CONJUNCTURE

The year 2015 marked the transition in official language from the *Millennium* Development Goals (MDGs) to the *Sustainable* Development Goals (SDGs). The lapse of time between 2000 and 2015 was not simply a decade and a half of assessment and reassessment of the MDGs – it was a decade and a half of cumulative awareness of serious environmental limits that, in turn, were exposing social and political limits associated with the organization and efficacy of the global food system. The UN Millennium Ecosystem Assessment (United Nations, 2005, p. 1) noted:

> Over the past 50 years, humans have changed ecosystems more rapidly and extensively than in any comparable period of time in human history . . . This has resulted in a substantial and largely irreversible loss in the diversity of life on Earth . . . These problems, unless addressed, will substantially diminish the benefits that future generations obtain from ecosystems.

In this vein, summarizing a long-standing global agrarian crisis of the neoliberal era, the International Assessment of Agricultural Knowledge, Science and Technology for Development (IAASTD) Report, informally subtitled as 'Agriculture at a Crossroads', observed that 'markets fail to adequately value environmental and social harm' (IAASTD, 2008, p. 20). Meanwhile, progress on global hunger reduction was faltering. The Millennium Goals Report 2010 (UNDESA, 2010, p. 11) stated:

> Since 1990, developing regions have made some progress towards the MDG target of halving the proportion of people suffering from hunger. The share of undernourished populations decreased from 20 per cent in 1990–1992 to 16 per cent in 2005–2007, the latest period with available data. However, progress has stalled since 2000–2002 . . . Food prices spiked in 2008 and falling income due to the financial crisis further worsened the situation. The Food and Agricultural Organization of the United Nations estimates that the number of people who were undernourished in 2008 may be as high as 915 million and exceed 1 billion in 2010.

Earlier, in 2007–8, with food prices spiking, food riots took place in 30 countries across the world – from Senegal through India to Argentina (Patel and McMichael, 2009). Biofuel expansion, spurred by government mandate and/or subsidies in the name of 'green fuels', were a proximate cause as crop and pasture land was corralled for fuel rather than food production, according to Howden: 'From the savannahs of West Africa to the rainforests of Congo, the plains of Tanzania and the wilderness of Ethiopia, governments are handing over huge tracts of fertile land to private companies aiming to convert biomass grown on large plantations into liquid fuels for export markets' (2008, p. 34).

This phenomenon became known as the 'land grab', and it extended through Asia to South America. Investors acquired land in response to food inflation and biofuel subsidies, accounting for almost 50 per cent of the rise in food prices as fuel crops replaced food crops (McMichael, 2010). As Borras et al., noted: 'The World Bank report on land grabs (or, as the Bank calls it, agricultural investment), released in September 2010, estimated this global phenomenon at 45 million hectares' (2011, p. 209). Since the 'food crisis' some land deals have 'backfired or failed for different reasons', such as water scarcity, lack of investor farming expertise, civil resistance, volatile financial and currency markets, and unstable governments and legal ambiguities regarding land tenure (GRAIN, 2016). Nevertheless, GRAIN reports many new deals are underway 'to expand the frontiers of industrial agriculture' and, beyond gaining access to food supplies, oil palm expansion beyond SE Asia into Africa complements 'a broader corporate strategy to profit from carbon markets, mineral resources, water resources, seeds, soil and environmental services' (ibid.). Oxfam claims more than 1,500 large-scale land deals have been signed since 2000, and that:

> We're entering a new and even more dangerous stage of the global land rush. The frenzied trade in millions of hectares of forests, coastlines and farmlands has led to murder, eviction and ethnocide. Land contracts are being signed and projects are breaking ground without the full consent of the communities living there. (Oxfam, 2016, p. 5)

Furthermore, such deals threaten a variety of other cultures unprotected from modern civilization, and capable, if adequately supported, of protecting landscapes and waterways:

> Half of the world's landmass is home to indigenous peoples and local communities that are its traditional owners. But they have no formally recognized ownership to 80% of this land ... often considered fair game for plunder, typically under the guise of 'economic development' ...
> There is a long list of benefits to securing people's rights to these lands. It would protect more than 5,000 human cultures, and 4,000 different languages, as well as 80 per cent of the planet's biodiversity. (Ibid.)

Under neoliberalism, with states beholden to investors and legitimacy tropes such as 'green fuels' and 'feeding the world', land has become a new 'financial asset' (Fairbairn, 2014). A report by *The Greens/European Free Alliance* in the European Parliament notes:

> The rush for land in Europe has a different character than for instance in Africa. Ordinarily, the concentration of land in the EU takes place legally ... [But] land has increasingly become an investment and an object of speculation and is no longer primarily the basis of small-scale farming. At the same time, agriculture is becoming more intensive and farms are getting bigger. This is a threat to biodiversity, the groundwater, our rural social structures, and the quality of food. Soil, grassland, and arable land are not a commodity but the livelihood of farmers. (Heubuch, 2015, p. 3)

The commandeering of land for intensive food and fuel production has major social and ecological consequences, where agro-industrialization deepens the ecological crisis of development – compromising ecosystems and accelerating global warming via GHG emissions associated with intensive agriculture. With the development of chemical agriculture and biotechnology, the growing abstraction of agriculture as an 'input–output process that has a beginning and an end' means that rather than a complex embedded in and regenerating local biological cycles, agriculture can in principle be relocated to specific locales anywhere on the planet as the 'intrinsic qualities of the land matter less' (Duncan, 1996, p. 123).

Agro-industrialization replicates the spatial mobility of manufacturing systems, including the subdivision of constituent processes into global commodity chains (such as the animal protein complex: feed crops, feed lots, factory farms and aquaculture). Given the key role of fossil fuels, petro-farming depletes soils and waterways by extending inputs of inorganic fertilizer, pesticides and herbicides. Through mechanization petro-farming increases demand for carbon-emitting fuels and inputs, at the same time releasing soil carbon into the atmosphere along with even more damaging nitrous oxide from fertilizer use, and from livestock waste in factory farming (Weis, 2010). The ensuing ecological crisis contributes to an active process of 'ecocide', which Zierler graphically depicted as: 'the environment being murdered by mankind . . . Our dense, amber air is a noxious emphysema agent; farming – antihusbandry – turns fertile soil into a poisoned wasteland; rivers are sewers, lakes cesspools, and our oceans are dying' (2011, p. 14).

Current acceleration of such processes of ecocide derives from an extractive economic rationality, combined with a renewed competition for increasingly scarce 'resources' as states and private investors pursue intensive development for legitimacy and profit, respectively. Even as the corporate world acknowledges ecosystem decline as the principal obstacle to future sustainability,[4] it maintains the development narrative's anthropocentric view of nature. This means disembedding natural processes, removing them from an economic calculus, and rendering them as 'environmental externalities'. As such, these 'externalities' are then subject to an artificial commodification as 'ecosystem services' via market environmentalism (as discussed in a later section).

Disregard for ecologically rational practices is the logical outcome of a development narrative premised on singular 'economic rationality', which consigns such cultures to pre-history. Here, 'development' reproduces modernity's trope of the irreversibility of time (Latour, 1991), rendering all that came before as pre-history and redundant. Rostow formalized this perspective in *The Stages of Economic Growth* (1960), generalizing a linear development transition for each nation-state through identifiable stages, from 'traditional' to 'high mass consumption society'. This trajectory combines ecological disembedding with wholesale commodification. It necessarily discounts future possibilities grounded in ecological practices, which might inform alternative modernities to sustain planetary health.

The supreme irony is that a singular, linear temporality is a trap, in two senses. First, it erases connection with ecological practices that continue to exist, but are deemed obsolete, and therefore scorned as impractical for a techno-future. Second, development's linear temporality is a trap insofar as its past now threatens the present and future. As Malm emphasizes:

> For every year global warming continues and temperatures soar higher, living conditions on earth will be determined more intensely by the emissions of yore, so that the grip of yesteryear on today intensifies – or, put differently, *the causal power of the past inexorably rises*, all the way up to the point when it is indeed 'too late'. The significance of that terrible destiny, so often warned of in climate change discourse, is the final *falling in of history on the present*. (2016, p. 9)

The consequence of this perilous legacy is that the development promise of improvement on the past is rendered hollow, precipitating widespread disillusionment with governments and the 'globalization project' (McMichael, 1996) on the one hand (as evident in the Brexit and Trump revolts of 2016), and a disturbing denialism by fossil fuel energy corporates on the other. On both counts, the conventional development paradigm has lost its *raison d'être*.

An alternative paradigm, of diversity, necessarily abandons 'the linearity of the Eurocentric conception of time and incorporates a different spatial and temporal frame into the analysis of cultural and territorial relations' (Leff, 2016, p. 261). It values coexistence of territories with distinct temporalities and particular ecological relations (for example Escobar, 2004). Above all, it recognizes that modernity has developed an ecological amnesia over the last two centuries. As Duncan (2007, p. 37) claims:

> . . . in the last hundred years we have had no idea what we were really doing on this planet . . . Instead of rethinking our possible role on the planet, instead of qualifying or revising our anthropocentric habits, we have shamelessly used the decline of theology relative to science as an excuse to elevate our own importance further. Logically we should have replaced theology with ecology, before enlarging the parameters of our behaviour by the heavy use of fossil fuels. Compared to the planet, our species has not been around for long, but compared to what historians or sociologists talk about, we certainly have . . . People who lived before agriculture have been condemned to what has been called, with breath taking arrogance: 'pre-history' [and] because historians in particular refused to consider humans in deep time, modern science has actually had no ecologically relevant cultural impact, at least not yet.

In regard to this, a recent monograph by an indigenous Australian (Pascoe, 2016) details the sophistication of Aboriginal peoples' economic and social practices as a complex civilization based in landscape and soil management for surplus-producing agriculture, underlining the ecological rationality of so-called 'pre-historic' people (many of whom continue such practices today). As Pascoe claims:

> One of the most fundamental differences between Aboriginal and non-Aboriginal people is the understanding of the relationship between people and land. Earth is the mother. Aboriginal people are born of the earth and individuals within the clan had responsibilities for particular streams, grasslands, trees, crops, animals and even seasons. The life of the clan was devoted to continuance. (Ibid., p. 145)

Pascoe's abiding point, echoing Duncan in situating such 'ecological rationality', is:

> Accepting the full history of the country has the benefit of discovering a whole new level of knowledge about sustainable harvests. Change may be required but it does not lead to a preference for wilderness or the withdrawal of productive lands. New ideas and new methods will arise out of the very oldest land use practices. (Ibid., p. 148)

EPISTEMIC SHIFT

New methods arising from old practices means not only revaluing such practised methods of landscape, soil and water management, but also shedding linear modernist epistemology. Recovering (and renewing) cultural practices deemed obsolete requires rejecting such a singular governing principle as the market is today. When the UK's *Stern Review on the Economics of Climate Change* (2006) proclaimed climate change to be 'the greatest market failure the world has ever seen', the implication was not simply that markets cannot value environmental harm, but also that the market episteme has a serious blind-spot – we did not see climate change coming. Linear thinking has left the world seriously threatened by the 'grip of yesteryear'.

Linear thought is not unique to modern liberalism. In critiquing the a-historical/linear categories of classical political economy, Marx's method of political economy (historicizing these categories) nevertheless reproduced a certain, cumulative linearity. His target was the bourgeois tendency to construct economic categories via a 'developmentalist' narrative, where the 'latest form regards the previous ones as steps leading up to itself, and ... it always conceives of them one-sidedly' (Marx,

1973, p. 106). Marx complicates this representation with his well-known methodological directive:

> Capital is the all-dominating economic power of bourgeois society. It must form the starting-point as well as the finishing-point, and must be dealt with before landed property ... It would therefore be unfeasible and wrong to let the economic categories follow one another in the same sequence as that in which they were historically decisive. Their sequence is determined, rather, by their relation to one another in modern bourgeois society, which is precisely the opposite of that which seems to be their natural order or which corresponds to historical development. (Ibid., p. 107)

Here, in *historicizing* landed property as now combined with, and in subordinate relation to, capital, the latter establishes directionality, specifically via ongoing accumulation (even as capitalism develops through periodic crises). To avoid conceiving of landed property one-sidedly, as the dominant social form prior to the capitalist era, Marx argues it must now be examined through the capital lens in order to resituate and understand its social function. It is not now so much a prior form, as it is subsumed by, or incorporated into, the relations of capital. A development narrative is reproduced here, insofar as this method suggests an inevitable 'obsolescence' of prior social forms – such as small-scale farming, fishing, forest-dwelling and pastoralism.

Arguably, this method permits a development narrative regarding the reproduction of capital via its subjection of landed relations to regimes of accumulation, which include trajectories of de-peasantization (cf. Kautsky, 1988; and Lenin, 1972). This formulation gives rise to an 'agrarian question' which objectifies the small-scale producer as remnant (Lenin) or a dependent (Kautsky) who is, therefore, devoid of historical subjectivity. At the same time, it invisibilizes the potential of ecological rationality in peasant farming (cf. Ploeg, 2013), enabling a capitalist economic rationality, premised on the elimination of localized farming systems. Land grabbing under colonialism was the measure of this, and of course continues today as a self-fulfilling prophecy of 'land improvement' via displacement of peasant communities (Liberti, 2013), or their incorporation into 'value chains'. Thus the director of Self Help Africa, which, with support from PepsiCo, works with cashew-nut farmers and processors in Benin to supply European markets, declared: 'Strengthening smallholder value chains is really about helping farmers to move from being subsistence based to enabling them to make a better profit' (*The Guardian*, 2012).

It was this 'productivist' vision of contract farming for global consumers that informed policy-makers at the FAO World Food Summit (2008), in the wake of the 'food crisis'. During the Summit, the International Planning Committee for Food Sovereignty (IPC) responded with the Terra Preta Declaration:

> The serious and urgent food and climate crises are being used by political and economic elites as opportunities to entrench corporate control of world agriculture and the ecological commons. At a time when chronic hunger, dispossession of food providers and workers, commodity and land speculation, and global warming are on the rise, governments, multilateral agencies and financial institutions are offering proposals that will only deepen these crises through more dangerous versions of policies that originally triggered the current situation [. . .] Small-scale food producers are feeding the planet, and we demand respect and support to continue. Only food sovereignty can offer long-term, sustainable, equitable and just solutions to the urgent food and climate crises. (IPC, 2008)

Even if small-scale producers are only feeding up to two-thirds of the planet (Action Group on Erosion, Technology and Concentration (ETC), 2009), the point here is that this mosaic of farming (across both rural and urban landscapes) has a key role to play, aside from farmers' rights to produce, and therefore to their lands. But human rights and cultural autonomy are secondary to the market solutions that framed the official response. In spite of pervasive evidence of a new threshold in a global food system that was neither equitable nor sustainable: 'agriculture at a crossroads' – as detailed in the IAASTD (2008), and the prior UN Millennium Ecosystem Assessment (United Nations, 2005) – could only be imagined by officialdom as a moment in which to double down and partner with the private sector in further capitalizing land and food production. The two decades-old neoliberal agenda of 'food security' as the 'right to purchase food', as supplied in the world market by grain traders and transnational food corporations, was to be recalibrated via public-private partnerships, including investment in value chains and land deals to consolidate the global food regime (McMichael, 2013b).

In this moment of substantial legitimacy crisis for the development institutions, the UN Food and Agricultural Organization's (FAO) Committee on World Food Security (CFS) invited the IPC to join the CFS as a Civil Society Mechanism (CSM) with non-voting, but participation, rights. This initiative acknowledged IPC advocacy for the salience of agrarian movements of food producers, landless workers and indigenous peoples in negotiating questions of food security – but from the perspective of 'food sovereignty'. This advocates for the rights of farmers to produce culturally appropriate food for local/domestic needs (vs standardized foods produced and processed for the global market). Given that such rights include farming systems geared to ecosystem integrity, the CSM's role has been to advocate an ecological rationality as counterpoint to the economic rationality that dominates debate in the CFS (McKeon, 2015).

THE ECOLOGICAL QUESTION

As above, the moment of general ecological crisis, which defines our time, is also a development crisis. In addition to deepening the urbanization of the countryside, and amplifying GHG emissions, the commandeering of land to expand the production of industrial foods, fuels and biomass is, at the same time, undermining the conditions of social reproduction of a significant proportion of humanity whose livelihoods depend on land, forests, rivers and mangroves for 'commoning' outside capital's commodity circuits (cf. Keyder, 2011).

'Ecological crisis' has a distinctive human dimension, notably over-urbanization and toxic contamination. Relatedly, there are growing concerns regarding 'population biology', characterized as a syndrome 'resulting from industrial farming and livestock operations, which multiply not only the number of human beings but the beings favoured in agro-food markets, all at the expense of the many beings and relationships in self-organizing ecosystems' (Friedmann, 2006, p. 464). The depletion of self-organizing ecosystems is considered a substantial risk as much by the authors of the UN Millennium Ecosystem Assessment (United Nations, 2005) as by the captains of industry (see note 4). It is exacerbated by wholesale enclosure and agro-industrialization, with serious social, ecological and public health consequences, rural dispossession and urban 'informalization' in excess of 50 per cent in Latin America, at 70 per cent in sub-Saharan Africa, and in India, 80 per cent of the workforce (Boyd, 2006).

As suggested, ecological crisis is in part a result of an epistemic crisis: the resistance to recognizing the ecological foundations of modern economy and the increasing irreversibility of human and planetary risk. The epistemic crisis stems from the 'ecological blind-spot' endemic to conventional development theory, as well as *orthodox* Marxism and its capital-centric method. Arguably we are in a historical moment where a new methodological directive is overdue, avoiding taking capital one-sidedly, given how this discounts ecological relations. Capital may still be the all-dominating economic power, but what does this mean in ecological terms beyond the proposition that capitalism is an 'ecological regime' (Moore, 2015)? As an 'ecological regime' capitalism involves exploitation of natural processes (both human and non-human). Marx made clear such exploitation is obscured by the 'fetishism of commodities', whereby commodity exchange relations abstract the human and natural relations involved in their production. How is it then possible to understand (and value) ecological processes through a capital lens, premised as it is on 'biophysical override' (Weis, 2007)? If 'development' is to have substantive meaning, it needs reformulation to revalue ecology, beyond the abstractions of the price form.[5]

Moore's concept of capitalism as an 'ecological regime' alters the methodological point of departure by rewriting the history of capital as governed by (moments of overcoming) environmental limits. Expanding commodity frontiers serve to sustain accumulation as capitalism abandons its degraded environments to incorporate new 'resource' complexes (Moore, 2015). Here, ecological appropriation is intrinsic to capital accumulation. Arguably, representing ecology as a relation of capital is ultimately limiting – Earth is constituted by self-forming ecological cycles, however compromised by capital (McMichael, 2012). The 'nemesis effect' (environmental feedback), for example, cannot be understood simply from the point of view of capital – biophysical processes are not only self-organizing, they are also historically cumulative, as evident in long-term processes of natural exhaustion and carbon emission.

Further, European capital's construction of an 'ecological regime' such as North American prairie farming in the late nineteenth century simultaneously undermined prior, and distinctive, ecological relations practised by Native Americans. That is, the new commodity frontier, responding to 'relative exhaustion of nature' in Europe, was premised on destruction of *extant* ecosystems variably produced and reproduced through the specific sedentary and/or nomadic relations of distinctive human cultures. The point here is that the condition of 'world-capitalist ecology' is the elimination or erasure of other self-organizing ecological relations.

The consequence of such erasure has been the progressive dependence of capitalist agriculture on energy-intensive methods of production supplied by chemical (petroleum-based) and mechanical inputs. Such 'biophysical override' masks the 'under-reproduction of nature' (Moore, 2015), where agro-inputs eliminate biodiversity and natural cycles that normally maintain soil and water cycle health. The erasure involves 'value override', by which capital fetishism discounts biodiversity and natural cycles. The two overrides are different sides of the same coin. Capitalist enclosure and its deepening 'metabolic rift'[6] simultaneously foreclose alternative ecologies (Schneider and McMichael, 2010).

Moore's concept of 'under-reproduction of nature' refers to the *relative* exhaustion of ecosystem services, accounting for the progressive colonization of new frontiers of accumulation as temporary solutions to accumulation crises. Here, capital habitually defers exhaustion of nature by under-reproducing ecosystems on particular frontiers, until such time as the frontier option disappears ('absolute exhaustion'). Arguably the capitalist world is approaching this time, as evidenced by the acceleration of land commandeering for industrial agriculture – not only contributing to mounting ecosystem degradation, but also to further climate change, both of which debilitate the remaining land.

The question is whether capital is a useful point of methodological departure for understanding this moment? As de Sousa Santos (and Einstein) would note, such modern problems no longer have modern solutions (Escobar, 2004), meaning adequate solutions must come from an alternative epistemology – drawing on values beyond the abstractions of the price form. While the price form represents the claim for universal value in the money commodity – a relational (economic) principle – an alternative, and equivalent (ecological) principle represents the unity of biological diversity (nature). Certainly, capital has attempted to subsume nature via ecological accounting, but this reproduces an artificial economy because ecological (interconnective) relations cannot be reduced to, or expressed in, singular standardized metrics. A produced tree plantation is no substitute for a living forest.

Establishing a new methodological directive is hardly straightforward. Taking a cue from Marx, we might identify the determinate condition as the general ecological crisis, which cannot be solved by capital (however much stock is put in 'market environmentalism', so to speak). A methodological directive then, paraphrasing Marx, might read 'Ecology, and its practice, is the ultimate determinant of the fate of human society. It must form the starting-point as well as the finishing point, and must be dealt with now before capital . . . It would therefore be unfeasible and wrong to let market, or economic categories remain decisive. Their presence is only determined by their ability to elide or externalize ecological relations. Their relation to ecology is precisely the opposite of that which seems to be their historical impact – rather they are formed, and ultimately governed, by ecological relations.'

Ecological relations include the exercise of human labour: the methodological starting point, as labour appropriates nature, converting raw materials into human sustenance. Marx recognized labour as an ecological relation when he claimed:

> It is not the unity of living and active humanity with the natural, inorganic conditions of their metabolic exchange with nature, and hence their appropriation of nature, which requires explanation, or is the result of a historic process, but rather the separation between these inorganic conditions of human existence and this active existence, a separation which is completely posited only in the relation of wage labour and capital. (1973, p. 489)

Such recognition of labour indicates how a capital-centric perspective subsequently erases this relation from value theoretic narrative. As Leff has noted: 'The problem [lies] mainly in the fact that neither nature's contribution to production nor the destructive effects of production on nature are valued' (2016, p. 254).

In explaining capitalist alienation of labour from the natural metabolic relation, Marx went on to critique the political economy of his time, privileging a labour theory of value at the expense of a conception of value embodying natural process. This was necessary to the critique, as a *methodological* intervention on Marx's part. Subsequently it has been interpreted by orthodoxy as a *theory* of history, and, as such, reproduces 'an ontology that, proceeding from the original fact of the metabolic rift, discounts alternative values such as ecological relations' (McMichael, 2012, p. 148). Since intensification of the metabolic rift is the result of capital's subordination of landed property, the latter is reconstituted as a value relation (expressed in price). Simultaneously there is a conversion in the structure of thought as well, superimposing a capital logic on history, as capital comes to order socio-economic relationships. I term this an 'epistemic rift' (ibid.).

A 'capital logic' theorizes history rather than historicizing theory. To historicize theory is to allow recovery of the socio-ecological presuppositions of the social/natural metabolism ruled out by 'metabolic rift' theory (ibid.). In other words, historicizing theory involves both situating theory (for example, critique of political economy) and reconstructing its premises. In regard to this, Tomich proposes going '*against the grain of Marx's classical theoretical presentation*', by moving from 'rational abstractions ... toward engagement, appropriation, and theoretical reconstruction of diverse historical relations excluded by the logic of Marx's presentation' (2004, p. 38). Thus the above quote from Marx regarding metabolism demonstrates how value theory (the capital/labour relation) separates social labour and nature – as ontologically distinct universes. As Taylor notes, this approach 'marginalizes how produced socio-ecologies are both productive and destructive of particular forms of life' (2015, p. 115). As such it elides the metabolic relation as a transformed and transforming relationship across time and space (as opposed to simply a one-time 'rift').

Malm's recent historical analysis of the rise of fossil fuels as 'a materialisation of social relations' (2016, p. 19) illustrates the method of historicizing theory, and thereby recovering the fundamental metabolic relationship of industrial capitalism:

> No piece of coal or drop of oil has yet turned itself into fuel, and no humans have yet engaged in systematic large-scale extraction of either to satisfy

subsistence needs: fossil fuels necessitate waged or forced labour – the power of some to direct the labour of others – as conditions of their very existence. (Ibid.)

In emphasizing the need to redefine modern capitalist ontology as indeed embedded in ecological relations, Malm goes on to state, in Marxian syntax: 'Natural scientists have so far interpreted global warming as a phenomenon in nature; the point, however, is to trace its human origins' (ibid.). In other words, social and scientific thought needs regrounding in ecological reality as a condition and consequence of human life. But it is not so easy from the perspective of economic rationality, as evident in contemporary forms of market environmentalism.

MARKET ENVIRONMENTALISM, 'SUSTAINABLE DEVELOPMENT', AND BEYOND

One measure of this is recent projects to revalue degraded land, in consequence of land grabbing. Where Moore argues capitalism develops precisely through biophysical crises (2011), Goldstein suggests that 'forest degradation is not an exhaustion of resource value or an obstacle to new forms of use and exchange value. Degradation is a productive reworking of economic value' (2014, p. 130). That is to say, in context of land grabbing, 'governments and investors are in the business of repurposing degraded tropical forests for export-oriented food and biofuel at the expense of local land users' (ibid., p. 131), deploying a 'marginal land narrative' (Nalepa and Bauer, 2012, p. 404). But as Goldstein points out 'incorporating degraded tropical forests into new circuits of resource production necessitates abstracting nonlinear ecologies into a single, simplified land use category' (2014, p. 132). Reworking of economic value, here, means assigning a generic price to particular ecologies, to facilitate market environmentalism.

Further, this process invokes an 'economy of repair' to complement resource conservation: 'The economy of repair is embedded within sustainability rhetoric but makes clear that unsustainable use in one location can be repaired by sustainable use somewhere else. Damage inflicted on nature, therefore, creates opportunities for new economic growth, through ecological repair or improvements' (ibid.). To render repair and improvement commensurable, 'science and policy work in tandem to create definitional and methodological equivalence across spaces . . . as generic abstractions that can then be brought into the realm of commodification' (ibid.). Goldstein's implication is that forest degradation, rendered as a 'commensurable abstraction', enables capitalization, or conservation,[7] through the application of economic value across an ecosystem universe, combining scientific and policy perspectives.

Such 'commensurable abstraction' threatens the override of particular ecologies, their self-organizing qualities, and perhaps practical knowledge of *extant* forest-dwellers in performing what have come to be known as 'ecosystem services'. As Goldstein suggests, such abstractions serve marketization initiatives, which default to measuring 'carbon stock as a primary guideline for determining whether a forest is worth protecting or rehabilitating through REDD+ schemes' (2014, p. 133). And carbon stock serves as a proxy measure for 'ecosystem services', investment in which enables indirect consumption of the environment, via offsets. That is, payment for ecosystem services 'relies on creating market mechanisms that attract investment from areas *requiring* ecosystem services – including maintenance of biodiversity – to areas *providing* these services, for example from urban to rural areas, and from the global "north" to the global "south"' (Sullivan, 2008). Once such a 'carbon market' is in place, given a calculus of economic scarcity (related to the exhaustion of nature), demand for ecosystem services increases their market value 'in ways that *outcompete* other forms and practices of value for the landscapes providing them' (ibid.). Thus market environmentalism creates a new economics of ecological accounting, now institutionalized as an industry in the UN-REDD+ Program: 'reducing emissions from deforestation and degradation in developing countries, and the role of conservation, sustainable management of forests, and enhancement of forest carbon stocks in developing countries'.

Whether calculations encourage land to be set aside for ecological restoration or converted for biofuels, measuring emissions accurately for purposes of standardization is problematic. The Intergovernmental Panel on Climate Change (IPCC) acknowledges 'CO_2 equivalences' are gross oversimplifications: 'the effects and lifetimes of different greenhouse gases in different parts of the atmosphere are so complex and multiple that any straightforward equation is impossible' (Lohmann, 2008, p. 360). *In*commensurability lies in the difference between a virtual fractionation of carbon units as a standardized means of regulating a carbon-based economy, and the actual interactive complexity of carbon cycles, both natural and 'unnatural' (fossil fuel release). 'Sustainable development', as such, is more about sustaining energy-intensive development through (repair or renew) offsets, rather than a wholesale substitution of 'ecological development'.

At the same time, there is the displacement effect, where in addition to attempting to internalize externalized environmental effects via an economy of repair, the ecology of human communities is also to all intents and purposes externalized, justifying resettlement. Thus: 'In many cases, lands perceived to be idle, under-utilised, marginal or abandoned by government and large private operators provide a vital basis for the liveli-hoods of poorer and vulnerable groups, including through crop farming, herding and gathering of wild products' (Cotula et al., 2008, pp. 22–3). Ethiopia is one such case, where the Ethiopian Investment Commission is making over 11 million hectares of land available for lease in the coming years. As Cazenave reports:

> The country intends to become one of the continent's largest exporters by favouring intensive agriculture destined to produce export crops such as rice, corn, oilseed crops as well as cane sugar and jatropha-based biofuel . . . bush, savannah and forest areas are presented as unoccupied. In reality they are often areas of traditional land for pastoralism and shifting cultivation. Ethiopia has adopted a villagization policy in order to empty these spaces . . . tens of thousands of peasants are seeing their natural resources confiscated in favour of a few, large commercial farms. (2016, p. 12)

Land grab-driven villagization in Africa, is the counterpart of China's elimination of over one million rural villages in the first decade of this century. By 2030, 300 million more Chinese peasants are to be 'urbanized', leading to the creation of one billion city dwellers (Shepard, 2015). China has taken the lead in anticipating food insecurity from climate change by purchasing or leasing large tracts of land in Africa and South America, 'introducing industrial agricultural practices that damage the soil, the water supply and the rivers' (Climate News Network, 2016). So a large-scale Chinese urbanization project depends, in part, on land grabbing offshore where a matching villagization process shows the global com-plementarities of the development narrative in an era of climate change. Not only is agro-industrialization itself a substantial contributor to GHG emissions, but such enclosure contributes to an unequal redistribution of food security. Both effects constitute the current development crisis.

PRECARIOUS DEVELOPMENT AND FOOD INSECURITY

A centrepiece of modern development has been the effective 'decoupling' of urbanization from industrialization, with the familiar 'planet of slums' mushrooming across the global South (Davis, 2006). A rural-urban migra-tion script assumed an unlimited supply of labour for urban industrial development (Lewis, 1954; Rostow, 1960). While this relationship may have held for initial generations in the nineteenth and twentieth centuries, technological change (resulting in farmer eviction, and capital-intensive manufacturing) and growing capital mobility in search of cheaper global labour have spawned informal urban economies as people lose secure means of livelihood. Neoliberal policies of economic austerity have in turn shorn these populations of public amenities.

Recent intensification of land acquisition by investors and financial houses attests to how the 'food security' trope is driving current development initiatives. Land deals are framed by discourses of population growth, 'yield gaps' in rural areas of the global South, market access for 'smallholders', and 'green revolution' techno-politics. Land grabs, promoted by investors and governments separately and together, expand large-scale industrial agriculture with standardized inputs to produce for global markets, at the expense of low-input farming communities and domestic food security,[8] and deepening industrial agriculture's climate change impacts.[9]

The parallel process of rural depopulation contributes to the making of a global labour force – living in the interstices of cities (slums) and the relational spaces of urban-rural seasonal migration, and the remittance economy, as migrant labourers send money back to their villages. Such precarious existence for working people has intensified across the world, as states and firms pursue 'comparative advantage' in cheap labour sourcing. While regional trajectories may diverge, a common assumption is that small-scale farming systems need replacing, rather than revitalizing. This perspective informs the UN High Level Panel (formed in conjunction with the UN's new Sustainable Development Goals initiative), which stated:

> The world is now more urban than rural, thanks to internal migration. By 2030 there will be over one billion more urban residents and, for the first time ever, the number of rural residents will be starting to shrink. This matters because inclusive growth emanates from vibrant and sustainable cities, the only locale where it is possible to generate the number of good jobs that young people seek. (UNDESA, 2010)

The High Level Panel went on to observe that 'environment and development were never properly brought together', leading to a questionable proposal that 'because we "treasure what we measure" an important part of properly valuing earth's natural abundance is to incorporate it into accounting systems'. Such a vision extends control over nature in the name of private interest, foreclosing other meanings and uses of land, and privileging investor rights over land-user rights in the name of 'feeding the world'. Ironically, not only does this threaten the food security of over two billion humans dependent on small-scale farming systems across the global South, but also this vision would threaten to erase low-input farming practices that can limit climate change and ecosystem depletion (De Schutter, 2011). This is a question of livelihood and cultural rights as much as of retaining more agro-ecological farming practices.

In this context, counter-trends of 're-peasantization', involving elaboration of 'nested local markets', localized food systems, seed networks, and food sovereignty movements inform an alternative paradigm of food security (Ploeg, 2013; Andrée et al., 2014; Desmarais, 2015; Duncan, 2015). This paradigm depends on farmer/peasant persistence rather than an emptying countryside, and, as a corollary, advocates restoring landscape ecology rather than capitalizing land as a financial asset (for example Hart et al., 2015). It rests on an emerging consensus that organic/agro-ecological farming, if adequately supported, could indeed provision an expanding global population at the same time as it would reduce chemical use, and restore soil and water health (Pretty et al., 2005; Badgley et al., 2007; Perfecto et al., 2009). It would model 'sustainability' as an alternative ecological practice to the market or 'economic rationality' of the development paradigm.

The food sovereignty movement gives voice to this ecological sensibility. Unlike the 'food security' dictates of the food regime, 'food sovereignty' is not a vision premised on an abstracted concept of value. Rather than privileging a universal (reductionist) metric of price to value social and ecological relationships, the movement anticipates a political ontology directly valuing self-organizing ecological practice through networks of cooperation (Holt-Giménez, 2006), including repairing the so-called 'metabolic rift' (Schneider and McMichael, 2010). Thus, Jésus León Santos, the head of a Mixtex organization known as CEDICAM (Mexico), characterized *milpa* agriculture: 'It's not a way of improving nature – it's a way of getting closer to the processes of nature, getting as close as possible to what nature does' (quoted in Canby, 2010, p. 36).

Emulating natural processes, at this juncture, combines refining farming knowledge (agro-ecology) with resistance to both the methods and impacts of industrial agriculture.[10] Across the world there is a growing recognition of the significance *and persistence* of smallholder agriculture, termed the 'return of the peasants': 'In countries like Ethiopia, India or the Democratic Republic of Congo the number of small farms has doubled during the last three decades, because people had no alternative' (Hoering, 2008, p. 7). It is estimated that there are upwards of 500 million small farms accounting for two billion people, 80 per cent of the land used for agriculture, and providing 50 per cent of the world's food (ibid., p. 8; ETC, 2009). According to Ploeg's research in Europe, China and Latin America, 're-peasantization' is a reality today – understood as a form of resistance to the indebtedness and de-skilling impacts of commodity farming (2013, pp. 127–9).

Such resistance is expressed in progressive elimination of commercial inputs (fertilizers, seeds, pesticides) as a debt-reduction strategy and bid for autonomy from market-driven relationships that subordinate farming to standardized (and increasingly expensive) inputs and outputs. In Ploeg's terms, decommodification of farming allows enlargement of the farmer's 'ecological capital', by which s/he restores and renews biological farming. Increased pluri-activity serves as a supplementary source of income, contributing to agricultural multi-functionality (with implications for rural economic vitality). Self-organization provides an alternative paradigm to the value relations of the agribusiness complex, or 'food empires' (Ploeg, 2009). Fundamental to this process is the 'return to nature', with agro-ecology reflecting and informing newly emerging practices of husbanding ecological capital (ibid., p. 71). Ecological capital is strengthened not simply via resources, but also via 'the relations and networks that govern their mobilization, use and valorization' (ibid., p. 31) such as farmer exchanges of seed and cooperative engagement in ecosystem management (Da Già, 2012).

Arguably, the peasant mobilization of the last two decades is one significant response to the deterioration of ecosystems and the redistribution of food security towards global consumers and agro-mercantilist states (McMichael, 2013a). It has inspired a food sovereignty movement that reaches beyond rural communities into urban centres, where urban gardening and reciprocal provisioning systems are consolidating with the goal of linking food security to soil and producer security (Patel, 2009; McMichael, 2014), and into global forums such as the FAO's Committee on World Food Security (Claeys, 2015; Duncan, 2015; McKeon, 2015).

While peasantries/small producers are destined to disappear in the development narrative, this new mobilization endeavours to recover ecological rationality and showcase it, inspiring an environmental and human rights activism across the world. It is this movement that prompts the inversion of the method of political economy insofar as it privileges a politics of agrarian reform, indigenous rights and 'land sovereignty' (Borras and Franco, 2012) aimed at restoring customary land rights and repairing ecosystems. That is, this broad counter-movement advocates socio-ecological reproduction, offering an alternative methodological directive – with ecology as the point of departure for a reformulated understanding of development.

CONCLUSION

As outlined above, the development narrative is deeply implicated in a contemporary ecological crisis. In material terms this is evidenced in ecosystem degradation and climate change. As Short characterizes it:

> One of the central ecological contradictions of capitalism is the exponential increase in the throughput of materials and energy needed by the relentless 'need' for growth and the natural limits of production. Disequilibrium exists between capitalism's ferocious pace in the throughput of energy and materials and nature's laws, temporal rhythms and metabolic cycles, which eventually provokes an inevitable shortage of materials and an accumulation crisis. (2016, p. 55)

In material terms, this crisis encourages 'extreme energy' exploration (Short, 2016), often requiring new bouts of land enclosure and toxification. In epistemic terms, this crisis generates climate denial and schemes to commodify nature – both expressing human alienation from natural process. As Kovel puts it:

> Our 'human nature' is to be both part of the whole of nature and also distinguished from it by what we do to it. This boundary is called *production*; it is the species-specific activity that defines us, and its outcome is the economy, the polity, our culture, religion and the way we inhabit our bodies . . . We do not have an environmental crisis, then, but an ecological crisis, in the course of which our bodies, ourselves, and the whole of external nature are undergoing severe perturbations. (2007, pp. 14–15)

Ultimately, then, our participation in a development crisis is by virtue of our ambivalent relation to non-human nature. And the way to resolve this conundrum is not only to reduce our ecological footprint, but also to progressively embrace a sentient episteme resituating our understanding of our place on Earth. This would approximate to what might be termed an 'ecology of development' in which humans learn to bend their extraordinary skills and earthly impact towards ensuring natural integrity, and social equality.

NOTES

1. Thanks are due to Marcus Taylor and Jenny Goldstein for helpful comments on a previous draft, and to Mary Hyland for her proofreading acumen. This work was supported by the Ministry of Education of the Republic of Korea and the National Research Foundation of Korea (NRF-2016S1A3A2924243).
2. This refers to the Jevons paradox, where greater efficiency of resource use does not

necessarily reduce resource use rather it tends to increase the rate of consumption of that resource.

3. Capital's extractive imperatives generate tension 'between economic time, which proceeds according to the quick rhythm imposed by capital circulation and the interest rate, and geochemical-biological time controlled by the rhythms of Nature ... expressed in the irreparable destruction of Nature and of local cultures which value its resources differently' (Martinez-Alier, 2002, p. 215).

4. Thus the World Economic Forum published a report entitled *Biodiversity and Business Risk*, noting that 'Global warming may dominate headlines today. Ecosystem degradation will do so tomorrow' – the damage in 2008 amounting to one-third of the profits of the 3,000 largest public companies (Jowit, 2010, p. 17).

5. Such as the proliferation of 'payment for environmental services' and carbon pricing – both of which have salience in regulating markets, but which are fictions since variable natural processes/cycles cannot be fractionated and standardized (McAfee, 2012).

6. The so-called 'metabolic rift' refers to the ongoing severing of nutrient cycles in agriculture as humans migrate from countryside to city (Foster, 1999), mixed farming is replaced by chemical farming as 'biophysical override' (Weis, 2007), and ecological farming practices disappear (Schneider and McMichael, 2010).

7. MacDonald's ethnography of the selection of conservation sites across the world by the International Union for Conservation of Nature (IUCN) comes to the conclusion that the commodification of nature renders 'conservation an instrument for the accumulation of capital and a vehicle through which capital interests could gain access to sites of "nature as capital"' (2013, p. 234).

8. Note that 'smallholders are a particular focus of [a commercialization] strategy because they comprise the majority of the world's farmers, occupy 60 per cent of arable land and produce more than 80 per cent of the food consumed in the developing world' (Taylor, 2015, p. 103).

9. Estimates vary according to what is counted, but a reasonable estimate is more than 20 per cent of GHG emissions (McMichael et al., 2007).

10. Note that this is not confined to small farmers, as practitioners of large-scale 'conventional' agriculture are replacing monocultures with crop rotations, nitrogen-fixing cover crops and so on (Levidow, 2015). And while the vast majority of small-scale producers reside in the global South, the US, the UK, France, the Netherlands and New Zealand for example have a percentage of small farms in the range of 10–25 per cent (Hilmi, 2012, p. 69).

REFERENCES

Andrée, P., J. Ayres, M.J. Bosia and M.-J. Massicotte (eds) (2014), *Globalization and Food Sovereignty: Global and local change in the new politics of food*. Toronto: University of Toronto Press.

Badgley, C., J. Moghtader, E. Quintero, E. Zakem, M.J. Chappell, K. Aviles-Vazquez, A. Samulon and I. Perfecto (2007), Organic agriculture and the global food supply. *Renewable Agriculture and Food Systems*, vol. **22** (2), pp. 86–108.

Borras, S.M. and J. Franco (2012), A 'Land Sovereignty' alternative? Towards a peoples' counterenclosure. TNI Agrarian Justice Programme Discussion Paper, July.

Borras, S.M. Jr., R. Hall, I. Scoones, B. White and W. Wolford (2011), Towards a better understanding of global land grabbing: an editorial introduction. *Journal of Peasant Studies*, vol. **38** (2).

Boyd, R. (2006), Labour's response to the informalization of work in the current restructuring of global capitalism: China, South Korea and South Africa. *Canadian Journal of Development Studies*, vol. **27** (4), pp. 487–502.

Canby, P. (2010), Retreat to subsistence. *The Nation*, 5 July, pp. 30–36.

Cazenave, C. (2016), *Land Inc*. Paris: Éditions Intervalles.

Claeys, P. (2015), *Human Rights and the Food Sovereignty Movement. Reclaiming Control*. London and New York: Routledge/Earthscan.

Climate News Network (2016), Food supply fears spark China land grab. Available at: https://climatenewsnetwork.net/food-supply-china-land-grab/.

Cotula, L., N. Dyer and S. Vermeulen (2008), Fuelling Exclusion? The Biofuels Boom and Poor People's Access to Land. International Institute for Environment and Development (IIED) and Food and Agricultural Organization (FAO).

Da Già, E. (2012), Seed diversity, farmers' rights, and the politics of repeasantization. *International Journal of Sociology of Agriculture and Food*, vol. **19** (2), pp. 229–42.

Davis, M. (2006), *Planet of Slums*. London: Verso.

De Schutter, O. (2011), Agroecology and the Right to Food. Report presented at 16th Session of the United Nations Human Rights Council [A/HRC/16/49]. Available at: http://www.ohchr.org/en/NewsEvents/Pages/DisplayNews.aspx?NewsID=10819&LangID=E.

Desmarais, A.A. (2015), The gift of food sovereignty. *Canadian Food Studies*, vol. **2** (2), pp. 154–63.

Duncan, C. (1996), *The Centrality of Agriculture. Between Humankind and the Rest of Nature*. Montreal and Kingston: McGill-Queens University Press.

Duncan, C. (2007), The practical equivalent of war? Or, using rapid massive climate change to ease the great transition towards a new sustainable anthropocentrism. Available at: http://globetrotter.berkeley.edu/GreenGovernance/papers/Rapid%20Climate%20Change. pdf (accessed 17 September 2008).

Duncan, J. (2015), *Global Food Security Governance. Civil Society Engagement in the Reformed Committee on World Food Security*. London and New York: Routledge/ Earthscan.

Escobar, A. (2004), Beyond the Third World: imperial globality, global coloniality and anti-globalisation social movements. *Third World Quarterly*, vol. **25** (1), pp. 207–30.

ETC (2009). Who Will Feed Us? ETC Group Communiqué, 102. Available at: www.etcgroup. org.

Fairbairn, M. (2014), 'Like gold with yield': evolving intersections between farmland and finance. *Journal of Peasant Studies*, vol. **41** (5), pp. 777–95.

Foster, J.B. (1999), Marx's theory of the metabolic rift: classical foundations for environmental sociology. *American Journal of Sociology*, vol. **105** (2), pp. 366–405.

Friedmann, H. (2006), A comment on Henry Bernstein's 'Is there an agrarian question in the 21st century'? *Canadian Journal of Development Studies*, vol. **XXVII** (4), pp. 461–6.

Goldstein, J.E. (2014), The afterlife of degraded tropical forests. New value for conservation and development. *Environment and Society. Advances in Research*, vol. **5**, pp. 124–40.

GRAIN (2016), The global farmland land grab in 2016: How big, how bad? Available at: https://www.grain.org/article/entries/5492-the-global-farmland-grab-in-2016-how-big-how-bad.

Hart, A.K., P. McMichael, J.C. Milder and S.J. Scherr (2015), Multi-functional landscapes from the grassroots? The role of rural producer movements. *Agriculture and Human Values*. doi:10.1007/s10460-015-9611-1

Heubuch, M. (2015), *Landrush. The Sellout of Europe's Farmland*. Greens/European Free Alliance.

Hilmi, A. (2012), Agricultural transition. A different logic. The more and better network. Available at: http://ag-transition.org/pdf/Agricultural_Transition_en.pdf.

Hoering, U. (2008), *Who Feeds the World? The Future is in Small Scale Agriculture*. Bonn: EED Church Development Service.

Holt-Giménez, E. (2006), *Campesino-a-Campesino. Voices from Latin America's Farmer to Farmer Movement for Sustainable Agriculture*. Oakland: Food First Books.

Howden, D. (2008), Africans unite in calling for immediate moratorium on switch from food to fuel, *The Independent*, 16 February. Available at: http://www.independent.co.uk/news/world/africa/africans-unite-in-calling-for-immediate-moratorium-on-switchfrom-food-to-fuel-783011.html.

International Assessment of Agricultural Knowledge, Science and Technology for Development (IAASTD) (2008), Executive summary of the synthesis report. Available at: www.agassess ment.org/docs/SR_Exec_Sum_280508_English.pdf.

International Planning Committee for Food Sovereignty (IPC) (2008), Civil society declaration of Terra Preta forum. 6 June. Available at: http://viacampesina.org.en/index.php/main-issues-mainmenu-27/food-sovereignty-and-trade-mainmenu-38/534-civil-society-declara tion-of-the-terra-preta-forum.

Jowit, J. (2010), Trillion-dollar cost of global pollution. *Guardian Weekly*, 26, 17 February.

Kautsky, K. ([1899] 1988) *The Agrarian Question*, vol. 2. London: Zwan Publications.

Kenis, A. and M. Lievens (2015), *The Limits of the Green Economy. From Reinventing Capitalism to Repoliticising the Present*. London: Routledge.

Keyder, C. (2011), Crisis, underconsumption and social policy, in *The Roots of the Global Financial Meltdown*, eds C. Calhoun and G. Derluguian, pp. 159–84. New York: New York University Press.

Kovel, J. (2007), *The Enemy of Nature: The End of Capitalism or the End of the World?* London: Zed Books.

Latour, B. (1991), *We Have Never Been Modern*. Cambridge, MA: Harvard University Press.

Leff, E. (2016), From the persistence of the peasantry in capitalism to the environmentalism of indigenous peoples and the sustainability of life, in *Peasant Poverty and Persistence in the 21st Century. Theories, Debates, Realities and Policies*, eds J. Boltvinik and S. Mann, pp. 247–68. London: Zed Books.

Lenin, V.I. ([1899] 1972) *The Development of Capitalism in Russia*. Moscow: Progress Publishers.

Levidow, L. (2015), European transitions towards a corporate-environmental food regime: agroecological incorporation of contestation? *Journal of Rural Studies*, vol. **40**, pp. 76–89.

Lewis, W.A. (1954), Economic development with unlimited supplies of labour. *The Manchester School*, vol. **22** (2), pp. 139–91.

Liberti, S. (2013), *Land Grabbing. Journeys in the New Colonialism*. London: Verso.

Lohmann, L. (2008), Carbon trading, climate justice and the production of ignorance: ten examples. *Development*, vol. **51**, pp. 359–65.

MacDonald, K.I. (2013), Nature for money: the configuration of transnational institutional space for environment governance, in *The Gloss of Harmony. The Politics of Policy-Making in Multilateral Organizations*, ed. B. Müller, pp. 227–54. London: Pluto Press.

Malm, A. (2016), *Fossil Capital. The Rise of Steam Power and the Roots of Global Warming*. London and New York: Verso Books.

Martinez-Alier, J. (2002), *The Environmentalism of the Poor. A Study of Ecological Conflicts and Valuation*. Cheltenham, UK and Northampton, MA, USA: Edward Elgar Publishing.

Marx, K. (1973), *Grundrisse*. New York: Vintage.

McAfee, K. (2012), The contradictory logic of global ecosystem services markets. *Development and Change*, vol. **43** (1), pp. 105–31.

McKeon, N. (2015), *Food Security Governance: Empowering Communities, Regulating Corporations*. London: Routledge.

McMichael, A.J., J.W. Powles, C.D. Butler and R. Uauy (2007), Food, livestock production, energy, climate change, and health. *Lancet*, **13**, September.

McMichael, P. (1996), *Development and Social Change. A Global Perspective*. Thousand Oaks, CA: Sage (1st edition).

McMichael, P. (2010), Agrofuels in the food regime. *Journal of Peasant Studies*, vol. **37** (4), pp. 609–29.

McMichael, P. (2012), In the short run are we all dead? A political ecology of the develop-ment climate, in *The Longue Dureé and World-Systems Analysis*, ed. R. Lee, pp. 137–60. Albany: SUNY Press.

McMichael, P. (2013a), Land grabbing as security mercantilism in international relations. *Globalizations*, vol. **10** (1), pp. 47–64.

McMichael, P. (2013b), *Food Regimes and Agrarian Questions*. Halifax: Fernwood Press.

McMichael, P. (2014), The land question in the food sovereignty project. *Globalizations*, vol. **12** (4), pp. 434–51.

Moore, J.W. (2011), Ecology, capital, and the nature of our times: accumulation and crisis in the capitalist world-economy. *Journal of World-Systems Research*, vol. **XVII** (1), pp. 107–46.

Moore, J.W. (2015), *Capitalism in the Web of Life: Ecology and the accumulation of capital*. London and New York: Verso.

Nalepa, R. and D.M. Bauer (2012), Marginal lands: the role of remote sensing in constructing landscapes for agrofuel development. *Journal of Peasant Studies*, vol. **39** (2), pp. 403–22.

Oxfam (2016), *Custodians of the Land, Defenders of our Future. A New Era of the Global Land Rush*. Oxford: Oxfam.

Pascoe, B. (2016), *Dark Emu. Black Seeds: Agriculture or accident?* Broome, WA: Magabala Books.

Patel, R. (2009), What does food sovereignty look like? *Journal of Peasant Studies*, vol. **36** (3), pp. 663–706.

Patel, R. and P. McMichael (2009), A political economy of the food riot. *REVIEW*, vol. **32** (1), pp. 9–35.

Perfecto, I., J. Vandermeer and A. Wilson (2009), *Nature's Matrix: Linking Agriculture, Conservation and Food Sovereignty*. London: Earthscan.

Ploeg, J.D. (2009), *The New Peasantries. Struggles for Autonomy and Sustainability in an Era of Empire and Globalization*. London: Earthscan.

Ploeg, J.D. (2013), *Peasants and the Art of Farming. A Chayanovian Manifesto*. Halifax, Nova Scotia: Fernwood.

Pretty, J., A.D. Noble, D. Bossio, J. Dixon, R.E. Hine, F.W.T. Penning de Vries and J.I.L. Morison (2005), Resource-conserving agriculture increases yields in developing countries. *Environmental Science and Technology*, vol. **40**, pp. 1114–19.

Rostow, W.W. (1960), *The Stages of Economic Growth: A Non-Communist Manifesto*. Cambridge: Cambridge University Press.

Schneider, M. and P. McMichael (2010), Deepening and repairing the metabolic rift. *Journal of Peasant Studies*, vol. **37** (3), pp. 461–84.

Shepard, W. (2015), *Ghost Cities of China*. London: Zed Books.

Short, D. (2016), *Redefining Genocide; Settler Colonialism, Social Death and Ecocide*. London: Zed Books.

Sullivan, S. (2008), Markets for Biodiversity and Ecosystems: Reframing Nature for Capitalist Expansion? Event organized by the International Institute for Environment and Development, and the IUCN Commission on Environmental, Economic, and Social Policy, Fourth World Conservation Congress, Barcelona.

Taylor, M. (2015), *The Political Ecology of Climate Change Adaptation*. London: Routledge/Earthscan.

Tomich, D. (2004), *Through the Prism of Slavery. Labor, Capital and the World Economy*. Lanham, MD: Rowman and Littlefield.

UNDESA (2010), The Millennium Development Goals Report 2010. Available at: http://www.unfpa.org/public/site/global/lang/en/pid/6090.

United Nations (2005), *Ecosystems and Human Well-being. Millennium Ecosystem Assessment*. Washington, DC: Island Press.

Weis, T. (2007), *The Global Food Economy: The battle for the future of farming*. London: Zed Books.

Weis, T. (2010), The accelerating biophysical contradictions of industrial capitalist agriculture. *Journal of Agrarian Change*, vol. **10** (3), pp. 315–41.

Zierler, D. (2011), *The Invention of Ecocide: Agent Orange, Vietnam and the scientists who changed the way we think about the environment*. Athens, GA: University of Georgia Press.

3. Development and imperialism: rethinking old concepts for a new age
Rowan Lubbock

INTRODUCTION

At the turn of the millennium, on 8 September 2000 in the United Nations headquarters in New York, the world's political leaders officially pledged to tackle a number of pressing socio-economic issues, including poverty, hunger and gender inequality, among others. Thus, the Millennium Development Goals (MDGs) were signed into history as a significant political effort at the global level to tackle the long-standing problems of international development. The projected time frame for the MDGs was 15 years after their signing, with 2015 marking the crucial measure of progress. Yet from the publication of the UN's 2015 MDG report last year, it appears that the last decade and a half have produced, at best, mixed results (United Nations, 2015). Interestingly, the preambular chapter to the report, entitled 'Measure what we treasure: sustainable data for sustainable development', emphasizes the crucial role of data collection, monitoring and analysis for tackling global development initiatives. Without progress in this area, the report notes, 'the poorest people in these countries often remain invisible' (ibid., p. 11). And yet, as other scholars have demonstrated, the use of data and statistics in measuring poverty, hunger and other indicators depends, to a significant degree, on the ways in which policy experts frame these problems. From the ad hoc manipulation of time frames (retroactive measuring) or 'rock-bottom' measures of poverty (the dollar-a-day paradigm), to the more general trend of simplifying or reifying social phenomena (the 'GDP illusion'), those in control of information, knowledge and discourse remain in a position of considerable power and privilege with respect to exactly what is measured and treasured (Saith, 2006; Fukuda-Parr et al., 2014; Hickel, 2016). The sum total of these distortions is that, *by its own statistical standards*, many of the social indicators measured by the MDG framework have actually *worsened* (Hickel, 2016).

In this chapter, I will argue that one way to think about the current impasse of global development is through a longer historical view of how the 'idea' of development has evolved during the epoch of 'modernity'.

This is not an arbitrary scholastic choice, but rather a window into the deeper connections between power and knowledge that has significantly shaped the geopolitical relations between what we have come to call the Global 'North' and 'South'. In short, thinking through the geographical distribution of poverty and plenty requires a concerted focus on the phenomenon of *imperialism* as a specific material dynamic and organizing principle of international relations.

The social sciences (at least among critical approaches) have long argued that the process of imperialism has been the key mechanism in forging the modern-day geography of 'centre-periphery' (Wallerstein, 1980; Arrighi, 1983), 'first world and third world' (Petras, 1980; Furedi, 1994) or zones of 'development and underdevelopment' (Frank, 1969; Kay, 1975). More mainstream approaches, which to varying degrees carry greater affinity (and institutional proximity) with the corridors of power and decision-making, have naturally sought to view this process of developmental divergence through more ideologically acceptable terminology, such as 'stages of development' and 'take-off' (Rostow, 1960), 'killer apps' (Ferguson, 2012) or 'political order' (Fukuyama, 2015).

With the proliferation of Western-led military interventions in the Middle East region at the turn of the twenty-first century, mainstream scholarship displayed an increasing ease with the term 'imperialism' and 'empire' as a way of grasping the nature of international relations in the new millennium (Cooper, 2002; Ignatieff, 2003; Ferguson, 2004). However, as I will show in this chapter, we cannot simply reduce imperialism to the use of overt coercive power against other, less powerful states or societies. To do so would be to miss, not only the *changing forms* assumed by imperialism over the centuries but, more crucially, the ways in which imperial geopolitics have historically come to shape, and continue to shape, the very problems of development that the UN is attempting to solve (cf. Jahn, 2005).

In order to open up this deeper relationship between development and imperialism, the chapter will proceed through several sections. The first section (Dreams of empire, dreams of progress: origins of 'modern' development) will firstly briefly unpack what the 'modern' discourse of development entails, and what consequences this has carried for the evolution of international relations over the past few centuries. What distinguishes this historical 'moment' from all other geopolitical orders is the inherently linear perspective adopted by early modern philosophers and political economists, which entailed notions of 'progress' without temporal or spatial limits. The second section (The development of imperialism and the imperialism of development) will then examine some of the first explicit theories of imperialism which emerged during the late nineteenth century. These thinkers, most of whom arose out of the newly formed international communist movement, sought to concretely link the dynamics of capitalist development with the geopolitical relations between European states (imperialist competition), and between Europe and the non-European world (imperialist domination). In section three (Global Cold War: the imperialism of development perfected), we will see how the Cold War bifurcation after 1945, between the communist 'East' centred on the Soviet Union, and the capitalist 'West' centred on the US, perpetuated this dynamic even further, though this time under the dominance of 'developmentalism'. Section four (Post-Cold War (dis)order and the rise of neoliberal discipline) will then look at how the dynamic of development and imperialism substantially altered with the collapse of the Soviet Union, after which the practice and discourse of 'neoliberalism' came to occupy an undeniably hegemonic position through the re-articulation of state-market relations and the (re)emergence of finance. Section five (Capitalism with a human face: towards the post-Washington consensus) will show how the power of Western-dominated forms of development has steadily diluted over the past two decades. From the largely independent development path sought by China to the rise of the 'post-Washington Consensus', the contemporary geography of development has recently taken a more autonomous role. The final section will then examine this neo-developmental turn in the context of Latin America's new left. And while this process has forged new ideas and practices that attend to the specific challenges faced by the Global South, the persistence of imperialism continues to complicate the struggle against the 'empire of capital' (Wood, 2005).

Before we embark on our investigation, we are faced with the unenviable task of specifying conceptual definitions. I would argue, at least for the sake of brevity, that 'development' is a word so general (the basic process in the 'movement of change' governing an object or system of objects) that we can simply sharpen our understanding of 'development' as and when the social or historical context requires. With 'imperialism', however, matters become more complicated. As the historian Bernard Porter notes, 'Whole books have been written simply on the way the term's meanings have changed' (Porter, 2004, p. 8). This, of course, is complicated by the fact that one's semantic interpretation will be heavily guided by the theories and concepts one already intends to pursue. Let me therefore offer at least a *generalized* understanding of imperialism, from which we will be better able to track its historically specific forms. I will take 'empire' and 'imperialism' to simply refer to the static and dynamic aspects of geopolitical hierarchy (cf. Colás, 2007). In this sense, 'imperialism' is the *process* by which social relations between different territorial communities (of whichever type) come to be formed in a hierarchal structure; the territorial *extent* of this hierarchy, the 'empire', is therefore always constituted by some 'imperial centre', as the very seat of empire. As we will come to see, this geopolitical hierarchy need not always entail direct territorial management of subordinate territories, while the changing forms of imperialism and empire tend to move in relation to the variable social struggles, material conditions and discursive structures that underpin the evolving notions of 'development'.

DREAMS OF EMPIRE, DREAMS OF PROGRESS: ORIGINS OF 'MODERN' DEVELOPMENT

The idea of development in what we now call 'the West' has an especially long lineage, going back to Ancient Greek thought and the philosophy of St Augustine (Rist, 2008, pp. 28–34).[1] Yet it was not until the slow and protracted emergence of 'modernity' during the fourteenth and fifteenth centuries that the notion of development became a distinctly *human* concern. The rise of Protestantism in particular enabled a new vision of human agency within Christian Europe, which conceived human (manual) labour not as the antithesis of a virtuous life (as with Aristotle), nor as some atonement for 'original sin' (as with Augustine), but rather as a specific way of serving both God and the community (Peet and Hartwick, 2009, p. 25; cf. Busch, 2000, pp. 13–14). Moreover, the new intellectual and scientific context of early modernity conceived the notion of 'development' through the prism of *cumulative progress*, and the steady accumulation of knowledge, technology, 'reason' and, ultimately, power (Dupré, 2004, p. 188). Henceforth, 'development' would be no longer hemmed in by nature's bounds, nor God's will, but set free towards the *infinite horizon* of intellectual discovery and geographical expansion.

None of this, however, should imply a supposed superiority or divine uniqueness of European development. As many authors have argued, Euro-centric notions of modernity have systematically obscured the significant roles played by the Eastern and Islamic civilizations in Europe's emergence (Goody, 1996; Hallo, 1996; Hobson, 2004; Anievas and Nişancıoğlu, 2015). There can be no doubt that by the sixteenth century Europe was the ultimate 'periphery' of the great pan-Eurasian trade network centred on China (Abu-Lughod, 1989). Many of Europe's scientific 'discoveries', on the other hand, were intimately bound up with the importation of Islamic scientific advances and the Indian number system (Swetz, 1989; Saliba, 2007). Nevertheless, we can discern some of the unique characteristics of Europe's expansion during the early modern era, which provided the background for the emergence of 'Enlightenment' discourses of development (Duchesne, 2011); these would include the ocean-borne quests for precious metals (with which to trade with the more developed East) and the steady militarization of commercial traffic and financial intermediation (Arrighi, 1994; Vilar, 2011), all of which became predicated upon the *quantifiable* nature of everyday life, and hence the rise of *abstraction* as the organizing discourse of modernity (Crosby, 1997).

Yet the colonial encounter with other peoples and societies posed a problem for European empires: how could God's kingdom, deemed universal and infinite, accommodate those who had no knowledge of God, nor the 'pious' conception of industrious labour and 'scientific discovery'? Francis Bacon, variably deemed the 'father' of secular science, would resolve this problem by reducing the contrast between Europe and its colonial 'Other' to developmental standards: 'Consider the abyss which separates the life of men in some highly civilized region of Europe from that of some savage . . . this is the effect not of soil, not of climate, not of physique, but of the arts' (Bacon, cited in Busch, 2000, p. 14). Categories of ethnic 'pseudo-speciation' were therefore seen, not as immutable characteristics, but rather as coordinates of geopolitical 'Othering' that seemingly necessitated colonial domination for the sake of raising the civilizational standard for non-European peoples. Thus, from John Locke in the seventeenth century to Rudyard Kipling in the late nineteenth, transplanting European ideas of 'individual property' towards the rest of the world became a necessary 'burden' of the white-settler West in its pursuit of 'developing' colonial subjects, and in the process making a 'paradise' of the world (cf. Duchesne, 2011, pp. 1–2; van der Pijl, 2014, p. 1).

THE DEVELOPMENT OF IMPERIALISM AND THE IMPERIALISM OF DEVELOPMENT

The rise of 'national economies', as the central unit of classical political economy, was from the start fundamentally premised on the geopolitical subjugation of other peoples and societies. In carrying forward the older practice of colonial conquest based on the extension of trade networks or the rush for precious metals, the non-Western world would go on to become the material foundation of the Atlantic world's developmental trajectory (Bairoch, 1993, pp. 85–6),[2] as well as the battleground for inter-imperialist competition during the latter part of the nineteenth century.

It is at this moment that we find one of the earliest systematic analyses (and critiques) of European imperialism, in the work of liberal economist John A. Hobson ([1902] 2005). Hobson traced the emergence of capitalist imperialism to the 'parasites' of modern industry: arms manufacturers keen for war, industrial combinations seeking new markets, and financiers with idle funds looking abroad for better returns than they could find at home (ibid., p. 61). Yet, while Hobson heaped scorn upon the capitalist class and 'insane' forms of colonial exploitation, he possessed all of the prejudices of his social class of that time. Hence, his anti-imperialist defence of the Boers against British domination effortlessly slipped into an explicit anti-Semitism (see Cowen and Shenton, 1996, pp. 259–60); on the other hand, while deploring the depredations of militaristic colonial rule, Hobson's view of non-European cultures was couched in the 'modern' European discourse of paternalistic guidance in the development of 'lower races' (Hobson, 2005, p. 229).

With the emergence of 'Marxism' – as both a system of critique of capitalist imperialism, and as a form of anti-imperialist organization in the shape of the international communist movement – the dynamic of capital accumulation and its geopolitical expression *qua* imperialism was explicitly condemned as a vicious hindrance to humanity's *free development*. Thus, while many of the early Marxist critiques of imperialism shared at least a shade of commonality with Hobson's early study (Hobson, 2005, pp. 75–9; cf. Bukharin, [1917] 1929, pp. 108–9; Lenin, [1917] 1999, p. 92; Luxemburg, [1913] 2003, chapter 31), their philosophical premises led to radically different political conclusions. What distinguished Marxist analyses of capitalist imperialism was the way in which they located the driving force of social and geopolitical dynamics in the specific class antagonisms constituent of them.[3] Thus, the exploitation of living labour, the systematic degradation of the ecological landscape, and the ceaseless forces of economic and geopolitical competition driving the urge to accumulate capital without end entailed not only suffering of the great majority of the world's population, but the continual recurrence of economic crisis and inter-state war. For Rosa Luxemburg, the contradictions of capitalism meant that '[a]t a certain stage of development there will be no other way out than the application of socialist principles' (Luxemburg, 2003, p. 447). This was, in effect, the central rallying cry for the international communist movement, despite its various internal debates and divisions.

At the conclusion of the first great inter-imperialist conflict, World War One, US President Woodrow Wilson would draft his Fourteen Points programme for the structural reorganization of Europe's political geography – from territorial empires to independent nation-states, representing smaller nationalities – and in the process set the stage for an epochal shift in the relationship between development and imperialism. Wilson's promotion of national independence partially coincided with Lenin's argument for self-determination, yet each led to irreconcilable political stances. According to Wilson's vision, 'every people should be left free to determine its own polity, its own way of development, unhindered, unthreatened, unafraid, the little along with the great and powerful' (Wilson, cited in van der Pijl, 2014, p. 63). Yet this was more than an exercise in liberal utopianism; rather, it was a geopolitical reaction to the communist revolution in Russia (Gardner, 1984), which threatened to derail the Western world's regime of 'sovereign-equality' (superintended by unequal socio-economic relations) by offering the peoples of the world the same opportunity for both self-determination and 'the satisfaction of toiling humanity's wants' (Luxemburg, 2003, p. 447), rather than the mere accumulation of capital.

Despite the promise of the international communist movement, however, the consequences of uneven development (both within Russia and throughout the world system), and the added pressures of civil war in Russia (with counter-revolutionary forces actively backed by Western states), led to the implosion of the communist dream in the newly christened Soviet Union, which subsequently 'degenerated' into something unique: not quite a capitalist state in the conventional sense, and certainly not the personification of the communist vision (see van der Linden, 2007). However one characterizes the Soviet Union, it had, by the time of Stalin's ascension to power, firmly entrenched the linear view of historical development (stagism), as well as a more imperialistic turn that in many ways mimicked the capitalist variety, even if on a smaller scale (Cliff, 1970). Hence, the Soviet Union seemed to internalize many of the hallmarks associated with the Western bourgeois civilization it so stridently denounced. We can therefore view the period between the late nineteenth century and the mid-twentieth century as a cumulative transformation from the development of imperialism towards the imperialism of development.

GLOBAL COLD WAR: THE IMPERIALISM OF DEVELOPMENT PERFECTED

At the close of World War Two, the US was the undisputed leader of the capitalist liberal order. Though post-war geopolitics is usually framed as a 'bi-polar' international system split between capitalist West and communist East, the world was in fact split into three. The 'Third World' thus stood in contrast to the first (Western) and second (Soviet) segments of the global system (Tomlinson, 2003). Yet it was the presence of the communist 'second world', which (despite its many flaws) represented an alternative development model to the peoples of the 'Third World'. In contrast to the Western vision of the 'invisible hand' of the market guiding the process of capital accumulation, the communist approach put the 'strong state' at the centre of its development model, whereby the strengthening of the social fabric (housing, health care, education, and so on) would be consciously planned, rather than left to the chance of market forces. For US policy makers, maintaining an adequate defence against the 'communist menace' was therefore premised on the fundamental success of its own (capitalist) development model; this is precisely what was meant when George Kennan, in his famous 'X' article for *Foreign Affairs*, wrote, 'the palsied decrepitude of the capitalist world is the keystone of Communist philosophy' (Kennan, 1947, p. 581).

This type of strategic thinking was, at least initially, entirely concentrated on the European theatre (referred to by Truman as the 'forefront of civilization'), with the preparation of the Marshall Plan and the construction of NATO – in effect, the economic and military planks in Truman's anti-communist strategy. It was almost by chance that a low-level staffer suggested to Truman the importance of including the non-Western countries in his post-war planning agenda (Rist, 2008, p. 70). Thus, Truman's 'Point Four' of his inaugural address seemingly ushered in a new phase in the discourse and practice of international development. As he proclaimed:

> More than half the people of the world are living in conditions approaching misery. Their food is inadequate. They are victims of disease. Their economic life is primitive and stagnant. Their poverty is a handicap and a threat both to them and to more prosperous areas. (Truman, 1949)

He continued: 'For the first time in history humanity possess the knowledge and skill to relieve the suffering of these people', a feat that would be accomplished with the 'imponderable resources in technical knowledge [which] are constantly growing and are inexhaustible' (ibid.).

In these few words, we find the key to unravelling the imperialist mindset during the post-war era. Peoples of the non-Western world are 'victims of disease' (with no regard to how this disease is constantly reproduced through colonial encounters); their poverty becomes a 'threat' (opening up the possibility of *securitizing* or *militarizing* the relations between North and South); while the West's 'imponderable resources' in technical knowhow can provide the solution to poverty in the Global South (though without acknowledging the possibility that the material foundation for this technological infrastructure was built through the exploitation of the non-Western world). As Arturo Escobar noted in his *Encountering Development* (1995), this 'development discourse' became a virtual science and branch of technical specialization within the wider hegemonic constellation of the Cold War order.

As such, the discourse of development had effectively become synonymous with the practice of imperialism. At least in the Asian region, it was through the reassertion of 'traditional' (military) imperialism that the US would seek to maintain Vietnam within the Western orbit through its subordinated position under the 'flying-geese' regional development model, centred on Japan (Kojima, 2000). And yet, despite the numerous imperial 'interventions' exacted by the US military throughout the Global South during the Cold War decades (see Blum, 2004; Westad, 2005), the era of US 'empire' was qualitatively different from that of its predecessors. For what the US sought was the perfection of Wilson's earlier (yet failed) vision of an international system composed of 'equal' sovereign states enmeshed within the transnational flows of 'global' (Western) capital. This latter success can be partially attributed to the establishment of a more substantial infrastructure of 'global governance', embodied within the International Monetary Fund (IMF), the World Bank, GATT (now the World Trade Organization), not to mention the multitude of development bodies working out of the United Nations (UN). Thus, in 1961 the UN had declared the beginning of the 'Decade of Development', necessitated by the fact that, for the whole of the 1950s, and 'in spite of the efforts made', the gap in per capita incomes between the North and South had steadily widened (United Nations, 1961). John F. Kennedy's famed 'Alliance for Progress', launched in the same year, sought to implement the more cooperative side of US development goals in the Latin American countryside, albeit coupled with an imperialistic 'fist of steel' (Smith, 1991, p. 76).[4] Yet, even these efforts were in vain, as 'the results for many developing countries were so disappointing that a second Decade was proclaimed for the 1970s' (Calvert and Calvert, 2007, p. 49). What accounted for such persistent economic weakness among the states of the Global South?

It was precisely this question that prompted the formation of many of the most influential theories of development today. For the 'structuralist' approach to international political economy, based around the leadership of Raúl Prebisch at the UN Economic Commission for Latin America and the Caribbean (ECLAC), the constant deterioration in the terms of trade between manufactures from the centre, and agricultural products from the periphery, of the world economy negated the possibility for national development for the Third World through export policies alone. Peripheral states thus needed to ensure a level of state-led protectionism of their infant industries in order to acquire critical mass. Though eliciting the ire of US policy makers (Bracarense, 2012), structuralist thought at the ECLAC did not fundamentally diverge from the basic tenets of capitalist development. The state was conceived as an autonomous terrain of action that could sporadically intervene in the market place in order to iron out imbalances and sustain social welfare. As a consequence, the ECLAC failed to grasp the *class nature* of the state, the ways in which state institutions reproduced (or attempted to transform) specific class relationships and the geopolitical dynamics that interweave these social struggles (Grigera, 2015). It is therefore of little surprise that the emergence of the famed 'New International Economic Order' (NIEO), proposed by the Group of 77 (G77) states at the UN General Assembly in 1974, would ultimately founder on the unacknowledged contradictions of capitalist development, which the G77 did not fundamentally question, in its drive to secure a (slightly) more favourable share of global wealth.

Dependency theory, however, represented a more radical yet essentially homologous framework to that of the ECLAC. André Gunder Frank became one of dependency theory's most recognizable figures, and his concept of the 'development of underdevelopment' became a cornerstone of 1970s' radical social theory. Yet Frank was not without his critics (see Larrain, 1989, pp. 175–93): Ernesto Laclau offered an early and influential critique of Frank's notion of a dependent periphery by pointing out the inadequacy of starting from the point of view of the relations of circulation between centre and periphery, rather than the truly 'Marxist' approach that would begin with the class structures specific to a given country (Laclau, 1977). Beyond this somewhat scholastic critique, a wider set of debates within Marxist approaches to Third World development would come to question the precise relationship between imperialism and the development of the Global South. This principally took the form of a somewhat controversial argument put forward by Bill Warren (1980), which claimed that imperialism was, in fact, a positive force in the development of peripheral states. Although we cannot rehearse the dimensions and data bound up with Warren's thesis (see Brewer, 1990, pp. 272–84), what is fundamentally at issue in this debate is *what* is being measured, and *how* that measurement is ultimately interpreted (cf. Ayres and Clark, 1998). Thus, even if significant rates of growth could be registered for developing economies during the post-war era, this fails to account for both the unevenness with which this pattern unfolds at the world scale (for example between East Asia and Latin America) and how the replication of the Western development model impacts upon the ecological world. These are two aspects that were at least acknowledged by the early structuralist school of the ECLAC, yet overlooked in Warren's account.

In any event, the shifting contours of the capitalist world economy would soon leave such debates essentially moot. For the resurgence of Western power over the Global South would alter the terms of the debate over imperialist domination from one of dependence to one of discipline.

POST-COLD WAR (DIS)ORDER AND THE RISE OF NEOLIBERAL DISCIPLINE

The onset of neoliberalism was, in many ways, a highly contingent affair, rather than the inevitable triumph of market rationalism, as is implied in Thatcher's phrase, 'there is no alternative'. Through a combination of a systematic fall in the rate of profit across the three nodes of global capitalism (US, Western Germany and Japan), and an explosion of class struggles throughout both the Global North and South, the conjunctural conditions had been laid for the rise of *neoliberal discipline* (Soderberg, 2004a) as the new organizing principle of society across the world. Broadly conceived, neoliberalism can be understood as 'the extension and installation of competitive markets into all areas of life, including the economy, politics, and society' (Birch, 2015, p. 572). Through the universalization of market competition, '[n]eoliberalism thus naturalizes capitalist relations by taking the economic definition of man/woman as the starting point for an integral social science' (van der Pijl, 2006, p. 29). However, such a seemingly benign image of society in fact implies its own immanent violence.

The imposition of neoliberalism took a strikingly brutal turn during its formative period in the Latin American region. Having been dismayed at the rise of Salvadore Allende on the back of a strong worker-peasant class alliance, Chile's right-wing military cadre, led by General Augusto Pinochet and with significant backing from the US State Department, instigated a military coup against the Allende regime for the purpose of fighting 'communism' in the region. This pattern was soon followed in Argentina and Uruguay through the US-sponsored 'anti-communist' terror network known as 'Operation Condor' (McSherry, 2005). As with the neoliberal revolution in the West, the Latin American transition towards this new form of social discipline engendered a radically altered balance of class power, in which the national bourgeoisie (in conjunction with Western transnational capital) would be fully supported by the strong arm of the state against working classes in both the city and countryside.

The more invisible forms of neoliberal violence, however, became instantiated through the rise of *finance*, aided principally by Richard Nixon's de-linking of the US dollar from gold in 1971 in an effort to stave off devaluation as a result of declining profit rates in the US, and thereby tying the monetary base of the world economy to the US currency (the 'dollar standard'). Added to this was an increase in the US real interest rate from around -2 per cent (1979) to an average of 7.5 per cent (1981–5) (Brenner, 2002, p. 50). This fulfilled the desire to re-discipline labour through massive lay-offs: the 'Volcker recession', which followed the interest rate hike, saw a doubling of the US unemployment rate (from 5 to

10 per cent) between 1979 and 1982 (Glyn, 2006, p. 26).[5] The consequence of this shift in US monetary policy was an enormous debt burden heaped on the shoulders of the Global South, which now faced increased rates of interest on its outstanding (dollar denominated) loans. This paved the way for Western finance capital to re-subordinate the periphery of the world economy to the dictates of market discipline. The 'Baker Plan' of 1985 entailed extended credits from the World Bank (in order to service debt payments to private lenders) in exchange for recipient countries undergoing 'Structural Adjustment Programmes' (SAPs). These SAPs included measures that lifted protection from infant industry development, removed price subsidies, reduced social welfare entitlement and saw the rapid rise of domestic interest rates for the sake of inflation control. It was during a US Congressional hearing that the economist John Williamson would testify to the effect that the parameters of the Brady Plan were both desirable and entirely necessary for the economic health of Latin America. In 1989, he presented a conference paper in which his now (in)famous 'Washington Consensus' made its first appearance. By the end of 1992 the World Bank had approved around 267 SAPs, with virtually no change whatsoever in the overall health of the target countries (Soderberg, 2006, p. 110).

Thus, in contrast to the more 'scientific' racist discourse of development during the early twentieth century, and the negotiated corporate-liberal development of the post-war era, neoliberal development manifested itself through the very circuits of finance capital itself, whether via the transfer of funds through international financial institutions or through the global network of private financial entities. Concretely, the dominance of finance can be seen as a crucial mechanism of imperial domination during the post-Cold War years, whose principle effect was periodic and recurring *financial crises*. As Christopher Rude underscores, instability and crisis formation emerge from the inherent economic nature of financial liberalization and speculation that is itself *mediated through fragmented territorial spaces of differing national currencies*, thus forming 'an "imperial chain" of more powerful and less powerful national banking and financial systems' (Rude, 2008, p. 203). Again, the frequency of these crises speaks to the very nature of neoliberal capitalism, and not simply a reflection of mismanagement; as *The Economist* magazine once quipped, '[f]inancial crises seem now to happen with almost monotonous regularity' (*The Economist*, 1999). As systemic crises moved their way through the imperial chain, the opportunities to restructure national economies consequently sprang up with a roughly equivalent regularity.

By the turn of the twenty-first century, geopolitical domination would soon revert to the older forms of imperialism. With the attacks against the US on 11 September 2001, new opportunities had opened for implementing a long-held goal to re-engineer (through military force) the 'troublesome', yet strategically central, Middle East region. Beginning with the bombing of Afghanistan in 2001 and the subsequent invasion and occupation of Iraq in 2003, the Bush administration's turn to 'global policing' (mobilized through the discursive frame of 'pre-emptive' wars) engendered both security concerns with 'rogue states' *and* the further integration of these territories into the circuits of global capital (Harvey, 2003; Roberts et al., 2003).[6] But this did not mean that the Bush administration had abandoned subtler forms of development tutelage perfected throughout the Cold War and neoliberal eras. Rather, security and developmental concerns, repackaged by the Bush administration as the 'Millennium Challenge Account' (MCA), had by this time effortlessly fused into a broader strategy for policing world order (cf. Duffield, 2001; Brainard et al., 2003, p. 8). As Susanne Soderberg (2004b) notes, the MCA was (like the military dimension of Bush's foreign policy) couched in terms of 'pre-emptive development', as recipient countries were now issued development grants that could be withheld until specific quantitative criteria had been satisfactorily achieved, such as liberalization, social investment and good governance.

However, the structures of global development were beginning to move beyond the well-laid plans of Western imperial states. Remarkable rates of economic growth seen in Brazil, Russia, India and especially China (known as the BRIC countries) had formed a new multi-polar structure of the world economy. And the manner in which these economies had climbed the global ladder of wealth and power signalled the inherent fallibility of Washington's way.

CAPITALISM WITH A HUMAN FACE: TOWARDS THE POST-WASHINGTON CONSENSUS

Even before the Bush administration's more muscular approaches to geopolitics and development, the relative failure of neoliberalism's record in the 1980s had in fact prompted a soul-searching exercise among the international financial institutions. This took place during the 1990s in the face of mounting evidence of the limitations of neoliberal orthodoxy – successful state intervention in the Asian region, lagging growth in Africa and Latin America, and steadily widening inequality both within and between states (Öniş and Şenses, 2005, pp. 266–7). A number of prominent economists, among them Joseph Stiglitz, urged a renewed role for the state in directing market economies, hemming in the potential harm of financial flows, and providing a host of public goods (Stiglitz, 1998).

Thus, the 'post-Washington Consensus' reflected a relative rejection of Western policy prescriptions in light of the achievements of economic development and growth seen throughout the so-called BRIC countries. Brazil's many travails during the period of neoliberal restructuring in the 1990s gave way to the arrival of the more progressive 'neo-developmentalist front' with the election of Lula da Silva in 2002, which brought about new supports for the poorest Brazilians, while actively supporting Brazilian capital (Boito and Berringer, 2014). Russia's high growth rates, on the other hand, derived largely from the commodity price spike of the 2000s, allowing the Russian economy to exploit its vast oil and gas reserves, thus super-charging its domestic economy, and moving from services to technology research. India and China – the two 'giants' of the developing world – have enjoyed the highest rates of growth over the past decade, through specialization in service sectors, high-technology design and industrial expansion (Winters and Yusuf, 2007). Moreover, the development of China and India has contributed to an actual fall in the global level of poverty over the past two decades (though it should be noted that if these two countries are taken out of the picture, global poverty levels have actually increased (Kiely, 2008)).

Nevertheless, even these remarkable economic indicators serve to reveal the continuing geo-economic power exerted by the North. As Arrighi et al. (2003) demonstrate, while the Global South (particularly East Asia) has actually overtaken the North in terms of industrial output, it has failed to achieve similar progress in comparable levels of *national income*. Both Ray Kiely (2014) and John Smith (2016) also point out that increased manufacturing in the Global South continuously transfers value to larger capitals in the North, constituting one of the main dynamics of imperialism in the twenty-first century.[7] This again underscores the ways in which certain empirical measurements are touted and celebrated: the GDP 'illusion', for instance (Smith, 2016), which hides the fact that a great deal of the value 'produced' by a developed country is actually generated by the exploitation of workers in the Global South.

Thus, while more autonomous routes have been opened up by the post-Washington Consensus, the turn to 'statist' economic development shares many of the weaknesses seen in the classical structuralist accounts of international economics, as well as in the geopolitical project of NIEO, launched by the G77. In each case, the very political economy of capitalism as a system of exploitative social/ecological relations was never brought into serious question. As such, even the poster child of contemporary development (China) is beginning to enter into a systemic contradiction characteristic of all capitalist development (over-accumulation), with a concomitant rise in the number and frequency of protests and strike waves (Ho-Fung, 2008). Despite the uneven progress throughout the Global

South during the post-Washington Consensus years, the balance of power in the world economy was beginning to shift. Led primarily by the dramatic rise of China, the world economy of the 2000s entered a 'commodity super cycle', which lifted the economies of the Global South, and, in the process, helped underwrite one of the most remarkable political changes of the past 50 years.

POST-LIBERAL DEVELOPMENT AND THE CONTRADICTIONS OF THE NEW LATIN AMERICAN LEFT

The social dislocations exacted upon Latin America during the neoliberal era had in fact created the very conditions for its demise. During the 1990s, a wave of anti-systemic movements spread across the continent, from the *caracazo* riots in Venezuela (1989), to the Zapatista uprising in Mexico (1994), and the 'water wars' in Bolivia (2000) (see Silva, 2009). Each of these brought in their wake new political discourses and electoral parties that sought to express the mood of popular hope for a world beyond neoliberal discipline and US hegemony. A common feature of Latin American states during the twenty-first century was their general antipathy to the Bush administration's unilateralism, as well as a general embrace of the post-Washington Consensus in what some scholars have dubbed the 'post-liberal' turn (Chodor and McCarthy-Jones, 2013). Yet the discourse and practice of anti-imperial geopolitics was most clearly invoked by the late Venezuelan president, Hugo Chávez Frías, especially in relation to the US-backed hemispheric neoliberal project that sought to more fully subordinate the region in the form of the Free Trade Area of the Americas. It was in this context that Chávez, along with Cuban president Fidel Castro, created the Bolivarian Alliance for the Peoples of our America (ALBA), envisaged as an alternative regional institution that would promote the principles of cooperation, solidarity and complementarity over and above those of competition, exploitation and uneven development (ALBA, 2004). Now with 11 member states, the ALBA regional space has launched numerous initiatives, from the development of popular access to higher education, to the formation of 'Grandnational Enterprises', oriented towards satisfying human need, rather than the pursuit of profit (Muhr, 2011; Califano, 2013).

However, Latin America's left and its development strategies remain in a highly contradictory position with respect to the wider capitalist world system. It was the onset of the 'commodities super cycle' of the 2000s that created the central condition of possibility for those countries' high levels of public spending. Due to their specific political projects favouring the popular classes, the region's more left-wing states clustered within the ALBA bloc (particularly Bolivia, Ecuador and Venezuela) have been better able to retain surplus profits from the extraction of their natural wealth than have other states in the region (Higginbottom, 2013). Yet the very fact that these popular forms of development are so heavily dependent upon the exploitation of natural resources has led many to view contemporary Latin America as stuck in a kind of 'new extractivism' (Gudynas, 2010; Veltmeyer and Petras, 2014). Two aspects of the new extractivism in particular severely complicate the stated aim of the ALBA states to achieve a type of 'socialism in the twenty-first century'. Firstly, the capture of surplus profits from the extraction of mineral wealth is ultimately tied to the dynamics of the international capitalist system. In other words, the level of 'ground rent' that extractivist states are able to capture depends fundamentally upon the dynamics of accumulation (and thus levels of demand) that take places in other states. With the onset of the world economic crisis in 2008, rates of accumulation (even in the traditional power-houses such as China) severely diminished, and thus negatively impacted on the magnitude of ground rent available to resource-dependent states. Secondly, the very nature of mining extraction, being territorially sensitive to resource location, often brings the process of production into direct conflict with the integrity of ecological and human landscapes. Thus, both environmental degradation and the threat to indigenous peoples' territorial rights tend to be the contradictory conditions of anti-imperialist/socialist development (Bebbington, 2012).

Venezuela is a stark example of both these structural contradictions of twenty-first century socialism. Firstly, the 'enduring legacy' (Tinker Salas, 2009) of petroleum on Venezuelan society creates a major obstacle in any attempt to move away from oil dependence. While Chávez's 'Bolivarian revolution' sought economic diversification, the contingency of class struggle during the formative years of the Bolivarian Republic led to a series of policy measures that produced a number of unintended consequences. In order to stave off a right-wing offensive in the form of massive capital flight, currency controls were introduced which kept the nation's hard currency under state control, and sold to the private sector at preferential currency rates for the purpose of importing consumer or capital goods. More often than not, however, Venezuela's commercial sectors either import key consumables (notably food staples) and re-sell them at vastly inflated prices, hoard consumer goods for the sake of inflation-fed price speculation, or even engineer fictitious imports (empty containers) for the purpose of maintaining dollars as a store of value (see Yaffe, 2015).[8] Thus, the health of the Venezuelan economy is supported by the continual injection of dollars from ground rent generated by the oil-demand from the rest of the world market. With the recent drop in global petroleum prices, Venezuela can no longer count on this support mechanism in its battle against the 'inflation-depreciation spiral'.[9]

Secondly, Venezuela has, until now, seen fewer tensions between development projects and indigenous communities/social movements in comparison to Bolivia and Ecuador. However, with the fall in oil revenues, the Maduro administration has now sought to exploit the country's natural resources (from gold mining to forestry), which has elicited a concerted outcry from various local communities and social movements (Angarita, 2016; *El Mundo*, 2016). Broadly speaking, whether the production of wealth is predominantly in the form of petroleum or other mineral resources, such forms of uneven development inevitably produce a series of social dislocations that seriously threaten the sustainability of twenty-first century socialism.

CONCLUSION

There are many ways in which this chapter could have been written. Perhaps focusing intensely on a small number of themes in order to draw out their deep and complex inner connections, or narrowing in on a geographically specific area of the world (Latin America has, after all, been a favoured laboratory for the hypothesizing of determinations between development and imperialism). However, I consciously opted for a broad historical approach to the relationship between development and imperialism. This choice was, as noted in the introduction, largely prompted by the desire to show how the various twists and turns of world history have demonstrated a striking constant: that the manner in which we use the language of 'development' significantly shapes and reflects the material processes that bind the world's many societies, states or empires. This is central to an understanding of the interrelations between the idea of development and the practice of imperialism.

The current notion of linear development, and its surrogate of endless progress, thus marked out the rise of the 'modern' epoch, couched in the understanding of *human labour* as the source of moral rectitude and, ultimately, 'value'. These ideas have led effortlessly to broader concepts about humanity itself, and how the European 'Self' has sought to relate to the non-European 'Other'. Such notions of racial dividing lines, and the 'standard of civilization' mobilized by the West at the turn of the twentieth century (Gong, 1984), constituted the founding edifice of international relations as an academic discipline (Vitalis, 2010). The emergent international communist movement would go on to challenge the West's self-proclamation as the guardian of human development, by holding up the principle of self-determination against the hypocrisy of the League of Nations' colonial mandate system. And yet, through a strange twist of fate, the Soviet Union would later go on to become the ultimate 'empire of the periphery' (Kagarlitsky, 2008), with its own imperial interventions into East Germany, Czechoslovakia and Hungary in order to quell popular, working-class rebellions.

With the international system's 'bi-polar' order firmly in place by 1945, the Western ('first') world had to elevate its concept of human civilization to the level of a fully-fledged science for the sake of routing the Soviet 'second world', primarily in waging the battle of ideas over the developmental direction of the 'Third World'. Although always punctuated by military interventions, the Cold War era was most clearly characterized by the scientifically 'objective', and thus politically 'neutral', prognostications of 'modernization theory', which saw its culmination in various geopolitical projects, from the UN's 'Decade of Development' to Kennedy's 'Alliance for Progress'. What these initiatives signalled, however, was not the end of imperialism, but a more perfect instantiation of it, in which the much older claim of 'universal' happiness, wrought by Anglo-Saxon domination, could, at least, fetch a modicum of feasibility behind the new institutions of sovereign equality and national self-determination. And while the structuralist political economy, espoused by various UN intellectuals, would come to challenge the orthodoxy of Western modernization theory, the absence of *class* as an analytical referent in the work of Prebisch and his colleagues would ultimately reflect the demise of the 'Third World' dream of a new international economic order.

From the systemic crisis of the capitalist world economy beginning in the late 1960s, an entirely new class project would be launched as a means of disciplining the unwieldy subjects of the world system, namely, the industrial working class of the Global North. Discursively structured around the sovereignty of the market, and the ontological primacy of *homo economicus*, 'neoliberalism' claimed to be following in the footsteps of the great classical thinkers such as Adam Smith; yet the reality was that, in contrast to Smith's moral philosophy which was based around the primacy of *society*, the neoliberal turn was more fully reflected in Thatcher's early quip that 'there is no such thing as society' (cf. Watson, 2006). Structural Adjustment Programmes, pushed by the Anglo-Atlantic world through the international institutions at their disposal (the IMF and the World Bank), significantly limited the ability of the Global South to act in its own *social* interests.

When seen from a macro-historical perspective, each of these three phases of capitalist 'civilization' ('scientific' racist, liberal/corporate, neo-liberal) can be seen as the steady construction of a type of *global governance*, though one exacted through unequal relationships established between the West and 'the rest'.[10] As Craig Murphy notes, 'Liberal arguments in favor of continued colonization always rely on some argument about a specific, temporary infirmity of the people in question, some reason why they are not, at this time, ready for self-rule' (Murphy, 2005, p. 95). Geopolitical domination could be justified for a whole range of reasons. If it was not because of the 'scientifically' determined backwardness of the non-white races, it was because of the dangerous rejection among some nations in the Global South of the 'objective' measures of modernization theory, or it was necessary to impose financial controls from without until the subservient country got its (fiscal) house in order.

Only with the relatively autonomous rise of China and the BRIC countries and the more radical experiments in popular democracy in Latin America has the Washington Consensus come into question. It is not only the more state-led development drives that have forced a type of auto-critique of many ex-neoliberal thinkers. Neoliberalism's failure to live up to its own claims has given rise to a number of ideological moderations: as the IMF recently noted in a report outlining the failure of liberalized capital flows and fiscal austerity, 'Policymakers, and institutions like the IMF that advise them, must be guided not by faith, but by evidence of what has worked' (Ostry et al., 2016, p. 41). This, then, brings us back to the original problem highlighted at the beginning of this chapter: how do we come to understand 'what works', and what metrics do we use to measure it? Perhaps more importantly, *who is in the position to make and impose these claims in the first place?* These questions, I suggest, help to reveal the inherent relations of conflict, power and authority in the social world, conflicts which today have arguably reached a catastrophic proportion. For even if we record high GDP growth here, and a relative lowering of poverty there, these metrics tell us next to nothing about the problems of social alienation, economic exploitation, consumerism and ecological degradation, factors that have been reproduced throughout the developing world, but whose effects are overwhelmingly suffered by the least powerful. This (often obscured) reality brings into relief once more Luxemburg's claim that, '[a]t a certain stage of development there will be no other way out than the application of socialist principles' (Luxemburg, 2003, p. 447). With the constant warnings pumped out by the scientific community concerning the various thresholds of ecological sustainability humanity has now surpassed, it seems there is little option left other than a radical transformation from an imperialism of development towards the free development of all.

NOTES

1. This Western-centric focus is due to the fact that the chapter's historical rereading is intended to shed light on the *contemporary* international order, which is itself *dominated* by the Western (Atlanticist) world. Such a reading, of course, brackets many other interesting examples of non-Western imperial thought on the nature of humanity and its development, for instance with the ancient Chinese notion of 'All-under-heaven' and the concept of 'family-ness' of the entire world population (see Tingyang, 2006).

2. This often amounted to the conscious destruction of the colonial territory's own domestic industries. The decimation of India's cotton manufacturers, which was a deliberate British policy, ensured that India's place in the international division of labour would be merely to satisfy Britain's interests in acquiring raw cotton, and as a guaranteed market for finished cotton products (Arrighi, [1994] 2010, p. 270). This historical pattern would later inspire the notion of the 'development of underdevelopment'.

3. This difference serves to illustrate the absolute contradiction of Hobson's bourgeois mode of thought. For in locating the organic source of imperialist expansion in the competition within capitalist industry, Hobson suggests that 'an intelligent *laissez-faire* democracy' that effectively underwrote free competition without favouritism to specific special interests would 'soon discard Imperialism' (Hobson, 2005, p. 47). Hence, the solution to imperialism, which springs from capitalist competition, is to ensure . . . capitalist competition!

4. Kennedy was carrying forth an earlier instantiation of US discourse in which 'development' became a major component in its foreign relations. The immediate impact of the Cuban Revolution led Eisenhower's ambassador to the UN, Henry Cabot Lodge, to argue that 'We should focus on the Declaration of Independence rather than on the Communist Manifesto where [the focus] has been . . . and in doing so we should not endeavour to sell the specific word "Capitalism" which is beyond rehabilitation in the minds of the non-white world' (cited in LeFeber, 1993, p. 14). In turn, Kennedy proclaimed to be building 'a hemisphere where all men can hope for a suitable standard of living and all can live out their lives in dignity and in freedom . . . Let us once again transform the American Continent into a vast crucible of revolutionary ideas and efforts' (cited in Grandin, 2007, p. 47). The discursive appropriation of the trope 'revolution' helped to infuse a popular idiom with the hidden metaphorical undertone of the *capitalist* revolution.

5. For a recent study of the relationship between class power and monetary policy-making across 23 OECD countries, see Ho-Fung and Thompson (2016).

6. This strategy ultimately harked back to the earlier time of US imperialism under the presidency of Theodore Roosevelt, which heralded the distinctly (North) American turn to 'anti-imperialist' imperialism (see Holmes, 2007).

7. One of the main socio-spatial arrangements through which this process of value transfer takes place is through the operation of global commodity chains, which has become a widely-debated topic in international political economy circles (see Starosta, 2010).

8. This incentive for fraud or black market transactions has also afflicted a significant number of state-led industries as well.

9. For a good summary of what is often a complex topic, yet one that is central to understanding the crisis in Venezuela today, see Mallett-Outtrim (2016).

10. Though I would not want to draw too fine a dividing line between each of these phases, given that historical change always tends to carry traces of the old within the new. Today's global (neoliberal? Post-Washington Consensus?) order has certainly not rid itself of various racialized contours of oppression, not to mention those of gender or sexuality.

REFERENCES

Abu-Lughod, Janet L. (1989), *Before European Hegemony*, Oxford: Oxford University Press.
ALBA (2004), 'Venezuela-Cuba Joint Declaration', I Summit, Havana, Cuba, 14 December, http://alba-tcp.org/en/contenido/joint-declaration-venezuela-cuba (accessed 14 December 2016).
Angarita, Yamileth (2016), 'Maduro: Over 130 companies interested in mining projects in Venezuela', *El Universal*, http://www.eluniversal.com/economia/160225/maduro-over-130-companies-interested-in-mining-projects-in-venezuela (accessed 10 March 2017).
Anievas, Alexander and Kerem Nişancıoğlu (2015), *How the West Came to Rule: The Geopolitical Origins of Capitalism*, London: Pluto Press.
Arrighi, Giovanni (1983), *The Geometry of Imperialism*, London: Verso.
Arrighi, Giovanni ([1994] 2010), *The Long Twentieth Century: Money, Power and the Origins of our Times*, London: Verso.
Arrighi, Giovanni, Beverly J. Silver and Benjamin D. Brewer (2003), 'Industrial Convergence, Globalization, and the Persistence of the North-South Divide', *Studies in Comparative International Development*, **38** (1), 3–31.
Ayres, Ron and David Clark (1998), 'Capitalism, Industrialisation and Development in Latin America: The Dependency Paradigm Revisited', *Capital & Class*, **64**, 89–118.
Bairoch, Paul (1993), *Economics and World History: Myths and Paradoxes*, Chicago: Chicago University Press.
Bebbington, Anthony (2012), *Social Conflict, Economic Development and Extractive Industry: Evidence from South America*, London, New York: Routledge.
Birch, Kean (2015), 'Neoliberalism: The Whys and Wherefores . . . and Future Directions', *Social Compass*, **9** (7), 571–84.
Blum, William (2004), *Killing Hope: U.S. Military and CIA Interventions since World War II*, London: Zed Books.
Boito, Armando and Tatiana Berringer (2014), 'Social Classes, Neodevelopmentalism, and Brazilian Foreign Policy under Presidents Lula and Dilma', *Latin American Perspectives*, **41** (50), 94–109.
Bracarense, Natália M. (2012), 'Development Theory and the Cold War: The Influence of Politics on Latin American Structuralism', *Review of Political Economy*, **24** (3), 375–98.
Brainard, Lael, Carol Graham, Nigel Purvis, Steven Radelet and Gayle E. Smith (2003), *The Other War: Global Poverty and the Millennium Challenge Account*, Washington, DC: Brookings Institute.
Brenner, Robert (2002), *The Boom and the Bubble*, London: Verso.
Brewer, Anthony (1990), *Marxist Theories of Imperialism: A Critical Survey*, London, New York: Routledge.
Bukharin, Nikolai ([1917] 1929), *Imperialism and World Economy*, London: Martin Lawrence Ltd.
Busch, Lawrence (2000), *The Eclipse of Morality: Science, State, and Market*, New York: Aldine de Gruyter.
Califano, Andrea (2013), 'Las Empresas Grannacionales. Algunas notas aclaratorias', in Maribel Aponte García and Gloria Amézquita Puntiel (eds), *El ALBA-TCP: Origen y Fruto del Nuevo Regionalismo Latinoamericano y Caribeño*, Buenos Aires: CLACSO, 109–46.
Calvert, Peter and Susan Calvert (2007), *Politics and Society in the Developing World*, Harlow: Pearson Longman.
Chodor, Tom and Anthea McCarthy-Jones (2013), 'Post-Liberal Regionalism in Latin America and the Influence of Hugo Chávez', *Journal of Iberian and Latin American Research*, **19** (2), 211–23.
Cliff, Tony (1970), *Russia: A Marxist Analysis*, London: Pluto Press.
Colás, Alejandro (2007), *Empire*, Cambridge: Polity.
Cooper, Robert (2002), 'The New Liberal Imperialism', *The Guardian*, https://www.the guardian.com/world/2002/apr/07/1 (accessed 9 March 2017).

Cowen, M. P. and R. W. Shenton (1996), *Doctrines of Development*, London, New York: Routledge.

Crosby, Alfred W. (1997), *The Measure of Reality: Quantification and Western Society, 1250–1600*, Cambridge: Cambridge University Press.

Duchesne, Ricardo (2011), *The Uniqueness of Western Civilization*, Leiden, Boston: Brill.

Duffield, Mark (2001), *Global Governance and the New Wars: The Merging of Development and Security*, London: Zed Books.

Dupré, Louis (2004), *The Enlightenment and the Intellectual Foundations of Modern Culture*, New Haven, London: Yale University Press.

The Economist (1999), 'The Price of Uncertainty', 10 June, http://www.economist.com/node/345991 (accessed 10 March 2017).

El Mundo (2016), 'Empresas de China y Venezuela evalúan potencial agroforestal de Mérida', 25 May, http://www.elmundo.com.ve/noticias/economia/industrias/empresas-de-china-y-venezuela-evaluan-potencial-ag.aspx (accessed 10 March 2017).

Escobar, Arturo (1995), *Encountering Development: The Making and Unmaking of the Third World*, Princeton, NJ: Princeton University Press.

Ferguson, Niall (2004), *Colossus: The Rise and Fall of American Empire*, London: Penguin Books.

Ferguson, Niall (2012), *Civilization: The Six Killer Apps of Western Power*, London: Penguin Books.

Frank, Andrew Gunder (1969), *Latin America: Underdevelopment or Revolution*, New York: Monthly Review Books.

Fukuda-Parr, Sakiko, Alicia Ely Yamin and Joshua Greenstein (2014), 'The Power of Numbers: A Critical Review of Millennium Development Goal Targets for Human Development and Human Rights', *Journal of Human Development and Capabilities*, 15 (2–3), 105–17.

Fukuyama, Francis (2015), *Political Order and Political Decay: From the Industrial Revolution to the Globalisation of Democracy*, London: Profile Books.

Furedi, Frank (1994), *Colonial Wars and the Politics of Third World Nationalism*, London: Tauris.

Gardner, Lloyd C. (1984), *Safe for Democracy: The Anglo-American Response to Revolution, 1913–1923*, New York, Oxford: Oxford University Press.

Glyn, Andrew (2006), *Capitalism Unleashed: Finance, Globalization and Welfare*, Oxford: Oxford University Press.

Gong, Gerrit W. (1984), *The Standard of 'Civilization' in International Society*, Oxford: Clarendon Press.

Goody, Jack (1996), *The East in the West*, Cambridge: Cambridge University Press.

Grandin, Greg (2007), *Empire's Workshop: Latin America, The United States, and the Rise of the New Imperialism*, New York: Holt.

Grigera, Juan (2015), 'Conspicuous Silences: State and Class in Structuralist and Neostructuralist Thought', in Jeffery R. Webber and Susan Spronk (eds), *Crisis and Contradiction: Marxist Perspectives on Latin America in the Global Political Economy*, Leiden: Brill, 193–210.

Gudynas, Eduardo (2010), 'The New Extractivism of the 21st Century: Ten Urgent Theses about Extractivism in Relation to Current South American Progressivism', *Americas Program Report*, Washington, DC: Center for International Policy.

Hallo, William W. (1996), *Origins: The Ancient Near Eastern Backgrounds of Some Modern Western Institutions*, Leiden: Brill.

Harvey, D. (2003), *The New Imperialism*, Oxford: Oxford University Press.

Hickel, Jason (2016), 'The True Extent of Global Poverty and Hunger: Questioning the Good News Narrative of the Millennium Development Goals', *Third World Quarterly*, 37 (5), 749–67.

Higginbottom, Andy (2013), 'The Political Economy of Foreign Investment in Latin America: Dependency Revisited', *Latin American Perspectives*, 40 (3), 184–206.

Hobson, John A. ([1902] 2005), *Imperialism: A Study*, New York: Cosimo Classics.

Hobson, John M. (2004), *The Eastern Origins of Western Civilization*, Cambridge: Cambridge University Press.
Ho-Fung, Hung (2008), 'Rise of China and the Global Overaccumulation Crisis', *Review of International Political Economy*, **15** (2), 149–79.
Ho-Fung, Hung and Daniel Thompson (2016), 'Money Supply, Class Power, and Inflation: Monetarism Reassessed', *American Sociological Review*, **81** (3), 447–66.
Holmes, James R. (2007), *Theodore Roosevelt and World Order*, Washington, DC: Potomac Books, Inc.
Ignatieff, Michael (2003), *Emipre Lite*, London: Vintage.
Jahn, Beate (2005), 'Kant, Mill, and Illiberal Legacies in International Affairs', *International Organization*, **59** (1), 117–207.
Kagarlitsky, Boris (2008), *Empire of the Periphery: Russia and the World System*, London: Pluto Press.
Kay, Cristobal (1975), *Development and Underdevelopment*, London: Macmillan.
Kennan, George [X] (1947), 'The Sources of Soviet Conduct', *Foreign Affairs*, **25** (4), 566–82.
Kiely, Ray (2008), '"Poverty's Fall"/China's Rise: Global Convergence or New Forms of Uneven Development?', *Journal of Contemporary Asia*, **38** (3), 353–72.
Kiely, Ray (2014), 'Imperialism or Globalisation? . . . Or Imperialism and Globalisation: Theorising the International after Rosenberg's "Post-Mortem"', *Journal of International Relations and Development*, **17**, 274–300.
Kojima, Kiyoshi (2000), 'The "Flying Geese" Model of Asian Economic Development: Origin, Theoretical Extensions, and Regional Policy Implications', *Journal of Asian Economics*, **11**, 375–401.
Laclau, Ernesto (1977), 'Feudalism and Capitalism in Latin America', *New Left Review*, **I** (67), 19–38.
Larrain, Jorge (1989), *Theories of Development: Capitalism, Colonialism and Dependency*, Cambridge: Polity Press.
LeFeber, Walter (1993), *Inevitable Revolutions: The United States in Central America*, New York: W. W. Norton & Company.
Lenin, Vladimir I. ([1917] 1999), *Imperialism: The Highest Stage of Capitalism*, Sydney: Resistance Books.
Linden, Marcel van der (2007), *Western Marxism and the Soviet Union: A Survey of Critical Theories and Debates since 1917*, Leiden: Brill.
Luxemburg, Rosa ([1913] 2003), *The Accumulation of Capital* [trans. Agnes Scharzchild], London, New York: Routledge.
Mallett-Outtrim, Ryan (2016), 'Does Venezuela's Crisis Prove Socialism Doesn't Work?', *Counterpunch*, 25 May, http://www.counterpunch.org/2016/05/25/does-venezuelas-crisis-prove-socialism-doesnt-work/ (accessed 10 March 2017).
McSherry, J. Patrice (2005), *Predatory States: Operation Condor and Covert War in Latin America*, Maryland: Rowman & Littlefield.
Muhr, Thomas (2011), *Venezuela and the ALBA: Counter-Hegemony, Geographies of Integration and Development, and Higher Education for All*, Saarbrücken: VDM Verlag.
Murphy, Craig N. (2005), *Global Institutions, Marginalization, and Development*, London, New York: Routledge.
Öniş, Ziya and Fikret Şenses (2005), 'Rethinking the Emerging Post-Washington Consensus', *Development and Change*, **36** (2), 263–90.
Ostry, Jonathan D., Prakash Loungani and Davide Furceri (2016), 'Neoliberalism: Oversold?', *Finance & Development*, June, 38–41.
Peet, Richard and Elaine Hartwick (2009), *Theories of Development: Contentions, Arguments, Alternatives*, New York, London: The Guilford Press.
Petras, James (1980), *Critical Perspectives on Imperialism and Social Class in the Third World*, New York: Monthly Review Press.
Pijl, Kees van der (2006), 'A Lockean Europe?', *New Left Review* **II** (37), 9–37.
Pijl, Kees van der (2014), *The Discipline of Western Supremacy: Modes of Foreign Relations and Political Economy, Volume III*, London: Pluto Press.

Porter, Bernard (2004), *The Absent-Minded Imperialists: Empire, Society, and Culture in Britain*, Oxford: Oxford University Press.

Rist, Gilbert (2008), *The History of Development: From Western Origin to Global Faith*, London: Zed Books.

Roberts, Susan, Anna Secor and Matthew Sparke (2003), 'Neoliberal Geopolitics', *Antipode*, **35** (5), 886–97.

Rostow, Walt W. (1960), *The Stages of Economic Growth: A Non-Communist Manifesto*, Cambridge: Cambridge University Press.

Rude, Christopher (2008), 'The Role of Financial Discipline in Imperial Strategy', in Leo Panitch and Martijn Konings (eds), *American Empire and the Political Economy of Global Finance*, New York: Palgrave Macmillan, 198–222.

Saith, Ashwani (2006), 'From Universal Values to Millennium Development Goals: Lost in Translation', *Development and Change*, **37** (6), 1169–99.

Saliba, George (2007), *Islamic Science and the Making of the European Renaissance*, Cambridge, MA: The MIT Press.

Silva, Eduardo (2009), *Challenging Neoliberalism in Latin America*, Cambridge: Cambridge University Press.

Smith, John (2016), *Imperialism in the Twenty-First Century: Globalization, Super-Exploitation, and Capitalism's Final Crisis*, New York: Monthly Review Press.

Smith, Tony (1991), 'The Alliance for Progress: The 1960s', in Abraham F. Lowenthal (ed.), *Exporting Democracy: The United States and Latin America*, Baltimore: The Johns Hopkins University Press, 71–89.

Soderberg, Susanne (2004a), *The Politics of the New International Financial Architecture: Reimposing Neoliberal Domination in the Global South*, London: Zed Books.

Soderberg, Susanne (2004b), 'American Empire and "Excluded States": The Millennium Challenge Account and the Shift to Pre-emptive Development', *Third World Quarterly*, **25** (2), 279–302.

Soderberg, Susanne (2006), *Global Governance in Question: Empire, Class, and the New Common Sense in Managing North-South Relations*, London: Pluto Press.

Starosta, Guido (2010), 'Global Commodity Chains and the Marxian Law of Value', *Antipode*, **42** (2), 433–65.

Stiglitz, Joseph (1998), 'More Instruments and Broader Goals: Moving Toward the Post Washington Consensus', WIDER Annual Lecture, Helsinki, 7 January, https://www.wider.unu.edu/sites/default/files/AL02-1998.pdf (accessed 18 October 2017).

Swetz, Frank天下1989), *Capitalism and Arithmetic*, La Salle, IL: Open Court.

Tingyang, Zhao (2006), 'Rethinking Empire from a Chinese Concept "All-under-Heaven" (Tian-xia,   )', *Social Identities*, **12** (1), 29–41.

Tinker Salas, Miguel (2009), *The Enduring Legacy: Oil, Culture, and Society in Venezuela*, Durham, London: Duke University Press.

Tomlinson, B. R. (2003), 'What was the Third World?', *Journal of Contemporary History*, **38** (2), 307–21.

Truman, Harry S. (1949), 'Truman's Inauguration Address', 20 January, https://www.truman library.org/whistlestop/50yr_archive/inagural20jan1949.htm (accessed 10 March 2017).

United Nations (1961), 'United Nations Development Decade', Res. 1715 (XVI), 19 December, http://www.un.org/en/ga/search/view_doc.asp?symbol=A/RES/1715%28XVI%29 (accessed 10 March 2017).

United Nations (2015), *The Millennium Development Goals Report 2015*, New York: United Nations.

Veltmeyer, Henry and James Petras (2014), *The New Extractivism: A Post-Neoliberal Development Model or Imperialism of the 21st Century*, London: Zed Books.

Vilar, Pierre (2011), *A History of Gold and Money*, London: Verso.

Vitalis, Robert (2010), 'The Noble American Science of Imperial Relations and its Laws of Race Development', *Comparative Studies in Society and History*, **52** (4), 909–38.

Wallerstein, Immanuel (1980), *The Modern World System II: Mercantilism and the Consolidation of the European World-Economy, 1600–1750*, New York: Academic Press.

Warren, Bill (1980), *Imperialism, Pioneer of Capitalism*, London: New Left Books.
Watson, Matthew (2006), 'Civilizing Market Standards and the Moral Self', in Brett Bowden and Leonard Seabrooke (eds), *Global Standards of Market Civilization*, London, New York: Routledge, 45–60.
Westad, Odd Arne (2005), *The Global Cold War: Third World Interventions and the Making of Our Times*, Cambridge: Cambridge University Press.
Winters, L. Alan and Shahid Yusuf (2007), *Dancing with Giants: China, India, and the Global Economy*, Washington, DC, Singapore: World Bank/IPS.
Wood, Ellen Meiksins (2005), *The Empire of Capital*, London: Verso.
Yaffe, Helen (2015), 'Venezuela: Building a Socialist Communal Economy?', *International Critical Thought*, **5** (1), 23–41.

4. Development and the private sector: the challenge of extractives-led development in Uganda

Laura Smith, Anne Tallontire and James Van Alstine

INTRODUCTION

International development discourse, as expressed in the Sustainable Development Goals (SDGs) for example, regards the private sector as a vital development actor. Bertrand Bardre, former managing director of the World Bank writes that: 'The SDGs cannot be achieved without the help of the private sector . . . There is no alternative' (Badre, 2017). The Addis Ababa Action Agenda (2015, p. 3), which provides the foundation for implementing the goals, calls for 'unlocking the transformative potential of the private sector', not only in financing development but in the areas of technology, trade, social protection, health and capacity building. The idea that business has the potential to be 'architects and builders of sustainable development and social inclusion' through 'creating shared value' (Nelson et al., 2015, p. 1) marks a significant discursive shift in the role of business in development. In just four decades the discourse has changed from one of Western Multinational Corporations (MNCs) as detrimental to development, to one which embraces MNCs as key development partners (Van Alstine and Barkemeyer, 2014), and Corporate Social Responsibility (CSR) as a delivery mechanism (Hopkins, 2007).

The way in which the private sector has been assigned the role of vital development actor over the last two decades is inherently linked to how business increasingly has moved into the international development sphere. The UN Global Compact, launched in 2000, has been instrumental in bringing the human development agenda into business, and providing the platform for business to demonstrate good corporate citizenship (Gregoratti, 2010). Jane Nelson, writing in *Optima* magazine's special edition for the 2002 World Summit on Sustainable Development, lists major global corporations engaging in development issues such as climate change, health, fair trade, micro-finance and bridging the 'digital divide'. Companies such as Coca-Cola, BP and Daimler Chrysler have used their 'marketing competencies and their community outreach programs' to tackle complex development challenges, such as the HIV crisis in Africa (Nelson, 2002, p. 84). An important driver of business involvement in development is the business case, that is, the instrumental benefits accruing to companies (Edward and Tallontire, 2009). A 'development case' is also increasingly articulated by large NGOs, such as Oxfam and CARE who stress the 'critical role' and 'great potential' of the private sector in poverty reduction. But as Frynas (2008) notes, while private sector development initiatives can be beneficial to specific firms, we know relatively little about their developmental benefits.

This chapter explores the private sector-development nexus, with a particular focus on the extractive industries.[1] Extractives-led development strategies, promoted by development agents such as International Finance Institutions, are predicated upon the benefits that extractive firms (such as oil, gas and mining MNCs) provide to host countries and communities. However, the tools with which the private sector engages in development in extractive contexts are the subject of intense criticism and scrutiny. We use the case of oil exploration in Uganda to illustrate both the issues around the tools used to address community development, and also how the wider political economic context in which the companies operate serves to limit the effectiveness of corporate-community development initiatives. We highlight the importance of continued debate about corporate accountability and the role of government, community and civil society actors in fostering broad-based development benefits from private sector activities

We begin by exploring the ways in which business engages as a development actor. We then look at how CSR in extractive contexts is used both as a tool for development and as a way to ensure legitimacy of the sector. The final section draws on a case study of multinational oil companies in Uganda to highlight challenges for the CSR agenda in bringing about development that is more inclusive.

Data collection for the chapter took place in Uganda in Hoima District, where Tullow Oil (UK/Ireland) and CNOOC (China) are operating companies. Over 80 semi-structured interviews were carried out between 2014 and 2016 in Hoima town, and in villages in Hoima district covering local community residents, as well as oil company representatives, local government officials, and civil society organizations.

THE PRIVATE SECTOR AS DEVELOPMENT ACTOR

By definition, the private sector contributes to development through wealth generation, job creation and the provision of goods and services.

Corporate philanthropy by manufacturers such as Rowntree and Cadbury in the UK, and Carnegie in the US, has existed since the Industrial Revolution, as has the idea that corporations should create wider societal value and not engage in exploitative practices (Djelic and Etchanchu, 2015). However, we have now entered an era where business is asked to be a conscious and deliberate development actor (Blowfield and Dolan, 2010). The resources, reach and know-how of business are highly relevant in what has been a general configuration of new alliances in development financing and intervention in recent years (Richey and Ponte, 2014).

By the late 1990s, the 'retreat of the state' (Strange, 1996) through economic restructuring associated with neoliberalism and accelerated globalization, led to the emergence of new centres of authority. In the move towards what Duffield (2001) has termed networked relations of governance, involving non-territorial decision-making by both state and non-state entities, the private sector is an important and powerful actor. Huge increases in Foreign Direct Investment (FDI), facilitated by deregulation and privatization, meant that the private sector expanded its reach and impact into the far corners of the globe. Western MNCs were seen as both the main drivers and main beneficiaries of an economic globalization which was creating inequalities, environmental harm and increased poverty. The growing momentum of public concern about unbridled corporate power and apparent disregard for social and environmental issues found expression in the anti-globalization protests in Seattle in 1999 (Stiglitz, 2002). Pressure was placed on businesses to reflect on their wider societal impacts and accept responsibility for their actions, particularly those MNCs operating in developing countries, where they were subject to less scrutiny.

The scandal involving Shell in Nigeria in the mid-1990s is a case in point. Initially the company refused to take a position on what it deemed to be the internal politics of the country: the dictatorship's hanging of nine Ogoni activists (HRW, 1999). Subsequently, intense international public pressure caused Shell to revise this stance to one that embraced its broader responsibilities to defend human rights and protect the environment. This incident was instrumental in bringing about a fundamental change in corporate strategy in one of the world's largest companies (Wheeler et al., 2002).

More generally, public and consumer pressure led to the introduction of new norms, standards and codes of conduct on industries, to address issues around value chain governance, working conditions, pollution and child labour (Levy and Newell, 2006). A key instrument for this new approach was the UN Global Compact, announced in 1999 by Kofi Annan, then Secretary-General of the UN. The Global Compact promotes business conduct around nine universal principles and is regarded as a way of reconciling corporate activities with social values (Ruggie, 2002). It seeks to (re)build legitimacy for responsible business practices and good corporate citizenship (Gregoratti, 2010), to develop CSR.

While the term CSR is a contested one, it generally refers to a corporation's commitment to adding positive value to society, through incorporating social and environmental concerns into its business operations and its interactions with stakeholders (United Nations Industrial Development Organization, n.d.). Essentially, CSR is a form of self-regulation, and has become a way for companies to improve their social and environmental performance without external regulation. At the outset, bilateral and multilateral development agencies and international institutions were hugely optimistic about the possible value of CSR in development terms. It was thought that socially responsible business could contribute to more inclusive development and fill key 'governance gaps' that had arisen through globalization (Blowfield and Frynas, 2005). Also, given that by the early 2000s FDI by transnational corporations had outpaced Official Development Assistance (ODA) threefold (Jenkins, 2005), the private sector was seen as a key resource for development.

However, while official development agencies embraced CSR as the bridge between business and development, many NGOs remained sceptical. For example, in 2004 Christian Aid voiced a concern that CSR was an insufficient response to the detrimental impact of MNCs. Further, the voluntarism that is CSR's core defining feature (Moon, 2007) is seen to be insufficient and a way to deflect attention from a requirement for more stringent regulation to ensure MNCs' accountability. Critiques of CSR also came from academics who were concerned that corporate-led approaches to CSR were technical and generic, and ignored local contexts and political structures. CSR's reliance on the stakeholder model is considered to be particularly problematic (Sharp, 2006). The stakeholder approach aims to achieve a more equitable distribution of the benefits of a corporation's activities by building relationships with its stakeholders (Maitland, 2001). It is seen as complementing CSR by offering a practical means of addressing the issue of to whom the corporation is accountable (Jamali, 2008), but ultimately it is linked to maximizing shareholder value over time (Freeman, 1984). Stakeholders are identified by the corporation and questions arise as to who is considered to be a legitimate stakeholder and included in engagement processes. Managers give priority to competing stakeholder claims (Mitchell et al., 1997) and the intended beneficiaries of CSR initiatives either are not adequately involved or are completely left out of the process (Blowfield, 2005; Blowfield and Frynas, 2005; Prieto-Carron et al., 2006), sometimes by virtue of their poverty and

marginalization (Jenkins, 2005). This is because the stakeholder engagement model on which CSR relies is not rooted in local needs and does not
sufficiently take account of those whose voice is weakly articulated.

The 2000s saw the emergence of more proactive market-led approaches
to development by the private sector. These initiatives promised 'win-
win' scenarios for both the private sector and the poor, and included the
mainstreaming of fair trade, micro-finance, and 'bottom of the pyramid'
selling. This latter approach (Prahalad and Hart, 2002) is one of 'inclusive
capitalism', whereby the poor are treated as consumers, rather than
recipients of charity. The assumption underlying 'bottom of the pyramid'
initiatives is that the poor and marginalized can directly benefit from
business engagement in development (Blowfield and Dolan, 2010; Richey
and Ponte, 2014).

This period also saw former adversaries coming together as development partners, as the private sector entered into partnerships with NGOs
and civil society actors to deliver development. This marked a new era
which saw the resources and reach of the private sector and the 'local
knowledge' of the NGO harnessed in a collective effort to address global
development challenges (Rajak, 2011). The NGO Christian Aid shifted
from its previous adversarial stance to one of 'seeking to build strong
partnerships with businesses – collaborating, connecting, championing
and challenging each other – to bring lasting solutions for the poor'
(Christian Aid, n.d.). This followed the lead of Oxfam, which had entered
into partnerships with MNCs such as Unilever (Clay, 2005) and, latterly,
Marks & Spencer. Thus, in less than a decade, the private sector had not
only been legitimized as a development actor but was actively partnering
with development 'experts'.

SHAPING THE MEANING OF DEVELOPMENT?

Although the notion that 'what is good for business is good for development' appears to have gained currency, there is considerable concern that
private sector involvement in development has led to development being
(re)defined according to the interests of corporate actors (Blowfield, 2005;
Blowfield and Dolan, 2010; Rajak, 2011). Indeed, the idea of a win-win
scenario for business and development indicates a specific vision of
development as one of development through access to markets, and by
which alternative visions of development tend to be marginalized (Rajak,
2011). The ways in which the private sector understands poverty and 'the
poor' is another cause for concern. 'Bottom of the pyramid' approaches
to development restructure the development/poverty relationship as one

of opportunity rather than one of dependence, so that 'the very notions of the poor, poverty, beneficiary, and development worthiness are being constructed around what is material, instrumental and comprehensible to business' (Blowfield and Dolan, 2010, p. 35).

There is also concern about the capacity of private sector/NGO partnerships to deliver development. The power imbalances in these relationships can compromise development principles, and NGO reliance on private sector funding to meet organizational goals can compromise their critical stance (Rajak, 2011). Indeed, alternative visions of development that might have been the domain of NGOs disappear at the same time as 'the demands of social and environmental justice require the development movement to challenge rather than endorse corporate interests' (Rajak, 2011, p. 19). Orok suggests that the activist-driven CSR movement has been appropriated by global corporations and now stands as a new meta-narrative of contemporary capitalism, buoyed by the neoliberal ideology of markets and profits being in the interests of all. This permits the coexistence of a discourse of corporate responsibility alongside irresponsible activity.

After a decade of analysis of private sector involvement – particularly CSR practice – in development contexts, there is still too little known about how, and under what circumstances, business has the potential to bring about development change. CSR discourse fails to see CSR as a political process (Edward and Tallontire, 2009), and neglects the importance of power in the relationship between corporations and the communities in which they invest (Garvey and Newell, 2005). Local voices and perspectives are marginalized (Blowfield, 2005; Blowfield and Frynas, 2005; Frynas, 2005; Prieto-Carron et al., 2006) and development discourse is reshaped by the moral discourse of corporate responsibility. Yet, as we will see in the next section, the CSR model and its corollary stakeholder engagement continues to be pursued by international oil, gas and mining companies to deliver local development benefits.

EXTRACTIVE INDUSTRIES AND PRIVATE SECTOR DEVELOPMENT

How the extractive industries can contribute to development continues to be the subject of much debate (Van Alstine et al., 2014). The global commodities boom during the early 2000s, and the growing demand for fossil fuels from newly emerging markets, strengthened the case for extractives-based development as a route out of poverty (World Bank, 2010). Debates about 'new extractivism' suggested the potential for a new era of a more equitable extractives model in Latin America, while the 2009 Africa Mining Vision promoted the harnessing of Africa's natural resource wealth as the key to Africa's development (Africa Mining Vision, 2009). Investment in the extractive industries remains the most important driver of FDI to Africa (World Investment Report, 2013). However, the experiences of many post-colonial resource-producing states have highlighted an apparent paradox in the relationship between natural resource wealth and development. In many cases, political conflict and social inequalities have increased, and democratization processes have reversed, generating a considerable literature about what is popularly termed the 'resource curse' (Auty, 1993; Yates, 1996; Ross, 2004; Collier, 2007).

Studies have shown that existing development challenges are frequently exacerbated by external and structural factors that are unique to extractive industries, and especially to oil. As Karl has argued: '[C]ountries that depend on oil for their livelihood eventually become among the most economically troubled, the most authoritarian, and the most conflict-ridden in the world' (2004, p. 662).

While mainstream scholarship has focused on the importance of institutions for the effective management of resource-related challenges, some scholars have highlighted the role of the international oil industry in perpetuating these challenges. For example, the work of Ferguson (2005) has shown that frequently investments in oil activities are concentrated in secured enclaves, with little or no economic linkages to the local community. Indeed, frequently corporate extractive enclaves are quite literally walled-off from national society, providing little or no benefit to the wider locality. Further, extraction within enclaves engenders particular sorts of capitalism which 'pose a challenge to customary forms of community authority, inter-ethnic relations and local state institutions' (Watts, 2005, p. 54). Conflicts between extractive firms and communities are increasing (Davis and Franks, 2014) as not only are local communities excluded from benefits, but they suffer the adverse social, economic and environmental impacts associated with extractive projects such as in-migration, rising living costs and pollution. Watts (2008) has shown that oil capital coexists with violent environments, meaning that security, surveillance and militarization are also characteristics of extractive enclaves.

The World Bank now acknowledges that governments and communities are applying increased pressure to ensure that project benefits are shared with communities, including jobs, infrastructure and community development (World Bank, 2012). In some cases this pressure has involved direct local action which has had cost implications for companies. Protests, blockages and vandalism have led to expensive stoppage time. In Nigeria, to cite an extreme but not isolated example, stoppages due to community sabotage and militia attacks can cost the industry billions of dollars a day. Canadian mining company Barrick Gold is one of numerous mines that have had operations interrupted or closed after local protests over the unfair distribution of costs and benefits escalated to the global scale. Thus, oil and mining companies are operating under increased scrutiny, and with increasingly vocal demands from local communities for local benefits (Bebbington et al., 2008).

Meanwhile the private sector is suffering a crisis of legitimacy in its position as a development actor. Industry assessments of the role of the extractive industries particularly, such as the Extractive Industries Review and the Global Mining Initiative, have encouraged greater CSR in the sector to address the issue of legitimacy (Gilberthorpe, 2013). Initiatives such as the 'social licence to operate', which denotes the acceptance of the company by the local community, have been put in place and are being embraced by industry (Owen and Kemp, 2012). A number of international norms and performance standards for industry have also been put in place that seek to guide companies in acquiring the social licence to operate. These include the Voluntary Principles on Security and Human Rights, the Extractive Industries Transparency Initiative (EITI), the Global Reporting Initiative (GRI), the International Finance Corporation (IFC) performance standards, and the Equator Principles (Slack, 2012). These are part of a package of self-regulatory measures for the extractive industries which have been agreed by governments, industry and NGOs as oversight and governance have increasingly shifted from the public to the private sector.

Campbell (2012) sees this shift as one consequence of the liberalization of the extractives sector in Africa. She has shown that public functions of the state, including service delivery and rule setting and implementation, are increasingly being delegated to private operators. Companies are unable to say that they are fulfilling responsibilities by adhering to national laws and legal requirements; states are too weak, or too complicit, to monitor activities, so corporations have to self-govern through CSR (Campbell, 2012). In some contexts, extractive firms have had to fill 'development voids' left by the failure of structural adjustment policies (Maconachie and Hilson, 2013). Oil MNCs have effectively taken over some government functions where the state is either incapable, as in Nigeria (Frynas, 2008), or unwilling, as in Chad (Cash, 2012). This blurring of responsibilities goes some way to explaining why companies may find themselves dealing with the demands and expectations of communities. In Papua New Guinea, Imbun (2007) has shown that local communities have become shrewd negotiators in their demands for benefits and projects from mining companies. Some communities present a development 'shopping list' of demands to extractive MNCs – generally in the 'public good' areas of health infrastructure, education, roads, income projects – highlighting the lack of these services in communities. Indeed, some scholars have argued that, in many cases, CSR projects delivered by extractives companies provide essential social development investment to isolated or marginalized communities (Kemp and Owen, 2013) and serve as a form of compensation for mining activities (Imbun, 2007).

Yet, overall, the mechanism of CSR does not have a good record as a means of delivering development benefits and improving the legitimacy of the sector. Evidence from developing country contexts overwhelmingly points to it having a minimal impact, and in some situations creating more problems for local communities. There is evidence that ineffective community engagement practices have exacerbated existing social tensions and caused divisions within communities (Gilberthorpe and Banks, 2012). Although community relations and CSR are now core concerns for business, research indicates that these functions are frequently 'tacked on', rather than part of the core business (Hilson, 2012; Owen and Kemp, 2012). Moreover, the use of Western and international standards as a blueprint for sustainable operations can serve to decontextualize local development needs. Ironically, the weakness and inadequacy of some CSR programmes actually exacerbate, rather than relieve, the social risk and legitimacy issues for the corporations that these standards seek to address (Gilberthorpe and Banks, 2012).

In research into the community development activities of 20 oil companies, Frynas (2009) found that they were motivated to engage in community development for reasons such as reputation management and acquisition of social licence, with benefits to communities being of much less importance. He found that community development projects often are driven by short-term expediencies rather than by the long-term development needs of a community. All 20 companies supported education initiatives and 18 companies supported health initiatives aimed at local communities. However, there was a wide variation in the scope of initiatives and the level of integration – for example initiatives ranged from the construction of a hospital to a donation of equipment. Reporting on progress was very weak, with reports of financial inputs but no measure of effectiveness, meaning there is no way to identify or measure benefits for local people. Although Frynas acknowledges that, in many cases, social service investment is vital for local communities, he concludes that 'for all the money that oil companies have spent on development initiatives, there are surprisingly few tangible benefits for local stakeholders' (Frynas, 2009, p. 189).

CSR programmes are most often the result of externally-driven initiatives, rather than ideas emanating from a domestic policy process and as integral parts of locally owned public policies (Campbell, 2012). So while CSR efforts are aiming to resolve problems of legitimacy faced by extractive companies, where they are based on top-down technical approaches, they fail to address issues that can be the manifestation of much deeper structural problems (Campbell, 2012). Indeed, one of the reasons why CSR has been unsuccessful in some contexts is that grievances are often deep-rooted and have historical or cultural origins that pre-date the entrance of extractive activity into a community (Idemudia, 2011). Another reason is the inherent contradiction between companies' commitments to social responsibility and the likely massive social and environmental impacts of the activities of extractive industries. In order to gain the social licence to operate, companies tend to downplay the costs and overplay the benefits (Slack, 2012).

OIL IN UGANDA

As a 'new extractive' context, Uganda is an interesting case study through which to explore some of the issues that surround the relationship between business and development. Uganda's oil industry is being developed by a joint venture partnership of international oil companies – China National Offshore Oil Corporation (CNOOC), Total of France and the Ireland-based Tullow Oil. Total became the lead partner after Tullow sold the majority of its share to Total in 2017. Although oil was discovered in 2006, the development of the industry has been drawn out and dogged by delays, with international oil companies not receiving production licences until 2013 (CNOOC) and 2016 (Tullow and Total).

Similar to all major international oil companies, the discourses of sustainable development and corporate citizenship shape the mission statements of the joint venture partners. Neoliberal ideas of 'creating shared prosperity' (Tullow Oil) and 'win-win' (CNOOC) are mirrored in oil company rhetoric regarding their operations in Uganda. This discourse is operationalized under the banner of the companies' CSR commitments, which include social investment projects and community engagement efforts that have been ongoing during the exploration period.

Like many developing country extractive contexts, the area of Uganda's oil discoveries is physically isolated and economically marginalized (Van Alstine et al., 2014). Oil deposits are to be found in the Albertine Graben part of the East African rift system in the western region of Uganda, which is one of the poorest in the country (Oil in Uganda, 2012). The region is undergoing significant transformation as it is developed into a site for international oil industry investment. In resource peripheries like

Uganda, such transformations require a new and proactive role for the state, which manages the enclosure and privatization of land (Glassman, 2007; Bridge, 2014). Indeed, the expansion of state power into the Graben can be seen through processes of displacement, dispossession, securitization and militarization. In 2012, over 7,000 people were moved from their homes and land by the government to make way for the oil refinery site. Inevitably, there are interruptions to local subsistence livelihoods, as well as increased land conflict and land grabbing as oil speculation intensifies (Smith and Van Alstine, forthcoming). At the same time, international oil companies are engaging in CSR activities that aim to build legitimacy for oil development and provide some benefits to local communities.

CSR AS DEVELOPMENT IN UGANDA

Tullow and Heritage Oil (which sold its Uganda assets to Tullow in 2010) were the earliest companies to engage in CSR in Uganda, from around 2005. CNOOC began its engagement with CSR in Uganda in 2013. Typical of extractives CSR, both Tullow and CNOOC implement CSR in the broad areas of health, education and the environment. Project investment varies greatly – Tullow has built schools and a hospital, while CNOOC has donated equipment to schools and health centres and supported workers' salaries. Other projects include educational scholarships, tree planting, HIV testing and distribution of condoms and provision of mosquito nets and school books. Tullow also implemented an agribusiness project that trained and supported local farmers to supply fresh produce to the oil worker camps.

A local government official suggested that CSR by international oil companies is expected, in the same way that NGOs are expected to deliver development projects: 'just like the big NGOs that come here, they have to give us something'. Oil MNCs are seen to carry on the work of development through external organizations, teaming up with international NGOs or local community organizations, for example. Tullow initially worked with international aid organizations to deliver health and HIV awareness training in some of the communities. CNOOC on the other hand, which entered the oil industry eight years after Tullow, chose to work more closely with local government and local community-based organizations.

Although some locals criticized Tullow Oil for working with external or 'high level' organizations to deliver CSR, others suggested that it used international NGOs because there were no local ones. This lack of local development partners for CSR is one challenge of the 'frontier' locations for new oil and gas discoveries. From 2012, Tullow used an international consultancy to shape and professionalize its CSR programme, linking it more to Tullow's strategic objectives. This moved Tullow away from CSR projects that were based directly in the communities, and more towards market-oriented agribusiness and agroforestry programmes with a regional focus.

Most of the CSR projects in Uganda implemented by Tullow and CNOOC are subject to review and evaluation by external consultancies. The requirement to demonstrate impact and justify the business case is a significant limitation on the developmental potential of projects. In carrying out the research that informs this chapter, we found that a number of potentially impactful projects (for example HIV programmes and scholarships for vocational skills training) were on hold waiting for review, or waiting (in vain, as it turned out) for the 'second phase' of a project, which local representatives claimed was promised and then was retracted.

It is clear that CSR as a development tool is precarious in the extractives sector, which is subject to the political economy of the industry. For example, Tullow's production licence was delayed, and during this time the company entered into a drawn-out court case around tax owed for the Heritage Oil sale. Tullow senior executives were accused of bribing Ugandan ministers, and the oil price dropped, all of which conspired to put the company into financial crisis. The financial constraints and industry uncertainty had a direct impact on CSR funding, which was withdrawn, and cuts to staffing levels had a knock-on effect on the agribusiness programme. As the numbers of workers in the camps dropped, so too did the demand for produce, leaving many of the farmers with no market for the increased produce committed to under the programme. Other CSR programmes, for which Tullow had won a CSR award, were simply pulled overnight. Several locals expressed their frustration that the CSR projects that 'were for our development' were taken away. Communities recalled the company use of the term 'neighbours' to describe their relationship with the community, which made the removal of the projects more confusing as it did not sit with the idea of neighbourly behaviour.

However, representatives of Civil Society Organizations (CSOs) and of local government noted the benefits at local level from some of the CSR programmes. New schools, plus new health centres and the hospital constructed by Tullow are some of the benefits reported. Other individuals noted the health initiatives implemented by Tullow and CNOOC in villages, such as HIV awareness raising and testing. Although not a CSR initiative per se, infrastructure projects such as road building were noted to have reduced travel times to major towns and the capital city Kampala, and to have enabled some to benefit from increased trade (community interviews, 2012, 2013). CNOOC's Best Performers Award distributed several thousand shillings among local schools in the district, based on the performance of the students. Although this was an award to individuals, the education office claimed that the scheme was having an impact on the levels of reading and attainment. Other CSR projects were praised for bringing social services closer to communities, for example the schools and health centres built close to the oil wells have reduced the time and cost for people to reach these services.

But even in situations where there were notable benefits to the community, there were many difficulties. CSR is voluntary and discretionary, and the communities that receive investment are selected by the oil companies. The projects were generally implemented without meaningful consultation with the communities. Although leaders were informed, this was more of a token meeting rather than a community consultation. Communities eligible for CSR projects were selected on the basis of their proximity to oil operations, so some villages received CSR investment and others did not. Commitment to CSR is underpinned by the need to forward business goals and to secure the social licence to operate. Thus, it is strategically linked to developments in the industry and the project cycle.

Interviews with oil company personnel demonstrate the ways in which the discourse of win-win is operationalized. Tullow personnel explained that their 'corporate responsibility' strategy has moved away from philanthropy towards a 'business case focus', with a requirement that development projects for communities must also meet strategic business objectives. In Uganda, now that the project is moving into the production phase, 'CSR is driven towards impact mitigation and social issues management' (2014 interview with Tullow Oil representative, Hoima); in other words, CSR investment shifts to address key operational requirements. Similarly, CNOOC's on-the-ground CSR is geared towards social impact mitigation. A CNOOC representative explained that their initial CSR projects around health and education were aimed at 'gaining entry into the community' (2014 interview with CNOOC representative, Hoima). Thus, any long-term developmental benefits from CSR are compromised by the win-win strategy, which is ultimately tied to strategic business decisions.

THE CHALLENGES OF PRIVATE SECTOR LED DEVELOPMENT

The issues raised in the Uganda case study are reflective of the wider CSR debates and critiques, and highlight an important concern about the reliance on business actors to deliver community development benefits.

The way in which community development was conceived and implemented has followed the typical patterns of CSR in extractive industries, in terms of being driven by a win-win philosophy (that is, the business case) and following the stakeholder model. Development is not rooted in local needs, but is based on being a stakeholder or belonging to an 'affected community', and so those not included as stakeholders nor considered to be affected by the project are neglected. This results in divisions between those communities receiving CSR investment and those not. As Gilberthorpe and Banks (2012) have shown, extractive industry operations are rooted in specific localities and in a developing country context each of the diverse 'impacted communities' is characterized by pre-existing inequalities and power relationships, and therefore socially uneven access to benefits can produce complex patterns of inclusion and exclusion.

CSR is a voluntary and corporate-driven form of self-regulation, which selectively engages with some sections of society with the aim of securing 'the social licence to operate'. In this Ugandan case study, extractive industry corporate staff were explicit in interviews about the link of CSR activities to legitimacy and risk reduction. Campbell (2012) has argued that CSR must be understood as being tied up with 'resource curse' prevention; in other words, it should mitigate against the potentially harmful impacts of resource-led growth. However, the 'structural nature' of such legitimacy issues continues to be ignored by those designing CSR programmes (Campbell, 2012).

The broader political economy issues of the oil industry make CSR vulnerable to its exigencies and uncertainties. Extractives capital is highly mobile and extractives MNCs can take advantage of different legal and institutional environments to shift profits across countries and to engage in capital flight in the form of tax avoidance (African Progress Report, 2013). The mechanics of the enclave mean that profits are repatriated in MNCs' home countries rather than flowing to, or around, a local economy (Ferguson, 2005). The Uganda case demonstrates that CSR is tied to capital and the short termism of the industry – projects were cut during the time of financial crisis and industry slow-down. Although extractives are territorially based and firms have to go to where the resources are located, mergers and acquisitions between companies mean that leadership and management change, and along with them approaches to community development change too. In early 2017 Tullow sold the majority of its assets to Total, which will now take over Tullow's block. The current focus of CSR as community development is not geared towards addressing these wider macro issues.

Industry best practice standards such as the IFC performance standards and Voluntary Principles on Human Rights have been important in raising human rights issues and promoting the importance of trust building between companies and local communities (Shift, 2013). Much of the international best practice guidance relies on 'effective stakeholder engagement' based on inclusion and two-way dialogue, with an aspiration for local community input into development decisions. However, as we have shown, this is not the reality of CSR as it is practised on the ground. International best practice calls for inclusive stakeholder engagement, yet there may be different understandings of this concept at different levels of a company. As Kapelus (2002) has shown, stakeholder engagement as imagined by MNCs' senior executives may not be how it is implemented far away from the boardroom, at a local level. Often there are cultural and/or context-specific reasons why certain groups do not participate or are not consulted. In our research, women rarely attended stakeholder engagement meetings organized by the company, as in many cases oil was said to be 'men's business', and women also reported feeling intimidated by meetings, or being too busy working or doing household chores.

Some scholars and NGOs advocate for Free Prior and Informed Consent (FPIC) to apply to all local communities to protect their liveli-hoods from the negative impacts of extractive industry on their land and resources (Greenspan, 2014). FPIC is one of the key principles of international human rights law that protects the rights, culture and way of life of indigenous peoples. It is a requirement for extractive companies to seek such consent when their activities may impact on indigenous people. In light of the continued challenges facing extractives companies' com-munity engagement, Buxton and Wilson (2013) note that FPIC can also benefit industry, and have called for the principle to be implemented by companies as a way to secure social licence to operate.

Other community-focused initiatives include Community Development Agreements (CDAs). These are formal agreements between private and public actors which aim to minimize industry impacts and ensure benefits to communities (O'Faircheallaigh, 2013). However, O'Faircheallaigh notes that while CDAs represent an important mechanism in seeking to ensure that communities benefit from development, unequal power rela-tions between actors in negotiations can impact their effectiveness.

A focus on industry accountability and the rights of communities must be part of the discussion if development benefits are to be realized in an inclusive way. Transparency must go hand in hand with accountability, and in order to truly address legitimacy issues CSR should shift towards accountability that is directed upwards from communities (Newell, 2005; Utting, 2008). Yet, the inequalities and imbalances of power in the con-texts in which CSR seeks to be a development tool, or where the private sector seeks to be a development actor, remain a considerable barrier to notions of accountability. Empirical research has shown that the success of accountability processes is determined by the relationship between community, company and the state (Garvey and Newell, 2005; Utting, 2008). Communities impacted by extractives are often economically and politically marginalized, and a community's lack of relative power impacts on its ability to secure effective mechanisms of enforceability (Garvey and Newell, 2005). The role of civil society is important, but also there is a role for the state and institutions to uphold rights and support actors to bargain on a more level playing field (Utting, 2008).

This is certainly the case in Uganda where CSOs are restricted by the state, and also struggle to gain recognition from the communities as legitimate representatives. The Public Order Management Bill and the NGO Bill are two pieces of legislation which have been passed in Uganda in recent years and which are seen as directly targeting CSOs working on oil issues (Smith and Van Alstine, forthcoming). Under this legislation, CSOs are required to seek permission from the state to enter the oil regions and must share work plans with state security representatives. Meanwhile, another important actor in the oil regions, local government, has been effectively sidelined from oil developments during the exploration period (Manyindo et al., 2014). Support needs to be better directed towards local institutions to enable them to articulate needs and hold industry and other actors to account to ensure that underdevelopment is not perpetuated.

The operations of multinational companies in the Ugandan oil sector demonstrate the limitations of businesses' contribution to development. The fundamentals of business are not compatible with an inclusive negotiated approach to development. Investments in development projects have taken place, but they have been led by company priorities and project cycles; they are poorly linked to community needs; and they are weakly embedded in the local economy and institutions. Mechanisms for accountability are lacking at the local level, with local actors only tangentially connected to the emerging international transparency and best practice initiatives. A multi-partnered approach to governance is called for, in order to deliver the SDGs. Relying on the private sector alone – although an important development actor – is not a viable strategy for inclusive development. CSR, which continues to be tied to the business case, must be expanded to account for the wider and structural impacts of industries and, at the local level, it must be redirected towards relationships of accountability in order for development benefits to be realized.

NOTE

1. Extractive industries are processes that involve the extraction of raw materials from the earth to be used by consumers. Examples of extractive processes include oil and gas extraction, mining, dredging and quarrying.

REFERENCES

Addis Ababa Action Agenda (2015), Addis Ababa Action Agenda of the Third International Conference on Financing for Development, accessed 27 April at: www.un.org/esa/ffd/wp-content/uploads/2015/08/AAAA_Outcome.pdf.

Africa Mining Vision (2009), African Mining Vision February 2009, African Union, accessed 12 May at: www.africaminingvision.org/amv_resources/AMV/Africa_Mining_Vision_English.pdf.

African Progress Report (2013), Equity in Extractives Stewarding Africa's Natural Resources for All, accessed 15 May at: www.africaprogresspanel.org/wp-content/uploads/2013/08/2013_APR_Equity_in_Extractives_25062013_ENG_HR.pdf.

Auty, Richard (1993), *Sustaining Development in Mineral Economies: The Resource Curse Thesis*, London: Routledge.

Badre, Bertrand (2017), To tackle global challenges, the public and private sectors must join forces. Here's why, accessed 20 April 2017 at: www.weforum.org/agenda/2017/02/public-private-cooperation/.

Bebbington, Anthony, Leonith Hinojosa, Denise Humphreys Bebbington, Maria Luisa Burneo and Ximena Warnaars (2008), Contention and ambiguity: mining and the possibilities of development, *Development and Change* 39, 6, 887–914.

Blowfield, Michael (2005), Corporate Social Responsibility: reinventing the meaning of development? *International Affairs* 81, 515–24.

Blowfield, Michael and Catherine Dolan (2010), Business as a development agent: evidence of possibility and improbability, *Third World Quarterly* 35, 1, 22–42.

Blowfield, Michael and Jedrzej George Frynas (2005), Setting new agendas: critical perspectives on Corporate Social Responsibility in the developing world, *International Affairs* 81, 499–513.

Bridge, G. (2014), Resource geographies II: the resource-state nexus, Progress report, *Progress in Human Geography* 38, 1, 118–30.

Buxton, Abbi and Emma Wilson (2013), FPIC and the Extractive Industries: A Guide to Applying the Spirit of Free, Prior and Informed Consent in Industrial Projects, International Institute for Environment and Development, London.

Campbell, Bonnie (2012), Corporate Social Responsibility and development in Africa: redefining the roles and responsibilities of public and private actors in the mining sector, *Resources Policy* 37, 138–43.

Cash, Aubrey (2012), Corporate social responsibility and petroleum development in sub-Saharan Africa: the case of Chad, *Resources Policy* 37, 2, 144–51.

Christian Aid (2004), Behind the Mask. The Real Face of Corporate Social Responsibility, accessed 12 May 2017 at: www.st-andrews.ac.uk/media/csear/app2practice-docs/CSEAR_behind-the-mask.pdf.

Christian Aid (n.d.), accessed 30 April 2017 at: www.cymorthcristnogol.org.uk/getinvolved/private-sector/index.aspx.

Clay, Jason (2005), Exploring the Links between International Business and Poverty Reduction: A Case Study of Unilever in Indonesia, Oxford: Oxfam, accessed 27 April 2017 at: www.policy-practice.oxfam.org.uk/publications/exploring-the-links-between-international-business-and-poverty-reduction-a-case-112492.

Collier, Paul (2007), *The Bottom Billion: Why the Poorest Countries are Failing and What Can Be Done About It*, Oxford, UK and New York, USA: Oxford University Press.

Davis, Rachel and Daniel Franks (2014), Cost of Company-Conflict in the Extractive Sector. CSR Initiative, Harvard Kennedy School, accessed at: https://sites.hks.harvard.edu/m-rcbg/CSRI/research/Costs of Conflict_Davis Franks.pdf.

Djelic, Marie-Laurie and Helen Etchanchu (2015), Contextualizing corporate political responsibilities: neoliberal CSR in historical perspective, *Journal of Business Ethics*. DOI: 10.1007/s10551-015-2879-7.

Duffield, Mark (2001), *Global Governance and the New Wars: The Merging of Development and Security*, London: Zed Books.

Edward, Peter and Anne Tallontire (2009), Business and development – Towards re-politicisation, *Journal of International Development* 21, 819–33. DOI: 10.1002/jid.1614.

Ferguson, James (2005), Seeing like an oil company, *American Anthropologist* 107, 3 (Sept), 377–82.

Freeman, Edward (1984), *Strategic Management: A Stakeholder Approach*, Cambridge: Cambridge University Press.

Frynas, Jedrzej George (2005), The false developmental promise of Corporate Social Responsibility: evidence from multinational oil companies, *International Affairs* 81, 3, 581–98.

Frynas, Jedrzej George (2008), Corporate Social Responsibility and international develop-ment: a critical assessment, *Corporate Governance* 16, 4, 274–81.

Frynas, Jedrzej George (2009), Corporate Social Responsibility in the oil and gas sector, *Journal of World Energy Law & Business* 2, 3, 178–95.

Garvey, Niamh and Peter Newell (2005), Corporate accountability to the poor? Assessing the effectiveness of community-based strategies, *Development in Practice* 15, 3–4, 389–404.

Gilberthorpe, Emma (2013), Community development in Ok Tedi, Papua New Guinea: the role of anthropology in the extractive industries, *Community Development Journal* 48, 3, 466–83.

Gilberthorpe, Emma and Glenn Banks (2012), Development on whose terms? CSR discourse and social realities in Papua New Guinea's extractive industries sector, *Resources Policy* 37, 185–93.

Glassman, Jim (2007), Neoliberal primitive accumulation, in Nik Heynen, James McCarthy, Scott Prudham and Paul Robbins (eds) *Neoliberal Environments: False Promises and Unnatural Consequences*, Abingdon: Routledge, pp. 94–8.

Greenspan, Emily (2014), Free, Prior, and Informed Consent in Africa: An Emerging Standard for Extractive Industry Projects, Oxfam America Research Backgrounder series, accessed 24 May 2017 at: www.oxfamamerica.org/publications/fpic-in-africa.

Gregoratti, Catia (2010), Growing sustainable business in Eastern Africa: the potential and limits of partnerships for development, in Peter Utting and Jose Carlos Marques (eds) *Corporate Social Responsibility and Regulatory Governance: Towards Inclusive Development?* Basingstoke: Palgrave, pp. 203–24.

Hilson, Gavin (2012), Corporate Social Responsibility in the extractive industries: experi-ences from developing countries, *Resources Policy* 37, 131–7.

Hopkins, Michael (2007), *Corporate Social Responsibility and International Development: Is Business the Solution?* Oxford: Earthscan.

HRW (1999), The Price of Oil: Corporate Responsibility and Human Rights Violations in Nigeria's Oil Producing Communities, Human Rights Watch, New York.

Idemudia, Uwafiokun (2011), Corporate social responsibility and developing countries: moving the critical CSR research agenda in Africa forward, *Progress in Development Studies* 11, 1, 1–18.

Imbun, Benedict Young (2007), Cannot manage without the 'significant other': mining, corporate social responsibility and local communities in Papua New Guinea, *Journal of Business Ethics* 73, 2, 177–92.

Jamali, Dima (2008), A stakeholder spproach to Corporate Social Responsibility: a fresh perspective into theory and practice, *Journal of Business Ethics* 82, 213–31.

Jenkins, Rhys (2005), Globalization, Corporate Social Responsibility and poverty, *International Affairs* 81, 525–40.

Kapelus, Paul (2002), Mining, Corporate Social Responsibility and the 'community': the case of Rio Tinto, Richards Bay Minerals and the Mbonambi, *Journal of Business Ethics* 39, 3, 275–96.

Karl, Terry Lynn (2004), Oil-led development: social, political, and economic consequences, in Cutler Cleveland and Robert Ayres (eds) *Encyclopaedia of Energy Volume 4*, Amsterdam: Elsevier, pp. 661–72.

Kemp, Deanna and John Owen (2013), Community relations and mining: core to business but not 'core business', *Resources Policy* 38, 4, 523–31.

Levy, David and Peter Newell (2006), Multinationals in global governance, in Suchil Vachani (ed.) *Transformations in Global Governance: Implications for Multinationals and Other Stakeholders*, Cheltenham, UK and Northampton, MA, USA: Edward Elgar Publishing.

Maconachie, Roy and Gavin Hilson (2013), Editorial introduction: the extractive industries, community development and livelihood change in developing countries, *Community Development Journal* 48, 3, 347–59.

Maitland, Ian (2001), Distributive justice in firms: do the rules of corporate governance matter? *Business Ethics Quarterly* 11, 1, 129–43.

Manyindo, Jacob, James Van Alstine, Ivan Amaniga Ruhanga, Emmanuelle Mukuru, Laura Smith, Christine Nantongo and Jennifer Dyer (2014), *The Governance of Hydrocarbons in Uganda: Creating Opportunities for Multi-Stakeholder Engagement*, Maendeleo ya Jamii, Kampala, Uganda.

Mitchell, Ronald, Bradley Agle and Donna Wood (1997), Toward a theory of stakeholder identification and salience: defining the principle of who and what really counts, *The Academy of Management Review* 22, 4, 853–86.

Moon, Jeremy (2007), The contribution of CSR to sustainable development, *Sustainable Development* 15, 5, 296–306.

Nelson, Jane (2002), World poverty and the private sector, *Optima*, Special Edition for the World Summit on Sustainable Development, September 2002.

Nelson, Jane, Beth Jenkins and Richard Gilbert (2015), Business and the Sustainable Development Goals: building blocks for success at scale, accessed at: http://www.igdleaders.org/wp-content/uploads/BusinessandSDGs.pdf.

Newell, Peter (2005), Citizenship, accountability and community: the limits of the CSR agenda, *International Affairs* 81, 3, 541–57.

O'Faircheallaigh, Ciaran (2013), Community development agreements in the mining industry: an emerging global phenomenon, *Community Development*, 44, 2, 222–38.

Oil in Uganda (2012), Oil in Uganda Newsletter, August 2012, Issue 2, accessed 27 April 2017 at: http://www.oilinuganda.org/wp-content/plugins/downloads-manager/upload/OIL%20IN%20UGANDA%20ISSUE%202%20(AUGUST%202012).pdf.

Owen, John and Deanna Kemp (2012), Social license and mining: a critical perspective, *Resources Policy* 38, 1, 28–35.

Prahalad, Coimbatore Krishnarao and Stuart Hart (2002), The fortune at the bottom of the pyramid, *Strategy and Business* 26, 2–14.

Prieto-Carron, Marina, Peter Lund-Thomsen, Anita Chan, Ana Muro and Chandra Bhushan (2006), Critical perspectives on CSR and development: what we know, what we don't know, and what we need to know, *International Affairs* 82, 977–87.

Rajak, Dinak (2011), Theatres of virtue: collaboration, consensus and the social life of corporate social responsibility, *Journal of Global and Historical Anthropology* 60, 9–20.

Richey, Lisa Ann and Stefano Ponte (2014) New actors and alliances in development, *Third World Quarterly*, 35, 1, 1–21.

Ross, Michael (2004), What do we know about natural resources and civil war? *Journal of Peace Research* 41, 3, 337–56.

Ruggie, John Gerard (2002), Taking embedded liberalism global: the corporate connection, in David Held and Mathias Koenig-Archibugi (eds) *Taming Globalization: Frontiers of Governance*, Cambridge: Polity Press, pp. 93–129.

Sharp, John (2006), Corporate social responsibility and development: an anthropological perspective, *Development Southern Africa* 23, 2, 213–22.

Shift (2013), Bringing a Human Rights Lens to Stakeholder Engagement, Shift workshop report No. 3, August 2013, accessed 12 May 2017 at: www.shiftproject.org/media/resources/docs/Shift_stakeholderengagement2013.pdf.

Slack, Keith (2012), Mission impossible? Adopting a CSR-based business model for extractive industries in developing countries, *Resources Policy* 37, 179–84.

Smith, Laura and James Van Alstine (forthcoming), Neoliberal oil development in Uganda: centralisation, accumulation and exclusion, in J. Weigratz et al. (eds) *Uganda: The Political Economy of State and Capital*, London: Zed Books.

Stiglitz, Joseph (2002), *Globalisation and its Discontents*, New York, USA and London, UK: Penguin Books.

Strange, Susan (1996), *The Retreat of the State: The Diffusion of Power in the World Economy*, Cambridge: Cambridge University Press.

United Nations Industrial Development Organization (n.d.), What is CSR?, accessed 4 May 2017 at: www.unido.org/csr/o72054.html.

Utting, Peter (2008), The struggle for corporate accountability, *Development and Change* 39, 6, 959–75.

Van Alstine, James and Ralph Barkemeyer (2014) Business and development: changing discourses in the extractive industries, *Resources Policy* 40, C, 4–16.

Van Alstine, James, Jacob Manyindo, Laura Smith, Jami Dixon and Ivan Amaniga Ruhanga (2014), Resource governance dynamics: the challenge of 'new oil' in Uganda, *Resources Policy* 40, 1, 48–58.

Watts, Michael (2005), Resource curse? Governmentality, oil and power in the Niger Delta, *Geopolitics* 9, 1, 50–80.

Watts, Michael (2008), Imperial Oil: The Anatomy of a Nigerian Oil Insurgency, Working Paper No. 17, Berkeley: University of California.

Wheeler, David, Heike Fabig and Richard Boele (2002), Paradoxes and dilemmas for stakeholder responsive forms in the extractive sector: lessons from the case of Shell and the Ogoni, *Journal of Business Ethics* 39, 3, 297.

World Bank (2010), The World Bank Group in Extractive Industries 2010 Annual Review, accessed 12 May 2017 at: www.siteresources.worldbank.org/EXTOGMC/Resources/336929-1233337886428/WBG_Extractive_Industries_Annual_Review_2010.pdf.

World Bank (2012), World Bank Mining Community Development Agreements Source Book, The World Bank, March 2012, accessed 12 May at: www.siteresources.worldbank.org/INTOGMC/Resources/mining_community.pdf.

World Investment Report (2013), Global Value Chains: Investment and Trade for Development, United Nations, accessed 3 May 2017 at: www.unctad.org/en/PublicationsLibrary/wir2013_en.pdf.

Yates, Douglas (1996), *The Rentier State in Africa: Oil Rent Dependency and Neo-colonialism in the Republic of Gabon*, London: Africa World Press.

5. Financialization and development: issues and perspectives
Cecilia Allami and Alan Cibils

INTRODUCTION

The end of the Bretton Woods international monetary system in the early 1970s brought about a series of profound transformations in domestic economies and in the world economy. Keynesian demand management and welfare state policies were increasingly abandoned in the industrialized world, as were import substitution industrialization policies in the periphery. Domestic and international financial regulation and capital controls were dismantled to give way to financial liberalization policies. This resulted in a process of ever-increasing trade and finance integration and, with it, a massive increase in international capital flows, increased volatility and economic instability.

One result of this process of deregulation and integration is what heterodox economists and critical social scientists have labelled 'financialization'. Since the 1990s, it has become increasingly present in heterodox economics publications. Interestingly, it is also an issue studied in other branches of the social sciences, making debates richer and broader than would otherwise be the case (Engelen, 2008). However, in spite of a rapidly growing body of literature, there is no single generally agreed definition. Rather, there is a set of what one could consider broadly complementary definitions. As Dore (2008, p. 1097) astutely observes, '"[f]inancialization" is a bit like "globalization"—a convenient word for a bundle of more or less discrete structural changes in the economies of the industrialized world'.

Dore's observation points to an additional issue with financialization: most of the original writings on the subject focused almost exclusively on the industrialized world and the effect on centre economic structures of the rise and dominance of finance capital. However, increasingly research has focused on the impacts of financialization on periphery countries, the different forms it takes and the channels through which it works. General definitions for financialization in the periphery are not available or even desirable, since different levels of development of productive and financial sectors impose specificities which make generalizations difficult.

89

Given this, what is the impact of the different forms of financialization on the prospects for development in the periphery? This chapter sets out to provide a comprehensive picture of the range of views in the literature rather than attempting to provide definitive answers. In the second section (Financialization: definitions and issues) we present the variety of definitions of financialization used in centre (global North) countries to describe the ascendance of finance capital. In the third section (Financialization in periphery countries), we consider the different forms that financialization has taken in the periphery (global South) according to a wide range of studies. We focus specifically on two aspects of financialization that have had a broad impact on the periphery: the accumulation of international reserves by central banks that has occurred since the crises of the 1990s, and the financialization of commodity markets, the main exports of many periphery countries. The chapter concludes with some preliminary reflections on the impact of financialization on the prospects for development in the periphery.

FINANCIALIZATION: DEFINITIONS AND ISSUES[1]

According to Foster (2007), 'financialization' is a term that was first used in 1993.[2] Since then, it has been used with increasing frequency.[3] In general terms, it is used to denote the growing ascendance of finance capital over industrial capital, or the financial over the 'real' economy since the end of the Bretton Woods system. The most widely cited definition is the one put forth by Epstein in 2005: 'Financialization is the increasing role of financial motives, financial markets, financial actors and financial institutions in the operation of the domestic and international economies' (Epstein, 2005, p. 3).[4]

Epstein (2015) classifies the ever-growing body of research on financialization into three categories. The first focuses on clarifying the definition of financialization with the purpose of determining whether it is a new phase of capitalist development or a new accumulation regime. The second focuses more on the effects of financialization, with a view to determining, through theoretical models and empirical analyses, the impact of financialization on productive investment, wages, distribution and crises. The third research category is more policy oriented, seeking to determine what policies are needed to curb the effects of financialization and to increase policy space for progressive macroeconomic policies.

Van der Zwan (2014) adopts a different classification of the literature, identifying three broad approaches to financialization. The first she identifies as the French regulationist approach, which sees financialization as a new regime of accumulation. This group includes not only regulationist but also some post-Keynesian and radical political economists. They view the emergence of the finance-led or finance-dominated regime of accumulation as a response to the fall in productivity of the late 1960s (Boyer, 2000). The second approach identifies financialization with the emergence of shareholder value as the main guiding principle for corporate behaviour. In other words, they posit that the main objective of the financialized corporation is to generate quarterly profits for its shareholders, producing substantial changes in corporate behaviour and investment horizons (Aglietta, 2000; Crotty, 2002). A third approach focuses on the financialization of everyday life. Research which takes this approach questions policies aimed at including every sector of society into the financial sphere, especially low- and middle-income segments.

Focusing on the definition of financialization, Krippner (2005) has identified four different definitions commonly used in the literature. First, financialization is sometimes used to describe the dominant place that shareholder value has taken in non-financial corporate governance.[5] Second, some use the term to refer to the growing role of capital markets in financial markets, displacing banks and other financial institutions.[6] Third, some follow Hilferding's finance capital usage to highlight the growing financial and economic power of financial capitalists or rentiers.[7] Finally, some use the term to refer to the explosion of financial trading and innovation in financial markets that has taken place in the last decade.

According to Krippner, the definitions used above and in much of the literature on financialization are centred on economic activity, often making it difficult to determine the existence of a financialization process. Based on the work of Arrighi (1994), Krippner argues that financialization is a 'particular pattern of accumulation in which profit-making occurs increasingly through financial channels, rather than through trade and commodity production' (2005, p. 181). In other words, it is necessary to study the evolution of sectoral profits and changes in their composition over time to be able to fully grasp the process of financialization.

In some cases, financialization is defined in such a way as to combine elements of all of the above definitions. For example, Lapavitsas (2013) describes it as 'a systemic transformation of capitalist economies' with three distinguishing features. First, relations between large non-financial corporations and banks have been altered, as the former have come to rely heavily on internal finance, while seeking external finance in open markets. Second, banks have consequently transformed themselves. Specifically, they have turned towards mediating transactions in open markets, thus earning fees, commissions and trading profits. They have also turned from corporations to individuals in terms of lending and handling financial assets. Third, individual workers and households have been led into the financial system with regard to both borrowing and holding financial assets. Stagnant real wages and the retreat of public provision in housing, health, education, pensions, and so on, have facilitated the financialization of individual income (Lapavitsas, 2013, pp. 70–71).

Most empirical research on financialization can broadly be classified under two headings – microeconomic and macroeconomic. Microeconomic research includes studies that focus on the activities of large industrial corporations, using firm-level data to identify the ways in which investment and growth are impacted by firms diverting funds to financial assets rather than in productive capacity. Examples of this are Orhangazi's (2007) research on financialization in the US economy, Demir's (2007) research on a sample of several peripheral countries, Plihon and Miotti's (2001) study of the relationship between financialization and bank crises, and Stockhammer's (2004, 2006, 2008) study of the impact of firm-level financialization on accumulation.

Macroeconomic-focused research uses aggregate sectoral, financial and macroeconomic data to explore mechanisms of financialization, integrating strategies of a broad number of economic actors. We can broadly classify them according to the economic school of thought authors subscribe to in regulationist (Boyer, 1999, 2000), post-Keynesian (Palley, 2007) and radical (Epstein 2002, 2005; Krippner, 2005; Lapavitsas, 2009a, 2009b).

There is a smaller number of theoretical studies on financialization, both at the macroeconomic and firm levels. Examples of theoretical models of financialization are Skott and Ryoo (2007), van Treeck (2007, 2009) and Orhangazi (2007).

What then has been the impact of financialization? In general, the research, as discussed above, concludes that financial liberalization and financialization have resulted in the following set of local and global economic transformations:[8]

1. monetary policy oriented almost exclusively to price stability (inflation targeting);
2. a significant increase in the volume of international financial flows;
3. a large expansion of consumer credit, resulting in large increases of household debt;
4. a reorientation of large corporation objectives toward the short-term interests of shareholders, and away from long-term investment in productive capacity;
5. a greater influence of the international financial institutions in the global economy;
6. a significant increase in economic instability;

7. an increased short-term orientation of key economic decisions;
8. an increase in income and wealth inequality.

In sum, financialization has transformed the functioning of economic systems at both the macro and micro levels. According to Palley (2007, p. 2) its principal impacts have been to:

1. elevate the significance of the financial sector relative to the real sector;
2. transfer income from the real sector to the financial sector;
3. increase income inequality and contribute to wage stagnation.

Despite the volume of literature on financialization, there are key questions that do not have single, clear-cut answers but are open to interpretation.[9] For example, when did the process of financialization begin? Some authors place the beginning of financialization in the early 1970s, due to the transformations in the world capitalist system,[10] while others believe that the process started around 1980,[11] and still others see it as a long-run evolutionary process inherent in the development of market relations.[12]

This leads us back then to the question of the causes of financialization. Is it due to the liberalization of financial markets starting in the 1980s, or is it a consequence of reduced profitability and stagnation in the real economy? Thus, is financialization the product of financial deregulation or do its causes lie in the deeper structures of contemporary capitalism?[13] These are not questions that can be easily or categorically answered but we need to pose them.

Finally, the overarching question is: what is the relationship between financialization, globalization and neoliberalism? In the literature, financialization is frequently presented as almost a second stage of financial liberalization. According to Epstein (2015, p. 5), this topic ultimately cannot be resolved since these phenomena have all arisen more or less together since the 1980s. Therefore, it might be impossible to settle this debate.

FINANCIALIZATION IN PERIPHERY COUNTRIES

Most of the early work on financialization, and a considerable part of what came after, focuses on the industrialized world. The same is true for empirical work where, with few exceptions, research focuses on Western Europe and the US. The role of the US as world hegemon, and the great availability of data account for this, at least in part.

The study of financialization in the periphery is more recent and more varied in approach. Financialization can be seen to have different effects on different economies, especially when comparing centre and periphery countries. According to Palley's 2007 analysis of US data, financialization operates through three different conduits: changes in the structure and operation of financial markets, changes in the behaviour of non-financial corporations, and changes in economic policy. How do these changes in the centre affect the periphery? What are the transmission channels from financialized centre countries to those in the periphery? Does financialization manifest itself in the same way in the periphery as it does in the centre? Is there a variety of periphery financializations?

These questions have been increasingly addressed by social scientists working in this field of research. Some have investigated the range of channels through which financialization impacts the periphery,[14] others have addressed specific issues such as the financialization of microfinance[15] or the effects of capital account liberalization and capital flows, while still others have examined the financialization process as it operates in specific periphery countries.[16]

According to Bonizzi financialization is 'not a linear process and assumes different forms in developing countries vis-à-vis advanced economies, as well as country specific forms' (2014, p. 85). Bonizzi's study identifies a number of different manifestations of financialization in peripheral countries, of which the first is non-financial corporation investment decisions, which increasingly favour investment in financial assets over production. Research on this particular form of financialization uses firm-level data to track investment decisions. Demir (2007, 2009), using data from Argentina, Mexico and Turkey, has found greater financialization in terms of non-financial corporations increasingly engaging in financial over productive investment, using this approach.

A second approach to financialization in the periphery, related to the first approach above, focuses on how the availability of high-return short-term financial investments has resulted in decreased productive investment and also a decrease in its share of GDP.[17] High-return assets are often the result of inflation-targeting monetary policy or public debt policies. In other words, official macroeconomic policy can be an important contributor to financialization, impacting negatively on growth and macroeconomic sustainability.

A third approach to periphery financialization focuses on transformations of banking systems and the financial sector more generally. According to a study of large transnational banks by dos Santos (2009), bank profits are increasingly generated from loans to individuals, from financial investments and from services, including investment banking. Thus, bank profits have shifted from the sphere of production to the sphere of circulation. Thus, it is not capitalist profits that are the main source of financial sector profits, but worker salaries (Lapavitsas, 2009a). Due to ever-growing financial globalization and transnationalization since the early 1990s, periphery banking systems have either been taken over by foreign banks, or have adopted international bank behaviour in order to compete.[18] This has had a profound impact on periphery banking and on household financial behaviour and indebtedness.[19] A particularly innovative aspect of financialization has been the incorporation of even the poorest households and individuals into the financialized banking system through policies of 'financial inclusion' and microfinance.[20]

Since the end of Bretton Woods, and especially since the 1990s, deregulation of domestic and international capital markets has resulted in massive increases in capital flows worldwide, greatly contributing to the volatility and instability of the world economy and especially the economies of developing countries. Financial flows move around the globe, seeking high returns and low risk. Low-risk markets, typically in the US or Europe, are generally not as profitable as riskier periphery country or 'emerging' markets, where high real interests compete to attract foreign capital. When flows are attracted, they are usually short term, and capital flight is easily triggered by domestic or foreign events, often with devastating effects. According to Lapavitsas (2009b), the links between domestic financialization in developed countries and international financialization affecting developing countries derive in large part from these capital flows.

Becker et al. (2010, p. 228) identify two forms of financialization: 'financialization based on the take-off of a second circuit of "fictitious capital" . . . i.e. securities, and financialization based on interest-bearing capital and thus, on high interest rates'. This second form of financialization is related to a key feature of financialization in periphery countries which is its dependence on foreign exchange and therefore capital inflows. Policies geared towards attracting foreign flows can include overvalued exchange rates coupled with high interest rates, which often allow banks to appropriate a considerable share of the surplus while promoting financial speculation over productive investment.

Levy-Orlik (2013b, p. 206), analysing the effects of post-Bretton Woods financial and productive globalization, characterizes financialization as having three central aspects: a new organization of production, a new way of profit appropriation, and a change in the behaviour of economic agents. The transnationalization of production and the consequent decoupling of demand and supply has led to the growth of imbalances within, and between, countries and regions. Centre countries have the role of liquidity providers and demanders of goods and services resulting in structural current account deficits and capital account surpluses. Periphery countries have adopted export promotion policies but do not always manage to achieve a current account surplus and face difficulties attracting capital flows to balance their external sector. They are therefore forced to offer increasingly higher financial returns and repress real wages[21] in order to compete (Levy-Orlik, 2013a, pp. 109–10). This structural characteristic of the globalization era has led to increasing financialization in the periphery, especially in Latin America.[22]

The ability of periphery countries to borrow has also been impacted by financialization. According to Hardie (2011, p. 141), investors 'reward or punish governments for policy decisions directly through the cost and availability of financing. The more a government can borrow, the greater its immediate ability to carry out its chosen policies.' Defining financialization as the ability of investors to trade in emerging government bond markets, Hardie asks whether increasing financialization enhances or diminishes a government's ability to borrow. He concludes that 'the more (less) financialized an emerging government bond market, the lower (higher) the capacity of governments to borrow on a sustainable basis. In emerging markets, financialized markets are debt intolerant markets' (ibid., pp. 142–3).

The Accumulation of International Reserves

A new characteristic of the past few decades has been the increase in the amount of foreign reserves held by central banks in periphery countries. Since the late 1990s, following a series of substantial financial crises in periphery countries,[23] international reserve accumulation has become even more marked.[24] According to the literature, there are three reasons for this development. First, countries have needed to increase international reserves due to the increase in trade (as a percentage of GDP).[25] Second, the international monetary system has become more unstable since the 1980s, making reserve accumulation by periphery countries a necessity to protect themselves from sudden capital flow reversals. And third, reserves are accumulated for exchange rate stability.[26] The last two reasons for international reserve accumulation are directly linked to the growth of financial globalization and financialization in the global capitalist economy.

Reserve accumulation requires net flows of capital from developing to developed countries. This resource transfer carries significant costs for periphery countries: rather than putting received funds to productive use, they sit idle in case a crisis eventually occurs. According to Lapavitsas, the precise composition of international reserves is not known, but there is little doubt that the bulk – about two thirds – are US dollars. The

Table 5.1   International reserve accumulation (in billions of dollars)

	Net international reserve increase 1998–2013	Increase in international reserves 1998–2013 (as a % of GDP)
Advanced economies	2.762	0.5%
Major advanced economies (G7)	1.076	0.2%
Emerging market and developing economies	7.355	3%
Latin America and the Caribbean	634	1%
Emerging and developing Asia	4.469	5%

Source: Authors' calculations based on the IMF's World Economic Outlook database.

policy of reserve accumulation thus amounts to developing countries storing dollars – a total reserve equivalent of about US$6 trillion in 2008 (Lapavitsas, 2009b, pp. 119–20). Their accumulation is nothing short of a very substantial loan to the US.

Table 5.1 shows international reserve accumulation for different groups of countries (IMF country classification). Data clearly show how reserve accumulation for the years 1998–2013, both in absolute value and as a percentage of GDP, has been substantially higher for countries in the periphery than in the centre. Although reserves provide some return,[27] the cost of holding reserves is the difference between the opportunity cost and the real return on reserves. The portion of reserves held as interest bearing deposits, or as the short-term government debt of the US, will typically earn a small positive real rate of interest (1 to 2 per cent); whereas reserves held as gold, currency or in non-interest bearing accounts will provide no real return. Given the mix of assets held as reserves, the average return is probably around 1 per cent (Baker and Walentin, 2001). On the other hand, periphery countries issue short-term debt from abroad at substantially higher commercial rates of interest, increasing the cost of international reserve holdings.

There are various estimates of the costs to periphery countries of holding international reserves. Rodrik (2006) estimated the social cost of this policy at 1 per cent of developing country GDP; Baker and Walentin (2001) estimate the cost to be 1 to 2 per cent of GDP for most periphery countries, while Akyüz (2008) estimates the annual cost to be US$100 billion.[28]

Parallel to reserve accumulation there has been a very substantial growth of periphery country public debt, mostly due to monetary sterilization needed to offset the inflationary impact of foreign capital inflows.[29] Domestic bond markets have grown strongly in periphery countries since the mid-1990s. The liabilities issued by central banks in these countries typically have significantly higher rates of return than the official rates on the foreign public assets also acquired by central banks. This rate of return differential adds to the periphery's costs (Lapavitsas, 2009b).

In other words, the periphery's accumulation of reserves as protection, due largely to the increase in financialization, has generated direct costs resulting from the difference in the interest rate on reserves and what must be paid for public debt. It has also generated indirect costs, as accumulated reserves sit idle and cannot be put to productive use for development.[30]

Periphery country costs have a counterpart in gains for the US economy, since the dollar is the main reserve currency. According to Lapavitsas:

> [. . .] the international arrangements of capital flows and world money have created an unprecedented source of gain for the US economy. Developing countries have been implicitly subsidizing the hegemonic power in the world economy purely because it issues the dominant form of (valueless) quasi-world-money. (Lapavitsas, 2009a, p. 121)

The negative impacts of these aspects of financialization have led to heterodox economists highlighting regulation alternatives for periphery countries that would allow a greater control of capital flows, providing greater policy space for development. These alternatives include strategies such as capital controls of various types, financial transactions taxes and financial asset reserve requirements among others.[31]

Financialization – which has already resulted in an increase in volatility, short-term orientation and financial fragility in periphery economies – has forced these countries to accumulate reserves with substantial costs due to interest rate differentials. Meanwhile, there are substantial stocks of foreign reserves being kept as 'crisis insurance' that could be put to work for more socially beneficial development purposes.

The Financialization of Commodities

As a result of the spread of financial deregulation, and of the 'market friendly' policies implemented since the end of Bretton Woods, many periphery countries have experienced a process of de-industrialization and increased dependence on primary sector (commodity) exports. Since Raúl Prebisch and Hans Singer first studied this issue in the late 1950s, the impact of terms of trade of commodity exports on periphery economies has been widely studied.

In recent years, a relatively new phenomenon has emerged, generally

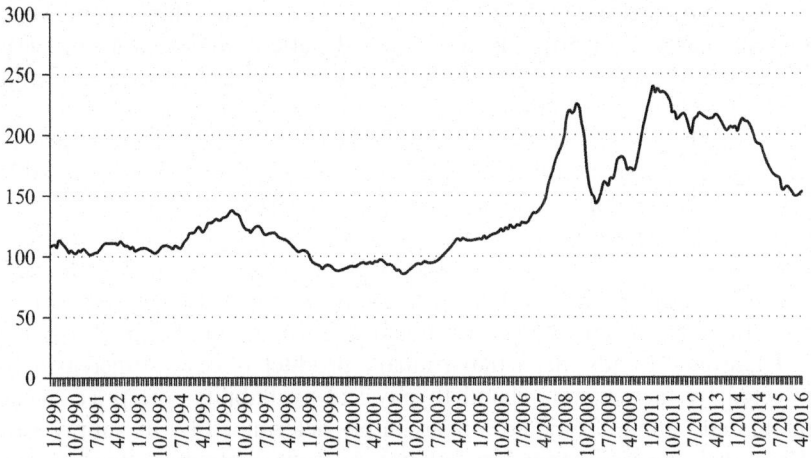

Source: Authors' calculations based on FAO data.

Figure 5.1   FAO Food Price Index 1990–2016 (Base: 2002–2004 = 100)

referred to as the financialization of commodities, due to a financial logic that increasingly permeates commodity markets. This has meant that prices have become heavily influenced by financial phenomena and less so by the 'real' economy, leading to much greater commodity world price volatility (Figure 5.1).

The links between commodities and finance go back a few centuries, to the early stages of agricultural product futures markets when credit, and other financing instruments, were issued by banks. This continued throughout the nineteenth and twentieth centuries. Futures agricultural markets[32] were used to hedge against weather and price variations, thus protecting producers from risks in physical markets. In this way, futures markets served as market, price and profit stabilizers, aiding forward budgetary planning (Murphy et al., 2012, p. 29; Gras, 2013, pp. 31–2).

In recent decades, significant changes have occurred in the relationship between commodities and finance due to financialization. Since the commodity price boom that began in 2000, investors have begun to take financial positions in futures markets as a way to increase returns, diversify portfolios and reduce risks. This process was aided by the deregulation of Chicago's futures markets and the creation of new financial instruments, such as derivatives. Furthermore, since the 1990s, new commodity markets have emerged in which hedge funds and investment banks can transact future contracts with no limitations or controls (Gras, 2013).

In this way, more recent financial deregulation has resulted in more intense and intricate links between commodity and financial markets. In some cases, derivatives have combined agriculture-based assets with assets based on other primary products linking commodity markets for all types of primary production (agriculture, livestock, mining, and so on). In addition, the volumes of exchange traded on commodity futures markets has increased exponentially. According to Bichetti and Maystre (2012, pp. 3–4), the volumes of exchange-traded derivatives on commodity markets are now 20 to 30 times greater than physical production. Furthermore, in the 1990s, financial investors accounted for less than 25 per cent of all market participants; today financial investors represent more than 85 per cent of all commodity futures market participants (ibid.).

These new trends mean that primary product prices are increasingly affected by factors not related to physical availability; the price of an individual commodity is no longer simply determined by its supply and demand. Whether financial speculation in commodity markets is one of these factors has been the subject of considerable debate in recent years. However, there is a degree of unanimity on the fact that such financial speculation has, at the very least, a short-run impact on the price of food.

Other factors found to have an impact on the determination of commodity prices are the aggregate risk appetite for financial assets and the investment behaviour of diversified commodity index investors. According to Tang and Xiong (2010, p. 4), on one hand the presence of these investors can lead to a more efficient sharing of commodity price risk but, on the other, their portfolio rebalancing can bring spillover of price volatility from outside into commodities markets and also across different commodities. Belke et al. (2013) found that financialization of commodities has led to a large flow of investment into commodity markets, especially into index investments. They contend that the rising volumes of financial investments in commodity derivatives markets have led to a synchronized boom and bust of seemingly unrelated commodity prices, thus driving commodity prices away from levels justified by commodity market fundamentals. Similarly, the United Nations Conference on Trade and Development (UNCTAD, 2011) found that increased speculation has probably accelerated and amplified price fluctuations. Tang and Xiong (2010) also point out that, concurrent with the rapidly growing index investment in commodities markets since the early 2000s, futures prices of different commodities in the US became increasingly correlated with each other.[33]

The main effect of financialization is uncertainty and potential destabilization of commodity markets. Consequently, those who suffer most from commodity market financialization are commodity-producing periphery countries. Those periphery countries most dependent on commodity production and export are the most exposed to external destabilizing factors, such as inflation, trade deficits, currency devaluations, and so on (Bichetti and Maystre, 2012, p. 28).

The new sources of instability and uncertainty especially impact the most vulnerable segments of the population, for example small producers at the end of the production chain. The very nature of financialization in an already complex agri-food system is often obscured, so that the role and impact of financial actors is not visible or clearly understood. This ambiguity is amplified by multilateral development bank promotion of financial deepening that is the liberalization of financial markets in periphery countries, and the use of financial inclusion measures, through the promotion of derivative products to smallholder farmers, as development strategies (Brooks, 2016, p. 769).

According to the Food and Agriculture Organization of the United Nations (FAO) (2011, p. 7), food price uncertainty and volatility affects the poor most intensely – especially the urban poor – who can spend up to 75 per cent of their income on food. High food prices reduce the quantity and quality of the food they can consume, threatening food security and generating malnutrition. According to the FAO, the 2007–8 food price increase resulted in an increase of world poverty. Robles et al. (2008) estimated that the 2006–8 price increases generated 21 million new poor in Latin American middle-income countries.

CONCLUSION

The survey presented in this chapter aims to underscore the wide, if complementary, variety of definitions and interpretations of the financialization phenomenon. It also aims to highlight the differences and varieties of financialization experiences in periphery countries. Given the wide range of economic, social and political structures in periphery countries, it makes eminent sense that this variety of definitions and interpretations exist and that we work with them.

Financialization poses a series of questions for the development prospects of periphery countries. How does the financialization that spreads from the centre affect the various periphery structures and through what channels? Does financialization aid or impede development? How do financial cycles in the industrialized countries impact financialization in the periphery? In fact, is development even possible in this financialized and globalized economy?

We are not yet in a position to fully answer these complex questions. Our aim here is to put forward some reflections that can be taken up in future research. To this end, Dasgupta's (2013, p. 5) observations are a good starting point:

> Financialization as a process is much more than the dominance by finance capital and rentier class in the economy. The uniqueness of the present financialization process lies in finance capital's hegemonic presence in almost every sphere of economic decision-making of firms, institutions, governments and societies, world over. Even the idea of economic development is now related to finance, in particular in the South, today as the prerequisite of any development is conditioned by foreign financial capital flows to a nation in this age of neoliberalism.

As we have seen in the preceding sections, financialization in the centre has had a substantial, if mixed, impact on the periphery. For example, monetary policies aimed exclusively at controlling inflation have resulted in high interest rates with a wide range of consequences for both domestic and international agents. Non-financial corporation and bank behaviour have shifted from long-run to short-run objectives, with substantial impacts on capital accumulation, economic growth and household debt.

Furthermore, productive and financial globalization have had a substantial impact on periphery productive structures, resulting in a return to dependence on primary production and exports and low value-added activities which compete on the basis of reducing labour costs. These transformations have resulted in a return to the cycles of foreign exchange shortages, public debt accumulation with attendant inevitable crises, and inefficient reserve accumulation by central banks as 'crisis insurance'. The large increase in financialization has led to the periphery's accumulation of reserves as protection, and has generated direct costs due to the difference in the interest rate on reserves and what must be paid for public debt. It has also generated indirect costs, as accumulated reserves sit idle and cannot be put to productive use for development.

In this context of globalization and reprimarization, the financialization of commodity markets has resulted in greater uncertainty and potential destabilization of commodity markets. Consequently, those who suffer most from commodity market financialization are commodity-producing periphery countries. Given the periphery's high dependence on commodity exports, commodity price volatility has substantial macroeconomic impacts through inflation, trade deficits and currency devaluations.

Financialization is additionally transmitted through the transnationalization of the banking sector and the adoption by local banks of practices typical of large transnational banks with profound impacts on domestic credit markets.[34] Furthermore, so-called policies of financial inclusion have sought to include even the poorest of the poor in financial markets, leaving no segment of society untouched by financialization. Periphery public debt, issued in centre financial markets, denominated in foreign currency and with rates of return set according to centre conditions, provides another transmission channel for financialization. Transnational corporations that operate on a global scale take their financialized practices to the multiple locations in which they operate. Finally, monetary policy in periphery countries, geared to controlling inflation and attracting foreign capital inflows, is also a key piece in the global financialization puzzle.

Thus, financialization's multiple impacts, together with the globalization of production and finance, impose strong restrictions on the periphery's development possibilities. The capacity of the state to intervene in favour of full employment, income distribution and the development of the internal market has been significantly eroded. This is because, to a large extent, the processes that have given rise to the new financialized world economy are mostly beyond a national state's reach. Thus, the state's ability to set trade policy, fiscal and monetary policies, and labour regulation, has become strongly constrained by the free mobility of financial and productive capital.

In sum, financialization, in its multiple forms, has resulted in an erosion of the possibility of interventions at the national level to address the problems of production, income distribution and development more generally. In this way, the capacity to articulate and implement policies aimed at the periphery's modernization and the achievement of a more egalitarian society has been all but lost. Recovering this capacity depends on our ability to develop a new global monetary and financial architecture which prioritizes the ability to implement egalitarian and full employment policies over financial-sector profits and financial speculation.

NOTES

1. This section is based on Cibils and Allami (2013).
2. According to Foster, Kevin Phillips first used the term 'financialization' in his *Boiling Point* (New York: Random House, 1993) and a year later devoted a chapter of his *Arrogant Capital* to the 'Financialization of America', defining financialization as 'a *prolonged* split between the divergent real and financial economies' (New York: Little, Brown, and Co., 1994). In 1994 Giovanni Arrighi used the concept in an analysis of international hegemonic transition in *The Long Twentieth Century*. According to Engelen (2008), the earliest academic publications using 'financialization' are from 1999, while Montgomerie and Williams (2009) place the 'genesis of this literature' in 2000.
3. For example, Chesnais (1999), Crotty (2002, 2005), Epstein (2002, 2005, 2015), Stockhammer (2004), Krippner (2005), Demir (2007), Orhangazi (2007), Palley (2007), Skott and Ryoo (2007), Kotz (2008), Lapavitsas (2009a, 2009b) and Van der Zwan (2014), among others.

4. See also Epstein (2002), Palley (2007) and Kotz (2008).
5. For example, Crotty (2002, 2005).
6. For example, Ertürk and Özgür (2009) and Pollin (1995) among others.
7. See, for example, Epstein (2002), Demir (2007).
8. For example, Skott and Ryoo (2007) and Palley (2007) among others.
9. These questions are formulated by Epstein (2015).
10. Lapavitsas (2008, 2011).
11. Sawyer (2013).
12. Vercelli (2013).
13. See also Lapavitsas (2013).
14. For example, Lapavitsas (2009b), Becker et al. (2010), Bonizzi (2014).
15. See Aitken (2013), Bond (2013) Mader (2013, 2014), Soderberg (2013), among many others.
16. For example, Levy-Orlik (2013a) for Mexico; Marois (2011) for a comparative study of financialization in Turkey and Mexico; Karacimen (2014) for Turkey; Cibils and Allami (2013) for Argentina; Kaltenbrunner (2010), Araújo et al. (2012) for the case of Brazil; Liang (2010), Rethel (2010), Caroll and Jarvis (2014) for various Asian countries; Gabor (2011), Ó Riain (2012) and Gambarotto et al. (2015) for studies on European periphery countries.
17. See Bonizzi (2014, pp. 89–90) for references on different country case studies using this approach.
18. See Tonveronachi (2006) for a case study of the Argentine banking system in the 1990s.
19. Bonizzi (2014, pp. 89–93) cites many periphery country studies that document different forms of financialization resulting from financial system transformations. See also Cibils and Allami (2013) for the case of Argentina.
20. Aitken (2013), Bond (2013), Mader (2013, 2014), Soderberg (2013).
21. Becker et al. (2010) point out that real wage repression often results in growing household debt, adding to the financialization process.
22. See also Cibils and Pinazo (2016) for a complementary account of productive transformation in the periphery in the era of globalization.
23. There were crises in Mexico (1994), Southeast Asia (1997), Russia (1999), Brazil (1999), Turkey (2001) and Argentina (2001–2).
24. See Mendoza (2004).
25. See Baker and Walentin (2001).
26. See Painceira (2009).
27. See Baker and Walentin (2001) and Rodrik (2006).
28. See also Mendoza (2004, p. 73).
29. 'Sterilization is the practice of issuing public debt by the Treasury or the central bank with the aim of absorbing increases in domestic liquidity (the money supply) due to surpluses of foreign exchange' (Painceira 2009, p.13).
30. Cruz (2006) evaluates theses costs for the Mexican case, as does Singh (2006) for India.
31. See Allami and Cibils (2010) for a survey of such proposals.
32. These markets, of which the Chicago Mercantile Exchange, founded in 1898, is the oldest, allow those who want to reduce risks to transfer them to others who are willing to take them on. In this way, contracts are drawn up between those who wish to buy or sell at some future time for an agreed price. These markets were typically used by wholesalers and food industry producers to hedge against risks (Gras, 2013, pp. 31–2).
33. According to the FAO, the transfer of financial market price increases to domestic food markets varies by country. For most developing countries, international commodity price increases in 2007–8 resulted in domestic food price increases, although in some cases with considerable lags. Furthermore, the subsequent drop in international prices was only partially transmitted to domestic food markets (FAO, 2011, pp. 10–11).
34. On this particular topic, Chick and Dow's (1988) work on the impact of financial liberalization on the prospects of regional development is highly relevant.

REFERENCES

Aglietta, Michel (2000), 'Shareholder and corporate governance: Some tricky questions', *Economy and Society* 29(1), 146–59.

Aitken, Rob (2013), 'The financialization of micro-credit', *Development and Change* 44(3), 473–99.

Akyüz, Yilmaz (2008), Managing Financial Instability in Emerging Markets: A Keynesian Perspective. Turkish Economic Association Discussion Paper No. 4. Ankara: Turkish Economic Association.

Allami, Cecilia and Alan Cibils (2010), 'Crisis financieras y regulación: Propuestas hetero-doxas', *Política y Cultura* 34, 57–85.

Araújo, Eliane, Miguel Bruno and Débora Pimentel (2012), 'Financialization against indus-trialization: A regulationist approach of the Brazilian paradox', *Revue de la Régulation* 11.

Arrighi, Giovanni (1994), *The Long Twentieth Century: Money, Power, and the Origins of our Times*. London: Verso.

Baker, Dean and Karl Walentin (2001), Money for Nothing: The Increasing Cost of Foreign Reserve Holdings to Developing Nations, Center for Economic Policy and Research Briefing Paper, Washington DC, November.

Becker, Joachim, Johannes Jäger, Bernhard Leubolt and Rudy Weissenbacher (2010), 'Peripheral financialization and vulnerability to crisis: A Regulationist perspective,' *Competition and Change* 14(3–4), 225–47.

Belke, Ansgar, Ingo Bordon and Ulrich Volz (2013), 'Effects of global liquidity on commod-ity and food prices', *World Development* 44, 31–43.

Bichetti, David and Nicolas Maystre (2012), The Synchronized and Long-lasting Structural Change on Commodity Markets: Evidence from High Frequency Data. Munich Personal RePEc Archive Paper No. 37486.

Bond, Patrick (2013), 'Debt, uneven development and capitalist crisis in South Africa: From Moody's macroeconomic monitoring to Marikana microfinance *mahonisas*', *Third World Quarterly* 34(4), 569–92.

Bonizzi, Bruno (2014), 'Financialization in developing and emerging countries: A survey', *International Journal of Polittical Economy* 42(4), 83–107.

Boyer, Robert (1999), 'Two challenges for the twenty-first century: achieving financial discipline and putting the internationalization process in order', *CEPAL Review* 69, 31–49.

Boyer, Robert (2000), 'Is a finance-led growth regime a viable alternative to Fordism? A preliminary analysis', *Economy and Society* 29(1), 111–45.

Brooks, Sally (2016), 'Inducing food insecurity: Financialisation and development in the post-2015 era', *Third World Quarterly* 37(5), 768–80.

Caroll, Toby and Darryl Jarvis (2014), 'Introduction: financialisation and development in Asia under late capitalism', *Asian Studies Review* 38(4), 533–43.

Chesnais, François (ed.) (1999), *La mundialización financiera: Génesis, costos y desafíos*. Buenos Aires: Losada.

Chick, Victoria and Sheila Dow (1988), 'A post-Keynesian perspective on the relation between banking and regional development', in Philip Arestis, ed., *Post-Keynesian Monetary Economics: New Approaches to Financial Modelling*. Aldershot, UK and Brookfield, VT, USA: Edward Elgar Publishing.

Cibils, Alan and Cecilia Allami (2013), 'Financialization vs. development finance: The case of the post-crisis Argentine banking system', *Revue de la Régulation* 13.

Cibils, Alan and Germán Pinazo (2016), 'The periphery in the productive globalization: A new dependency?', in Noemí Levy-Orlik and Etelberto Ortiz, eds, *The Financialization Response to Economic Disequilibria: European and Latin American Experiences*. Cheltenham, UK and Northampton, MA, USA: Edward Elgar Publishing.

Crotty, James (2002), The Effects of Increased Market Competition and Changes in Financial Markets and the Structure of Nonfinancial Corporations in the Neoliberal Era. University of Massachusetts, Amherst: Political Economy Research Institute, Working Paper No. 44.

Crotty, James (2005), 'The neoliberal paradox: The impact of destructive product market competition and "modern" financial markets on non-financial corporation performance in the neoliberal era', in Gerald Epstein, ed., *Financialisation and the World Economy*. Cheltenham, UK and Northampton, MA, USA: Edward Elgar Publishing.

Cruz, Moritz (2006), ¿Pueden las reservas internacionales contribuir al crecimiento mexicano?, *Economía UNAM* 3(8), 115–24.

Dasgupta, Byasdeb (2013), Financialization, Labour Market Flexibility, Global Crisis and New Imperialism – A Marxist Perspective, Working Paper, Fondation Maison des sciences de l'homme, Paris.

Demir, Firat (2007), 'The rise of rentier capitalism and the financialization of real sectors in developing countries', *Review of Radical Political Economics* 39(3), 351–9.

Demir, Firat (2009), 'Financial liberalization, private investment and portfolio choice: Financialization of real sectors in emerging markets', *Journal of Development Economics* 88(2), 314–24.

Dore, Ronald (2008), 'Financialization of the global economy', *Industrial and Corporate Change* 17(6), 1097–1112.

dos Santos, Paulo (2009), 'On the content of banking in contemporary capitalism', *Historical Materialism* 17(2), 180–213.

Engelen, Ewald (2008), 'The case for financialization', *Competition & Change* 12(2), 111–19.

Epstein, Gerald (2002), Financialisation, Rentier Interests, and Central Bank Policy. University of Massachusetts, Amherst: Political Economy Research Institute. Paper prepared for conference 'Financialisation and the World Economy', University of Massachusetts, Amherst, 7–8 December 2001.

Epstein, Gerald (ed.) (2005), *Financialisation and the World Economy*. Cheltenham, UK and Northampton, MA, USA: Edward Elgar Publishing.

Epstein, Gerald (2015), Financialization: There's Something Happening Here. Political Economy Research Institute (PERI), Working Paper No. 394.

Ertürk, Korkut and Göcker Özgür (2009), 'What is Minsky all about, anyway?', *Real World Economics Review* 50, 3–15.

FAO (2011), *La volatilidad de los precios y la seguridad alimentaria*. Informe del Grupo de alto nivel de expertos en seguridad alimentaria y nutrición del Comité de Seguridad Alimentaria Mundial, Roma.

Foster, John Bellamy (2007), 'The financialization of capitalism', *Monthly Review* 58(11).

Gabor, Daniela (2011), *Central Banking and Financialization: A Romanian Account of How Eastern Europe Became Subprime*. Basingstoke: Palgrave Macmillan.

Gambarotto, Francesca, Marco Rangone and Stefano Solari (2015), 'Mediterranean capitalism in disarray: Financialization and deindustrialization in the European periphery'. Paper presented at the *Colloque International Recherche & Régulation 2015*, 12–15 June, Paris.

Gras, Carla (2013), Agronegocios en el Cono Sur Actores sociales, desigualdades y entrelazamientos transregionales. *desiguALdades.net* Working Paper Series 50.

Hardie, Iain (2011), 'How much can governments borrow? Financialization and emerging markets government borrowing capacity', *Review of International Political Economy* 18(2), 141–67.

Kaltenbrunner, Annina (2010), 'International financialization and depreciation: The Brazilian real in the international financial crisis', *Competition and Change* 14(3–4), 296–323.

Karacimen, Elif (2014), 'Financialization in Turkey: The case of consumer debt', *Journal of Balkan and Near Eastern Studies* 16(2), 161–80.

Kotz, David (2008), 'Neoliberalism and financialisation'. University of Massachusetts, Amherst: Department of Economics. Paper presented for the conference in honour of Jane D'Arista, Political Economy Research Institute, 2–3 May.

Krippner, Greta (2005), 'The financialisation of the American economy', *Socio-Economic Review* 3(2), 173–208.

Lapavitsas, Costas (2008), Financialised Capitalism: Direct Exploitation and Periodic Bubbles, Working Paper, Department of Economics School of Oriental and African Studies University of London, London.

Lapavitsas, Costas (2009a), 'Financialisation, or the search for profits in the sphere of circulation', *Ekonomiaz* 72(3).
Lapavitsas, Costas (2009b), Financialisation Embroils Developing Countries. School of Oriental and African Studies, Discussion Paper No. 14.
Lapavitsas, Costas (2011), 'Theorizing financialization', *Work, Employment and Society* 25(4), 611–26.
Lapavitsas, Costas (2013), 'Financialization and capitalist accumulation: A structural account of the 2007–09 crisis', in Kichiro Yagi et al., eds, *Crises in the Global Economy and the Future of Capitalism: Reviving Marxian Crisis Theory*. Abingdon: Routledge.
Levy-Orlik, Noemí (2013a), 'Financialization and economic growth in developing countries: The case of the Mexican economy', *International Journal of Political Economy* 42(4), 108–27.
Levy-Orlik, Noemí (2013b), *Dinero, Estructuras Financieras y Financiarización: Un Debate Teórico Institucional*. Ciudad de México: Editorial Itaca.
Liang, Yan (2010), 'Interdependency, decoupling and dependency: Asian economic development in the age of global financialization', *International Journal of Political Economy* 39(1), 28–53.
Mader, Philip (2013), 'Explaining and quantifying the extractive success of financial systems: Microfinance and the financialization of poverty', *Economic Research-Ekonomska Istraživanja* 26(1).
Mader, Philip (2014), 'Financialisation through microfinance: civil society and market-building in India', *Asian Studies Review* 38(4), 601–19.
Marois, Thomas (2011), 'Emerging market bank rescues in an era of finance-led neoliberalism: A comparison of Turkey and Mexico', *Review of International Political Economy* 18(2), 168–96.
Mendoza, R. U. (2004), 'International reserve-holding in the developing world: Self-insurance in a crisis-prone era?', *Emerging Markets Review* 5(1), 61–82.
Montgomerie, Johanna and Karel Williams (2009), 'Financialised capitalism: After the crisis and beyond neoliberalism', *Competition & Change* 13(2), 99–107.
Murphy, Sophia, David Burch and Jennifer Clapp (2012), *El lado oscuro del comercio mundial de cereales. El impacto de las cuatro grandes comercializadoras sobre la agricultura mundial*. Oxford: Informes de investigación de Oxfam.
Ó Riain, Seán (2012), 'The crisis of financialization in Ireland', *The Economic and Social Review* 43(4), 497–533.
Orhangazi, Özgür (2007), Financialisation and Capital Accumulation in the Non-financial Corporate Sector: A Theoretical and Empirical Investigation of the US Economy 1973–2003. University of Massachusetts, Amherst: Political Economy Research Institute, Working Paper No. 149.
Painceira, Juan Pablo (2009), Developing Countries in the Era of Financialization: From Deficit Accumulation to Reserve Accumulation. Research on Money and Finance Discussion Paper No. 4. London: School of Oriental and African Studies.
Palley, Thomas (2007), Financialisation: What it is and Why it Matters. Annandale-on-Hudson, NY: The Levy Economics Institute of Bard College, Working Paper No. 525.
Plihon, Dominique and Louis Miotti (2001), 'Libéralisation financière, spéculation et crises bancaires', *Revue d'économie internationale*, 85, 3–36.
Pollin, Robert (1995), Financial Structures and Egalitarian Economic Policy. University of Massachusetts, Amherst: Political Economy Research Institute, Working Paper No. 182.
Rethel, Lena (2010), 'Financialisation and the Malaysian political economy', *Globalizations* 7(4), 489–506.
Robles, M. J., S. Cuesta, T. Duryea, A. Enamorado and V. Rodríguez (2008), 'Rising food prices and poverty in Latin America: Effects of the 2006–2008 price surge'. Inter-American Development Bank, Washington DC.
Rodrik, Dani (2006), The Social Cost of Foreign Exchange Reserves. NBER Working Paper Series No. 11952.

Sawyer, Malcolm (2013), 'What is financialization?', *International Journal of Political Economy* 42(4), 5–18.
Singh, Charan (2006), 'Should India use foreign exchange reserves to finance infrastructure?', *Economic and Political Weekly* 41, 11 February.
Skott, Peter and Soon Ryoo (2007), Macroeconomic Implications of Financialisation. University of Massachusetts, Amherst: Department of Economics Working Paper 2007–8.
Soderberg, Susanne (2013), 'Universalising financial inclusion and the securitisation of development', *Third World Quarterly* 34(4), 593–612.
Stockhammer, Engelbert (2004), 'Financialisation and the slowdown of accumulation', *Cambridge Journal of Economics* 28(5), 719–41.
Stockhammer, Engelbert (2006), 'Shareholder value-orientation and the investment-profit puzzle', *Journal of Post Keynesian Economics* 28(2), 193–215.
Stockhammer, Englebert (2008), 'Stylized facts on the finance-dominated accumulation regime', *Competition and Change* 12(2), 189–207.
Tang, Ke and Wei Xiong (2010), Index Investing and the Financialization of Commodities. National Bureau of Economic Research Working Paper No. 16385.
Tonveronachi, Mario (2006), 'The role of foreign banks in emerging countries: The case of Argentina 1993–2006', *Investigación económica*, LXV(255), 15–60.
UNCTAD (2011), *Price Formation in Financialized Commodity Markets: The Role of Information*. New York and Geneva: United Nations.
Van der Zwan, Natascha (2014), 'Making sense of financialization', *Socio-Economic Review* 12(1), 99–129.
Van Treeck, Till (2007), A Synthetic Stock-flow Consistent Model of Financialisation. Düsseldorf: Institut für Macroökomie (IMK), Working Paper No. 6/2007.
Van Treeck, Till (2009), 'The political economy debate on "financialisation" – A macroeconomic perspective', *Review of International Political Economy* 16(5), 907–44.
Vercelli, Alessandro (2013), 'Financialization in a long-run perspective: An evolutionary approach', *International Journal of Political Economy* 42(4), 19–46.

6. Development and regionalism
Philippe De Lombaerde, Stephen Kingah,
Liliana Lizarazo Rodríguez and Stefano
Palestini

INTRODUCTION

This chapter deals with the contribution of (international or supra-national) regions to development. Regional integration projects always have development objectives, but whether these objectives are achieved is an empirical question (Schiff and Winters, 2003). We will focus on the role of regions and Regional Organizations (ROs) in the design and implementation of social development policies, including: regional redistributive policies, regional promotion and protection of democracy, and regional protection of Human Rights (HRs). We will not deal with the traditional concerns of regionalism, that is, economics and security.

The scope of our chapter is inspired by, but goes beyond, the analytical framework of Deacon and colleagues. They argue that Regional Social Policy (RSP) should take account of redistribution mechanisms, regional social and labour regulations, regional supra-national social rights (Yeates and Deacon, 2006; Deacon, 2011), and, in addition, regional intergovernmental cooperation in social policy (Deacon, 2007). Regional social rights refer to the manner in which regional entities are engaged in providing for and defending social rights. Such rights may relate to access to affordable healthcare, the right to education and also the right to shelter. Regional redistribution mechanisms seek to address gross inequalities within and between given regions and countries. Regional regulations cover the variety of primary and secondary norms and principles or guidelines that are put in place to deal with policy issues, such as labour rights for example.

But how definitive can we be in making a linkage between regional integration and development? For Van Langenhove and De Lombaerde (2007), regional integration is important, as they see the regional level as being key in the provision of regional public goods, especially for smaller countries. So regional integration may provide scale for the creation of an 'internal market, for reaching a minimum level of policy autonomy, and for handling border-crossing problems, such as economic migration and environmental threats, (but) we cannot dismiss the possibility that regional integration processes end up favouring the relatively richer and bigger players in the region in the absence of cohesion policies' (Van Langenhove and De Lombaerde, 2007, pp. 383–4). Van Langenhove and Macovei (2010) argue that the effects of regional integration on national social policy are mixed and unclear. For Yeates and Deacon some challenges with RSP include its 'elite origins and orientations of regional formations; competition from trans-continental and bilateral trading arrangements; financing; and long term policy-making' (2010, p. 36). But the overall effects of RSP are seen as positive, especially the locking in of standards (Van Langenhove and Macovei, 2010, p. 21).

While this chapter takes a somewhat broader perspective than Deacon's, it adopts a largely similar categorization. In the second section (Regional development finance) we consider how regional organizations are contributing to financing development policies and projects. The third section (Regional redistributive policies) discusses how regions serve as redistributing platforms, section four (Regional promotion of democracy) assesses the contribution of regions to the promotion and protection of democracy and section five (Regional protection of rights) investigates how regional arrangements and courts are playing a role in the protection of HRs. The chapter concludes with a presentation of some possible ways forward.

REGIONAL DEVELOPMENT FINANCE

The role of ROs in the design, financing and implementation of developmental policies has undergone change throughout history, alongside changes in economic ideas and policy paradigms. Those ROs created in the 1960s and 1970s focused primarily on issues of economic and social development. Cases in point were the first three regional development banks (RDBs): the Inter-American Development Bank (IDB) in 1959; the African Development Bank (AfDB) in 1964; and the Asian Development Bank (ADB) in 1966; all of which were established on the basis that multilateral institutions could help to promote the development of poor countries (Sloan, 1971; Dosman, 2006; Helleiner, 2009). This idea initially faced resistance from the governments of global and regional powers, such as the United States (US) and Japan, but was eventually embraced, largely because of two factors. First, channelling development finance through a multilateral institution came to be perceived by global and post-colonial powers as a means to increase and legitimize their influence in Latin America, Southeast Asia and Africa at the time of the Cuban Revolution, the Vietnam War and the African independence movements (Krasner, 1981; Tussie, 1995; Dutt, 2001). Second, the UN Economic Commissions promoted the creation of regional development institutions, underpinning the demand of developing states. The three regional commissions – ECLA (later ECLAC), UNECA and ECAFE (later ESCAP) – transferred policy ideas from the academic and intellectual spheres to the political corridors in Washington, thus paving the way for the development of regional financial institutions (Prebisch, 1963; Sloan, 1971).

The idea that ROs should coordinate and finance the modernization of their member states became outdated by the end of the 1970s. For neoliberal economists working for the International Financial Institutions (IFIs), old-fashioned developmental policies were at the root of the external debt crisis of the 1980s, as suggested by two influential World Bank reports of the time, the *Berg Report* (1981) and *The East Asian Miracle* (1993). According to neoliberal theory, economic and social development would be the result of a 'trickle-down effect' of competitive and liberalized markets. From this viewpoint, regional market-making required liberalizing of trade and prices, and elimination of public interventions. Old ROs, such as the Association of Southeast Asian Nations (ASEAN) (1967) and the Andean Pact (1969) were reformed, and new ones, such as APEC (1989) and the Common Market of the South (MERCOSUR) (1991), were created, according to a new paradigm of multilateral liberalization that became known as 'new' or 'open' regionalism (Bhagwati, 1993; ECLAC, 1994).

Within this paradigm, there was little room for developmental policies. Regional integration organizations such as the ASEAN Free Trade Area (AFTA) and MERCOSUR were mainly oriented towards achieving 'negative integration' (that is, the reduction of tariff and non-tariff barriers), at the expense of 'positive integration' (that is, the coordination of common policies and institutions) (Tinbergen, 1965). The RDBs, in turn, were reoriented towards supporting poverty alleviation and financing structural adjustment policies (Babb, 2009). In Europe, a new RDB was created under the leadership of France and Germany. This was the European Bank for Reconstruction and Development (EBRD) which was explicitly mandated to foster the transition of former Soviet states from post-socialist economies to liberal-market economies (Bronstone, 1999). The EBRD is a case in point of this neoliberal generation of ROs. Newly capitalist governments were highly receptive to overtures from the economists of the EBRD, aware that the potential outcome of such contact was the delivery of major Foreign Direct Investment (FDI) to their countries (Culpeper, 1997; Park and Strand, 2016).

Regional initiatives created since the new millennium differ from both the 'old' and 'new' regionalisms. Most of them are oriented to upgrade public institutions *and* private-market actors in order to foster competitiveness in global markets (Bruszt and Palestini, 2016). Competitiveness in this approach is not a result of comparative advantages, but is rather an outcome of public-private investment, regulatory harmonization and the provision of 'regional public goods' such as cross-national infrastructure, energy market integration, and even RSPs in health and education (Estevadeordal et al., 2004; Bruszt and McDermott, 2009; Bianculli and Ribeiro Hoffmann, 2016).

As we move through the current decade, RDBs have reverted to a more developmental agenda, becoming key players in regional development governance initiatives. Concepts such as 'public-private partnerships' and 'regional public goods' are central to the new vocabulary of the IDB, the ADB and the AfDB. As Mingst (2016) observes, RDBs' regional integration strategies go beyond the mere provision of cheap credit, they are becoming partners and brokers between states, international organizations and private actors, helping to design and implement developmental policies. For example, the AfDB provides the headquarters for the Infrastructure Project Facilities of the New Partnership for Africa's Development (NEPAD), in the same way that the IDB and Corporación Andina de Fomento (CAF) coordinated the Initiative for the Integration of the Regional Infrastructure of South America (IIRSA) in South America, and the ADB coordinated the Growth Triangles in Southeast Asia (Palestini, 2016). Such change in the RDBs approach can be explained by their need to justify their *raison d'être,* not only vis-à-vis donor countries, but also vis-à-vis borrower countries. Some of the latter countries have even created new RDBs which challenge the existing ones (for example, Eurasian Development Bank, Bank of the South, New Development Bank, Asian Infrastructure Investment Bank), thus contributing to the 'regime complexity' of the field of development finance (Palestini, 2016).

REGIONAL REDISTRIBUTIVE POLICIES

The manner in which RSP is articulated in regions around the world varies. This is especially the case for redistribution, a function which is absent in many regions, or only implicitly present through differentiated financial contributions to ROs. In other regions explicit redistribution mechanisms have been designed (Bruszt and Palestini, 2016).

It is likely the case that many of these initiatives drew normative and institutional inspiration from the structural funds and cohesion policies of the European Community (EC) and the European Union (EU). The assumption that underlies these policies is that market integration can enhance the development of asymmetries among national and local economies, creating both winners and losers, and producing potential negative effects for the entire integration project that need to be tackled through regional development policies (Delors, 1989). Special funds have been in existence since the birth of the European Economic Community. With the advent of newer members into the organization in 2004 the redistribution mechanisms that had been in place and geared at countries such as Greece, Ireland, Portugal and Spain were expanded.

In Africa, the African Union (AU), through NEPAD, has sought to source funds from international partners to improve the economies of laggard states. The AfDB and the African Development Fund are also important in fostering development, reducing gaps within, and between, African countries. At the sub-regional level in the Economic Community of West African States (ECOWAS), Southern African Development Community (SADC) and the East African Community (EAC) the organizations have all created regional development funds. Compensation mechanisms have also been established to assuage the plight of countries that have been adversely affected by regional trade liberalization. Such schemes have been created in West and Southern Africa especially within the context of the West African Economic and Monetary Union (WAEMU or UEMOA) and the Southern African Customs Union (SACU).

Latin America has also been a theatre for redistributive policies. MERCOSUR, for example, has its common fund, *Fondo de Convergencia Estructural del MERCOSUR* (FOCEM) (Riesco, 2010). FOCEM was created in 2004 to support less developed members and regions and to foster structural convergence. It focuses on four areas: structural convergence; competitiveness; social cohesion; and the fortification of the institutional structure and integration process as a whole (Correa, 2010). Within the Andean Community (CAN) there is an important community development fund.

In the wake of the Asian financial crisis in 1997, the Initiative for ASEAN Integration (IAI) was launched with the aim to coordinate and implement a portfolio of projects of transport connectivity, human resources development, information and communication technology, and economic integration. An ASEAN Development Fund was created in 2006 to finance the Vientiane Action Plan (Chavez, 2007, 2010). In the context of the South Asian Association for Regional Cooperation (SAARC) it is critical that, in spite of bitter rivalries between some of the countries, the region did come together to forge the SAARC Development Fund (Chavez, 2010). It is also important to note here the central role played by the ADB, which has bankrolled important infrastructure programmes such as the Central Asian Regional Economic Cooperation (CAREC) Program.

REGIONAL PROMOTION OF DEMOCRACY

Traditionally, questions related to respect for democracy and the rule of law have been considered as internal political issues, intimately related to national sovereignty and, therefore, beyond the realm of international politics. However, since the 1990s, and in tandem with the *third wave* of democratization, ROs have increasingly adopted norms and procedures to promote and defend democracy in their member states (Börzel and van Hüllen, 2015; Pevehouse, 2016). Thus, we find democratic standards, not only in ROs composed exclusively of formal democracies (for example, the Organization of American States (OAS) or the EU), but also in ROs that include non-democratic members (for example, the AU or the CIS). However, the degree of institutionalization of the norms, the precision of the procedures, and the capacity to enforce them vary considerably from one RO to another (Legler and Tieku, 2010; Van der Vleuten and Ribeiro Hoffmann, 2010; Closa et al., 2016).

ROs have developed instruments to both promote and protect democracy. Examples of the former are electoral monitoring and capacity-building programmes. Democracy protection instruments include formalized rules and procedures whereby ROs can organize diplomatic missions or impose sanctions against the government of a member state. Where these protection mechanisms are codified in an instrument of international law, we typically refer to a democratic clause, by which ROs require, as a condition of membership, that *states should be* and *should remain* democracies (Schnably, 2000, 2005; Genna and Hiroi, 2015; Closa et al., 2016).

The literature in international relations offers different theoretical explanations as to why states have adopted these norms of democracy promotion and protection at the regional level. Scholars, puzzled by the synchronized timing of the institutionalization of democratic standards in different regions, have hypothesized that a number of diffusion mechanisms are in place (Franck, 1992; Börzel and Stapel, 2015). Other explanations focus on the functional needs of newly established democracies, which expect that multilateral commitments (such as a democratic clause) will help to dissuade non-democratic domestic actors and, thus, increase the probability of democratic regime survival (Moravcsik, 2000; Pevehouse, 2005; Mansfield and Pevehouse, 2006; Genna and Hiroi, 2015). A third strand of literature is more sceptical of the intentions of governments adopting these norms at the regional level. It has been suggested that authoritarian, or semi-authoritarian, regimes aim to legitimize their regimes by the adoption of democracy promotion or protection instruments, signalling to the international community their commitment to 'Western principles' while fending-off possible external interventions.

This would be the case especially in ROs with a high proportion of non-democratic member states (Ambrosio, 2008), but a similar phenomenon is also observed in more democratic regional settings (Closa and Palestini, 2015).

In Europe, ROs contain a wide array of both democracy promotion and protection mechanisms. Furthermore, European ROs are unique among ROs in that they apply some of these mechanisms to non-member states as part of their external relations policies (Schimmelfennig and Scholtz, 2008; Youngs, 2009). In terms of democracy promotion, the EU, the Organization for Security and Co-operation in Europe (OSCE) and the Council of Europe have developed monitoring capacities to observe and assist the elections of political representatives in member and non-member countries. In terms of capacity-building, the Council of Europe has developed a wide array of programmes targeting citizens and civil society. European ROs have also adopted democracy protection mechanisms. Article 7 TEU outlines the basic structure of the sanctions that the EU is allowed to apply though, to date, the EU has never invoked Article 7. Instead the European Commission has established infringement procedures against the governments of Hungary, Romania and Poland for alleged breaches of the rule of law (Sedelmeier, 2014; Closa et al., 2016).

Several (overlapping) ROs in the Americas and the Caribbean have adopted some democracy promotion and protection norms. With the end of the Cold War, the OAS began a process of modernization and revision of its commitment to democracy. In 2001, it adopted an Inter-American Democratic Charter that encompasses mechanisms for democracy promotion and protection. It has also developed electoral cooperation and observation missions and capacity-building programmes (Cooper and Legler, 2001; Levitt, 2006; Duxbury, 2011; Herz, 2012). The sub-regional ROs have also adopted democratic clauses but these remain less precise in their definitions and highly intergovernmental in their design and enforcement, when compared with the Inter-American Democratic Charter (Closa and Palestini, 2015; Closa et al., 2016;). The Caribbean Community (CARICOM), MERCOSUR and, more recently, UNASUR have played an important role as mediators in many democratic crises, ranging from *coups d'état* to episodes of political violence and revolt.

In Africa, the commitment to democracy and, for that matter, HRs is more recent than in Europe and the Americas. The African Charter on Elections, Governance and Democracy was approved by the AU in 2007, and entered into force in 2012. This Charter lays out the AU's promotion and protection mechanisms. Previous declarations and protocols allowed the AU to intervene in cases of unconstitutional change of government (UCG). The ECOWAS was the first to move, adopting a Protocol on

Democracy and Good Governance in 2001, under the leadership of Nigeria (Souaré, 2014; Lehninger, 2015). Military, or civil, *coups d'états* have been systematically censured with the suspension of membership rights and, in some cases, with the imposition of economic, and even military, punitive measures (Hartmann, 2016; Striebinger, 2016).

Asia, Eurasia and the Middle East are regions where regional democracy governance has been less institutionalized by ROs. The variety of types of non-democratic regimes that characterize member states of these ROs has probably prevented the development of democracy promotion and protection mechanisms. Nonetheless, some developments have taken place. In 2007, after 15 years of debate, ASEAN adopted norms for the protection of HRs that could perhaps pave the way to democratic governance mechanisms in the future (Ciorciari, 2012). The Commonwealth of Independent States (CIS) has adopted democracy promotion instruments, including the Democratic Election Convention in 2002 and the International Institute of Monitoring of Development of Democracy four years later. However, these instruments are not binding and face serious problems of enforcement (Libman, 2014).

REGIONAL PROTECTION OF RIGHTS

The role played by regional institutions in the protection of rights is conceptually linked to the Human Rights-Based Approach to Development (HRBAD) which covers national, regional, international and transnational aspects, and which is therefore considered as a cosmopolitan approach to HRs (Reyntjens, 1988; de Souza Santos, 2009). This approach seeks to identify and promote the links between development programmes and compliance with International HRs Law (IHRL). Multilateral, social and cultural agencies and regional banks have also been integrating this approach into their development programmes (Gauri and Gloppen, 2012).

Although the HRBAD refers to all rights, the realization of economic, social and cultural rights (ESCR) and collective rights are of particular relevance, because they are directly linked with the satisfaction of basic needs and the respect for a minimum threshold for each right (Reyntjens, 1988). It is a concept that evolved towards the core content of a right, understood as the 'definition of the absolute minimum needed, without which the right would be unrecognizable or meaningless' (ICJ, 2008, p. 39).

HRBAD has also had its own regional dynamics, the most developed being those of Europe, America and Sub-Saharan Africa. Regional systems have been created in Europe by the Council of Europe mainly by means of the Convention for the Protection of HR and Fundamental Freedoms (1950) and the European Social Charter (1963), and by the European Union and the Charter of Fundamental Rights of the European Union (2000) incorporated through the Treaty of Lisbon (2007). Systems have been established in America by the OAS, through the Protocol of San Salvador (1988) and in Africa by the Organization of Africa Unity (OAU), today the AU, which adopted the Banjul Charter in 1981.

In Europe two systems co-exist that are more or less coordinated. In the framework of the European Convention on HRs and Fundamental Freedoms, the Council of Europe has created the European Court of HRs (ECHR), the European Committee of Social Rights and the Commissioner for HRs (Van Der Plancke et al., 2016). The ECHR has been actively protecting HRs by the application of the horizontal effects of HRs treaties, that is, they can be applied not only to relations between individuals and the state but also to relations among individuals. In some cases they also recognize the extra-territorial jurisdiction for HRs violations outside Europe (Van Der Plancke et al., 2016). The European Committee of Social Rights (ECSR) also plays a role through the implementation of the system of collective complaints (Van Der Plancke et al., 2016). The Strasbourg Court has been very active in pushing the boundaries of protection for economic and social rights through a string of recent cases pertaining to the socio-economic rights guarantees for citizens (*Orsus* v. *Croatia*, 2010) and even for asylum seekers (*MSS* v. *Greece and Belgium*, 2011; *Hirsi Jamaa and Others* v. *Italy*, 2012; and especially in the case of children, *Tarakhel* v. *Switzerland*, 2014).

The EU has also created the European Instrument for Democracy and HRs (EIDHR) to intervene in concrete HRs situations (Benedek et al., 2010) and the European Fundamental Rights Agency as an advisory body of the EU and of the member states in respect of fundamental rights when they are implementing EU law (Benedek et al., 2010). Of course, the Court of Justice of the EU has also played a role in the protection of HRs, particularly after the incorporation of the EU Charter of Fundamental Rights by the Treaty of Lisbon. In the EU, the doctrine of direct effect (enforcement of rights in EU law through national courts) can also be applied to social rights. If rights in terms of free movement are violated, the EU also has services for recourse such as Europe Direct and its Citizen Signpost Service that responds to questions with cross-border implications. SOLVIT is a mechanism to solve smaller rights problems without going through the courts (Threlfall, 2010).

In an effort to develop a coherent and unitary system of protection of HRs, the members of the Council of Europe and the European Commission opened negotiations on the accession of the EU to the ECHR. However, the Court of Justice of the EU rejected this option in 2014 because the European Convention of HRs would be a binding convention for purposes of EU law. As a result, the EU and its institutions would be subject to the control of the ECHR bodies, particularly to the ECHR, which was considered a threat to the autonomy and the effectiveness of the preliminary ruling procedure of the EU. In addition to these systems of protection of HRs, the EU also has an extensive body of primary and secondary norms which include regulations, directives and decisions on many aspects of life, including consumer protection, maternity leave, labour rights and a clean environment.

In Africa, the system is complex because the Banjul Charter created the African Commission on Human and Peoples' Rights and the African Court on Human and Peoples' Rights in 2004, but this system shares jurisdiction with sub-regional courts (Kingah, 2013; Molano Cruz and Kingah, 2014). The African Commission has been actively promoting an HRBAD, including the creation of a Working Group on Economic, Social and Cultural Rights, and through progressive adjudication in favour of indigenous rights and minorities (see, the *Endorois* decision). However, the decisions of these bodies are not binding (Van Der Plancke et al., 2016). The African Court has more scope to rule in favour of HRs, but as of 2016 only seven states had granted direct access to the Court to individuals. The Commission is still the main way for NGOs and individuals to protect their rights (Van Der Plancke et al., 2016, p. 154).

Since 2005, the ECOWAS Community Court of Justice has had jurisdiction over individual complaints against HRs violations in its member states, even if national protection mechanisms have not been exhausted (Van Der Plancke et al., 2016). The SADC Tribunal had also the competence to apply HRs to individual complaints. However, it was suspended in 2010 and disbanded in 2012 because it made a progressive ruling against Zimbabwe. The Court of the EAC also includes, as a fundamental principle, the protection of the African Charter, and since 2005 it admits individual complaints with a 'progressive attitude towards human rights' (Van Der Plancke et al., 2016, p. 159). The role of the COMESA Court of Justice in actively protecting HRs is less prominent (Van Der Plancke et al., 2016).

Thus, the situation in Africa is becoming ever more complex as both the African Court and the Commission, created by the Banjul Charter, lose their regional adjudicative monopoly on HRs because of the active adjudication of sub-regional courts. In fact, forum shopping is emerging between national tribunals, the African Court and these regional tribunals in cases of HRs complaints. In Africa, there is also a growing body of regulations on social protection that are overseen by ROs, especially those at the sub-regional level such as ECOWAS, the EAC and SADC, but also the AU (Deacon, 2010).

In the Americas, the Inter-American System of HRs is composed of the Inter-American Commission on HRs (IACHR), and the Inter-American Court of HRs. This system has been the most progressive in the protection of all HRs, and also in addressing corporate-related HRs violations (Van Der Plancke et al., 2016) and actively protecting the rights of Afro-descendants and indigenous peoples. It is true that both entities have been more active in addressing gross violations of civil and political rights (for example, extrajudicial killings and disappearances: *Velasquez Rodriguez* v. *Honduras*; *Barrios Altos* v. *Peru*; *Almonacide Arellano* v. *Chile*; *Gomes Lund*; *La Rochella*; *El Mozote* v. *El Salvador*). However, the Commission and the Court have also been active in adjudicating on important cases impinging on the rights of indigenous communities in places such as Brazil and Paraguay (for example, *Sawhoyamaxa Indigenous Community* v. *Paraguay*). Instruments such as the precautionary measures or the conventionality control have increased the effectiveness of this mechanism. The conventionality control ensures that national authorities incorporate the American Convention on HRs in the execution of their respective competences. This measure has faced resistance from some Latin-American countries, on the basis that their constitutions are based on the principles of the 'self-determination of the peoples' and 'non-interference with the internal affairs of sovereign states'. These precise principles were referenced by Venezuela when it denounced the American Convention on HRs in 2012 (Couso, 2015).

Some sub-regional courts share jurisdiction with the Inter-American System of HR protection, even if they are not prominently enforcing HRs. However, some mechanisms or rulings could be considered as a way to follow an HRBAD. The CAN adopted the Andean Charter for the Promotion and Protection of HRs, but it is not a binding instrument and the Andean Tribunal of Justice (ATJ) has not applied it as a formal convention. In 1999, the Andean Social Charter was enacted seeking the universalization of all rights, including ESCR. In 2012, the Andean Parliament sought to give it binding character, but until now it remains a declaration of intentions (Lizarazo and De Lombaerde, 2015). Although the ATJ has also been basically dealing with trade issues of CAN, the ATJ has a relevant role in intellectual property rights (IPR) issues and it has tried to balance IPR in favour of access to medicines, but with the pressures of the trade-related aspects of intellectual property rights (TRIPS) and the Colombian and Peruvian FTAs, this position is being weakened at the cost of public health (Uribe, 2007; Helfer and Alter, 2014; Lizarazo and De Lombaerde, 2015).

The Caribbean Court of Justice (CCJ) of CARICOM has increased its relevance by means of the creation of the appellate jurisdiction, or court of last resort in civil and criminal cases from the member states. Although it does not have jurisdiction to hear individual complaints of HRs abuses, these matters have been part of the appeals in civil and criminal matters. However, only three member states (Barbados, Belize and Guyana) have adopted this mechanism, but some rulings are referred to as progressive in the protection of rights (see, *King* v. *Reyes et al.*, [CCJ Appeal No. CV 3 of 2011]) (Maharajh, 2014).

The Central American Court of Justice was created in the Central American Integration System, having as its main objectives peace, liberty, democracy and development, together with the respect and protection of HRs. This Court admits individual claims affected by a SICA agreement or actor (Statute of the Central American Court of Justice, art. 22). However, its statute excludes jurisdiction over HRs matters, recognizing the exclusivity of the Inter-American Court of HRs.

MERCOSUR has instruments like the Protocol of Asunción on the Commitment to the Promotion and Protection of HRs in MERCOSUR; the Social-Labour Declaration; the Agreement on the Regularisation of Internal Migration; the Agreement against Illicit Traffic of Migrants; the Agreement on Regional Cooperation for the Protection of Children in Situations of Vulnerability; and the Agreement on the Implementation of Shared Databases of Children in Situations of Vulnerability in MERCOSUR and Associated States (Lixinski, 2010). MERCOSUR also has a Social Charter (MERCOSUR, 2000).

In the Arab World, the Declaration on HRs in Islam (CDHRI), held by the member states of the Organization of the Islamic Conference in 1990, sought to present the Islamic perspective on HRs and to ratify Islamic Sharia as a legal source. This declaration has also been seen as a reaction to the Universal Declaration on Human Rights (UDHR), as it has come out against some civil freedoms and anti-discrimination positions. In addition, regional mechanisms to protect HRs have not been developed due to geographical, cultural and religious complexities.

Although two courts exist in the Arab world, the Court of Justice of the Arab Maghreb Union (AMU) and the Judicial Tribunal of the Organization of Arab Petroleum Exporting Countries, they do not have jurisdiction on HRs matters. But the Arab Charter of HRs was enacted in 2004 and the Arab Committee of HRs was created in 2009 by the League of Arab States. However, the preamble of the Arab Charter refers not only to the UDHR, the International Covenant on Civil and Political Rights (ICCPR) and the International Covenant on Economic, Social and Cultural Rights (ICESCR) but also to the controversial Cairo Declaration on HRs.

In Asia, there has been no regional system of HRs protection up to now. The Asian Human Rights Commission (NGO) promoted the adoption of the Asian Human Rights Charter in 1998 while the Bangkok Declaration of 1993 is also considered to be a relevant document. The signing parties expressed their agreement with the principles of the UN Charter and the UDHR but also articulated the importance of the principles of sovereignty and self-determination and the need for Asian values to be considered (Ghai, 2000; Twining, 2007; Chavez, 2010). However, in 2009 ASEAN established an Intergovernmental Commission on Human Rights, and in 2012 it adopted the ASEAN Human Rights Declaration, albeit without a formal convention or a court. This ASEAN mechanism appears to be the most practicable solution in the Asia-Pacific region but it clearly privileges non-interference in internal affairs over HRs approaches to development (Benedek et al., 2010).

Little progress has been made in the SAARC where the differences between India and Pakistan continue to complicate any structured regional political cooperation on matters of HRs. That being said, it is noteworthy that SAARC has a Social Charter of 2004 and an SAARC Convention on Child Welfare (Chavez, 2010, p. 153).

CONCLUSIONS AND WAYS FORWARD

This chapter has highlighted the increasing role of regions in mobilizing financial resources for development, in complementing national social policies by regional actions, in promoting and 'locking in' democracy in member states, and in complementing national legal systems with regional instruments and courts to protect HRs more effectively. The (potential) value added of regional institutions lies in their scale, their capacity to tackle cross-border issues, their (possible) relative autonomy vis-à-vis domestic interests, and their capacity to interact with third countries and actors.

Let us add a few additional considerations, pointing to the observed challenges for the policy practices in the distinct regions, as well as to the opportunities they imply for the academic research agenda.

Regional Development Finance

Regionalism and developmental policy have always been intertwined, but in many different ways, depending on prevalent policy ideas and geopolitical interests. The recent initiatives of regional development governance involve a mix of ideas, taken from the old developmental regionalism (for example, the importance of policy coordination and the role of public authority and public investment), and also from neoliberal theory (for example, the importance of private and foreign investment).

Meanwhile, there are three important challenges for both academics and practitioners which need to be addressed in future research. First, the interplay between extra-regional and intra-regional development finance must be examined. While the concept of 'regional development governance' (Bruszt and Palestini, 2016) suggests that intra-regional actors are increasingly more relevant in the design, financing and implementation of developmental policies, the interaction between external and internal financial actors must be elucidated empirically. Second, most citizens are not aware that the projects that perhaps benefit them and their communities were designed and implemented by ROs. Hence, there is a problem of information and accountability that ROs need to take into account. Third and most important, there is a lack of academic and policy research into the redistributive effects of developmental policies implemented by ROs. Further research is needed to both identify and measure the benefits, and also the potential negative externalities of developmental policies and programmes designed by ROs.

Regional Redistributive Policies

On redistribution, one can argue that this element provides the ready-made empirical test of the regional demos, to actually pacify the needs of the most vulnerable. It is also arguable that the redistributive component of RSP is the one that is often first hit or affected in the context of deep economic challenges. But the manner in which RDBs can be engaged in this regard in partnership with the conventional regional entities is still to be fully explored. Deacon and Macovei show how all RDBs, other than the Islamic Development Bank, place emphasis on regional integration in social policies. Some of the areas of social policy they dwell on include communicable diseases, preventing human trafficking of women and children, social protection, and social security transferability (Deacon and Macovei, 2010, p. 45).

Given the numerous flash points around the world and the challenges various countries are facing in dealing with migrants, it is hard to contemplate a greater urge and concrete support for RSP in various capitals. While it may be normatively sound (Kingah, 2014a), it is not politically attractive to evoke RSP in a context where sentiments about foreigners have hit a trough. However what regions can do in the areas of health (Kingah, 2014b; Amaya et al., 2015), unemployment mitigation (Kingah, 2014c) and education (Riesco, 2010) should not be minimized.

Regional Promotion of Democracy

The promotion and protection of democracy by ROs presents a number of challenges. One of these stems from the overlap of mandates and membership among ROs. Overlap, per se, is not necessarily a bad thing when it is managed through coordination and division of labour between ROs (for example, in the Americas the OAS organized fact-finding and diplomatic missions alongside the CARICOM and SICA in the democratic crises in Haiti in 2004 and in Honduras in 2009). However, there is also evidence of increasing competition among overlapping ROs. Electoral monitoring missions organized by the CIS have clashed on several occasions with electoral missions of the EU and the OSCE, showing a strong division between the CIS and 'Western observers' (Kelley, 2010; Libman, 2014). A consequence of this overlapping regionalism is *forum shopping* (Helfer, 1999; Busch, 2007), a situation in which states with multiple memberships choose the RO that better serves their normative or material preferences. In the ongoing political crisis in Venezuela, for instance, the incumbent government has constantly preferred UNASUR as the political mediator, rather than the OAS, even though (or maybe because?) the latter has greater experience in democracy promotion and protection (Closa and Palestini, 2015).

Forum shopping brings us to a second challenge that ROs face: the legitimacy deficit. There are significant flaws in the institutional design of ROs democratic accountability procedures. This creates the paradoxical situation of the 'promotors of democracy' not being themselves 'democratic'. The literature on the democratic deficit has been particularly prolific in the context of the EU, even though the EU claims to be the RO with the most developed democratic procedures (Schmitter, 2000; Schmidt, 2006; Ribeiro-Hoffmann and Van der Vleuten, 2007; Rittberger and Schröder, 2016). ROs in other regions have considerably less delegation of competences to third parties, concentrating the decision-making process on intergovernmental bodies and frequently conferring on the affected government a privileged role in the activation of protection mechanisms. In the ROs of the Americas, for example, affected governments are supposed to activate the democratic clauses generating a sort of intervention 'by invitation' (Legler and Tieku, 2010). Supra-state bodies such as the General Secretariats and the Regional Courts have practically no role; civil society organizations are also completely excluded from the enforcement of democracy protection mechanisms (Closa et al., 2016). The underlying assumption is that governments can be *only* victims, and not the *perpetrators*, of democratic breaches, which supports the hypothesis that governments use ROs and democratic clauses as instruments for regime survival and self-protection (Closa and Palestini, 2015).

The third challenge relates to the permeability of ROs' democratic norms to domestic changes in member states. This is an issue not only for ROs which look like 'authoritarian clubs' (Pevehouse, 2016) but also for ROs which traditionally have been considered as 'democratic clubs', such as the EU. The arrival of governments that claim to be truly 'European', while at the same time showing little respect for the rule of law and the rights of minorities and vulnerable groups in their societies, posits an unprecedented challenge to the European regionalist project and its hitherto undisputed democratic identity.

Regional Protection of Rights

HRs litigation is one of the clear manifestations of the HRBAD, and the fact that (some) regional systems include the protection of HRs is seen as a positive development (Zumbansen, 2014). However, these systems have not been strong enough to enforce HRs law vis-à-vis trade and investment regulations. Adjudication bodies, such as the WTO Dispute Settlement Body and the International Centre for Settlement of Investment Disputes (ICSID), do not consider that they should apply international or regional HRs law. In addition, neither regional HRs bodies nor the UN institutions are conceived to hold non-state actors accountable. This could explain why states often prefer to comply with trade and investment regulations at the cost of HRs duties (Van Hees, 2004).

It is notable that Africa has the most regional courts to protect HRs. It is also remarkable that Europe, America and Africa have used the regional HRs systems as a framework to protect constitutionalism (Wiebusch, 2016). Such regional systems can be seen as a way to support the national constitutional courts that actively look after the protection of fundamental rights (Grey, 2003; Ginsburg, 2008; Alviar et al., 2015).

This judicial protection is being consolidated despite objections based on the vagueness of the contents of ESCR, or on the lack of capacity and legal competences of the judiciary to adjudicate on issues of social policies (ICJ, 2008; Landau, 2011). Judicial enforcement of ESCR is justified by the lack of capacity of the victims of violations of ESCR to obtain remedies and reparations, and by the lack of accountability and determination of the state to implement these rights (ICJ, 2008). In practice, many countries have been using international legal standards when interpreting national rules or, in other cases, national judiciaries have applied them directly (ICJ, 2008). Progress has been recognized particularly in Latin America, but also in countries such as India and South Africa (López, 2004; Cottrell and Ghai, 2004; ICJ, 2008; Bonilla, 2013; Kingah et al., 2014; Roux, 2014). The use of comparative experiences and regional case law to encourage judicial activism in the defence of ESCR is therefore promoted (ICJ, 2008).

Another pending topic to be supported by the regional systems of HRs protection is the creation of mechanisms to hold non-state actors accountable for HRs violations. An important avenue for this to occur would be through better control of the regional development agencies, regional NGOs and regional businesses.

With the proliferation of declarations and treaties on sustainable development, the regional systems are also concerned with the enforcement of the third generation of HRs, also known as group rights, collective rights or solidarity rights, looking to empower and protect vulnerable groups such as women, children and especially indigenous communities, consumers and/or populations affected by environmental damage. These populations have received unequal regional treatment. For instance, the rights of indigenous populations have been recognized in most of the constitutions in Latin America and, to a lesser extent, in those of the US, Canada, Australia and New Zealand. The Inter-American system has been particularly sensitive to the protection of indigenous rights. Consumer rights are strongly protected in the US and Europe, and the protection of minorities is a growing concern in Europe, particularly in light of recent migration waves (Wilken, 2008; Roald, 2011).

As is clear from what precedes, the connections between regionalism and development are multiple and dynamic. In the area of social policy there are very good theoretical and practical arguments to defend an increasing role for regional organizations and regional governance. Various regions have experimented with policy initiatives and with the creation of new institutions for that purpose. These have, led, in many cases, to real and significant impacts for citizens in the enjoyment of their rights. At the same time, developmental regionalism is under stress and is contested in an epoch of economic crisis and new nationalist reflexes.

REFERENCES

Alviar, H., K.K. García and L.A. Williams (2015), *Social and Economic Rights in Theory and Practice*, London: Routledge.

Amaya, A., V. Rollet and S. Kingah (2015), 'What is in a Word? The Framing of Health at the Regional Level: ASEAN, EU, SADC and UNASUR', *Global Social Policy*, 15(3), 229–60.

Ambrosio, T. (2008), 'Catching the "Shanghai Spirit": How the Shanghai Cooperation Organization Promotes Authoritarian Norms in Central Asia', *Europe-Asia Studies*, 60(8), 1321–44.

Babb, S. (2009), *Behind the Development Banks*, Chicago: University of Chicago Press.

Benedek, W. et al. (2010), 'The Role of Regional Human Rights Mechanisms', Brussels: European Parliament (EXPO/B/DROI/2009/25).

Berg, E. (1981) Accelerated Development in Sub-Saharan Africa, World Bank.

Bhagwati, J. (1993), 'Regionalism and Multilateralism: An Overview', in J. De Melo and A. Panagariya (eds), *New Dimensions in Regional Integration*, Cambridge: Cambridge University Press, pp. 22–50.

Bianculli, A.C. and A. Ribeiro Hoffmann (2016), 'Regional Organizations and Social Policy: The Missing Link', in A.C. Bianculli and A. Ribeiro Hoffmann (eds), *Regional Organizations and Social Policy in Europe and Latin America*, London: Palgrave, pp. 1–22.

Bonilla Maldonado, D. (ed.) (2013), *Constitutionalism of the Global South. The Activist Tribunals of India, South Africa, and Colombia*, New York: Cambridge University Press.

Börzel, T.A. and S. Stapel (2015), 'Mapping Governance Transfer by 12 Regional Organizations: A Global Script in Regional Colors', in T. Börzel and V. van Hüllen (eds), *Governance Transfer by Regional Organizations*, Basingstoke: Palgrave, pp. 22–48.

Börzel, T.A. and V. van Hüllen (eds) (2015), *Governance Transfer by Regional Organizations: Patching Together a Global Script*, Basingstoke: Palgrave.

Bronstone, A. (1999), *The European Bank for Reconstruction and Development*, Manchester: Manchester University Press.

Bruszt, L. and G.A. McDermott (2009), 'Transnational Integration Regimes as Development Programmes', in L. Bruszt and R. Holzhacker (eds), *The Transnationalization of Economies, States and Civil Societies. New Challenges for Governance in Europe*, London: Springer, pp. 23–59.

Bruszt, L. and S. Palestini (2016), 'Regional Development Governance', in T. Börzel and T. Risse (eds), *The Oxford Handbook of Comparative Regionalism*, Oxford: Oxford University Press, pp. 374–404.

Busch, M.L. (2007), 'Overlapping Institutions, Forum Shopping, and Dispute Settlement in International Trade', *International Organization*, 61(4), 735–61.

Chavez, J.J. (2007), 'Social Policy in ASEAN: The Prospect for Integrating Migrant Labour Rights and Protection', *Global Social Policy*, 7(3), 358–78.

Chavez, J.J. (2010), 'Regional Social Policies in Asia: Prospects and Challenges from the ASEAN and SAARC Experiences', in B. Deacon et al. (eds), *World-Regional Social Policy and Global Governance*, London: Routledge, pp. 140–61.

Ciorciari, J. (2012), 'Institutionalizing Human Rights in Southeast Asia', *Human Rights Quarterly*, 34, 695–725.

Closa, C. and S. Palestini (2015), 'Between Democratic Protection and Self-defense: The case of Unasur and Venezuela', EUI Working Paper (2015/93).

Closa, C., S. Palestini and P. Castillo (2016), *Regional Organisations and Mechanisms for Democracy Protection in Latin America, the Caribbean, and the European Union*, Hamburg: EU-LAC Foundation.

Cooper, A.F. and T. Legler (2001), 'The OAS Democratic Solidarity Paradigm: Questions of Collective and National Leadership', *Latin American Politics and Society*, 43(1), 103–26.

Correa, F. (2010), 'A Legal/Institutional Analysis of FOCEM, the MERCOSUR Fund for Structural Convergence', in M.T. Franca, L. Lixinski and M.B. Olmos (eds), *The Law of MERCOSUR*, Oxford: Hart Publishing, pp. 395–412.

Cottrell, J. and Y. Ghai (2004), *Economic, Social and Cultural Rights in Practice: The Role of Judges in Implementing Economic, Social and Cultural Rights*, London: Interrights.

Couso, J. (2015), *Back to the Future? The Return of Sovereignty and the 'Principle of Non-intervention in the Internal Affairs of the States' in Latin America's 'Radical Constitutionalism'*, Utrecht: Montaigne Centre.

Culpeper, R. (1997), *Titans or Behemoths?*, London: Lynne Rienner.

Deacon, B. (2007), *Global Social Policy and Governance*, London: Sage.

Deacon, B. (2010), 'Regional Social Policies in Africa: Declarations Abound', in B. Deacon et al. (eds), *World-Regional Social Policy and Global Governance*, London: Routledge, pp. 162–87.

Deacon, B. (2011), 'Influencing Regional Social Policies from Above: Case Study of Sub-Saharan Africa', UNU-CRIS Working Paper (02).

Deacon, B. and M.C. Macovei (2010), 'Regional Social Policy from Above: International Organizations and Regional Social Policy', in B. Deacon et al. (eds), *World-Regional Social Policy and Global Governance*, London: Routledge, pp. 41–62.

Delors, J. (1989), *Report on Economic and Monetary Union in the European Community*, Brussels: European Commission.

de Souza Santos, B. (2009), 'Toward a Multicultural Conception of Human Rights', in F. Gómez and K. De Feyter (eds), *International Human Rights Law in a Global Context*, Bilbao: University of Deusto, pp. 97–121.

Dosman, E. (2006), *Raúl Prebsch: Power, Principle and the Ethics of Development*, Buenos Aires: INTAL.

Dutt, N. (2001), 'The US and the Asian Development Bank: Origins, Structure and Lending Operations', *Journal of Contemporary Asia*, 31(2), 241–61.

Duxbury, A. (2011), *The Participation of States in International Organizations. The Role of Human Rights and Democracy*, Cambridge: Cambridge University Press.

ECLAC (1994), *Open Regionalism in Latin America and the Caribbean*, Santiago: ECLAC.

Estevadeordal, A., B. Frantz and T. Nguyen (2004), *Regional Public Goods: From Theory to Practice*, Washington, DC: IDB and ADB.

Franck, T.M. (1992), 'The Emerging Right to Democratic Governance', *American Journal of International Law*, 86(1), 46–91.

Gauri, V. and S. Gloppen (2012), 'Human Rights Based Approaches to Development: Concepts, Evidence, and Policy', Policy Research Working Paper (5938), World Bank.

Genna, G.M. and T. Hiroi (2015), *Regional Integration and Democratic Conditionality: How Democracy Clauses Help Democratic Consolidation and Deepening*, New York: Routledge.

Ghai, Y. (2000), 'Human Rights and Governance: The Asia Debate', *Asia Pacific Journal on Human Rights and The Law*, 1(1), 9–52.

Ginsburg, T. (2008), 'The Global Spread of Constitutional Review', in K. Whittington and D. Keleman (eds), *Oxford Handbook of Law and Politics*, Oxford: Oxford University Press, pp. 81–98.

Grey, T.C. (2003), 'Judicial Review and Legal Pragmatism', *Wake Forest Law Review*, 38 (May), 473–511.

Hartmann, C. (2016), 'Sub-Saharan Africa', in T. Börzel and T. Risse (eds), *The Oxford Handbook of Comparative Regionalism,* Oxford: Oxford University Press, pp. 271–98.

Helfer, L.R. (1999), 'Forum Shopping for Human Rights', *University of Pennsylvania Law Review*, 148(2), 285–400.

Helfer, L.R. and K.J. Alter (2014), 'The Influence of the Andean Intellectual Property Regime on Access to Medicines in Latin America', in R. Dreyfuss and C. Rodríguez-Garavito (eds), *Balancing Wealth and Health: Global Administrative Law and the Battle over Intellectual Property and Access to Medicines in Latin America*, New York: Oxford University Press, pp. 247–62.

Helleiner, E. (2009), 'The Development Mandate of International Institutions: Where Did It Come From?', *Studies in Comparative International Development*, 44(3), 189–211.

Herz, M. (2012), 'The Organization of American States and Democratization', in J. Haynes (ed.), *Routledge Handbook of Democratization*, Abingdon: Routledge, pp. 337–50.

ICJ (2008), *Courts and the Legal Enforcement of Economic, Social and Cultural Rights: Comparative Experiences of Justiciability*, Geneva: International Commission of Jurists.

Kelley, J. (2010), 'Election Observers and their Biases', *Journal of Democracy*, 21(3), 158–72.

Kingah, S. (2013), 'Regional Courts and Human Rights in the Developing World', UNU-CRIS Working Papers (W-2013/11).

Kingah, S. (2014a), 'Regionalising Global Social Policy in Times of Crises: Comparing the European Union and the Common Market of the South', *Regions and Cohesion*, 4(1), 3–28.

Kingah, S. (2014b), 'Sit Up or Shut Up: Regional Organizations and Health', *Africa Health Journal*, 37(1), 16.

Kingah, S. (2014c), 'Regional Strategies to Mitigate Unemployment in the Wake of Crises: Comparing the EU in Greece and MERCOSUR in Paraguay', *Centre for European Law and Legal Studies (CELLS) On-line Papers*, 3(5).

Kingah, S., L. Lizarazo and P. De Lombaerde (2014), 'Constitutional Courts as Bulwarks against the Erosion of Social and Economic Rights through Free Trade Agreements: Colombia and South Africa Compared', *Manchester Journal of International Economic Law*, 11(3), 331–66.

Krasner, S.D. (1981), 'Power Structures and Regional Development Banks', *International Organization*, 35(2), 303–28.

Landau, D. (2011), 'The Reality of Social Rights Enforcement', *Harvard International Law Journal*, 53(1), 452–59.

Legler, T. and T.K. Tieku (2010), 'What Difference Can a Path Make? Regional Democracy Promotion Regimes in the Americas and Africa', *Democratization*, 17(3), 37–41.

Lehninger, J. (2015), 'Against All Odds: Strong Democratic Norms in the African Union', in T. Börzel and V. Van Hüllen (eds), *Governance Transfer by Regional Organizations. Patching Together a Global Script*, Basingstoke: Palgrave, pp. 51–67.

Levitt, B.S. (2006), 'A Desultory Defense of Democracy: OAS Resolution 1080 and the Inter-American Democratic Charter', *Latin American Politics & Society*, 48(3), 93–123.

Libman, A. (2014), 'Commonwealth of Independent States and Eurasian Economic Community', in L. Levi, G. Finizio and N. Vallinoto (eds), *The Democratization of International Institutions. First International Democracy Report*, Abingdon: Routledge, pp. 435–49.

Lixinski, L. (2010), 'Human Rights in MERCOSUR', in M.T. Franca, L. Lixinski and M.B. Olmos (eds), *The Law of MERCOSUR*, Oxford: Hart Publishing, pp. 351–64.

Lizarazo Rodríguez, L. and P. De Lombaerde (2015), 'Regional and Inter-Regional Economic Rules and the Enforcement of the Right to Health: The Case of Colombia', *Global Social Policy*, 15(3), 296–312.

López, M.D. (2004), *Teoría Impura del Derecho: La transformación de la cultura jurídica latinoamericana*, Bogotá: Legis.

Maharajh, A.N. (2014), 'The Caribbean Court of Justice: A Horizontally and Vertically Comparative Study of the Caribbean's First Independent and Interdependent Court', *Cornell International Law Journal*, 47(3), 735–66.

Mansfield, E.D. and J.C. Pevehouse (2006), 'Democratization and International Organizations', *International Organization*, 60(1), 137–67.

MERCOSUR (2000), *Charter of Buenos Aires on Social Commitment in MERCOSUR, Bolivia and Chile*, Washington, DC: MERCOSUR.

Mingst, K. (2016), 'The African Development Bank: From Follower to Broker and Partner', in J. Strand and S. Park (eds), *Global Economic Governance and the Development Practices of the Multilateral Development Banks*, New York: Routledge, pp. 80–98.

Molano Cruz, G. and S. Kingah (2014), 'Addressing Human Rights in the Court of Justice of the Andean Community and the Tribunal of the Southern African Development Community', *Colombia Internacional*, 81, 99–127.

Moravcsik, A. (2000) 'The Origins of Human Rights Regimes: Democratic Delegation in Postwar Europe', *International Organization*, 54(2), 217–52.

Palestini, S. (2016), 'Development Banks and Regional Powers: An Analytical Framework', Working Paper FFG The Transformative Power of Europe (77).

Park, S. and J.R. Strand (2016), *Global Economic Governance and the Development Practices of the Multilateral Development Banks*, London: Routledge.

Pevehouse, J. (2005), *Democracy from Above. Regional Organizations and Democratization*, Cambridge: Cambridge University Press.

Pevehouse, J. (2016), 'Regional Governance of Democracy and Human Rights', in T. Börzel and T. Risse (eds), *The Oxford Handbook of Comparative Regionalism*, Oxford: Oxford University Press, pp. 579–99.

Prebisch, R. (1963), *Towards a Dynamic Development Policy for Latin America*, New York: CEPAL.

Reyntjens, F. (1988), 'The Growing Role of Human Rights in Development Cooperation', in D. Van Den Bulcke (ed.), *Recent Trends in International Development*, Antwerp: College for Developing Countries, pp. 143–63.

Ribeiro Hoffmann, A. and A. van der Vleuten (2007), *Closing or Widening the Gap? Legitimacy and Democracy in Regional Integration Organizations*, Farnham: Ashgate.

Riesco, M. (2010), 'Regional Social Policies in Latin America: Binding Material for a Young Giant?', in B. Deacon et al. (eds), *World-Regional Social Policy and Global Governance*, London: Routledge, pp. 108–39.

Rittberger, B. and Ph. Schröder (2016), 'The Legitimacy of Regional Institutions', in T. Börzel and T. Risse (eds), *The Oxford Handbook of Comparative Regionalism*, Oxford: Oxford University Press.

Roald, A.S. (2011), 'Multiculturalism and Pluralism in Secular Society: Individual or Collective Rights?', *Ars Disputandi: The Online Journal for Philosophy of Religion*, 5, 147–63.

Roux, T. (2014), 'Assessing the Social Transformation Performance of the South African Constitutional Court: From Totalitarianism to the Rule of Law', in C. Jenkins and M. du Plessis (eds), *Law, Nation-Building and Transformation: The South African Experience in Perspective*, Antwerp: Intersentia, pp. 223–40.

Schiff, M. and L.A. Winters (2003), *Regional Integration and Development*, Washington, DC: The World Bank.

Schimmelfennig, F. and H. Scholtz (2008), 'EU Democracy Promotion in the European Neighbourhood', *European Union Politics*, 9(2), 187–215.

Schmidt, V. (2006), *Democracy in Europe: The EU and National Polities*, Oxford: Oxford University Press.

Schmitter, P.C. (2000), *How to Democratize the European Union: And Why Bother?*, Lanham, MD: Rowman & Littlefield.

Schnably, S.J. (2000), 'American System', in G. Fox and B. Roth (eds), *Democratic Governance and International Law*, Cambridge: Cambridge University Press, pp. 155–98.

Schnably, S.J. (2005), 'The OAS and Constitutionalism: Lessons from Recent West African Experience', *Syracuse Journal of International Law and Commerce*, 33, 263–76.

Sedelmeier, U. (2014), 'Anchoring Democracy from Above? The European Union and Democratic Backsliding in Hungary and Romania after Accession', *Journal of Common Market Studies*, 52(1), 105–21.

Sloan, J.W. (1971), 'The Strategy of Developmental Regionalism: Benefits, Distribution, Obstacles, and Capabilities', *Journal of Common Market Studies*, 10(2), 138–62.

Souaré, I.K. (2014), 'The African Union as a Norm Entrepreneur on Military Coups d'État in Africa (1952–2012): An Empirical Assessment', *The Journal of Modern African Studies*, 52(1), 69–94.

Striebinger, K. (2016), 'Coordination between the African Union and the Regional Economic Communities', Working Paper, International IDEA.

Threlfall, M. (2010), 'Social Policies and Rights in the European Union and the Council of Europe', in B. Deacon et al. (eds), *World-Regional Social Policy and Global Governance*, London: Routledge, pp. 85–107.

Tinbergen, J. (1965), *International Economic Integration*, Amsterdam: Elsevier.

Tussie, D. (1995), *The Inter-America Development Bank*, London: Lynne Rienner.

Twining, W. (2007), 'Human Rights: Southern Voices. F. Deng, A. An-Na'im, Y. Ghai and U. Baxi', *Law, Social Justice & Global Development Journal*, 1. Available at: http://www.go.warwick.ac.uk/elj/lgd/2007_1/twining.

Uribe, A.M. (2007), 'Los "Beneficios" del TLC: Las Consecuencias para la Biodiversidad y el Sistema de Propiedad Intelectual de Colombia', *Revista Pensamiento Jurídico*, (18), 103–23.

Van Der Plancke, V., V. Van Goethem, G. Paul and E. Wrzoncki (2016), *Corporate Accountability for Human Rights Abuses*, Paris: FIDH (3rd edn).

Van der Vleuten, A. and A. Ribeiro Hoffmann (2010), 'Explaining the Enforcement of Democracy by Regional Organizations: Comparing EU, Mercosur and SADC', *Journal of Common Market Studies*, 48(3), 737–58.

Van Hees, F. (2004), *Protection v. Protectionism. The Use of Human Rights Arguments in the Debate for and against the Liberalisation of Trade*, Åbo: Åbo Akademi.

Van Langenhove, L. and P. De Lombaerde (2007), 'Regional Integration and Development', *Global Social Policy*, 7(3), 379–385.

Van Langenhove, L. and M.C. Macovei (2010), 'Regional Formations and Global Governance', in B. Deacon et al. (eds), *World-Regional Social Policy and Global Governance*, London: Routledge, pp. 9–26.

Wiebusch, M. (2016), 'The Role of Regional Organizations in the Protection of Constitutionalism', IDEA Discussion Paper (17).

Wilken, L. (2008), 'Are Rights Universal? The Development of Minority Rights in Europe', in K. De Feyter and G. Pavlakos (eds), *The Tension between Group Rights and Human Rights: A Multi-Disciplinary Approach*, London: Hart Publishers, pp. 89–104.

Yeates, N. and B. Deacon (2006), 'Globalisation, Regionalism and Social Policy: Framing the Debate', UNU-CRIS Occasional Paper (O-2006/6).

Yeates, N. and B. Deacon (2010), 'Globalization, Regional Integration and Social Policy', in B. Deacon et al. (eds), *World-Regional Social Policy and Global Governance*, London: Routledge, pp. 27–39.

Youngs, R. (2009), 'Democracy Promotion as External Governance?', *Journal of European Public Policy*, 16(6), 895–915.

Zumbansen, P.C. (2014), 'Transnational Law, Evolving', King's College London Law School Research Paper (29).

7. Small loans, big problems: the rise and fall of microcredit as development policy
Milford Bateman

INTRODUCTION

After many false starts in the post-war period, the international development community announced in the 1980s that it had, finally, found the perfect solution to the problem of global poverty. This solution was microcredit, the provision of a microloan to the poor that could be used to establish a tiny income-generating business activity.[1] With the income derived from this business activity, it was envisaged that a poor individual could escape poverty, educate children, reinvest and build household assets, and generally become a more 'empowered' member of the local community. With the decisive turn to neoliberalism following the election of Margaret Thatcher in the UK in 1979, and then Ronald Reagan in the US a year later, the individualistic, self-help and market-affirming simplicity of the microcredit model resonated almost perfectly with the new global zeitgeist. It was no surprise, therefore, that the microcredit model caught on within neoliberal-oriented policy-making circles in key Western governments and in the international development community. Very soon microcredit was being described as a poverty reduction and local economic development panacea, a market-driven private sector intervention that, according to its leading light and future Nobel Peace Prize recipient (2006), Dr Muhammad Yunus, would 'eradicate poverty in a generation'. Governments in the global south were instructed to liberalize, privatize and deregulate their local financial systems in order to provide the best possible 'enabling environment' for a local microcredit industry to take root. Progress along these lines was very rapid indeed, and the resulting growth was exponential. By mid-2000 the provision of microcredit to the global poor was probably the highest-profile and most widely celebrated anti-poverty policy of all time.

But then, beginning in 2007, in one of the most dramatic about-turns in international development history, an astonishing wave of bad news began to destroy the entire legitimacy of microcredit as a development and social policy. Within just a few years, in fact, many institutions within the international development community and a growing number of developing country governments began to abandon the microcredit model. Fearing its entire collapse, the World Bank took the lead in mounting a rescue operation, which involved rebadging microcredit as one of the main components of its new 'financial inclusion' agenda. This move attests to the microcredit model's immense value to a number of narrow political and financial constituencies, but not to the global poor effectively forced into engaging with microcredit, which the evidence now shows have been severely disadvantaged in a multitude of ways.

The focus of this chapter is to briefly explain this turn of events. The first section (Historical twists and turns) charts the heady rise to fame of the microcredit model following its 'discovery' in Bangladesh in the 1980s. Section two (But then the downfall begins) then provides a summary of the key milestones in its rapid transition after 2007 into a failed development intervention, ultimately requiring its incorporation within the financial inclusion movement to help keep it alive. The third section (Three fundamental flaws of the microcredit model) first describes the two fundamental flaws in the basic microcredit model, before going on to point out the very significant flaws created by the turn to a new commercialized, or 'neoliberalized', microcredit model in the 1990s. The final section provides a brief conclusion.

HISTORICAL TWISTS AND TURNS

The Early Years

The basic microcredit model appears to have many similarities with a good number of financial innovations throughout history designed to collectively empower the poor, such as savings clubs, revolving credit schemes, and member-based financial cooperatives and credit unions. However, this similarity is deceptive. This is because the contemporary microcredit model actually has its origins, put simply, in an attempt by an elite to maintain its power over the poor majority.

The microcredit model was first conceived in the 1960s as a component part of a US government foreign policy approach designed to prop up friendly Latin American governments (at the time including many military dictatorships), thereby ensuring continued US political and economic domination in the region. The thinking was that the small number of microcredit recipients able to make some sort of a business success with their microcredit would begin to see themselves as a new class of 'entrepreneurial poor'. Eventually, it was hoped, this new class would begin to mobilize and seek to defend their individualized gains in the face of claims that wider collective action – for example, peasant movements, leftist political parties, and church-based movements espousing 'liberation theology' – would be a far better option for the poor overall.[2] In 1972, as part of this 'divide and conquer' effort, the US government's aid arm – USAID – helped establish a number of microcredit programmes in the region, starting with the first genuine microcredit programme in Latin America, in the city of Recife in Brazil. Similar programmes soon began to emerge with US government support right across the continent. The global microcredit industry had effectively been launched.

In the 1980s, the growing global interest in microcredit shifted focus to Bangladesh, and specifically to the US trained Bangladesh economist, Dr Muhammad Yunus. Having arrived back in Bangladesh after a prolonged period of PhD research and teaching in the US, Yunus was keen to do something about the horrendous levels of poverty and deprivation he saw all around him in the aftermath of a bitter civil war. Yunus examined a number of the microcredit programmes then operating in the region, especially the 'Comilla Model' pioneered in East Pakistan (later to become Bangladesh) by Akhter Hameed Khan. Following a number of his own experiments in the village of Jobra near Chittagong, and the introduction of a novel form of group-lending based on one's social capital rather than physical collateral, Yunus began to argue that even the very poorest could successfully engage in tiny entrepreneurial activities and, in so doing, could repay high interest rate microloans. Thenceforth the poor were deemed to be 'bankable'. Inevitably, these claims enamoured the microcredit model to the US government and to a number of right-wing US foundations. Yunus's central message to the international development community – that it was possible to 'bring down capitalism to the poor' – was a very enticing one indeed.

At the same time, Yunus managed to convince many people that he had found an answer not just to Bangladesh's poverty and underdevelopment, but to poverty everywhere. With financial and technical support increasingly forthcoming from many quarters, in 1983 Yunus was able to establish the now iconic Grameen Bank, which he was to go on to control almost single-handedly for the next 40 years. Support for other Microcredit Institutions (hereafter MCIs) to become established in Bangladesh also followed. Very soon Bangladesh was being held up as the global 'role model' that all other poor countries should emulate in order to address poverty. After only a very short period of operation, Yunus began to claim that microcredit and the Grameen Bank represented a poverty reduction panacea (see Hulme, 2008, p. 6). The international donor community was now more convinced than ever of the value that the microcredit model could bring to the effort to reconceptualize poverty interventions in an acceptable individualistic and market-affirming direction. With growing international donor support, Grameen Bank 'clones' soon began to pop up all over Asia and then Africa.

The Microcredit Model is 'Neoliberalized'

Even as the microcredit sector began to mushroom all around the global south in the 1980s, neoliberal policy-making elites still saw a fundamental operational flaw in the microcredit model that, they felt, had to be corrected. This was the fact that virtually all of the world's MCIs at the time, notably including the Grameen Bank itself, funded their operations with a variety of subsidies provided by the international donor community, host governments, private foundations, and other sources. But with neoliberalism now the guide to acceptable policies everywhere, the very idea that the microcredit industry would be reliant on state subsidies was anathema. Moreover, even with very generous state subsidies, it was realized that the microcredit industry would never be able to achieve the scale envisaged by the international development community as necessary to reach into every community in the global south.

Accordingly, the international development community was forced to abandon its support for the original subsidy-dependent Grameen Bank-style microcredit model. Under World Bank and USAID tutelage, it turned instead to supporting a new for-profit highly commercialized business model, one that prioritized above all else the profitability and the financial self-sufficiency ('full cost recovery') of the MCI (CGAP, 1995; Robinson, 2001). All new MCIs had to be of the commercialized variety, while existing MCIs were instructed to convert over to commercialized respectability.[3] Crucially, with far-reaching negative consequences as we shall see, many of Wall Street's most innovative (and destructive) operating methodologies were introduced. This included, for instance, the operational freedom for CEOs to award themselves high salaries and bonuses, the use of performance bonuses for loan officers to bring in as many new clients as possible, the securitization of loan portfolios, and a much greater emphasis upon attracting commercial investment from the leading global financial corporations. To help matters, the World Bank pushed even harder than ever for more deregulation (that is, self-regulation) of the microcredit industry, seeing this as the way to further 'free up' the average MCI to get on with the business of providing as much microcredit to the poor as possible.

Thanks to all of these moves, the supply of microcredit did indeed rapidly increase all across the global south. This was no more so than in

Bolivia, which in the early 1980s the World Bank used as the 'test-bed' for the newly commercialized microcredit model (Rhyne, 2001). Such was the progress that, by the early 2000s, a growing number of countries and regions had achieved the microfinance industry's 'holy grail' – every single poor individual wishing to access microcredit could now very easily do so; in fact, was being implored to do so (as we shall see below). By 2008, the most saturated countries included the two pioneering developing countries – Bangladesh and Bolivia – and were joined by a long list of other developing countries, including Mexico, Peru and Cambodia, and a set of post-communist countries from Eastern Europe, notably Bosnia and Mongolia (Bateman, 2011, p. 6).

The feeling in the international development community was now very clear indeed: the rapid growth of the global microcredit sector represented a fantastic achievement. Leading commercialization advocates, Otero and Rhyne (1994) claimed that the commercialized microcredit model was about to usher in a 'new world' of massive poverty reduction and human progress. The UN was successfully petitioned from both the right wing and left wing of politics to recognize this supposed progress, which it did when it agreed to designate 2005 as the 'UN Year of Microcredit'. And then the apotheosis arrived in 2006 when it was announced that Muhammad Yunus and the Grameen Bank he founded were to be the co-recipients of the Nobel Peace Prize.

By then the market-driven microcredit model was seen as one of the most popular international development policies of all time, and it was certainly the most important when it came to the specific issue of poverty reduction and local economic development. As the International Labour Organization's (ILO) then head of social finance, Bernd Balkenhol, famously remarked, by the mid-2000s the international development community was in full agreement that microcredit was 'the strategy for poverty reduction par excellence' (Balkenhol, 2006, underlining in the original). Not surprisingly, resources and technical support began to shift even faster into establishing and expanding MCIs and microcredit programmes, with the funds to achieve this very often raised by scaling down support for other types of local intervention, such as support for SME financing and development programmes. But even with support for other local development interventions being scaled back as a result (a seriously problematic development in the case of financing for formal SMEs, as we shall see), the rosy future predicted for the global microcredit model was such that, at the time, few were really concerned.

BUT THEN THE DOWNFALL BEGINS

The Commercialization of Microcredit Precipitates an Explosion of Greed and Unethical Behaviour

Those individuals and institutions promoting the commercialization of the microcredit model in the 1990s were convinced, and they convinced many others, that the newly commercialized microcredit industry would continue to lend responsibly to the global poor. But this hope turned out to be a forlorn one. The Wall Street-style changes made to the global microcredit model in the 1990s predictably created instead a wave of Wall Street-style 'blowback' outcomes and disasters, a misstep of such magnitude that it soon plunged the once unimpeachable reputation of the global microcredit sector to a new low.

One event in April 2007 in Mexico is widely noted as being the precursor of all the bad commercialization-driven outcomes that were soon to follow. This was the Initial Public Offering (IPO) of Banco Compartamos, the one-time non-governmental microcredit organization funded with grants from the US government and other sources. Thanks to commercial savvy and to quietly charging their very poor clients ultra-high interest rates (at most times nearly 100 per cent, and up to as much as 195 per cent on some loan products), Banco Compartamos was able to grow very rapidly, and by the early 2000s it was Mexico's largest microcredit bank. But then the IPO process inadvertently revealed to the public how Banco Compartamos really worked, and on whose behalf. Rather than demonstrating that microcredit had been able to reduce the grinding poverty in the poor Mexican communities in which it worked – there was then and still is today (see Angelucci et al., 2015) no real evidence for this – the IPO process revealed instead a quite spectacular level of greed and wilful profiteering by those closest to the institution. It started with Banco Compartamos' own senior management, several of whom became multi-millionaires following the sale of their shares at the time of the IPO. External investors also did very well indeed, including ACCION, the US-based microcredit advocacy and investment body that had provided a few thousand dollars of initial investment capital to get Compartamos started and then saw this turned into a shareholding valued at $270 million (Sinclair, 2012, p. 75).

But even more important to the fate of the global microcredit model was that the Banco Compartamos IPO episode revealed to others in the microcredit community just how easy it was to get rich. Those who supplied microcredit could generate and appropriate great wealth for themselves at the expense of the poor and desperate individuals and communities that demanded microcredit in an often all-too-unsuccessful attempt to escape poverty. Instead of seeing Banco Compartamos as a lesson in what not to do, the message received by a large number of savvy and unethical individuals attached to the microcredit sector was that Banco Compartamos was the 'role model' they needed to emulate in order to secure their own private enrichment under cover of 'helping the poor'. Similar private enrichment episodes thus began to emerge as the norm all over the global south, effectively confirming that the microcredit model had not just been thoroughly 'Wall Street-ized' in the 1990s but it was now producing predictable Wall Street-style results.

In many respects the deregulated and profit-driven global microcredit industry has been overwhelmed by a wave of what Black (2005) has termed 'control fraud' – a fraud committed against an organization by those employed and in control of it.[4] In the new 'financialization' era ushered in with the turn to neoliberalism in the 1980s, the CEOs and senior management of many MCIs are increasingly individually incentivized and free, because of deregulation/self-regulation, to take control of that MCI. But they seek such a position not in order to promote poverty reduction, but largely in order to maximize their own short-term rewards, taken out as high salaries, bonuses, share allocations, interest free loans, private business activities funded and promoted by the MCI, and so on. In many cases, the CEO is free to continue down this personal enrichment route even though this very much increases the possibility of destroying the MCI and/or the entire microcredit sector in the longer run,[5] which indeed has been the outcome in a growing number of cases (see below).

As many long-time advocates, now critics, began to lament increasingly (for example Harper, 2011; Sinclair, 2012; Waterfield, 2016; see also Bateman and Maclean, 2017), by the late 2000s it was becoming clear to all that the social mission of the microcredit industry had been completely subverted. To all intents and purposes, the global microcredit industry had been taken over by greedy individuals, opportunistic so-called social entrepreneurs, aggressive private banks and hard-nosed investors. The inevitable result was that the global poor are no longer the primary benefi-ciaries of the commercialized microcredit sector, but are involved as much as possible merely in order to serve as its hapless victims.

The Evidence Long Said to Confirm the Power of Microcredit is Debunked

The very widespread feeling in international development circles and among academic economists from the 1980s onwards was essentially that microcredit 'worked' just as its proponents claimed. Numerous impact evaluations produced in the 1990s and early 2000s by academic economists and professional evaluators all appeared to confirm this (see the summary by Odell, 2010). Moreover, a major survey in Bangladesh by then World Bank economists, Pitt and Khandker (1998), appeared to provide robust evidence of numerous positive impacts in the spiritual home of microcredit, most especially of reduced poverty among female clients. Many microcredit advocates thereafter used the results of this survey to justify the microcredit model, most notably and consistently Yunus himself.[6]

However, one inevitable result of the fierce criticism levelled at the microcredit industry in the wake of the 'Compartamos scandal', was a renewed interest in the veracity of the accumulated evidence purporting to confirm a positive impact. The feeling was that if the suppliers of microcredit were making so much money for themselves, it was more than ever important to confirm that the global poor were also benefitting. And almost immediately, a number of once sympathetic analysts began to find problems with the claims that microcredit successfully addressed poverty (Dichter and Harper, 2007). Some went on to claim that the evidence actually showed that microcredit did not 'work' at all (Bateman, 2010; Bateman and Chang, 2012; Chang, 2010). Pitt and Khandker's influential study was revisited by a number of researchers who found that it seriously exaggerated and distorted the evidence in order to produce the important finding of a positive impact of microcredit in Bangladesh (see Duvendack and Palmer-Jones, 2012; Roodman and Morduch, 2013; see also Bateman, 2013a).

By the early 2010s, the veracity of the accumulated evidence base in favour of microcredit was being called into question on an almost daily basis. By far the most important of the many new outputs re-evaluating the evidence in favour of microcredit was the systematic review undertaken by Duvendack et al. (2011). This UK government-funded systematic review provided a comprehensive denunciation of the accumulated evidence base long purported to confirm the positive impact of microcredit. It concluded, from a careful study of 2,643 impact evaluations that, thanks to problematic methodologies, flawed assumptions and outright bias, as few as 58 of the impact evaluations studied could be counted as robust, and that even in those cases there was insufficient evidence to conclude anything other than that there was no real evidence to confirm that the microcredit model worked. Their conclusion, that the global microcredit movement had effectively been 'constructed upon foundations of sand' (ibid., p. 76) sent shock waves through the microcredit industry. Subsequently, a summary of six of the leading Randomized Control Trial (RCT)-based impact evaluations of microcredit, a supposedly more accurate form of evaluation, could only conclude that microcredit had very little to no positive impact on the ground, summarizing that, 'The studies do not find clear evidence, or even much in the way of suggestive evidence, of reductions in poverty or substantial improvements in living standards. Nor is there robust evidence of improvements in social indicators' (Banerjee et al., 2015, p. 13). This, from a number of high-profile academics, several of whom had essentially built a good part of their academic reputation on their outspoken support for the microcredit model, was quite dramatic.

Microcredit Creates Mass Over-indebtedness and 'Microcredit Meltdowns'

Streeck (2014) is just one of many analysts arguing that neoliberal-oriented politicians and the business sector have seen rising private indebtedness as the only acceptable way of forestalling an otherwise inevitable under-consumption-driven crisis in capitalism.[7] Playing its part in the construction of this worrying scenario, and one of the defining features of the microcredit model in recent years, is the growing ubiquity of serious individual over-indebtedness wherever the microcredit sector has gained a significant foothold (Bateman, 2010, pp. 140–41; Guérin et al., 2013, Guérin et al., 2015).

The most important aspect of this destructive over-indebtedness trend is that it very often involves moving from microcredit being used for income-generation specifically to its use as a prop for consumption spending over the short term (Bateman, 2010, pp. 135–40).[8] Increasingly, in the absence of a regular income the poor are trapped into maintaining the bare minimum of consumption by accessing more and more microcredit, often at very high interest rates and often from more than one MCI. Such a survival tactic represents an extremely risky and ultimately destructive way of attempting to survive from one day to the next. The end game is all too often the seizure by an MCI of vital household assets, such as land and housing, taken as the final repayment on a growing bundle of microcredits that a poor client could not otherwise repay. Soederberg (2014) explains this dangerous trend as programmatically giving rise to what she terms 'the debtfare state', a new proactive configuration within contemporary capitalism, involving the wilful construction of forms of microdebt-based exploitation of the poor that are designed to benefit the well-connected financial elite. For example, it is surely no coincidence that those MCIs most involved in driving forward the growth of consumer microcredit across the global south are the same MCIs shown to have reaped quite stratospheric financial rewards, notably in South Africa (Bateman, 2015).

Further to this, and largely, though not exclusively, because of the over-indebtedness issue, a long and growing list of developing countries have gone on to encounter a destructive 'microcredit meltdown' phenomenon, among them Bolivia, Bosnia and Herzegovina, India (Andhra Pradesh state), Morocco, Nicaragua, Senegal, Pakistan, South Africa and Uganda. Like the sub-prime lending-driven financial crisis that occurred in the US in 2008, the typical 'microcredit meltdown' inflicts very serious damage on the overall economy and society, but particularly on the lives of the poor. Pointedly, thanks to the intervention of the international development community fearful that the global microcredit industry could not survive a full-blown crisis in its spiritual homeland, Bangladesh is noted for having only just averted a major meltdown in 2009–10 – what the CEO of one of the leading MCIs in Bangladesh otherwise called 'an approaching train wreck' (Chen and Rutherford, 2013). Many analysts are now raising the distinct possibility that a full-blown over-indebtedness crisis is on the cards for a number of 'at-risk' countries, including Cambodia, Colombia, Kyrgyzstan, Mexico, Mongolia, Peru and, once again, India.

The Microcredit Industry Is Rescued by the Financial Inclusion Movement

By the late 2000s, it had become clear within the international development community that the microcredit model was in very serious trouble. However, it was also clear that, for two very important reasons, the collapse of the microcredit movement would not be permitted. First, it plays an important role in the international development community's self-designated task of validating and operationalizing individual entrepreneurship and self-help within global capitalism, turning, it is hoped, even those struggling to survive in the informal sector into 'card-carrying capitalists' (see Harvey, 2014, pp. 182–98). Second, the microcredit model, once commercialized in the 1990s, opened the way for a narrow financial elite to enjoy huge financial rewards by programmatically draining the wealth from the very poorest communities. Mader (2015, p. 118) estimates that microcredit is responsible for the withdrawal of up to $125 billion from poor communities in the global south since 1995, due to their repayment of interest on microloans. Given that it has been shown that microcredit has had no real positive impact on poverty in the short term, and a seriously deleterious impact into the longer term by undermining and blocking the process of sustainable development, this extraction of wealth essentially serves no function other than to enrich the narrow financial elite that owns and controls the microcredit industry.

The approach taken to deal with the mounting problems of microcredit was to reposition it within a wider new development agenda termed 'financial inclusion', defined as the drive to endow the poor in developing countries with all of the most basic financial tools – microcredit, microsavings, bank accounts, payment cards, mobile money systems, and so on. With uplifting rhetoric and a seemingly renewed passion for facilitating pro-poor change, and in spite of almost zero evidence to confirm that financial inclusion might work as proposed by the international development community (see Mader, 2016), the financial inclusion movement has successfully kept the microcredit model alive. Indeed, thanks to new digital technologies and internet-based payment systems, the global south stands ready to be flooded with microcredit (Klapper and Singer, 2014).

THREE FUNDAMENTAL FLAWS OF THE MICROCREDIT MODEL

The Basic Microcredit Model Was Founded on a Fallacy

The global microcredit model was founded on the belief that, through a greatly increased number of informal microenterprises and self-employment ventures, it could significantly reduce poverty in the global south. As Muhammad Yunus (1989, p. 156) most famously put it, a 'Grameen-type credit program opens up the door for limitless self-employment, and it can effectively do it in a pocket of poverty amidst prosperity, or in a massive poverty situation'. This statement was based on the assumption that the poor individuals helped by microcredit to get into such activities would never encounter a local demand barrier. That is, it was widely believed that the poor could establish an informal microenterprise in their own village or community and then, at a price sufficient to make a profit, they would be able to sell virtually any amount of basic goods and services to their equally poor neighbours.

This fundamental assumption was wrong. Those who constructed the microcredit model, above all Muhammad Yunus, had actually fallen victim to one of the most famous fallacies in economics – Say's law, the mistaken idea that supply creates its own demand. As Amsden (2010) argued, poverty in the global south this last 30 or so years has not been caused by an insufficient supply of the basic goods and services needed by the poor to survive. Poverty has arisen more because of the lack of purchasing power (effective demand) that is necessary for the poor to obtain these necessary things. This goes a long way to explaining why the microcredit model has not reduced poverty anywhere near as much as its supporters claimed that it would: a microcredit-induced increase in the supply of goods and services in a local community requires an automatic uptick in local demand, but there is no automatic mechanism to ensure this.[9] The result is that a microcredit-induced increase in local supply all too often (1) depresses the local price of the goods and services produced by the poor, and (2) contributes toward a reduction in turnover per individual microenterprise (as demand is shared out among the increased number of informal microenterprises) that directly depresses incomes, wages and profits. The overall result of such ultra-competitive microcredit-induced dynamics, as Breman (2003) and Davis (2006) and many others richly document, is that the global poor are increasingly forced to inhabit a 'race-to-the-bottom' world where incomes are competed down to the bare subsistence level,[10] and where heightened exploitation and inequality, worsening working conditions, fewer public services, and rising levels of violence and business 'turf wars' in the community are the inevitable social consequences.

In addition, as Nightingale and Coad (2014) emphasize, the job creation impact of microcredit is also much less than is typically argued by the microcredit industry. Two largely predictable adverse impacts on employment are responsible for depressing the real number of jobs created. First, the high (microcredit-induced) levels of new microenterprise entry in poor communities are typically followed by high levels of job displacement, whereby a comparable number of the existing jobs in incumbent microenterprises are lost following the entry of these new microenterprises. Second, there is the problem of exit, which is the situation where incumbent microenterprises are forced to close down due to the increased (microcredit-induced) competition coming from new entrant microenterprises. And the pattern repeats itself again and again. This combination of high levels of displacement and exit – known as 'job churn' – results in far fewer sustainable local employment opportunities being realized through informal microenterprises and self-employment ventures than the entry figures would suggest. And the claim by the microcredit industry that it instantly creates a quite large number of self-employment opportunities – yes, but most are extremely short-lived, heavily debt burdened and with the potential to ultimately wipe out a poor household's entire bundle of valuable assets.

Microcredit Is Inimical to Longer-run Local Economic Development

Economic history demonstrates that development and growth are largely a function of rising productivity (Krugman, 1994). This makes it incumbent on any country to construct and maintain a financial system that, in so far as is possible, ensures that the most productive enterprises enjoy the greatest access to financial resources (and other forms of support). As King and Levine (1993) demonstrated, a developmentally effective financial system can be defined as one which increases the quantity and quality of capital available for investment in the enterprise sector. However, in the light of the most recent spectacular development successes in Vietnam, China, Brazil and elsewhere, this definition is now recognized as being incomplete (Bateman, 2013b), a fact that has major implications for the validity of the microcredit model.

A developmentally effective financial system is not just about the volume of investment being channelled into the enterprise sector per se, which ideally should be maximized, as King and Levine argue; it is also about which enterprises within the range of possible attributes (size, use of technology, product and process sophistication, innovative potential, and so on) are prioritized and, by the same token, which are relatively ignored if they do not possess these important attributes. A developmentally effective financial system can therefore be defined as one that possesses particular institutions, organizations, incentive structures and regulatory frameworks that can combine to proactively 'guide' capital investment into the best potentially growth-oriented individual enterprises (individually, in clusters and in sectors), while also denying capital to the least productive enterprises, which should really be discouraged and forced to exit. Importantly, as Foster et al. (2008) point out, functioning enterprises should also be able to grow fast through accessing more capital, thus helping them to absorb market share from the least productive enterprises, which should be pushed to exit as soon as possible and their remaining assets recombined into the more successful enterprises.

To gain a greater understanding of the financial structures, specific institutions and regulatory requirements which can successfully 'guide' capital in such a manner, and also to understand what these 'right' enterprises are, we can turn to those working within the 'developmental statist' paradigm (for example, see Wade, 1990; Evans, 1995; Amsden, 2001; Chang, 2006). A core argument here was that only particular types of enterprise drive growth, economic development and eventual poverty reduction; namely those enterprises big enough, flexible enough, innovative enough, connected enough and sophisticated enough to be able to take part in a process of increasing technological and institutional capability upgrading and continuous learning. If we distil the historical evidence, we find that the 'right' type of enterprise is a small, medium or large enterprise that has some or all of the following characteristics:

1. it is formally registered and operating according to all legal requirements;
2. it operates at, or well above, the minimum efficient scale;
3. it is as much as possible operating on the technology frontier;
4. it is innovation and skills-driven rather than (just) low labour cost-driven;

5. it is horizontally (clusters, networks) and vertically (subcontracting, supply chains, public procurement links) connected to other organizations;
6. it is able to continually facilitate the creation of new organizational routines and capabilities.

By the same token, the 'wrong' enterprises to support financially are clearly those enterprises which do not possess any of the important productivity-raising characteristics listed above; that is, informal microenterprises and self-employment ventures (Bateman, 2010; Pagés, 2010; Bateman and Chang, 2012). Baumol (1990) discusses forms of entrepreneurship that, while conferring some advantages on the owner(s), greatly disadvantage the community as a whole, giving rise to his concept of 'productive' and 'unproductive' entrepreneurship. Nor can the 'job churn' phenomenon, discussed above, be realistically portrayed as some sort of Schumpeterian 'creative destruction' process that might lead to increased productivity. The 'job churn' outcome involves almost none of the known valuable features whereby new better enterprises displace old inefficient ones (Bateman, 2010, p. 65). We must also discount the myth that the informal microenterprise sector serves as the foundation, or 'breeding ground', for larger and higher-productivity SMEs. As La Porta and Shleifer (2008) and Shane (2009) emphasize, all but a tiny number of the vast bulk of formal SMEs start out as formal SMEs, not informal microenterprises. Promoting the entry of larger numbers of informal microenterprises is thus very unlikely to add to the eventual supply of productive formal SMEs.

Raising productivity and promoting development is something that is simply not in the gift of the informal microenterprise or self-employment venture (Chang, 2010). Instead, the rapid proliferation of informal microenterprises and self-employment ventures has, all too often, created a set of adverse 'initial conditions' that, through a number of different mechanisms and feedback loops, tend to frustrate and prohibit sustainable local economic development. Reinert (2007) provides one of the best explanations as to why this might be so. He has argued that the programmed expansion of ultra-low productivity and diminishing returns' activities (which is almost the definition of the informal sector) can only combine to deindustrialize, primitivize and informalize the local economy. Such an outcome is the inevitable result whenever important scale economies are lost, technologies suitable at certain volumes of activity are abandoned, and important efficiency-enhancing vertical and horizontal inter-enterprise connections are inoperable. Reinert (2007, p. 171) effectively sums up the problem:

Systems based on increasing returns, synergies and systematic effects all require a critical mass; the need for scale and volume creates a 'minimum efficient size'. When the process of expansion is put in reverse and the necessary mass and scale disappears the system will collapse.

Crucially, the general retrogression process that Reinert describes is exactly what we are seeing in all locations – at national, regional and local level – where the microcredit model has gained the strongest foothold. If the best enterprises begin to lose out in the struggle for capital investment, and if they are also increasingly surrounded by informal microenterprise and self-employment ventures that possess certain temporary competitive advantages (do not pay tax, can exploit workers, do not invest in order to adhere to environmental and health regulations, etc.) that allow them to unfairly gain market share, the retrogression process raised by Reinert becomes the reality. By actively shepherding scarce financial resources into promoting the least productive enterprises, the microcredit model succeeds only in deindustrializing, primitivizing, informalizing and disconnecting the local enterprise structure, and helping to permanently 'lock in' a state of under-development and poverty.

Commercialized Microcredit is a Destructive Sub-prime Style of Finance

The moves to commercialize and deregulate the microcredit industry in the 1990s were initially a response to the fact that the microcredit model made famous by Muhammad Yunus relied upon subsidies of one kind or another. This was intolerable to the neoliberal policy-making community that generally agreed with Robinson's (2001) notion that a 'healthy' MCI must necessarily be a financially self-sustaining one. Furthermore, those policy makers that most aggressively promoted the commercialization of microcredit – notably Robinson, Maria Otero and Elizabeth Rhyne – also believed in the supreme value of profit incentives and largely unregulated market competition in the financial sector. They held the view that only by commercializing microcredit and ensuring a deregulated (that is, self-regulated) business environment would an MCI strive to be bigger and better, and so generate the most positive impact with regard to the poor. However, they gravely misunderstood the all too often destructive nature of financial markets and profit incentives under capitalism. This miscalculation was to have a disastrous impact on the global poor.

All markets suffer from a tendency to over-supply or under-supply. However, if regulatory structures are deliberately kept minimal and weak, and if incentive structures are tied to the rapid expansion of a financial institution, history shows that it is actually very difficult indeed to ensure that a financial institution will lend responsibly. The Great Depression in the 1930s, the Savings and Loans Crisis in the US in the 1990s, and the global financial crisis of 2008, all involved reckless lending emerging in the wake of a major deregulatory exercise and a general willingness to incentivize and reward senior management for achieving short-term growth at the expense of longer-term sustainability (Minsky, 1986; Black, 2005; Galbraith, 2014).

Therefore, it should have been no surprise that when similar 'enabling conditions' were applied to the global microcredit sector in the 1990s as a result of the drive to commercialize the sector, this incentivized many MCIs to indulge in reckless lending. These reckless lending exercises were principally designed to immediately enrich the CEO and senior management but also, later, the shareholders. Accordingly, reckless lending has become one of the major factors in precipitating mass individual over-indebtedness in the global south, and the related tendency for regular 'microcredit meltdowns' to occur.[11] Appropriately, the first such episode of over-indebtedness and crisis took place in the very first developing country to agree to the commercialization of its microcredit sector – Bolivia (see Rhyne, 2001) – but since then a whole host of the 'role model' countries in the global south have followed suit (see Bateman, 2010; Guérin et al., 2015).

The major structural flaws and contradictions which have destroyed much of the functioning and legitimacy of the global neoliberal model of 'financialization' (Mirowski, 2013), have thus also contributed to destroying the functioning and legitimacy of the commercialized global microcredit model. Moreover, with a growing volume of developed country foreign direct investment and funds for on-lending channelled into the microcredit sectors in the global south, significant outflows of capital are now being generated through dividends, profits, management fees and capital appreciation, all of which can be repatriated to head office. In a very real sense, MCIs regard the earnings of informal microenterprises as a flow of funds that can be used to repay high interest rate microloans, thus allowing the MCI and its investors to capture a large part of the economic surplus of a poor community.

CONCLUSION

Long described in popular renditions of development as a 'bottom-up' success story, notably in the work of Jeffrey Sachs (2005), the common understanding of the developmental role of microcredit is almost entirely wrong. It is now increasingly recognized that microcredit has played no real role in poverty reduction. Further to this, the evidence points to the longer-term impact of the increased supply of microcredit having been to compete wages and incomes down to subsistence levels and, in the process of doing this, creating a hyper-competitive 'dog-eat-dog' local economy that destroys the potential for sustainable local economic and social development. As Davis (2006) remarks, the growing phenomenon of (microcredit-induced) hyper-competition at the local economy level does not represent one of the solutions to poverty in the global south, but rather one of the ugliest manifestations of it. Meanwhile, the only identifiable beneficiaries of the microcredit model are actually those individuals and institutions choosing to supply microcredit to the global poor, not the poor communities that are its recipients.

NOTES

1. Note that another term – microfinance – has long been used to describe microcredit. Strictly speaking, however, the term microfinance now covers a whole range of micro-financial interventions, such as micro-insurance, microsavings, micro-leasing, as well as microcredit.
2. This broad idea was extensively promoted in the region through a number of individuals and institutions financially supported by the US government, perhaps most famously by Peruvian economist Hernando de Soto (1986).
3. The Grameen Bank itself finally gave in to the pressure in 2001 and, thanks to what it called the 'Grameen II Project', it was converted into a for-profit model (Hulme, 2008).
4. It is important to note that 'control fraud' may be entirely legal, though illegality typically follows in most cases (for example, see Galbraith, 2014).
5. Akerlof and Romer (1994) famously demonstrated that CEOs and the senior management in a financial institution operating within a weakly regulated financial system are very often willing and able to deliberately drive their own institution into bankruptcy, since this will maximize their own individual financial returns in the interim.
6. Based on the data produced by Pitt and Khandker, Muhammad Yunus would, for many years, deploy a famous quote – '5 per cent of Grameen borrowers escape poverty every year' – which was only very much later shown to have been false (see next paragraph).
7. According to the International Institute of Finance (IIF, 2015), household debt has exploded in recent years, rising by \$7.7 trillion between 2007 and 2015, the bulk of which (\$6.2 trillion) is associated with emerging markets.
8. In South Africa, to give just one example, as much as 96 per cent of microcredit is now taken out for simple consumption spending applications (Bateman, 2015).
9. Another way to understand the fundamental problem here is to see it as akin to the error made by those who long argued that famines were caused by 'a lack of food' and that 'more food availability' would quickly remedy the problem. This 'common sense' was then overturned by Amartya Sen (1981) who showed that the core problem behind famines was actually the limited purchasing power of the poor that prevented them from buying the food that was often quite widely available in a famine region.
10. As Galbraith ([1967] 1978) pointed out, the common idea that perfect competition competes away all profits/wages is a necessary fiction in the world of big business, but it is generally the painful reality in the world of small businesses.
11. Many governments in the global south are aware of the problem, but remain relatively sanguine, at least partly because they hope that the inevitable repayment crisis will take place well into the future or, at a minimum, that it will confront the next government to come to power.

REFERENCES

Akerlof, G.A. and P.M. Romer (1994), 'Looting: The Economic Underworld of Bankruptcy for Profit' (April). NBER Working Paper, R1869.

Amsden, A.H. (2001), *The Rise of 'The Rest': Challenges to the West from Late-Industrializing Economies*. Oxford: Oxford University Press.

Amsden, A.H. (2010), 'Say's law, poverty persistence, and employment neglect', *Journal of Human Development and Capabilities*, 1(1): 57–66.

Angelucci, M., D. Karlan and J. Zinman (2015), 'Microcredit impacts: Evidence from a randomized microcredit program placement experiment by Compartamos Banco', *American Economic Journal: Applied Economics*, 7(1): 151–82.

Balkenhol, B. (2006), 'The Impact of Microfinance on Employment: What do we know?' Paper presented to the Global Microcredit Summit. Halifax, Canada, 12–16 November.

Banerjee, A., D. Karlan and J. Zinman (2015), 'Six randomized evaluations of microcredit: Introduction and further steps', *American Economic Journal: Applied Economics*, 7(1): 1–21.

Bateman, M. (2010), *Why Doesn't Microfinance Work? The Destructive Rise of Local Neoliberalism*. London: Zed Books.

Bateman, M. (ed.) (2011), *Confronting Microfinance: Undermining Sustainable Development*. Sterling, VA: Kumarian Press.

Bateman, M. (2013a), 'The Art of Pointless and Misleading Microcredit Impact Evaluations'. Governance across borders, 29 May 2013. Available at: http://governancexborders.com/2013/05/29/the-art-of-pointless-and-misleading-microcredit-impact-evaluations/.

Bateman, M. (2013b), 'Financing local economic development: In search of the optimal local financial system', in OFSE (ed.), *Private Sector Development – Ein neuer Businessplan fur Entwicklung?* Vienna: OFSE.

Bateman, M. (2015), 'South Africa's post-apartheid microcredit experiment: Moving from state-enforced to market-enforced exploitation'. Forum for Social Economics. DOI: 10.1080/07360932.2015.1056202.

Bateman, M. and H.-J. Chang (2012), 'Microfinance and the illusion of development: From Hubris to Nemesis in thirty years', *World Economic Review*, 1: 13–36.

Bateman, M. and K. Maclean (eds) (2017) *Seduced and Betrayed: Exposing the Contemporary Microfinance Phenomenon*. Albuquerque and Santa Fe: University of New Mexico Press and School for Advanced Research.

Baumol, W. (1990), 'Entrepreneurship: Productive, unproductive, and destructive', *Journal of Political Economy*, 98(5): 893–921.

Black, W.K. (2005), *The Best Way to Rob a Bank is to Own One: How Corporate Executives and Politicians Looted the S&L Industry*. Austin: University of Texas Press.

Breman, J. (2003), *The Labouring Poor: Patterns of Exploitation, Subordination and Exclusion*. Oxford: Oxford University Press.

CGAP (1995), *Good Practice Guidelines for Funders of Microfinance* (1st edition). Washington, DC: CGAP, World Bank.

Chang, H.-J. (2006), *The East Asian Development Experience: The Miracle, the Crisis and the Future*. London: Zed Books and Third World Network.

Chang, H.-J. (2010), *23 Things they Don't Tell you about Capitalism*. New York: Bloomsbury Press.

Chen, G. and S. Rutherford (2013), 'A Microcredit Crisis Averted: The Case of Bangladesh'. Focus Note 87, July. Washington, DC: CGAP, World Bank.

Davis, M. (2006), *Planet of Slums*. London: Verso.

de Soto, H. (1986), *El otro sendero: La Revolución Informal*. Lima: Editorial El Barranco.

Dichter, T. and M. Harper (eds) (2007), *What's Wrong with Microfinance?* London: Practical Action Publishers.

Duvendack, M. and R. Palmer-Jones (2012), 'Response to Chemin and to Pitt', *Journal of Development Studies*, 48(12): 1892–7.

Duvendack, M., R. Palmer-Jones, J. Copestake, L. Hooper, Y. Loke and N. Rao (2011), *What is the Evidence of the Impact of Microfinance on the Well-being of Poor People?*

London: EPPI-Centre, Social Science Research Unit, Institute of Education, University of London.

Evans, P. (1995), *Embedded Autonomy: States and Industrial Transformation*. Princeton, NJ: Princeton University Press.

Foster L., J. Haltiwanger and C. Syverson (2008), 'Reallocation, firm turnover, and efficiency: Selection on productivity or profitability?', *American Economic Review*, 98(1): 394–425.

Galbraith, James K. (2014), *The End of Normal: The Great Crisis and the Future of Growth*. New York: Simon and Schuster.

Galbraith, John K. ([1967] 1978), *The New Industrial State* (3rd edition). Boston, MA: Houghton Mifflin.

Guérin, I., S. Morvant-Roux and M. Villarreal (eds) (2013), *Microfinance, Debt and Over-indebtedness: Juggling with Money*. London: Routledge.

Guérin, I., M. Labie and J.M. Servet (eds) (2015), *The Crises of Microcredit*. London: Zed Books.

Harper, M. (2011), 'The commercialisation of microfinance: Resolution or extension of poverty?', in M. Bateman (ed.), *Confronting Microfinance: Undermining Sustainable Development*. Sterling, VA: Kumarian Press, pp. 49–63.

Harvey, D. (2014), *Seventeen Contradictions and the End of Capitalism*. London: Profile Books.

Hulme, D. (2008), 'The Story of the Grameen Bank: From Subsidised Microcredit to Market-based Microfinance'. BWPI Working Paper, 60. Institute for Development Policy and Management, University of Manchester, November.

International Institute of Finance (2015), *Capital Markets Monitor: Key Issues* (November/December). International Institute of Finance.

King, R.G. and R. Levine (1993), 'Finance, entrepreneurship, and growth: Theory and evidence', *Journal of Monetary Economics*, 32(3): 513–42.

Klapper, L. and D. Singer (2014), *The Opportunities of Digitizing Payments*. Washington, DC: World Bank.

Krugman, P. (1994), *The Age of Diminished Expectations*. Cambridge, MA: The MIT Press.

La Porta, R. and A. Shleifer (2008), 'The Unofficial Economy and Economic Development'. National Bureau of Economic Research Working Papers, 14520. Washington, DC: NBER.

Mader, P. (2015), *The Political Economy of Microfinance: Financialising Poverty*. London: Palgrave Macmillan.

Mader, P. (2016), 'Questioning Three Fundamental Assumptions in Financial Inclusion'. Evidence Report Number 176: Policy anticipation, response and evaluation, February. Brighton: Institute of Development Studies.

Minsky, H. (1986), *Stabilising an Unstable Economy*. New York: McGraw-Hill Professional.

Mirowski, P. (2013), *Never Let a Serious Crisis go to Waste: How Neoliberalism Survived the Financial Meltdown*. London: Verso.

Nightingale, P. and A. Coad (2014), 'Muppets and gazelles: Political and methodological biases in entrepreneurship research', *Industrial and Corporate Change*, 23(1): 113–43.

Odell, K. (2010), *Measuring the Impact of Microfinance*. Washington, DC: Grameen Foundation.

Otero, M. and E. Rhyne (eds) (1994), *The New World of Microenterprise Finance: Building Healthy Institutions for the Poor*. London: IT Publications.

Pagés, C. (ed.) (2010), *The Age of Productivity: Transforming Economies from the Bottom Up*. Washington, DC: Inter-American Development Bank.

Pitt, M. and S. Khandker (1998), 'The impact of group-based credit programs on poor households in Bangladesh: Does the gender of participants matter?', *Journal of Political Economy*, 106(5): 958–96.

Reinert, E. (2007), *How Rich Countries Became Rich, and Why Poor Countries Stay Poor*. London: Constable.

Rhyne, E. (2001), *Mainstreaming Microfinance: How Lending to the Poor Began, Grew, and Came of Age in Bolivia*. West Hartford, CT: Kumarian Press.

Robinson, M. (2001), *The Microfinance Revolution: Sustainable Finance for the Poor*, Washington, DC: World Bank.
Roodman, D. and J. Morduch (2013), 'The Impact of Microcredit on the Poor in Bangladesh: Revisiting the Evidence'. Financial Access Initiative, Working Paper 06/2103.
Sachs, J. (2005), *The End of Poverty: Economic Possibilities for Our Time*. London: Penguin.
Sen, A. (1981), 'Ingredients of famine analysis: Availability and entitlements', *The Quarterly Journal of Economics*, 96(3) (August): 433–64.
Shane, S. (2009), 'Why encouraging more people to become entrepreneurs is bad public policy', *Small Business Economics*, 33(2): 141–9.
Sinclair, H. (2012), *Confessions of a Microfinance Heretic: How Microlending Lost its Way and Betrayed the Poor*. San Francisco: Berrett-Koehler.
Soederberg, S. (2014), *Debtfare States and the Poverty Industry: Money, Discipline and the Surplus Population*. New York: Routledge.
Streeck, W. (2014), *Buying Time: The Delayed Crisis of Democratic Capitalism*. London: Verso.
Wade, R. (1990), *Governing the Market*. Princeton: Princeton University Press.
Waterfield, C. (2016), 'Opportunity International and MyBucks: A Dangerous Partnership Decision?', Next Billion Blog. Available at: http://nextbillion.net/opportunity-international-and-mybucks-a-dangerous-partnership-decision/ (accessed 1 July 2016).
Yunus, M. (1989), 'Grameen Bank: Organization and operation', in J. Levitsky (ed.), *Microenterprises in Developing Countries*. London: Intermediate Technology Publications.

8. 'A rising tide lifts us all; don't rock the boat!' Economic growth and the legitimation of inequality
Gareth Dale

A widely-held view on the relationship between poverty and inequality is that there isn't one.[1] Welfare, in this optic, is determined by economic growth, not distribution. How the poor fare has nothing to do with how well-heeled are the rich. What matters is not the pie's ingredients or how it is carved up, but the fact that tomorrow's delivery is bigger than today's. As the size of the average serving grows, all will reap the benefits.

To switch metaphor, the aphorism that encapsulates the case is 'a rising tide lifts all boats'. The 'rising tide' metaphor carries a distinctively modern charge. In this chapter I examine its qualities, as they relate in particular to the growth paradigm. By growth paradigm I refer to the idea that 'the economy' exists as an identifiable social sphere, that it possesses an inherent propensity to grow, that its growth is imperative, continuous (even limitless), and that growth is an acknowledged social goal and considered to be a fundamental social good – even, indeed, the principal remedy for a catalogue of social ills.

I shall discuss four aspects of the 'rising tide' image. Three are attributes of the metaphor itself: it envisages 'the economy' as, like the sea, a law-governed natural phenomenon; it moves (or rises) as a whole and in a manner that is perceptible and measurable; and all human livelihoods rest on a single socio-economic basis, much as vessels on the ocean. The fourth pertains to the conjuncture in which the aphorism first gained popularity: in a speech by John F. Kennedy in which he laid out his Smithian-Keynesian version of the growth paradigm.

'THE ECONOMY' AS A LAW-GOVERNED ENTITY

If the study of various aspects of economic behaviour – including policies, ethics and the dynamics of certain processes of production and trade – is ancient, it was not until the middle of the last millennium that 'the economy' as a discrete, law-governed realm came to be studied in a systematic way. The breakthrough was striking in Western Europe. In

151

the medieval era, economic behaviour was considered an indissoluble aspect of the social totality, with economic interests deemed to be subordinate to the real business of life, which was salvation. God administered worldly affairs, and no sense existed of an economic realm independent of the service of the clerics and the nobles, having its autonomy and its own laws as a part of nature. The prevailing ideas held natural laws to be part of a comprehensively *graded* order consisting of hierarchies nested within hierarchies, punctuated by contingencies and divine intervention. It was a tiered conception of the universe: thoroughly hierarchical, with God, angels, kings, priests, etc., each in their place. And it was static. There was little sense in searching for laws of motion (Borkenau, [1934] 1971).

From around the sixteenth century that began to change. The new era was fascinated by motion and circulation. Copernicus had theorised the circular motion of heavenly bodies. Physiology was reinvented as the study of fluid hydraulics and forces, with the body conceived as a hydraulic machine of circulating fluids, and sickness and health understood as a matter of the equilibrium among the body's 'humours' (fluids) (Christensen, 1994, p. 252). These developments rubbed off on social discourse. Relations of economic value began to be discussed under a similar rubric to the laws of motion, and with similar metaphors. The circulation of commodities and money came to be explicated using the vocabulary of astronomy and mathematics, anatomy and pathology, and accounting: the *quantity* theory of money, the *balance* of trade (from the weighing apparatus, via accounting), and so on (Harris, 2004). The mercantilist economist Edward Misselden was far from alone in resorting to geometric and hydrological metaphor to depict the balance of trade. Whereas international trade marks 'the *Periphery or Circumference of the Circle of Commerce*', the balance of trade constitutes 'the very *Center* of this *Circle*', and if conceived thus, all the mysteries of exchange will resolve themselves. For, just 'as a paire of Scales or Ballance, is an Invention to shew us the waight of things' so the balance of trade is 'an excellent and politique Invention, to shew us the difference of waight in the *Commerce* of one Kingdome with another'. All the 'rivers of Trade' he concludes, 'spring out of this source, and empt themselves againe into this *Ocean*. All the waight of Trade falle's to this *Center,* & come's within the circuit of this *Circle*' (Misselden, [1623] 1995, p. 211).

The seventeenth-century mercantilists were interested in questions of growth, production and distribution, but their focus, more than that of their successors, was on the 'circular flow of economic life', the maintenance of which was deemed essential to the preservation of a stable commonwealth, and which helped writers to conceptualise the interdependence among diverse phenomena such as price levels, specie flows and the quantity of money (McNally, 1988, pp. 29–34). Out of this project, the 'circulatory model' of economic behaviour was to evolve.

The metaphor of 'circulation' originated in husbandry (agricultural production), and in this it is of a piece with Thomas Mun's conceptualisation of the investment of bullion in foreign trade ventures as a kind of 'advance', like the planting of seed, which would yield a profitable 'harvest' (McNally, 1988, p. 33). Metaphors from biology and anatomy were also attracting attention, such as theories of the circulation of celestial bodies, and Claude Perrault's study of the circulation of sap in plants. Another was William Harvey's studies of the circulation of blood, which appeared in 1616. The understanding that prevailed before Harvey posited the key anatomical relations as those between each individual bodily part and the whole – for example, the Hippocratic notion of harmonic equilibrium among bodily humours. With Harvey, a new mechanical understanding emerged, of organs affecting one another through the flow of blood (Finkelstein, 2000). Harvey cited the mechanism of a water pump as an analogy for blood circulation (Borkenau, 1971), but Ernest Gilman's thesis is also suggestive: that the context was provided by the privateering ventures of Francis Drake and his ilk. Harvey, he writes:

> specifies the idea of bodily circulation by opening a 'passage' between the arterial and venous systems for the flow of blood (moving in vessels, coincidentally) to unite the most distant points in the body with the heart . . . In the 'lesser world' of man, Harvey remapped the global voyages of the great circumnavigators. (Harris, 2004, p. 161)

There was a close fit between the scientific revolution and the invention of the economy as a law-governed system; the ascent of mechanical philosophy coincided with that of the market mechanism, and the concomitant sundering of 'economy' from 'society'. From the conception of the universe as a machine it was a short step to envisaging society and economy likewise – as determined by lawful regularities that are akin to those that govern the natural world.

From the mid-seventeenth century onward, the idea prevailed that commerce 'is a field of social regularities' that should receive extensive support from, but not the detailed intrusion of, human law. By the late 1660s, Child already possessed 'a clear idea of the explanatory value of the simple fact that commodities tend to seek the most advantageous market' (Schumpeter, 1955, p. 368), being drawn by expectations of profit, and the related idea that trade is by *nature* free. He believed that the laws of money, with their 'foundation in nature' will ensure a downward trend to interest rates and a correlative upward trend to economic growth – in which respect he quotes William Petty: 'nature must and will have its course' (Child, [1668/1690] 1751, p. 10). Davenant, in 1696, argued similarly:

> Trade is in its Nature Free, finds its own Channel, and best directeth its own Course: and all Laws to give it Rules, and Directions, and to Limit, and Circumscribe it, may serve the Particular Ends of Private Men, but are seldom Advantagious to the Publick. Governments in Relation to it, are to take a Providential Care of the Whole, but generally to let Second Causes work their own way. (Hont, 2005, p. 216)

In Locke, the idea of the natural laws of trade finds a still more sophisticated form, with an explicit proposal that the laws of trade are different in character from, and thus independent of, laws of governments; that the exchange process possesses an independent causal character, with all prices determined by the universal forces of supply and demand, and the exchange mechanism of a free market 'generating an operation of its own, one which is independent of most of the characteristics of the participants' (Brown, 1984, p. 59).

Another key figure in developing the case that natural laws of economic phenomena exist which defy political control was North. He was the first, according to Letwin, to construct an analysis founded on a few general axioms, which enabled him 'to provide a mechanistic explanation of an economic process, and to reach policy conclusions that are deducible strictly from the premises' (Letwin, 1963, p. 198). This is most apparent with respect to his theorisation of the supply and demand for money. 'This ebbing and flowing of Money', he wrote, 'supplies and accommodates itself, without any aid of Politicians. For when Money grows scarce, and begins to be hoarded, then forthwith the Mint works, till the occasion be filled up again' (Brown, 1984, p. 60). Might the tidal allusion have been inspired by Isaac Newton's discovery, a few years earlier, that the tides are influenced by the Moon, as set out in his 'Equilibrium Theory of Tides'? Be that as it may, North's perspective is that the laws of trade form elements of a self-equilibrating system. The law he describes works through individuals – they take coins to the Mint for melting down, and so on – but in so acting not one of them is aiming to maintain the money supply in equilibrium. From this economic 'law', North deduces the laissez-faire conclusion that prices should not be set by government. There exists a self-adjusting mechanism which maintains the money supply within the required limits, a homeostatic process with which political regulation would interfere (Brown, 1984, p. 60). North thereby propounded an 'equilibrium vision' – a supply and demand theory of price formation. As mentioned above, he also identified the pursuit of profit as the driving force of economic activity, the notion that free market exchange is conducive to general economic welfare, and the idea that a self-regulating order emerges from the process of exchange between profit-driven individuals (Tieben, 2012). His arguments for laissez-faire policies, including towards the labour market – entailing abolition of the Elizabethan Poor Law – invoked self-regulating mechanisms (Finkelstein, 2000).

The market, according to post-mercantilist economists such as North (and, later, Richard Cantillon and Adam Smith) operates as a self-equilibrating system with, at its heart, the self-adjusting price mechanism functioning to maintain the supply of commodities (including money) in balance with demand. The economic 'machine', they postulated, works in an orderly and predictable manner to produce results that could be defined as subject to *laws* – in the novel, seventeenth-century sense of 'regularities' – and which therefore constituted a proper field of enquiry for the social scientist (Brown, 1984). The laws of the market are different in character from those of government, and intervention by government would interfere with the self-adjusting mechanism.

THE ECONOMY AS SUBJECT TO GROWTH AND MEASUREMENT

To become constituted as an object or process, the movement of which can be clearly apprehended (like a tide), economic affairs had to be subjected to rigorous measurement. Here too, the sixteenth and seventeenth centuries marked a watershed. In previous civilisations, arithmetical calculation was a normal and necessary part of economic life, particularly where money was involved. It was in some societies regarded as indispensable to justice and civic peace. Amon weighed the deeds of the ancient Egyptians in his scales, as did Archangel Michael for the Christians (Kula, 1986). 'The discovery of calculation (*logismos*) ended civil conflict and increased concord', proposed Archytas of Tarentum in the fourth century BC. 'For when there is calculation there is no unfair advantage, and there is equality, for it is by calculation that we come to agreement in our transactions' (Seaford, 2004, p. 269). But, on the whole, and certainly in pre-modern Europe, the standardisation of weights and measures remained relatively haphazard, and land was viewed through the prism of its purpose rather than against the slide rule of abstraction. 'The *lan* of barren soil in Poland was larger than the *lan* of fertile soil', the historian Witold Kula informs us, while the bushel for measuring oats was larger than that used for selling wheat. In France, similarly, the *arpent* was the area one farmer with two oxen or horses could plough in a day. One department had nine sizes of *arpent,* the largest was five times the size of the smallest. The unit of measure in both cases varied tremendously according to the value of the measured object – and often deliberately so, for in the feudal order price was regarded as an inherent attribute of a commodity, its alteration as sinful. Hence, different measures were necessary: merchants would apply one when buying and another when selling – the profit lay in the difference (Kula, 1986, pp. 29, 70, 103).

The picture changed dramatically with the rise of capitalism – and its associated culture of 'agricultural improvement' – and European colonialism. Colonial expansion and capitalist agriculture generated a demand for a type of science that could present reality as objective, precise, quantifiable. This was especially striking in seventeenth-century England. There, writes historian Sarah Irving, the discourse in which the natural environment was understood:

> became more quantitative and meticulous. It needed to, in order to render colonial knowledge useful. Natural philosophy became more theorized, experimental and regulated as a result of the exigencies of effective planting. Political arithmetic produced the kind of knowledge which colonization demanded: quantifiable, and encased in a claim of epistemological reliability. (2008, p. 67)

The system of 'political arithmetic' devised by Petty to statistically assess the economic potential of England and its Irish colony was important here. It tabulated assets in quantified form, enabling the process of assessment to appear 'objective and disinterested' (Irving, 2008, p. 66).

With this, Petty made a seminal contribution both to the political arts of economic administration (statistics) and to the conceptualisation of 'the economy' as a distinct field subject to scientific study and accurate measurement. The latter assured him recognition by *The Economist* as 'the man who invented economics' (Anonymous, 2013). Marx acknowledged him as the originator of English political economy – although, Hugh Goodacre points out, the more accurate moniker would be 'the political economist *par excellence* of the period of primitive accumulation' (2013). He planted quantification at the heart of scientific economics, crafted to the purposes of English empire and deployed in ideological form, making the most of the sheen of objectivity with which economic statistics – or 'political arithmetic' as he termed it – comes coated. Moreover, he played a significant part in priming the growth paradigm. In England before Petty, it could hardly have existed, for the simple reason that, as Paul Slack points out, no one knew the nation's territory, population or income (Slack, 2016, p. 2). But by the time of his death these had all been calculated:

> within acceptable margins of error and were widely known; they could be related to one another, so that average incomes per head and the distribution

of population and taxable wealth could be determined; and they could be compared with data from other countries and from the past . . . New information enabled England's improvement, its material progress, to be measured. (McCormick 2009, p. 178)

For Petty, the quest to frame economic potential in scientific terms necessitated the reduction of all relevant phenomena to 'number, weight and measure'. To modern ears, this phrase has connotations of empiricism and logic but, in his time, it also connoted justice, authority and sovereignty – to all of which, for millennia, number, weight and measure had been seen as essential attributes. Indeed, 'number, weight and measure' is itself a scriptural quote that was much cherished by Petty – and, not coincidentally, by Francis Bacon, Blaise Pascal, Robert Hooke and Newton too – because it states that the substance of God's creation is revealed in the form of 'number, weight and measure' and is thereby discernible most clearly to mathematicians and natural philosophers such as they.

The purpose of Petty's political arithmetic was not just actuarial but political; it was, as Ted McCormick describes, 'not simply to describe the nation's lands and hands but to show the sovereign how to manipulate them' (McCormick, 2009, p. 178). Hence, it was not precise numbers that obsessed Petty so much as ratios. They provide information of the greatest relevance to the management of population, such as the ratio of an acreage of land to the number of mouths it feeds, or that of Protestants to Catholics in Ireland, or that of the labour required for the provision of the workers' necessary consumption to that which can be creamed off by landlords and the state: surplus labour (Aspromourgos, 1988; McCormick, 2009). The scientific authority that numbers conveyed, moreover, was less in their precision than in the procedure through which they are produced. Arguments based on 'number, weight and measure', in Petty's view (here paraphrased by Mary Poovey) 'would compel assent as surely as mathematics did – especially if the King was willing to back the knowledge that the supposedly disinterested numbers expert produced' (Verran, 2012, p. 114). The aspiration to 'disinterest' was central to the emergent discipline of economics. As Till Düppe has argued, economics ever since Petty has gained scientificity (and thus, in a scientific age, epistemic authority) less through 'objectivism' – e.g. the meticulous accounting of individuals' productive acts and consumer needs – than through 'formalism', and the belief that 'the economy' has an independent existence 'was not made by means of the objectification of economic life, but by means of the formalization of an a-subjective structure' (Düppe, 2011, p. 48).

Petty's claim to originality is usually thought of in connection with his adumbration of a 'national accounting' model of the economy. His presentation of estimates of income, expenditure, stock of land and other physical assets in an integrated set of accounts for the whole economy of England and Wales make him, according to a hagiography in *The Economist,* the man who 'came up with the idea of how to measure GDP' (Anonymous, 2013). But in establishing aggregated data as the raw material of economics, he also helped to steer the attention of scientific economics toward the aim of 'maximizing quantities like the total wealth of a nation', an approving stance toward economic growth *in the abstract,* with the occlusion of 'issues of distributive justice' (Olson, 1993, p. 65). As has been widely noted, in Petty's work 'the millenarian conquest of nature and the idea of nature as a machine (and hence of society as a machine) blended to produce a new concept of wealth as resources and the product- ive power to harness them' with the nation conceived 'as a productive engine' (Finkelstein, 2000, p. 254), an economic collectivity that serves the interests of English power projection (Fioramonti, 2013). His assessments of national income were dedicated not to the blue skies of social science but to improving the state's wartime tax-collecting capability by supplying it with a 'quantitative framework for effective implementation of fiscal policy and mobilization of resources' (Maddison, 2007, p. 5). In these ways, Petty helped to found economics as a positivist 'science of wealth'; one that gave methodological expression to commodity fetishism – for example the idea that the economy is a system that functions with similar law-governed regularities as are found in the natural world. The new discipline was infused with the spirit of scientific optimism, and the assumption that epistemological and material progress march arm in arm. It promised to seal the 'open link', as Düppe has put it, 'between science and economic growth' (Düppe, 2011, p. 101).

THE RISING TIDE LIFTS US ALL; DON'T ROCK THE BOAT!

In Petty's day, sustained economic growth did not exist as a reality, and the growth paradigm did not exist as a discernible ideology or mental construct. In the following century, the eighteenth, its contours began to become apparent, and this was, in part, in the form of the legitimation of inequality.

The context (at least in Britain, the focus of this chapter) was formed by political and ideological responses to a social transition. An older social arrangement, in which all forms of inequality are sanctioned by God and custom, in which the ruling classes were rigidly and culturally separated from the producing classes, and in which the latter were highly dispersed and fragmented (geographically and culturally), was giving way to a new order. The principle of legal equality was gaining ground and was associated with a levelling of the status order and a pervasive societal democratisation. Mentalities of subjecthood and deference were beginning to yield to those of citizenship and equality. Government was beginning to bargain with the legislature for the authorisation to tax, and with citizens over the delivery of taxes. Together with a revolution in transport, communications, media and literacy, all this contributed to a mobilisation of the citizenry. The producing classes were increasingly educated and socially mobilised – massing in workplaces and urban conurbations, and beginning to push their demands through organised public displays on the national scale. The two great revolutions of the period under consideration, in 1640s England and in 1789 in France, raised the spectre of popular sovereignty.

These transformations raised the question, in a new way, of how to legitimate economic inequality. Of course, the old ideologies – religious, patrimonialist, and so on – could be adapted to the task, but traditional conceptions of a fixed hierarchy of social rank were harder to maintain in the new order, pulsing as it was to ideas of individual self-interest, social change (progress, economic growth and revolution) and popular sovereignty (democracy and nationalism). However, might there be a way in which the new ideas, of individualism, nationalism and progress/growth, could be knitted together in a way that supports hierarchy and class division? The thinker who answered this question with particular originality and influence was Smith.

In *The Wealth of Nations*, Smith's starting point is self-interested commercial activity, as the engine of that natural social process of self-sustaining growth, the advance of 'opulence'. In his words, 'The uniform, constant, and uninterrupted effort of every man to better his condition, the principle from which publick and national, as well as private opulence is originally derived, is frequently powerful enough to maintain the natural progress of things toward improvement' (Smith, [1776] 1993, p. 205).

Material progress redounds to the good of the community as a whole, in terms of higher living standards (a greater quantity of goods sold at lower prices), such that class inequality tends to diminish. As axioms, Smith postulates a direct and automatic relationship between the welfare of the nation and the quantity of goods and services produced (relative to population), and that the increase of capital is synonymous with the increase of national wealth. 'Every individual', he writes in a famous passage, endeavours 'to employ his capital in the support of domestic industry, and so to direct that industry that its produce may be of the greatest value'. Hence, 'every individual necessarily labours to render the annual revenue of the society as great as he can'. In acting thus, 'he intends only his own gain, and he is in this . . . led by an invisible hand to promote an end which was no part of his intention' (Smith, 1993, p. 477). Note in this passage the elision of capitalists and the population at large ('every individual' invests 'his capital') and the notion that each capitalist-individual is an active, if unwitting, agent of the growth imperative.

At times, Smith portrays the rich as the key source of demand (he even imagines that they serve the poor in a familial, 'hand-me-down' manner).

> The houses, the furniture, the clothing of the rich, in a little time, become useful to the inferior and middling ranks of people. They are able to purchase them when their superiors grow weary of them; and the general accommodation of the whole people is thus gradually improved. (Smith, 1993, p. 143)

Elsewhere, and equally memorably, he identifies 'butchers, brewers, and bakers', and indeed labourers, as a prodigious source of demand, and even defines wealth in terms of the level of consumption of the majority of society, the labouring poor (McNally, 1988). One of his justifications of economic growth, moreover, is linked to his assumption that it leads to rising real wages, and he is adamant that the most thriving and felicitous state – especially for its working masses – is not the wealthiest but the one that is growing most rapidly, as measured by output and the average wage. (These go hand in hand: higher wages are the necessary effect' of 'increasing national wealth'.) 'An augmentation of fortune', he argues, 'is the means by which *the greater part of men* propose and wish to better their condition . . . and the most likely way of augmenting their fortune is to save and accumulate some part of what they acquire' (Smith, 1993, p. 203).

In having provided grounds for both the rich and the poor to hitch their wagon to economic growth – the rich, as the principal creators of demand and the enlightened stewards of the civilisation process; the poor, as beneficiaries of growth, through rising living standards – Smith's ideas were amenable to interpretation by two quite different traditions of political economy. A conservative-liberal route proceeded via Burke and Ricardo to Hayek and Samuelson; a radical route wended via Paine and Sismondi to the Smithian socialism of William Thompson and Karl Polanyi. Relatedly, Smith's argument that economic growth raises wages was seized upon by radicals and liberals alike. For radicals, it justified demands for wage rises, and, much later, served to endorse social democracy's embrace of the capitalist system. For conservatives and liberals, it was rolled out whenever the poor needed to be put in their place.

A critical period was the 1790s, a decade of social turbulence, as the lower orders found inspiration in the French Revolution. For philosophers and political economists, it appeared imperative to remind readers of the need to keep the hoi polloi in their place. Burke's view, as laid out in *Thoughts and Details on Scarcity*, was that the deity and science, in alliance, ensured that the poor shall and must remain poor. The laws of commerce, after all, 'are the laws of nature, and consequently the laws of God' (Stanlis, [1958] 2009, p. 58). The mutual benefit that arises from the pursuit of individual selfish interest, he argued, depends upon the universal acceptance of the natural chain of subordination: of beast and plough to labourer, of labourer to farmer, and so on (Macpherson, 1980). A similar argument was put by Archdeacon Paley – a utilitarian philosopher, admirer of Smith, and one of the two dominant theological figures of the age – in a two-pence anti-revolutionary pamphlet of 1792. How lucky they are, he reminded the poor, given that God had created frugality as 'a pleasure' (Paley, [1793] 1849, p. 931). Workers should 'learn the art of contentment', and should accept their role as one of God-given duty – for 'the labour of the world is carried on by *service*, that is, by one man working under another man's direction' (Paley, 1849, p. 931). The crass inequality of wealth that obtained across Europe, he argued, was dispiriting but was the by-product of a system that, by fostering industry and the arts, was, considered in the round, beneficial to all. In his ideal society, 'a laborious frugal people [ministered] to the demands of an opulent, luxurious nation' (Bellon, 2014, p. 102). He warned the lower classes who were enchanted by events in Paris that:

> The change, and the only change, to be desired, is that gradual and progressive improvement of our circumstance which is the natural fruit of successful industry; when each year is something better than the last; when we are enabled to add to our little household one article after another of new comfort or conveniency, as our profits increase, or our burden becomes less.

This, he cautioned, 'may be looked forward to, and is practicable, by great numbers in a state of public order and quiet; it is absolutely impossible in any other'.[2]

In ways such as these, traditional norms of deference (to rulers, to God, to the social hierarchy) were reinvented for the new times. They slotted neatly into the nationalist framework, affirming that, although in a sense equals before the law, the political community could, like a family, act together as an ordered unit, with individual differences seen as either functional or irrelevant. They could be alloyed to the idea of material and social progress: if each accepts their place in the nation's hierarchy, all will benefit from the 'gradual and progressive improvement' that ensues. This may not have constituted 'grand' ideology, in the sense of a population swept up in fervent support for a set of beliefs. It was perfectly compatible with a grumbling pragmatic apathy towards the social order and its rules. Nonetheless, it was vitally ideological. It said, in effect: the rising tide will lift us all; so don't rock the boat!

THE RISING TIDE AND THE GROWTH TAKE-OFF

The heyday of the growth paradigm arrived in the twentieth century. In its early decades, a shift occurred, from a vague sense – long prevalent – that government should preside over economic 'improvement' and 'material progress' to a conviction that promoting growth is a matter of national priority. Factors behind the shift included intensified geopolitical rivalry, and the increasing 'muscularity' of states, with expanded bureaucratic apparatuses, surveillance systems and welfare provision. In some countries the expansion of the suffrage was an additional factor: rights were extended and an infrastructure and ideology of 'national belonging' was constructed with the aim of incorporating the lower orders as citizens into the body politic. National accounting techniques were systematised. In 1932, the US Congress commissioned the economist Simon Kuznets to devise a means by which to measure the nation's output. Gross domestic product (GDP) was the result. Another 1930s' milestone was the publication of Keynes' *General Theory*.

Keynesian ideas, developed in parallel, and/or in dialogue with Michał Kalecki, Joan Robinson and Keynes' former student Roy Harrod, among others, responded to, and fed into, the mid-century transformation of the world economy towards corporatism and state capitalism. For social democratic parties in particular, Keynesian theory offered a strategic ideology that provided justification for their aspiration to, or assumption of, a role as a party of government within a capitalist environment. Following success in winning legal status in Western Europe and elsewhere, it sought to marshal its followers behind goals – economic growth, welfare spending and war – that can be pursued within a capitalist framework. The paradigmatic case was Sweden's Social Democratic Party, which, in the inter-war period abandoned the quest for 'equal rewards' and economic democracy in favour of aspirations to economic growth and 'democratised opportunities', neatly wrapped in a Keynesian compact with the corporate sector. Keynesianism offered something precious to social democracy. As Adam Przeworski explains, it:

> granted a universalistic status to the interests of workers. Earlier, all demands for increased consumption were viewed as inimical to the national interest: higher wages meant lower profits and hence a reduced opportunity for investment and future development . . . But in the logic of Keynes' theory, higher wages . . . meant an increase of aggregate demand, which implied increased expectations of profit, increased investment, and hence economic stimulation. The significance of increasing wages changed from being viewed as an impediment to national economic development to being its stimulus. Corporatist defence of the interests of workers, a policy social democrats had pursued during the 'twenties . . . now found ideological justification in a technical economic theory. (Przeworski, 1980, p. 122)

In short, Keynesianism furnished social democracy with new tools with which to claim that the corporatist defence of workers' material interests was synonymous with the interests of the nation as a whole. Economic growth would enable rich and poor to flourish together. This helped to ensure the marginalisation of some of the left's traditional agenda, notably workers' control, economic planning and radical redistribution. In the US, for example, the left and the union movement in the 1940s dropped such demands in favour of support for a government-led programme of economic growth. In her history of the period, Elizabeth Fones-Wolf describes the emergence of a capital-labour accord:

> with unions abandoning their quest for industrial control in return for periodic wage and benefit increases. In politics, labor shelved its earlier commitment to economic planning and social solidarity for a program emphasizing 'sustained growth and productivity gain-sharing' with a small expansion of the welfare state. (Fones-Wolf, 1994, p. 3)

This went hand in hand with the expulsion of communists from the unions, undermining militancy, and limiting labour's ability to act as an independent political force. Writing of the same period, Steve Fraser (2015) has described how US unions bargained away control over the shop floor in exchange for employment security and wage growth. A comparatively affluent age ensued, but the spirit of solidarity declined, with organised labour taking its place within the prevailing culture of acquisitiveness and individualism.

By the mid-point of the century, growth had firmly established itself in industrial societies, whether capitalist or communist, as a 'secular religion', in Daniel Bell's phrase, supplying 'the source of individual motivation, the basis of political solidarity' and the justification for mobilising society behind a common purpose (Bell, [1976] 2008, p. 237). Growth was increasingly understood as a goal (as much as a means), with the economy conceived as an entity essentially divorced from a natural resource base and defined by its momentum of growth (Lane, 2014). It became an integral part of social life throughout the world, and played a decisive part in binding 'civil society' into capitalist hegemonic structures. It came to be seen as a proxy for the profitability of national economies and as a magic wand to achieve all sorts of goals: to abolish the danger of returning to Depression, to soothe class tensions, to reduce the gap between 'developed' and 'developing' countries, to carve a path to international recognition, and so on. The greater the rate of growth, it was universally supposed, the lesser the economic, social and political challenges, and the more secure the regime. There was a military angle too. The Cold War rivals identified growth as the elixir of geopolitical success. 'If we lack a first-rate growing economy', as John F. Kennedy declaimed on the campaign trail, 'we cannot maintain a first-rate defence' (Kennedy, 1960a).

The US in the 1950s saw the growth paradigm achieve its acme. In 1952 William Paley's report *Resources for Freedom: Foundations for Growth and Security* declared that it shares 'the belief of the American people in the principle of growth', for growth seems preferable to its every conceivable antithesis, all of which imply 'stagnation and decay' (Lane, 2013, p. 3). In 1958, the Republican plutocrats Nelson and Laurence Rockefeller recruited Henry Kissinger to prepare a report on *The Challenge of the Future*. Heading a panel comprised of economists associated with large corporations and major universities, Kissinger produced a book, *The Key Importance of Growth to Achieve National Goals*, which identified growth as *the* solution to the continuous pressure of competing claims on national income (the arms race, public infrastructure, education, etc.). Growth, it argued, not only brings 'dignity, freedom, and purpose' but promises to expand 'the opportunities for individual fulfilment, multiply the incentives for enterprise, enable us to improve our educational system, permit us to increase our protection against economic hardship, make possible rising standards of national health and open new vistas of cultural achievement' (Andrew, 1998; Purdey, 2010, p. 80).

In this context, the notion of the economy as a tide that raises all boats appeared common-sensical. The idiom itself entered popular discourse thanks to Kennedy. He first used it in 1960, on the campaign trail in Ohio. His campaign was oriented around questions of the arms race, social justice, and above all growth – one of his campaign promises was to hike the GDP growth rate to an annual rate of 5 per cent. In his Ohio speech Kennedy asks rhetorically: how can we 'move this country ahead'?; how can we 'provide full employment, [and] develop the natural resources'? The answer he gives is: 'We must attempt to stimulate the growth of the United States' and 'we must develop our natural resources' (Kennedy, 1960b). He related these points specifically to the building of the St. Lawrence Seaway. This was a project for which he was proud to have voted in the Senate, for, even though his base was Massachusetts, which did not stand to benefit, the scheme would be 'a national asset, and a rising tide lifts all boats'.[3] This was, in essence, a Smithian-Keynesian formulation of the growth paradigm: Smithian in its assumption that the extension of commerce is of universal benefit, and in its denigration of protectionism and pork-barrel politics; Keynesian in its emphasis on full employment as the goal and public infrastructure investment as the means.

It was little wonder, then, that Kennedy was impressed by the work of Walt Rostow, a leading purveyor of growth economics, along neoclassical/

Keynesian lines. Rostow's theory was based on neoclassical assumptions, and focused on the 'supply side' conditions for growth (population, savings, innovation, capital accumulation). However, he paid close attention to social and institutional factors, and, although never a card-carrying Keynesian, did think that Keynes had essentially solved the problem of economic volatility (Rostow, 1990). Rostow enthused:

> There is every reason to believe . . . that the sluggish and timid policies of the 1920s and 1930s with respect to the level of unemployment will no longer be tolerated in Western societies. And now the technical tricks of the trade – due to the Keynesian revolution – are widely understood. It should not be forgotten that Keynes set himself the task of defeating Marx's prognosis about the course of unemployment under capitalism; and he largely succeeded. (Meszaros, 2008, p. 100)

Rostow's own neoclassical/Keynesian box of tricks proved influential within the new politics of 'development' that arose in the post-1948 conjuncture, in which Cold War rivalry extended to the newly independent nations of the South. US administrations, from Truman to Kennedy and Johnson, were keen to associate themselves with the 'modernisation' of their Third World allies, and development economists were recruited to advise on the project. Academics would 'swarm into Washington', with much talk of nation-building and 'self-sustaining growth' recalls George Ball, Under Secretary of State from 1961 to 1966, in his memoirs.[4] In 1958, Kennedy met Rostow, and the modernisation theorist entered his inner circle of advisors.

The alliance of Rostow's *Stages* and Kennedy-Johnson foreign policy ushered in the heyday of modernisation theory, during an era in which development became synonymous with rapid GDP growth, to the service of which an industry was called into being to advise the US and other major powers on how to develop the Third World (much as 'developers' develop real estate).[5] Rostovian theory – with its postulate that, once liberated from their traditional customs and institutions, poor countries will enjoy rapid capitalist growth – was transparently aligned with a long-standing but newly revitalised US mission to remake the Third World in its interests, establishing thriving zones of Western capitalism, secured against the threats of leftist nationalism or communist insurgency. But Rostow's influence extends beyond 'development', to the theory of growth, and to the propagation of the growth paradigm. In his magisterial treatise on the age of ecology, Joachim Radkau goes so far as to refer to Rostow as *the* principal source of 'the growth obsession of the economic sciences' (Radkau, 2011, p. 487).

CONCLUSION

The growth paradigm serves to naturalise and justify the prevailing social order, applying ideological gloss to the true goal of capitalist production: the self-expansion of capital. Capitalists and the social layers that support them would prefer their interests not to be seen in these terms. In other words, as a system of competition, capitalism depends on the growth of capital, but as a class system it depends on obscuring the sources of that growth. In this, the ideology of growth is pivotal. It enables accumulation to be understood as something of general interest – growth – rather than as a process of exploitation that depends upon structural inequality. In this sense, growth is central to the justification of capitalism. As the economist Joseph Schumpeter argued in the 1940s, capitalist economic growth produces 'avalanches of consumer goods' which 'progressively raise the standard of life of the masses' – and if sustained, moreover, will surely abolish poverty (Schumpeter, 1954, pp. 66–8). The system, as Joan Robinson paraphrased Schumpeter's case, is 'cruel, unjust, turbulent, but it does deliver the goods, and, damn it all, it's the goods that you want' (Castoriadis, 1996, p. 66).

The growth paradigm enjoyed its heyday during the *trentes glorieuses*. Since then, storm clouds have gathered, from several directions. One concerns the growth paradigm in its own terms. Per capita growth rates, at the global level and especially in the richer countries, have declined, decade by decade. This poses a problem for systemic legitimacy, for 'performance legitimacy', based on popular approval of a regime's success in bringing about economic growth and satisfying popular demand for goods and services, has over the decades become the norm. In a context of lower growth, the notion of a 'social contract' between the state and the citizenry suffers attrition. States rely more heavily on techniques of repression and of divide and rule. The symptoms are manifest in the form of alienation, electoral volatility, anti-politics, and so forth. Increasing numbers feel excluded. As a modern proverb of uncertain origin puts it, 'A rising tide that lifts all boats drowns those who have no vessel' (Higgs, 2014, p. 63).

Secondly, various forms of growth scepticism are on the march. Some emphasise the disconnect between economic growth and social well-being. As numerous scholars have argued – perhaps most notably Richard Wilkinson and Kate Pickett in *The Spirit Level* (2010) – the relationship between per capita GDP and well-being is limited, and such correlation between them as does exist tends to decline after a certain point (for the sake of argument, when the former hits $15,000). As national income increases beyond a certain level it ceases to translate into improvements in health or general well-being. Instead, the critical variable is the degree of equality.

Another source of growth scepticism concerns the impact of growth on supplies of non-renewable resources and on the natural environment. Recognition of the hazardous effects of climate change in particular have transformed the debate on growth. For the most powerful pro-growth argument is an argument from freedom. It has been put with particular eloquence by Arthur Lewis. The advantage of economic growth, he proposed,

> is not that wealth increases happiness, but that it increases the range of human choice ... What distinguishes men from pigs is that men have greater control over their environment; not that they are more happy. And on this test, economic growth is greatly to be desired. The case for economic growth is that it gives man greater control over his environment, and thereby increases his freedom. (Lewis, 2007, p.71)

This argument from freedom is becoming less convincing with each passing season. Certainly, growth gives human beings the *potential* for greater control over our environment, and greater *actual* control over certain *aspects* of it. But partial control can create blowback, and enhanced control of some part of the system can undermine our ability to shape the whole.

Think for example of our ability to 'tame rivers'. This, as Fred Pearce shows in *When the Rivers Run Dry*, often involves the exercise of short-term, localised and merely instrumental control that doesn't consider the long term, or for the entire course of the river let alone other affected ecosystems. The successful 'taming' of a river may generate all manner of problems downstream – geographically or temporally (Pearce, 2006). Specific cases such as this may erode but do not destroy Lewis' argument. Climate change, however, is on an altogether different scale. A momentous example of humanity learning the laws of nature but failing to apply them judiciously, it attests to economic growth *actually decreasing* humanity's ability to control the natural environment, as the planet careers towards feedback-fuelled runaway warming.

And at that point, the rising tide will no longer be a metaphor.

NOTES

1. The research for this chapter was funded by a British Academy Mid-Career Fellowship (2013–14, project title 'Economic growth as ideology: Origins, evolution and dilemmas of the "growth paradigm"'). The chapter itself was first presented at the British International Studies Association (BISA) annual conference, London, June 2015, and at the BISA International Political Economy Working Group conference, University of Manchester, October 2015.

2. Paley, William ([1793] 1849) 'Reasons for Contentment, addressed to the labouring part of the British public', in *The Works of William Paley*, Wm Orr & Co, p. 933. A reply to Paley, penned by an anonymous 'poor labourer', rebutted his arguments point by point. What reasons, it began, 'could be given why we labourers ought to be contented, by a man who never worked in his life, and how he who never felt the anguish of dividing a mouldy crust among his famished children could presume to offer arguments to convince us that we were unreasonable because such a state did not afford us content?'. Paley's aim, it concluded, 'was not to lessen the hardships of the labourer, but to secure to the rich and powerful their luxuries, extorted from the toil and miseries of the poor!' A Poor Labourer (1793) *A letter to William Paley, M.A., Archdeacon of Carlisle, from a poor labourer in answer to his reasons for contentment*, J. Ridgway, pp. 2–3.
3. The St. Lawrence Seaway had long stood as an emblem of pork-barrel disputation between New York and the Lake States. See, e.g., Lippmann, Walter ([1937] 2005) *The Good Society*, Transaction, p. 79.
4. The development decade – Development Doctrine and Modernization Theory. Available at: http://www.americanforeignrelations.com/A-D/Development-Doctrine-and-Moderni zation-Theory-The-development- decade.html#ixzz1c5bAIQVv.
5. The development decade – Development Doctrine and Modernization Theory. Available at: http://www.americanforeignrelations.com/A-D/Development-Doctrine-and-Moderni zation-Theory-The-development- decade.html#ixzz1c5bAIQVv.

REFERENCES

Andrew, J. (1998), 'Cracks in the Consensus: The Rockefeller Brothers Fund Special Studies Project and Eisenhower's America'. Available at: www.thefreelibrary.com/.
Anonymous (2013), 'Petty Impressive', *The Economist*, 21 December.
Aspromourgos, T. (1988), 'The life of William Petty in relation to his economics: A tercentenary interpretation', *History of Political Economy*, Vol. 20, No. 3, p. 346.
Bell, D. ([1976] 2008), *The Cultural Contradictions of Capitalism*, Basic Books.
Bellon, R.D. (2014), *A Sincere and Teachable Heart: Self-Denying Virtue in British Intellectual Life, 1736–1859*, Brill.
Borkenau, F. ([1934] 1971), *Der Übergang vom feudalen zum bürgerlichen Weltbild: Studien zur Geschichte der Philosophie der Manufakturperiode*, Wissenschaftliche Buchgesellschaft.
Brown, R. (1984), *The Nature of Social Laws: From Machiavelli to Mill*, Cambridge University Press.
Castoriadis, C. (1996), 'The "Rationality" of Capitalism'. Available at: https://southdowns commune.wordpress.com.
Child, J. ([1668/1690] 1751), *A New Discourse of Trade*, Robert and Andrew Foulis.
Christensen, P. (1994), 'Fire, motion, and productivity: The proto-energetics of nature and economy in François Quesnay', in Philip Mirowski, ed., *Natural Images in Economic Thought: Markets Read in Tooth and Claw*, Cambridge University Press.
Düppe, T. (2011), *The Making of the Economy: A Phenomenology of Economic Science*, Lexington.
Finkelstein, A. (2000), *Harmony and the Balance: An Intellectual History of Seventeenth-century English Economic Thought*, The University of Michigan Press.
Fioramonti, L. (2013), *Gross Domestic Problem: The Politics Behind the World's Most Powerful Number*, Zed Books.
Fones-Wolf, E. (1994), *Selling Free Enterprise: The Business Assault on Labor and Liberalism, 1945-60,* University of Illinois Press.
Fraser, S. (2015), *The Age of Acquiescence: The Life and Death of American Resistance to Organized Wealth and Power*, Little, Brown.
Goodacre, H. (2013), 'The William Petty problem and the Whig history of economics', *Cambridge Journal of Economics*, Advance Access published 9 May.

Harris, J.G. (2004), *Sick Economies: Drama, Mercantilism, and Disease in Shakespeare's England*, University of Pennsylvania Press.

Higgs, K. (2014), *Collision Course: Endless Growth on a Finite Planet*, The MIT Press.

Hont, I. (2005), *Jealousy of Trade: International Competition and the Nation-state in Historical Perspective*, Harvard University Press.

Irving, S. (2008), *Natural Science and the Origins of the British Empire*, Pickering & Chatto.

Kennedy, J.F. (1960a), 'Remarks at Fund-Raising Dinner, Philadelphia', 31 October. Available at: www.jfklibrary.org/Research/Research-Aids/JFK-Speeches/Philadelphia-PA_19601031-Funding-Raising-Dinner.aspx.

Kennedy, J.F. (1960b), 'Remarks at Municipal Auditorium, Canton, Ohio', 27 September. Available at: www.jfklibrary.org/Research/Research-Aids/JFK-Speeches/Canton-OH_1960 0927.aspx.

Kula, W. (1986), *Measures and Men*, Princeton University Press.

Lane, R. (2013), 'The nature of growth: The postwar history of the economy, energy and the environment', Ph.D. in International Relations, University of Sussex.

Lane, R. (2014), 'Resources for the future, resources for growth: The making of the 1975 growth ban', in Benjamin Stephan and Richard Lane, eds, *The Politics of Carbon Markets*, Routledge.

Letwin, W. (1963), *The Origins of Scientific Economics: English Economic Thought, 1660–1776*, Methuen.

Lewis, W.A. (2007), *The Theory of Economic Growth*, Routledge Taylor and Francis Group.

Lippmann, W. ([1937] 2005), *The Good Society*, Transaction.

Macpherson, C.B. (1980), *Burke*, Oxford University Press.

Maddison, A. (2007), *Contours of the World Economy, 1–2030 AD: Essays in Macro-economic History*, Oxford University Press.

McCormick, T. (2009), *William Petty and the Ambitions of Political Arithmetic*, Oxford University Press.

McNally, D. (1988), *Political Economy and the Rise of Capitalism: A Reinterpretation*, University of California Press.

Meszaros, I. (2008), *The Challenge and Burden of Historical Time: Socialism in the Twenty-First Century*, Monthly Review Press.

Misselden, E. ([1623] 1995), 'The Circle of Commerce or the Ballance of Trade', in Lars Magnusson, ed., *Mercantilism, Volume 1*, Psychology Press.

Olson, R. (1993), *The Emergence of the Social Sciences, 1642–1792*, Twayne Publishers.

Paley, W. ([1793] 1849), 'Reasons for Contentment, addressed to the labouring part of the British public', in *The Works of William Paley*, Wm S. Orr and Co.

Pearce, F. (2006), *When the Rivers Run Dry: Water – the Defining Crisis of the Twenty-First Century*, Beacon Press.

Przeworski, A. (1980), 'Social democracy as a historical phenomenon', *New Left Review* I/122, July–August. Available at: https://newleftreview.org/I/122/adam-przeworski-social-democracy-as-a-historical-phenomenon.

Purdey, Stephen (2010), *Economic Growth, the Environment and International Relations*, Routledge.

Radkau, J. (2011), *Die Ära der Ökologie: Eine Weltgeschichte*, C.H. Beck.

Rostow, W. (1990), *Theories of Economic Growth from David Hume to the Present*, Oxford University Press.

Schumpeter, J. (1954), *Capitalism, Socialism, Democracy*, Unwin.

Schumpeter, J. (1955), *History of Economic Analysis*, Allen & Unwin.

Seaford, R. (2004), *Money and the Early Greek Mind: Homer, Philosophy, Tragedy*, Cambridge University Press.

Smith, A. ([1776] 1993), *An Inquiry into the Nature and Causes of the Wealth of Nations*, Oxford University Press.

Slack, P. (2016), *Paul Slack, The Invention of Improvement: Information and Material Progress in Seventeenth-century England*, Oxford University Press.

Stanlis, P. ([1958] 2009), *Edmund Burke and the Natural Law*, Transaction.

Tieben, B. (2012), *The Concept of Equilibrium in Different Economic Traditions: An Historical Investigation*, Edward Elgar Publishing.
Verran, H. (2012), 'Number', in Celia Lury and Nina Wakeford, eds, *Inventive Methods: The Happening of the Social*, Routledge.
Wilkinson, R. and K. Pickett (2010), *The Spirit Level: Why Equality is Better for Everyone*, Penguin Books.

PART II

POLITICAL ASPECTS

9. Developing democracy, democratizing development: a backlash against hegemonic norms and practice?
Matthew Louis Bishop

INTRODUCTION

One of the most remarkable recent developments in global politics has surely been the election of Donald Trump as President of the United States. It is intriguing for many reasons. On the one hand, much of his support came from the so-called 'left behind' who had plainly become frustrated with the enduring failure – as they perceived it – of liberal democracy and a highly marketized economy to deliver decent living standards. Trump entered office promising to 'drain' the supposedly corrupt and venal Washington 'swamp' and thereby finally deliver meaningful development to areas of the US that had suffered decades of pronounced economic and industrial decline. Yet, on the other hand, the presidential election itself highlights some thorny problems with US democracy: a self-funded billionaire political neophyte with no experience of government, a highly controversial, utterly confused and contradictory policy platform, spouting outright falsehoods unchallenged by large sections of the media, still made it to the White House even though he won *three million fewer* votes – over 2 per cent of the total – than the runner-up, Hillary Clinton, because of a voting system designed in, and for the context of, the eighteenth century.

Democracies, in contrast to authoritarian regimes, are supposed to be the very highest form of human political organization. They should be inclusive, accessible, rational, and facilitate the rising of the cream to the top. People – not simply men – of serious purpose and great ability, from all backgrounds, are meant to be able to participate in governing a well-ordered and effective state bureaucracy that generates policy, facilitative of ongoing improvements in economic development and social well-being. That Trump personifies the exact opposite of many of the characteristics of his predecessor – with whom we might sharply contrast him – is one thing. That a large rump of people might think him the solution to the myriad ills afflicting the contemporary US is quite another. What is frequently missed in the disparaging media portrayals of Trump's supporters, and of the man himself, is the underlying reason why he engendered so much support: this is that the central failure in the neoliberal era, as in all Western countries, has been a slow, and often hidden, but nevertheless perceptible deterioration in the quality of both the democracy and the development that is increasingly (not) being delivered to large segments of the population. If large parts of Trump's analysis – that democracy was failing to deliver development – seemed to resonate with people, it is because there was a large grain of truth to it.

The purpose of this chapter is to engage with this debate in a broader fashion. Many assume a tightly constituted link between democracy and development, but this is far more contested and contingent than it usually appears, and particularly so in the contemporary era when a great many challenges are now ranged against the neoliberal certitudes of the past few decades. Indeed, it is partly the hubris of those who have imposed a particular, Western-centric view of what it is to be 'developed' or 'democratized' that is responsible for, what I term here, the emerging backlash against hegemonic norms and practice. However, what is perhaps different today is that the criticisms that have long been made in the less developed or democratized parts of the world are increasingly coming to animate public discourse in the West, too. The chapter unfolds in the following way. In the first section, I sketch the outline of the essentially liberal account of why development and democracy are believed to go together, before asking why, if this is the case, there has been a backlash against attempts to promote them. Then, in the second, I explain in greater detail the genesis of the backlash itself. In the final substantive section, I reflect on the wider implications for global liberalism in the contemporary era, focusing on three broad patterns of change: reassertions of state sovereignty, the rise of economically nationalist rhetoric, and the undermining of multilateral institutions. The chapter concludes by briefly considering the significance of the argument for broader processes of global governance.

DEMOCRACY AND DEVELOPMENT IN TENSION

There is little doubt that, in terms of their 'essence', both democracy and development are positive phenomena to which people and societies quite rightly aspire. But they are also considerably more problematic – in both a conceptual and practical sense – than we might intuitively expect. Several specific related points are worth making in this regard. First, a broad – but inconclusive – consensus exists that they are 'good things' in and of themselves, and in many cases mutually supportive. Put crudely, this implies that more development leads to more democracy, and democratic countries are better at delivering the growth and progress associated with successful development. This is, of course, true from time to time, but not always. Second, the positively correlated relationship between them – in terms of causation – is less clear than is often suggested. Third, they are not reducible to each other. This may seem obvious, but it is worth reiterating: as contested concepts, with a variety of definitions and interpretations that depend on specific foundational assumptions about the nature of the world, they can mean very different things to different people. Moreover, there are plenty of places and cases where one exists without the other, or is even inimical to it. Democratization, in other words, can destabilize processes of development, and rapid development does not necessarily lead to democracy.

I could say more here about the thorny debate on the relationship between democracy and development (and have done elsewhere: see Bishop, 2016a). However, the key point to make for the purpose of the analysis at hand is that large numbers of people, particularly in the West, have come to accept the notion that it is actually – and intrinsically – one of mutual reinforcement, when, in reality, it is a relationship that, at times, does not even exist, and when it does it is replete with contingencies. The reason this matters is because, following the three points above, the modern 'common sense' on the subject actually derives from a particular (neo-)liberal viewpoint regarding both the perceived desirability and essential necessity – even inevitability – of market-led growth and development, and liberal forms of democracy, both of which imply a restricted role for the state. Rather than being seen as particular historically and contextually bounded expressions *of* democracy and development that exist in a specific place and time – and therefore represent, by implication, just one example of many possible forms – the kinds of liberal, and, increasingly, neoliberal forms that exist in the contemporary West in general, and the Anglosphere in particular, have come to be conflated *with* democracy and development *themselves* (see Grugel and Bishop, 2013). This is obviously highly reductive: it narrows the conceptual essence of both ideas, and consequently the kinds of distinctive variants that different societies may claim as reflective of them. But crucially, because of this, it operates as a powerful myth that not only reduces the space for alternatives, but posits Western neoliberals as the undisputed defenders of democracy and development writ large (when it is just their interpretation of them). This, in turn, legitimizes all manner of pressure and intervention to correct the supposed deficiencies of those societies that do not live up to the ideal. For, if democracy and development have reached their apotheosis in the West, there can – almost by definition – be no real alternative. It may even completely eviscerate their emancipatory potential (Grugel, 2003).

So, why is there an emerging backlash against the hegemonic variants of these ideas and practices? The problem is threefold. The myth itself is highly teleological: there is an assumption that exists within all liberal accounts of modernization and progress that Western countries have achieved an end-point that others are yet to achieve (Leftwich, 2000; Payne and Phillips, 2010). This was just about defensible in previous eras, but as many other societies have closed the relative development gap – often with quasi-authoritarian, yet highly performing governing regimes and institutions that contrast strongly with both the kleptocracies of the past and the perfect liberal states that exist only in textbooks – it is considerably less so. Moreover, the space between myth and reality in the West itself is arguably larger than at any time in the recent past: what Andrew Gamble (2014) has called 'the crisis without end' has revealed the depth of the deterioration in living standards for much of the working and middle classes that has been ongoing since the 1970s, and this has been accompanied by a discernible hollowing out of the substance of democracy in much of North America and Europe (Crouch, 2004; Mair, 2013). This not only matters in and of itself: for the myth has consequently legitimized interventions to impose forms of democracy and development at the very moment that they appear most emaciated and are subject to their most sustained contestation. Therefore, while we might instinctively consider ourselves democrats and broadly in favour of development in general, large numbers of people – in all parts of the world – are increasingly suspicious of their prevailing contemporary variants which seem all too frequently to be captured by elite, and even oligarchic, interests (Winters, 2011; Mount, 2012), and also unable to deliver growth and progress that is spread with a reasonable degree of equity throughout society, rather than accruing relentlessly to those very elites (Piketty, 2014).

A myth only survives as a dominant account of reality for as long as it appears to have sufficient purchase on that reality. Once dominant typologies break down, as, for example, enough people come to see that the form of democracy is belied by its meagre content, or the gap between liberal rhetoric and both the practice and performance of Western states vis-à-vis their authoritarian counterparts against which they define themselves is far shorter and fuzzier than originally conceived, contestation is only likely to intensify. This is particularly so, given that, in the post-9/11 security context, neoliberalism has displayed a much harsher – even 'authoritarian' (Tansel, 2017) – character. This evidently takes myriad forms, but the broad argument made by those emphasizing it is that in an era of capitalist crisis, neoliberalism as both ideology and practice has been compelled to find ever-more aggressive methods of reproduction. The liberal promise of human freedom is, in short, abrogated by the brutal imposition of various subtle and insidious forms of unfreedom. For example, one aspect of this process is the way in which a crisis *of* neoliberalism has actually been utilized as a way of intensifying its invasion and marketization of the public sphere (Mirowski, 2013). This carries with it a range of malign effects, such as the consistent race to the bottom in environmental standards, democratic oversight of international capital, the undermining of the tax bases of states, as well as diminishing social security and employment protection. At their most overt, these processes are reproduced in genuinely violent fashion, as Western attempts to remake world order rest on the imposition of deficient, hollowed-out forms of liberal democracy and development, amid great bloodshed and catastrophic human consequences. This is, as Naomi Klein (2007) put it in her harrowing book, *The Shock Doctrine,* nothing less than 'disaster capitalism' writ large.

THE EMERGING BACKLASH

The reason all of this matters is because both democracy and development are in question in ways that have perhaps never before been the case. One aspect of this is generalized hubris on the part of the neoliberal West. David Runciman (2014) has explored this in great detail, arguing that the problem with the established democracies themselves is that their very resilience represents their most fundamental and enduring weakness: because they have survived a series of crises – the Great Depression, World Wars, the disintegration of Communism, even, so far, the contemporary Global Financial Crisis – this has not induced hard-headed critical reflection regarding the extent to which such a state of affairs may continue, but rather has led to complacency and myopia. 'Democracy is trapped', he argues 'by the nature of its own success' (Runciman, 2014, p. xiii). This is especially problematic at the current juncture, because Western countries are not only struggling with the fallout from the 2008 crisis and the messy aftermath of the wars in Iraq and Afghanistan, but a pathology of over-confidence represents the worst possible mindset with which to approach the truly epochal challenges of massive debt burdens, China's rise, climate change and the War on Terror. Yet the broader problem with democracy and development is not simply – or even – a Western story alone. The backlash against both has been brewing for some time elsewhere in the world.

For much of the 1990s, as the 'good governance' agenda became more deeply embedded in the thinking and practice of the international financial institutions (IFIs), underpinned by the idea that liberal democracy – itself reduced to a scrawny hotchpotch of processes and institutions like elections and party competition, but not always a great deal of substance – was now the only game in town, its promotion increasingly became an active component of policy. In certain respects this was less controversial than others: the European Union (EU), for example, was highly effective at using what Levitsky and Way (2007) have termed 'linkages' – that is, dense patterns of diplomatic, media and economic connections – to induce democratization in the many Central and Eastern European countries that wished to accede to the EU. But this was also accompanied, particularly in places where linkages were less dense, by what they term 'leverage', characterized by the susceptibility of different countries to Western, and, especially, US, pressure to change. This was especially contentious during the 1990s and 2000s, since many states had already undertaken a degree of political liberalization, usually amid great tension, and this tended to rest on a range of complicated and fragile social compromises, particularly among elites. In the terms favoured by specialists, they had, nevertheless, not completed or 'consolidated' their 'transition to' democracy, and therefore required 'assistance'. However, what was often not realized was that these so-called 'hybrid regimes' (Levitsky and Way, 2010), which embodied both authoritarian and democratic features simultaneously, could actually be seen to represent distinctive entities in their own right, rather than simply 'failed' or 'stalled' transitions as per the teleological assumptions that animated much of the field of democratization studies (see Grugel and Bishop, 2013).

This can be seen clearly with the example of the 'Color Revolutions' that took place in the mid-2000s. The Orange Revolution in Ukraine was possibly the most spectacular of the period, and it was preceded by huge amounts of European and American money and support for pro-democracy organizations. However, contrary to engendering a meaningful process of democratization, the past decade has witnessed the gradual reassertion of Russian influence over Ukraine, including the annexation of Crimea, to the extent that democracy is as far away as ever. It would, of course, be too glib – and wrong – to blame the West for failures such as this (which were repeated elsewhere in Eastern Europe and Central Asia). However, they do illustrate the limits of what democracy promotion can achieve. The promise of rapid – even revolutionary – democratic change led to nervousness on the part of semi-authoritarian elites, encouraging them to limit civil society activity, including its ability to access international support. Moreover, Western influence in Kiev was seen as highly provocative by Russia, further ratcheting up tensions and ultimately leading to a tough response once the opportunity to seize the initiative presented itself (see Sakwa, 2015).

A similar story can, perhaps, be told regarding the Arab Spring. As the dominoes began to fall during 2011, many Western countries at first responded by betraying their supposed democratic credentials: as Dixon (2011, p. 310) suggests, the 'image of Western governments as defenders and promoters of democracy and development fractures before a fumbling, reticent reaction to mass democratic movements confronting authoritarian rule'. France even offered the Tunisian autocrat, Zine El Abidine Ben Ali, weapons and logistical support to put down the protests (Noueihed and Warren, 2012, p. 65). Yet the broader problem was not simply that Western support for democratization was generally subordinated to strategic objectives of *Realpolitik* (Berger, 2011). The catastrophe in Syria, the disintegration of Libya, and the strong backing for Abdel Fattah el-Sisi in Egypt, the country's new military ruler, attest to this thorny challenge. The issue is that democracy promotion was generally perpetuated in a piecemeal and disingenuously partial way. It also simply did not work very well. As in the previous example, the US has spent decades providing support to opposition movements in much of the Middle East, with relatively little success, regularly even making things worse. In Iran, democracy promotion during the 1990s so incensed the government that it facilitated a purge of moderates by hardliners, setting reform efforts back years (see Tezcür, 2012). In Iraq, the kind of democracy that has been imposed from outside has rested on an emaciated state, utterly unable to sustain it: enduring sectarian warfare, generations of people traumatized by violence, and deficient institutions have provided a fertile context for the growth of networks that fuse criminal gangsterism and terrorism, of which Islamic State (ISIS) is only the most recent example.

It is, therefore, not difficult to see why the past decade has witnessed a discernible 'backlash' (Carothers, 2006, 2010) against democracy promotion activities and other attempts to engender 'good governance'. Even in societies which are not marred by a complete breakdown of political and social institutions, or the most pernicious forms of authoritarianism, these agendas are highly contentious. In much of Africa, for example, 'democratization' became largely a reflection of the leverage of international agencies and Western mores (Harrison, 2010). Some countries – such as Ghana – have achieved a significant degree of success in engendering more responsive democratic institutions, but arguably this is more about effective leadership and long-term internal processes of change than anything else. Normally, the kind of conditionality that marks external pressure fails to realize its objectives, for several reasons. First, it is often only partially implemented and generative of cosmetic change – for benchmarking and evaluation – rather than meaningful, long-term democratization (Lynch and Crawford, 2011). Second, human rights and pro-democracy policies are often subordinated to strategic goals in countries that are central to Western interests. Third, democracy through conditionality is visited primarily, or at least most thoroughly, on the poorest countries that are least able to resist Western leverage. Aid sanctions have been applied primarily in the parts of sub-Saharan Africa with the lowest levels of development and the weakest and most fragmented states, where they have generally undermined social cohesion rather than stimulating the creation of deeply-rooted democracies (Harrison, 2010).

Semi-authoritarian states, which claim to be moving towards embedding greater democracy – a process that took Western countries centuries, waxing and waning over time in response to pronounced patterns of internal contestation and changes in class structure and culture – are, as Carothers (2006, p. 64) has argued, inevitably uneasy with 'the whole body of US democracy-building programs, no matter how routine or uncontroversial the programs once were'. External support works only when it is accompanied by genuine consent internally. Where there are strong domestic foundations conducive to democratic change, pro-democracy policies from outside can help to embed and deepen it. But it is unrealistic to expect either conscious pro-democracy policies or brash assertions regarding the inevitable 'triumph of democracy' to transform what, in many cases, are centuries-old authoritarian cultures and practices, especially not overnight. It may even be the case, as Laurence Whitehead (2010, p. 25) has contended, that radical forms of democracy promotion have, in fact, retarded and undermined the prospects for greater political opening around the world: because 'liberal internationalists lost their sense of reality in their hubristic desire to remake the entire world in accordance with their utopia'. He argues that this resulted in a 'backlash which will last for a substantial period'. Moreover, not only is it unrealistic to expect such externally imposed change, it is arguably not desirable in many cases: democracy is not – or certainly not always – a panacea for development, particularly if it implies a weakened state.

The case of contemporary Rwanda is, in fact, instructive. Since the genocide of 1994, the country has been one of the major recipients of Western aid in sub-Saharan Africa. Along with Belgium, the British government took a particular interest in its reconstruction (Hayman, 2010). Huge amounts of money, people and expertise have been poured into the country over the past decade or more by the UK Department for International Development (DfID), with state-building the principal objective. However, as Beswick (2011) argues, this has left London both more hegemonic in Rwanda than other donors, as well as considerably more implicated in the behaviour of the government. The intriguing thing is that this extensive financial and diplomatic support has not facilitated a meaningful – or, to use the teleological language of completion favoured in parts of the literature, fully 'consolidated' – transition to democracy: Paul Kagame, the military commander who brought the genocide to an end, had, at the time of writing in early 2017, served as president for *17* years. He has also been dogged by accusations of authoritarianism, suppression of political opposition, and human rights abuses. So, it is certainly true that 'the UK has effectively minimized its ability to support the positive trajectory it seeks to promote' (Beswick, 2011, p. 1927). But equally, Kagame does not appear to be a wild kleptocrat: he is widely viewed as a serious leader who has, in fact, constructed a highly powerful set of state institutions that are able to set out a clear developmental path. As Laura Mann and Marie Berry (2016) have noted, a pronounced level of control and development go hand in hand: by prioritizing growth, the space has been subsequently opened up to stabilize the country, and create new development imaginaries that transcend the enduring ethnic and social cleavages that still bubble under the surface. This is, moreover, a process underway in a number of African states today: greater numbers of leaders with developmentalist aspirations are increasingly rejecting orthodox policy advice, building powerful state apparatuses, embedding them more forcefully in the economy, and seeking to effect deeper patterns of change than the simple creation of free markets (see Booth et al., 2015).

The broader issue here, of course, relates to the critical role of the state in development. Early in the neoliberal era, the importance of states was essentially denied as structural adjustment continued apace in North and South alike. Yet even as this gave way to the more sensitive post-Washington Consensus period, attempts to institute 'good governance' were broadly about seeking to institutionalize market-friendly, liberal democratic political systems which were, as Anthony Payne and Nicola Phillips (2010, p. 97) suggest, fundamentally 'apolitical'. What they mean by this is that they essentially denied the crucial *political* role of the state in driving forward a distinctive – even radical – development strategy, viewing it as little more than an *administrative* carrier of external programmes and preferences (see Leftwich, 2000, 2005). It barely needs saying that this was, as suggested above, highly problematic – and even dangerous – in contexts where the state was unable to carry out the myriad compromises of democracy, let alone set out a meaningful development path (Grugel and Bishop, 2013). But thankfully this era is now beginning to pass. Intellectually, numerous thinkers have stressed the notion of *stateness* as a critical attribute necessary for the exercise of power and the adoption of the necessary institutional paraphernalia of modern systems of governance. Consequently, any democratizing reforms are increasingly considered to require proper 'sequencing' if they are to be successfully adopted (Fukuyama, 2005; Møller and Skaaning, 2011).

The exemplar of these processes *par excellence* can surely be found in the so-called 'rise' of China, a country that has enjoyed an astonishing and rapid developmental expansion over the past four decades – its economy is presently *five times* the size of India's – and quite evocatively challenges a number of key planks of the hegemonic neoliberal consensus on development. First, China has undergone a genuine developmental *transformation* (see Bishop, 2016b). It ignored free-market sages who recommended early opening up to forms of free trade that would have neutered nascent sectors and therefore kept its economy operating at a far lower level of comparative advantage, rather than experiencing, as it has, successive stages of relentless industrial upgrading and ongoing transformations of its panorama of developmental possibility (Lin, 2011). Second, it has achieved this with a highly penetrating state apparatus, which has, in a careful and controlled way, sequenced economic reforms, and taken a central role in shaping and distorting markets to achieve developmental ends, much as was the case in the earlier so-called 'Asian Tigers' (Breslin, 2011). Third, China has resolutely resisted – until now, at least – Western-style liberal democratic political reform, which is arguably a large part of the explanation for its success, given a history of external intervention and a massive, and in many respects fragmented, state that has still not fully consolidated its rule over its enormous territory. Some do worry, though, about the inevitable slowdown and rebalancing which has now begun, particularly in terms of whether pronounced economic restructuring may induce a wider political crisis. However, equally, because of the breadth and depth of China's transformation, a softer landing is an equally plausible scenario (see Bishop, 2017).

The lessons, therefore, seem obvious. As Tony Heron (2017) has suggested, these are not a simplistic and superficial presupposition that state-led development is inherently superior to market-led development, and that the two are not mutually exclusive. Similarly, authoritarianism is not inherently preferable to democracy, and in many ways is considerably worse. Rather, a powerful, strategic, developmentally-minded state is crucial, particularly in the early stages of the development process, and this may well not be democratic (Leftwich, 2000). This also does not, of course, mean that authoritarian states always deliver development. As Francis Fukuyama (2011, p. 311) has put it: 'For every Lee Kuan Yew [of Singapore] there are probably half a dozen authoritarians like North Korea's Kim Jong-il, Zaire's Mobutu Sese Seko, or Zimbabwe's Robert Mugabe, who drive their economies into the ground while enriching themselves and their followers.' But, by the same token, weak states can neither bear democracy nor engender meaningful development. Strong states can do both, but may do one or neither. This may sound like a discussion of semantics, but it matters. The approach taken by China, although it has many undesirable dimensions – not least heavy repression and environmental degradation – is desirable for the very fact that the lessons it offers appear to work, are reasonably easy to grasp, and are potentially implementable by all states wishing to effect a substantive transformation (see Lin, 2014). Moreover, they do not preclude further gradual liberalization: China's growth is as much about (controlled) market opening and globalization as it is about protectionism and economic nationalism, and there is no reason to suspect that political opening of some kind (and widespread environmental renewal) will not eventually be sequenced into its reform process down the line.

THE FUTURE OF THE LIBERAL ORDER

We have now witnessed a definitive return of the state to development, a rejection of external intervention in democratization, and greater suspicion towards dominant ideologies, with some going so far as to suggest that the liberal order itself is under threat. However, the backlash against hegemonic norms was not against liberal forms of democracy and development per se. It was – and remains – antagonistic to the emaciated, hollowed-out variants which have passed for them in recent decades, and which have been imposed, often viciously, on different societies.

The promise of liberal democracy and global interdependence – for example growth, rising living standards, multilateral solutions, equality between states, equity within societies, efficiently operating market economies, universal human rights, well-functioning democracies that deliver substantive rights and citizenship, and so on – is certainly significant. But when it is betrayed by variants of a neoliberal market fundamentalism that actually delivers crises and austerity, economic stagnation, rampaging inequality, depressed growth, belligerent warmongering, deficient, exclusionary and oligarchic forms of democracy, oligopolistic rentier-dominated rigged markets, the asset-stripping of the public realm, diminishing levels of social capital, and a partial – even racist – commitment to human rights, the myth alluded to earlier becomes difficult to sustain. Furthermore, despite the rhetoric, it also becomes far easier for critics to decry the failures of liberalism, and proclaim the superiority – certainly in terms of performance – of illiberal ways of doing things. This is clearly evident in three broader, interlinked processes of change that are beginning to make themselves apparent.

First, the reassertion of state sovereignty has, as already noted, improved the developmental prospects of many parts of the world. In some respects, this is not a new story: the most excitable early accounts of globalization and the challenge it posed to the state were soon countered by arguments that emphasized its enduring power (e.g. Weiss, 1998). More recently, critical scholars have pointed out that what has actually happened is that, rather than simply being 'rolled back', states have often been reconfigured in complex ways such that they increasingly operate as conduits for international capital via specific forms of 'arm's length' regulation (Cerny, 2010). The key point is that, even though they may not necessarily have been undermined in a simplistic or uniform fashion – although, of course, in many cases they may well have been weakened dramatically by structural rearrangements imposed from outside – neoliberal reform, in general, whether applied to richer or poorer, weaker or more powerful, larger or smaller states, does imply the kinds of hollowing-out of the public realm and anomic marketization that impoverishes society and the substantiveness of democracy (Crouch, 2013; Mair, 2013).

The problem, though, is that, for a broadly open, liberal order to survive, a balance needs to be struck between the egoistic behaviour of states and the broader needs of the global community. The election of Donald Trump to the US Presidency is extremely troubling in this regard, particularly given both the travails in which the EU finds itself – coping with the fallout from Brexit, the refugee crisis, and enduring economic stagnation in southern Europe – and increased Russian bellicosity. As Ivan Krastev and Stephen Holmes (2017) have put it: 'Trump is positioning himself as the global leader of an anti-global movement that is anti-elite, anti-establishment, anti-liberal, and nationalistic.' It is one thing to hope for an end to global market fundamentalism and a return to a more managed, equitable form of globalization that balances liberal ideals with substantive social democratic content. It is quite another to want to bring down the entire edifice of a painstakingly constructed global political economy. However, again, it is instructive to consider that Trump can only convince large sections of the American electorate to support his agenda *because of* the very stagnation of their living standards, and the debasement of their democratic voice that has systematically occurred during the neoliberal era.

This brings us to the second, related issue, which is the broader rise of economically nationalist rhetoric and, potentially, practice. The disavowal of the state's *political* role in development, particularly in the crucial early stages of industrialization, is both historically illiterate (Chang, 2002) and, again, thankfully on the retreat. Relatively benign forms of economic nationalism, in states as diverse as the East Asian 'Tigers' of the 1970s, China and Vietnam today, or indeed a number of African states, are clearly generating high levels of growth and rapid industrial expansion. However, the danger comes from the fact that all countries cannot pursue mercantilist policies – or even just export-oriented growth strategies – simultaneously. The dangerous accumulation of global imbalances is something about which we have been acutely aware, at least since Keynes was alive, but it takes on new salience in the contemporary period. This is because the major powers – and especially the US under Trump – are becoming alive to the possibilities of greater protectionism, not just those seeking to catch up. It is actually unsurprising that this should be occurring, given the pronounced crisis – which is, at root, a *development* crisis, even though that language is rarely deployed to describe countries in the North when it really should be (see Payne, 2005) – into which many have fallen since 2008. This in turn raises the spectre that not only will Southern countries catch up developmentally, but they may even go beyond this, such that the already-wealthy may not, as Mark Blyth (2013) has put it, 'stay on top' over the coming decades. This explains why China now appears to be the greatest defender of globalization among the most powerful states, as, like all dominant economies (for example Britain in the eighteenth century, the US in the twentieth century), it has the most to gain from open trade.

This realignment need not be especially troublesome were it embedded in a flexible system of international governance of the kind that Keynes, again, advocated long ago. However – and this represents the other problem – it is quite plausible that any Trumpian attempt to engage in protectionist policy is likely to be dramatic, ill-thought-out, haphazard and highly destabilizing. Rather than a balanced form of re-embedding of developmentally minded states within national and international economies which seeks to correct the excesses of the neoliberal era, we may well see countries tip into outright nationalist provocations. It is not as if there are no other Trumps waiting in the wings, particularly in European countries where, before the crisis, the emergence of hard-right nationalists to a position where they could genuinely compete to win elections (as in France) or decisively shape national policy (as in the Brexit-era UK) would have seemed, at best, implausible. A broader turn to economic nationalism, then, will not necessarily be benign; the embeddedly liberal baby may well be thrown out with the neoliberal bathwater.

Finally, huge question marks consequently hang over the existing edifice of multilateralism that has governed – albeit imperfectly – the international order since 1945. For a period, it appeared that, as Daniel Drezner (2016) has put it, 'the system worked' and the major institutions of liberal internationalism stabilized the system after the 2008 crisis, preventing a much bigger disaster. This is certainly true in a narrow sense: we have still not (yet) seen a return to the kind of rampant protectionism that haunted the 1930s (Siles-Brügge, 2013). However, if recent rhetoric is any guide, this may now be brewing and, if the argument advanced in this chapter has merit, simply saving an increasingly discredited system is not sufficient: not only do market fundamentalist variants of neoliberalism not really provide answers to the myriad political and developmental problems faced by different societies today – hence the search for often-radical alternatives – but they have also effectively undermined the broader appeal of more emollient, equitable and negotiated forms of liberalism that could plausibly have been realized in the recent past.

Part of the problem is the lack of inclusiveness of many multilateral arrangements: the World Trade Organization (WTO), to give one obvious example, has broadly failed to institutionalize a meaningful 'social purpose' that can underpin a kind of global trade politics that takes seriously the distinct needs and challenges of countries with drastically varied levels of development and, therefore, diverse needs and a differentiated capacity to participate (Muzaka and Bishop, 2015). As the collapse of the Doha Round in 2015 revealed clearly, the dogmatic pursuit of forms of liberalization that would have disproportionately benefited the powerful may ultimately have diminished the WTO, perhaps even irretrievably. Again, neoliberals have been their own worst enemy: as Dani Rodrik (2016) has argued, too many have resisted the kinds of state intervention that characterized the post-war period in the West and downplayed the distributional costs of free trade. Again, the backlash against these hegemonic norms, from societies – including now the most powerful – demanding greater policy space should not come as a shock. Other examples could easily support the argument: the Group of 20 (G20) was upgraded as the premier forum for global politicking immediately after the crisis, with a mandate to broaden the shoulders on which rested the management of the global economy. However, this process itself was inherently exclusionary as it consciously omitted the participation of the vast majority of the world's states, and it has fallen prey to a narrowing of its mission and an inability to seriously institutionalize a coherent agenda for coordinating global economic management (Payne, 2010, 2014).

CONCLUSION

Overall, then, we appear to be left with an apparently decaying liberal order that was designed in and for a previous era, and support for its key tenets – in large part because of the decadent, arrogant overreach of the neoliberals – has wavered significantly. It did not, of course, have to be this way. The response to the crisis could have been more radical, and could have engendered the creation of new institutions embodying a meaningful multilateralism, just like in 1945, to meet the challenges of today. In doing so, it may have effectively rebooted the shared global governance of international order in ways that were more balanced, equitable, and with the kind of differentiated distribution of gains from globalization that could have corrected historical, social and economic inequalities of all kinds. That this has not happened suggests that we have been left with, as Eric Helleiner (2014) describes it, an enduring 'status quo crisis' characterized by a world poorly equipped to meet the challenges of the future, and which cannot easily bind the majority of states and societies willingly to a shared global vision that facilitates us living together peacefully on one planet.

If liberal internationalism is to be saved, it is not sufficient to demonize those alternatives, which, despite their many evident problems, appear to be delivering growth and improved living standards in many parts of the world. There are a great many different forms of illiberalism: from outright kleptocracies to forms of authoritarian developmentalist economic nationalism of a variety of flavours and intensities. Of course, few people wish to live under dictatorship. But that is just as true of a variant of market fundamentalism that privileges elites, impoverishes large numbers of people, atomizes society, and continually reduces the substance and significance of political choice. The backlash described in this chapter is not against democracy and development per se. It is against the tendency of neoliberalism to narrow and hollow out their meaning and the substantive forms that they embody when delivered to the world, along with the disavowal of all potential alternative versions of them. Democracy and development cannot simply be aspired to in the abstract. Their quality genuinely matters. If liberalism is to prevail it must achieve its victories on its own merits; by winning hearts and minds – not through bullets and bombs – and showing that it represents an authentically superior, flexible framework for organizing societies and delivering widely shared development and meaningful democratic participation, all the while accommodating many different variants, recipes and blueprints. This can only happen with greater development of democracy, and more democratized forms of development.

REFERENCES

Berger, L. (2011), The Missing Link? US Policy and the International Dimensions of Failed Democratic Transitions in the Arab World. *Political Studies*, *59*(1), 38–55.

Beswick, D. (2011), Aiding State Building and Sacrificing Peace Building? The Rwanda–UK Relationship 1994–2011. *Third World Quarterly*, *32*(10), 1911–30.

Bishop, M. L. (2016a), Democracy and Development: A Relationship of Harmony or Tension? In J. Grugel and D. Hammett (eds), *The Palgrave Handbook of International Development* (pp. 77–98). London: Palgrave Macmillan.

Bishop, M. L. (2016b), Rethinking the political economy of development beyond 'The Rise of the BRICS'. Sheffield Political Economy Research Institute Paper No. 30. Retrieved from: http://speri.dept.shef.ac.uk/wp-content/uploads/2016/07/Beyond-the-Rise-of-the-BRICS.pdf.

Bishop, M. L. (2017), China Crisis? In C. Hay and T. Hunt (eds), *The Coming Crisis*. London: Palgrave Macmillan.

Blyth, M. (2013), This Time it Really is Different: Europe, the Financial Crisis, 'Staying on Top in the Twenty-First Century'. In D. Breznitz and J. Zysman (eds), *The Third Globalization: Can Wealthy Nations Stay Rich in the Twenty-first Century?* (pp. 207–31). Oxford: Oxford University Press.

Booth, D., Dietz, T., Golooba-Mutebi, F., Helmy Fuady, A., Henley, D., Kelsall, T., Lelivald, A. H. M. and van Donge, J. K. (2015), *Development Regimes in Africa: Synthesis Report*. London: Overseas Development Institute.

Breslin, S. (2011), The 'China Model' and the Global Crisis: From Friedrich List to a Chinese Mode of Governance? *International Affairs*, *87*(6), 1323–43.

Carothers, T. (2006), The Backlash Against Democracy Promotion. *Foreign Affairs*, *85*(2), 55–68.

Carothers, T. (2010), The Continuing Backlash Against Democracy Promotion. In P. J. Burnell and R. Youngs (eds), *New Challenges to Democratization* (pp. 59–72). London: Routledge.

Cerny, P. G. (2010), *Rethinking World Politics: A Theory of Transnational Neopluralism*. New York: Oxford University Press.

Chang, H.-J. (2002), *Kicking Away the Ladder*. London: Anthem Press.

Crouch, C. (2004), *Post-Democracy*. Cambridge: Polity Press.

Crouch, C. (2013), *The Strange Non-Death of Neoliberalism*. Cambridge: Polity Press.

Dixon, M. (2011), An Arab Spring. *Review of African Political Economy*, *38*(128), 309–16.

Drezner, D. W. (2016), *The System Worked: How the World Stopped Another Great Depression*. Oxford: Oxford University Press.

Fukuyama, F. (2005), 'Stateness' First. *Journal of Democracy*, *16*(1), 84–8.

Fukuyama, F. (2011), Is There a Proper Sequence in Democratic Transitions? *Current History*, *110*(739), 308–11.

Gamble, A. (2014), *Crisis Without End?: The Unravelling of Western Prosperity*. Basingstoke: Palgrave Macmillan.

Grugel, J. (2003), Democratisation Studies Globalisation: The Coming of Age of a Paradigm. *The British Journal of Politics and International Relations*, *5*(2), 258–83.

Grugel, J. and Bishop, M. L. (2013), *Democratization: A Critical Introduction*. Basingstoke: Palgrave Macmillan, 2nd edition.

Harrison, G. (2010), *Neoliberal Africa: The Impact of Global Social Engineering*. London: Zed Books.

Hayman, R. (2010), Abandoned Orphan, Wayward Child: The United Kingdom and Belgium in Rwanda Since 1994. *Journal of Eastern African Studies*, *4*(2), 341–60.

Helleiner, E. (2014), *The Status Quo Crisis: Global Financial Governance After the 2008 Meltdown*. Oxford: Oxford University Press.

Heron, T. (2017), Governing the Formal Economy: The Convergence of Theory and Divergence of Practice. In J. Grugel and D. Hammett (eds), *The Palgrave Handbook of International Development* (pp. 169–84). London: Palgrave Macmillan.

Klein, N. (2007), *The Shock Doctrine: The Rise of Disaster Capitalism*. London: Allen Lane.

Krastev, I. and Holmes, S. (2017), The Kremlin is Starting to Worry About Trump. Retrieved from: http://foreignpolicy.com/2017/02/13/the-kremlin-is-starting-to-worry-about-trump/ (accessed 29 March 2017).

Leftwich, A. (2000), *States of Development: On the Primacy of Politics in Development*. Cambridge: Polity Press.

Leftwich, A. (2005), Politics in Command: Development Studies and the Rediscovery of Social Science. *New Political Economy*, *10*(4), 573–607.

Levitsky, S. and Way, L. A. (2007), Linkage, Leverage, and the Post-Communist Divide. *East European Politics and Societies, 21*(1), 48–66.

Levitsky, S. and Way, L. A. (2010), *Competitive Authoritarianism: Hybrid Regimes After the Cold War*. Cambridge: Cambridge University Press.

Lin, J. Y. (2011), *Demystifying the Chinese Economy*. Cambridge: Cambridge University Press.

Lin, J. Y. (2014), *The Quest for Prosperity: How Developing Economies Can Take Off*. Princeton, NJ: Princeton University Press.

Lynch, G. and Crawford, G. (2011), Democratization in Africa 1990–2010: An Assessment. *Democratization, 18*(2), 275–310.

Mair, P. (2013), *Ruling the Void: The Hollowing of Western Democracy*. London: Verso Books.

Mann, L. and Berry, M. (2016), Understanding the Political Motivations That Shape Rwanda's Emergent Developmental State. *New Political Economy, 21*(1), 119–44.

Mirowski, P. (2013), *Never Let a Serious Crisis Go to Waste: How Neoliberalism Survived the Financial Meltdown*. New York: Verso.

Møller, J. and Skaaning, S.-E. (2011), Stateness First? *Democratization, 18*(1), 1–24.

Mount, F. (2012), *The New Few: Or a Very British Oligarchy*. London: Simon and Schuster.

Muzaka, V. and Bishop, M. L. (2015), Doha Stalemate: The End of Trade Multilateralism? *Review of International Studies, 41*(2), 383–406.

Noueihed, L. and Warren, A. (2012), *The Battle for the Arab Spring: Revolution, Counter-Revolution and the Making of a New Era*. New Haven, CT: Yale University Press.

Payne, A. (2005), *The Global Politics of Unequal Development*. Basingstoke: Palgrave Macmillan.

Payne, A. (2010), How Many Gs are there in 'Global Governance' After the Crisis? The Perspectives of the 'Marginal Majority' of the World's States. *International Affairs, 86*(3), 729–40.

Payne, A. (2014), Steering into the Great Uncertainity: The G20 as Global Governance. *Caribbean Journal of International Relations and Diplomacy, 2*(3), 73–85.

Payne, A. and Phillips, N. (2010), *Development*. Cambridge: Polity Press.

Piketty, T. (2014), *Capital in the Twenty First Century*. Cambridge, MA: Harvard University Press.

Rodrik, D. (2016), Straight Talk on Trade. Retrieved from: https://www.project-syndicate.org/commentary/trump-win-economists-responsible-by-dani-rodrik-2016-11?barrier=accessreg (accessed 29 March 2017).

Runciman, D. (2014), *The Confidence Trap: A History of Democracy in Crisis from World War I to the Present*. Princeton, NJ: Princeton University Press.

Sakwa, R. (2015), *Frontline Ukraine: Crisis in the Borderlands*. London: IB Tauris.

Siles-Brügge, G. (2013), Explaining the Resilience of Free Trade: The Smoot–Hawley Myth and the Crisis. *Review of International Political Economy, 21*(3), 535–74.

Tansel, C. B. (2017), Authoritarian Neoliberalism: Towards a New Research Agenda. In C. B. Tansel (ed.), *States of Discipline: Authoritarian Neoliberalism and the Contested Reproduction of Capitalist Order* (pp. 1–28). London: Rowman and Littlefield.

Tezcür, G. M. (2012), Democracy Promotion, Authoritarian Resiliency, and Political Unrest in Iran. *Democratization, 19*(1), 120–40.

Weiss, L. (1998), *The Myth of the Powerless State: Governing the Economy in a Global Era*. Cambridge: Polity Press.

Whitehead, L. (2010), State Sovereignty and Democracy: An Awkward Coupling. In P. J. Burnell and R. Youngs (eds), *New Challenges to Democratization* (pp. 23–41). London: Routledge.

Winters, J. A. (2011), *Oligarchy*. New York: Cambridge University Press.

10. Development NGOs, civil society and social change
Su-ming Khoo

INTRODUCTION: LOOSE DEFINITIONS AND CHANGING CONTEXTS

In order to understand development-focused Non-Governmental Organizations (NGOs), it is useful to situate them in terms of their role in civil society and, more generally, in relation to the global historical context of social change. The three main elements of this contribution – NGOs, civil society and social change – are hard to define, dynamic and contested. NGOs are difficult to define and classify, and the lack of an agreed definitional framework poses ongoing difficulties for understanding and analysis. The term 'NGO' merely defines what they are not, leaving an extremely broad canvas of differing origins, motivations, organizational and funding structures. NGOs may have exogenous or endogenous origins, and are usually associated with voluntarism, 'private' constitution and non-profit orientation. The definitional dilemma surrounding NGOs is not merely a theoretical or conceptual problem; it also presents practical obstacles for understanding and learning. The literature defines them as Private Voluntary Organizations (PVOs), or Non-Profit Organizations (NPOs) (Salamon, 1994; Vakil, 1997). Development NGOs are those associated with the delivery of humanitarian relief, rehabilitation and development programmes. They are typically financed through a mix of voluntary private donations and funding from donor agencies, including private and public or official governmental and intergovernmental aid. The definition of NGOs as being autonomous and independent of local, national and/or international state actors is therefore partly inaccurate. NGO work is often justified as being more altruistic, benevolent, efficient and effective in pursuing public purposes than state agencies. However, NGOs have been increasingly influenced by and dependent upon donor policies since the late 1990s, and the predominant analysis and understanding of NGOs has tended to reflect the influence of changing macroeconomic ideologies, rather than being grounded in evidence-based research (Wallace, 2003, 2004).

Recent histories of NGOs (Khagram et al., 2002; Davies, 2013) point to the continuities with much earlier forms of religious and collective activism and action. Including religious organizations in 'NGOs' makes them eight or nine hundred years old (Davies, 2013), a far more ancient pedigree than 'governments'. Their history potentially spans from their 'prehistory' (Davies, 2013) through to the 'hypercollective action' era, which began in the latter half of the 1990s (Severino and Ray, 2009). Korten notes that 'NGOs' are, by definition, a much older phenomenon than states, if we consider how communities organized for mutual protection and self-help even before governments came into existence (Korten, 1991). Davies argues that older, as well as non-Western organizations, have tended to be neglected, while Barnett's history of humanitarianism problematizes an evolutionary view of NGOs, which 'is rooted in Western history and globalized in ways that were largely responsive to interests and ideas emanating from the West' (Barnett, 2011, p. 16). Scholars taking a more long-term, global view tend to see NGO development not as linear expansion, but contingent, complex and possibly following cyclical, dialectical patterns of global expansion, retrenchment and fragmentation.

NGOs are often understood as synonymous with 'civil society', representing a 'third sector' distinct from both the public state sector and the private market sector. They are especially associated with 'development', and most of the literature tends to exclude purely business-oriented organizations, as well as some non-profit ones such as trade unions, professional groupings, recreational, cultural and exclusively religious bodies. Vakil considers 'development' to be the central defining aspect of NGOs, but there is a lack of agreement about the definition of 'development', although most commentators accept that economic and social development are now core defining features of NGOs (Gorman, 1984; Salamon and Anheier, 1992). The coexistence of definite and fuzzy defining criteria makes more sense when NGOs are set within the context of neoliberal transformations of global development. This situates NGOs within the active and changing reconfiguration of the relative roles of the state, the market and civil society – focusing on the role of states before the 1980s, promoting the role of markets in the 1980s and 1990s and pointing to market failures after the mid-1990s (Wallace, 2004). Thus, the rise of NGOs reflects ideological undercurrents concerning global development and poverty reduction that have come to prominence since the 1980s (Hulme, 2013).

Two major debates have emerged through the attempts to define NGOs: one around the extent to which NGOs can be said to act on behalf of civil society and the second concerning the relationship between the NGO sector and the state (Vakil, 1997, p. 2059). 'Civil society' remains an elusive concept, having gained different meanings and inflections as it emerged and evolved through the nineteenth, twentieth and now twenty-first centuries. In the early 1820s, the philosopher G.W.F. Hegel theorized 'civil society' as the necessary precondition for state-formation. The French aristocrat Alexis de Tocqueville saw civil society in quite a different light in his observations of American democracy in the 1830s – as a sphere of private, civil affairs separate from the state. Having experienced both the terror of the French Revolution and the Bonapartism that followed (Chakrabarti, 2016), de Tocqueville was attracted by the independent quality of American civil society and idealized independent civic association as a bulwark against the potential despotism of a centralized administrative state. Marx, writing in the 1840s, saw civil society as the source of power for a bourgeois state, an idea that Gramsci reworked in his Prison Notebooks of the 1920s. Gramsci saw civil society as the space where hegemony was achieved as an alliance between the state and dominant classes (Chandoke, 2010, p. 177). Civil society included 'private' institutions such as trade unions, churches and the education system, which generated popular consent for political rule by the state. However, this consent was a dynamic and unfinished process and therefore civil society could also provide the arena in which non-dominant, or 'subaltern', classes could forge social alliances and begin to articulate alternatives or counter-hegemony.

What we see today, a century and a half after de Tocqueville is a largely Tocquevillian view of civil society, but in a very different context. The contemporary understanding of civil society has its recent history in the breakdown of the totalitarian state in Eastern Europe in the 1980s. Civil society came to be equated with the rejection of dominating, state-oriented and single party-based mass politics, in favour of individualism and a more liberal orientation based on democratization and civil and political freedoms, along with an implicit welcome for the arrival of market forces. The concept of civil society that was reborn in 1980s' Eastern Europe was translated into a welcome for civil society as a good thing in and of itself, particularly in the context of African development in the 1990s (Ilal et al., 2014). Proponents of global civil society tend to see NGOs as expressions of it, even to the extent of being synonymous with it (Anheier et al., 2001, pp. 4, 15).

The third element for discussion here, social change, may involve two kinds of processes, adaptation or transformation. It can involve different 'units' of change and we need to be able to think in quite a flexible way about how different actors (persons, movements or organizations) exercise agency in bringing about change (Dwyer and Minnegal, 2010).

Kaldor distinguishes the activist 'Post-Marxist' perspective on civil society which emerged from oppositional forces in Central Europe in the 1970s and 1980s from a neoliberal version of it. The collapse of the Soviet bloc in 1989 offered a watershed for redefining 'associational life' as the non-profit, voluntary 'third' sector. Kaldor further identifies a 'post-modern' civil society, an arena of contestation and pluralism that may be characterized by incivility as well as civility (Kaldor, 2003, pp. 6–12). The next section looks at the rise to influence of NGOs in international and national political processes in the decades leading up to the 1990s, reflecting a shift in political thinking away from 'government' and towards 'governance' in a market-dominated global system.

THEMES AND TENSIONS IN NGO ACTIVISM

The long-run history of NGOs highlights two intertwined themes: the universalizing push towards a global spread of humanitarianism and internationalism, and a contradictory push-and-pull of politicization and depoliticization.

Davies' (2013) new history identifies three main phases of NGO development since ancient times, with the early 1930s and late 1990s marking exceptional peaks in transnational NGO activism. 'Modern' NGOs emerged in the age of political enlightenment and revolution after the 1760s, and from then on NGOs underwent processes of internation-alization, diversification and specialization. The early twentieth century saw a second period of major international NGO (INGO) expansion. Notable NGOs of this period included the Carnegie and Rockefeller Foundations which sought to solve international problems using univer-salistic scientific approaches. However, many transnational actors of the early twentieth century were 'uncivil' in the sense of promoting aggressive nationalism and imperialism, and contributing to the deterioration of peaceful international relations (ibid., p. 76). Many organizations 'became increasingly exploited by governments, and fragmented along the geopolitical divisions of the period' (ibid., p. 107). Internationalism expanded as a cause during the early decades of the twentieth century, largely in response to growing nationalism and political ideological competition, world war and the need for economic and social renewal wrought by the Great Depression.

Political-ideological rivalry declined with the end of the Cold War in 1989, leading to a new boom for NGOs. The closing decades of the twentieth century are sometimes described as a period of 'associational revolution' (Salamon, 1994). This period saw the growth of humanitarian assistance, the rapid rise of voluntary, non-profit organizations and their coalescence as a 'sector'. Development NGOs emerged in this context of broad-based expansion of voluntary, non-profit organizations 'pursuing public purposes outside the formal apparatus of the state' (ibid., p. 109). The collapse of authoritarian regimes, the re-emergence of 'civil society' and a major shift in conceptualizing 'development' came together, according NGOs greater prominence as development's key actor. Civil society gained a renewed significance in a world of 'transition', where capitalism no longer had to contend with a rival political ideology. Yet it still retained a subversive connotation as it was identified with popular mobilization challenging state authoritarianism and claiming civil and political rights (Chandoke, 2010).

However, the spread of neoliberalism meant that it was no longer subversive to subvert the state, since the roll-back of state power was implied in neoliberal policies of deregulation, structural adjustment, privatization and market expansion. NGOs supplement the reduced and transformed role of the state under neoliberalism, as enabler and regulator of private sector-led development, rather than acting as provider and producer of public goods (Wallace, 1997).

The expanded role for NGOs in the 1990s saw them becoming the key actors, supporting a largely unchallenged consensus in the global development sector or 'industry' (Lewis, 2008). This put NGOs in a contradictory position. Banks et al. (2015) and others point out that the rise of development NGOs as a whole 'sector' was based on the premise that they provide means to achieve alternative development, including transformative missions of empowerment and social justice. The NGO sector was brought in to widen the real participation of civil society in development, increasing the inputs of poor people into, and their responsibility for, planning and implementing development. Yet this expansion sucked NGOs into managerialist, top-down approaches and enhanced the advantages of larger more 'corporatized' NGO players over smaller organizations that might have held stronger pro-poor and participatory values (Wallace, 2003).

These trends may actually undermine local and national movements for structural change and benefits to the poor, while serving, and remaining complicit with, state and private sector interests (Lang, 2013). This underpins the radical argument that the dramatic expansion of the NGO sector over the past three decades has failed to produce a stronger, more vibrant civil society capable of tackling issues of power and inequality head on, thus generating real transformative change. This critique is valid, but it should be seen in the context of new dilemmas of funding, accountability and influence, which significantly relate to questions of scale but also to the connection between development and politicization or depoliticization.

NGOs, THE UN AND GLOBAL CIVIL SOCIETY

The post-1945 period saw NGOs becoming involved in emerging structures of global governance and starting to become identified as the agents
of 'global civil society'. Over the following decades, NGOs were able to
attain influence within the UN structure of global governance, by gaining
official status and inclusion in the work of the UN Economic and Social
Council (ECOSOC), the UN organ responsible for coordinating the work
of the UN specialized agencies and commissions. ECOSOC designation
resulted in the emergence of different categories of NGOs with differing
opportunities to participate, as NGOs continued to expand, proliferate,
specialize, professionalize and represent the emerging demands of new and
different actors.

NGOs' identity and position in international law and global governance
is broadly accepted, but remains rather flexible, as there is no single agreed
international legal definition. Article 71 of the UN Charter defines NGOs
as organizations that are independent from government influence and
not-for-profit, and in 1950 UN ECOSOC defined NGOs, for the purposes
of establishing consultative arrangements, as 'any international organization which is not created by an intergovernmental agreement'. In practice,
a wide range of organizations have used various UN meetings both to
further international causes and to make their views known to government
representatives (Seary, 1996, p. 27). The position of NGOs within the
international system ranges from one of formal consultative status with
intergovernmental bodies and instruments, to purely informal bilateral
contacts. New developments point to increasing NGO involvement as
recently introduced measures include NGO membership of regional
bodies such as the African Union and more participation by NGOs
in UN organs; streamlined and depoliticized accreditation procedures
within the UN; renewed self-regulation and self-organization of NGOs
in their relations with the UN; innovative participatory status for NGOs
in the Council of Europe; and informal participation and administrative
facilitation of NGOs in various EU meetings. These measures reflect the
assumption that NGOs constitute 'civil society participation', which is
increasingly perceived as a parameter for international organizations' own
efforts to do 'good governance' (Dupuy and Vierucci, 2008, p. 9).

The Cold War both politicized and depoliticized NGOs, as organizations were drawn into complex East–West and inter-state rivalries, leading
to controversies over their purpose and status (de Frouville, 2008). These
controversies persist to an extent today, complicating the difficulties of
meaning and interpretation accompanying the term 'NGO'. The question
of NGO inclusion and regulation in the international order reflects a

tension between an idealist view of NGOs as normative, advocacy-focused organizations and the instrumental, pragmatic view of NGOs as efficient service deliverers. International law, regulation and voluntary standards for self-regulation may be seen as self-evident, value-neutral and objective. Alternatively, we can see emerging international standards as the result of a mix of problem solving and contestation, with a variety of actors trying to maximize different and, possibly competing, values (Higgins, 1994). The politicization of NGO participation and acceptance of their role could lead to what de Frouville criticizes as a 'servile society', where NGOs serve narrow state interests and domesticate the public, rather than constituting and robustly contesting the broader 'public interest' (de Frouville, 2008). While the World Bank has embraced 'participation' and NGOs since the 1990s, critics argue that this has not led to sufficient NGO influence on the World Bank to change its model of development. In practice, despite NGO involvement, development policies remained basically at variance with the values and advocacy messages that they claimed to embody (Nelson, 1995; Wallace, 2004).

UN-NGO relations have evolved in three phases (Hill, 2004). In the first phase, up to the end of the Cold War, they tended to be at arm's length and largely formal and ceremonial. Key exceptions to this were the 1972 Stockholm Conference on the Human Environment, and the International Coalition for Development Action's (ICDA) work under the auspices of UNCTAD on the North-South Dialogue for a New International Economic Order from the 1970s to the early 1980s. The second phase, in the 1990s, saw the fuller emergence of 'global civil society' and the consolidation of global governance, incorporating new ideas and practices of democratic governance. In this phase, greater emphasis was placed on the need for ongoing participation by citizens and citizen organizations in governance processes. This phase focused on a number of World Conferences and Summits where NGOs sought to engage more directly in intergovernmental deliberations. NGOs developed more sophisticated advocacy and mobilization work to influence the outcomes of these meetings and global NGO alliances and coalitions became more prominent. Examining a mixture of reports and resolutions on the consultative relationship between NGOs and intergovernmental organizations, Rebasti (2008, pp. 23–37) finds that NGO consultative status is inadequate to control and facilitate participation, as there is a 'gap between the factual and legal dimensions' of NGOs' role. The trend is towards the institutionalization of arrangements, via ECOSOC, the Commission on Sustainable Development, and the Joint United Nations Programme, for example. Rebasti notes significantly that the prevalence of informality is likely to work against, rather than in favour of, the smallest and least well-resourced organizations. At the same time, the 1990s also saw the increasing presence and influence of the private sector at the UN (Hill, 2004).

The 1992 Rio Conference proved to be a watershed as concerted attempts by NGOs to participate in the Rio process led to ECOSOC's adoption of Resolution 1996/31 as a formal, legal framework for UN-NGO relations. Resolution 1996/31 explicitly opened UN consultative status to national NGOs. These efforts were opposed by an alliance of established 'first generation' INGOs and reluctant member states who wanted to prevent the opening of governance spaces to include national and regional NGOs. Despite these efforts at blocking, a 'second generation' of UN-NGO relations emerged, incorporating larger-scale NGO presence across the UN system. This involved more diverse organizations including national, regional and international NGOs, networks, coalitions and alliances, to bring a greater diversity of issues and positions to the table. The 'second generation' of UN-NGO relations was more political, since NGOs were better integrated into the institutional architecture of global governance. Greater politicization expanded the ideological spectrum within the UN system, and conservative and largely UN-sceptical national NGOs crowded in as a means to curtail the reach of UN agreements, especially in the areas of women's reproductive rights, arms control, pre-emptive military action and climate change.

Since the 1990s the 'second generation' of UN-NGO relations has seen a significant increase in operational cooperation between the UN Secretariats and agencies and NGOs, to collectively fund non-governmental projects and activities, both development focused and humanitarian in scope, in the global South. In addition to contractual cooperation, many forms of voluntary and consultative joint action have emerged between NGOs and UN secretariats. For example there have been hearings in the run-up to UNCTAD meetings, and the International Planning Committee, constituted by NGOs and allied groups and movements such as Via Campesina, have engaged with following up UN summits. There have also been more efforts at cooperation and coordination between UN field offices and information centres in developing countries and the local and regional NGOs.

Hill speculated that a third generation of UN-Civil Society relations had begun to emerge by the early 2000s. This third generation had two forms: like-minded coalitions of governments and civil society (for example the International Criminal Court and Landmine Convention); and multi-stakeholder, public-private, public policy networks and partnerships, such as the Global Compact and GAVI, plus the literally hundreds of 'Track II' partnership agreements that emerged after the 2002 Johannesburg World Summit on Sustainable Development. These new forms of partnership relations embody both continuities and tensions with the second generation advocacy, which was largely political in nature.

The second generation saw a change in the UN, from an organization in which only governments spoke to other governments, to one that, in the third generation, brings the political power of governments together with the economic power of the corporate sector, the 'public opinion' power of civil society, and the influence of (also corporate and highly monopolistic) global communication and information media (Hill, 2004). By the end of the 1990s, it had become possible to surmise that the NGOs were now part of a world of 'hypercollective action' – 'a whole new ball game' – of donor and organizational proliferation and fragmentation, 'a phase of international policies where thousands of actors are playing different ball games in the same field – with no referee!' (Severino and Ray, 2009, p. 11).

In a recent debate at the London School of Tropical Medicine, the editor of the *Lancet* journal, Richard Horton, suggested that a myth of pure virtue veils NGO action in the area of global health (Horton, 2016). Horton's critique provoked a powerful rejoinder from NGO advocates, who argued that criticisms should be levelled at government and market, rather than 'stigmatising' NGOs (Sarriot et al., 2016). However, some NGOs have become powerful political actors who can fight back. There are now estimated to be some ten million NGOs and it is suggested that if all NGOs were one economy, they would be the fifth largest economy in the world (OnGood, 2016). Horton argues that NGOs' power begs critical questions about whose interests they serve and who really benefits from their interventions. Frequently, they may fragment services, promote unsustainable projects and remain unaccountable. To be fair, the same criticisms could be levelled at both government and private sector actors who don't want a vigorous NGO sector that can challenge their authority.

TRENDS OF MANAGERIALISM AND 'NGO-IZATION'

The increasing role of institutional donors from the end of the 1980s coincided with the significant increase in the establishment and support of NGOs to channel increasing official aid budgets. At the same time, new priorities and methods and cycles of growth and decline in aid flows resulted in larger NGOs expanding and relying more on institutional funding from official aid donor programmes, and then innovating to stay competitive in a now increasingly competitive development industry. Growing budgets and stringent donor demands led NGOs to embrace managerial concepts and tools commonly used in the private sector, ushering in an era of managerialism (Wallace, 1997, p. 35; Lewis, 2008) and 'NGO-ization' (Lang, 2013). The growth in aid budgets in the late 1980s and early 1990s meant that donor agencies responded to growing demands for public accountability by imposing logical frameworks, and frameworks for evaluation and performance management, in order to demonstrate the legitimacy and impact of their work. The private sector gained greater cultural, as well as material, influence within national and international governance and this influenced language and ways of working:

> 'Contract' is the modus operandi, with a focus on 'deliverables', measurable performance indicators and the achievement of targets against which people can potentially be called to account. The assumption is usually that the process is at least partly under control. Financiers look for value defined in financial terms and in terms of efficiency. The perspective is often short term. Rational and deductive project models and quantitative planning tools fit best in this sort of framework: Logical Framework Analysis (LFA) and Cost-Benefit Analysis (CBA) are increasingly common. (Wallace, 1997, p. 37; see also Riddell, 1996)

Successful NGOs began to grow considerably and their increasing size, complexity and desire for further growth resulted in their embracing standardized and bureaucratic systems of financial and management performance and quality control. Some donors introduced new competing actors in the landscape, for example the Department for International Development 'groomed' several selected UK organizations to enter the sector that had not previously been part of it, including the Trades Union Congress (TUC) and the General Medical Council (GMC). Donor funding volatility, short timelines and complex bid processes tended to favour big NGOs, or coalitions of big NGOs, and many smaller and medium-sized NGOs found themselves excluded or overstretched in applying for new bids that required intensive inputs of staff time, capacity and expertise (Wallace, 2003, p. 565). The growing size and complexity of 'winning' big NGOs (BINGOs) and the competitiveness of the development market, especially when donor funding changed or targeted new priorities, were key factors pushing NGOs towards managerialism and 'NGO-ization'. NGO-ization' is:

> [a] . . . process by which social movements professionalize, institutionalize and bureaucratize in vertically structured, policy outcome-oriented organizations that focus on generating issue-specific and, to some degree, marketable expert knowledge or services. Emphasis is placed on organizational reproduction and in the cultivation of funding sources. It frequently results in increased recognition and insider status in NGO's issue-specific policy circles. One effect might be the containment and reframing of more radical messages; another effect might be an orientation toward institutional advocacy and away from public displays of dissent. (Lang, 2013, pp. 63–4)

NGO-ization has some clear advantages. The focus on professional expertise and getting more resources can result in more stable organizations that are able to support their moral claims with research, evidence and facts. Being seen as expert and competent may increase an organization's access to institutional settings and help to inform and improve NGOs' strategies and success. However, the downside might be a narrowing of NGOs' constituencies as they become more donor facing and less focused on the constituencies that they are supposed to stand for, and benefit (ibid., pp. 86–96). Larger NGOs increasingly use the services of commercial marketing and public relations firms to 'sell' their messages to donors and the public. The concern is that this leads to a 'flattened-out' version of civil society (Chandoke, 2003, p. 9), susceptible to publicity takeovers and 'greenwashing' (Lang, 2013, p. 89). While the introduction of corporate methods has enabled slicker, appealing and arguably 'effective' publicity campaigns, for example recruiting celebrities to further development causes, it signals the tendency to practise 'speaking for' instead of 'engaging with' (ibid., p. 91).

CRITIQUES OF EUROCENTRISM AND THE SEARCH FOR ALTERNATIVE APPROACHES

The critical analyses of NGOs coming from NGO voices themselves are joined by loud and distinct critiques of the 'Western-centred orientation' of the study of NGOs and civil society. Some critics point to the restrictive reading of 'civil society' in the Southern context, which downplays much of the grass-roots social interaction because they are deemed 'uncivil' a priori, and thus excluded from understandings of civil society (Ilal et al., 2014). Viewed from a Southern perspective, a Eurocentric or Northern reading of civil society and NGOs becomes empirically dubious and difficult to justify. The fact is that the majority of NGOs are located in the majority world, but Southern-based NGOs and networks are far less frequently studied. In India alone, one 2008 study estimated that there were as many as 3.3 million NGOs, a figure outnumbering the primary schools and primary health centres in that country (Shukla, 2010). The same study also noted that the Indian government provided the largest proportion of the funding for these 'social sector' NGOs, almost double the amount contributed by foreign sources.

From an African perspective, there are critiques of the underrepresentation and 'underweighting' of the distinctive features of African civil society in the literature analysing global civil society (Fowler, 2012). Some complain about the quest for civil society unfolding amid a widespread disillusionment with both idea and reality, noting that social citizenship is being eroded everywhere. Meanwhile, Obadare argues that the dilemma of African civil society is straightforwardly political – a question of how to reinvent the post-colonial state as part of new economic development and political accountability strategies (Obadare, 2011, p. 434), or from a South African perspective through democratizing development through a democratic politics of socioeconomic rights (Jones and Stokke, 2005). What Africa needed was the kind of civil society that acts as a civil sphere (Alexander, 2006), imposing limits on the ability of both the state and the economy to colonize the lifeworld and foster individual and collective self-determination (Young, 2000, p. 189). What it got instead was civil society organizations, especially NGOs. Following the scathing decolonial-critical analysis of Issa Shivji, NGOs could be seen as 'inextricably imbricated in the neoliberal offensive, which follows on the heels of the crisis of the national project' and acting as 'the ideological footsoldiers of imperialism' (Obadare, 2011, pp. 434–5). In that context, the quest by donors and NGOs to measure, assess and evaluate the efficacy of civil society in Africa is, in Obadare's view, a quixotic venture. As an alternative, Fowler argues for the adoption of an Afrocentric epistemology to civil society, which would inform African self-understanding, draw on endogenous research, address the context and substance and take a practical and citizen-centred perspective on power relations (Fowler, 2012, pp. 21–2).

Studies of Chinese civil society point to a divergence from the Tocquevillian assumption about civil society and empirical alignment between Chinese statism and the realities of NGO-ization. While

> the typical Western concept of a civil society [implies] opposing state power . . . the purpose of early Chinese civil society was not to confront the government, but rather to harmonize the relations between society and the government, providing autonomy to assist government. This point was mutually accepted by both the government and society. (Ma, 1995, p. 287)

Though China's single party-state system and its long tradition of government control of all social organizations have caused commentators to see Chinese NGOs as lacking autonomy, that merely mirrors the trends for Northern donors to turn to NGOs to disburse development aid and implement development. Chinese NGOs have less autonomy than NGOs in democratic countries, but the practice of government influence through funding occurs in many Western countries. Thus Ma asks whether the Chinese government's influence is more questionable than that of others (Ma, 2002, p. 122). In fact, the 'Chinese' model for autonomous, but state-assisting, NGOs is structurally similar to that of 'Western' NGDOs (Non-Governmental Development Organizations) particularly after the mid-1990s, when structural adjustment policies were replaced with the return of the state's role to the centre of development. This time it was with an explicit focus on 'good governance' (Banks et al., 2015, p. 708) that incorporated NGO expertise and values to speak for civil society while also delivering necessary goods and services to those denied them by market failures.

Despite this reality on the ground, the development sector industry takes a narrow, depoliticized and top-down definition of civil society, conflating it with a professionalized, elite cohort of NGOs who can connect with, and satisfy strict accountability processes to, governments, Northern NGOs, philanthropists, and other donors. The main distinction that should be made is between 'intermediary NGOs' and membership-based organizations. Many NGOs lack the attributes of membership-based organizations, and this limits their potential to act as countervailing powers against dominant state and market interests.

This explains why development NGOs have made less transformative progress and social change than might be expected. The argument is that, on the whole, the majority of development NGOs have weak roots in civil society, in the countries they work in and in which they generate resources. This weakness limits how much they can drive social change. Secondly, over the past decade, the NGO world has become permeated with technocratic reform and this has narrowed its work to focus on more limited, donor-oriented service delivery, or mere astroturfed 'democracy promotion', rather than authentic, deep-rooted transformation (Bebbington, 1997; Kamstra et al., 2013). In fact, this astroturfing threatens to erode the kind of vibrant civil society that is necessary for structural change. Trends in national and international political environments continue to constrain NGO activities, through defunding, repression and selectivity.

THE POSSIBILITIES AND DISAPPOINTMENTS OF HUMAN RIGHTS

This complexity and fragmentation of development governance has led some international development research, policy and practice actors to voluntarily seek to reground their development practice within a human rights agenda. Since the rise of ethical approaches to development (Goulet, 1971; Gasper, 2004), and the critique of development's failures in light of the Rwanda genocide (Uvin, 1998), numerous attempts have been made to inform development with human rights concerns, align development agendas with human rights frameworks and integrate human rights in practice via the adoption of 'rights based approaches' to development (United Nations Development Programme, 2000). Yet, recent research suggests that human rights have actually lost traction since the formulation of the post-2015 development consensus of 'sustainable development goals' (Brolan et al., 2015). These findings examined the global agenda-setting process for global health, arguably the most advanced domain of rights in practice, and a fundamental underpinning for global struggles for development and justice. A rights-based approach, grounded in the Right to Development, foregrounds the importance of 'meaningful participation' and benefit in development practice (Sengupta, 2002). This aligns with NGO work and a conception of civil society that is actively participatory and 'engaging with', rather than 'speaking for'. Noting that the development process is prone to the contradictory push-pull of politicization and depoliticization, a rights-based approach looks to enact processes of democratizing development through a democratic politics of socioeconomic rights (Jones and Stokke, 2005, p. 2).

Human rights offers a serious alternative possibility of de-commodified approaches to development in an increasingly market-dominated world. It offers a normatively grounded understanding of what development is about, how it might be practised and, ultimately, what it is for. The global, managerial and marketized version of NGO action risks becoming a Trojan horse for processes of commodification, accumulation and inequality, fought on the terrain of 'development'. A contending global vision of development can be constructed, based on de-commodified visions of social and economic rights that prohibit inequality and discrimination. However, it is disappointing, but unsurprising, that many critical assessments of NGO-ization and managerialism list human rights-based approaches as examples of the problem, rather than the solution. The concept of development based on human rights principles seems to have receded from the forefront of donor funding and NGO priorities in recent years, while funding, and the agenda, for humanitarian relief have grown. This is largely due to the expanded and protracted nature of conflict, the frequency of natural disasters, the increased targeting of humanitarian facilities in contravention of international law, and the blending of humanitarian relief with developmental goals, as humanitarian activities move towards longer-term disaster preparedness, prevention and resilience. Some of this expansion may help to meet immediate human needs where development has failed. However, the questions remain: has the development community left human rights behind as a project and a principle, as it moves to embrace new pragmatic interests? Can human rights advocates and practitioners re-engage with development in practice, or do human rights and development remain as 'ships passing in the night', destined to pass each other in conditions of mutual unfamiliarity and incomprehension (Alston, 2005)?

CONCLUSIONS – NGO ACCOUNTABILITY IN A WORLD OF NARROWING PUBLIC SPACES

Even as we survey the critical challenges for NGOs detailed herein, it is already becoming apparent that NGOs are entering a new era. Arguably, they face even deeper challenges today than they have faced since they began their latest wave of expansion three decades ago. So perhaps a new era of retrenchment and fragmentation has begun, as predicted by the long-run analysis. Regular reports by NGOs document tightening political restrictions on the way they work, while the OECD's Busan partnership principles for development cooperation accorded official parity of esteem to private, for-profit actors in development assistance (OECD Development Assistance Committee, 2012). At the same time, the space for human rights, arguably the most hopeful and coherent alternative discourse and underpinning set of values for NGO work, is shrinking. 'This global wave of restrictions has a rapidity and breadth to its spread we've not seen before, that arguably represents a seismic shift and closing down of human rights space not seen in a generation' (Savage, 2015). Political elites across the world are increasingly seeking to control, command and restrict NGOs. More than 60 governments have enacted new and more restrictive legislation to control the operations of international and national NGOs, and in 96 countries NGO staff have reported experiencing vilification, funding restrictions, administrative harassment, closure and expulsion (Houghton, 2016).

Historically, INGOs maintained primary accountability in the countries in which they were headquartered and had secondary accountability in the countries in which they operated. In the former, they had significant freedom to publicly advocate, and even challenge, their governments to advance their interests overseas. In the countries in which INGOs work, large variations in freedom or restriction applied to local civil society organizations (CSOs). But major shifts in power and discourse have taken place and these variations in freedom are becoming the default experience, even for large INGOs. Today, most African, Asian and Latin American governments no longer look exclusively to European and North American donors and push back vocally against donor demands and conditionalities. Governments are becoming more openly confrontational and frank about potential conflicts of interest and there has been a turn away from internationalism and liberal cooperation across many countries regardless of 'global North' or 'global South' provenance.

Donor governments in Europe and North America are themselves turning to modes of engagement that are less idealized or normatively internationalist and more instrumental and 'realist'. Governments are increasingly reframing development assistance within the envelope of trade facilitation, and are more unambiguous about geopolitical and commercial interests, even if old discourses of assistance and cooperation have not entirely disappeared. Overseas development assistance has become more complex, multi-modal and unpredictable. NGOs may have to change in order to be empowered to challenge the shrinking political space for their work, while inequalities continue to widen and market failures continue. Houghton points to five specific areas that must be addressed if NGOs are to adapt to these new conditions. Firstly, the pattern of resource concentration must change. Most of the development resources are currently retained in the global North. Less than 2 per cent of the US$150 billion of development funds spent by INGOs is directed to local CSOs in-country. Such inequity shows the bureaucratic and professional practices of the organizations to be self-serving and not disinterested. It is unfair to concentrate power in the head office, while withholding resources and influence from local development actors.

Secondly, the tendency towards elitism encourages conservatism and a culture of risk aversion. Neither expatriate nor in-country elites have the legitimacy needed to challenge local elites when the latter start to close down democratic spaces. This leads to Houghton's third point, that NGOS should shift the emphasis towards building solidarity with local interests and communities and support them to become empowered to undertake their own governance oversight and self-regulation. Fourthly, INGOs must themselves implement more visibly representative forms of governance. Sixty-four per cent of those in positions of governance and 63 per cent of the CEOs of the top 500 NGOs are drawn from the Western world, according to https://www.ngoadvisor.net. Only 4 per cent of CEOs are of African origin. Where they are African, the likelihood is that they have been recruited from the most privileged domestic top '1 per cent'. Houghton's fifth, and final, point is that the supposition that NGOs can fully control, plan, measure and evaluate the world must be challenged. Development is an emergent and contested concept and openness, unpredictability and messiness are essential aspects of the work. The critique of the coloniality of NGOs and aid as largely Western, Eurocentric and focused on the desires or needs of those in wealthy countries cannot be dismissed. The critique points to a continuity between the colonial roots of 'development' as resource exploitation and the self-interested nature of contemporary international aid. Most accounts of NGOs continue to express an overly elitist, ethnocentric and narrow view. Western NGOs, and scholars alike, who are seeking to become more 'global' in their governance and identities, still exhibit a lack of awareness about the diversity of organizations that already exist around the world. They must learn from, and even link up with, these historical organizations and movements (Gaventa, 2015) if they really wish to be more global and cosmopolitan in a connected, rather than an imperialistic, manner.

The dilemmas of NGO and civil society action reflect the dilemmas of globalization itself. Globalization processes have intensified questions about the limitations of state power, the definitive form of political power in the international realm since the birth of modern international politics (Mann, 1997). States no longer hold the monopoly where global power is concerned. In terms of economic power, only 37 of the world's 100 largest economies are countries, the majority, 63, are corporations, a fact which tips the balance of global power away from the political and towards economic forms of power. While there are elements of a global architecture in place, in the form of UN and customary international law, this falls far short of comprising a world government. In the absence of a world state, it remains unclear what actors ought to represent 'public power' on the global scale (Buckinx, 2012). Cosmopolitan global optimists (Kaldor, 2003; Archibugi, 2008) see the rise of global civil society organizations as a democratizing force for global governance. However, in truth these organizations represent a variety of different values, rationales and world views: from secular to religious; egalitarian to paternalistic. CSOs or NGOs may work through, with or against markets; and they may regard people as active participants to be engaged or as passive beneficiaries to be spoken for. While many NGOs are generally benevolent and their actions beneficial, Buckinx argues that they are not 'properly public' and therefore should not seek to replace public authorities in performing certain key tasks, such as protecting liberties, or carrying out global distribution, regulation or administration. She observes that global actors of all kinds are frequently oppressive and cause harm to the individual with whom they interact – transnational corporations may pollute the environment, governments may attack their own populations, international financial bodies may dictate financial and economic policies that depress growth and reduce welfare provision. NGOs, when compared to this, may be rather benign and possibly quite effective global actors, but that does not mean that they should be pushed to the forefront of global governance (Buckinx, 2012, p. 536). They still lack the properties needed to be fully 'public' actors. NGOs are private actors and are expected to behave, and be constituted, differently from public actors. This is why NGOs should not be asked to take on public tasks directly, tasks such as administering public programmes or regulation of other actors' behaviour in society. By their very nature, the scope of NGOs does not extend to all of the polity. Nor are NGOs subject to the kind of scrutiny and democratic accountability that we can expect from state-based politics. There are few tools currently available to exert control over them, beyond self-regulation and the normative pull of collective voluntary agreements. Thus they are not in a position to serve, speak for, or represent the public as a whole. Instead, they should be recognized as acting on behalf of the specific interests that they represent.

The transformative ambitions of development cannot be understood through a limited analysis of how well civil society 'works', but rather require an understanding and ethical response to the changing ideology of largely Northern-based organizations and institutions. Pragmatism and opportunism have played a large role in determining NGOs' choices and will likely continue to do so. It is almost two decades since Wallace and her co-researchers began setting out a research agenda for the study of NGOs (Wallace, 1997). Their research findings keep pointing to questions of power and values. Will NGOs retain their historic capacities to do work based on values beyond that of cost-efficiency, to do what is right rather than what is cheapest? Can smaller and medium-sized NGOs remain more flexible, and less 'corporate' than their larger BINGO counterparts? Must the latter inevitably succumb to problems of bureaucracy and managerialist and market-based solutions as they increase in size? What kind of NGOs actually use resources most prudently? Do smaller and medium-sized NGOs work more equally or more effectively with partners? Does the combination of donor dependence and need for marketing appeal mean that NGOs have essentially lost their independence?

An important emerging conundrum is the systemic trend towards donor bias favouring fewer, large NGOs as a result of the neoliberal ethos of competition that forces NGOs to compete against each other for not only funds, but also influence and 'a seat at the table'. The preference for 'policy focused advocacy' means that NGOs may make donors their primary constituency and development 'beneficiaries' needs and aspirations may take second place, as, ironically, NGOs 'succeed' in representing them. The trend is towards a 'winner takes all' logic that has been marginalizing small and medium-sized NGOs, which have to turn to charity and direct fundraising such as Comic Relief in the UK (Wallace, 2003). These large NGOs then operate very much in the mode of 'speaking for' rather than 'engaging with'. It seems clear that the market-influenced competition impedes the learning of harder and more critical lessons, as the fear of losing funding, influence and position leads to the erosion of openness and trust between funders and the funded, at all levels. The accountability sought through reporting and evaluation are increasingly self-censoring and self-fulfilling, reduced to proving that donor conditions, with their myriad demands for transparency and effectiveness, are met. A very different notion of accountability is required that can engage with the more difficult ethical questions. The political philosopher Judith Butler, in *Giving an Account of Oneself*, argues that the failure to give a coherent and final account of oneself does not mean that ethical responsibility has evaporated. We have to live in a complex and contradictory world full of competing ethical claims and demands. Ultimately, NGOs must make themselves intelligible to themselves and to the public, but not on terms of their own making. They must respond to the ethical questions of others, and broader understandings and language that exist in the world (Butler, 2005). In Butler's ethical philosophy, ethical failures are unavoidable but also hopeful. Failures of accountability have ethical value as it is such failures in the act of accountability to others that point us towards the possibilities of a more just political reality.

REFERENCES

Alexander, J. (2006), *The Civil Sphere*, Oxford: Oxford University Press.
Alston, P. (2005), Ships passing in the night: the current state of the human rights and development debate seen through the lens of the Millennium Development Goals, *Human Rights Quarterly*, vol. **27** (3), pp. 755–829.
Anheier, H., M. Glasius and M. Kaldor (2001), Introducing global civil society. In H. Anheier, M. Glasius and M. Kaldor (eds) *Global Civil Society*, Oxford: Oxford University Press, pp. 3–20.
Archibugi, D. (2008), *The Global Commonwealth of Citizens: Toward Cosmopolitan Democracy*, Princeton: Princeton University Press.
Banks, N., D. Hulme and M. Edwards (2015), NGOs, states, and donors revisited: still too close for comfort?, *World Development*, vol. **66**, pp. 707–18.
Barnett, M. (2011), *Empire of Humanity: A History of Humanitarianism*, Ithaca: Cornell University Press.
Bebbington, A.J. (1997), New states, new NGOs? Crises and transitions among rural development NGOs in the Andean region, *World Development*, vol. **25** (11), pp. 1755–65.
Brolan, C.E., P.S. Hill and G. Ooms (2015), 'Everywhere but not specifically somewhere': a qualitative study on why the right to health is not explicit in the post-2015 negotiations, *BMC International Health and Human Rights*, vol. **15** (22).
Buckinx, B. (2012), Global actors and public power, *Critical Review of International Social and Political Philosophy*, vol. **15** (5), pp. 535–51.
Butler, J. (2005), *Giving an Account of Oneself*, New York: Forham University Press.
Chakrabarti, A. (2016), Democracy as civil religion: Reading Alexis De Tocqueville in India, *Journal of Human Values*, vol. **22** (1), pp. 14–25.
Chandoke, N. (2003), *The Conceits of Civil Society*, New York: Oxford University Press.
Chandoke, N. (2010), Civil Society. In A. Cornwall and D. Eade (eds) *Deconstructing Development Discourse: Buzzwords and Fuzzwords*, Bourton-on-Dunsmore: Practical Action Publishing, pp. 175–84.
Davies, T. (2013), *NGOs: A New History of Transnational Civil Society*, London: Hurst and Company.
de Frouville, O. (2008), Domesticating civil society at the United nations. In P. Dupuy and V. Luisa (eds) *NGOs in International Law: Efficiency in Flexibility?*, Cheltenham, UK and Northampton, MA, USA: Edward Elgar Publishing, pp. 71–115.
Dupuy, P. and L. Vierucci (eds) (2008), *NGOs in International Law: Efficiency in Flexibility?*, Cheltenham, UK and Northampton, MA, USA: Edward Elgar Publishing.

Dwyer, P.D. and M. Minnegal (2010), Theorizing social change, *The Journal of the Royal Anthropological Institute*, vol. **16** (3), pp. 629–45.

Fowler, A. (2012), Measuring civil society: perspective on Afro-centrism, *Voluntas*, vol. **23**, pp. 5–25.

Gasper, D. (2004), *Development Ethics*, Edinburgh: Edinburgh University Press.

Gaventa, J. (2015), Review of NGOs: a new history of transnational civil society by Davies Thomas, *Journal of Global History*, vol. **10** (3), pp. 502–3.

Gorman, R. (1984) *Private Voluntary Organizations as Agents of Development*, Boulder: Westview Press.

Goulet, D. (1971), The Cruel Choice: A new concept in the theory of development. s.l.: s.n.

Higgins, R. (1994), *Problems and Process: International Law and How We Use It*, Oxford: Clarendon Press.

Hill, T. (2004), *Three Generations of UN-Civil Society Relations*, Geneva: Global Policy Forum.

Horton, R. (2016), Offline: uncivil society, *The Lancet*, vol. **387** (10023), p. 1041.

Houghton, I. (2016), International CSOs in a differentiated, globalised and networked world – five traits they must drop. (Online.) Available at: https://irunguh.wordpress.com/2016/09/23/international-csos-in-a-differentiated-globalised-and-networked-world-five-traits-they-must-drop/ (accessed 10 October 2016).

Hulme, D. (2013), Poverty and development thinking: synthesis or uneasy compromise? BWPI Working Paper 180, Manchester: Brooks World Poverty Institute.

Ilal, A., T. Kelibl and R. Munck (2014), *Interrogating Civil Society: A View from Mozambique*. s.l.: s.n.

Jones, P. and K. Stokke (2005), *Democratising Development: The Politics of Socio-economic Rights in Africa*, Cambridge: Cambridge University Press.

Kaldor, M. (2003), *Global Civil Society: An Answer to War*, Cambridge: Polity.

Kamstra, J., L. Knippenberg and L. Schulpen (2013), Cut from a different cloth? Comparing democracy-promoting NGOs in Ghana and Indonesia, *Journal of Civil Society*, vol. **9** (1), pp. 1–20.

Khagram, S., J.V. Riker and K. Sikkink (2002), *Restructuring World Politics: Transnational Social Movements, Networks and Norms*, Minneapolis: University of Minnesota Press.

Korten, D.C. (1991), The role of nongovernmental organizations in development: changing patterns and perspectives. In P. Samuel and I. Arturo (eds) *Nongovernmental Organizations and the World Bank*, Washington, DC: The World Bank, pp. 1–18.

Lang, S. (2013), *NGOs, Civil Society and the Public Sphere*, Cambridge: Cambridge University Press.

Lewis, D. (2008), Nongovernmentalism and the reorganization of public action. In S. Dar and B. Cooke (eds) *The New Development Management*, London: Zed Books, pp. 41–55.

Ma, Q. (1995), *Guan shang zijian: shehui jubian zhong de jidai shenshang* [*Between Government and Merchants: Modern Gentry-merchants During Social Transition*], Tianjin: Tianjin People's Publishing House.

Ma, Q. (2002), Defining Chinese Nongovernmental Organizations. *Voluntas: International Journal of Voluntary and Nonprofit Organizations*, vol. **13** (2), pp. 113–30.

Mann, M. (1997), Has globalization ended the rise and rise of the nation-state? *Review of International Political Economy*, vol. **4** (3), pp. 472–96.

Nelson, P.J. (1995), *The World Bank and Non-governmental Organizations: The Limits of Apolitical Development*, London: Macmillan.

Obadare, E. (2011), Revalorizing the political: towards a new intellectual agenda for African civil society discourse, *Journal of Civil Society*, vol. **7** (4), pp. 427–42.

OECD Development Assistance Committee (2012), *The Busan Partnership for Effective Development Co-operation*, Busan: OECD.

OnGood (2016), Facts and stats about NGOs worldwide. (Online.) Available at: www.ongood.ngo (accessed 6 October 2016).

Rebasti, E. (2008), Beyond consultative status: which legal framework for an enhanced interaction between NGOs and intergovernmental organizations. In P. Dupuy and

L. Vierucci (eds) *NGOs in International Law: Efficiency in Flexibility?*, Cheltenham, UK and Northampton, MA, USA: Edward Elgar Publishing, pp. 23–37.

Riddell, R. (1996), *Linking Costs and Benefit in NGO Projects*, London: Overseas Development Institute.

Salamon, L.M. (1994), The rise of the nonprofit sector, *Foreign Affairs*, July/August, pp. 109–22.

Salamon, L. and H. Anheier (1992), *In Search of the Nonprofit Sector 1: The Search for Definitions*, Baltimore: Johns Hopkins University Press.

Sarriot, E.G., K. LeBan, E. Sacks and S. Christine (2016), Uncivil and skewed language on civil society?, *The Lancet*, vol. **387**, p. 2377.

Savage, J. (2015), Amnesty International Annual Report 2015, s.l.: s.n.

Seary, B. (1996), The early history: from the Congress of Vienna to the San Francisco Conference. In P. Willetts (ed.) *The Conscience of the World: The Influence of Non-governmental Organizations in the UN System*, Washington, DC: The Brookings Institution, pp. 15–30.

Sengupta, A. (2002), On the theory and practice of the Right to Development, *Human Rights Quarterly*, vol. **24**, pp. 837–89.

Severino, J.-M. and O. Ray (2009), *The End of ODA: Death and Rebirth of a Global Public Policy*, s.l.: Center for Global Development.

Shukla, A. (2010), First official estimate: an NGO for every 400 people in India, *Indian Express*, 7 July.

United Nations Development Programme (2000), *Human Development Report 2000: Human Rights and Human Development*, New York: Oxford University Press.

Uvin, P. (1998), *Aiding Violence: Development Enterprise in Rwanda*, s.l.: Lynne Rienner Publishers.

Vakil, A.C. (1997), Confronting the classification problem: toward a taxonomy of NGOs, *World Development*, vol. **25** (12), pp. 2057–70.

Wallace, T. (1997), New development agendas: changes in UK NGO policies and procedures, *Review of African Political Economy*, vol. **24** (71), pp. 35–55.

Wallace, T. (2003), Trends in UK NGOs: a research note, *Development in Practice*, vol. **13** (5), pp. 564–9.

Wallace, T. (2004), NGO dilemmas: Trojan horses for global neoliberalism?, *Socialist Register*, pp. 202–19.

Young, I.M. (2000), *Inclusion and Democracy*, Oxford: Oxford University Press.

11. The Developmental State Paradigm in the age of financialization
Ben Fine and Gabriel Pollen

INTRODUCTION[1]

This chapter is concerned with the shifting fortunes of the Developmental State Paradigm (DSP) and how it does, or does not, have continuing presence and relevance. The DSP has undergone a dual trajectory in terms of its own intellectual content on the one hand, and how this has responded to an evolving set of global and national circumstances on the other. In this light, we show that the DSP has increasingly diverged in understanding of, and in policymaking for, the conditions that it needs to confront. There are two main reasons for this: the first is the long-standing neglect, or more appropriately, shallow notion and treatment, of labour (Chang 2013). The second is the absence of financialization within its continuing framing, despite the enhanced power and presence of finance as key characteristics of the past 30 years of neo-liberalism. Whilst, in the post-war boom, the DSP offered some purchase on material realities and the prospects for policymaking, this has been eroded by financialization. Unless both finance and labour are satisfactorily incorporated analytically, the DSP will remain what it has become policy-wise, marginal to development theory and practice.

Despite longer origins in the experiences of developed economies,[2] the DSP was initially and primarily tied to the fortunes of the East Asian Newly Industrialized Countries (NICs). As such, it was at its height of prominence and influence during the age of the East Asian miracle, particularly through its opposition to the dogmas of the Washington Consensus that emerged in the 1980s. However, by the time the East Asian crisis of 1997–8 took place the DSP was in decline. Subsequently, its purpose has been diluted and broadened, from offering a strategy and conditions for latecomer, catch-up industrialization to one where the notion of the developmental state is deployed increasingly to refer to any successful, piecemeal intervention by the state, as opposed to transformational interventions and the conditions necessary to underpin them. We suggest that the DSP has now become a 'buzz' and 'fuzz' concept,[3] freely applied across a wide range of diverse contexts, without reference to long-standing traditions and experiences and to broader and deeper causal factors and goals.

In the following section (The Development State Paradigm) we present DSP as middle-range theory, involving the integration of theory and empirical research. We chart its shifting content as such by highlighting what it does, and does not, incorporate within its explanatory framework and scope of analysis. This leads to a discussion in the next section (How the DSP treats labour) of how labour has been neglected within the DSP. The fourth section (The DSP in times of financialization) examines the nature of financialization and its relationship to neo-liberalism (and the problems this poses for the DSP). The chapter concludes with the assertion that financialization, and the transformation of labour relations under neo-liberalism, have eroded the presence and content of the DSP.

THE DEVELOPMENTAL STATE PARADIGM

Although not acknowledging itself as such, the DSP can be classified as an almost ideal example of what Robert K. Merton defined as middle-range theory.[4] This offers an integration of the theoretical and the empirical, situating itself somewhere between grand theory and case study, and it is marked by its workability in explaining social outcomes by reference to underlying causal factors, without being either unduly deterministic or insensitive to diversity and specificity. The DSP became prominent by the 1980s as the spearhead of opposition to the Washington Consensus in both theoretical and empirical terms. For, theoretically in the inductive traditions of modernization theory associated with the old or classical development economics, the DSP sought, successfully, to show that the East Asian miracles had been the consequence of extensive state intervention, especially industrial policies. In other words, developmental success depended upon rejection of the Washington Consensus, and the analyses and prescriptions associated with it.[5]

Consider the targets for the DSP as it shot to prominence in opposition to the Washington Consensus. First and foremost, it was concerned with the circumstances and the policies that make for latecomer, catch-up industrialization. Each of these terms is important in defining the scope of the DSP, and in projecting its significance through history (from Alexander Hamilton and US protectionism, through Friedrich List and German industrialization, to Latin American ISI and beyond to East Asian miracles) and to future prospects. But latecomer, catch-up industrialization is only one broad stage in the process of industrialization. Thus, for example, the DSP has generally overlooked the earliest stages of industrialization,[6] that is the transition from agrarian society, as well as the later stages, which involve moving beyond, and not just to, the technological frontiers of developed economies Also, until lately, for reasons that will become apparent, the DSP has tended to have very little to say about economic activity other than through the lens of industrialization and/or industrial policy. Apart from agriculture, it has neglected areas such as health, education and welfare for example.

This begs the question of the approach's empirical scope of application across stages of development and in terms of the notion of development itself. Defining these narrowly was, to some extent, convenient for advocates of the DSP in their conflict with the Washington Consensus over the virtues of state intervention. As exemplified by the East Asian NICs, its industrial successes were not matched by achievements in social policy (and democratization). Indeed, these were sub-contracted and ghettoized to that other critical tradition that emerged at the same time – adjustment with a human face – with few points of contact between them.

There is also the issue of what middle ground is occupied by the DSP as theory. Are its principles confined, by accident or design, to a limited phase of industrialization? Should they apply more widely, and, if so, does this indicate their strengths or weaknesses? Of course, such questions cannot be answered without interrogating DSP theory itself. Broadly, though, we can identify what we have termed two schools within the DSP literature, the economic and the political.[7] The economic school places emphasis on the role of state interventionism in correcting systemic market failures associated with economies of scale and scope, coordination of complementary investments, targeting finance for investment, and so on. For the economic school, the developmental state is exemplified by the South Korean Pohang Iron and Steel Company (POSCO), initially a state-owned corporation, built against World Bank advice on grounds of comparative advantage, and spearhead of the country's subsequent industrialization.

Whilst the economic school has self-selected interventionist successes, the focus of the political school of thought is upon whether the state is characterized by political or other conditions that allow it to be developmental without questioning what this means in policy and practice.[8] The symbolic mantra of the political school is summed up in – 'embedded autonomy' – reflecting the idea that the state is both engaged and independent in pursuit of its goals.

Market imperfections and embedded autonomy are ideal examples of middle-range concepts. As theoretical principles they are universal, bordering on the ahistorical and asocial, and not confined to either latecomer, catch-up or, indeed, any form of industrialization. Thus, for example, the transition from agrarian to industrial society is surely as much a matter of market imperfections as it is at later stages.

By confining itself to latecomer, catch-up industrialization, the DSP's middle-range carelessness in relation to its scope of application across history and development is indicative of three critical weaknesses, equally applicable to its own preferred sphere of application. First is how the DSP is structured by taking the state-market dichotomy (possibly complemented by civil society) as foundational. This is understandable given the goal of countering the Washington Consensus on its own terms of market versus state, if coming down on the opposite side of the divide in the debate. But, on longer and alternative views of development, from least developed to most advanced countries, the state-market dichotomy appears much less appealing, once addressing the nature and causes of major economic and social transformations. These are far from reducible to, nor run along the lines of, the state-market dichotomy. This is especially so of class interests, and of economic, political and ideological interests more generally, as these evolve and are represented through both the state and the market. In any case, the state is itself a major player in and upon the market.

Second, whilst class interests are not absent from the DSP they tend to be confined to consideration of capitalists alone, involving a double reduction in not only focusing solely on capital but also on its relationships to the state as more or less exclusively constituted out of the latter's embedded autonomy in administering industrial policy on capital's behalf and in its collective interest. Most obviously, this means conceiving the state in terms of the ministries, institutions, networks and personnel for making policy, at the expense of broader considerations of the politics of (inter- and intra-) class conflicts and the sources and exercise of power and associated hierarchies. On the longer view, this reinforces the failure to address how class structure is transformed by development, with the emergence of new (fractions of) classes and shifts in the balance and forms of power between them. This is taken up below in a slightly more detailed discussion with reference to financialization and labour.

Third, the DSP is grounded in methodological nationalism and, in particular, in the idea that each and every nation-state can develop, subject to the adoption of appropriate policies.[9] This is not to suggest that the global is overlooked by the DSP, since much can be made of how to relate to international capital in trade, finance and access to technology. What is characteristic of the DSP, though, is to overlook the systemic functioning of the world economy in which each nation-state is an integral, rather than independent, part. As Gray (2011b, p. 118) puts it in the context of South Korea:[10]

Most analyses have adopted either an approach that analyses state transformation in terms of changes in the underlying domestic social relations of production, or have viewed neo-liberal state transformation as stemming from international factors, namely the pervasive nature of neo-liberal ideology and/or the coercive manoeuvrings of the US along with the international financial institutions. The argument . . . [here] is not simply that both 'levels of analysis' are important in the explanation of the state transformation, but that these 'levels' in fact need to be understood as inter-related and mutually constitutive.

Thus, as Gray (2011a, p. 587) observes for the birth of the East Asian NICs in general, 'As with Japan and South Korea, the US had deliberately sought to nurture economic growth and self-sufficiency in Taiwan as part of the wider geopolitical aims in East Asia.'[11]

In making these points, reference has already been made to the demise of developmental states themselves, not least those of the East Asian NICs, although those that came earlier in Latin America, primarily through Import Substitution Industrialization (ISI), are also perceived already to have suffered such a fate. Meanwhile, there has also been an evolution in the literature of the DSP. This has consisted of a number of strands, both broadening and shifting its content. First has been the response to the supposed demise or death of the developmental state by acknowledging a number of separate elements or influences. Most obvious was the impact of the East Asian crisis of 1997–8, especially as it came on top of a revisionist literature that had suggested the region's miracle had been a myth, as popularized by Krugman (1994). Also important for the decline of the DSP was the move from Washington to post-Washington Consensus (PWC), allowing, in principle, for limited and piecemeal concessions on state interventionism in response to identifiable market and/or institutional imperfections (without ever acknowledging that this shift had in part been provoked by the critical contributions of the DSP, which never warrants a mention in the PWC universe).

But, equally, prior to both the 1997–8 crisis and the emergence of the more state-friendly PWC, doubts were being expressed about the continuing viability of the East Asian NICs as developmental states on the grounds that the embedded autonomy required for their success would be undermined by that success. For latecomer, catch-up industrialization brings with it a class of industrialists who are increasingly powerful enough not to be inclined to be subject to state control. More generally, successful industrialization also creates other demands from other classes that derive from the associated strains of economic and social development, whether it be for higher wages and welfare (from organized labour and social movements in Latin America) or democratization. Significantly, the understanding of the developmental state as 'its own gravedigger', to coin a phrase, offered an unwitting acknowledgement and a return of some of those factors that had been omitted in establishing the DSP. This is clearly the case in terms of incorporating the role of evolving classes and class interests as underpinning the relationship between state and market. In the context of the East Asian NICs particularly, it involved due deference to the impact of systemic global factors, not least as domestic capitals sought to gain access to international financial markets and, thereby, free themselves from state controls in terms of sources and application of funds.

This is indicative of that feature in the DSP literature that sees it draw upon a necessarily cumulative set of case studies both by country and by stage and nature of industrialization (or development more broadly). For the economic school, given its self-selection bias towards success, this is much more muted than for the political school. The latter is more able to accommodate both success and failure in terms of meeting, or not, the conditions for an increasingly qualified notion of autonomy with, in the first instance, the addition of the moniker, embedded, to form the 'oxymoron', embedded autonomy. This has been merely the first step in the process of accumulating political or other criteria for a state to be developmental.[12] As a result, we are subsequently offered different ideal types to suit different types of developmental states, from the networked for Ireland,[13] through to the neo-liberal for Singapore, and, for Botswana, the development-oriented gate-keeping state (Hillbom, 2012).[14] Further, not only is there an accumulation of ideal types of developmental states, these are complemented by an ever-expanding range of explanatory factors across social, cultural, political and institutional variables.

There is a strand in the literature which questions whether the developmental state is dead after all, especially as the East Asian crisis becomes less a distant memory and is seen more as an obstacle that is overcome through the renewal of state-supported growth[15] as well as a greater ability to ride out the 2008–9 crisis. This in part reflects the heterogeneity attached to continuing state intervention in the neo-liberal era as opposed to the presumed loss, or lesser autonomy, of the state relative to an increasingly powerful class of capitalists. It dovetails with another distinct but closely related literature that claims that industrial policy is alive and well.

A majority of middle-income countries – in Latin America, sub-Saharan Africa, the Middle East and North Africa, and South Asia – have fallen behind the West in relative average income since the 1980s. Many are now seeing their manufacturing sectors stagnate or shrink in the face of East Asian competition. Some are pressing the World Bank to give more assistance in industrial policy . . . this may turn out to be an early phase in the emergence of a new set of global policy norms in favour of a more 'developmental' state, qualifying the near-consensus around the norms of a 'regulatory' state (Wade, 2012, p. 224).

This is unduly optimistic since, as Wade (2012) acknowledges, support for more extensive industrial policy, even of a limited kind, has minimal support within the World Bank. Indeed, even its major proponent, Justin Lin (the Bank's Chief Economist until June 2012), suggested that 'less than 10% of World Bank economists are sympathetic to his arguments' (Wade, 2012, p. 225). As argued by Fine and Van Waeyenberge (2013), Lin is more realistically interpreted as seeking to constrain, rather than to promote, state intervention as far as industrial policy is concerned.

The notion that the developmental state is alive and well, or has been resuscitated in East Asia or elsewhere, is far from confined to an empirically grounded account of industrial policy. Indeed, as argued in Fine (2013) following Cornwall and Eade (2010), currently the 'developmental state' is best understood as a failed buzzword (and fuzzword) within development discourse. It is a buzzword in the sense that, in combining together the other strands in the DSP literature and deploying them across many issues within development, the concept has lost its original roots in explaining systemic industrialization. Instead, it ranges freely across many topics, however narrow or broad and however distant from industrial policy. In this respect, it is like other buzzwords such as participation, citizenship, empowerment, sustainability, transparency, accountability, corruption and governance. In effect, wherever there is an example of successful state intervention, it can be interpreted as indicative of the presence of a developmental state, whether in relation to a sector or across any aspect of economic and social functioning more generally. The attachment of development and the state to economic and social transformation in general, and to industrialization in particular, is suspended, other than at some piecemeal micro level. Whilst rendering the concept of the developmental state as wide-ranging as possible, it is reduced to an ethos of just favouring some degree of state intervention more than allowed for by current, neo-liberal orthodoxy. That is why the developmental state is a failed buzzword since success, or wide-scale use of the fuzz and buzz, depends upon its adoption, by the World Bank, so dominant is the latter in development discourse both in setting the analytical agenda and skewing content within that agenda. As far as the World Bank is concerned, the developmental state might just as well never have existed, whether in the literature or the real world itself.[16]

In short, the DSP has become marginalized in effecting its core mission of promoting state intervention in the form of industrial policy as a means to development. It has become too widely spread across a broad and diffuse range of applications. To what extent, however, does this reflect the reduced opportunities to prosper for, what might be deemed to be, potential developmental states? Initially, the idea of non-replicability by other states of East Asia was strong, and indeed promulgated by the World Bank (1993). This served as a second line of defence amongst those begrudgingly accepting the evidence of industrial policy as a source of East Asian success. But it has subsequently given way to doubts within the DSP camp itself over whether global conditions remain conducive to developmental states, along the lines experienced by those of the past. Thus, for Evans (2008), drawing incoherently and superficially upon new growth theory, new institutional economics and the capability approach, the developmental state of the twenty-first century will be oriented toward the knowledge economy, as opposed to manufacturing, with opportunity for broader participation and rewards than those confined to an industrializing elite coordinated by a state bureaucracy.[17] Here Evans arguably reinforces weaknesses in the DSP, with regard to labour and finance, to which we turn in the following sections.

HOW THE DSP TREATS LABOUR

The DSP does not ignore labour, but how it engages with labour is problematic in developing an understanding of its transformative role in development and social change. The DSP's lacklustre theorization of labour is a consequence of its taking the Washington Consensus as the critical point of departure, with the state-market dichotomy as starting point, at the expense of a class-centred analysis. This approach perceives labour through the prism of state-society relations: on the one hand, society is reduced to the role of promoter of business interests, with labour presumed as merely the beneficiary of development; on the other hand, the theory of the state sees it limited to a set of coordinating institutions (for industrial policy), thereby failing to take account of its broader economic and social character. In short, weak theorization of both state and society has underpinned and reduced how the DSP has understood labour.

Whilst it can claim to incorporate class analysis, particularly when conceptualizing state autonomy, it only does so in ways that are incongruent with class-centred analyses of the state. The state is seen as interacting with capital primarily, and interaction with labour is very much secondary and thus its role in capital-labour relations tends to be disregarded. This has serious implications, not just for the DSP in its original form, but also for the lessons it can provide for those seeking inspiration within and beyond contemporary conditions.

The tendency to silence labour, as made explicit for instance with an appeal for 'depoliticized' labour, can be seen as holding the key to (Japan's) developmental success (Johnson, 1995, p. 49). Conceiving labour as, at most, obstructive enabled the DSP to focus on how the state interacted with capital, adjudicating over its allocation, accumulation and distribution without disruption from opposition. Consequently, labour's interests simply became synonymous with, or subordinate to, those of capital, those interests being unquestioned as national goals of economic development and corporate expansion, and represented and promoted in class-neutral terms – from another era and place, 'what is good for General Motors is good for America'.[18]

Consequently, the developmental state is modelled in such a fashion that bilateral interests between the state and private capital have more in common than those between the state and labour or between private capital and labour. This facilitates the de facto arrangement that exists between the state and private enterprises in repressing the labouring classes (Kohli, 1999) whose goals and interests are at most realized through the passive consequences of development. This, and similar arguments, led Chang to fault the DSP's grasp of the role of labour in development, contending that 'the concept of the developmental state can be derived only with a particular understanding of labour that is disempowered and depoliticised' (2013, p. 85). Nor is this simply a matter of whether labour promotes or obstructs development, but of how it is integrated into the complex determination of various economic and social processes, as for example clearly brought out by Fishwick's (2015) comparative study of ISI between Chile and Argentina and Selwyn's (2012) comparative study of viniculture within Brazil.[19]

Precisely because national interests, expressed in development policy in general and industrial policy in particular, are perceived to be crafted, coordinated, managed and supervised by an (almost) omniscient state through highly intelligent and gifted state bureaucrats, labour's interests are simply presumed to be safeguarded. These bureaucrats have access to innumerable sources of information, and possess the capacity to sift through data for planning and implementation of the state's agenda. Not only are they exceptionally talented, they possess unwavering commitment to national development policy, thereby insulating the state against seizure by other interests. Paradoxically, in this way, the state has the capacity both to work with capital and to remain autonomous from it, such that labour challenges to the state (and hence to capital) represent undesirable disruptions (with the demise of erstwhile Latin American developmental states, following uncontrolled populist demands for economic and social wage levels seen as decisive evidence). In this context, government disciplining of labour becomes a positive attribute, and a further indication of its resolve and autonomy.

Indeed, these capacities and autonomy are how the state is perceived to relate to capital, at least where the state plays a coordinating, as opposed to a disciplining, role. Nonetheless, tensions are observed in the state's relations with capital, much more than with labour. Amsden points out that, although the Korean state insisted on export targets for corporations as a commitment to developmentalism, its role incorporates biases and social ties to businesses in that:

> Discipline has taken the form of refusal on the part of the government to bail out relatively large scale, badly managed, bankrupt firms in otherwise healthy industries. The bail-out process has been highly politicized insofar as the government has typically chosen friends to do the taking over of troubled enterprises . . . (yet) the government's friends . . . have undoubtedly been bailed out on at least one occasion. (1989, pp. 15–16)

In short, as the developmental state itself is seen as the management of capitalists by an autonomous state, so the understanding of industrialization is one which tends to exclude consideration of labour and capital-labour relations, even where the rescue of troubled enterprises is subject to job loss and contestation.

Capital's attitude towards labour is seen mainly through employment policy, which tends to be framed as though organized labour's industrial-related actions are disruptive rather than progressive. Labour is stripped of its power (through organization and protest) by the ability and capacity of employers to structure and manage employment policy in a manner that tramples labour's representation of its own interests. Reducing the interaction of the state with capital-labour relations to those between the state and capital alone is questionable from any perspective. Both in other academic literature and in popular discourse, capital-labour relations, and the role of the state within them, have, at times, been seen as critical to success in late-industrializing countries. For example, and especially in Japan, emphasis has been placed on just-in-time, Toyota, systems of production, and, further back, post-war Japan's prosperity was seen as conditioned upon labour's loyalty through seniority wage systems and lifetime employment systems, both ensuring labour had a stake in business success.

Whilst the above identifies how capital-labour relations mediated by the state can be conducive to development and mutual gains, as is generally interpreted within the social compacting paradigm as characteristic of the post-war boom,[20] this does not preclude the role of capital-labour conflict as a positive in development. Significantly, just as for industrialization itself, classical DSP contributions (Wade, 1988; Amsden, 1989; Johnson, 1995) tend to see improvements in worker conditions, and their positive consequences for development, as the result of the state's interventions, possibly finding it necessary to discipline capital to promote improvement in workers' conditions. This appears unidirectional, simply a reflection of state's policy and ideology; in effect, the autonomous and developmentally beneficial and benevolent state is seen to deliver education, skills, training, social development and more, either directly or through its influence on capital, just as it delivers industrialization. By contrast, as Chang (2013) has shown, it has been labour's struggles for the economic and social wage that have often underpinned the state's policies in these regards. In short, more rounded historical and theoretical accounts of Japan, Korea and Taiwan have confronted the disenfranchised and depoliticized treatment of labour in the DSP. These reveal how the DSP misinterprets the relationship between capital, labour and the state in general, and in particular by reducing the presence of labour in these relationships.

THE DSP IN TIMES OF FINANCIALIZATION

Evans' (2008) approach raises his own middle-range theory of bringing the state (and its preferred, contested and, to considerable degree, misinterpreted elements in growth, institutions and capabilities) back in to grand theory, whilst overlooking what has been a considerably more important factor in determining what has to be negotiated in twentieth-century (state) developmentalism. This is the extraordinary growth of finance over the past 30 years, something which Evans distortedly takes, at most, as indicative of the need to be service- and not manufacturing-oriented in the twenty-first century.[21] On the contrary, the role of finance has increasingly been to limit the prospects for development. Such is best understood by reference to financialization. Across a new but rapidly expanding, predominantly heterodox literature, the notion of financialization has pointed to a number of different features of contemporary capitalism, mainly drawing upon the US and the UK as its leading sites.

According to Fine (2011) financialization has involved:

> The phenomenal expansion of financial assets relative to real activity (by three times over the last thirty years); the proliferation of types of assets, from derivatives through to futures markets with a corresponding explosion of acronyms; the absolute and relative expansion of speculative, as opposed to or at the expense of, real investment; a shift in the balance of productive to financial imperatives within the private sector, whether financial or not; increasing inequality in income, arising out of weight of financial rewards; consumer-led booms based on credit; the penetration of finance into ever more areas of economic and social life such as pensions, education, health, and provision of economic and social infrastructure; the emergence of a neo-liberal culture of reliance upon markets and private capital and a corresponding increase in

anti-statism, despite the extent to which the rewards to private finance have in part derived from state finance itself. Financialization is also associated with the continued role of the US dollar as world money despite, at least in the 2008–9 crisis, the US deficits in trade, capital account, the fiscus, and consumer spending, and minimal rates of interest.[22]

However financialization is characterized, its consequences have been: reductions in overall levels and efficacy of real investment as financial instruments and activities expand at its expense, even if excessive investment does take place in particular sectors at particular times (as with the dotcom bubble of a decade ago); prioritizing shareholder value, or financial worth, over other economic and social values; pushing of policies towards conservatism and commercialization in all respects; extending influence of finance more broadly, both directly and indirectly, over economic and social policy; and placing more aspects of economic and social life at the risk of volatility from financial instability and, conversely, placing the economy and social life at risk of crises from triggers within particular markets (as with the food and energy crises that preceded the financial crisis). Whilst, then, financialization is a single word, it is attached to a wide variety of different forms and effects of finance. And, even if exposed in acute form by the current crisis, its expansion over the last few decades has been at the expense of the real economy, despite otherwise extraordinarily favourable 'fundamentals' for capitalist economies in terms of availabilities of new technologies, expansion in supplies of labour, weakening of labour, slow increases in economic and social wages under the influence of neo-liberal policy, and the end of the Cold War. (Fine, 2011, pp. 3–4)

In these terms, the role of financialization in the Asian crisis and the presumed demise, at least temporarily, of the East Asian developmental states, is apparent. To a great extent, those who regret the demise perceive it in terms either of the liberalization (and internationalization) of domestic finance or the undermining of coordinated industrial policy. But both of these were operative and were mutually reinforcing. As Rethel suggests:

As the East Asian economies became increasingly integrated with the world economy, it was more difficult to afford the insulation necessary to maintain the developmental state system of old. Similarly, capital markets increasingly competed with banks as main sources of funding. Major pillars of the old developmental state system were gone. (2010, p. 499)

He further notes, 'While in the developmental state model of old, the consumption needs of households had been subordinated to the financing needs of economic transformation, since the crisis, private consumption is increasingly seen as an important driver of domestic growth' (ibid., p. 510). This is all perceived as having drawn the NICs towards the Anglo-American forms of financial architecture and governance, something that was accelerated by the East Asian crisis and the responses to it (eventually giving rise to so-called 'neo-liberal developmental states'). Further, it is not simply that financialization has eroded or transformed existing developmental states; it has also constrained or, more exactly, transformed and conditioned how they can be achieved, by way of exception, as opposed to universally (as suggested by the optimism attached to methodological nationalism in the face of neo-liberal globalization pessimism). This is because financialization is associated with the strengthening and/or emergence of national financial elites, and the increasing integration of such elites with international finance. The result has been to reduce levels and efficacy of investment, and not only to subordinate policy to short-run financial gains but also to change the nature of the way in which policy is made, with a shift towards the interests of finance and forms of governance that reflect this. In terms of the DSP vernacular, financialization involves an embedded (or should that be disembedded?) autonomy in which the interests of finance come to the fore, and for which developmental gains are accidental or incidental rather than integral.[23]

Such observations are drawn much too generally, of course, and should be seen more as setting the conditions under which developmental states do or do not emerge. In the case of China, and in much development of a more systematic or systemic kind, a necessary condition is the extent of insulation from financialization, particularly the extent to which finance for investment continues to be subject to state direction. On the other hand, for Ireland, the dysfunctional forms taken by its financialization as a developmental state (Celtic Tiger) were sharply revealed by the global financial crisis.

CONCLUSION

Drawn by the ceaseless winds of globalization, multinational corporations have responded by moving to 'restructure operations and workforces across regions and countries' (Peters, 2011, p. 84), with the effects of financialization reaching labourers in their distant workplaces, albeit in diverse and indirect ways. The DSP's appeal, particularly at its height, implicitly depended on a kind of labour that was necessary to drive the 'real' economy and that could serve as an agent for socio-economic change through collective organization. For the DSP, the idea of developmentalism became confined to catch-up, latecomer industrialization, underpinned by (physical) capital accumulation and coordination of capital by the state with labour and, to a lesser extent, finance confined to a residual role. Today, corporate success, in terms of maximization of shareholder value for example, continues to depend on material accumulation, but the effect of financialization on business strategies, including on labour relations, must be noted. Further, in examining business strategies and corresponding enterprise structure, Thompson (2013) sees the role of global value chains and production networks as imperative. Whilst industrial policy is apparently back on the agenda, generally seeking to finesse the twin pressures of globalization and financialization, policies of austerity in the wake of the global crisis have undermined the capacity and presence of social policy and domestic production for domestic needs as core strategies for development (Fine, 2011, 2014), contingent though they may be on challenging the powers underpinning those pressures.

So whilst the strengths, weaknesses and trajectory of the DSP have been highlighted here, development now faces very different conditions than did the East Asian NICs, not least the conditions of globalized and financialized neo-liberalism, as opposed to the Keynesian post-war boom, quite apart from the weakening of labour and its presence in social compacting.[24] Rather than building on its strengths, and resolving its weaknesses, to address these issues in theory and in practice the DSP has declined into an amorphous commitment to defend progressive if piecemeal interventions by the state.

NOTES

1. This chapter draws on parts of Fine (2016).
2. On which see Ha-Joon Chang (1994, 2002, 2007, 2010).
3. See Cornwall and Eade (2010).
4. Neatly, in terms of what follows, his son, Robert C., was awarded the Nobel Prize in Economics in 1997, together with Myron S. Scholes, for discovering 'a new method to determine the value of derivatives', the Black–Scholes(-Merton) formula. See http://www.nobelprize.org/nobel_prizes/economics/laureates/1997/.
5. Although eventually eschewing reference to the DSP as such, Ha-Joon Chang (1994, 2002, 2007, 2010) has been at the forefront of this sort of continuing assault on the Washington Consensus, with a corresponding convergence towards more mainstream market imperfections and institutional economics, with affinities to the post-Washington Consensus (Fine and Van Waeyenberge, 2013).
6. See Frangie (2011) for a rare juxtaposition of the developmental state with 'primitive accumulation' and the process of state formation itself.
7. For previous work on the DSP in general in this vein, see Fine (2003, 2006) and Fine et al. (2013).
8. For a useful, if unwitting, overview of the political school with no mention of financialization and neo-liberalism as such, see Routley (2012, 2014).
9. See Pradella (2014) for methodological nationalism as the long-standing basis for the DSP.
10. See also Gray's (2011a, p. 595) study for Taiwan, 'moving beyond attempts to understand transformation through national comparative ideal type models', and also Song (2011, p. 297) for South Korea, in light of the putative demise of its developmental state and in drawing on world systems theory and the state derivationist approach.
11. See also the discussion of Chinese and US struggle for hegemony in the region, especially with the putative demise of the Taiwanese developmental state and the apparently irresistible attraction of the Chinese mainland for Taiwanese investment (Gray, 2011a, p. 590).
12. See Mkandawire (2012, p. 18) for observing that, 'Peter Evans coined . . . the oxymoron-like expression "embedded autonomy"'.

13. For an account see Breznitz (2012, p. 106), who takes a constructivist ideational approach, interrogating how an ideology across neo-liberalism and developmentalism reconciled these in practice.
14. See Tsukamoto (2012) for Japan's, equally neo-oxymoronic, neo-liberalized developmental state, and Liow (2012) for Singapore.
15. For Petropoulos (2011), this can involve the substitution of expanding and furnishing domestic demand through state intervention across the East Asian NICs and especially in China.
16. Thus, for example, in his proposal for a new development economics there is no reference by Lin (2012), even by way of critical departure, to the DSP (apart from a title in references) despite his putative shift towards embracing industrial policy.
17. See also his contribution in Williams (2014), a collection that might be interpreted, largely inadvertently, to illustrate the propositions offered here, both in general and for South Africa in particular. Interestingly, in contrast to Evans, those such as Lin (2012) who disregard the DSP altogether continue to regard industrialization and industrial policy as central to development (and Lin even suggests light targeting of industries a decade ahead in the process of development, as revealed by those who are to be emulated); see Fine and Van Waeyenberge (2013) for a critique.
18. This is a quote that has been attributed to General Motors President Charles E. Wilson at his confirmation hearings for Secretary of Defence in 1953. What he actually said was '. . . for years I thought what was good for our country was good for General Motors, and vice versa'. Cf. https://blogs.loc.gov/inside_adams/2016/04/when-a-quote-is-not-exactly-a-quote-general-motors/.
19. For restoration of class struggle and labour into analysis of development, see the collection introduced by Campling et al. (2016).
20. For the social compacting paradigm and its affinities as well as its difference with the DSP see Fine (2016), the most important contrast being how social compacting places labour relations at the heart of its analysis in explaining comparative economic performance.
21. To be fair, Evans does not seem to have the benefit of the global crisis by which to assess the role of finance and its implications for development.
22. We observe here, in passing and for future reference, that the policies adopted by the US and some other developed countries have been exactly the opposite of those advised – or should that be imposed – on developing countries experiencing similar crises in the past. As Ha-Joon Chang has been at the forefront of arguing in the context of historical paths to development, those that have traversed it insist, 'Do not do as we did, do as we say', to which should be added the nostrum, 'Do not do as we do, do as we say.'
23. Significantly, Leftwich (2010), a leading member of the DSP's political school, bemoans the lack of attention to agency, and despite his focus being on the role of elites in creating developmental aspirations, or not, there is not a single reference to finance! The single exception that proves the rule is to be found on page 102:

> It is in this context that the role of agency becomes critical, at least in the world of real politics, that is in shaping institutional responses to political, economic and social challenges – such as the financial crisis of 2008–2009, political instability and violence in the context of failed or unconsolidated states, or the threat of nationwide HIV/AIDS epidemics that currently ravage many countries in the south.

Finance, or its crisis, is merely something to which elites need to be able to respond developmentally (as opposed to being seen as both causal and, in large measure, beneficiary). This is of significance for how finance confronts labour.
24. See also Fine and Saad Filho (2016).

REFERENCES

Amsden, A. (1989), *Asia's Next Giant: South Korea and Late Industrialization*. New York: Oxford University Press.

Breznitz, D. (2012), 'Ideas, Structure, State Action and Economic Growth: Rethinking the Irish Miracle'. *Review of International Political Economy* 19 (1), 87–111.

Campling, L., Miyamura, S., Pattenden, J. and Selwyn, B. (2016) 'Class Dynamics of Development: A Methodological Note'. *Third World Quarterly* 37 (10), 1745–67.

Chang, D.-O. (2013), 'Labour and "Developmental State": A Critique of the Developmental State Theory of Labour'. In *Beyond The Development State: Industrial Policy into the Twenty-First Century*, ed. by Fine, B., Saraswati, J. and Tavasci, D. London: Pluto Press, pp. 85–109.

Chang, H.-J. (1994), *The Political Economy of Industrial Policy*. Basingstoke: Macmillan.

Chang, H.-J. (2002), *Kicking Away the Ladder – Development Strategy in Historical Perspective*. London: Anthem Press.

Chang, H.-J. (2007), *Bad Samaritans Rich Nations, Poor Policies, and the Threat to the Developing World*. London: Random House.

Chang, H.-J. (2010), *23 Things They Don't Tell You About Capitalism*. London: Allen Lane (Penguin).

Cornwall, A. and Eade, D. (eds) (2010), *Deconstructing Development Discourse: Buzzwords and Fuzzwords*. Oxfam and Rugby: Practical Action Publishing.

Evans, P.B. (2008), 'In Search of the 21st Century Developmental State'. The Centre for Global Political Economy, University of Sussex [online] Centre for Global Political Economy Working Paper Series (Working Paper No. 4). Available at: http://www.sussex.ac.uk/cgpe/research/publications/workingpapers.

Fine, B. (2003), 'Beyond the Developmental State: Towards a Political Economy of Development'. In *Beyond Market-Driven Development: A New Stream of Political Economy of Development*, ed. by Hirakawa, H., Noguchi, M. and Sano, M. Tokyo: Nihon Hyoron Sha, in Japanese, pp. 21–43.

Fine, B. (2006), 'The Developmental State and the Political Economy of Development'. In *The New Development Economics After the Wasington Consensus*, ed. by Jomo, K.S. and Fine, B. New Delhi/London: Tulika Books/Zed Books, pp. 101–22.

Fine, B. (2011), 'Locating the Developmental State and Industrial and Social Policy after the Crisis'. In *The Least Developed Countries Report 2011: The Potential Role of South-South Cooperation for Inclusive and Sustainable Development* [online], ed. by UNCTAD. Background Paper No. 3, 2011. Available at: http://www.unctad.org/Sections/ldc_dir/docs/ldcr2011_Fine_en.pdf.

Fine, B. (2013), 'Beyond the Developmental State: An Introduction'. In *Beyond The Development State: Industrial Policy into the Twenty-first Century*, ed. by Fine, B., Saraswati, J. and Tavasci, D. London: Pluto Press, pp. 85–109.

Fine, B. (2014), *The Continuing Enigmas of Social Policy* [online]. UNRISD project on Towards Universal Social Security in Emerging Economies (UNRISD Working Paper 2014). Available at: http://www.unrisd.org/Fine.

Fine, B. (2016), Across Developmental State and Social Compacting: The Peculiar Case of South Africa [online]. ISER Working Paper No. 2016/1. Grahamstown: Institute of Social and Economic Research, Rhodes University. Available at: https://www.ru.ac.za/media/rhodesuniversity/content/iser/documents/ISER%20Working%20Paper%20No.%202016.01.pdf.

Fine, B. and Saad Filho, A. (2016), 'Thirteen Things You Need to Know about Neoliberalism'. *Critical Sociology* 43 (4–5), 685–706.

Fine, B. and Van Waeyenberge, E. (2013), 'A Paradigm Shift that Never Was: Justin Lin's New Structural Economics'. *Competition and Change* 17 (4), 355–71.

Fine, B., Saraswati, J. and Tavasci, D. (eds) (2013), *Beyond The Development State: Industrial Policy into the Twenty-first Century*. London: Pluto Press.

Fishwick, A. (2015), Industrialisation and the Working Class: The Contested Trajectories of ISI in Chile and Argentina. Unpublished PhD dissertation. University of Sussex.

Frangie, S. (2011), 'Post-Development, Developmental State and Genealogy: Condemned to Develop?' *Third World Quarterly* 32 (7), 1183–98.

Gray, K. (2011a), 'Taiwan and the Geopolitics of Late Development'. *The Pacific Review* 24 (5), 577–99.

Gray, K. (2011b), 'The Social and Geopolitical Origins of State Transformation: The Case of South Korea'. *New Political Economy* 16 (3), 303–22.

Hillbom, E. (2012), 'Botswana: A Development-Oriented Gate-Keeping State'. *African Affairs* 111 (442), 67–89.

Johnson, C. (1995), *Japan: Who Governs? The Rise of the Developmental State*. New York and London: W.W. Norton & Company.

Kohli, A. (1999), 'Where Do High-Growth Political Economies Come From? The Japanese Lineage of Korea's "Developmental State"'. In *The Developmental State*, ed. by Woo-Cumings, M. Ithaca and London: Cornell University Press, pp. 93–136.

Krugman, P. (1994), 'The Myth of Asia's Miracle'. *Foreign Affairs* 73 (6), 62–8.

Leftwich, A. (2010), 'Beyond Institutions: Rethinking the Role of Leaders, Elites and Coalitions in the Institutional Formation of Developmental States and Strategies'. *Forum for Development Studies* 37 (1), 93–111.

Lin, J. (2012), *New Structural Economics: A Framework for Rethinking Development and Policy* [online]. Washington: World Bank. Available at: http://siteresources.worldbank.org/DEC/Resources/84797-1104785060319/598886-1104951889260/NSE-Book.pdf.

Liow, E. (2012), 'The Neoliberal-Developmental State: Singapore as Case Study'. *Critical Sociology* 38 (2), 241–64.

Mkandawire, T. (2012), Building the African State in the Age of Globalisation: The Role of Social Compacts and Lessons for South Africa [online]. Mapungubwe Institute for Strategic Reflection, Inaugural Annual Lecture, MISTRA. Available at: http://www.mistra.org.za/MediaDocs/The%20role%20of%20social%20compacts.pdf.

Peters, J. (2011), 'The Rise of Finance and the Decline of Organised Labour in the Advanced Capitalist Countries'. *New Political Economy* 16 (1), 73–99.

Petropoulos, S. (2011), 'The 2008 Global Crisis and the East Asian Developmental States Shifts of Export-Driven Strategies'. *European Journal of East Asian Studies* 10 (2), 181–202.

Pradella, L. (2014), 'New Developmentalism and the Origins of Methodological Nationalism'. *Competition and Change* 18 (2), 180–93.

Rethel, L. (2010), 'The New Financial Development Paradigm and Asian Bond Markets'. *New Political Economy* 15 (4), 493–517.

Routley, L. (2012), 'Developmental States in Africa? A Review of Ongoing Debates and Buzzwords'. *Development Policy Review* 32 (2), 159–77.

Routley, L. (2014), Developmental States: A Review of the Literature. ESID Working Paper No. 3. Manchester.

Selwyn, B. (2012), *Workers, State and Development in Brazil: Powers of Labour, Chains of Value*. Manchester: Manchester University Press.

Song, H.-Y. (2011), 'Theorising the Korean State beyond Institutionalism: Class Content and Form of "National" Development'. *New Political Economy* 16 (3), 281–302.

Thompson, P. (2013), 'Financialization and the Workplace: Extending and Applying the Disconnected Capitalism Thesis'. *Work, Employment & Society* 27 (3), 472–88.

Tsukamoto, T. (2012), 'Neoliberalization of the Developmental State: Tokyo's Bottom-Up Politics and State Rescaling in Japan'. *International Journal of Urban and Regional Research* 36 (1), 71–89.

Wade, R. (1988), 'State Intervention'. In *'Outward-Looking' Development: Neoclassical Theory and Taiwanese Practice*, ed. by White, G. London: Macmillan Press, pp. 30–67.

Wade, R. (2012), 'Return of Industrial Policy?' *International Review of Applied Economics* 26 (2), 223–39.

Williams, M. (ed.) (2014), *The End of the Developmental State?* London: Routledge.

World Bank (1993), *The East Asian Miracle: Economic Growth and Public Policy*. A World Bank Policy Research Report. Oxford: Oxford University Press.

12. Development and social change in Latin America
Raúl Delgado Wise and Henry Veltmeyer

INTRODUCTION

Latin American contributions to development theory have left an indelible mark on the field of development studies, giving it a more critical edge. These contributions relate not just to the vibrant debates on the development question, but to the activism of social movements and a history of experimentation with diverse forms and models of development.

The Cuban Revolution had a momentous impact on the development project which was launched in 1948 by Harry Truman in the form of a programme of development assistance and international cooperation. This programme was designed – and the associated idea of development was 'invented' – as a means of ensuring that the economically 'backward' countries of the Third World would not fall prey to the siren of communism, and would continue to follow the capitalist path towards national development.

In many ways, Latin American thinkers and practitioners have been rebels to the Northern, occidental, mainstream development route boosted by the US and its imperialist institutional arms: the World Bank (WB), the International Monetary Fund (IMF), and the World Trade Organization (WTO). Since the post-war period, development and social change in the region have followed a distinctive and critical path in search of avenues to overcome – and transcend – Latin America's asymmetrical and subordinated integration into the world capitalist system. The aim of this chapter is to assess that process from a critical perspective, in an attempt to envision what could be regarded as the Latin American legacy in the field.

THE EMERGENCE OF A SOUTHERN POSITION

In the 1950s and 1960s capitalist development, unfolding in the form of a process of productive and social transformation (the rural outmigration of the proletarianized peasantry of small landholding producers and their integration into the urban labour market), was theorized by mainstream

development economists as a matter of economic growth and modernization of the corresponding infrastructure and institutional framework.

This 'modernization theory' took form as the dynamics of economic
growth and institutional reform, but it was grounded in the idea of the
transformation into a modern industrial capitalist system of an agrarian
society and macroeconomic system, one based on pre-capitalist relations
of production and a traditional communalist culture. Notwithstanding
this, a fundamental paradigm shift took place at the time: Latin American
theorists, particularly those associated with the Economic Commission
for Latin America (ECLA – later, with the inclusion of the Caribbean,
ECLAC), made a major contribution to the theory and practice of development: a conceptualization rooted in what we might term a Southern
perspective. This contribution took the form of an analysis of the development dynamics of the structure of international economic relations
between countries at the centre of the system and those on the periphery
(Kay, 1989). The main theory advanced was that the centre-periphery
structure of North-South relations was disadvantageous for countries
on the periphery, leading, as it did, to a deterioration of the terms of
trade for these countries. However, the centre-periphery model was also
used to construct another theory with rather different and more radical
political implications: a dependency theory of underdevelopment – the
theory that the 'development' of economies at the centre of the system and
the underdevelopment of economies on the periphery were interrelated
(Frank, 1970). This theory was advanced in different permutations, but it
basically combined propositions advanced by economists at ECLAC and
neo-Marxists, namely that the structure of North-South relations repli-
cated the unequal exchange between capital and labour as a mechanism
for transferring the economic surplus (Kay, 1989).

DEPENDENCY THEORY

Dependency theory, as it came to be called, was elaborated in the late
1960s and early 1970s in three forms: (1) as the 'development of underdevelopment', a thesis advanced by André Gunder Frank with reference
to a metropolis-satellite model of the world capitalist system; (2) a
theory elaborated by three Brazilian Marxist scholars – Mauro Marini
(1973), Theotonio dos Santos (2003) and Vania Bambirra (1986) – which
argued that the centre-periphery (North-South) structure of the world
capitalist system functioned as a mechanism of super-exploitation, a
theory based on a neo-Marxist conception of US imperialism and the
dynamics of revolutionary change in Latin America; and (3) a theory

of associated dependent development proposed by Fernando Henrique Cardoso and Enzo Faletto (1969), which was constructed within the framework of the ECLA school of Latin American structuralism, associated with a reformist approach to social change (that is, predicated on capitalism rather than socialism).

Marini (1973) posited that dependent capitalism was a *sui generis* form of capitalism that could only be understood when analysed from the perspective of the system as a whole, both at the national and the international level. From this perspective, the diminished accumulation capacity of the peripheral economies was explained in terms of structural forces that resulted in a trend towards growing trade deficits, internal market thinness, and an oversupply of labour. These structural conditions resulted from the asymmetric and subordinated integration of peripheral economies into the world capitalist system. This 'dependency theory' was constructed within the framework of the centre-periphery model which was used by the economists at ECLAC as scaffolding in their construction of a rather different theory based on a reformist approach to social change.

These neo-Marxist theorists of dependency argued that the structure of North-South relations resembled the capital-labour relation, in that it was based on the appropriation of the economic surplus – a series of mechanisms for extracting surplus value from the wealth generated by the working class and the direct producers in the peripheral economy. Also, these theorists did not share the faith of the ECLA theorists in a model of import-substitution industrialization, based on the agency of the national bourgeoisie. They did, however, agree with Prebisch's diagnosis of the origins of underdevelopment and Celso Furtado's thesis regarding the adverse impact of the labour supply on wages (Furtado, 1970). But they did not agree with ECLA theorists that the structural imbalances of the centre-periphery relation could be resolved by means of institutional and social reforms and bourgeois modernization policies. Marini, for example, praised the theoretical findings of ECLAC economists but questioned their beliefs regarding the possibility of autonomous capitalist development in Latin America by reforming the system or via a bigger dose of foreign investment (Marini, 1973). The only solution was to abandon capitalism, that is, overthrow it in a process of revolutionary struggle. Like Bambirra and Dos Santos, Marini also criticized the failure of ECLA economists to understand the role played by the region in the accumulation of capital in the central economies, and the role of the state in this process. These Marxist dependency theorists rejected ECLAC's presentation of the state as an artefact and agency of economic growth and autonomous industrialization, and criticised their ignorance of the state as an instrument of class domination and rule.

Dos Santos emphasized the role of multinational corporations as bearers of capital and as an agency of imperialism in the global integration of capital. He shared Samir Amin's (2013) diagnosis regarding the worldwide operation of the law of value in the sphere of international relations. He also concurred with Paul Baran and the *Monthly Review* school regarding US hegemony and the global dynamics of monopoly capital, particularly in regard to its relationship with surplus transferences from peripheral countries – the dialectical relationship between monopoly capital and uneven development – and its propensity towards crisis. Marini evaluated the dynamics of a downward trend in the rate of profit on the periphery, noting that the fall in profitability derives from the reduction of new living labour embodied in global capitalist production vis-à-vis dead labour objectified in raw materials and machinery. He argued that the inflow of capital from the centre to the periphery helped reduce the decline in core economies via the super-exploitation of both the workers and the small-scale agricultural producers on the periphery who were assigned the role of providing cheap food and supplies for metropolitan industry. Apart from the transfer of surpluses and the negative implications of the crisis from the centre to the periphery, Marini stressed the adverse effect on the consumption capacity in countries with lower wages, thus inhibiting the growth of a middle class, seen by many as a necessary condition (and outcome) of economic development (Marini, 1973).

This theory of dependency in its diverse permutations, but especially in the formulation by André Gunder Frank and other 'world system theorists', had considerable currency in academe in the 1970s, effectively displacing Modernization Theory as a framework for the analysis of the dynamics of (capitalist) development. Emmanuel Wallerstein, for one, famously announced the death of Modernization Theory. With the simultaneous emergence of the phenomenon of 'Newly Industrialized Countries' (NICs) on the Asian periphery of the system, which contradicted the expectations and conclusions derived from it, Modernization Theory was subjected to a reality test that led to a major internal debate, an abandonment of the theory in some circles, and a serious rethinking of its central propositions in others. Although the announcement of its demise was somewhat premature, the theory suffered a near-death, which led to a series of reformulations, including transformation into what its exponents termed 'world systems theory'.

THE NEOLIBERAL COUNTER-REVOLUTION

The 1980s opened with a conservative counter-revolution, focused on halting the incremental, but steady, gains made in earlier decades by the working class within the institutional framework of the welfare-development state. The main institutional mechanism for this – for reactivating the capital accumulation process, the motor and driving force of economic growth – was a programme of market-oriented or friendly 'structural reforms' designed to bring about a 'free market' form of capitalism. The reforms included opening up the economies in the region to the global economy (globalization, as it came to be called); privatization of the means of production and economic enterprise; deregulation of product, capital and labour markets; liberalization of the flow of investment capital and trade; and administrative decentralization (Petras and Veltmeyer, 2002).

By the beginning of the decade both the labour movement and the struggle for land in the countryside (the latter in the form of diverse armies of national liberation) had been defeated. This was by a combination of state repression and a strategy of integrated rural development designed to turn the rural poor – the masses of dispossessed peasant families forced by the capitalist development of agriculture to abandon their rural livelihoods and communities – away from the confrontational politics of the social movements seeking revolutionary change. The defeat of these revolutionary movements, together with the dynamics of an accumulated and expanding external debt, created conditions that allowed the major operating agencies of the system to impose on the national governments in the region a programme of structural adjustment to their macroeconomic policies, initiating what David Harvey (2005) dubbed the 'neoliberal era'.

A major aim, and one of the stated goals of the Washington Consensus and neoliberal policy reform agenda, was to liberate the 'forces of economic freedom' from the regulatory constraints of the development state. But the immediate outcome of these structural reforms was the advance of capital in both the cities and the countryside, resulting in the destruction of the productive forces in both agriculture and industry, and a virtual collapse and involution of the labour market. This, in turn, forced the growing mass of displaced urban workers and rural migrants to work 'on their own account' on the streets, rather than exchange their labour for a living wage in the industrial plants or factories. Economists and sociologists at the Regional Programme of Employment for Latin America and the Caribbean (PREALC in Spanish) and ECLAC estimated that, in this context, up to 80 per cent of new jobs or employment generated in the 1980s were formed in what was termed the 'informal sector' (Portes and Benton, 1987; Klein and Tokman, 1988; Tokman, 1991).

But the development community, that is the theorists and practitioners associated with the project of international cooperation in the war against global poverty, focused their concern and attention, not on these and other structural changes, but rather on the deterioration of the social condition of people in the urban centres, many of whom had replaced rural poverty with a new form of poverty. The diagnosis of what the New World Order had brought about – a deepening of social inequalities and increased poverty – was reflected in the common phrase of 'a decade lost to development'.

What was almost entirely lost in diverse theoretical reflections on this process was the strategic and political response of the urban poor. This response took the form of the creation of soup kitchens and other such collective actions and solidarity organizations to assist the poor in coping with the forces of capitalist development and to survive in the new conditions (Petras and Leiva, 1994). In some cases, this led to the formation of a vibrant social economy within the expanding cities of slums on the Latin American periphery (Davis, 2006). This was particularly advanced in Chile and Peru, as well as in Mexico, where an earthquake, measuring 8.0 on the Richter scale and resulting in at least 10,000 deaths, led to a proliferation of non-governmental organizations stepping into the breach of a retreating state and the construction of a social economy based on self-help, mutual support and social solidarity (Veltmeyer, 2007).

Construction of a social economy based on a culture of social solidarity, and the emergence and mushrooming growth of 'civil society', based on an associational type of non-governmental organization, resulted from a convergence of diverse forces. But this was only one of several responses to these forces and changing conditions. Another was widespread protest and resistance. At first, in the late 1970s and much of the 1980s, these protests and this resistance against the neoliberal reform agenda – in the form of what were then dubbed 'IMF protests' – was spontaneous and unorganized (Walton and Ragin, 1990). At the time, the primary target of the protests was IMF-dictated austerity measures, such as cuts in government spending and the removal of subsidies on public services and utilities, which raised the cost of transportation, fuel, electricity, water, food, and so on, beyond the reach of the urban poor. In the 1990s, however, the resistance – directed against the WB's neoliberal agenda of structural reform rather than the IMF's austerity measures – became more organized. The agency of this resistance was found in the new social movements formed by the peasantry, the rural landless or semi-proletarianized workers, and the indigenous communities. This new wave of social movements against the advance of capital and the government's neoliberal policy agenda began in Ecuador with an uprising in 1990 orchestrated by the Confederation of Indigenous Nationalities of Ecuador (CONAIE) – a confederation of several dozen indigenous nationalities (Petras and Veltmeyer, 2013).

With the upsurge of CONAIE and other such peasant and indigenous movements across the region – most notably the Zapatista Army of National Liberation (EZLN) – the 1990s were dubbed by some as a 'golden age' of resistance, with reference to the power of these movements to halt the neoliberal policy reform agenda in its tracks, and place neoliberalism on the defensive – so much so as to bring about its eventual demise. By the end of the decade, to all intents and purposes, the neoliberal agenda was dead in the water, leading to a sea-tide of regime change – the emergence of a progressive cycle in Latin American politics that can be traced back to the activism of the peasant social movements (Petras and Veltmeyer, 2013).

NEOLIBERALISM WITH A 'HUMAN FACE' – THE 1990s

In the 1980s the neoliberal policy agenda was advanced with a programme of structural reforms and austerity measures designed by economists at the WB and the IMF: the Structural Adjustment Program (SAP). The theory underlying this programme was that these policy reforms would create the necessary conditions for activating a process of stable economic growth, in particular the control of runaway inflation. The paradigmatic case of this development was Bolivia. The WB and the IMF, together with other development agencies, commissioned a series of studies into the outcome and economic impact of the structural adjustment programmes that were established as loan conditionalities and the price for accessing capital in restructuring the debt (Morley, 1995). Most of these studies were never published because they tended to show that, notwithstanding the success of these programmes in controlling inflation, they did not place the countries at issue on a stable growth path. On the contrary, Chossudovsky (1997) argued, they created conditions such as increased inequalities and poverty, social discontent and political protests, which tended to destabilize the democratic neoliberal regimes formed in the 1980s. This led to the forging of a new consensus around a 'new social policy' focused on poverty reduction, the need for inclusionary state activism (getting right not prices, but the balance between state and market) and decentralized 'good governance' with social or popular participation (the engagement of 'civil society' in the development process). This was as well as a new 'comprehensive development framework' in which 'structural adjustment' as a one-size-fits-all approach would be replaced by a new policy in which each country would 'own' its own poverty reduction programme (World Bank, 2001).

By 1989, barely six years into the neoliberal structural reform agenda, it was already evident that 'free market' capitalism was not working. Rather than activating a process of capital accumulation and economic growth, the 'bold reforms' instituted under the Washington Consensus had brought about a 'decade lost to development' with consequences that threatened to destabilize the fragile democratic regimes formed in conditions of the New World Order. The end result was a new consensus on the need to establish a better balance between the state and the market, and promote a more inclusive form of development based on a 'new social policy' of poverty reduction (Fine, Lapavitsas and Pincus, 2001; World Bank, 2007; Infante and Sunkel, 2009). Within the framework of this consensus, economists at ECLAC constructed a new paradigm and development theory that was essentially an amalgam of Latin American structuralism and neoliberalism – neostructuralism (Leiva, 2008) – that would be used to establish the institutional and policy framework for the 'new developmentalism' (Bresser-Pereria, 2007, 2009).

A key landmark of the neoliberal era, underlying the myth of 'free market' capitalism, is what Samir Amin (2013) refers to as a 'generalized monopoly capitalism [that is] imploding before our eyes'. The overwhelming expansion and restructuring of monopoly capital has engendered new contradictions within the world capitalist system and new modalities of unequal exchange that, it has been argued, are at the core of the development question in Latin America today.

NEOSTRUCTURALISM AND NEO-DEVELOPMENTALISM

In the vortex of neoliberal structural reform and diverse forces of social change in the 1990s Latin American development theory evolved in a number of different directions. Within the mainstream of development theory, economists and sociologists at ECLAC, headed by Osvaldo Sunkel, sought a theoretical convergence between Latin American structuralism and a theory of market-friendly structural reform. This would take the form of neostructuralism, which combines a sociocentric conception of development, a structural analysis of North-South relations, and a policy agenda aligned with the post-Washington Consensus on the need for a more inclusive form of development – the new developmentalism, as it is now termed (Bresser-Pereira, 2007, 2009; Leiva, 2008).

Local Development Dynamics of the Social Economy and the Cooperative Movement

In Latin America, the search for alternative forms of development, promoted by the turn of many governments towards neoliberalism as a 'new economic model', led to a spate of theorizing about the dynamics of alternative forms of community-based local development and how to construct a social economy 'from below'. This theorizing, and the associated debate, took place within the framework of a 'new development paradigm' but it has been closely associated with the cooperative movement, which can be traced back to the early years of the twentieth century, although it did not begin to take shape and exercise a significant influence on national life until after the 1930s, with the consolidation of the Mexican Revolution (Fabra Ribas, 1943).

There were a number of experiments and diverse experiences with what were understood at the time as exemplars of popular power – particularly in Bolivia, Chile, Peru and Brazil (Veltmeyer, 2016). The significance of these, and other such experiments in popular power, and experiences with cooperativism and unionism, is that they were all closely tied to dynamics of capitalist development and can only be understood in this context. Thus, although the history of cooperativism in Latin America is very complex, with a different experience in each country, its main aim was to prevent countries on the periphery of the world capitalist system from taking a socialist path towards development, and to turn the rural poor away from revolutionary social movements.

With the support of an appropriate institutional framework of decentralized governance, a new social policy focused on poverty reduction, international cooperation in the form of microfinance, and social participation, that is the engagement of civil society in the development process. The strategy devised was for the rural poor to diversify their source of household income, enabling them to remain in, and develop, their rural communities. The solution – a survival strategy rather than a local development strategy – was to combine the following sources of household income: agriculture, labour, remittances, micro-development finance and projects, and conditional cash transfers from the government to poor households (Kay, 2008). Some rural sociologists such as Cristobal Kay and others associated with Revista Latinoamericana de Estudios Rurales have theorized this development as the 'new rurality' (ibid.).

Economists at ECLAC, armed with a sociocentric and neostructuralist conception of national development based on the agency of the state with international cooperation and social cooperation, conceptualized the new model alternatively as 'development within' (Sunkel, 1993), the 'new developmentalism' (Bresser-Pereira, 2007, 2009), and 'inclusive development' (Infante and Sunkel, 2009).

NEW APPROACHES

The 1990s have been described as the golden age of the resistance – with reference to the neoliberal policy agenda and the formation of anti-neoliberal movements with their social base in the semi-proletarianized peasantry (Petras and Veltmeyer, 2005, 2013; Munck, 2015). By the end of the decade, the political activism of these movements had placed a number of the governments that were pursuing this agenda on the defensive, so much so, that observers and analysts began to write and theorize about the end of the neoliberal era. Be that as it may, the activism of these new social movements created conditions that led to a left turn in several countries in the Southern Cone, a cycle of 'progressive' post-neoliberal regimes and, with it, a rethinking of alternative pathways towards 'development' and a new economic model to guide policy in a progressive direction. The conjunction of this shift towards what has been described as 'inclusionary state activism' – the emergence of post-neoliberal regimes concerned with bringing about a more inclusive form of national development – with several significant changes in the geo-economics of capital in the region, created an entirely new context for the capitalist development process and for rethinking the role of Latin America in it.

In the vortex of these forces of change, we can identify two basic schools of thought. The first we might describe as the economics and politics of alternative development within the institutional and policy framework of the operating capitalist system. Advocates of this way of thinking challenge neoliberalism and US hegemony but are concerned to preserve the social and institutional structure of capitalism. Some have described this approach as 'left neoliberalism'. The second stream is associated with a new wave of critical development thinking that assumed diverse forms, but is based on the agency of grass-roots organization and the activism of anti-systemic social movements that share an anti-capitalist vision and reject developmentalism in all its forms.

At the level of the global economy, what precipitated this development and facilitated the appearance of a new progressive cycle in Latin American politics was the rise of China as an economic power, and a consequent primary commodities boom fuelled by the demand for natural resources and energy. In response to this demand, a number of governments in South America turned towards extractivism – the extraction of natural resources and their exportation in primary commodity form – as a model of national development (Gudynas, 2015). Combined with a push towards inclusionary state activism and the search for a more inclusive form of development (the new developmentalism), these regimes pursued what some theorists and analysts have dubbed 'new extractivism' – a mode of national development constructed on the base of two pillars: an extractive form of capitalist development, and inclusionary state activism (the use of resource ground rents to finance a programme of poverty reduction).

The 'new extractivism' (see Veltmeyer and Petras, 2014) has generated a wave of rethinking both in regard to the fundamental contradictions of capitalism in this phase of its development and the 'new dependency' brought about by the new geo-economics of extractive capital in conditions of a new progressive cycle in Latin American politics. The irony is that this progressive cycle includes the quest of the progressive regimes formed under these conditions – Argentina, Bolivia, Brazil, Ecuador and Venezuela – for independence from the yoke of US imperialism, but led to the subsequent new dependency on foreign direct investment in the extractive sector.

NEO-DEPENDENCY THEORY

The emergence of new trends in both the geo-economics and the geo-politics of capital in the region has also led to a serious rethinking of their development implications – what might be described as 'critical development studies', a critical assessment of what can be described as the new geo-economics of capital in the region and its development implications. This assessment has taken various forms, including a revival and reformulation of Dependency Theory, which today – as in its original formulation – is more a school of thought than a theory. In any case, this 'new dependency' theory is a response to the new relation of dependency associated with the latest advance in the process of capitalist development in the form of extractivism and globalization (Sotelo, 2005; Borón, 2008; Osorio, 2009; Martins, 2011). The proponents of this theory argue that the latest advance of capital on a global scale has created a neo-colonial system of global production in which countries on the (Latin American) periphery are forced into a new relationship of dependency around the export of primary commodities and the influx of 'resource seeking' capital (Sotelo, 2005; Osorio, 2009). The renewed dependency of governments and economies in the region on both the export of the social product in primary commodity form and large-scale foreign direct investments has generated a vibrant and heated debate on the nature of this dependency.

One outcome of this debate is the emergence of what has been described as post-dependency. This current of thought is described by Atilio Borón (2008) and Claudio Katz (2016) in the following terms: in the twenty-first century, under conditions of a major reconfiguration of economic power in the global economy and the advance of capitalism towards the end of the neoliberal era, there emerged a new current of post-dependency thought that postulated the emergence in Latin America of another indus-trialization process, one based on a new industrial policy designed to take advantage of the opportunities provided by the region's integration into the global economy (Guillén, 2007; Dos Santos, 2010). But some scholars (for example, Sunkel 2013) are not so sanguine; indeed, they are rather pessimistic regarding the opportunities for national development provided by the global economy, and Latin America's integration into it, on the basis of the rules governing the current world order. Others, oriented towards a neo-Marxist reformulation of dependency theory, entirely reject this post-dependency theory with reference to a reconstructed Marxist theory of monopoly capitalism (on this see Delgado Wise, 2013). From this perspective, monopoly capital, more than ever, has become a central player in the global economy. Through mega-mergers and strategic alli-ances, this fraction of capital has reached unparalleled levels of concentra-tion and centralization: the top 500 largest multinational corporations now concentrate between 35 and 40 per cent of world income (Foster, McChesney and Jonna, 2011).

As the proponents of this neo-Marxist theory of the new dependency see it, the new scenario is characterized by global networks of monopoly capital through which large multinational corporations can expand their services, as well as productive and commercial activities, via mechanisms such as outsourcing or subcontracting to peripheral regions in search of cheap and flexible labour forces through labour arbitrage (Márquez and Delgado Wise, 2011; Delgado Wise and Martin, 2015). Extractivism and neo-extractivism, through the creation of export platforms that operate as enclaves in peripheral countries, are also part of this scenario. But, from the perspective of these analysts, more relevant is the extension of monopoly capital towards the sphere of scientific and technological innovation. By accessing a mobile and highly qualified workforce formed on the periphery, the large multinational corporations that dominate the world system have managed to lower labour costs, transfer risk and liability coverage, and capitalize visible benefits through the concentration of patents (Delgado Wise, Chávez and Rodriguez, 2016).

Another pillar of this new global architecture of monopoly capital is financialization, which involves a growing reliance on fictitious or speculative capital rather than on productive capital, a venture that also encompasses sovereign wealth funds, public budgets, pension funds and investment funds formed in the Global South (Amin, 2010). This generates short-term profits that distort the functioning of the so-called real economy and leads to massive fraud and recurrent crises, as well as the concentration and centralization of capital.

An inescapable feature of capitalism in this form is the deepening of unequal development. The global and national dynamics of capitalist development, the international division of labour supported by a system of international power relations, together with the dynamics of extractive capital, have rendered economic, social, political, and cultural polarization more extreme than ever before in human history, leading to what Joseph Stiglitz – chief economist at the WB until 2000[1] – terms 'the great divide'. As Walden Bello (2006) has argued, it also leads to a profound multifaceted crisis, which undermines the main sources of wealth creation – labour and nature – to the point of a potentially catastrophic outcome.

Post-development as Critique – Buen Vivir as Alternative

The sea-tide of regime change in the first decade of the new millennium, and an associated progressive cycle in Latin American politics, brought to the fore new ways of thinking about development. One particular new counterpoint of critical development thought relates to the indigenous Quechua concept of Sumak Kawsay, translated in Spanish as 'Buen Vivir' (Ecuador) or 'Vivir Bien' (Bolivia). This concept is notoriously difficult to render into English (see Solón, 2012), but it is taken by Eduardo Gudynas to describe a condition of living in social solidarity and in harmony with nature (see also Dávalos, 2008; Acosta, 2012). As Gudynas sees it Vivir Bien or Buen Vivir is a form of post-development thought constructed within a 'non-capitalist paradigm' (also see Albó, 2009; Farah and Vasapollo, 2011; Wanderley, 2015; Barkin, 2017). He formulates this idea as follows: 'post-development as critique, Vivir Bien as alternative' (Gudynas, 2015). This interpretation involves a deep-rooted critique of capitalist modernity, and the rejection of the simplistic parallelism between development and economic growth. Buen Vivir is thus conceived as the practical application of post-development, an alternative to development, that is as an anti-capitalist, anti-colonialist and post-development approach to social change.

At issue in this debate – and it has spawned a voluminous literature – is the economic model used by the governments of Bolivia and Ecuador to bring about an alternative form of national development (Acosta, 2012). The model is constructed on the base of two pillars: (1) neo-developmentalism, an approach based on the post-Washington Consensus on the need for a more inclusive form of development; and (2) neo-extractivism – 'inclusionary state activism' regarding the extraction of the society's natural wealth and the channelling by the government of the resource rents collected from this process into a poverty reduction social programme (Veltmeyer and Petras, 2014; Gudynas, 2015).

Socialism of the Twenty-first Century

In January 2005 at the World Social Forum, Hugo Chávez explicitly called for the reinventing of socialism – different from that which had existed in the Soviet Union. 'We must reclaim socialism as a thesis, a project and a path, but a new type of socialism, a humanist one, which puts humans and not machines or the state ahead of everything' (Chávez, 2005).

Six months later, Chávez argued the importance of building a new communal system of production and consumption – in which there is an exchange of activities determined by communal needs and communal purposes, not just what Marx described as the 'cash nexus' or the profit motive, the incentive to make money, and accumulate capital. For Chávez, 'We have to help to create it, from the popular bases, with the participation of the communities, through the community organizations, the cooperatives, self-management and different ways to create this system' (http://motores constituyentes.blogspot.mx/2007/07/5-motores-constituyentes-de-la.html).

The occasion was the creation of a new institution – the Empresas de Producción Social (EPS), which invites comparison with the 'Socially Responsible Enterprises' (SREs), identified by Rafael Betancourt and Julia Sagebien (2013) as the key operational units of a social and solidarity economy – and an organizational pathway towards achieving 'inclusive growth'. Drawn from a number of sources – existing cooperatives pledged to commit themselves to the community rather than only collective self-interest, smaller state enterprises, and private firms anxious to obtain access to state business and favourable credit terms – these new enterprises of social production were to be committed both to serving community needs and incorporating worker participation.

On Chávez's re-election in December 2006, a new building block was added: communal councils (based upon 200 to 400 families in existing urban neighbourhoods and 20 to 50 in the rural areas). These were established to diagnose democratically community needs and priorities. With the shift of resources from municipal levels to the community level, the support of new communal banks for local projects, and a size which permits the general assembly, rather than elected representatives, to be the supreme decision-making body, the councils were envisioned as a basis not only for the transformation of people in the course of changing circumstances, but also for productive activity based upon communal needs and communal purposes.

These new councils were identified as the fundamental cell of Bolivarian socialism and the basis for a new state. 'All power to the communal councils!' Chávez declared. An 'explosion in communal power', designated as the fifth of 'five motors' driving the path toward socialism. The logic is one of a profound decentralization of decision-making and power.

Without denying the obstacles, both internal and external, faced by this development alternative since its inception, we cannot ignore the increasing difficulties faced by the Bolivarian Republic of Venezuela to transform its productive matrix and overcome its crucial dependency on oil exports (Wilpert, 2007). The death of Chávez and the turn to the right of a number of governments in the Southern Cone of the region have called into question this alternative path for social change. However, as Marta Harnecker (2010) has posited, 'heaven cannot be taken by storm . . . a long historical period is needed to make the transition from capitalism to a socialist society' (p. 104). She adds: 'Some talk in terms of decades . . . still others think that socialism is the goal we must pursue but that perhaps we may never completely reach' (ibid., p. 91).

Theorizing from Below and from Within the Social Movements: The Politics of Anti-neoliberal and Anti-capitalist Resistance

The capitalist development of the forces of production has always been accompanied by the mobilization of the forces of resistance generated in the process, most often in the form of social movements and a class struggle. But in the current context the social movements which have mobilized the forces of resistance to the expansion of capitalism have acquired certain cutting-edge features characterized by a concern for territorial autonomy (material and political sovereignty), and the right of access of all communities and peoples to the global commons of land and water; direct or participatory democracy (to command by obeying); a recovery and reaffirmation by indigenous nationalities of their cultural identity and integrity, and the need to create their own education and health systems; a cooperative and horizontal organization of work that is free from all forms of exploitation, discrimination, exclusion and contempt; and encouragement of new forms of development based on relations of social solidarity and harmony with nature (Zibechi, 2008).

These ideas are regarded by the constellation of social movements and coalitions spawned by the resistance to neoliberalism, extractivism and capitalism as fundamental principles. Other theoretical contributions made from within the social movements relate to ideas advanced by the

Zapatistas as to how to 'confront the capitalist hydra' (EZLN Sexta Comisión, 2015). They include the idea of a fourth world war – based on an analysis of the current global crisis – fought against the human species. From this, surges the need for radical change – to confront the capitalist system and its assault not just on labour, livelihoods, culture and civilization, but on nature and life itself. In its drive for private profit, capital seeks to convert, not only the land and the means of social production into commodities, but water and other elements of the commons that are vital for the very survival of humankind. To respond to this civilizationary challenge and confront the 'capitalist hydra' the forces of resistance, both those negatively affected by the workings of the capitalist system and the excluded, must come together in a common struggle waged 'from below' and 'from and towards the left' (Aguirre Rojas, 2015; EZLN Sexta Comisión, 2015). This struggle will need to engage a new 'way of doing politics' based on a new vision of power, direct democracy and radical autonomy (Aguirre Rojas, 2015, p. 251; Zibechi, 2015, p. 236). It means the emancipation from all forms of exploitation and exclusion, and the construction of new forms of resistance organized from within and below. It means an alternative modernity, a new world that encompasses many worlds (Echeverría, 2011).

CONCLUSION

Our analysis of six-and-a-half decades of development and social change in Latin America highlights the indelible mark that the region has left in this field of theory and practice. ECLAC's structural school introduced a fundamental paradigmatic shift in the field; for the first time the theory and practice of development was analysed from a Southern perspective. This paradigmatic turn did not simply imply a negation of the North, but rather a negation of the negation in dialectical terms, that is a search for a more systematic analysis of the dynamics of development and underdevelopment, and a more equitable form of development or post-development. With the advent of the dependency school, an emancipatory anti-systemic angle was incorporated into the debate – the necessity to transcend the limits of capitalism.

After 20 years of the neoliberal counter-revolution, a new wave of critical thought arose in the region, revisiting and updating the legacy of the dependency school. It did not only entail a Southern and critical perspective on the development process but a rethinking of its dynamics 'from below', based on ideas advanced by and from within the social movements.

The main features of the development project envisioned in this new wave of critical thought are not simply an abstract model of socialism or post-capitalism. The sources of inspiration of the social transformation project pursued were diverse and based on a wide range of experiences derived from the practice – and theory – of social movements in the region. Included here is a recovery of indigenous values such as social solidarity and harmony with nature, the envisioning of new modes of communal systems of production and consumption, the recovery and preservation of the commons, and the construction of a non-homogeneous and non-hegemonizing new world.

From this new observation post new and radical modalities of social transformation are envisioned. They reveal that the route for social change is not straightforward; nor is it around the corner, but they also show that within capitalism the pathways, or the road paved by the mainstream agencies of development, inevitably lead to the preservation of the status quo, and thus imply the need for a fundamental reframing of the development question today. This is where critical development studies from a Latin American standpoint come in.

NOTE

1. The significance of Stiglitz's study is that he shows very clearly that the yawning inequalities of our time are not simply the result of the structural forces generated by the contradictions of capitalism, but are the cumulative result of unjust policies and misguided priorities in the interest of the economically dominant ruling class.

REFERENCES

Acosta, Alberto (2012), 'El buen vivir en la senda del posdesarrollo'. In *Renunciar al bien común. Ezxtractivismo y (pos) desarrollo en América Latina*, 282–323. Buenos Aires: Mardulce.
Aguirre Rojas, Carlos (2015), 'La contribución del neozapatismo mexicano al desarrollo del pensamiento crítico contemporáneo'. In *El Pensamiento Crítico frente a la Hidra Capitalista III*, 237–58. Mexico: EZLN.
Albó, Xabier (2009), 'Suma qamaña = el buen convivir'. *Revista Obets* No. 4: 25–40.
Amin, Samir (2010), *Global History: A View from the South*. Oxford: Pambazuka Press.
Amin, Samir (2013), *The Implosion of Contemporary Capitalism*. London: Pluto Press.
Bambirra, Vania (1986), *El capitalismo dependiente latinoamericano*. Mexico: Siglo XXI.
Barkin, David (2017), 'Ecological Economics from Below'. In *The Essential Guide to Critical Development Studies*, edited by Henry Veltmeyer and Paul Bowles. London: Routledge.
Bello, Walden (2006), 'The Capitalist Conjuncture: Over-accumulation, Financial Crises, and the Threat from Globalisation'. *Third World Quarterly* 8 (27): 1345–68.
Betancourt, Rafael and Julia Sagebien (2013), 'Para un crecimiento inclusivo: empresas no estatales responsables en Cuba'. *Temas* No. 75: 58–65.

Borón, Atilio (2008), *Socialismo siglo XXI. ¿Hay vida después del neoliberalismo?* Buenos Aires: Ediciones Luxemburg.

Bresser-Pereira, Luiz C. (2007), 'Estado y mercado en el nuevo desarrollismo'. *Nueva Sociedad* No. 210: 110–25.

Bresser-Pereira, Luiz C. (2009), *Developing Brazil: Overcoming the Failure of the Washington Consensus.* Boulder, CO: Lynne Rienner Publishers.

Cardoso, Fernando H. and Enzo Faletto (1969), *Desarrollo y dependencia en América Latina. Ensayo de interpretación sociológica.* Buenos Aires: Siglo XXI.

Chávez, Hugo (2005), Discurso del presidente Hugo Chávez en foro social mundial de porto alegre, Brasil. 30 January 2005, p. 5. Available at: https://issuu.com/picoyespuelavocesliber tarias-97.3fm/docs/discurso_del_presidente_hugo_ch__ve.

Chossudovsky, Michel (1997), *The Globalisation of Poverty. Impacts of IMF and World Bank Reforms.* London: Zed Books.

Dávalos, Pablo (2008), 'El sumak kawsai (Buen Vivir) y las cesuras del desarrollo'. ALAI, América en Movimiento. Available at: http://www.alainet.org/es/active/23920 (accessed 13 April 2015).

Davis, Mike (2006), *Planet of Slums.* London: Verso.

Delgado Wise, Raúl (2013), 'The Migration and Labor Question Today: Imperialism, Unequal Development, and Forced Migration'. *Monthly Review* 64 (9): 25–38.

Delgado Wise, Raúl and David Martin (2015), 'The Political Economy of Global Labour Arbitrage'. In *The International Political Economy of Production*, edited by Kees van der Pijl, 59–75. Cheltenham, UK and Northampton, MA, USA: Edward Elgar Publishing.

Delgado Wise, Raúl, Mónica Chávez and Héctor Rodríguez (2016), 'La Innovación y la Migración calificada en la Encrucijada: Reflexiones a partir de la Experiencia Mexicana'. *Revista Interdisciplinar da Mobilidade Humana* 47 (3): 153–74.

Dos Santos, Theotonio (2003), *La teoría de la dependencia: balance y perspectivas.* Buenos Aires: Plaza Janés.

Dos Santos, Theotonio (2010), *Economía mundial. Integración regional y desarrollo sustentable: Las nuevas tendencias y la integración latinoamericana.* Lima: Infodem.

Echeverría, Bolívar (2011), *Crítica de la modernidad capitalista.* La Paz: Vicepresidencia del Estado Plurinacional de Bolivia.

EZLN Sexta Comisión (2015), *El pensamiento crítico frente a la hidra capitalista.* Vol. 1. Available at: http://enlacezapatista.ezln.org.mx/2015/07/13/indice-volumen-uno-participaci ones-de-la-comision-sexta-del-ezln-en-el-seminario-el-pensamiento-critico-frente-a-la-hidra-capitalista (accessed 13 April 2015).

Fabra Ribas, Antonio (1943), *The Cooperative Movement in Latin America: Its Significance in Memisphere Solidarity.* Albuquerque: The University of New Mexico Press.

Farah, Ivonne and Luciano Vasapollo (eds) (2011), *Vivir Bien: ¿Paradigma no capitalista?* La Paz: Universidad Mayor de San Andrés (CIDES-UMSA) y Departamento de Economía de la Universidad de Roma La Sapienza.

Fine, Ben, Costas Lapavitsas and Jonathan Pincus (2001), *Development Policy in the Twenty-First Century: Beyond the Post-Washington Consensus.* London and New York: Routledge.

Foster, John B., Robert W. McChesney and Jamil Jonna (2011), 'The Internationalization of Monopoly Capital'. *Monthly Review* 63 (2): 3–18.

Frank, André G. (1970), *Capitalismo y subdesarrollo en América Latina.* Buenos Aires: Siglo XXI.

Furtado, Celso (1970), *Obstacles to Development in Latin America.* New York: Anchor Books/Doubleday.

Gudynas, Eduardo (2015), *Extractivismos. Ecología, economía y política de un modo de entender el desarrollo y la Naturaleza.* Bolivia: CEDIB.

Guillén, Héctor (2007), *México frente a la mundialización neoliberal.* Mexico: Era.

Harnecker, Marta (2010), 'II. Twenty-First Century Socialism'. *Monthly Review* 62 (3): 89–105.

Harvey, David (2005), *A Brief History of Neoliberalism.* Oxford: Oxford University Press.

Infante, Ricardo B. and Osvaldo Sunkel (2009), 'Chile: hacia un desarrollo inclusivo'. *Revista CEPAL* 10 (97): 135–54.
Katz, Claudio (2016), 'Centro y periferia en el marxismo de posguerra'. Available at: http://katz. lahaine.org/b2-img/CENTROYPERIFERIAENELMARXISMODEPOSGUERRA.pdf (accessed 13 April 2015).
Kay, Cristóbal (1989), *Latin American Theories of Development and Underdevelopment*. London: Routledge.
Kay, Cristóbal (2008), 'Reflections on Latin American Rural Studies in the Neoliberal Globalization Period: A New Rurality?' *Development and Change* 39 (6): 915–43.
Klein, Emilio and Víctor Tokman (1988), 'Sector informal: una forma de utilizar como consecuencia de la manera de producir y no viceversa. A propósito de Portes y Benton'. *Estudios Sociológicos* 16 (6): 205–12.
Leiva, Fernando (2008), 'Toward a Critique of Latin American Neostructuralism'. *Latin American Politics and Society* 4 (5): 1–25.
Marini, Ruy M. (1973), *Dialéctica de la dependencia.* Mexico: ERA.
Márquez, Humberto and Raúl Delgado Wise (2011), 'Signos vitales del capitalism neoliberal: imperialismo, crisis y transformación social'. *Estudios Críticos del Desarrollo* 1 (1): 11–50.
Martins, Carlos E. (2011), *Globalizacao, Dependencia e Neoliberalismo na América Latina*. Sao Paulo: Boitempo.
Morley, Samuel A. (1995), 'Structural Adjustment and Determinants of Poverty in Latin America'. In *Coping with Austerity: Poverty and Inequality in Latin America*, edited by Nora Luisting, 42–70. Washington, DC: The Brookings Institution.
Munck, Ronaldo (2015), *Rethinking Latin America: Development, Hegemony and Social Transformation*. New York: Palgrave Macmillan.
Osorio, Jaime (2009), *Explotación redoblada y actualidad de la revolución*. México. UAM-X.
Petras, James and Fernando Leiva (1994), *Democracy and Poverty in Chile: The Limits of Electoral Politics*. Boulder, CO: Westview Press.
Petras, James and Henry Veltmeyer (2002), 'Auto-gestión de trabajadores en una perspectiva histórica'. In *Produciendo Realidad. Las Empresas Comunitarias*, edited by Enrique Carpintero and Mario Hernandez. Buenos Aires: Ediciones.
Petras, James and Henry Veltmeyer (2005), *Social Movements and the State: Argentina, Bolivia, Brazil, Ecuador*. London: Pluto.
Petras, James and Henry Veltmeyer (2013), *Social Movements in Latin America: Neoliberalism and Popular Resistance*. Basingstoke: Palgrave Macmillan.
Portes, Alejandro and Lauren Benton (1987), 'Desarrollo industrial y absorción laboral: una reinterpretación'. *Estudios Sociológicos* (13) 5: 111–37.
Solón, Pablo (ed.) (2012), *¿Es posible Vivir Bien?* La Paz: Fundación Solón.
Sotelo, Adrián (2005), *América Latina. De crisis y paradigmas*. México: Plaza y Valdes.
Sunkel, Osvaldo (1993), *Development from Within: Toward a Neostructuralist Approach for Latin America*. Boulder, CO: Lynne Rienner.
Sunkel, Osvaldo (2013), 'Democracy and the Socioeconomic and Political Consequences of Neoliberalism'. In *Development in an Era of Neoliberal Globalization*, edited by Henry Veltmeyer. London and New York: Routledge.
Tokman, Víctor (1991), 'El Enfoque PREALC'. In *El Sector Informal en América Latina, dos décadas de análisis*, edited by Víctor Tokman. Mexico: CONACULTA.
Veltmeyer, Henry (2007), *On the Move: The Politics of Social Change in Latin America*. Toronto: University of Toronto Press.
Veltmeyer, Henry (2016), 'The Social Economy in Latin America: Alter- or Post-Development? Rethinking Latin America: Towards a New Paradigm'. Keynote address. University Seminar – Prospects for a Sustainable and Equitable Transition. Juraj Dobrila at Pula University, Pula, Croatia, 16–17 June.
Veltmeyer, Henry and James Petras (2014), *The New Extractivism: A Post-Neoliberal Development Model or Imperialism of the Twenty-First Century?* London: Zed Books.
Walton, John and Charles Ragin (1990), 'Global and National Sources of Political Protest: Third World Responses to the Debt Crisis'. *American Sociological Review* 55 (6): 876–90.

Wanderley, Fernanda (ed.) (2015), *La economía solidaria en la economía plural: Discursos, prácticas y resultados en Bolivia.* La Paz: CIDES-UMSA.

Wilpert, Gregory (2007), *Changing Venezuela by Taking Power: The History and Policies of the Chavez Government.* London: Verso.

World Bank (2001), *Reviewing Poverty Reduction Strategy Program.* Washington, DC: World Bank.

World Bank (2007), *Meeting the Challenges of Global Development.* Washington, DC: World Bank.

Zibechi, Raúl (2008), *Autonomías y emancipaciones. América Latina en movimiento.* México: Bajo Tierra.

Zibechi, Raúl (2015), 'Participación de Raúl Zibechi'. In *El Pensamiento Crítico frente a la Hidra Capitalista III*, 228–36. Mexico: EZLN.

13. Development in Africa as the global commodity super-cycle ends: African uprisings during and after 'Africa Rising'
Patrick Bond

INTRODUCTION: AFRICANS UPRISING

The conditions for reproduction of daily life in Africa have not improved as a result of the frenetic expansion of global capitalism, given that this process has, for the past third of a century: entailed structural adjustment austerity imposed by the Bretton Woods Institutions; has been carried out by dictatorships or, at best, semi-democratic regimes; has had the effect of deepening Resource Curses due to extractive industry exploitation and has amplified other political, economic and ecological injustices.

The period of so-called 'secular stagnation' which the world entered in 2007, but whose roots go back several decades, has exacerbated all these problems. As a result, contrary to 'Africa Rising' rhetoric, from late 2010 a new wave of protests arose across the continent. The African Development Bank (AfDB) commissions annual measurements, based upon journalistic data, which suggest that major public protests rose from an index level of 100 in 2000 to nearly 450 in 2011. Much of the turmoil in Africa prior to the 2011 upsurge took place in the vicinity of mines and mineral wealth (Berman et al., 2014). After the so-called Arab Spring – especially acute in Tunisia, Egypt and Morocco – the index of protests rose higher still, to 520 in 2012, as Algeria, Angola, Burkina Faso, Chad, Gabon, Morocco, Nigeria, South Africa and Uganda maintained the momentum of 2011 (African Development Bank et al., 2013). In 2013, the index rose still higher, to 550 (African Development Bank et al., 2014). From that peak level, there was an ebb, declining to the 350 index level by 2016. The AfDB and its co-authors found that, by then, the main causes of protest had shifted to socio-economic injustices:

> unemployment remains the most pressing issue for African citizens. Citizens think governments should address this issue and also spend more money on it. Healthcare and education are respectively the second and third most mentioned problems. At the same time, expectations for better infrastructure have been on the rise since 2008 ... African citizens tend to have low net satisfaction rates with their public services compared with the rest of the world. (African Development Bank et al., 2015, p. 129)

African uncivil society activists – those willing to express frustration in means other than what are often termed the 'invited spaces' of official participation – have been protesting at an increasing rate. There are various ways to measure this activity, including police statistics, journalistic accounts and business executive surveys. According to (Pentagon-sponsored 'Minerva') research carried out at the Universities of Sussex and Texas, protest incidents rose dramatically in 2010–11 and stayed at remarkably high levels in many African cities.

In 2010, the Armed Conflict Location and Event Data (ACLED) database recorded scores of violent protests, or riots, in Cairo and Alexandria, Mogadishu, Nairobi, the cities and towns on the Gulf of Guinea – especially in Nigeria – and the four largest South African cities: Johannesburg-Pretoria, Cape Town, Durban and Port Elizabeth (see Figure 13.1). In

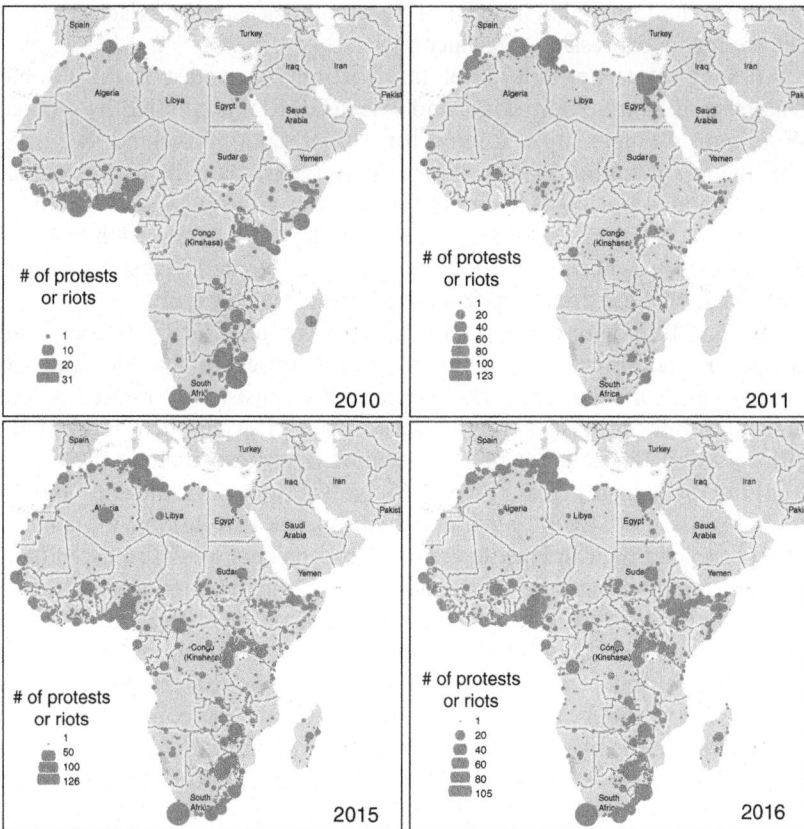

Figure 13.1   Protests and riots (armed conflict location and event data)

2011, the dozens of protests in these cities continued but Tunis, Algiers and Cairo were now measured as hosting more than 100 protests each. In the 2015–16 measurements, the continent had even more intense protest sites across North Africa, Nigeria and South Africa. In addition, Southern Africa witnessed high levels of protests in Harare, Zimbabwe and in Kinshasa and Goma, in the Democratic Republic of the Congo, and in Zambia and Madagascar with the capitals of Lusaka and Antananarivo recording substantial increases compared to 2011. East Africa and the Horn witnessed scores of protests: in Nairobi, Kenya; Kampala, Uganda; Bujumbura, Burundi; Khartoum, Sudan; and in Ethiopia, Addis Ababa and surrounding towns. West African protests were led by Nigerians but there were many other scattered sites of social unrest in the Gulf of Guinea. In North Africa in 2016, there were new rounds of protests in the main 2011 sites: Tunisia, Egypt, Libya and Algeria. Although the counter-revolution had prevailed in most of these countries, the activists were not deterred from expressing grievances.

Another interesting source of information on protest is the Global Database of Events, Language, and Tone (GDELT), initiated by George Washington University's Center for Cyber and Homeland Security, drawing upon millions of media reports. Latest data from November 2016 show that hot-spots included Tunisia, Libya, Nigeria, Côte d'Ivoire, Cameroon, Tanzania, Malawi, Zambia and South Africa. Other world protest sites that month included the US, due to Donald Trump's election, and India, where currency restructuring was extremely painful.

The AfDB and its partners also measure protests, using Reuters and Agence France Press reports, and, in 2017, observed that demand for higher wages and better working conditions consistently ranked as the main reason for protests in recent years (African Development Bank et al., 2015, p. 129). These types of socio-economic protests include the fabled Tunisian revolt in 2011, catalysed by Mohamed Bouazizi's self-immolation. Both Tunisia and Egypt generated such intense revolutionary bursts of energy because their independent labour movements were also ascendant. Notwithstanding extreme unevenness across and within the continent's trade unions, Africa is ripe for a renewed focus on class struggle.

Indeed, as socio-economic conditions continue to deteriorate, the World Economic Forum's (WEF's) annual *Global Competitiveness Reports* – an annual survey of 14,000 business executives in 138 countries – have ranked the continent's workers as the least cooperative on earth (see Table 13.1). In 2016, workforces from South Africa (the world's most militant every year since 2012), Chad, Tunisia, Liberia, Mozambique, Morocco, Lesotho, Ethiopia, Tanzania, Algeria and Burundi were in the top 25 most confrontational proletariats (World Economic Forum, 2013) while the most cooperative workers were in Norway, Switzerland, Singapore, Denmark and Sweden.

With GDP declining (to just 1.4 per cent in 2016), commodity prices remaining low and declining levels of transnational corporate investment increasingly exploiting the continent, the contradictions may well lead to more socio-political explosions. The idea of a 'double-movement' – that is, social resistance against marketization, as suggested by Karl Polanyi ([1944] 1957) in *The Great Transformation* – has long applied to Africa. International Monetary Fund (IMF) austerity and subsequent 'IMF Riots' spread across the continent during the 1980s and, to some extent, catalysed democratization movements during the early 1990s, but failed, in the main, to establish durable liberal political regimes. With the spoils of commodity markets going to unaccountable elites, another intense protest wave began in 2011.

Indeed, the current conjuncture is one we can consider as 'Africans *uprising* against the "Africa Rising" myth'. But where the protests go depends upon whether a corresponding ideology, hostile to corporate power, emerges from the ashes, and whether the fragile middle classes unite with the masses in universalistic social and economic policies. This uprising is by no means a revolutionary situation, nor even a sustained rebellion. One of the main reasons for this is the failure of protesters to become a movement, one with a coherent ideology to face the problems of their times with the stamina and insight required.

This is not necessarily a permanent problem, but it is one that Frantz Fanon complained of in *Toward the African Revolution:* 'For my part the deeper I enter into the cultures and the political circles, the surer I am that the great danger that threatens Africa is the absence of ideology' (1967, p. 186). In his 1966 speech 'The weapon of theory,' Amilcar Cabral agreed:

> The ideological deficiency within the national liberation movements, not to say the total lack of ideology – reflecting as this does an ignorance of the historical reality which these movements claim to transform – makes for one of the greatest weaknesses in our struggle against imperialism, if not the greatest weakness of all.

Ironically, as the uprisings gathered steam, the era was being advertised in the mainstream press as 'Africa Rising' (for example, Perry, 2012; Robertson, 2013). Per capita Gross Domestic Product (GDP) levels rose rapidly, with most of the gains occurring from 1999 to 2008. There was even a hoax-type claim from the AfDB's economist, Mthuli Ncube, in April 2011, endorsed by the *The Wall Street Journal,* that 'one in three Africans is middle class' with the absolute number varying from 313 to 350 million (m) (Ncube, 2013). Ncube defined 'middle class' as those who

Table 13.1   Labour militancy of working classes, measured by reputation among corporations
In your country, how do you characterize labour employer relations? [1 = generally confrontational; 7 = generally cooperative]

Rank	Country	Score
1	Norway	6.2
2	Switzerland	6.2
3	Singapore	6.2
4	Denmark	6.1
5	Sweden	6.1
6	Netherlands	5.9
7	Japan	5.8
8	Austria	5.7
9	New Zealand	5.7
10	United Arab Emirates	5.7
11	Luxembourg	5.6
12	Iceland	5.6
13	Qatar	5.5
14	Hong Kong SAR	5.5
15	United Kingdom	5.4
16	Taiwan, China	5.4
17	Malaysia	5.3
18	Rwanda	5.3
19	Ireland	5.3
20	Canada	5.2
21	Bahrain	5.2
22	Finland	5.2
23	Estonia	5.2
24	Costa Rica	5.2
25	Germany	5.1
26	Bhutan	5.1
27	Philippines	5.1
28	Guatemala	5.1
29	Albania	5.1
30	United States	5.0
31	Israel	5.0
32	Malta	4.9
33	Saudi Arabia	4.9
34	Latvia	4.8
35	Mauritius	4.8
36	Thailand	4.8
37	Belgium	4.8

Table 13.1   (continued)

Rank	Country	Score
38	Honduras	4.8
39	Armenia	4.7
40	Panama	4.7
41	Jordan	4.7
42	Brunei Darussalam	4.7
43	Tajikistan	4.7
44	Czech Republic	4.7
45	Indonesia	4.7
46	Lao PDR	4.6
47	China	4.6
48	Colombia	4.6
49	Uganda	4.6
50	Azerbaijan	4.6
51	Portugal	4.6
52	Mexico	4.6
53	Sri Lanka	4.6
54	Australia	4.6
55	Oman	4.5
56	Kuwait	4.5
57	Chile	4.5
58	Côte d'lvoire	4.5
59	Ghana	4.5
60	Kazakhstan	4.5
61	Lithuania	4.5
62	Namibia	4.4
63	Mauritania	4.4
64	Ecuador	4.4
65	Cyprus	4.4
66	Gambia, The	4.4
67	India	4.4
68	Mongolia	4.4
69	Botswana	4.4
70	Cambodia	4.4
71	Nicaragua	4.4
72	Dominican Republic	4.4
73	Zambia	4.3
75	Peru	4.3
76	Barbados	4.3
77	Senegal	4.3
78	Paraguay	4.3
79	Vietnam	4.3
80	Spain	4.3

Table 13.1   (continued)

Rank	Country	Score
81	Macedonia, FYR	4.3
82	Hungary	4.3
83	Jamaica	4.3
84	Mali	4.2
85	Lebanon	4.2
86	Nigeria	4.2
87	Slovak Republic	4.2
88	Congo, Democratic Rep.	4.2
89	Georgia	4.2
90	Ukraine	4.2
91	Bangladesh	4.2
92	Bulgaria	4.2
93	Poland	4.2
94	Madagascar	4.2
95	Kenya	4.2
96	Egypt	4.1
97	Moldova	4.1
98	Gabon	4.1
99	Kyrgyz Republic	4.1
100	Cameroon	4.1
101	Benin	4.1
102	Malawi	4.1
103	Russian Federation	4.1
104	Sierra Leone	4.1
105	Greece	4.0
106	Romania	4.0
107	Cape Verde	4.0
108	Zimbabwe	4.0
109	El Salvador	4.0
110	France	3.9
111	Italy	3.9
112	Montenegro	3.9
113	Yemen	3.9
114	Burundi	3.8
115	Algeria	3.8
116	Tanzania	3.8
117	Ethiopia	3.8
118	Brazil	3.8
119	Turkey	3.8
120	Lesotho	3.7
121	Argentina	3.7
122	Morocco	3.7

Table 13.1   (continued)

Rank	Country	Score
123	Mozambique	3.7
124	Iran, Islamic Rep.	3.7
125	Bosnia and Herzegovina	3.7
126	Serbia	3.7
127	Liberia	3.7
128	Tunisia	3.6
129	Venezuela	3.6
130	Chad	3.5
131	Nepal	3.5
132	Croatia	3.5
133	Bolivia	3.5
134	Pakistan	3.4
135	Korea, Rep.	3.4
136	Uruguay	3.4
137	Trinidad and Tobago	3.2
138	South Africa	2.5

Source: World Economic Forum, *Global Competitiveness Report 2016–17.*

spend between US$2 (*sic*) and US$20 per day, with 20 per cent in the US$2 to US$4 per day range and 13 per cent from US$4 to US$20. Both ranges are poverty-level in most African cities whose price levels place them amongst the world's most expensive.

One of the central reasons for the disconnect between 'Africa Rising' and the poverty experienced by the continent's majority is looting: Illicit Financial Flows (IFFs), as well as *legal* financial outflows, in the form of profits and dividends sent to Transnational Corporate (TNC) headquarters. These profits are mainly drawn from minerals and oil taken from the African soil. In 2015, Global Financial Integrity measured the IFFs from 2004 to 2013 as costing US$18 billion (bn) annually to Nigeria, while sub-Saharan Africa, as a whole, lost 6.1 per cent of GDP annually to IFFs. This was more than 50 per cent higher than the rate for poor countries overall (Kar and Spanjers, 2015, pp. 8–9, 23). Although South African figures have been distorted by the way gold is measured, enormous illicit sums – probably exceeding US$10 bn annually – are assumed to have been spirited out of the country, especially as exchange controls were progressively relaxed and as the country's reputation as the world's leading site of white-collar crime grew.

A general case can be made against TNCs, based on their excessive profiteering and distortion of African economies. The worst form of Foreign Direct Investment (FDI) tends to come solely in search of raw materials. However, the dramatic crash of commodity prices in 2014–15 has served to reduce this type of investment. The crash saw an immediate drop in: oil by 50 per cent; iron ore by 40 per cent; coal by 20 per cent; and copper, gold and platinum by 10 per cent (International Monetary Fund, 2015). Far greater falls can be traced to prior peaks in 2011. Although an uptick occurred in 2016, lower longer-term commodity prices are likely to prevail.

The ebbing of FDI inflows is promising, in part because following the 2002–11 commodity super-cycle, the extractive industries' extreme pressures on people and environments will eventually slow. In some cases, however, corporate desperation will intensify site-specific extractive industry malpractices, as shareholders demand sustained profits, based not on the former high-price regime, but on lower prices and higher extractive volumes. In turn that will generate more extreme forms of ecological degradation, social depravity and labour exploitation, and fewer resources for corporate social responsibility. Traumatic job losses are on the cards – with the Anglo American Corporation (the largest on the continent over most of the twentieth century) announcing in late 2015 that it would scale down mining employment by more than 50 per cent, and sell most South African operations to Vedanta (the super-exploitative Indian firm). On the positive side, that could also mean less financial looting of Africa, as was the case in 2008–10 when prices and profits were also lower.

To gauge the extent of the problem we consider the following lines of argument: excessive profits are exiting Africa as IFFs; *licit* (legal) financial flows are also worthy of more concern; FDI continues to leave Africa poorer; the need to pay TNCs their profits and dividends in hard currency recently raised Africa's foreign debt to unprecedented heights; South African sub-imperial accumulation is worsening; new subsidized infrastructure and financing will exacerbate African underdevelopment; uncompensated mineral and oil/gas ('natural capital') depletion continues; land grabs, militarization and climate change are all growing threats to the continent; and the 2017 German finance ministry's G20 strategy – the G20 Compact with Africa – will exacerbate all these tendencies. Finally, only more social resistance – but with stronger ideological orientations – can halt and reverse these trends.

ILLICIT FINANCIAL FLOWS

The IFFs reflect many of the corrupt ways in which wealth is withdrawn from Africa, mostly in the extractives sector. These TNC tactics include mis-invoicing inputs, transfer pricing and other trading scams, tax avoidance and evasion of royalties, bribery, 'round-tripping' investment through tax havens, and simple theft of profits via myriad gimmicks aimed at removing resources from Africa. Examples abound:

- in South Africa, Sarah Bracking and Khadija Sharife (2014) reported that De Beers mis-invoiced US$2.83 bn of diamonds over six years;
- the Alternative Information and Development Centre (2014) showed that Lonmin's platinum operations – notorious at Marikana not far from Johannesburg, where the firm was complicit in a massacre of 34 of its wildcat-striking mineworkers in 2012 – has spirited hundreds of millions of dollars offshore to Bermuda since 2000;
- the Chief Executive of the Indian mining house, Vedanta, bragged at a Bangalore meeting that he bought Zambia's Konkola Copper Mines (Africa's largest), for US$25 m in 2006 and then reaped at least US$500 m profits from it annually, apparently through an accounting scam (*Lusaka Times*, 2014).

The most detailed analysis of IFFs at continental scale has been carried out by Burundian political economist Leonce Ndikumana who, with colleagues James Boyce and Adeth Ndyiaye in 2014, showed that, largely due to exploitation, Africa is now 'more integrated but more marginalised' in world trade. Ndikumana subsequently authored a UN Conference on Trade and Development (2015) critique of extractive industries, and the South African and Zambian cases generated intense rebuttals from mining industry representatives about poor statistical quality. While this has required a recalculation, especially of copper and gold exports, the overall critique of IFFs remains intact. There are also policy-oriented NGOs working against IFFs across Africa and the south, including several with northern roots like Trust Africa's 'Stop the Bleeding' campaign, Global Financial Integrity, Tax Justice Network, Publish What You Pay and Eurodad. IFFs are a subject of research and economic critique that give hope to many who want Africa's scarce revenues to be recirculated inside poor countries, not siphoned away to offshore financial centres.

Nevertheless, the implicit theory of change adopted by the head offices of some such NGOs is dubious: because *transparency* is like a harsh light that can *disinfect* corruption, their task is mainly a matter of making capitalism cleaner by bringing problems like IFFs to the public's and regulators' attention. To their credit, many NGOs and allied funders and grass-roots activists generated sufficient advocacy pressure to compel the African Union and UN Economic Commission on Africa to commission an IFF study led by former South African president Thabo Mbeki (2015).

Reporting in mid-2015 and using a conservative methodology updated in 2016, his estimate is that IFFs from Africa exceed US$80 bn a year. The IFF looting is mostly – but not entirely – related to the extractive industries. In an even more narrow accounting than Mbeki's, the AfDB and allies' *African Economic Outlook* (African Development Bank et al., 2015) estimated that US$319 bn was robbed from 2001–10, with the most theft in metals, US$84 bn; oil, US$79 bn; natural gas, US$34 bn; minerals, US$33 bn; petroleum and coal products, US$20 bn; crops, US$17 bn; food products, US$17 bn; machinery, US$17 bn; clothing, US$14 bn; and iron and steel, US$13 bn. The charge that Africa is 'resource cursed' fits the data well.

FROM IFFs TO LICIT FINANCAL FLOWS

Even if IFFs were reduced, another reason that FDI leaves Africa much poorer is what can be termed *Licit* Financial Flows (LFFs). These are legal profits and dividends sent home to TNC headquarters after FDI begins to pay off. They are hard to pin down, but can be found within what's called the 'current account', along with trade. According to the IMF's *Regional Economic Outlook* (2017) the last 15 years or so witnessed trade surpluses between sub-Saharan African countries and the rest of the world reaching 5.6 per cent of GDP in 2011, followed by smaller net surpluses and then, in 2015–16, deficits of 3.1 and 2.0 per cent of GDP, respectively, with more deficits projected into the future.

But the current account measures not only whether imports are greater than exports, but also the flows of profits, dividends and interest. Sub-Saharan Africa had a fair balance (and even in 2004–8 an average surplus of 2.1 per cent of GDP). But, since 2011, it has rapidly fallen into the danger zone, with a current account deficit of 4.0 per cent of GDP in 2016, led by Mozambique (–38 per cent), the Republic of the Congo (–29 per cent) and Liberia (–25 per cent). Adding North African countries, the full continent's current account deficit was 6.5 per cent of GDP in 2016, as a result of the fall in oil prices to a low of US$26 a barrel in early 2016.

FDI IN RETREAT

Partly due to the extended low prices of commodities, the difficulty in raising new hard currency to pay profits and dividends rises as FDI falls. From a US$66 bn peak annual inflow in 2008 to a 2016 level of US$56 bn, FDI remains the second major inflow of hard currency, trailing only labour remittances, which were US$65 bn in 2016 (up from an average annual US$42 bn from 2005–9). Globally, annual FDI was US$1.56 trillion (tn) in 2011, fell to US$1.23 tn in 2014, rose to US$1.75 tn in 2015 and then receded to US$1.52 tn in 2016 (UN Conference on Trade and Development, 2016). The largest 2016 inflows of FDI to particular countries – the US with US$385 bn, China (including Hong Kong) with US$231 bn and Britain with US$179 bn – each outstrip Africa, with Singapore and Brazil following, both at US$50 bn of inflows in 2016.

The failure to sustain accumulation through FDI is due, in part, to shrinking commodities markets and the end of the Chinese growth miracle. UNCTAD also records 'an overall increasing share of regulatory and restrictive policies in total investment policy measures over the last decade' as a result of 'a new realism about the economic and social costs of unregulated market forces' although this may also represent, in part, 'investment protectionism' (United Nations Conference on Trade and Development, 2015, p. 128). This applies less in Africa, although South Africa has become more restrictive about trade as a result of deindustrialization, as well as cancelling Bilateral Investment Treaties because they conflict with the country's Black Economic Empowerment policy.

FOREIGN DEBT EXPLODES

The current account deficit in turn requires that state elites attract yet more new FDI, so as to have hard currency on hand to pay back old FDI (usually as profit and dividend outflows), or if that is less available, as now appears the case, to take on new foreign borrowings. So as to cover the payments deficits and slight trade deficit, Africa's foreign debt is soaring. For sub-Saharan Africa, what was a foreign debt in the US$170–210 bn range from 1995 to 2005 (when G7 debt relief lowered it by 10 per cent) rose to nearly US$400 bn by 2015.

In the case of the largest African debtor, South Africa, foreign debt rose from US$25 bn in 1995 to US$35 bn in 2005 and then soared to US$150 bn in 2017, that is, from 20 per cent of GDP in 2005 to more than 50 per cent in 2017. The last time this ratio was reached was in 1985, and the result – thanks also to anti-apartheid activist sanctions' pressure against bankers – was that South African president P.W. Botha defaulted on US$13 bn of short-term debt coming due and imposed exchange controls. The move signalled to the English-speaking capitalist class that the end of apartheid was near and thus, they should hasten to make favourable post-apartheid arrangements with the African National Congress (then in exile). Unfortunately, those arrangements entailed drawing South Africa much deeper into the world economy, and there were at least ten decisions (sometimes termed 'Faustian Pacts') taken by the presidency, finance ministers and reserve bank governors during the 1990s (see following list). Of these the first, the decision to repay US$25 bn of apartheid-era debt, was most damaging:

- repay US$25 bn of inherited apartheid-era foreign debt (October 1993);
- give the South African Reserve Bank 'independence' in the interim constitution (November 1993);
- borrow US$850 m from the IMF with tough neoliberal conditions (December 1993);
- reappoint apartheid-era finance minister Derek Keys and South African Reserve Bank governor Chris Stals after firm IMF advice (May 1994);
- join the General Agreement on Tariffs and Trade (later renamed the World Trade Organization) on highly disadvantageous terms (August 1994);
- lower primary corporate taxes from 48 per cent to 29 per cent and maintain the most important of apartheid privileges for white people and corporations (1994–9);
- privatize peripheral parts of the state and demutualize two huge insurance companies, Old Mutual and Sanlam (1995–9);
- relax exchange controls (the 'finrand') and, as a result of capital flight within a year, raise interest rates to historic levels (March 1995);
- adopt the neoliberal Growth, Employment and Redistribution ('Gear') strategy and a variety of other neoliberal economic, social and environmental policies (June 1996); and
- grant permission to South Africa's largest companies to move their financial headquarters and primary stock market listings to London and New York (1999).

EXPLOITATION ALSO COMES FROM WITHIN AFRICA

More nuance is important in terms of *which* firms are doing the looting. Western TNCs looted Africa for centuries, and continue to do so. But the single biggest country-based source of FDI in Africa is internal, coming from South Africa. A dozen companies with Johannesburg Stock Exchange listings draw out very high levels of FDI profits: British

American Tobacco, SABMiller breweries, the MTN and Vodacom cell phone networks, Naspers newspapers, four banks (Standard, Barclays, Nedbank and FirstRand), the Sasol oil company and the local residues of the Anglo American Corporation empire.

The result is the systematic internal exploitation of the rest of Africa by South African capital, especially as the main retail chains – for example, Walmart-owned Massmart and its affiliates – use the larger market in the south to achieve production economies of scale, production that then swamps and destroys Africa's residual basic-needs manufacturing sector. This is a form of looting also based on the IFF strategies used against South Africa by TNCs. Amongst others, South Africa's MTN cell phone service was reported by the Amabhungane (2015) investigative journalist network to have Mauritian and Dubai financial offices which systematically skim profits for dubious tax-avoidance purposes from high-profit operations in Nigeria, Uganda and South Africa (Mauritian company taxes are 3 per cent with no capital gains). This was a blatant practice when MTN's chairperson was Cyril Ramaphosa, subsequently South Africa's deputy president from 2014. He was also a 9 per cent owner of Lonmin when similar Bermuda platinum 'marketing' operations were a source of tax-avoidance payments (Alternative Information and Development Centre, 2014). More than US$100 m in a World Bank credit line raised by Lonmin in 2007 was meant to construct more than 5,000 housing units, but just three were built, under Ramaphosa's direct responsibility.

When in November 2015 MTN was fined more than US$4 bn by Abuja authorities for its failure to disconnect more than five million unregistered Nigerian customers during the state's attempt to crack down on cell phone use by Boko Haram terrorists, there were few defenders of the firm. Indeed, when South African capital flows elsewhere in Africa, it carries the baggage of its home base, and so when xenophobia broke out in 2015 there were many branch plants of Johannesburg firms that became targets of protest by Nigerians, Zimbabweans, Malawians, Mozambicans and Zambians, concerned about their relatives' safety.

Hostility to Johannesburg capital is logical because its leadership was named the world's most corrupt according to several crucial indicators compiled by PwC in 2014, as 80 per cent of managers admitted to the firm that they commit economic crimes and South African firms were the 'world leaders in money-laundering, bribery and corruption, procurement fraud, asset misappropriation and cyber-crime' (Hosken, 2014, p .1).

At the same time, since the late 1990s, South Africa's current account deficit has soared because the country's biggest companies, almost without exception, relocated to London or New York, and took LFFs with them: Anglo American and its historic partner De Beers, plus SABMiller,

Investec bank, Old Mutual insurance, Didata IT, Mondi paper, Liberty life insurance, Gencor (BHP Billiton) and a few others. As a result, in mid-2015, the South African Reserve Bank (2015) revealed that Johannesburg firms were, in 2012–14, drawing in only half as much in internationally-sourced profits ('dividend receipts') as TNCs were taking out of South Africa. But that was an improvement from the 2009–11 period, when local TNCs pulled in only a third of what foreigners took out. One reason for this is that Johannesburg firms have been busier in the rest of Africa in the past few years, as mining, cell phones, banking, brewing, construction, tobacco, tourism and other services from South Africa became more available up-continent.

INCLEMENT PUBLIC SUBSIDIZATION AND PRIVATE FINANCING OF DESTRUCTIVE FDI

A continual threat to the continent is more frenetic mining and petroleum extraction, as a result of state subsidies, notwithstanding falling prices. The largest will go to the Programme for Infrastructure Development in Africa (PIDA). The donor-supported, trillion-dollar strategy is mainly aimed at extraction. New roads, railroads, pipelines and bridges are planned, but they largely emanate from mines, oil/gas rigs and plantations, and are mainly directed towards ports. Electricity generation is overwhelmingly biased towards projected mining and smelting needs, although the case of Eskom – which faced load-shedding in early 2015 – is illustrative, as demand for its product fell at least 5 per cent in late 2015 as shafts and foundries were shuttered due to adverse economic conditions.

Subsidies of the sort envisaged in PIDA could bring back the worst of the FDI, especially from BRICS (Brazil, Russia, India, China, South Africa) companies like Brazil's Vale mining (in Mozambique), Russia's Rosatom nuclear (in a proposed US$100 bn deal with Pretoria), India's Vedanta (extremely exploitative in Zambia), various Chinese parastatals, and the profusion of unethical Johannesburg firms (to illustrate, the military has looted Zimbabwe's diamonds and the largest dam builder was banned by the World Bank in 2014 due to African bribery). One route through which they anticipate receiving indirect financing subsidies – that is, loans at preferential rates – is via the BRICS New Development Bank. For example, one new director, South Africa's Tito Mboweni, had earlier derided the NDB as 'very costly' and yet just after his appointment he told Bloomberg that nuclear financing 'falls squarely within the mandate of the NDB' (Bloomberg, 2015).

Potentially, any new public institution should be welcome if it grapples with market failures, especially related to development finance. For example, private financing from South Africa is becoming instrumental to extraction across the continent, now that the South African Reserve Bank is liberalizing exchange controls with the rest of Africa in mind. But as the climate campaigning group 350.org Africa (2014) points out, 'South African banks are greenwashing their work while funding Africa's growing addiction to fossil fuels at the same time', by targeting 'massive coal power stations, oil refineries and drilling rigs'. These include Nedbank, Barclays (owner of ABSA) and Standard Bank which, together, invested more than US$1 bn in coal projects alone in the period 2005–13. It is fair to predict that the BRICS NDB and PIDA will amplify the problems given the prevailing power structure.

UNCOMPENSATED NATURAL CAPITAL DEPLETION

The financing and FDI aimed at extraction are responsible for depletion of non-renewable resources without the kinds of reinvestment that are more common in sites like Norway, Australia and Canada, whose economies are also resource-based but not nearly so 'resource cursed' as Africa. This is in large part because they host headquarters of mining and petroleum TNCs. Many BRICS corporations appear oriented to rapid depletion of Africa's 'natural capital', a term used by economists to describe natural resource endowments. Although the end of the commodity super-cycle will mean a lower rate of extraction, this should not blind Africans to the continent's residual colonial-era bias towards the removal of non-renewable minerals, oil and gas, the exploitation of which leaves Africa far poorer in net terms than anywhere else on earth. That bias towards non-renewable resource depletion without reinvestment meant the continent's net wealth fell rapidly after 2001.

Even the World Bank admits, in its *Wealth of Nations* series (2011, 2014), that 88 per cent of sub-Saharan African countries suffered net negative wealth accumulation in 2010. In contrast, what is termed 'Adjusted Net Savings' rose in Latin America and East Asia.

THE CRISIS CONTINUES THROUGH LAND GRABS, CLIMATE CHANGE AND MILITARIZATION

There are several other devastating features of contemporary African political economy and political ecology, in the form of land grabs, militarization and climate change. The most immediate threats face the African peasantry, especially women, and especially those in areas attractive to foreign investors. Already, small farmers are being displaced in areas of Ethiopia and Mozambique as a result of land grabs by Middle Eastern countries and India, South Africa and China (Ferrando, 2013). The growing role of the US military's Africa Command in dozens of African countries bears testimony to Washington's overlapping desire to maintain control amidst rising Islamic fundamentalism from the Sahel to Kenya, areas which are, coincidentally, theatres of war in the vicinity of large petroleum reserves (Turse, 2014).

Climate change will affect the most vulnerable Africans in the poorest countries, who are already subject to extreme stress as a result of war-torn socio-economic fabrics in West Africa, the Great Lakes and the Horn of Africa. The Pentagon-funded University of Texas's Strauss Center is acutely concerned about the extent to which social unrest will emerge, as a result.

ENDING THE LOOTING AND ROASTING OF AFRICA

Finally, to halt the uncompensated depletion, to address climate change properly (for example, with systematic demands for climate debt reparations to be paid to African climate victims), and to prevent the BRICS from adopting explicitly sub-imperial accumulation strategies will require more coherence from those engaged in a variety of African uprisings, especially those referenced in the first section of this chapter.

To take the most auspicious example, much labour movement activism is still rooted in micro-shop floor and industry-level sectoral demands. Shifting to a broader ideological terrain, to national policy contestation and to Africa-wide solidarity are huge tasks. The South African working-class turn to xenophobia in 2008, 2010 and 2015 (and in between) shows that even the most advanced, militant proletariat can revert to Othering rather than adopting continental and internationalist solidarity.

Still, once organized labour – in unison with community, environmental, women's and other groups – take the lead in the 'Africans uprising' against the 'Africa Rising' constituency of extractive industries and neoliberal policy managers, a different set of policies will be advocated. An egalitarian economic argument will be increasingly easier to make now that global capitalism is forcing Africa towards rebalancing. That will compel, ultimately, a much more courageous economic policy which will, according to Bond and Garcia (2015):

- in the short term, re-impose exchange controls to better control both illicit and licit financial flows; lower interest rates to boost growth; audit 'odious debt' before further repayment; and better control imports and exports;
- adopt an ecologically sensitive industrial policy aimed at import substitution, sectoral re-balancing, social needs and true sustainability;
- increase state social spending paid for by higher corporate taxes, cross-subsidization and more domestic borrowing;
- reorient infrastructure to meet unmet basic needs and expand/maintain/improve the energy grid, sanitation, public transport, clinics, schools, recreational facilities and the internet; and
- in places like South Africa and Nigeria, rife with fossil fuels, adopt 'Million Climate Jobs' strategies to generate employment for a genuinely green 'Just Transition'.

These are radical-sounding policies. But assuming state power can be won in a democratic election, they are attractive to those Africans with even a 'Keynesian' world view, aiming to rescue capitalism from its most self-destructive instincts. Indeed, John Maynard Keynes was the most brilliant economist of the last century when it came to saving capitalism from its worst excesses. As Keynes (1933, p. 756) put it in his *Yale Review* 'National Self-Sufficiency' essay:

> I sympathise with those who would minimise, rather than with those who would maximise, economic entanglement among nations. Ideas, knowledge, science, hospitality, travel – these are the things which should of their nature be international. But let goods be homespun whenever it is reasonably and conveniently possible and, above all, let finance be primarily national.

Today we might term this the 'globalization of people and deglobalization of capital', and it is a perfect way to sloganize a sound short-term economic strategy appropriate for Africa. Samir Amin, the continent's greatest political economist, has argued for this sort of delinking strategy since the 1960s. It is time those arguments were dusted off and put to work, to help Africans continue to rise against the 'Africa Rising' meme and all that it represents.

Those who would dispute this line of argument must confront evidence of the futility of Africa's export-led economic fantasies, whether via the West or BRICS economies, in view of the continuing Great Recession, the dramatic downturn in world trade over the past year, the decline in rich country GDP to a 2 per cent annual level, and recessionary conditions in emerging markets. And, finally, there is also a political-ecological imperative to reboot the fossil fuel-addicted sectors of the economy as the world necessarily moves to post-carbon life. The Naomi Klein book *This Changes Everything* (2014) bears witness to the need to restructure a great many areas of life:

- energy (oil/coal to renewables);
- transport (private to public, shipping to local production);
- urban form (from sprawling suburbs to compact cities);
- housing/services (from hedonism to socio-ecological);
- agriculture/food (from semi-feudal, sugar-saturated, carbon-intensive, plantation grown to organic, cooperative and vegetarian-centric);
- production (from multinational-corporate capitalist logic to 'Just Transition' localization, eco-social planning and cooperation);
- consumption (from advertisement-driven, high-carbon, import-intensive and materialistic to de-commodified basic-needs guarantees and eco-socially sound consumption norms);
- disposal (from planned obsolescence to 'zero-waste');
- health, education, arts and social policy (from capitalist-determined to post-carbon, post-capitalist);
- social/private space (from durable race/class/gender segregation to public space, recreation, desegregation and human liberation).

This, then, is the major challenge for Africans who rise up against injustice, especially those forms which can generate solidarity with the rest of the world's progressive people, and even their own middle classes. It is only in sketching out contradictions and opportunities that we can project forward several decades. But at this critical juncture, as the commodity super-cycle's denouement makes obvious the need for change, at least it is evident that Africans are not lying down. After the 2011 peak of the commodity super-cycle, it was simply illogical to proclaim that Africa was 'rising' given its economies' dependence on primary exports and with most major mining houses' value crashing on the world's stock exchanges. Not even the more intensive corporate exploitation of Africa can disguise the crisis. This case requires continuous revisiting, given how damaging the neoliberal export-orientated strategy (and middle-class rising myth with it) has been to genuine popular development, gender equity and Africa's natural environment.

REFERENCES

350.org Africa (2014), 350 Africa.org Launches Fossil Free Africa Campaign with Call on Dirty South African Banks to Stop Financing Fossil Fuel Projects, Johannesburg. Available at:

http://350africa.org/2014/11/26/350-africa-org-launches-fossil-free-africa-campaign-with-call-on-dirty-south-african-banks-to-stop-financing-fossil-fuel-projects/.

African Development Bank, OECD Development Centre, UN Development Programme and Economic Commission for Africa (2013), *African Economic Outlook*, Tunis. Available at: http://www.undp.org/content/dam/rba/docs/Reports/African%20Economic%20Outlook%202013%20En.pdf.

African Development Bank, OECD Development Centre, UN Development Programme and Economic Commission for Africa (2014), *African Economic Outlook*, Tunis. Available at: http://www.undp.org/content/dam/rba/docs/Reports/African%20Economic%20Outlook%202014%20En.pdf.

African Development Bank, OECD Development Centre, UN Development Programme and Economic Commission for Africa (2015), *African Economic Outlook*, Tunis. Available at: http://www.undp.org/content/dam/rba/docs/Reports/African%20Economic%20Outlook%202015%20En.pdf.

Alternative Information and Development Centre (2014), Lonmin, the Marikana Massacre and the Bermuda Connection, Cape Town. Available at: http://aidc.org.za/lonmin-the-marikana-massacre-and-the-bermuda-connection-seminar-and-press-conference/.

Amabhungane (2015), Ramaphosa and MTN's Offshore Stash. *Mail & Guardian*, 8 October. Available at: http://amabhungane.co.za/article/2015-10-08-ramaphosa-and-mtns-offshore-stash.

Berman, N., M. Couttenier, D. Rohner and M. Thoenig (2014), This Mine is Mine! How Minerals Fuel Conflicts in Africa, *American Economic Review* 107, 6: 1564–1610.

Bloomberg (2015), '$100billion BRICS lender more keen on risk World Bank', 10 July. Available at: https://www.bloomberg.com/news/articles/2015-07-10/brics-100-billion-lender-seeks-riskier-projects-than-world-bank.

Bond, P. and A. Garcia (2015), *BRICS: An Anti-Capitalist Critique*, London: Pluto Press.

Bracking, S. and K. Sharife (2014), Rough and Polished. Manchester University Leverhulme Centre for the Study of Value. Available at: http://thestudyofvalue.org/wp-content/uploads/2014/05/WP4-Bracking-Sharife-Rough-and-polished-15May.pdf.

Fanon, F. (1967) *Toward the African Revolution – Political Essays*. New York: Grove Press.

Ferrando, T. (2013), BRICS, BITs and Land Grabbing: Are South-South Relationships Really Different? Unpublished paper, Paris: Sciences Po Law School.

Hosken, G. (2014), World Fraud Champs, *The Times*, 19 February. Available at: https://www.pressreader.com/south-africa/the-times-south-africa/20140219/281479274320165.

International Monetary Fund (2015), *Regional Economic Outlook: Africa*. Washington, DC. Available at: http://www.imf.org/external/pubs/ft/reo/2015/afr/eng/pdf/sreo0415.pdf.

International Monetary Fund (2017), *Regional Economic Outlook: Africa*, Washington DC, http://www.imf.org/external/pubs/ft/reo/2017/afr/eng/pdf/sreo0415.pdf.

Kar, D. and J. Spanjers (2015), *Illicit Financial Flows from Developing Countries: 2004–2013*. Washington, DC: Global Financial Integrity.

Keynes, J.M. (1933), National Self-Sufficiency. *Yale Review*, Summer. Available at: http://www.panarchy.org/keynes/national.1933.html.

Klein, N. (2014), *This Changes Everything*. New York: Simon and Schuster.

Lusaka Times (2014), Video – Vedanta Boss Saying KCM Makes $500 Million Profit Per Year, Lusaka, 13 May. Available at: https://www.lusakatimes.com/2014/05/13/video-vedanta-boss-saying-kcm-makes-500-million-profit-per-year/.

Mbeki, T. (2015), Track it! Stop it! Get it! Illicit Financial Flow, Report of the High Level Panel on Illicit Financial Flows from Africa, United Nations Economic Commission on Africa, Addis Ababa. Available at: http://www.uneca.org/iff.

Ncube, M. (2013), *The Middle of the Pyramid: Dynamics of the African Middle Class*, Tunis, African Development Bank. Available at: http://www.afdb.org/fileadmin/uploads/afdb/Documents/Publications/The%20Middle%20of%20the%20Pyramid_The%20Middle%20of%20the%20Pyramid.pdf.

Ndikumana, L. (2015), Integrated Yet Marginalized: Implications of Globalization for African Development. University of Massachusetts/Amherst Political Economy Research Institute.

Available at: http://www.peri.umass.edu/236/hash/b3af64ea1d53b2a932a8b6cd57e45e6d/publication/653/.

Ndikumana, L., J. Boyce and A. Ndyiaye (2014), Capital Flight: Measurement and Drivers. University of Massachusetts/Amherst Political Economy Research Institute. Available at: http://www.peri.umass.edu/236/hash/b3af64ea1d53b2a932a8b6cd57e45e6d/publication/653/.

Perry, A. (2012), Africa Rising. *Time*, 3 December.

Polanyi, K. ([1944] 1957), *The Great Transformation: The Political and Economic Origins of Our Time*. Boston: Beacon Press.

Robertson, C. (2013), Why Africa Will Rule the 21st Century. *African Business*, 7 January 2013. Available at: http://africanbusinessmagazine.com/features/profile/why-africa-will-rule-the-21st-century.

South African Reserve Bank (2015), *Quarterly Bulletin* (June 2015), Pretoria. Available at: https://www.resbank.co.za/Publications/Detail-Item-View/Pages/Publications.aspx?sarbweb=3b6aa07d-92ab-441f-b7bf-bb7dfb1bedb4&sarblist=21b5222e-7125-4e55-bb65-56fd3333371e&sarbitem=6776.

Turse, N. (2014), AFRICOM Becomes a 'War-Fighting Combatant Command'. Available at: http://www.tomdispatch.com/blog/175830/tomgram%3A_nick_turse,_africom_becomes_a_%22war-fighting_combatant_command%22.

United Nations Conference on Trade and Development (UNCTAD) (2015), *World Investment Report 2015*, Geneva. Available at: http://unctad.org/en/PublicationsLibrary/webdiaepcb2013d11_en.pdf.

United Nations Conference on Trade and Development (UNCTAD) (2016), *Global Investments Trends Monitor* No. 22. Available at: http://unctad.org/en/PublicationsLibrary/webdiaeia2016d1_en.pdf.

World Bank (2011), *The Changing Wealth of Nations*. Washington, DC: World Bank.

World Bank (2014), *Little Green Data Book*. Washington, DC: World Bank.

World Economic Forum (2013), *Global Competitiveness Report, 2013–2014*, Davos. Available at: http://www.weforum.org/issues/global-competitiveness.

14. Tracing the emergence of Sino-capitalism: social change and development in contemporary China
Christopher A. McNally

INTRODUCTION

China provides an incisive example of a society that experimented during the twentieth century with perhaps every major social development model in existence at that time. Throughout the late nineteenth and early twentieth centuries, the monarchic Qing Dynasty sought to transform itself while facing increasing encroachment from Western powers and later Japan. Within-system reform of the Imperial Confucian system failed, and China began its first experiment with republicanism and modern Western constitutionalism after the 1911 Xinhai Revolution. Following a prolonged period of warlordism and internal strife, Chiang Kai-shek's regime veered towards fascism and the state-centred national development models in vogue during the early 1930s. But yet again, this experiment was arrested by Japan's invasion and subsequent occupation of northern, eastern and central China during the 1930s and the Second World War.

After Japan's surrender in 1945, another period of civil war was followed by the establishment of the People's Republic of China (PRC) in 1949. With this, for the first time during the twentieth century, a regime powerful enough to effectively govern all of mainland China came into existence. In its early years, the Chinese Communist Party (CCP) adopted, more or less wholesale, the Soviet model based on totalitarian social governance and central economic planning. But as with China's other social development experiments, this one did not last long. By 1956 Mao Tse-tung had decided to leave the Soviet model behind and engage in some of the most radical socio-economic experiments of the twentieth century. The Great Leap Forward from 1958 to 1962 ended in an economic disaster of massive proportions, causing the largest man-made famine in history. The Cultural Revolution, which began several years later, ended fewer lives, but ravished Chinese society with its lurch into radical socialist revolutionary ideology. By 1979, communist social engineering had fundamentally transformed most institutional vestiges of Confucianism in China, including the role of women and family.

In an ironic twist, the Cultural Revolution created a cultural and moral *tabula rasa* that provided 'an opportunity for Western capitalism to press forth into China without being hindered by traditional factors' (Ku, 2010, p. 35). Capitalism with its insatiable drive for profit and accumulation faced little religious, cultural, or socio-political resistance, but, nonetheless, was never adapted wholesale from the West. Even as its advance in China was amplified by the advent of neoliberal globalization, it took on uniquely Chinese characteristics. Capitalism in China emerged as a hegemonic state project by the CCP to sustain its domination over society and reject Western liberal democracy.

The form of capitalism that evolved in China after 1979 – Sino-capitalism – assimilates residues of the Imperial political economy, as well as those of China's twentieth-century social and economic experiments. Historical layers of Imperial state-society relations, the colonial influences of Western capitalism, especially in the treaty port of Shanghai and the British colony of Hong Kong, the Republican trials with state-led indigenous economic development in the early 1930s, and the establishment of a socialist centrally planned economy during the PRC's early years, are all present under Sino-capitalism. Yet, despite this unique historical background, Sino-capitalism follows earlier examples along the rather well-trodden path of late capitalist development under state tutelage.

The focus of this chapter is on the social experiment of capitalist development begun after Deng Xiaoping ushered in the 'reform and open door' policy. As Ronaldo Munck lays out in his introductory chapter, social development in the contemporary era is historically and analytically coupled with the European experience of the Industrial Revolution. Hence, understanding modernity itself, including China's rapid economic re-emergence, involves the study of the social, economic and cultural quandaries that all societies experience with the advent of industrialization and capitalism.

Capitalism is conceived of as a socio-economic system encompassing three dynamic elements: first, an unceasing drive to accumulate capital; second, the emergence of market society, including increased international economic integration, that ultimately tends to commodify every conceivable good and service; and, finally, the rise of capital-holding social strata to socio-political prominence, transforming, constraining, and empowering the modern state (Heilbroner, 1985; Ingham, 2008; McNally, 2008). Capitalism, moreover, differs from all prior social systems in that it relies on, and fosters, constant change, the creative destruction and reinvention of all socio-economic institutions over time (Schumpeter, 1950). In the contemporary era, there is perhaps no better example of this constant transformation of society and economy than the emergence of Sino-capitalism.

Contemporary China has seen the most expansive, rapid and sustained industrialization in human history, creating opportunities for massive wealth accumulation. But in the same historical time span, Chinese break-neck growth has created some of the largest socio-economic inequalities on earth, massive environmental degradation, and a cultural no man's land of materialism and consumerism in the world's oldest continuous civilization. Perhaps most intriguingly, China's experiences have not corresponded to the standard Western prescriptions for economic development based on liberal markets and politics; neither have they adapted the insights of the post-development and post-globalization perspectives to inspire a new course of development.

The crucial case of China makes clear that there is no standard model of capitalist development, only certain Grundrisse (outlines) of its dynamics. Social change is not a linear cumulative process with a simple teleological path, but is one riddled with complexity, discontinuity, and heterogeneity. We must thus retain a healthy scepticism toward metanar-ratives that posit development as unfolding according to a set recipe leading to a predefined end. Capitalism's trajectory is always driven by historically embedded forces that are unique both in terms of space and time. Nonetheless, this analysis attempts to uncover some of the common analytical facets of late capitalist development, while noting the unique dynamics of Sino-capitalism that are increasingly reshaping the global capitalist system itself.

I start with tracing the emergence of Sino-capitalism in China after 1980, focusing on three elements: late capitalist development under state guidance; the bottom-up dynamics of China's network capitalism; and the influences of neoliberal globalization. The third part analyses the institutional characteristics of Sino-capitalism, noting the unique dialectic characterizing Sino-capitalism's reproduction and the role of China's Leninist party-state. The fourth part looks at the socio-economic consequences of Sino-capitalism in the PRC, especially increased social stratification and the 'Polanyian gamble' (Bowles, 2011) that CCP leaders have attempted since the mid-2000s. The conclusion comes back to the major themes of this *Handbook* and uses the crucial case of China to highlight theoretical implications for the study of social development and change.

THE EMERGENCE OF SINO-CAPITALISM

Capitalist development did not just 'happen' in China. The critical juncture occurred in 1978–9, as the CCP faced a loss of political legitimacy due to the revulsions of the Cultural Revolution and gnawing economic stagnation (Naughton, 1995). Party leaders, first and foremost Deng Xiaoping, realized with shock how far other East Asian economies, including three majority-Chinese societies (Taiwan, Hong Kong, and Singapore), had managed to undertake great spurts of industrialization (Cumings, 1989). Capitalist development thus constituted a deliberate policy choice by the CCP elites. It reversed the radical policies of the Maoist era and began to draw upon a variety of existing development models and historical legacies. As a result, the form of capitalism that emerged in China combines China's historical legacy with Western, Asian developmental, socialist, and modern Chinese reform elements. It is also deeply influenced by China's enormous size and its exposure to the forces of neoliberal globalization from the 1980s onwards. The result of this layering of historical legacies has been to produce a hybrid form of capitalism with unique dynamics – Sino-capitalism.

One of the deepest historical reservoirs on which Sino-capitalism rests is China's Imperial political economy, especially from the Sung Dynasty onwards until the last days of the Qing Dynasty in the early twentieth century. During these dynasties, the state tended to stifle autonomous capital-owning strata, reinforcing a reliance on reciprocal personal ties – guanxi – to undertake business dealings. Rather than the sanctity of contracts and the rule of law, 'ritual and patronage had a strong place in Chinese business institutions' (Faure, 2006, p. 5). A preference for interpersonal accommodation thus hindered the development of bureaucracies, with formalized and universally applicable rules, to govern the economy and foster autonomous capital accumulation (Gates, 1996; Faure, 2006).

Hill Gates (1996) notes how the Imperial Chinese political economy generated a sizeable class of small merchants and producers with often considerable local economic influence. However, what accumulation took place was never for purely private reasons, but always harnessed by the Imperial regime for statist purposes. A dominant state-managed tributary system oversaw a system of commodity production by kin corporations (Gates, 1996). Under this duality, the scholar officialdom harnessed both capital and markets for its own purposes – the maintenance of ritual order.

In essence, China's Imperial political economy generated substantial amounts of private commerce and entrepreneurship, but all under the tutelage of a dominant state. While history does not repeat itself, China's political economy continues to display these historical roots. Capital accumulation is enabled, but ultimately harnessed for state purposes. A vibrant entrepreneurial class is tolerated, but eventually circumscribed by a hegemonic state.

State-led Development

As is the case generally with late developers who have succeeded in rapid industrial catch-up, China has undertaken a form of state-guided capitalist development (McNally, 2012). The PRC constitutes a classical example of a 'latecomer' to the global capitalist system. Gerschenkron's work (1962) highlights the crucial role of the state in late development and its potential to harness the comparative advantages of backwardness to enable rapid catch-up industrialization. East Asian industrialization in Japan, South Korea, Singapore, and Taiwan clearly displayed these dynamics, generating what have been termed 'developmental states' (Johnson, 1982; Wade, 1990; Amsden, 1989; Evans, 1995; McNally and Chu, 2006). Similarly, the more eclectic approaches of the Comparative Capitalisms literature propose that the state fulfils a central role in guiding and, ultimately, enabling capital accumulation and the class compromises sustaining it (Coates, 2000; Boyer, 2005; Schmidt, 2009).

The Chinese experience very much resonates with these analyses. State direction and intervention have played crucial roles in China's capitalist transition and structured the very logic of Sino-capitalism. In practically every sphere of the economy, the CCP party-state remains a major force shaping national, local, and firm-level institutions (Naughton and Tsai, 2015). Although highly powerful in comparative perspective, the Chinese central state is neither omnipotent nor especially efficient. Due to its size, bureaucratic fragmentation, and local autonomies, it faces great challenges in effectively implementing policy measures.

Local initiatives, therefore, have played a crucial role in teasing out policy solutions. Throughout the reform era the CCP has implemented experimental and gradual, yet ultimately, far-reaching reforms. These relied on strengthening and legitimizing already existing autonomies at the local level that gave local cadres political space for a variety of ever bolder economic trials. Indeed, the CCP nomenklatura system – the system that is responsible for party personnel appointments – was employed in the 1980s and 1990s to create strong incentives for local cadres to foster economic growth above all else in their jurisdictions.

The Chinese state itself also reformed over time. By the mid-2000s, several phases of restructuring had generated a state bureaucracy much better suited to the demands of a globalizing market economy (Yang, 2004; Zheng, 2004). Yet even in its reformed structure, the Chinese state retains enormous leeway to intervene in the economy. It has preserved key institutions to implement industrial policy, to influence cadre incentives, and to exert ownership control over state enterprises controlling the commanding heights of industry and finance.

Despite its wide array of policy levers, the Chinese state's role in guiding the political economy comes nowhere near the ideal-type of a 'developmental state' that can effectively implement industrial upgrading policies (Johnson, 1982; Amsden, 1989; Wade, 1990). Bureaucratic fragmentation, China's large size, and overlapping and incongruous features of the state apparatus have created a jumble of authority relations that allow local government interventions to run counter to central policies (Howell, 2006). On the positive side, though, increased autonomies at the local level have created the political space for economic experiments and innovations. These, in turn, have sustained the reform process and facilitated the ever-churning nature of capitalism.

In summary, state-guided late capitalist development forms a central element of Sino-capitalism. As in Germany, Russia, and Japan at the end of the nineteenth century, the role of the state in China was essential for breaking through socio-political barriers and establishing the institutional infrastructure for capitalist accumulation. And as in earlier instances, the pace of development in China has accelerated once more (cf. Gerschenkron, 1962). Chinese economic growth, industrialization, and infrastructure development are outpacing that of previous late capitalist developers, even those in East Asia just a generation earlier.

China's Astonishing Network Economy

China is undoubtedly developing a form of capitalism, but it is of a hybrid nature, a fact that has generated much conceptual confusion. One of the most conceptually confounding aspects of Sino-capitalism is the unique juxtaposition of state coordination from above with networked private entrepreneurial capital accumulation from below. Keynes' 'managed capitalism' meets Schumpeter's 'heroic entrepreneurs', producing a distinct dialectic of state hegemony, interacting with chaotic market-based entrepreneurialism that reproduces Sino-capitalism over time.

Albeit starting from the basis of a socialist centrally planned economy (Kornai, 1992), China experienced few of the pitfalls that Eastern European transition economies, and the successor republics of the Soviet Union, did. There was never a sustained decline in living standards or long periods of high inflation. How was this possible? Historical factors and China's gradualist and experimental state policies (Naughton, 1995) enabled social groups within and without the Chinese party-state to form local alliances in pursuit of breakneck economic growth. These 'growth alliances' overcame internal obstacles and established economic spaces outside the centrally planned system, fostering rapid and relatively smooth marketization.

A central element of these growth alliances were Township and Village Enterprises (TVEs) and other locally owned collective firms. These firms mostly grew out of Maoist policies striving for local economic autarky in the early 1970s. Paradoxically, these industries intended for autarky would later form the backbone of China's light industrial export boom. Initial agricultural reforms, which gave land back to farmers in long-term leases and fostered markets for agricultural goods, increased agricultural productivity and incomes. The rural consumer boom that followed in the early 1980s benefited TVEs enormously, just as local cadres gained sufficient autonomy to promote local industrial development. Not burdened with the social obligations of larger state firms and able to implement flexible labour practices, TVEs boomed and eroded the monopoly profits of the state sector during the late 1980s (Naughton, 1992).

The rise of TVEs and other quasi-private enterprises allowed China to 'outgrow the plan' (Naughton, 1995), and fostered a host of institutional innovations (Tsai, 2007). Different types of entrepreneurs, various branches of local government, and often overseas investors, formed entrepreneurial alliances that created China's light industrial export success. Sino-capitalism was thus, in part, generated by bottom-up processes of networked entrepreneurship or guanxi capitalism (McNally, 2011; Nee and Opper, 2012). The rapid growth of network capitalism, without explicit state support, expresses the centrality of personal networks in Chinese society throughout history. These networks, based on guanxi, allowed private entrepreneurs to link up with each other and state officials, creating a more certain business environment in China's tumultuous transition economy.

Since these growth alliances depended on the local autonomies granted by the CCP, considerable local variation continues to characterize China's network capitalism. By the late 1990s, however, TVEs and other collective enterprises were being rapidly privatized by their local government owners. By 1999 almost 90 per cent of these firms had transferred their shares to private entrepreneurs, partially or completely (Li and Rozelle, 2003). Much of this happened via insider privatization, whereby former managers bought out the business. TVE privatization represents perhaps the biggest such episode experienced by any transition economy. Subsequently, the legal standing of private firms was continuously strengthened by legislation and constitutional amendments. The culmination of this gradual evolution was the promulgation of the Property Law (Wuquan Fa) in March 2007. This law codified earlier constitutional changes to afford equal protection to state and private property.

Despite these remarkable advances under a still nominally communist regime, private entrepreneurs in China continue to face institutional uncertainty and other obstacles in their business ventures. This institutional ambiguity, however, is often compensated for by guanxi, the flexibility and nimbleness of private firms, as well as their increasing technological sophistication. By now, most competitive sectors in the Chinese economy, such as retail, technology, construction, real estate, and much of manufacturing, are dominated by private (both foreign and domestic) or hybrid ownership ventures. Privately-directed manufacturers have played a crucial role in capital accumulation and have profoundly changed China's industrial landscape (Lardy, 2014). In fact, over the course of the 2000s, the CCP has begun to foster the needs and interests of private capital accumulation to a considerable extent (Dickson, 2008).

Sino-capitalism therefore is by no means a pure form of state capitalism. It encompasses strong bottom-up dynamics of capital accumulation, based on informal institutional adaptations and the use of family and guanxi networks. One typical phenomenon is 'swarming'. Private Chinese bosses tend to hastily invest in similar manufacturing fields, competing with each other cut-throat. Such swarming has created rapid phases of expansion in certain manufacturing sectors, often followed by industrial overcapacity. Late phases of swarming thus tend to be characterized by painful sectoral shakeouts involving mergers, bankruptcies, and restructurings. These shakeouts display Schumpeterian creative destruction at its most vivid, though they remain juxtaposed with the more stable and staid Chinese state sector.

Swarming cycles force Chinese entrepreneurs to carve out cost advantages while generating adaptive and innovative capacities in the process. To survive, entrepreneurs enter multi-firm networks in which technology development becomes multidirectional and embedded in global production networks (Steinfeld and Nahm, 2014). Sino-capitalism's dynamics thus represent a new development model: bottom-up networks facilitate creative destruction almost by design, leading to domestically-driven, yet globally integrated and intensely competitive industrial upgrading (Brandt and Thun, 2015).

In this manner, China's network capitalism has already emerged as a key component of the Western-led economic order (Steinfeld, 2010). It is central to the business models of large global corporations like Apple and Walmart, and by now it constitutes a key link in most international value chains. It is in this manner that the forces of neoliberal globalization have shaped China's reform process outside-in, permeating Sino-capitalism's bottom-up network capitalism and, to a lesser extent, state-led accumulation efforts.

The Influences of Neoliberal Globalization

China's entry into the international capitalist system occurred just as neoliberal globalization, the policy advocacy of market liberalization, privatization, deregulation and financialization, was taking off. This stands in marked contrast to what the economies of Japan, South Korea, and Taiwan experienced. These late developers in East Asia benefited from being front-line states in the Cold War, obtaining privileged access to US markets and technology, but facing few pressures to open up their domestic markets to international investment and trade (Stubbs, 1999). China, on the other hand, had fewer such direct privileges. Rather, the strengthening forces of globalization offered new opportunities and challenges.

Therefore, compared to earlier cases of Asian capitalist development, China adopted more free-market principles (Ten Brink, 2010; So and Chu, 2016). These principles include substantial access by foreign capital to China's manufacturing and retail sectors; the relatively rapid development of stock markets and intensive use of Hong Kong's internationalized capital markets to take large state firms public; and a set of developments that rapidly increased labour market flexibility, especially the hiring and dismissal of employees. In particular, China's opening to foreign direct investment is noteworthy. At the beginning, overseas Chinese capital played a crucial role (Hsing, 1998), but soon more globalized players used China's eastern seaboard as a low-cost manufacturing platform. China therefore developed a highly-internationalized export sector very rapidly.

Neoliberal globalization can be understood to have prodded the Chinese government to develop one of the highest 'absorption capacities' for the forces of globalization among developing economies. In other respects, however, China quite closely followed Japan, Taiwan, and South Korea in their development strategies. For instance, China has used programmes of subsidized investment in 'strategic industries', pursued an export-led growth strategy, and suppressed domestic consumption, while encouraging high savings and investment rates. China also has followed its Asian predecessors by employing exchange rate controls to maintain an under-valued currency that fosters export performance. Despite some liberal impulses, therefore, Sino-capitalism features a substantial role for the state and emphasizes the development of domestic industry and technology.

In retrospect, China would have faced enormous costs in seeking to insulate itself from globalization. As a result, Chinese policies have openly endorsed certain aspects of neoliberalism. Concerted local government efforts to attract multinational manufacturing interests stand out, as does the establishment of myriad export industrial zones with good infrastructure, but few regulatory strings, and flexible, but often brutal, labour markets.

China has, therefore, aggressively embraced the global capitalist system and absorbed considerable industrial, technological, and financial capacities from abroad. In the process, it had to radically restructure its domestic economy to more market-like control systems and adapt a host of liberal policy measures, culminating in its entry into the World Trade Organization in 2001. Nonetheless, Sino-capitalism's global integration also relies on the proliferation of business networks, based on interpersonal relationships that find their origin in Chinese culture. To some extent, China has been able to select those aspects of globalization beneficial to its development, while excluding those aspects seen as dangerous to economic and political stability. Its size, ultimately, played a crucial role in allowing it to pick and choose. Neoliberal globalization might have opened China to the world, but on Chinese terms.

As neoliberal globalization has been losing its lustre in the aftermath of the global financial crisis, its influences on China have been diminishing. At the same time, China's size and increasing economic weight are making it a rapidly rising global player. This, in turn, is giving China substantial measures of international economic influence. Historically, late developers have had very little influence over how the global capitalist system functioned and thus had to adjust to its rules, institutions, and power relations. China's aggregate economic heft means that the country's political economy is having a substantial impact on the global competitive landscape at an early developmental stage. Sino-capitalism is increasingly reshaping the neoliberal global capitalist system inside-out, opening up new policy spaces for more state-guided and network-based development solutions.

THE DYNAMICS OF REPRODUCING SINO-CAPITALISM

The calibration and reproduction of Sino-capitalism's institutional structure lies in how state-led development, network-based private capital accumulation, and the influences of neoliberal globalization interact. The dynamic interface of these three elements has created a unique dialectic that juxtaposes top-down state capitalist development with bottom-up market-based entrepreneurial private capital accumulation. At first sight it is clear that state guidance has played a crucial role in China's capitalist transition. The CCP led party-state controls finance and the commanding heights of industry, including crucial producer goods sectors and network industries, such as steel, oil and gas, telecoms, and airlines. Moreover, the Chinese state itself, even if not very efficiently, drives capital accumulation in the state sector, while providing infrastructure needed to engender private capital accumulation.

Set against state-led capital accumulation are economic sectors with strong market competitive pressures, such as retail and manufacturing. These all tend to be populated by privately directed firms, including a large stock of foreign-invested enterprises. Obviously, these two modes of capital accumulation are quite unalike. One relies on oligopolistic competition with enormous support from state agencies, especially in terms of financing and regulation; the other depends on the savvy of individual entrepreneurs, exposed to market pressures with little state aid. These two differing modes tend to meet at the lower levels of the state-administrative apparatus, where local cadres have played a crucial role in accommodating entrepreneurial capitalist practices (Hsing, 1998; Tsai, 2007). As a consequence, state-capital relations have been localized, creating considerable variation of political economic systems within China.

State-capital relations have also undergone considerable change over time. China's private sector has been able to move from being an object of state discrimination to forging a symbiosis with various individuals and agencies situated within the CCP party-state. This has changed the relative powers of state and capital over time: the power of the private sector has continuously increased, putting it in a stronger position to negotiate with the state. By now, many of China's private entrepreneurs, especially those in charge of the largest private firms, are embedded in the party-state (Dickson, 2003, 2008), blurring the lines between the state-owned and privately directed elements of Sino-capitalism. Nonetheless, CCP hegemony over the economy and society remains largely intact.

The evolution of Sino-capitalism clearly does not consist of the state solely retreating in favour of market-based forces. Neither is it a story of initial liberalization, followed by a state-led smothering of private entrepreneurship. The best way to understand Sino-capitalism's evolution and reproduction is to focus on how the development of private capital accumulation put pressure on the state to reform and adapt. State reforms in turn enabled further private sector development, while improving the ability of state agencies to govern and guide an increasingly sophisticated and internationally integrated capitalist political economy.

The reproduction of Sino-capitalism demonstrates how the notion of a zero-sum game, in which either state or market/private sector forces win, must be discarded. Neither the statist nature of Sino-capitalism, nor bottom-up entrepreneurship, fully represents China's developmental dynamics. Evolutionary reproduction is more akin to the 'mutual empowerment' of state and society (Kohli and Shue, 1994; Evans, 1995). China's capital accumulation has been driven by the mutual conditioning and strengthening of juxtaposed political economic realms. This created cycles of induced reforms, where each small step at restructuring created pressures for further modifications (Jefferson and Rawski, 1994; Naughton, 1995).

To sustain such induced reform cycles, an 'unusual combination of policy experimentation with long-term policy prioritization' (Heilmann, 2010, p. 109) has been employed. All-out liberalization according to a blueprint was consciously eschewed in favour of innovative experimentation and work-around solutions. Most importantly, at every juncture of the reform process, market liberalization and privatization have been experimentally paired with concerted efforts to keep state control intact. These processes have allowed policy makers to ameliorate the rigidity of state planning with localized experimentation in special zones. In virtually every major reform undertaking, the CCP has used such 'planned tinkering' to find developmental solutions, a dynamic process that is perhaps most clearly expressed by Deng Xiaoping's dictum of 'crossing the river by feeling the stones'.

This combination of localized experimentation with top-down developmental planning has undoubtedly contributed to China's economic success. Sino-capitalism's institutional dynamics thus do not conform to ideal-typical notions of how capitalism functions, especially liberal free-market capitalism. Instead, Sino-capitalism encompasses unique compensating institutional arrangements (cf. Crouch, 2005) that balance the strengths and weaknesses of different politico-economic realms.

Despite Sino-capitalism's experimentalism, global integration, and relentless creative destruction, the CCP led party-state has been able to adapt and retain its hegemony throughout the reform period (Brodsgaard and Zheng, 2006; Shambaugh, 2008). In particular, later phases of reform starting in the 1990s saw unswerving efforts to restructure and strengthen the central state and its governing capacity (Yang, 2004; Zheng, 2004). Reflecting China's historical legacies, the CCP itself can be seen as 'an entirely different breed of political party from those we can observe in the West: it is a transformed emperor' (Zheng, 2010, p. 16). And as in Imperial times, market, legal, and regulatory rules are only partially institutionalized, while state officials have considerable leeway to intervene in private firms and markets.

The CCP party-state's dominance in economic governance thus encourages a degree of 'deliberate ambiguity' in business dealings. Since most state officials and private entrepreneurs are likely to have committed some illegal act during their careers, the CCP party-state can easily find them guilty of a transgression, providing it with an effective deterrent to political challenges from economic elites and lower-ranked officials. Deliberate ambiguity is, in this manner, the glue that binds private capital to the state, assuring CCP social hegemony, while also introducing flexibility in economic governance (Ho, 2001; McNally, 2011). Since deliberate ambiguity fosters a reliance on interpersonal relations, the continued prevalence of family, guanxi, and other informal networks under Sino-capitalism is not surprising. According to Western standards, then, the rule of law is not fully developed. There is a lack of autonomous institutions outside the party-state's control to assure institutional certainty, such as an independent judiciary.

Evidently, Sino-capitalism's dialectical reproduction encompasses, simultaneously, deep tensions and symbiotic dynamics. Although the use of contracts, formal institutional arrangements, and modern corporate forms has proliferated in China's economy, a deep-seated ambiguity in rules and institutions persists. This ambiguity has allowed the CCP to retain control over China's society and economy, while private entrepreneurs have been able to translate wealth into political influence (Dickson, 2003; Tsai, 2007). As demonstrated by the expansion of governmental infrastructure, Sino-capitalism's state-capital symbiosis has enabled the CCP party-state to foster rapid capital accumulation by private interests, even as a part of the newly generated wealth is captured to assure the CCP's survival.

THE SOCIO-ECONOMIC CONSEQUENCES OF SINO-CAPITALISM

As capitalist development progressed, Chinese society became more deeply divided. The PRC now has one of the world's highest levels of income inequality. An early 2016 report by Peking University found that the richest 1 per cent of households owns about a third of the country's wealth, while the poorest 25 per cent own just 1 per cent. Statistical indicators for inequality reflect this situation, with the official Gini coefficient calculated by China's statistics bureau at 0.469 in 2014. This represents a slight fall from 0.477 in 2011, but a massive rise from roughly 0.3 in the 1980s (Wildau and Mitchell, 2016).

The Chinese case provides a crass reminder of how capitalist development can lift all boats, but at staggeringly different rates. The rough image of China's class structure is as follows: at the very top sits a small minority, most members of which are closely affiliated to, or deeply embedded in, the party-state, such as owners of medium and large private enterprises, and the technocratic state elite with its family members. This top tier is followed by a relatively small upper middle class, including managers in both foreign and private domestic enterprises, and various types of professionals, such as lawyers, accountants, financiers, engineers, and high-level state employees. Then come self-employed small-scale entrepreneurs and lower-level professionals, a large formal urban working class, and finally, in the expansive bottom part, rural migrants and Chinese farmers. Roughly 15 per cent of the population occupies the narrow upper levels, while the remaining 85 per cent form a wide base. In summary, Sino-capitalism has generated a highly polarized and stratified class structure (Chen, 2008; Wright, 2010).

How has this stratification occurred? Since the early 1990s China has embraced globalization and neoliberal policies, such as attracting multi-national capital with weak regulations, cheap land, and a comparatively quiescent and disciplined labour force. This has given unskilled Chinese labourers new chances for economic advancement, but exposed them to the vicissitudes of the global market. Globalization also provided Chinese entrepreneurs and skilled professionals with new economic opportunities. As in the large majority of capitalist political economies, globalization has increased returns on skills and connections, such as guanxi, leading to a widening wealth gap.

Capitalist development under globalization also influenced China's regional income gaps. Due to China's large size, different regions possess different endowments, especially in terms of access to foreign markets and capital. The more globally integrated a region, the wealthier it tends to be. And finally, China's status as a transition economy influenced growing wealth differentials. State sector reforms have focused on closing down, or selling off, loss-making enterprises. Rank and file state workers suffered considerably as a result, while skilled professionals and managers gained. Another socialist legacy, tough restrictions on the migration of farmers to cities based on residency permits (hukou), further contributes to large income gaps, since migrant farmers are not entitled to the same social welfare benefits that urban residents enjoy.

The development of China's industrial relations under Sino-capitalism reflects the broader trends toward social polarization. At the outset of reforms, farmers were tied to the land, while urban workers held the 'iron rice bowl' – a cradle to grave system that allocated jobs, housing, and welfare benefits. These socialist legacies have more or less disappeared during the reform period. Newly hired workers are on contracts and have lost the assurance of lifetime tenure, though higher paying jobs can still carry substantial fringe benefits. Even in the state sector, the hiring and dismissal of employees has become flexible. China therefore has utilized highly liberal, as well as repressive, elements to increase labour market flexibility, including a constitutional change in 1982 that abolished the right to strike.

Despite substantial differences among regions and industries, most firms are characterized by strong management control over basic working conditions. This is not much different from other examples of labour regimes in late developing East Asian economies. However, China distinguishes itself by the lack of any trade union organization that could act independently from state and capital (Lüthje, Luo and Zhang, 2013). The All-China Federation of Trade Unions (ACFTU), with its approximately 200 million members, does not act as an independent union. Its upper echelons are controlled by the CCP party-state, and cannot freely advocate the interests of workers, though there have been some efforts to strengthen collective bargaining rights and to make ACFTU branches more responsive to worker concerns.

Industrial relations are further characterized by a deep urban-rural divide. Migrant labour remains second tier, since permanent migration to cities is restricted by the hukou system. Rural migrant workers have, in this manner, emerged as a highly flexible buffer for China's export industries, since they can easily be laid off, sent back to their villages, and then rehired when conditions improve. China's industrial relations exhibit considerable segmentation and polarization of the workforce, along a line dividing better paid urban workers in core assembly plants from migrant workers with poor pay at the lower tiers of the supply chain. It is therefore unsurprising that the number of labour conflicts in China has been on the rise.

Class polarization, however, has not yet led to regime-threatening social unrest. The wealthy minority tends to fear the political empowerment of the poor, which could threaten their economic privileges (Chen, 2008). In fact, entrepreneurs and college-educated urban residents generally do not to seek to distance themselves from the CCP party-state, but rather view it as a flexible and relatively open collection of organizations and institutions, wherein individuals and social groups can expect to find some representation of their interests (Dickson, 2008; Wright, 2010). This implies that, so far, upper social strata have seen it as in their interest to perpetuate the political status quo.

The embeddedness of the wealthy in the party-state might suggest that the bottom strata of Chinese society is less inclined to support the CCP. However, this is generally not the case. While the poorer social strata tend to have many social grievances, there are really no viable political alternatives for these groups. Moreover, they still support 'socialist' economic ideals, something the CCP has nimbly exploited by retaining some commitment to socialist economic values. As a result, when relatively poor citizens engage in protest, rather than calling for an end to CCP rule, they urge the party to live up to its socialist rhetoric (Wright, 2010).

Given increasing social polarization and unrest as Sino-capitalism's profit-driven accumulation regime advanced, the CCP began in the mid-2000s, under the then new party secretary Hu Jintao, to take a variety of initiatives to address these threats. Concrete measures include the setting up of universal social security and health insurance systems, the building of large amounts of urban social housing, lifting restrictions on the hukou system to ease urban migration for farmers, and state-driven legal efforts to create better working conditions. Put together, these measures amount to Bejing's 'Polanyian gamble'. The CCP leadership is betting that it can 'contain and address the social and political pressures unleashed by 30 years of market-led economic reform' (Bowles, 2011, p. 126). Various institutional and redistributive measures have been put in place, top-down, to forestall the social upheaval that a bottom-up Polanyian 'counter-movement' could unleash.

As Ronaldo Munck (2006, p. 176) argues, 'counter movements' do not necessarily emanate from social groups feeling exploited and oppressed; they also can come from 'enlightened managers of capitalism' or from 'reactionary backward-looking forces'. As in Sino-capitalism's dialectic of reproducing state-capital relations, the CCP is dialectically balancing the liberalization and globalization of the economy with the maintenance of social harmony. Its leadership has at the highest level pledged to address inequality, including Chinese President Xi Jinping in 2014: 'We want to continuously enlarge the pie, while also making sure we divide the pie correctly. Chinese society has long held the value of, "Don't worry about the amount, worry that all have the same amount"' (Wildau and Mitchell, 2016).

While unrest and demands for social fairness create the urgency for policy change, the main agents in this Polanyian balancing act are CCP state elites. They are trying to ameliorate the market's most negative side-effects, especially its distributional outcomes. This 'counter-movement from above' has had some successes so far, especially in addressing rural incomes (Michelson, 2012). And as commodification and casualization of industrial labour have progressed, various legal changes have been implemented. For instance, the Labour Contract Law, introduced in 2008, aims to limit some of the worst consequences of employment flexibility on workers. Nevertheless, under deliberate ambiguity, contractual safeguards can be skirted by management in cahoots with local government.

Therefore, Beijing's Polanyian gamble still hangs in the balance; yet it is noteworthy how the progressive unleashing of markets and capital accumulation has been calibrated with a multitude of policies to protect society from exactly these forces. The goals of building a 'harmonious society', under Hu Jintao, have now evolved into Xi Jinping's policies to constrain the worst power abuses by CCP elites, via an 'anti-corruption campaign' and efforts to further improve the people's livelihood. The crucial rebalancing of China's political economy, away from low value added exports and state-driven investment towards domestic consumption and higher value-added activities, aims in large part to create a well-off and productive workforce that can populate new urban economies. Commodification and private capital accumulation are thus paired with gradual state-driven efforts to redistribute wealth and level the playing field, in the hope of forestalling revolutionary sentiments from below.

CONCLUSION

Conceptualizing Sino-capitalism relies on an open approach (Becker, 2014) that eschews the rigid confines of ideal-types (cf. Hall and Soskice, 2001) and metanarratives (cf. Rostow, 1960). Sino-capitalism is first and foremost a hybrid, combining liberal and statist elements plus clientelism, based on guanxi and other informal networks. As in other instances of late capitalist development, the state has played a leading role in strategically making use of China's 'advantages of backwardness' (Gerschenkron, 1962).

China also follows another of Gerschenkron's insights: the speed of industrialization and continental infrastructure development is outpacing that of earlier late capitalist developers. Moreover, China has been highly effective at rapidly copying institutions, business models, and technologies of more advanced economies, while adopting them to China's unique circumstances. Finally, given China's large size, industrialization has attained enormous economies of scale, implying that, for the first time since 1850, the Anglo-American liberal model of capitalism could be challenged at the global level.

Nonetheless, China has been deeply influenced by US-led neoliberal globalization. No formation of capitalism takes place independently of already developed global capitalist forces. These forces, such as multinational capital and liberal market ideology, have directly influenced China's development and reform approach, prodding greater openness to foreign direct investment, substantial economic liberalization, and, at a relatively early stage of development, an intensely global approach. Global influences, however, have been balanced by state guidance and indigenous bottom-up networks of entrepreneurs, allowing China to build national capacities in industry and technology.

Most analytically important is how Sino-capitalism highlights the structural role of the state in capitalist development. Vivien Schmidt (2009) has forcefully argued that the state must be systematically treated as an autonomous political-economic actor, deviating from many conceptions of capitalism, including those in most of the Comparative Capitalisms literature. Following Gerschenkron's thesis, this structural role of the state is further magnified under late capitalist development. Even more to the point, Sino-capitalism's seemingly contradictory coexistence of state-led development with neoliberal globalization is not atypical. State agency and market/private sector forces are complementary – they have to coexist and mutually strengthen each other for capitalist development to take place.

Capitalism, ultimately, relies on a 'particular historical coexistence and mutual dependence of two kinds of power: private economic power from the control of property and opportunities for profit-making, and the coercive territorial power of states' (Ingham, 2008, p. 175; cf. Heilbroner, 1985). When a dialectical struggle cum symbiosis between an emerging bureaucratic state and burgeoning capitalist classes takes place, capitalism can advance. This is Weber's ([1927] 1981) 'memorable alliance': it can only function if capitalists are provided with sufficient freedom to operate within and between states; the overwhelming dominance of either the state or capital can undermine the system's dynamism.

The misleading notion that a relatively weak state somehow aids capitalist development must be discarded. Massive evidence to the contrary shows how a strong bureaucratic state is necessary, albeit not sufficient. There is always the potential for state elites to subordinate capitalists and markets to their whims. Even more balanced alliances among state and business elites can lead to excessive exploitation, corruption, and monopoly capitalism. There is an extremely fine line to walk between an overly autonomous state that can ride roughshod over capital and society, and insufficient state autonomy that allows for state capture by special interests (Evans, 1995).

The state not only balances markets and private capital, but remains crucial in driving the top-down recomposition and reconstitution of capitalist relations of production. Beijing's gamble to restrain the excesses of market society and rebalance social relations while improving the economy's productivity reiterates the central position of state agency. As Munck notes in his introduction, a Polanyian view of capitalism's inherent social instability and complexity – the push and pull of disembedding and re-embedding the market in socio-cultural institutions – is a crucial element in analysing social change. The state is forever in a multi-pronged juggling act of fostering relentless capitalist accumulation, while simultaneously saving it from its own destructive tendencies.

Sino-capitalism illustrates that there is no uniform model of development, even of state-guided late capitalist development. Given Sino-capitalism's historical antecedents, it differs from Western conceptions of economy and polity (Jacques, 2009) and is unlike Anglo-American liberal capitalism, as well as continental European coordinated capitalism (McNally, 2012). A deep dialectic of state capitalist features juxtaposed with vibrant, often globally integrated entrepreneurial private capital accumulation, drives Sino-capitalism's reproduction. A careful listening to history and an exploration of the critical junctures, ruptures, complexities, and, even perhaps foremost, dialectical contradictions that accompany capitalist development, emerge in this manner as indispensable prerequisites for comparative analysis.

As a final point, Sino-capitalism's rise proves that development from the periphery is possible, but only under unique circumstances. In the post-2000 era, China is the only major developing economy that has successfully charted a course towards middle-income status with sustained industrial upgrading. Other examples of late catch-up industrialization in this era, such as India, Brazil, and Mexico, show more pronounced characteristics of uneven, halting, and fragmented development. Their industrial catch-up remains circumscribed. But even China is facing enormous challenges of rebalancing the economy. Excessive corporate debt and industrial overcapacity will have to be tackled, while continued social and technological upgrading needs to be fostered.

At the global level, Sino-capitalism's interaction with the dominant American-led neoliberal order has generated a dynamic mix of mutual dependence, symbiosis, competition, and friction. As Sino-capitalism gains in global heft, this precarious combination is starting to shift. Although no real post-neoliberal development agenda has emerged (Crouch, 2011), Sino-capitalism is nonetheless generating an increasingly potent in-system challenge to the neoliberal order. China's unique formation of capitalism highlights the key structural role that the state can play in development, even if more market-enabling and globally integrated. Perhaps in this manner, Sino-capitalism's growing international sway could mark the return of the state to a more consciously central role in managing capitalist political economies nationally and globally.

REFERENCES

Amsden, Alice H. (1989), *Asia's Next Giant: South Korea and Late Industrialization*. Oxford: Oxford University Press.
Becker, Uwe (ed.) (2014), *The BRICs and Emerging Economies in Comparative Perspective:*

Political Economy, Liberalisation and Institutional Change. London and New York: Routledge.

Bowles, Paul (2011), 'Beijing's Polanyian Gamble'. *Revista Estudios Criticos del Desarrollo* 1, no. 1: 125–50.

Boyer, Robert (2005), 'How and Why Capitalisms Differ'. *Economy and Society* 34, no. 4: 509–57.

Brandt, Loren and Eric Thun (2015), 'Competition and Upgrading in Chinese Industry', in Barry Naughton and Kellee S. Tsai (eds) *State Capitalism, Institutional Adaptation, and the Chinese Miracle*. New York: Cambridge University Press, 154–98.

Brodsgaard, Kjeld Erik and Zheng Yongnian (2006), 'Introduction: Whither the Chinese Communist Party', in Kjeld Erik Brodsgaard and Yongnian Zheng (eds) *The Chinese Communist Party in Reform*. New York and London: Routledge, 1–14.

Chen, An (2008), 'Why Does Capitalism Fail to Push China Towards Democracy', in Christopher A. McNally (ed.) *China's Emergent Political Economy – Capitalism in the Dragon's Lair*. New York and London: Routledge, 146–65.

Coates, David (2000), *Models of Capitalism: Growth and Stagnation in the Modern Era*. Cambridge: Polity Press.

Crouch, Colin (2005), 'Three Meanings of Complementarity'. *Socio-Economic Review* 3, no. 2: 359–63.

Crouch, Colin (2011), *The Strange Non-Death of Neo-liberalism*. London: Polity Press.

Cumings, Bruce (1989), 'The Political Economy of China's Turn Outward', in Samuel S. Kim (ed.) *China and the World: New Directions in Chinese Foreign Relations*. Boulder, CO: Westview Press, 203–36.

Dickson, Bruce J. (2003), *Red Capitalists in China*. Cambridge: Cambridge University Press.

Dickson, Bruce J. (2008), *Wealth into Power: The Communist Party's Embrace of China's Private Sector*. Cambridge: Cambridge University Press.

Evans, Peter B. (1995), *Embedded Autonomy: States and Industrial Transformation*. Princeton, NJ: Princeton University Press.

Faure, David (2006), *China and Capitalism: A History of Business Enterprise in Modern China*. Hong Kong: Hong Kong University Press.

Gates, Hill (1996), *China's Motor: A Thousand Years of Petty Capitalism*. Ithaca, NY: Cornell University Press.

Gerschenkron, Alexander (1962), *Economic Backwardness in Historical Perspective: A Book of Essays*. Cambridge, MA: Harvard University Press.

Hall, Peter A. and David W. Soskice (eds) (2001), *Varieties of Capitalism: The Institutional Foundations of Comparative Advantage*. Oxford: Oxford University Press.

Heilbroner, R. (1985), *The Nature and Logic of Capitalism*. New York: W. W. Norton.

Heilmann, Sebastian (2010), 'Economic Governance: Authoritarian Upgrading and Innovation Potential', in J. Fewsmith (ed.) *China Today, China Tomorrow: Domestic Politics, Economy and Society*. Lanham, MD: Rowman and Littlefield, 109–26.

Ho, Peter (2001), 'Who Owns China's Land? Policies, Property Rights and Deliberate Institutional Ambiguity'. *The China Quarterly* 166: 394–421.

Howell, Jude (2006), 'Reflections on the Chinese State'. *Development and Change* 37, no. 2: 273–97.

Hsing, You-tien (1998), *Making Capitalism in China*. New York: Oxford.

Ingham, Geoffrey (2008), *Capitalism*. Cambridge: Polity Press.

Jacques, Martin (2009), *When China Rules the World: The End of the Western World and the Birth of a New Global Order*. New York: Penguin Books.

Jefferson, Gary H. and Thomas G. Rawski (1994), 'Enterprise Reform in Chinese Industry'. *Journal of Economic Perspectives* 8, no. 2: 47–70.

Johnson, Chalmers (1982), *MITI and the Japanese Miracle*. Stanford, CA: Stanford University Press.

Kohli, Atul and Vivienne Shue (1994), 'State Power and Social Forces: On Political Contention and Accommodation in the Third World', in Joel S. Migdal, Atul Kohli and

Vivienne Shue (eds) *State Power and Social Forces – Domination and Transformation in the Third World*. Cambridge: Cambridge University Press, 293–326.

Kornai, Janos (1992), *The Socialist System: The Political Economy of Communism*. Princeton, NJ: Princeton University Press.

Ku, Chung-hwa (2010), 'The "Spirit" of Capitalism in China: Contemporary Meanings of Weber's Thought', in Yin-wah Chu (ed.) *Chinese Capitalisms: Historical Emergence and Political Implications*. Basingstoke: Palgrave Macmillan, 19–45.

Lardy, Nicholas R. (2014), *Markets Over Mao: The Rise of Private Business in China*. Washington, DC: Peterson Institute for International Economics.

Li, H. and S. Rozelle (2003), 'Privatizing Rural China: Insider Privatization, Innovative Contracts and the Performance of Township Enterprises'. *The China Quarterly* 176, December: 981–1005.

Lüthje, B., S. Luo and H. Zhang (2013), *Beyond the Iron Rice Bowl, Regimes of Production and Industrial Relations in China*. Frankfurt and New York: Campus.

McNally, Christopher A. (2008), 'Reflections on Capitalism and China's Emergent Political Economy', in Christopher A. McNally (ed.) *China's Emergent Political Economy – Capitalism in the Dragon's Lair*. New York and London: Routledge, 17–35.

McNally, Christopher A. (2011), 'China's Changing Guanxi Capitalism – Private Entrepreneurs between Leninist Control and Relentless Accumulation'. *Business and Politics* 13, no. 3.

McNally, Christopher A. (2012), 'Sino-Capitalism: China's Reemergence and the International Political Economy'. *World Politics* 64, no. 4, October: 741–76.

McNally, Christopher A. and Yin-wah Chu (2006), 'Exploring Capitalist Development in Greater China: A Synthesis'. *Asian Perspective* 30, no. 2: 31–64.

Michelson, Ethan (2012), 'Public Goods and State-Society Relations: An Impact Study of China's Rural Stimulus', in Dali L. Yang (ed.) *The Global Recession and China's Political Economy*. New York: Palgrave Macmillan, 131–57.

Munck, Ronaldo (2006), 'Globalization and Contestation: A Polanyian Problematic'. *Globalizations* 3, no. 2: 175–86.

Naughton, Barry (1992), 'Implications of the State Monopoly over Industry and its Relaxations'. *Modern China* 18, no. 1: 14–41.

Naughton, Barry (1995), *Growing Out of the Plan: Chinese Economic Reform, 1978–1990*. Cambridge: Cambridge University Press.

Naughton, Barry and Kellee S. Tsai (eds) (2015), *State Capitalism, Institutional Adaptation, and the Chinese Miracle*. New York: Cambridge University Press.

Nee, Victor and Sonja Opper (2012), *Capitalism from Below: Markets and Institutional Change in China*. Cambridge, MA: Harvard University Press.

Rostow, W. W. (1960), *The Stages of Economic Growth: A Non-Communist Manifesto*. Cambridge: Cambridge University Press.

Schmidt, Vivien A. (2009), 'Putting the Political Back into Political Economy by Bringing the State Back Yet Again'. *World Politics* 61, no. 3: 516–48.

Schumpeter, Joseph A. (1950), *Capitalism, Socialism and Democracy*. New York: Harper and Row.

Shambaugh, David (2008), *China's Communist Party: Atrophy and Adaptation*. Berkeley and Los Angeles, CA: University of California Press.

So, Alvyn, and Yin-wah Chu (2016), *The Global Rise of China*. Cambridge: Polity.

Steinfeld, Edward S. (2010), *Playing Our Game: Why China's Economic Rise Doesn't Threaten the West*. New York: Oxford University Press.

Steinfeld, Edward S. and Jonas Nahm (2014), 'Scale-up Nation: China's Specialization in Innovative Manufacturing'. *World Development* 54, February: 288–300.

Stubbs, Richard (1999), 'War and Economic Development: Export-Oriented Industrialization in East and Southeast Asia'. *Comparative Politics* 31, no. 3: 337–55.

Ten Brink, Tobias (2010, May), 'Structural Characteristics of Chinese Capitalism', mimeo, Max Planck Institute for the Study of Societies, Cologne, Germany.

Tsai, Kellee S. (2007), *Capitalism without Democracy: The Private Sector in Contemporary China*. Ithaca, NY: Cornell University Press.

Wade, Robert (1990), *Governing the Market: Economic Theory and the Role of Government in East Asian Industrialization*. Princeton, NJ: Princeton University Press.

Weber, Max ([1927] 1981), *General Economic History*. New Brunswick, NJ: Transaction Publishers.

Wildau, Gabriel and Tom Mitchell (2016), 'China Income Inequality among World's Worst'. *Financial Times*, 14 January. Available at: https://www.ft.com/content/3c521faa-baa6-11e5-a7cc-280dfe875e28 (accessed 26 September 2016).

Wright, Teresa (2010), *Accepting Authoritarianism: State-Society Relations in China's Reform Era*. Stanford, CA: Stanford University Press.

Yang, Dali (2004), *Remaking the Chinese Leviathan*. Stanford, CA: Stanford University Press.

Zheng, Yongnian (2004), *Globalization and State Transformation in China*. Cambridge: Cambridge University Press.

Zheng, Yongnian (2010), *The Chinese Communist Party as Organizational Emperor: Culture, Reproduction and Transformation*. London: Routledge.

15. Culture and development: contemporary debates and practices
Susanne Schech

INTRODUCTION

It is now well over two decades since critiques of development, informed by cultural studies and postcolonialism, have started to make their mark in teaching and research. The culture and development approach, or paradigm, as some suggest (Nederveen Pieterse, 2001), has been expounded in several books (for example, Allen, 1992; Skelton and Allen, 1999; Schech and Haggis, 2000; Radcliffe, 2006). A sign that it has become established is the fact that development studies reference books include 'culture and development' among the various conceptualizations of development as a process and phenomenon (Clark, 2006; Desai and Potter, 2008, 2014). The 'and' suggests a separateness between development viewed as a mainly economic process of change, and culture as the non-economic aspects of society or individuals that are affected by development, or actively constrain it. In the critical development literature, however, the two concepts are considered as intertwined in various ways.

What makes the culture and development approach difficult to delineate is that both concepts are impossible to pin down in a neat definition. Development is a concept with many meanings, but a useful distinction can be made between development as processes of social and economic change, and development as intention, the 'purposeful pursuit of economic, social and political goals through planned intervention' (Crewe and Axelby, 2013, p. 3). The Sustainable Development Goals are an expression of this intent – 17 aspirational goals to 'end poverty, protect the planet, and ensure prosperity for all' (United Nations, 2015), to be attained by 2030 through policies, programmes and projects designed by governments and other institutions or organizations. Culture is an even trickier word to define. It refers to the ordinary, everyday processes of human life and the human mind – subjectivities, identities, values, systems of belief, kinship patterns, modes of livelihoods – and also the forms of signification that circulate within a society. Words, images, material objects all function as signs or symbols which enable communication between social actors, and their circulation is influenced by states, institutions, corporations and other structures. The main point of examining the interconnections between culture and development is to acknowledge that cultural aspects of life, like religion and value systems, are as important as economic and political aspects, and are not separate. Thus, taking culture seriously can make development interventions more effective and beneficial to the people whose lives are being changed (Schech and Haggis, 2000).

My purpose in this chapter is twofold. First, I map how the culture and development approach has evolved, what impact it has had on the study of development, and what limitations and critiques have been raised. Having emerged in the 1990s at a time of crisis in development theory and praxis, how relevant is the culture and development approach today? The second part of the chapter examines the extent to which culture has been placed at the centre of development interventions, and how this has changed development practices and their critical analyses.

CULTURE AND DEVELOPMENT APPROACH – EMERGENCE AND CONTEMPORARY DEBATE

The interest in culture in the 1990s came at a time of crisis in development thinking, which, informed by Marxist or neoliberal theories of change, was widely considered to have failed to equip scholars with the conceptual tools to understand how countries develop, when and why, and to chart sustainable development paths. Development practice, too, was revealed as flawed, focused too much on economic goals and not enough on the lived experience of the people whose lives it had promised to improve. In-depth analysis of failed development projects highlighted how important factors had been left out of the picture – geographical and historical local circumstances, ethnic and gender inequalities in the community, indigenous knowledge, local values and meanings, the legacy of colonial development interventions (for example, Porter et al., 1991). These non-economic factors can be summed up as cultural factors in that they contribute to a more holistic understanding of people's lives and their agency, and developers were ignoring them at their peril. Some scholars went further, arguing that development was little more than a neo-colonial project to consolidate political and economic domination in the hands of the few. In the words of one such critic, 'Development (as a programme for collective happiness) no longer exists except as virtual reality, as a synthetic image in a full-length film of globalization' (Rist, 1997, p. 230). In comparing development to a cultural artefact and calling it a 'global faith', Rist suggested that development, as the purposeful pursuit of economic, social and political goals, was a cultural construct and a matter of belief, rather than a material reality. Thus, for the purposes of this chapter it is possible to distinguish two trends in the cultural and development approach – one that argues that 'culture matters' in development and cultural factors must be incorporated in the theories and practices of development, and another that calls for the idea of development, and the claims made under its mantle, to be critically examined as a cultural construct. These two trends will be briefly discussed in the following two sections.

Culture Matters

Culture's relevance to development has been explained both in terms of the ways culture affects what is of value in a society, and the ways in which culture influences the responses of individuals, communities, informal and formal institutions to developmental changes and opportunities. Development economist Amartya Sen (2004) argues that culture matters in development both as means and end. As means, culture influences economic behaviour by shaping attitudes to work, aspirations, entrepreneurialism and risk taking, and culture can generate economic growth through the production and marketing of arts, crafts and cultural tourism, for example. Cultural conditions can also shape how people participate in political processes. By influencing value formation, culture functions as a lens through which development interventions are perceived, received and enacted. The enjoyment of literature, art, music and other expressions of culture is an important part of human well-being, and therefore culture is also a constitutive part, or end, of development. A sense of belonging, community and social solidarity are important to well-being and often culturally based, though Sen points out that culture can also be an instrument of exclusion and discrimination. Culture matters along with many other social factors, like class, race and gender as well as political factors and institutions, and it is shaped by these factors. Hence culture is constantly changing and not internally homogeneous, and thus cannot be fixed, preserved or used as causal factors in development.

Sen's attempt to delineate the role of culture in development – too narrowly in the views of some – was a response to claims that culture plays a central role in determining whether a country is prosperous, politically stable and democratic. The central proposition of *Culture Matters*, an edited collection with contributors from the US and several developing countries, is that valuing efficiency, rationality, secularism and other so-called Western cultural traits is a prerequisite for economic growth, and that people in developing countries are keen to embrace these values. Culture explains the developmental success of South Korea, whose citizens 'valued thrift, investment, hard work, education, organization, and discipline', and the underdevelopment of Ghana, where cultural values are not compatible with modernization (Huntington, 2000, p. xiii). A culturally deterministic view implies that having the 'wrong' culture precludes a country from joining the 'developed' class, which Sen (2004, p. 38) considers politically and ethically repulsive. The *Culture Matters* argument is based on modernization theory which, as Watts has pointed out, considers development as culturally neutral and attributes culture to non-Western societies, where it can hinder or facilitate capitalist economic development (Watts, 2003, p. 434). Cultural practices are judged by how well they support the pursuit of material wealth. For example, when Landes claims that young Thai men reduce their obligatory stints in a Buddhist monastery, it is to get back to the 'real material world' where 'time is money' (Landes, 2000, p. 3).

Watts' point that the attention to culture in development is not new has contributed to direct attention back to the sociological and anthropological development literature of the 1950s to 1970s, when sociologists and anthropologists sought to broaden modernization theory from a focus on economic growth to a more holistic societal change. They viewed modernization as a systemic process of change in a country whereby 'economic development, cultural change, and political change go together in coherent and even, to some extent, predictable patterns' (Inglehart, 1997, p. 5). Numerous studies of this period focused on culture as a marker to distinguish modern from traditional societies, and even individuals. American sociologist Daniel Lerner's (1958) study of a small village in Turkey in the 1950s, for example, portrayed traditional man as a pious village chief, content with a modest lifestyle and his world restricted to the village. Modern man was represented by the village grocer, an ambitious man who dreamed of moving away and pursuing his dreams to be rich. Modernization involves dreaming of a different, more expansive world 'populated more actively with imaginings and fantasies' and 'hungering for whatever is different and unfamiliar' (Lerner, 1958, p. 23; cited in Schech and Haggis, 2000, p. 35). Similarly, Inkeles and Smith (1974; cited in Peet and Hartwick, 2009, pp. 125–6) described 'traditional man' and 'modern man' as opposites in terms of values, attitudes and behaviours, with the former rooted in tradition and oriented towards the past, unreceptive to new ideas and information, suspicious of technology and of people beyond the family, and deeply religious and fatalistic. This binary conceptualization of traditional/Western culture assumes that traditional culture is expected to dissolve or be cast aside through contact with Western modernity. Adopting modern values, attitudes and behaviours is expected to facilitate economic development, as the modernization perspective holds that '[t]he more thorough the disintegration of traditional elements, the more a society could absorb change and develop' (Peet and Hartwick, 2009, p. 122). From this perspective, societies will only succeed in their quest for development if they are willing to give up their traditional values, institutions and cultural practices, or if they happen to possess cultural traits that are favourable to modernization.

The modernization view of culture has been critiqued as both Eurocentric and imperialistic. It is Eurocentric because it assumes that development requires 'assuming the mental models of the West' and effectively, Western culture (ibid., p. 132), although the Western cultural moorings of development are often hidden under its universal claims. It is imperialistic because the centrality of the market and 'the worship of commodities' that underpin the modernization approach to development, facilitate the control of spaces, resources and people in developing countries through multinational corporations, international financial institutions, and foreign investment, policy imposition through global development institutions, and even development aid (ibid., p. 165). Modernization theory ignores colonialism and its impacts while creating the Third World as a space without history, where culture stands still and people are local, in contrast to the image of a 'self-contained', developed, modern and globalized First World (McEwan, 2009, p. 128). This cultural move has enabled the dominance of the West to be naturalized and imperial power relations to be continued into the present, supported by First World development policies and blueprints that are intended to guide the Third World.

Culture as a Changing Resource

One important critique of modernization theory is that its view of culture is bounded, static and ahistorical. As Sen and many other scholars have pointed out, cultures do not evolve in isolation or as separate boxes, but through interaction with other cultures. Cultural interconnections through migration, conquest, trade, travel and pilgrimage go far back into history, well before any notion of Europe or the West. In the current era of globalization, people's lived experience anywhere on the globe is influenced by an awareness of the circumstances, experiences, images, products, values and perspectives of others elsewhere. Nederveen Pieterse is one scholar who locates culture in the context of globalization. This enables a dynamic view of culture as changing, hybrid, historically layered, containing internal diversities and having temporal and spatial dimensions. Crucially, he argues, culture is an arena of struggle where multiple actors operate at local, national and global levels (Nederveen Pieterse, 2001, p. 60). The construction of national identity is a cultural struggle which involves the selective use and reinterpretation of cultural roots, as well as invention of cultural artefacts, as can be seen in the invention of a national language, for example, in Indonesia. Local cultures, too, are constructed, with Balinese culture described as 'a multiply authored invention, a historical formation, an enactment, a political construct, a shifting paradox, an ongoing translation, an emblem, a trademark, a non-consensual negotiation of contrastive identity, and more' (ibid., p. 64, citing Boon, 1990, p. ix). The way culture is constantly being reworked and reproduced is expressed well in Alan Pred's 1992 poem which evokes culture's interconnectedness with the uneven articulations of capitalist economic processes that are never just physical – labour, capital, goods, technologies and so on – but always take on cultural forms:

> Culture does not stand   isolated
>   on its own, immutable and uncontested.
> It is neither fixed, nor confined to the traditional,
>   neither completely stable, nor a unified monolith of coherence.
> It is not an autonomous entity,
>   existing in a territory of its own,
> beyond the realms of materiality and social reality.
> Culture is embodied and lived,
>   actively produced and expressed,
> through all social practices,
> through all that is concrete and everyday,
> through all that is enmeshed in power relations
>   and their associated discourses,
>   their associated representations and rhetorics . . . (1992, p. 109)

However, when it comes to development practice, this dynamic view of culture is overlooked, or set aside. Instead, culture is treated as if it existed 'out there', a resource to be tapped (Nederveen Pieterse, 2001). For some, cultural practices generate stuff that can be marketed to generate income, such as Indian Bollywood films or African 'world music'. Culture can also be employed to position a country in a competitive global market. For example, the 'Imagine India' campaign used attractive imagery of India's colourful culture to sell the country in the global market as 'a nation in tune with the neoliberal desires of a structurally adjusted world' (Kaur, 2012, p. 603). In other writing, culture is a resource that empowers locally based opposition and alternatives to capitalist development. Indian scientist and environmental activist Vandana Shiva argues that traditional indigenous knowledges about water and seeds can help communities resist pressures to privatize water and genetic plant material, and defend them as common public goods (Opel and Shiva, 2008). Also working with the notion of culture as a resource, Appadurai (2004) argues that cultural practices can empower the poor. His example is a pro-poor alliance of housing activists in India which uses housing exhibitions as a public space where poor people are able to discuss their housing needs with politicians, donor agencies, local planners, architects and professional builders. By employing what is essentially an upper-class cultural form and placing slum residents at its centre, the alliance enhances their visibility and recognition, as well as subverting the dominant class cultures in India (Schech, 2014, p. 44).

Seeing culture as a resource for desirable development outcomes has its pitfalls. It can romanticize indigenous knowledge, portraying these knowledge systems as somehow outside history, and ignoring the often uneven distribution of knowledge and power at the local level. Culture is seen as a matrix of meaning that belongs to a social group and in a particular space, as if isolated from other cultural influences and other spaces (Nederveen Pieterse, 2001, p. 69). Local aspirations and cultural rituals and practices are treated 'as a world unto itself' with little attention paid to how they might be influenced by 'the cultural map of aspirations' of others, particularly the rich and the trustees of development (Da Costa, 2010, p. 513). A critical engagement with capitalism shaping these aspirations and desires, so evident in Pred's (1992) poem on culture and development, is frequently missing. Culture as a resource leaves development untouched as a socio-economic and political process into which people can insert themselves through using their culture.

Development as a Cultural Construct

Development is cultural in the sense that it is 'embedded in "imaginaries of desirability", material culture, and social relations' (Radcliffe, 2006, p. 17). From this perspective, development itself is a construct, a set of culturally embedded practices and meanings that change over time and are contested. This view of culture and development pays close attention to discourse and power, whereby discourse refers to the social practices through which the world is made meaningful. Discourse is linked to power because discourses determine 'what it is possible to say, the criteria of "truth", who is allowed to speak with authority and where such speech can be spoken' (McEwan, 2009, p. 122). Studying development texts and how authors use language, rhetoric, images and metaphors to represent the world is one way of understanding how development interventions are understood and justified.

Arturo Escobar employed this approach in his analysis of development as a Western discourse which is globalized and constantly reproduced through powerful institutions. He takes the World Bank as an example, which uses statistics to rank countries from 'very high income' to 'low income' and 'least developed' and designates people with a low income as 'poor'. These acts of definition have established the West as the desirable endpoint of development and those regions of the world that do not conform to this image of prosperity as deficient and needing development interventions. The 'Third World', 'the Third World woman', 'the poor' and so on become stereotypes of the development industry's imagination that are produced and reproduced through development discourse. As Escobar notes, the development project 'was – and continues to be for the most part – a top-down, ethno-centric, and technocratic approach, which treated people and cultures as abstract concepts, statistical figures to be moved up and down the charts of "progress"' (1995, p. 44). He argues that development discourse has material impacts as it shapes the science and technology, planning and management that operate through the professional and institutional practices of development. These practices marginalize other modes of knowing and seeing the world, and, according to Escobar, 'even the most remote communities in the Third World are torn apart from their local context and redefined as "resources"' (Ibid., p. 194).

Escobar demonstrates that by studying the representational language of development texts, it is possible to reveal the cultural work of development discourse and how it constructs certain kinds of meaning. Efforts of this kind often draw on postcolonial studies and cultural studies. In his landmark contribution to postcolonial studies, Edward Said (1978) analyses Orientalism as not just a Western way of knowing the Orient but also as a Western style of dominating, restructuring and having authority over the Orient. He describes Orientalism as forms of communicative practice, such as travel writing, journalism, academic accounts and fine arts, which seek to present an objective analysis of Eastern phenomena to Western audiences. Yet these accounts have a tendency to dehumanize the Orient and present it as a fixed, unchanging Other. From a cultural studies perspective, Hall argues that European colonization involved not only economic and political domination of the New World but also cultural domination: 'Europe brought its own cultural categories, languages, images, and ideas into the New World in order to describe and represent it' (Hall, 1992, pp. 293–4). Colonial representations have long-lasting effects. They continue to frame how the world is seen through Western eyes and legitimize contemporary economic and geopolitical interventions, as Said's work on the media coverage of Islam and Middle East politics has shown (Said, 1997).

Development scholars have employed the analytical tools of cultural studies and postcolonialism to identify and problematize the negative stereotypes about people and places that development discourse has inherited and continues to propagate (McEwan, 2009). Critiques of representation have been included in undergraduate development textbooks to explain, for example, how developing areas have come to be associated with overpopulation, danger and illness (Williams et al., 2009). Studying discourses like Orientalism and Development can tell us more about Western culture and consciousness than about the cultures they seek to represent. The recognition that scientific knowledge is socially and culturally embedded, that development is a cultural practice, has turned researchers' attention onto the workings of their own disciplines. In development anthropology, for example, an analytical focus on knowledge and power reveals that much anthropological knowledge tells us more about the anthropologists' ethno-centric bias than about the culturally different communities they study (Crewe and Axelby, 2013, p. 38). As Nederveen Pieterse (2001, p. 71) notes, 'Development is intrinsically an intercultural transaction' where the aim is to develop cultural 'others'. However, he argues that, in studying development interventions, it would be simplistic to focus only on the lines of cultural difference between developed and developing countries/actors. There are multiple differences involved in development which cut across each other, and recognizing the cultural differences within the developed and the developing world is just as important. Viewing development as a politics of difference, he argues, offers a more nuanced lens for analysing how development is negotiated locally and globally, and opens a space for self-consciousness and a practice of reflexive development (ibid., pp. 71–2).

LOCATING CULTURE IN DEVELOPMENT POLICIES AND PRACTICES

While many development scholars are now paying more attention to culture and development, the extent to which policy makers and implementers in multilateral organizations, state institutions or NGOs do is a matter of debate. How can development policies and interventions become more culturally attuned? Rao and Walton (2004) argue that the cultures of development institutions themselves have to be scrutinized. They see a growing openness to scrutiny and self-awareness in multilateral development institutions like the World Bank and a shift away from imposing development interventions towards partnership and mutual learning. The mid-1990s' turn towards poverty reduction in the World Bank was underpinned by the partnership model, announced as a new global framework for development cooperation. This model, according to the OECD, would usher in a people-centred, participatory, sustainable development led by developing countries and facilitated by Northern donors (OECD, 1996). In contrast, Clammer (2012, p. 13) states that development policy makers remain reluctant to take culture into account and seek information on local socio-cultural conditions. Above all, they 'rarely want to be told that their proposed interventions are undesirable, will not work, or will simply generate yet more problems to be solved'. The following sections will analyse efforts by two multilateral organizations, the World Bank and UNESCO, to give culture a more central place in development policies, and what they understand by this.

The World Bank's Cultural Approach to Poverty

The World Bank is a leading development knowledge producer and policy maker. A brief analysis of how it operates shows that critical approaches have had diminishing impact. At first, there were some encouraging signs that the World Bank was taking on board some of the ideas advanced by critical culture and development research, such as the importance of participatory knowledge creation and listening to other voices in designing development interventions. To gather information for the *World Development Report 2000* on poverty, which fed into the Millennium Development Goals, the World Bank undertook a large-scale consultation with the poor, resulting in the much-cited three-volume summary report on the *Voices of the Poor*. Consulting with poor people enabled the Bank 'to know more about our clients as individuals' (Francis, 2001, p. 85, citing World Bank President James Wolfensohn), and gain their input as 'the true poverty experts' into poverty strategies that would properly reflect their experiences, priorities, reflections and recommendations (Narayan and Petesch, 2000, p. 2). The insights from an estimated 20,000 poor people in 23 countries certainly would contribute to a more sophisticated understanding of poverty. The report made a large impact on the international development community because it 'brought a glimpse of ordinary people's lives into the field of view of development actors, whose exposure to the realities of life in developing countries is often limited to expatriate enclaves and air-conditioned meeting rooms in five-star hotels' (Cornwall and Fujita, 2012, p. 1753).

The researchers leading the *Voices* study concede that to really understand the nature and root causes of poverty requires an understanding of the historical, political, social, cultural, ecological and economic contexts – a task well beyond the scope of the study which had to be completed within a short time frame. Hence they focused more narrowly on how poor people defined poverty, what their main problems and the most important institutions were in their daily lives, and how gender relations had changed over the past decade. However, researchers found that even the seemingly straightforward question of who was poor in their communities triggered lengthy discussions among the study participants, indicating that local communities did not have a shared understanding. In each site, study participants defined 'the poor' in different ways, often on an individual basis, and the majority who by the fact of their participation were categorized as poor by the researchers, did not consider themselves poor, but used the label to identify others, and many resisted the categorization. Cornwall and Fujita compared the *Voices* study with local site reports, showing how the diverse meanings of poverty were funnelled into a common definition of poverty through guidelines provided to the local research teams. These guidelines provided the concepts with which to categorize and frame the information provided by the research participants, concepts including 'vulnerability', 'social exclusion', 'gender' and 'the poor'. By imposing these value-laden concepts, the voices are editorialized so as to tune out any discordant sounds and present an overarching narrative that is in perfect harmony with the World Bank's own policies: their 'cries for change are harnessed to support a particular set of prescriptions' (ibid., p. 1761). When the *World Development Report 2000/2001: Attacking Poverty* (WDR 2000) is examined, it is clear that only a faint echo of the *Voices* study is incorporated to humanize and animate the report (World Bank, 2000). The decisions and policies set out in the WDR 2000 did not radically diverge from poverty policies pursued by the World Bank previously. In spite of this, the participatory strategy delivered two important advantages: it allowed the World Bank to present its revised policy framework as a global project, supported by a harmonious coalition of a wide range of poor and non-poor, powerful and powerless actors. And, second, by involving the poor in the background research the World Bank was able to present its policy recommendations as something the poor themselves requested, 'rendering its own interests, power and agency invisible in the process' (Schech and Vas Dev, 2007). Overall, analysing the World Bank's consultation with the poor has revealed a limited capacity to hear and respond to voices that present different understandings of development, despite a growing awareness in its ranks that development interventions should respond to local priorities, needs and aspirations.

Fast forward to 2015, the year in which the Sustainable Development Goals were finalized with the ambition to abolish extreme poverty by 2030. The *World Development Report* for 2015 (WDR 2015) focused on mind, society and behaviour, which are all shaped by culture (World Bank, 2015). This report considers why people behave and make decisions in ways that are often not rational, nor in their own best economic interest as predicted by neoclassical economic theory and policies. The aim of the World Bank is to shift people's decisions towards desirable goals through behavioural interventions. This requires understanding mental models, defined as the 'concepts, categories, identities, prototypes, stereotypes, causal narratives, and world views drawn from their communities' (ibid., p. 11). Another term for this is culture which, the WDR 2015 argues, 'influences individual decision-making because it serves as a set of interrelated schemes of meaning that people use when they act and make choices'. Some mental models and social networks are helpful for development, but others are not and may explain why poverty persists and rational economic policies fail. The report states that mental models can 'block choices that enhance agency and promote well-being' but fortunately mental models are 'somewhat malleable' and thus can be shifted through targeted interventions to promote development objectives (ibid., pp. 13, 20).

In this report the World Bank promotes behavioural interventions that aim to change people's mental models in ways that enable them to purpose their own goals, or at least those goals that the World Bank considers to be in their best interest. Rather than addressing structural causes of poverty, the World Bank sees the obstacles to development and poverty alleviation lying in the poor decision-making of individuals, which can be addressed through minor and low-cost policy changes that 'nudge' the poor towards choosing better options (Fine et al., 2016, p. 642). In the behavioural economics approach of the World Bank, human behaviour is shaped by social and cultural context, but 'the social nature or determinants of behaviour . . . are totally decontextualized, implicitly reflecting asocial, ahistorical and universal notions of human, as individual, behaviour' (ibid., p. 652). Social structures of power, race, class, conflict and gender are left out of the picture. Instead, people's poverty is the result of a mental model which makes them incapable of exercising self-control or developing aspirations, and these pathologies can be addressed through minor policy adjustments. By incorporating a limited notion of culture into its analysis, the World Bank is participating in an ongoing process of neoclassical economics colonizing other social sciences. In other words, the World Bank integrates culture into its 'arsenal of neo-liberal development rule' (Watts, 2006, p. 55). Watts uses this term to explain how development operates as a realm of expertise that enframes and shapes the conduct of people. In the WDR 2015, the World Bank seeks to reshape the mindsets of people to change the way they behave and make decisions. This is not a new approach, however, and socio-technical practices to expand the neoliberal economic arrangements have a long history. The World Bank, in supporting the Urban Property Rights Project in Peru, for example, assumed that making residents of informal neighbourhoods owners of the properties they had built would turn them into small entrepreneurs and lift them out of poverty (Mitchell, 2005). What these interventions share is an approach to culture as a separate sphere, as 'worlds unto themselves', which can be 'incorporated into another world of incentives, behaviours and values that is a priori designated as economic' (Da Costa, 2010, p. 509).

UNESCO's Conceptualization of Culture

A different perspective and policy approach to culture and development can be expected from UNESCO, given its central mission to protect and promote the diversity of cultural expression. Article 3 of the UNESCO Universal Declaration on Cultural Diversity states that cultural diversity is 'one of the roots of development, understood not simply in terms of economic growth, but also as a means to achieve a more satisfactory intellectual, emotional, moral and spiritual existence' (UNESCO, 2001). Development is always culturally constituted, or as Bandarin and his colleagues put it, '[t]he workings of culture are so intricately interwoven with and rooted in every aspect of economic, political, social and environmental activity that it is difficult to single them out and to measure their influence with precision' (Bandarin et al., 2011, p. 16). They argue that there is no contradiction between preserving culture and using it to create sustainable development because 'to preserve cultural and natural heritage for the enjoyment of future generations is also to tap into the creativity that is hallmark to the transformative power that brings about quality development' (ibid., p. 23).

Culture is also portrayed as a source of creativity, and cultural diversity must be defended and heritage preserved so that future generations can access the diversity of human experience and aspirations. At the same time, the Universal Declaration on Cultural Diversity acknowledges that culture takes different forms across space and time, and is therefore malleable, but cultural change is not explicitly mentioned. This tension has been identified by scholars who criticize the UNESCO conceptualization of culture as imprecise and contradictory (Eriksen, 2001; Isar and Pyykkönen, 2015). On the one hand, culture is conceptualized as a total and distinctive way of living for people in a particular society, which incorporates the economic. While this appears to be a holistic view, culture as a 'way of life' is then mainly applied to activities and people that are deemed exotic or different in the eyes of UNESCO, while the cultural dimension of modern phenomena is not explicitly recognized (Eriksen, 2001). This leads to a view of cultures as rooted, old, fragile and requiring respect and protection even when cultural practices curtail the rights of others. Eriksen argues that when referring to local arts, language, ideology, patriarchy, children's rights, food habits, ritual practices or local political structures, it would be better to use those or equivalent terms and jettison the deceptively cosy blanket of culture.

On the other hand, UNESCO understands culture as a resource – as arts and heritage that can be commodified and used to produce cultural goods and services for viable and competitive cultural industries (Isar and Pyykkönen, 2015, p. 17). The tension between these different conceptualizations can be seen to play out in relation to indigenous groups, for example, whose 'cultural logic' may not include marketization of cultural expressions (ibid.). Furthermore, their cultural expressions are often discouraged or actively repressed by governments if they are seen to challenge national unity. To understand how local cultural practices are selectively commodified, or why indigenous communities may resist pressures to market their culture, culture must be recognized as a site of struggle, not as essentialized difference (Nederveen Pieterse, 2001; Da Costa, 2010).

More recently, UNESCO has intervened in the discussion about the Sustainable Development Goals stating that 'culture should be placed at the heart of development policies' (UNESCO, n.d.). Global flows of labour, information and capital have 'a homogenizing influence on local culture' and 'a loss of uniqueness of local culture' which is counterproductive, as it leads to 'loss of identity, exclusion and conflict' particularly for 'traditional societies/communities exposed to modernisation models'. Putting culture at the heart of development policies should not fix or confine them but, rather, it would encourage investing in local culture and developing local resources, knowledge and skills 'to foster creativity and sustainable progress' and reduce poverty. UNESCO points out that many jobs and industries associated with the production and stewardship of culture are 'green by design' – sustainable tourism, music and local foods for example. Similar arguments that culture is good for the economy and poverty reduction have been made in relation to the Millennium Development Goals, for example world heritage sites providing employment for conservation workers, tour guides and craftspeople (Bandarin et al., 2011, p. 18). The problem with UNESCO's approach to culture in development policy is that it becomes a site for neoliberal market expansion, and thus lays itself open to the same criticisms levelled against the World Bank.

Reflexive Development Professionals?

These case studies of the World Bank and UNESCO suggest that multilateral institutions have incorporated culture in a limited and partial way, and have retreated since the early 2000s from efforts to broaden the range of knowledge and representation, like the *Voices of the Poor* study and the Universal Declaration on Cultural Diversity. There is little evidence of self-reflection in these powerful development organizations, at least not in any formal sense. This final section examines how development professionals have responded to the scholarship on culture and development.

In recent years, there has been a surge of self-reflective analysis by development professionals, many of whom have worked in universities as well as in development practice (Fechter and Hindman, 2011). Some of this work has been sparked by Raymond Apthorpe's writing about 'aidland', which he describes as a kind of bubble where the global development elite lives and works, largely oblivious of reality (Apthorpe, 2011). He argues that aid practices should be analysed within a broader context. This involves making 'we planners, administrators, human rights campaigners, development and humanitarian studies professors, researchers, aid-workers and others' the object of political, economic and social observation and analysis (ibid., p. 200).

Development practitioners are not merely providers of technical expertise and skills but also see themselves as engaged in cultural exchange. In a study of Nordic donor agents in Tanzania (Baaz, 2005), development workers saw themselves as exchanging culture, experience and values along with providing expertise and skills. Yet this cultural exchange was informed by the discourse of development which assigns the Northern development professionals a superior identity compared with their Southern partners (ibid., p. 110). The Nordic development workers in Baaz's study described themselves as active, reliable and innovative agents, but their effectiveness was compromised by Tanzanian partners who they constructed as passive and unreliable. This passivity was presented as the product of bad development aid practice. When Baaz's Nordic development actors questioned the Western modernity and Eurocentrism of the development discourse under which they were operating, the passivity of their partners became something to be admired. In this context, passivity was 'genuinely African', 'located within a traditional African culture and tradition' which contrasted favourably with the egocentrism, materialism and lack of spirituality of the West (ibid., p. 160). This self-reflective critique of development falls back on the same binary of the West and its others, with only the hierarchy reversed. What it doesn't do is question the foundation of the binary and how Western culture and Tanzanian culture are constructed. Thus the Western development workers construct the Third World other to suit their own image and desire, only as far as they want to know it, as bearers of 'a difference or an otherness that will not go so far as to question the foundation of their beings and makings' (Baaz, 2005, p. 162, citing Trinh 1989; see also McEwan, 2009, p. 129).

Many development practitioners yearn for 'effective and ethical relationships' that can replace old power hierarchies, develop trust between development actors and enable genuine dialogue (Hinton and Groves, 2004, p. 9). Such 'active partnerships require ongoing negotiation, sharing ideas and skills, and learning by trial and error' (Lewis, 1998, p. 506). Some argue that strong personal relationships are crucial to being able to bridge power and knowledge gaps between partners, and create space for joint problem solving (Lister, 2000; Eyben, 2014). Today this optimistic view of partnerships is no longer widely held. The concept of partnership has been so widely adopted and imbued with different meanings that it has lost all meaning. In practice, partnerships are often reduced to the instrumental purpose of 'getting things done' (Elbers, 2012), particularly in the context of Northern donor preoccupation with development effectiveness (Overton and Storey, 2004; Hatton and Schroeder, 2007). The 'ideal of "productivity", of getting more for less, permeates the aid sector to the point where bureaucrats and others can refer to it as the "aid industry" without a trace of irony' (Macintyre, 2012, p. 261). While donors hold the purse strings and call the shots, contractualized partnerships serve as a convenient mechanism for spreading risks and responsibilities among 'stakeholders' if things go wrong (Overton and Storey, 2004; Hatton and Schroeder, 2007).

Many development interventions now require the participation of the communities and people they are targeting because this is seen to enhance their effectiveness and sustainability. However, this engagement with those who are being developed is not a partnership of equals, where solutions to problems are jointly created, but rather a project of 'educating desires, habits, aspirations and beliefs; they are a form of government through (constructed) community' (Engel and Susilo, 2014, p. 159). Community is constructed through these interventions in the sense that they are imagined by the development professionals as homogeneous groups, without class, gender and ethnic divisions. In other words, culture is equated with otherness, and cross-cutting differences are ignored. Comparing a water and sanitation project in Java in the 2000s with a hygiene and sanitation project in the 1920s, Engel and Susilo conclude that both shared 'a process of governmentality' in which 'sanitation practices not conforming to (newly discovered) Western standards are condemned as filthy and backward' (ibid., p. 174). Participation is reduced to 'select from a menu of latrine designs and police their neighbours' sanitation habits' (ibid., p. 175). This form of governmentality is a one-size-fits-all approach to a development problem which is applied around the world without really engaging with local practices in their cultural, ecological, social, political and economic dimensions.

CONCLUSION

In this chapter I have argued that we can find different approaches to culture and development in the development literature, depending on how the two concepts are defined and theorized. One approach draws on a discourse of a national or territorially bounded culture, in which culture tends to be seen as separate from other social structures and practices. Culture is variously invoked as needing protection from 'outside' development processes, as a resource for development, or as a determinant of development outcomes. The latter perspective can lead to the argument that some countries, groups or individuals fail to develop because they have the wrong culture, a view that can be traced back to the modernization theory of the 1950s. In this view, adopting Western-style cultural traits and values is key to becoming modern and developed, and Western culture is simplified as a homogeneous system of values and behaviours. Culture matters in development in so far as it impacts on people's and countries' capacity to benefit from development interventions, as can be seen in the *World Development Report 2015*, and, on the positive side, culture can be a resource for economic growth, as claimed by UNESCO.

Another approach treats culture as fluid and changing, as a result of people interacting with cultural artefacts, ideas and practices from elsewhere. These intercultural connections have increased in recent decades as globalization has sped up and most, if not all, cultures today are hybrid and 'multicultural'. In this second approach, culture is seen as 'embodied and lived, actively produced and expressed, through all social practices, through all that is concrete and everyday' (Pred, 1992, p. 109). In other words, culture takes in processes and things that are not normally called culture, including class, gender, sovereignty, trade, politics and place (Apthorpe, 2005, p. 137). Development, in this approach, is cultural, and mainstream development discourse, or 'developmentalism' (Apthorpe, 2005), can be analysed as a cultural construct or as a global faith, just as the 'economy' and 'economics' – which looms so large in development discourse – as a stand-alone structure is a cultural construct that can be studied (Mitchell, 2005).

Culture cannot simply be added on to development policies and practices because it is already part of them. Careful analysis of development texts can uncover the workings of culture, and close attention to geographical and historical context can reveal the multiple truths that each culture contains. One common challenge emerging from attempts to integrate culture into development interventions is that these interventions are intended to be above the politics of culture – they are designed as global blueprints that can work anywhere. Multiple voices and special interests of diverse actors are not compatible with this approach. But many development actors are passionate about improving the lives of people, and many people want their lives improved – with the right kind of development. A critical perspective on culture and development needs to see not only culture as changing but also development. Rather than seeing development as a regime of truth based in Western modernity, we need to view and analyse it as set of hybrid, dynamic, cultural formations that emerge in different places, involve different relationships and often combine indigenous and modern concepts (Mosse, 2014).

REFERENCES

Allen, T. (1992), 'Taking culture seriously', in T. Allen and A. Thomas (eds), *Poverty and Development in the 1990s*, Oxford: Oxford University Press, pp. 331–46.

Appadurai, A. (2004), 'The capacity to aspire: culture and the terms of recognition', in V. Rao and M. Walton (eds), *Culture and Public Action*, Stanford: Stanford University Press, pp. 59–84.

Apthorpe, R. (2005), '"It's [the] culture, stupid!" Why "adding culture" is unlikely to make any serious difference to international developmentalism', *The Asia Pacific Journal of Anthropology*, 6(2), 130–41.

Apthorpe, R. (2011), 'With Alice in aidland: a seriously satirical allegory', in D. Mosse (ed.), *Adventures in Aidland: The Anthropology of Professionals in International Development*, Oxford: Berghahn, pp. 199–219.

Baaz, M. E. (2005), *The Paternalism of Partnership. A Postcolonial Reading of Identity in Development Aid*, London: Zed Books.

Bandarin, F., J. Hosagrahar and F. S. Albernaz (2011), 'Why development needs culture', *Journal of Cultural Heritage Management and Sustainable Development*, 1(1), 15–25.

Boon, J. A. (1990), *Affinities and Extremes*, Chicago: University of Chicago Press.

Clammer, J. R. (2012), *Culture, Development and Social Theory: Towards an Integrated Social Development*, London: Zed Books.

Clark, D. A. (ed.) (2006), *The Elgar Companion to Development Studies*, Cheltenham, UK and Northampton, MA, USA: Edward Elgar Publishing.

Cornwall, A. and M. Fujita (2012), 'Ventriloquising "the poor"? Of voices, choices and the politics of "participatory" knowledge production', *Third World Quarterly*, 33(9), 1751–65.

Crewe, E. and R. Axelby (2013), *Anthropology and Development: Culture, Morality and Politics in a Globalised World*, Cambridge: Cambridge University Press.

Da Costa, D. (2010), 'Introduction: relocating culture in development and development in culture', *Third World Quarterly*, 31(4), 501–22.

Desai, V. and R. B. Potter (eds) (2008), *The Companion to Development Studies* (2nd edn), London: Hodder Education.

Desai, V. and R. B. Potter (eds) (2014), *The Companion to Development Studies* (3rd edn), Abingdon: Routledge.

Elbers, W. (2012), *The Partnership Paradox: Principles and Practice in North-South NGO Relations*, Ontwerp: Ipskamp B.V.

Engel, S. and A. Susilo (2014), 'Shaming and sanitation in Indonesia: a return to colonial practices in Indonesia?', *Development and Change*, 45(1), 157–78. doi:10.1111/dech.12075

Eriksen, T. H. (2001), 'Between universalism and relativism: a critique of the UNESCO concept of culture', in J. K. Cowan, M.-B. Dembour and R. A. Wilson (eds), *Culture and Rights: Anthropological Perspectives*, Cambridge: Cambridge University Press, pp. 127–48.

Escobar, A. (1995), *Encountering Development: The Making and Unmaking of the Third World*, Princeton: Princeton University Press.

Eyben, R. (2014), *International Aid and the Making of a Better World*, London: Routledge.

Fechter, A.-M. and H. Hindman (eds) (2011), *Inside the Everyday Lives of Development Workers: The Challenges and Futures of Aidland*, Sterling, VA: Kumarian Press.

Fine, B., D. Johnston, A. C. Santos and E. V. Waeyenberge (2016), 'Nudging or fudging: the World Development Report 2015', *Development and Change*, 47(Forum 2016), 640–63.

Francis, P. (2001), 'Participatory development at the World Bank: the primacy of process', in B. Cook and U. Kothari (eds), *Participation: The New Tyranny?*, London: Zed Books, pp. 72–87.

Hall, S. (1992), 'The west and the rest: discourse and power', in S. Hall and B. Gieben (eds), *Formations of Modernity*, Cambridge: Polity Press/Open University Press, pp. 274–311.

Hatton, M. J. and K. Schroeder (2007), 'Partnership theory and practice: time for a new paradigm', *Canadian Journal of Development Studies*, 28(1), 157–62.

Hinton, R. and L. Groves (2004), 'The complexity of inclusive aid', in L. Groves and R. Hinton (eds), *Inclusive Aid: Changing Power and Relationships in International Development*, London: Earthscan, pp. 3–20.

Huntington, S. P. (2000), 'Foreword: cultures count', in L. E. Harrison and S. P. Huntington (eds), *Culture Matters: How Values Shape Human Progress*, New York: Basic Books, pp. xiii–xvi.

Inglehart, R. (1997), *Modernization and Postmodernization: Cultural, Economic, and Political Change in 43 Societies*, Princeton, NJ: Princeton University Press.

Inkeles, A. and D. H. Smith (1974), *Becoming Modern: Individual Change in Six Developing Countries*, Cambridge, MA: Harvard University Press.

Isar, Y. R. and M. Pyykkönen (2015), 'Confusing culture, polysemous diversity: "culture" and "cultural diversity" in and after the Convention', in D. D. Beukelaer, M. Pyykkönen and J. P. Singh (eds), *Globalization, Culture, and Development*, Palgrave Macmillan, pp. 13–28.

Kaur, R. (2012), 'Nation's two bodies: rethinking the idea of "new" India and its other', *Third World Quarterly*, 33(4), 603–21.

Landes, D. (2000), 'Culture makes almost all the difference', in L. E. Harrison and S. P. Huntington (eds), *Culture Matters: How Values Shape Human Progress*, New York: Basic Books, pp. 2–13.

Lerner, D. (1958), *The Passing of Traditional Society: Modernizing the Middle East*, New York: Free Press.

Lewis, D. (1998), 'Development NGOs and the challenge of partnership: changing relations between North and South', *Social Policy and Administration*, 32(5), 501–12.

Lister, S. (2000), 'Power in partnership? An analysis of an NGO's relationships with its partners', *Journal of International Development*, 12, 227–39.

Macintyre, M. (2012), 'Gender violence in Melanesia and the problem of Millennium Development Goal No. 3', in M. Jolly, C. Stewart with C. Brewer (eds), *Gender Violence in Melanesia*, Canberra: ANU E Press.

McEwan, C. (2009), *Post-Colonialism and Development*, London: Routledge.

Mitchell, T. (2005), 'The work of economics: how a discipline makes its world', *European Journal of Sociology*, 46, 297–320.

Mosse, D. (2014), 'Knowledge as relational: reflections on knowledge in international development', *Forum for Development Studies*, 41(3), 513–23. doi:http://www.tandfonline.com/action/showCitFormats?doi=10.1080/08039410.2014.959379.

Narayan, D. and P. L. Petesch (eds) (2000), *From Many Lands, Voices of the Poor*, Vol. 3, New York: Oxford University Press for the World Bank.

Nederveen Pieterse, J. (2001), *Development Theory* (1st edn), Thousand Oaks: Sage.

Opel, A. and V. Shiva (2008), 'From water crisis to water culture', *Cultural Studies*, 22(3–4), 498–509.

Organisation for Economic Co-operation and Development (OECD) (1996), *Shaping the 21st Century: The Contribution of Development Co-operation*, Paris: OECD.

Overton, J. and D. Storey (2004), 'Aid and partnerships: the effectiveness of relationships', *Development Bulletin*, 65, 30–44.

Peet, R. and E. Hartwick (2009), *Theories of Development: Contentions, Arguments, Alternatives* (2nd edn), New York: Guilford Press.

Porter, D., B. Allen and G. Thompson (1991), *Development in Practice: Paved with Good Intentions*, London: Routledge.

Pred, A. (1992), 'Capitalisms, crises, and cultures II: notes on local transformation and everyday cultural struggles', in A. Pred and M. J. Watts (eds), *Reworking Modernity: Capitalisms and Symbolic Discontent*, Brunswick: Rutgers University Press, pp. 106–17.

Radcliffe, S. A. (ed.) (2006), *Culture and Development in a Globalizing World: Geographies, Actors and Paradigms*, London: Routledge.

Rao, V. and M. Walton (2004), 'Conclusion: implications of a cultural lens for public policy and development thought', in V. Rao and M. Walton (eds), *Culture and Public Action*, Stanford: Stanford University Press, pp. 359–72.

Rist, G. (1997), *The History of Development. From Western Origins to Global Faith*, London: Zed Books.

Said, E. W. (1978), *Orientalism: Western Conceptions of the Orient*, New York: Pantheon Books.

Said, E. W. (1997), *Covering Islam: How the Media and the Experts Determine How we See the Rest of the World* (rev. edn), New York: Vintage Books.

Schech, S. (2014), 'Culture and development', in V. Desai and R. B. Potter (eds), *The Companion to Development Studies* (3rd edn), London: Routledge, pp. 42–6.

Schech, S. and J. Haggis (2000), *Culture and Development: A Critical Introduction*, Oxford: Blackwell.

Schech, S. and S. Vas Dev (2007), 'Governing through participation? The World Bank's new approach to the poor', in D. B. Moore (ed.), *The World Bank: Development, Poverty, Hegemony*, Durban: University of Natal Press, pp. 171–203.

Sen, A. (2004), 'How does culture matter?', in V. Rao and M. Walton (eds), *Culture and Public Action*, Stanford: Stanford University Press, pp. 37–58.

Skelton, T. and T. Allen (1999), *Culture and Global Change*, London: Routledge.

Trinh, Thi Minh-Ha (1989), *Woman, Native, Other: Writing Postcoloniality and Feminism*, Bloomington: Indiana University Press.

UNESCO (2001), *Universal Declaration on Cultural Diversity*, Paris: UNESCO.

UNESCO (n.d.), 'The future we want: the role of culture in sustainable development'. Retrieved from: http://www.unesco.org/new/en/culture/themes/culture-and-development/the-future-we-want-the-role-of-culture/.

United Nations (2015), 'Sustainable Development Goals: 17 goals to transform our world'. Retrieved from: http://www.un.org/sustainabledevelopment/sustainable-development-goals/.

Watts, M. J. (2003), 'Alternative modern – development as cultural geography', in K. Anderson (ed.), *Handbook of Cultural Geography*, Thousand Oaks: Sage, pp. 433–53.

Watts, M. J. (2006), 'Culture, development and global neoliberalism', in S. A. Radcliffe (ed.), *Culture and Development in a Globalising World*, London: Routledge, pp. 30–58.

Williams, G., P. Meth and K. Willis (2009), *Geographies of Developing Areas: The Global South in a Changing World*, London: Routledge.

World Bank (2000), *World Development Report 2000/2001 Attacking Poverty*, Washington, DC: World Bank.

World Bank (2015), *World Development Report 2015: Mind, Society, and Behavior*, Washington, DC: World Bank.

PART III

SOCIAL ASPECTS

16. The migration–development nexus: current challenges and future research agenda

Tanja Bastia[1]

INTRODUCTION

Since the turn of the century, the migration–development nexus has emerged as a key concern for policy-makers (United Nations, 2006; World Bank, 2006, Ratha and Shaw, 2007; United Nations Development Programme, 2009; Chappell, 2010) as well as for social scientists (Skeldon, 1997; Sørensen et al., 2002; de Haas, 2005, 2010; Bakewell, 2008; Piper, 2009; Glick Schiller and Faist, 2010; Faist et al., 2011; Brønden, 2012) and is now regularly discussed at high-level meetings (Martin et al., 2007). However, most of this literature is undifferentiated with regard to gender relations (Sørensen, 2005; Kunz, 2008), despite the availability of a considerable literature on gender and migration (Willis and Yeoh, 2000; Silvey, 2006; Piper, 2008) and the fact that today women constitute almost half of all migrants.

The purpose of this review is therefore twofold: first, to interrogate the migration–development nexus in relation to that which it excludes and, second, to bring the gender and migration – and to a lesser extent, the gender and development – literature to bear on migration–development nexus debates.

The review will trace the emergence of the migration–development nexus debates. While migration and development can be understood as referring to a broad area of interest in the relationship between migration and development, the recent emergence of the migration–development nexus is more closely associated with development understood as purposive intervention (see Cowen and Shenton, 1994; Radcliffe, 2006b) and, as I will argue, generally excludes the broader processes of social change that are also associated with migration. Moreover, the type of development privileged in the migration–development nexus relates to development as economic growth, marginalising the social dimensions of development (Piper, 2009). Writing from the premise that gender is a constituting factor in migration processes, this review will show that the migration–development nexus is generally gender blind (King et al.,

2006). When gender is included in these debates, this is usually done in the form of including women as 'better remitters', which, as has been shown elsewhere (Kunz, 2008), is infused with stereotypes. Such an approach is skewed, given that it focuses only on women, as opposed to focusing on gender relations (King, 2012). Moreover, it includes women solely on the basis of efficiency arguments, that is it includes women for the benefit of others, be it their households, communities or countries of origin.

While there is a large literature on the role of women in development, some of which also relates to migration – for example, work on women and globalisation (Wolf, 1990) or research on internal migration (Jelin, 1977; Townsend, 1995) – this is usually not considered to be part of the migration–development nexus because of the narrow definition of what 'development' means in these debates. There is clearly scope here for a broader understanding of development, which might include a move away from the normative framing of migration as being 'useful' for (economic) development towards a more comprehensive understanding of the ways in which multiple forms of movement across space are related with broader processes of socio-economic change. A more critical perspective would therefore challenge the unidirectional view of the benefits of migration flowing in the opposite direction to the movement of people (discussed below) but would also allow space for an interrogation of those who are able to participate and benefit from these movements.

On the basis of these critiques, this chapter argues for re-engaging feminist analyses with migration–development debates. This will include:

1. developing a better understanding of how gender relations influence migration as well as how gender relations change as a result of migration (Hondagneu-Sotelo, 1994; Donato et al., 2006; de Haas and van Rooij, 2010);
2. asking who benefits from migration, as opposed to including women on the basis of efficiency arguments (Kabeer, 1994; Jackson and Pearson, 1998);
3. including an appreciation of the importance of multiple axes of advantage and disadvantage (Bastia et al., 2011; Lutz et al., 2011; Riaño 2011).

THE EMERGENCE OF THE MIGRATION–DEVELOPMENT NEXUS

In the current historical juncture, we can observe six global migration trends: globalisation, acceleration, differentiation, feminisation, increased politicisation, and the proliferation of migration transitions (Castles and Miller, 2009; Samers, 2010). Debates around the potential migration holds for development are clearly related to these most recent trends. However, they are in no way new. Thomas Faist and Margit Fauser (2011) identify a first post-WWII phase, which spanned the 1950s and 1960s, where the focus was on remittances and return, specifically on filling labour gaps in the North – particularly in the US and Northern European countries. De Haas, who uses the analogy of a 'pendulum' to illustrate shifts in migration–development debates, describes this first phase as being predominantly optimistic (de Haas, 2012).

A second phase ran during the 1970s and 1980s and focused on underdevelopment and migration. Key themes during this phase were poverty and the brain drain; that is, poverty and underdevelopment as causes of migration and the ways in which brain drain was understood as exacerbating pre-existing poverty levels by depleting poor countries of much needed highly skilled workers, such as nurses and doctors (Özden and Schiff, 2006; Raghuram, 2009b; Faist and Fauser, 2011). This phase was predominantly pessimistic and portrayed migration as a problem for development (de Haas, 2012). According to Faist and Fauser (2011), we are currently in the third phase, which they identify as 'migration and co-development'. This phase is characterised by a celebration of transnational circulation, in which temporary and circular migration are seen as an ideal and are often portrayed as new measures that will facilitate the achievement of development, including community development and post-conflict reconstruction (ibid.; Skeldon 2012). 'Brain drain' therefore gives room to 'brain gain' and a move towards neo-optimism (Raghuram, 2009b; de Haas, 2012).

It is clear that the way in which development is understood in relation to migration reflects broader ideological shifts in dominant development theories (de Haas, 2012). For example, development is conceptualised as a possibility during the post-WWII period, particularly in the context of the welfare state and strong government intervention. On the other hand, more recent approaches reflect migrants taking increasingly individualised responsibilities for the development of their countries and communities of origin, in the context of dwindling amounts of foreign aid, a shrinking state and privatisation of social services following the implementation of structural adjustment programmes in much of the developing world (Glick Schiller and Faist, 2010; Glick Schiller, 2011). However, most of the most recent interest is firmly rooted in post-WWII understandings of development as progress, in which the 'Third World' is homogenised and seen as in need of development, albeit with the significant transfer of the responsibility for development from the nation-state to the individual migrant (Schuurman, 2000; see also Raghuram, 2009a).

Moreover, development in these debates is understood as purposive intervention as opposed to an immanent process of social change (Cowen and Shenton, 1994). The migration–development nexus is now an industry (Raghuram, 2009a), with a complex web of multiple actors at the local, regional and global levels, interested in fulfilling the 'development potential' of migration while mitigating its social costs. This framing of development has implications for the kinds of issues that are understood as falling under the migration–development nexus agenda. For example, while remittances for productive investment are of interest, those that are used to fund 'independence' movements are not (Raghuram, 2009a), given that development in this perspective is supposed to support the status quo and 'reinforce social economic and political processes within *statuted* spatialities' (ibid., p. 112; emphasis in original). The implication for feminist readings of migration and development is important, given feminist objectives of disrupting existing unequal gender relations.

The withdrawal of the developmental state therefore explains the current (neo-)optimism towards migrants. Migration became appealing because it is closely related to remittances, which are in turn associated with a number of positive consequences. First, remittances are often greater than the amount received in the form of aid or foreign direct investment (World Bank, 2006; Ratha and Shaw, 2007; United Nations Development Programme, 2009). As such, they can improve the balance of payments and provide key financial resources for investment in development. Moreover, they can be counter-cyclical (World Bank, 2006) and therefore smooth economic and financial troubles experienced in the country of origin. Second, at the meso and micro levels, it is believed that remittances will lead to 'development' through monetary transfers directly to those 'who need it most' (Skeldon, 1997; Kothari, 2002). This will improve the well-being of the household of origin through direct monetary transfers from the migrant to the relatives who stayed in the country of origin. Moreover, once achieved, it is believed that this increased level of development will also work towards stemming migration (de Haas, 2007).

These assumptions are largely disputed. For example, there is little evidence to suggest that increased development will decrease migration. In fact, the reverse is often true (de Haas, 2007). There is also ample evidence that migration requires access to financial, human and social capital (Kothari, 2003). Remittances might therefore be going to those who are already better off and contribute towards reproducing pre-existing social hierarchies (Bracking, 2003; Black et al., 2005). In fact, with most development efforts focusing on poverty alleviation, there has been little attention on the relationship between migration and inequality in the migration–development nexus (ibid.).

Moreover, the social dimension of the migration–development nexus needs further exploration (Piper, 2009). Remittances, for example, are not just economic. The migration literature has shown that remittances are also social (Levitt, 1998), while the social context of the receipt of economic remittances is also significant (Goldring, 2004).

There are therefore four key problems with this literature. First, it omits or pays little attention to the social dimension of development. Second, development is understood as purposive intervention as opposed to a broader process of social change. Third, women and gender are largely overlooked. Finally, there is little attention paid to the development of migrants themselves (Raghuram, 2009a). While referring to the first two, this review will focus largely on the last two points.

WHERE ARE THE WOMEN?

In much of this literature, the particular role of migrant women has been overlooked (King et al., 2006; Kunz 2008), which is partly a result of how the literature is framed. Migrant women have been largely absent, particularly during the earlier interest in migration and development, which, to some extent, reflects their absence from migration theories in general. During the 1960s and 1970s, women were usually seen as secondary migrants, that is not migrants in their own right but as wives accompanying the primary male migrant worker (Anthias, 1983; Phizacklea, 1983; Morokvasic, 1984). During the first phase, migration scholarship was notably gender blind, assuming that all migrants, particularly migrant workers, were men. There was very little attention paid to women migrants, despite early realisations of the role of women in migration (Ravenstein, 1885). This started to change only during the 1980s, when an emergent feminist critique of migration theories began making women migrants visible (Morokvasic, 1983; Phizacklea 1983).

The following decade moved the focus from women to gender relations and expanded our knowledge of how gender is a constituting factor in migration processes, influencing each stage of the migration journey (Grasmuck and Pessar, 1991; Hondagneu-Sotelo, 1994; Zinn et al., 1997; Kofman, 1999, 2000; Willis and Yeoh, 2000). Some of this work focused on developing countries (Chant, 1992; Radcliffe, 1993) and included research on internal migration (Gugler, 1997; Chant, 1998; Lawson, 1998); how migration is related to modernity (Mills, 1997); and sexuality (Constable, 1997). A significant amount of research was based on the Asian region, where women have been historically active in migration flows (Piper and Roces, 2003; Piper and Yamanaka, 2003; Piper, 2004).

Much of this literature clearly relates to development, for example, research on internal migration or processes of globalisation, such as work on the new international division of labour (for example, Wolf, 1990), or research that is more closely associated with regional patterns of cross-border or internal migration (for example Jelin, 1977; Townsend, 1995; Pessar, 2005). However, because of the narrow framing of the migration–development nexus discussed above, this research is not usually considered part of that nexus. The narrow framing of the debates often precludes the inclusion of broader processes of social change, and we clearly have much to learn by expanding the notion of what is meant by 'development' in the migration–development nexus.

At the turn of the century, work on gender and migration moved on to highlight migrant women's agency (Gardiner Barber, 2000), including work on migration decision-making (De Jong, 2000) and how the experience of migration challenges gender relations in communities of origin (Gamburd, 2000). Another strand of the literature aimed at making transnationalism more 'gender aware' (Mahler and Pessar, 2001; Pessar and Mahler, 2003; Pratt and Yeoh, 2003). Some research focused on particular sectors of work, such as domestic work, where migrant women often predominate (Anderson, 1993; Parreñas, 2001; Hondagneu-Sotelo, 2007). This literature sometimes crosses over into discussions of trafficking, which emerged since the ratification of the trafficking protocol in 2000 (Andrijasevic, 2003; Kempadoo et al., 2005; O'Connell Davidson, 2006, 2010).

Feminist geographers are leading the field in providing new understandings of social reproduction in globalised capitalism (Katz, 2001) and in identifying migration as 'mutually constituted with patterns of social reproduction' (Silvey, 2009, p. 510). While mainstream approaches to development, such as those included in the 2009 World Development Report, identify migration as a route out of poverty in rural areas, they also downplay existing connections, social networks and power relations that span different places (Silvey, 2009). A focus on social reproduction challenges current understandings of the migration–development nexus. As previously argued, the migration–development nexus conceptualises development benefits flowing through migrants and/or remittances from higher- to lower-income countries. A critical understanding of social reproduction, on the other hand, identifies low-income countries as delivering a direct subsidy to higher-income countries, given that migrants' countries of origin bear most of the costs associated with social reproduction (ibid.).

Care has also emerged as a dynamic area of enquiry for those working on migration. This began with Rhacel Salazar Parreñas's work on the 'international division of reproductive labour' (Parreñas, 2000) and the 'international transfer of caregiving' (Parreñas, 1998), which was popularised by Arlie Hochschild under the term 'care chains' (Hochschild, 2000). Since then, this literature has expanded to include many studies on domestic workers as carers (Parreñas, 2001; Gutierrez Rodriguez, 2010); caring across distances (Hondagneu-Sotelo and Avila, 1997); and the distribution of benefits across these care chains (Parreñas, 2012). However, most of these studies adopt the global as the most relevant level of analysis, with little attention to the genealogies of care in different places, the different institutions in the organisation of care (or the care diamond, see Razavi, 2007), or the recognition of the diversity of family forms (Raghuram, 2012). While this literature is not generally seen as being part of the migration–development nexus, for the reasons outlined above, once we expand the notion of migration–development to include broader processes of social change these studies clearly contribute to a better understanding of the reorganisation of care under the current process of neoliberalisation (see also Marchand and Sisson Runyan, 2011).

There is also an increasing interest in advancing a better understanding of undocumented migration, which is difficult to estimate (Koser, 2005, 2010; Anderson and Ruhs, 2010). Most of the data available are not sex-disaggregated (for an example see Koser, 2005). Studies based on apprehension rates identify young single men as making up the majority of irregular migrants (Jandl, 2007), while young men are also more prevalent as the subjects of undocumented moves in the popular imaginary (Andrijasevic, 2003). However, most reviews of irregular migration refer to women irregular migrants only exclusively in terms of being victims of trafficking (see for example, Koser, 2005). As many have shown, the sole focus of women migrants in potentially vulnerable situations as victims of trafficking is far from useful, obscuring the situations surrounding their migrations as well as devaluing their agency (Andrijasevic, 2003, 2007; Kempadoo et al., 2005; O'Connell Davidson 2006).

Most of this literature focuses on migrant women, but it does so by taking into account low-wage work and sectors of the labour market where women predominate, such as domestic work or sex work (Raghuram, 2008). As Raghuram (ibid.) argues, there is little research on migrant women who enter male-dominated sectors, such as ICT. Moving beyond feminised sectors of work and of migration as a strategy to overcome 'career blockages' is increasingly important given the expanding middle class globally, and the fact that work is increasingly part of middle-class women's identities in many parts of the world (ibid.).

The relevance and significance of gender relations for understanding migration were eventually also acknowledged in migration–development nexus debates. However, these were done with a particular view of the migrant woman in mind, one that supported the idea of development as economic growth and a path to modernisation. From the policy-makers' point of view, women became the 'better' remitters because of the view that (1) women tend to remit a larger proportion of their salaries, even when their salaries are generally lower than men's (Global Commission on International Migration (GCIM), 2005; Sørensen, 2005; Ribas, 2008) and (2) a belief that 'women make the most effective use of remittances' (GCIM, 2005, p. 28). Both assumptions can be challenged on the basis of existing empirical evidence (Kunz, 2008). However, women became the ultimate migrants of choice in some contexts, such as the Philippines, which began drawing up its migration policies on the basis of these stereotypes (Gardiner Barber, 2000, 2008; Parreñas, 2001, 2008). At the same time, while sometimes encouraged, women's migration also became increasingly associated with undesirable social consequences (Parreñas, 2005; Whitehead and Hashim, 2005). Those who take up opportunities abroad are not just young, single women, sending back remittances to their parents, but also mothers, some of whom have young children. Mothers who migrate generally rely on other female relatives or paid childminders, who look after their children during their often prolonged absences while working abroad, giving rise to the 'global care chains' and the vertical distribution of care across class and race (Ehrenreich and Hochschild, 2003), discussed earlier. While these long absences and the lack of the stable emotional care often provided by mothers raise real concerns for children's welfare (Parreñas, 2005), the reactions of policy-makers, as well as community leaders, can be characterised as a 'moral panic' (Cohen, 1972). This is not to say that policy-makers and other commentators raised concerns only about the migration of mothers. All women migrants, whether single, married, with or without children, give rise to moral concerns and speculations in a way that men's migrations do not. For example, the migration of single women is often associated with the corruption of their sexual character (Constable, 1997), while migrant mothers are characterised as irresponsible and greedy, who prefer to leave their children for financial gain instead of staying put and fulfilling their given mothering role (Parreñas, 2008; Bastia, 2013). In these debates, very little is said about the role that fathers could play in filling in for their partners' absence or the ways in which young women migrants are often the object of unwanted sexual attention.

In this newer round of interest in migration and development, therefore, women became the object of intense interest given the relatively higher benefits that their families or their communities of origin could gain from them. These views mimic and reuse what are known as the 'efficiency' arguments in the gender and development literature, in which women were seen as the objects of development policy only on the basis that their 'integration' in development would spur wider benefits for their children and/or the national economies (Boserup, 1970; Kabeer, 1994; Razavi, 1997). Such approaches, while focusing on women, place women centre stage only on the grounds that others can benefit from their inclusion in development and/or migration–development policies. Women become carriers of benefits for others, with very little attention or even interest to what these consequences might mean for the women themselves. Moreover, many of these policies fail to take into account the real costs of women's inclusion in development (Beneria, 2003; Rocha, 2007) and/or migration–development (Kunz, 2008).

It is clearly difficult to put a figure on suffering. But women's integration into the global economy – be it through development, by providing additional income-generating opportunities, or through migration – is often infused with suffering. This might be related to leaving children at home while working abroad for long periods of time or the types of jobs that women perform in the global economy – such as manual labour in export processing zones, care work, agricultural labour, and low-paid service sector work – where the emotional suffering is often coupled with labour exploitation, long working hours, isolation and sometimes servitude (Anderson, 1993; Lim, 1998; Parreñas, 2001; Ehrenreich and Hochschild, 2003). Some of these forms of movement can rightly be considered as a form of human trafficking (Kempadoo et al., 2005).

Therefore, while the children and other family members as well as the nation's coffers might benefit from the remittances that migrant women send home, women are seldom at the heart of policy-makers' concerns. In other words, one seldom hears the question being asked: who actually benefits from the migration of women?

MIGRATION, SOCIAL CHANGE AND MULTIPLE AXES OF DIFFERENTIATION

In an increasingly globalised and interconnected world, it is imperative that we pay attention to whether existing inequalities are exacerbated or challenged by the factors associated with globalisation and the so-called network society, such as migration. For women migrants, therefore, the challenge is to place women at the heart of our enquiry to better understand the extent to which they may also benefit from their migration. Feminist theories are well placed to help frame such an enquiry (Hondagneu-Sotelo, 2000; Bonifacio, 2012).

Feminism is inherently interested in promoting gender equity and achieving an equitable society where women and men enjoy not only the same opportunities but also equal status and worth. In migration, feminism helped shape an understanding of migration in which gender and migration are understood as constituting each other, that is representing a dialectical relationship in which gender relations influence migration and are in turn influenced by migration (Hondagneu-Sotelo, 1994; Kofman, 1999; Willis and Yeoh, 2000; Pessar, 2005; Curran et al., 2006; Mahler and Pessar, 2006; Piper, 2006; Silvey, 2006). Moreover, by following the critiques of the Black women's movement, postcolonial critics and those who have historically been misrepresented by feminist knowledge and scholarship (Mohanty, 1986; Radcliffe, 2006b; McEwan, 2009), it is clearly important to acknowledge the multiple forms of feminist organising (McEwan, 2001), as well as the multiple axes of disadvantage, which destabilise gender as the most important basis of unequal power relations. Some of these critiques have been taken up through the use of intersectionality, although this also carries its own set of problems (see below). It is clear that migration has the potential for promoting progressive social change. As migrants move from one place to another (whether within the same country or across national borders), they experience new cultures and ways of being that can lead them to question their own culture and society (Bastia, 2011), thereby leading them to challenge the status quo. However, most evidence suggests that migration reinforces existing social structures. De Haas for example, argues that 'Despite the often considerable benefits of migration and remittances for individuals and communities involved, migrants alone can generally not remove more structural development constraints and migration may actually contribute to development stagnation and reinforce the political status quo' (2012, p. 8).

This can be verified empirically but is also a logical conclusion if we take into account what we already know about migration: that the poorest generally lack the human, financial and social capital required to migrate (Skeldon, 1997; Kothari, 2002, 2003). Those who are able to migrate, if not the elites, are therefore generally better-off, and then reap even further benefits through migration and reinforce existing inequalities. Moreover, migration itself may also be an escape valve for societies in turmoil: by emigrating, migrants may be contributing to decreasing the overall levels of unemployment as well as weakening social and political demands on the state (Glick Schiller, 2011; de Haas, 2012). However, evidence to date is inconclusive (Black et al., 2005) and largely context-specific (de Haas, 2012).

For gender relations, the causal relationship is not so straightforward. While migration per se has the potential to disrupt existing gender-based ideology, it is unlikely to do so in the long term because women often trade any potential for disrupting gender relations for upward class mobility, a strategy they share with their partners (Bastia, 2011). In a context where women 'stay behind', that is where they do not migrate, they may engage in new activities as a result of their husbands' absence, but these may be seen as a burden rather than a source of empowerment (de Haas and van Rooij, 2010).

This brief overview of migration and social change already identifies multiple axes of differentiation as a key component of any feminist critique of migration and development, as opposed to focusing on gender alone. Over the past couple of decades, some have started integrating multiple axes of differentiation in a feminist analysis through the use of intersectionality. Intersectionality is credited to Crenshaw (1991) and emerged during the 1990s, promoted by feminist and critical race theorists who wished to critique the notion that gender, class, race and ethnicity are separate essentialist categories (Davis, 1981; hooks, 1984; Lorde, 1985; Hill Collins, 2009). Intersectionality is therefore used to draw attention to the interconnection of these categories of disadvantage (Burman, 2003; Brah and Phoenix, 2004; McCall, 2005; Valentine, 2007), with the aim of focusing on those who have been thus far excluded from mainstream feminist analysis (Anthias and Yuval-Davis, 1983; Nash, 2008). While race and gender constituted the 'quintessential intersection' (Nash, 2008, p. 1) and black women the 'quintessential intersectional subjects', with the proliferation of studies using intersectionality to look at migrant women, it would be possible to argue that migrant women are fast becoming the 'new quintessential intersectional subjects' (Bastia, forthcoming).

Over the last half-decade, there have been a number of studies of migration using intersectionality, particularly in the European context (Lutz et al., 2011; see also Burman, 2003; Buitelaar, 2006; Ludvig, 2006; Prins, 2006; Kosnik, 2011). These studies show that an intersectional approach can begin to redress some of the shortcomings in migration studies, for example by highlighting the importance of disaggregating analytical categories and revealing intra-group differences (for example, McIlwaine and Bermudez, 2011; Riaño, 2011). However, not everyone uses intersectionality from within a feminist perspective, and some have recently argued for the use of intersectionality for understanding other social inequalities in migration (Bürkner, 2012). Intersectionality is merely an approach, not a theoretical framework, and it is important to combine it with contextually sensitive historical analysis of power relations, of the type advanced by critical and postcolonial geographers (McEwan, 2001; Radcliffe, 2006a, 2006b; Andolina et al., 2009; Radcliffe and Rivers-Moore, 2009; Silvey, 2009) to avoid depoliticising it as, some have argued, has been the case with the implementation of 'gender mainstreaming' programmes (see Pearson, 2005).

CONCLUSION

This chapter began by reviewing the literature on the migration–development nexus, explaining its emergence and the way it has changed over the past decades. The migration–development nexus is firmly rooted in an understanding of development as economic growth, which privileges the productive dimension of migrants' lives and potential contribution to their countries of origin, marginalising social dimensions of development, including important areas such as social reproduction. The literature review identified key themes in the current phase of interest in the relationship between migration and development, particularly remittances and the ways in which this interest is linked to the retreat of the developmental state.

The review went on to highlight the lack of attention to gender relations, except for some interest in women as 'better' remitters than men, a stereotype that can be challenged on the basis of existing empirical evidence. It drew parallels between the lack of awareness of gender issues in the migration–development nexus literature and migration studies in general. It showed how migration studies moved from being gender blind to making women visible to finally understanding migration and gender as constituting each other. Taking into account the rich literature that exists on migration, for example that on internal migration or globalisation, would provide ample material for moving the debates forward within the migration–development nexus.

However, of critical importance here is what type of development we are referring to. Clearly, if we expand the notion that development does not refer solely to purposive action with the underlying assumption that it leads to progress and modernisation, but is rather a wider process of social change with the aim of creating more equal and just societies, we open up the possibility of including a number of areas of interest that are currently not thought of as being part of the migration–development nexus. In particular, the current retreat of the welfare state and the neoliberalisation of everyday life, including social reproduction, become of key importance, given that they disrupt the normative assumption that development benefits flow through migrants or remittances from richer to poorer countries. It opens up the possibility of recognising that social reproduction is borne by home countries and therefore represents 'a direct development subsidy to the economies of wealthy nations' (Silvey, 2009, p. 512).

Finally, the review also cautions against including women on the basis of efficiency arguments and argues for increased attention to be given to the 'winners' and 'losers' of migration (and development) or, to follow Raghuram 'migrants' own development' (2009a, p. 107). A feminist framework could provide the basis for such an analysis. However, it is important to qualify what is meant by 'feminism' and to integrate the historic critiques of the white, middle-class, Western feminism that was prevalent during the 1990s. Intersectionality emerged as part of these critiques and has been increasingly adopted for the study of migration. However, intersectionality is merely a framework, and this chapter argues that it should be combined with contextually sensitive, historical approaches with due attention to local power relations.

While it is necessarily valuable to include gender in the migration–development nexus, it is clearly as, or in fact more, important to, first, expand the notion of what development actually means. If we include gender in current conceptualisations of development, only as understood in the migration–development nexus, it will be difficult to move away from efficiency notions of women's integration in migration and development. A more critical approach to these debates calls for the expansion of what is meant by development so as to allow space for interrogating the notion of development and questioning who actually benefits from migration.

NOTE

1. This chapter was first published as an article in *Geography Compass*, 7 (7), pp. 464–477, and is reprinted here with permission from John Wiley and Sons. The author is grateful to the publisher for granting permission to reprint.

REFERENCES

Anderson, B. D. P. (1993), *Britain's secret slaves: an investigation into the plight of overseas domestic workers in the United Kingdom*. London: Anti-Slavery International.
Anderson, B. and Ruhs, M. (2010), Researching illegality and labour migration. *Population, Space and Place* 16, pp. 175–179.
Andolina, R., Laurie, N. and Radcliffe, S. A. (2009), *Indigenous development in the Andes: culture, power, and transnationalism*. Durham, NC: Duke University Press.
Andrijasevic, R. (2003), The difference borders make: (il)legality, migration and trafficking in Italy among Eastern European women in prostitution. In Ahmed, S., Castaneda, C., Fortier, A.-M. and Sheller, M. (eds) *Uprootings/regroundings: questions of home and migration*. Oxford and New York: Berg.
Andrijasevic, R. (2007), Beautiful dead bodies: gender, migration and representation in anti-trafficking campaigns. *Feminist Review* 86, pp. 24–44.
Anthias, F. (1983), Sexual divisions and ethnic adaptation: the case of Greek-Cypriot

women. In Phizacklea, A. (ed.) *One way ticket: migration and female labour*. London: Routledge and Kegan Paul.

Anthias, F. and Yuval-Davis, N. (1983), Contextualizing feminism: gender, ethnic and class divisions. *Feminist Review* 15, pp. 62–75.

Bakewell, O. (2008), 'Keeping them in their place': the ambivalent relationship between development and migration in Africa. *Third World Quarterly* 29, pp. 1341–1358.

Bastia, T. (2011), Migration as protest? Negotiating gender, class, and ethnicity in urban Bolivia. *Environment and Planning A* 43, pp. 1514–1529.

Bastia, T. (2013), 'I am going, with or without you': autonomy in Bolivian transnational migrations. *Gender, Place and Culture* 20 (2), pp. 160–177.

Bastia, T. (forthcoming), Intersectionality, migration and development. *Progress in Development Studies*.

Bastia, T., Piper, N. and Prieto Carròn, M. (2011), Geographies of migration, geographies of justice? Feminism, intersectionality, and rights. *Environment and Planning A* 43, pp. 1492–1498.

Beneria, L. (2003), *Gender, development, and globalization: economics as if all people mattered*. New York and London: Routledge.

Black, R., Natali, C. and Skinner, J. (2005), *Migration and inequality*. Washington, DC: World Bank.

Bonifacio, G. T. (2012), *Feminism and migration: cross-cultural engagements*. Dordrecht and London: Springer.

Boserup, E. (1970), *Woman's role in economic development*. London: Allen & Unwin.

Bracking, S. (2003), Sending money home: are remittances always beneficial to those who stay behind? *Journal of International Development* 15, pp. 633–644.

Brah, A. and Phoenix, A. (2004), Ain't I a woman? Revisiting intersectionality. *Journal of Women's International Studies* 5, pp. 75–86.

Brønden, B. M. (2012), Migration and development: the flavour of the 2000s. *International Migration* 50, pp. 2–7.

Buitelaar, M. (2006), 'I am the ultimate challenge'. *European Journal of Women's Studies* 13, pp. 259–276.

Bürkner, H.-J. (2012), Intersectionality: how gender studies might inspire the analysis of social inequality among migrants. *Population, Space and Place* 18, pp. 181–195.

Burman, E. (2003), From difference to intersectionality: challenges and resources. *European Journal of Psychotherapy and Counselling* 6, pp. 293–308.

Castles, S. and Miller, M. J. (2009), *The age of migration: international population movements in the modern world*. New York and London: Guilford Press.

Chant, S. (1998), Households, gender and rural–urban migration: reflections on linkages and considerations for policy. *Environment and Urbanization* 10, pp. 5–22.

Chant, S. H. (1992), *Gender and migration in developing countries*. London: Belhaven.

Chappell, L. (2010), *Development on the move: measuring and optimising migration's economic and social impacts: global project report*. London: GDN and Institute for Public Policy Research.

Cohen, S. (1972), *Folk devils and moral panics: the creation of the mods and rockers*. London: MacGibbon & Kee.

Constable, N. (1997), Sexuality and discipline among Filipina domestic workers in Hong Kong. *American Ethnologist* 24, pp. 539–558.

Cowen, M. and Shenton, R. (1994), *Doctrines of development*. London: Routledge.

Crenshaw, K. (1991), Mapping the margins: intersectionality, identity politics, and violence against women of color. *Stanford Law Review* 43, pp. 1241–1299.

Curran, S. R., Shafer, S., Donato, K. M. and Garip, F. (2006), Mapping gender and migration in sociological scholarship: is it segregation or integration? *International Migration Review* 40, pp. 199–223.

Davis, A. Y. (1981), *Women, race & class*. London: Women's Press.

de Haas, H. (2005), International migration, remittances and development: myths and facts. *Third World Quarterly* 26, pp. 1269–1284.

de Haas, H. (2007), Turning the tide? Why development will not stop migration. *Development and Change* 38, pp. 819–841.

de Haas, H. (2010), Migration and development: a theoretical perspective. *International Migration Review* 44, pp. 227–264.

de Haas, H. (2012), The migration and development pendulum: a critical view on research and policy. *International Migration* 50, pp. 8–25.

de Haas, H. and van Rooij, A. (2010), Migration as emancipation? The impact of internal and international migration on the position of women left behind in rural Morocco. *Oxford Development Studies* 38, pp. 43–62.

De Jong, G. F. (2000), Expectations, gender, and norms in migration decision-making. *Population Studies: A Journal of Demography* 54, pp. 307–319.

Donato, K. M., Gabaccia, D., Holdaway, J., Manalansan, M. and Pessar P. R. (2006), A glass half full? Gender in migration studies. *International Migration Review* 40, pp. 3–26.

Ehrenreich, B. and Hochschild, A. R. (2003), *Global woman: nannies, maids, and sex workers in the new economy.* New York: Metropolitan Books.

Faist, T. and Fauser, M. (2011), The migration–development nexus: towards a transnational perspective. In Faist, T., Fauser, M. and Kivisto, P. (eds) *The migration–development nexus: a transnational perspective.* Basingstoke: Palgrave Macmillan.

Faist, T., Fauser, M. and Kivisto, P. (2011). *The migration–development nexus: a transnational perspective.* Basingstoke: Palgrave Macmillan.

Gamburd, M. R. (2000), *The kitchen spoon's handle: transnationalism and Sri Lanka's migrant housemaids.* Ithaca, NY: Cornell University Press.

Gardiner Barber, P. (2000), Agency in Philippine women's labour migration and provisional diaspora. *Women's Studies International Forum* 23, pp. 399–411.

Gardiner Barber, P. (2008), The ideal immigrant? Gendered class subjects in Philippine–Canada migration. *Third World Quarterly* 29, pp. 1265–1285.

Glick Schiller, N. (2011), A global perspective on migration and development. In Faist, T., Fauser, M. and Kivisto, P. (eds) *The migration–development nexus: a transnational perspective.* Basingstoke: Palgrave Macmillan, pp. 29–56.

Glick Schiller, N. and Faist, T. (2010), *Migration, development, and transnationalization: a critical stance.* New York: Berghahn Books.

Global Commission on International Migration (GCIM) (2005), *Migration in an interconnected world: new directions for action.* Geneva: GCIM.

Goldring, L. (2004), Family and collective remittances to Mexico: a multi-dimensional typology. *Development and Change* 35, pp. 799–840.

Grasmuck, S. and Pessar, P. R. (1991), *Between two islands: Dominican international migration.* Berkeley, CA and Oxford: University of California Press.

Gugler, J. (1997), Gender and rural–urban migration: regional contrasts and the gender transition. In Fairhurst, U. J., Booysen, I. and Hattingh, P. S. (eds) *Migration and gender: place, time and people specific.* Pretoria: IGU Commission on Gender and Geography.

Gutierrez Rodriguez, E. (2010), *Migration, domestic work and affect: a decolonial approach on value and the feminization of labor.* London: Routledge.

Hill Collins, P. (2009). *Black feminist thought: knowledge, consciousness, and the politics of empowerment.* New York: Routledge.

Hochschild, A. (2000), Global care chains and emotional surplus value. In Hutton, W. and Guiddens, A. (eds) *On the edge: living with global capitalism.* London: Jonathan Cape, pp. 130–46.

Hondagneu-Sotelo, P. (1994), *Gendered transitions: Mexican experiences of immigration.* Berkeley, CA and London: University of California Press.

Hondagneu-Sotelo, P. (2000), Feminism and migration. *The Annals of the American Academy of Political and Social Science*, 571, pp. 107–120.

Hondagneu-Sotelo, P. (2007), *Doméstica: immigrant workers cleaning and caring in the shadows of affluence.* Berkeley, CA and London: University of California Press.

Hondagneu-Sotelo, P. and Avila, E. (1997), 'I'm here, but I'm there': the meanings of Latina transnational motherhood. *Gender and Society* 11, pp. 548–571.

hooks, b. (1984), *Feminist theory from margin to center*. Boston, MA: South End Press.

Jackson, C. and Pearson, R. (1998*)*, *Feminist visions of development: gender, analysis and policy*. London: Routledge.

Jandl, M. (2007), Irregular migration, human smuggling, and the eastern enlargement of the European Union. *International Migration Review* 41, pp. 291–315.

Jelin, E. (1977), Migration and labor force participation of Latin American women: the domestic servants in the cities. *Signs* 3 (1), pp. 129–141.

Kabeer, N. (1994), *Reversed realities: gender hierarchies in development thought*. New Delhi: Kali for Women, 1995.

Katz, C. (2001), Vagabond capitalism and the necessity of social reproduction. *Antipode* 33, pp. 709–728.

Kempadoo, K., Sanghera, J. and Pattanaik, B. (2005), *Trafficking and prostitution reconsidered: new perspectives on migration, sex work, and human rights*. Boulder, CO and London: Paradigm Publishers.

King, R. (2012), Geography and migration studies: retrospect and prospect. *Population Space Place* 18, pp. 134–153.

King, R., Dalipaj, M. and Mai, N. (2006), Gendering migration and remittances: evidence from London and Northern Albania. *Population Space Place* 12, pp. 409–434.

Kofman, E. (1999), Female 'birds of passage' a decade later: gender and immigration in the European Union. *International Migration Review* 33, pp. 269–299.

Kofman, E. (2000), *Gender and international migration in Europe: employment, welfare, and politics*. London: Routledge.

Koser, K. (2005), *Irregular migration, state security and human security*. Geneva: Global Commission on International Migration.

Koser, K. (2010), Dimensions and dynamics of irregular migration. *Population, Space and Place 16*, pp. 181–193.

Kosnik, K. (2011), Sexuality and migration studies: the invisible, the oxymoronic and heteronormative othering. In Lutz, H., Herrera Vivar, M. T. and Supik, L. (eds) *Framing intersectionality: debates on a multi-faceted concept in gender studies*. Farnham: Ashgate.

Kothari, U. (2002), *Migration and chronic poverty*. Manchester: Chronic Poverty Research Centre.

Kothari, U. (2003), Staying put and staying poor? *Journal of International Development* 15, pp. 645–657.

Kunz, R. (2008), 'Remittances are beautiful'? Gender implications of the new global remittances trend. *Third World Quarterly* 29, pp. 1389–1409.

Lawson, V. A. (1998), Hierarchical households and gendered migration in Latin America: feminist extensions to migration research. *Progress in Human Geography* 22, pp. 39–53.

Levitt, P. (1998), Social remittances: migration driven local-level forms of cultural diffusion. *International Migration Review* 32, pp. 926–948.

Lim, L. L. (1998), *The sex sector: the economic and social bases of prostitution in Southeast Asia*. Geneva: International Labour Office.

Lorde, A. (1985), *I am your sister: black women organizing across sexualities*. New York: Kitchen Table, Women of Color Press.

Ludvig, A. (2006), Differences between women? Intersecting voices in a female narrative. *European Journal of Women's Studies* 13, pp. 245–258.

Lutz, H., Herrera Vivar, M. T. and Supik, L. (2011), *Framing intersectionality: debates on a multi-faceted concept in gender studies*. Farnham: Ashgate.

Mahler, S. J. and Pessar, P. R. (2001), Gendered geographies of power: analyzing gender across transnational spaces. *Identities: Global Studies in Culture and Power* 7, pp. 441–459.

Mahler, S. J. and Pessar, P. R. (2006), Gender matters: ethnographers bring gender from the periphery toward the core of migration studies. *International Migration Review* 40, pp. 27–63.

Marchand, M. and Sisson Runyan, A. (2011), Introduction: feminist sightings of global restructuring. In Marchand, M. and Sisson Runyan, A. (eds) *Gender and global restructuring: sightings, sights and resistance* (2nd edn). London: Routledge.

Martin, P., Martin, S. and Cross, S. (2007), High-level dialogue on migration and development. *International Migration* 45, pp. 7–25.

McCall, L. (2005), The complexity of intersectionality. *Signs: Journal of Women in Culture and Society* 30 (3), pp. 1771–1800.

McEwan, C. (2001), Postcolonialism, feminism and development: intersections and dilemmas. *Progress in Development Studies* 1 (2), pp. 93–111.

McEwan, C. (2009), *Postcolonialism and development*. London: Routledge.

McIlwaine, C. and Bermudez, A. (2011), The gendering of political and civic participation among Colombian migrants in London. *Environment and Planning A* 43, pp. 1499–1513.

Mills, M. B. (1997), Contesting the margins of modernity: women, migration, and consumption in Thailand. *American Ethnologist* 24, pp. 37–61.

Mohanty, C. T. (1986), Under Western eyes: feminist scholarship and colonial discourses. *Boundary 2* 12 (3), pp. 333–358.

Morokvasic, M. (1983), Women in migration: beyond the reductionist outlook. In Phizacklea, A. (ed.) *One way ticket: migration and female labour*. London: Routledge and Kegan Paul.

Morokvasic, M. (1984), Birds of passage are also women. *International Migration Review* 18, pp. 886–907.

Nash, J. (2008), Re-thinking intersectionality. *Feminist Review* 89, pp. 1–15.

O'Connell Davidson, J. (2006), Will the real sex slave please stand up? *Feminist Review* 83, pp. 4–22.

O'Connell Davidson, J. (2010), New slavery, old binaries: human trafficking and the borders of 'freedom'. *Global Networks* 10, pp. 244–261.

Özden, Ç. and Schiff, M. W. (2006), *International migration, remittances, and the brain drain*. Washington, DC/Basingstoke: World Bank/Palgrave Macmillan.

Parreñas, R. S. (1998), The global servants: (im)migrant domestic workers in Rome and Los Angeles. PhD dissertation, Department of Ethnic Studies, University of California, Berkeley.

Parreñas, R. S. (2000), Migrant Filipina domestic workers and the international division of reproductive labour. *Gender and Society* 14 (4), pp. 560–580.

Parreñas, R. S. (2001), *Servants of globalization: women, migration and domestic work*. Stanford, CA: Stanford University Press.

Parreñas, R. S. (2005), *Children of global migration: transnational families and gendered woes*. Stanford, CA: Stanford University Press.

Parreñas, R. S. (2008), *The force of domesticity: Filipina migrants and globalization*. New York and London: New York University Press.

Parreñas, R. S. (2012), The reproductive labour of migrant workers. *Global Networks* 12 (2), pp. 269–275.

Pearson, R. (2005), The rise and rise of gender and development. In Kothari, U. (ed.) *A radical history of development studies: individuals, institutions and ideologies*. London and New York: Zed Books.

Pessar, P. R. (2005), *Women, gender, and international migration across and beyond the Americas: inequalities and limited empowerment*. Mexico City: UN, Population Division.

Pessar, P. R. and Mahler, S. J. (2003), Transnational migration: bringing gender in. *International Migration Review* 37, pp. 812–846.

Phizacklea, A. E. (1983), *One way ticket: migration and female labour*. London: R.K.P.

Piper, N. (2004). Gender and migration policies in Southeast and East Asia: legal protection and sociocultural empowerment of unskilled migrant women. *Singapore Journal of Tropical Geography* 25, pp. 216–231.

Piper, N. (2006), Gendering the politics of migration. *International Migration Review* 40, pp. 133–164.

Piper, N. (2008), *New perspectives on gender and migration: livelihood, rights and entitlements*. London: Routledge.

Piper, N. (2009), The complex interconnections of the migration–development nexus: a social perspective. *Population, Space and Place* 15, pp. 93–101.

Piper, N. and Roces, M. (2003), *Wife or worker? Asian women and migration*. Oxford and Lanham, MD: Rowman & Littlefield.

Piper, N. E. and Yamanaka, K. E. (2003), Gender, migration and governance in Asia. *Special issue of the Asia and Pacific Migration Journal* 12, pp. 1–2. Quezon City, Philippines: Scalabrini Migration Center.

Pratt, G. and Yeoh, B. (2003). Transnational (counter) topographies. *Gender, Place and Culture* 10, pp. 159–166.

Prins, B. (2006). Narrative accounts of origins. *European Journal of Women's Studies* 13, pp. 277–290.

Radcliffe, S. A. (1993), The role of gender in peasant migration: conceptual issues from the Peruvian Andes. In Momsen, J. K. (ed.) *Different places, different voices: gender and development in Africa, Asia and Latin America*. London: Routledge.

Radcliffe, S. A. (2006a), *Culture and development in a globalizing world: geographies, actors, and paradigms*. London: Routledge.

Radcliffe, S. A. (2006b), Development and geography: gendered subjects in development processes and interventions. *Progress in Human Geography* 30 (4), pp. 524–532.

Radcliffe, S. A. and Rivers-Moore, M. (2009), Gender and nationalism in Latin America: thoughts on recent trends. *Studies in Ethnicity and Nationalism* 9, pp. 139–145.

Raghuram, P. (2008), Migrant women in male-dominated sectors of the labour market: a research agenda. *Population, Space and Place*, 14, pp. 43–57.

Raghuram, P. (2009a), Which migration, what development? Unsettling the edifice of migration and development. *Population, Space and Place*, 15, pp. 103–117.

Raghuram, P. (2009b), Caring about 'brain drain' migration in a postcolonial world. *Geoforum* 40, pp. 25–33.

Raghuram, P. (2012), Global care, local configurations – challenges to conceptualizations of care. *Global Networks* 12 (2), pp. 155–174.

Ratha, D. and Shaw, W. (2007), *South–south migration and remittances*. Washington, DC: World Bank.

Ravenstein, E. G. (1885), The laws of migration. *Journal of the Royal Statistical Society* 48, pp. 167–227.

Razavi, S. (1997), Fitting gender into development institutions. *World Development* 25, pp. 1111–1125.

Razavi, S. (2007), The political and social economy of care in a development context: conceptual issues, research questions and policy options. Gender and Development Paper No. 3, UNRISD, Geneva.

Riaño, Y. (2011), Drawing new boundaries of participation: experiences and strategies of economic citizenship among skilled migrant women in Switzerland. *Environment and Planning A* 43, pp. 1530–1546.

Ribas, N. (2008), Gender, remittances and local rural development: the case of Filipino migration to Italy. Santo Domingo, IFAD, Filipino Women's Council and UN-INSTRAW.

Rocha, M. G. (2007), The construction of the myth of survival. *Development and Change* 38, pp. 45–66.

Samers, M. (2010), *Migration*. London: Routledge.

Schuurman, F. J. (2000), Paradigm lost, paradigm regained? Development studies in the twenty-first century. *Third World Quarterly* 21 (1), pp. 7–20.

Silvey, R. (2006), Geographies of gender and migration: spatializing social difference. *International Migration Review* 40, pp. 64–81.

Silvey, R. (2009), Development and geography: anxious times, anaemic geographies, and migration. *Progress in Human Geography* 33 (4), pp. 507–515.

Skeldon, R. (1997), *Migration and development: a global perspective*. Harlow: Longman.

Skeldon, R. (2012), Going round in circles: circular migration, poverty alleviation and marginality. *International Migration* 50, pp. 43–60.

Sørensen, N. N. (2005), *Migrant remittances, development and gender*. Copenhagen: Dansk Institut for Internationale Studier.

Sørensen, N. N., Hear N. V. and Engberg-Pedersen, P. (2002), The migration–development nexus: evidence and policy options. *International Migration* 40, pp. 49–73.

Townsend, J. (1995), *Women's voices from the forest*. London: Routledge.

United Nations (2006), *International migration and development*. New York: United Nations, General Assembly.

United Nations Development Programme (2009), *Overcoming barriers: human mobility and development*. UNDP.

Valentine, G. (2007), Theorizing and researching intersectionality: a challenge for feminist geography. *The Professional Geographer* 59, pp. 10–21.

Whitehead, A. and Hashim, I. (2005), Children and Migration. Retrieved 29 April 2013 from: http://www. childtrafficking.com/Docs/dfid_05_child_mig_bac_0408.pdf.

Willis, K. and Yeoh, B. S. A. (2000), *Gender and migration*. Cheltenham, UK and Northampton, MA, USA: Edward Elgar Publishing.

Wolf, D. L. (1990), Daughters, decisions and domination: an empirical and conceptual critique of household strategies. *Development and Change* 21 (1), pp. 43–74.

World Bank (2006), *World economic prospects: economic implications of remittances and migration*. Washington, DC: World Bank.

Zinn, M. B., Hondagneu-Sotelo, P. and Messner, M. A. (1997), *Through the prism of difference: readings on sex and gender*. Boston and London: Allyn and Bacon.

17. Requiem for the sustainable livelihoods approach?

A. Haroon Akram-Lodhi[1]

INTRODUCTION

Over the course of the last 25 years, rural development studies have witnessed the introduction of a framework that, for a time, came to dominate action-oriented research, policy analysis and advocacy. That framework is called the 'sustainable livelihoods' approach (SLA). This chapter will discuss the rise of the SLA and then identify its key salient features. Next, it will offer a critical perspective on the SLA, discussing both its strengths and its weaknesses. Finally, the chapter will examine why the SLA has gone into decline over the last decade.

ORIGIN OF THE SLA

Ian Scoones (2015) traces the origin of livelihoods theory back to the 1820s. He argues that Karl Marx utilized important aspects of the livelihoods approach in the *Grundrisse* and suggests that generations of social anthropologists, geographers and social theorists have, in essence, used key facets of livelihoods thinking in their analyses. In particular, Scoones (2015) notes that the village studies tradition, the examination of farming systems and intra-household labour allocation dynamics, as well as research into environmental change were important precursors to the SLA. However, it was not until the early 1990s that the phrase 'livelihood' started to be more widely used in the rural development studies literature (Bernstein et al., 1992). In 1992 Robert Chambers and Gordon Conway produced a working paper for the Institute of Development Studies (IDS) which offered a definition of a sustainable livelihood that, as we will see, has not essentially changed since that time (Scoones, 2015). Originally, the phrase 'livelihood' was used as an essentially descriptive device to show an understanding of the nuanced, complex and diverse specificity of rural life, in which rural people and communities undertook a set of varying and different productive and reproductive activities, of which only one might be farming, in order to fashion a standard of living (O'Laughlin, 2004). However, the election of the Labour government in the United Kingdom (UK) in 1997 resulted in the creation of the Department for International Development (DfID), and the commissioning of comparative multidisciplinary research into sustainable livelihoods. Drawing especially on ground-breaking work at IDS and the University of East Anglia (UEA), DfID produced a White Paper on international development that was explicitly committed to a livelihoods approach as 'a core development priority' (Scoones, 2015, p. 7). There can be little doubt that, as a brand-new department of state, DfID was seeking to make an intellectual, as well as a programmatic, statement. Thus, by the late 1990s, in the space of only a few years, and particularly following the publication of *Rural Livelihoods and Diversity in Developing Countries* (2000) by Frank Ellis, the SLA came to signify an overarching framework within which poverty analysis could be undertaken, one in which the 'assets' of poor people are identified and subsequently expanded, as a consequence of policy interventions, in order to foster poverty reduction.

SLA IN THEORY

The rise of the SLA coincided with innovative thinking around development processes and practices in the 1990s. Academics, practitioners and advocates in the UK and the northern European countries were extremely critical of the implications of the Washington Consensus[2] for developing countries, having produced important research on the failures of structural adjustment to improve the well-being of poor people around the world during the 1980s and early 1990s. In 1993 Douglass North won the Nobel Prize in Economic Sciences for his work on institutions, Amartya Sen won the same Prize in 1998 for his work on entitlements, social capital was an important area of economic research throughout the 1990s, and innovative work at UEA had given rise to political ecology as a means of understanding environmental and resource interactions and dynamics. Scoones makes the extremely important point, though, that despite this plurality of innovation in development thinking, as it rose in prominence the SLA was increasingly located within 'disciplinary economics' terms' which 'emphasized the economic attributes of livelihoods as mediated by social-institutional processes' (2015, p. 8).

Thus, by the early 2000s 'sustainable livelihoods' had come to be understood as encompassing the capabilities, assets and activities a rural household can employ in order to make a living that enhances its well-being and is not detrimental to its resource entitlements; an understanding almost the same as that originally formulated by Chambers and Conway who had written:

A livelihood comprises the capabilities, assets (including both material and social resources) and activities for a means of living. A livelihood is sustainable when it can cope with and recover from stresses and shocks, maintain or enhance its capabilities and assets, while not undermining the natural resource base. (1992, p. 6)

The SLA thus came to be premised upon the proposition that poor people have assets. The assets available to people were seen to comprise:

- *natural* capital, such as land and water;
- *physical* capital, such as tools and equipment, infrastructure and transport, shelter, sanitation and energy;
- *financial* capital, such as income, savings and credit;
- *human* capital, such as education, skills, knowledge and health;
- *social* capital, such as households, networks, formal groups, institutions and information.

Within a particular context, people creatively employed these assets as inputs, to construct a 'livelihood strategy', designed to improve a household's means of making a living. In so doing, people would have to, in many cases, carry out a multiplicity of productive and reproductive activities which would be, of necessity, based upon the portfolio of assets under their control. Thus, people could, at an individual and at a household level, simultaneously undertake a range of different activities and seek to achieve a range of different goals, some of which may even conflict. The implication is explicit: people, and especially poor people, do not do just one activity, and nor are they passively defined within social and cultural frameworks. Rather, people are active agents who can articulate and seek to expand the boundaries of their capabilities, which can be defined as the effective freedom to make autonomous choices that are of importance to the individual. At the same time, however, the range of the agency available to people to construct a living is mediated by the institutions, policies and processes of civil society and the state, which, in turn, affects how people can use their livelihood assets. The core SLA approach is encapsulated in Figure 17.1.

Several implications flow from this, admittedly simplistic, account of the SLA. The first implication is that all people have assets. The second implication is that different types of assets are, from an analytical standpoint, identical in their importance. The third is that the relevant unit of analysis in livelihood studies is a well-defined social grouping: the individual, a household, a community, an ethnicity, a caste, an age group, gender, or class. The fourth is that, given the presence of well-defined social groups, there must be forms of social division in populations or

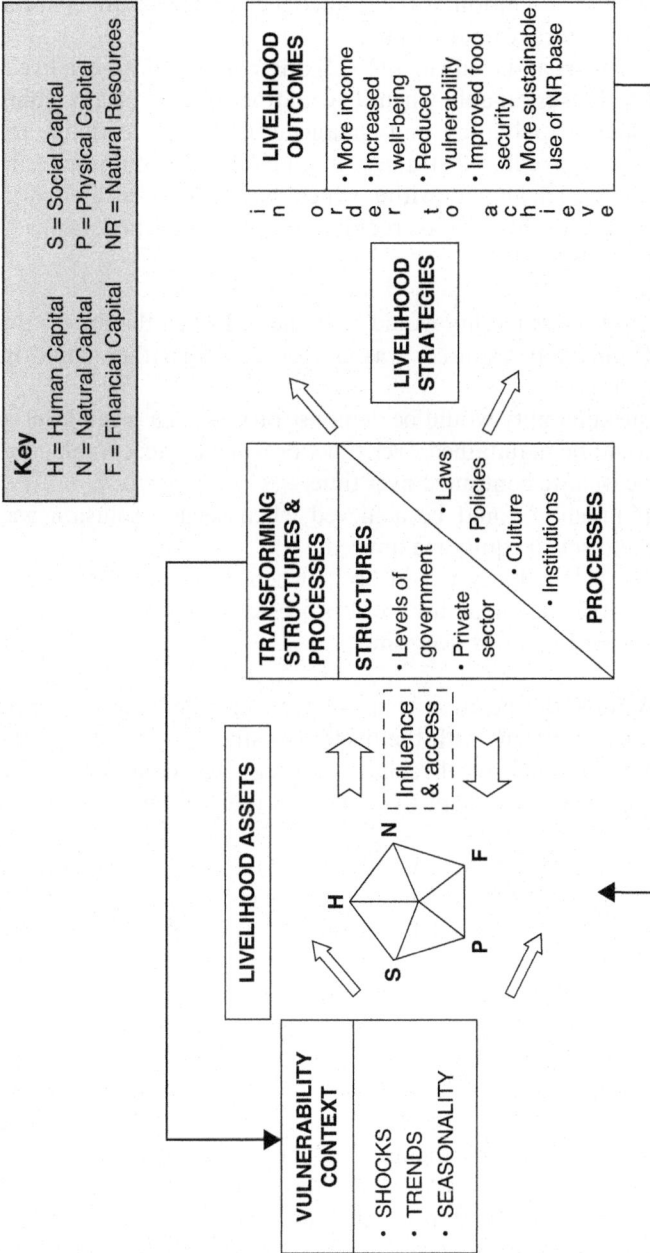

Key

H = Human Capital   S = Social Capital
N = Natural Capital   P = Physical Capital
F = Financial Capital   NR = Natural Resources

LIVELIHOOD OUTCOMES
- More income
- Increased well-being
- Reduced vulnerability
- Improved food security
- More sustainable use of NR base

LIVELIHOOD STRATEGIES

TRANSFORMING STRUCTURES & PROCESSES

STRUCTURES
- Levels of government
- Private sector

PROCESSES
- Laws
- Policies
- Culture
- Institutions

LIVELIHOOD ASSETS

Influence & access

H   N   S   P   F

VULNERABILITY CONTEXT
- SHOCKS
- TRENDS
- SEASONALITY

Source: DFID (1999) *Sustainable Livelihoods Guidance Sheets* Figure 1, taken from http://www.eldis.org/vfile/upload/1/document/0901/section2. pdf on 2 August 2017, under CC-BY 3.0 licence.

Figure 17.1 The sustainable livelihoods framework

within households themselves. With regard to this last point, many who adopted the SLA at the outset suggested that a particular strength of the SLA was its explicit recognition of the gendered character of much social inequality in contemporary poor countries.

As seen in Chambers and Conway's (1992) original formulation, a livelihood was said to be sustainable when it would be capable of absorbing shocks, maintaining capabilities, and enhancing the assets available for the construction of a livelihood strategy, in a manner that did not act to the detriment of the environment within which the livelihood strategy was constructed. Sustainable livelihoods required that four key dimensions of sustainability be addressed:

1. environmental sustainability would be witnessed when the productivity of environmental resources was enhanced so that they could be used in the future;
2. economic sustainability would be demonstrated when a given level of spending could be maintained over time, or when an acceptable level of economic welfare continued over time;
3. social sustainability would be achieved when social exclusion was minimized and social equity maximized;
4. institutional sustainability would occur when dominant formal and informal institutional structures and processes could perform livelihood-enhancing functions over time.

Thus, the SLA took the position that poverty reduction must operate in a way that was consistent with the livelihood strategies of people, the social setting within which the livelihood strategy was constructed and the capabilities of people to adapt to changes in the economic and social environment.

This had clear methodological implications. Research, policy advice and advocacy, using the SLA, had to analyse the components of people's livelihoods, and how these changed over time, stressing the way in which people themselves defined the strengths and the weaknesses of their livelihood strategy. Thus, there was an exceptionally strong relationship between the SLA and participatory research methodologies. The analysis that was undertaken had to be conducted in the context of a set of institutional arrangements and policy processes that impacted upon people's livelihood strategies and may not always have considered the economic and social agendas the of people themselves. Thus, the analysis had to seek to identify the livelihood goals of people, households and communities, and create an environment within which institutions and policy-making would take full account of these goals. The intellectual origins of the

SLA in the pioneering work of Robert Chambers, and particularly in his *Rural Development: Putting the Last First* (Chambers, 1983), cannot be overemphasized.

Between the late 1990s and the late 2000s, the SLA dominated rural development policy advice, research and advocacy. It was applied in a multitude of settings around the world, it generated a vast array of papers, toolkits and operational guides, and it became a core component of rural development programming. Part of the reason for its rapid rise to dominance was because of its explicit recognition that poverty is multidimensional and fosters creative responses to deprivation among poor people. These expressions of agency produced not only material incomes, but also meaning and values, capabilities and well-being. Thus, the SLA was an actor-oriented approach to rural development that eschewed 'magic bullets', but rather stressed diversity and difference within, and between, household members. In the aftermath of the Washington Consensus, this fit the tenor of the times; not only in its emphasis on grass-roots development, but also in according an important role to international and national non-governmental organizations (NGOs) that were seeking to promote small-scale development projects that would be pro-peasant, pro-poor, pro-gender equity and pro-environment. Note too, though, that in its rejection of grand theories of development, and in its accession to more micro-oriented theories of change, the SLA emphasized what could be gradually brought about from below by individuals and households with the resources that they had in the markets in which they participated, however 'imperfect' they might be. In this way too, it fit the tenor of the times, with a heavily decentralized state being given only a limited role in the construction of a market-oriented livelihood strategy, clearly reflecting the dominance of neoliberal thinking. Finally, it should also be noted that the rapid increase in funding for research, policy advice and advocacy that used the SLA had the effect of creating livelihood opportunities for livelihood consultants who jumped on the latest development bandwagon.

THE SLA IN ACTION: THE *ANISHNABEG* OF SLATE FALLS NATION

The power of the SLA can be most easily grasped through the use of an example. In 1934, the Rat Rapids Generating Station was built to the north-east of Lake St Joseph, some 225 km from Sioux Lookout in Northern Ontario, Canada. The construction of the generating station involved building a dam, which significantly altered the topography of Lake St Joseph, because the shoreline of the lake changed and the water levels of the lake rose, becoming irregular. At the time of construction, Lake St Joseph was the principal source of livelihood of the *Anishnabeg* (Ojibwa) peoples of what is now called Slate Falls Nation. Calling themselves the *Mishoganiniwuk* (Big Lake People, in reference to Lake St Joseph), Slate Falls Nation was a community of 87 at the time,[3] within three extended families (Sieciechowicz, 2010, p. 45), the Carpenters, Wesleys and Loons, who accounted for more than 50 per cent of those relying on Lake St Joseph for their livelihood (Sieciechowicz, 2010, p. 47).

Prior to 1934 the *Anishnabeg*, in common with most of the indigenous populations of the rest of Northern Ontario, were essentially a hunter-gatherer society. Small and mobile populations relied upon a diversity of naturally-occurring resources across expansive geographical territories, of which Lake St Joseph and its immediate hinterland were the focal point. These lands provided the Slate Falls people – who trapped, hunted, fished, gardened and gathered – with a diverse subsistence from abundant seasonal sources; in particular fresh, dried and smoked fish which was the main source of protein throughout the year. Trapping was the principle source of limited cash incomes for the Slate Falls people, who had been engaged in the fur trade since contact with Europeans and the commodity economy in the mid-eighteenth century. These activities were undertaken using an intimate knowledge of the lands they occupied, which had been acquired over a prolonged period of time, along with knowledge of the food sources, dangers and opportunities that existed within their territory.

Human Capital

Human capital refers to the education, skills and health of the members of the household who can facilitate the use of labour as a productive resource in supporting the livelihood of the household and the community (Ellis, 2000, p. 33). The Sieciechowicz Report stresses that prior to 1934, Slate Falls Nation displayed what anthropologists call 'situated practice' (2010, p. 163). This means that the construction of utilitarian practical knowledge and the understanding of intra-communal social skills as well as the implicit norms, values and rules of the community were an outcome of living as, and thus being one of, the Slate Falls people. For example, skills around trapping, hunting and fishing were practice-based, drawn from localized knowledge, experience and observation (Sieciechowicz, 2010, pp. 163–4). Economists call this 'learning by doing': the acquisition of knowledge or skills through the direct experience of carrying out a task. It means that the education and skills of the members of Slate Falls Nation – its human capital – were a function of being a member of Slate Falls Nation.

In large part, this was because life was communal and the cultural and technical knowledge and skills of individuals were widely and equally shared amongst the community. What one person knew and believed the entire community tended to know and believe because custom and tradition, which were learnt by imitation and hence 'being', determined behaviour and values. Custom, tradition, values and communal knowledge all contribute to the stock of social capital found within a community which, in turn, produces human capital.

Social Capital

Social capital is the 'reciprocity within communities and between households based on trust deriving from social ties' (Moser, 1998). Such localized reciprocity is typically a function of being a member of personal or family networks, such as near and remote kin as well as close friends (Ellis, 2000, p. 36). In order to be sustained over time, social capital requires investments of time, effort and resources.

As was noted earlier, according to the Sieciechowicz Report (2010) the human capital of Slate Falls Nation was a function of adhering to the social precepts and values of the Slate Falls people. In other words, if an individual acted in a way that society defined as being an *Anishnabeg* of the Slate Falls people then they were an *Anishnabeg* of the Slate Falls people. The Sieciechowicz Report identifies five ways of being *Anishnabeg* (2010, p. 68):

1. living off the land and achieving self-sufficiency;
2. moving over the land as needed to achieve self-sufficiency;
3. independence of action;
4. non-interference with others;
5. accommodation of others.

What is striking about these ways of being *Anishnabeg* is that, within the context of the ecosystem in which they lived, they could not be carried out autonomously. The localized knowledge and the environmentally-sensitive skills that individuals needed to be *Anishnabeg* required that individuals take part in, and contribute to, the social and economic roles required of them by their community if they and their community were to survive, let alone prosper. So, Slate Falls Nation witnessed reciprocal dependency, operating both across and within communities, suggesting that social relations and stocks of social capital strongly shaped individuals and their behaviour.

In many societies, immediate kinship, however defined, is the basis of the social roles assumed by individuals and the social capital arising out of individuals interacting with each other in their social networks. However, this was not the case in Slate Falls Nation prior to 1934: while being kin was, as in other societies, a 'serious matter' for individuals as it was the basis for helping or protecting others, kinship was bilateral, with little depth, and could easily be extended to unrelated individuals through, for example, adoption. Rather, within the Slate Falls people, social values – and thus social capital – determined the core meaning of kin relations. While kinship was strongly egalitarian and produced obligations, it was principally defined not through the affinities of 'genuine' kinship but through cohabitation, particularly in the winter and summer camps occupied temporarily but recurrently by families. The capabilities of individuals to meet the social and economic obligations placed upon them by the community, by following the community's implicit expectations, norms and values, together defined its stock of social capital. Consequently, within Slate Falls Nation, economics and residency could potentially override narrowly-defined genuine kinship in assigning people to social roles within their families and communities, based on their contribution to the stock of social capital (Sieciechowicz, 2010).

So stocks of social capital strongly shaped localized knowledge, interpersonal relations and the capacity to survive. In this regard, the role of Lake St Joseph for Slate Falls Nation prior to 1934 was pivotal in ways that would not necessarily be apparent if the focus of attention was solely on the economics of household and community livelihoods. Lake St Joseph was the key means for families to travel, to visit, to socialize and to sustain the social networks (Sieciechowicz, 2010) upon which investments in the stocks of social capital of Slate Falls Nation were built. Lake St Joseph's role in sustaining the social cohesion of the community was a vital, indeed critical, component of the stocks of social and human capital within the livelihood platform of the *Anishnabeg* of Slate Falls Nation. It was a source of the social capital of Slate Falls Nation.

Natural Capital

Natural capital consists of the lands, waters and biological resources used by households to produce a means of survival and sustenance (Ellis, 2000). Clearly then, prior to 1934, the waters of Lake St Joseph and the lands adjacent to it were the principal stock of natural capital for the livelihood platform of Slate Falls Nation and land occupancy and use were clearly associated with the social and economic life of Slate Falls Nation. While some of the lands of the *Anishnabeg* were sacred areas, and some were for common use, for the most part it was large tracts of land adjacent to Lake

St Joseph that were needed for the subsistence livelihood strategies of trapping, hunting, fishing, gathering and gardening (Sieciechowicz, 2010). Land would have been controlled by small groups of two to three 'core' extended families, or perhaps 15 to 25 people. These extended families need not necessarily be genuine kin, but could have been located within the extended group as a consequence of contributing to the stock of social capital of the Slate Falls people. Households outside the core families could obtain access to land controlled by the core families if they selected to include them in the extended family group because of the character of their inter-personal social relations, and thus their contribution to the stock of social capital. These autonomous groups then moved over land as necessary over the course of the year to obtain a livelihood. It was also an approach which served to achieve subsistence while maintaining environmental sustainability. All territories of the Slate Falls people were ultimately controlled by adjacent core extended family groups, and indeed extended groups were known by the lands under their control – but not all land that was controlled was used (Sieciechowicz, 2010).

This had two implications: first, no land was empty but, second, because land usage by extended groups of families was used to define a socially acceptable control of land, failure to use land under the control of extended groups over a period of years could lead to efforts to effect a transfer of usage or control of the unused land (Sieciechowicz, 2010). Thus, while socially-defined precepts of group autonomy meant that family groups would not interfere with the activities of others pursuing their livelihood, values of reciprocal dependency meant that they would have to consider accommodating the needs of other extended groups, particularly if land was being left unused and the group seeking accommodation was in difficulty. The main ways in which this came about were through permission to share lands, invitations to co-trap and negotiations to access unused land. Marriage was also, in part, a means of facilitating the transfer of land access. Males and females had equal rights to access land, and so marriage took place outside the extended family, often to gain access to land for those in-marrying. In this way, land fed back directly into wider community social relations and thus into the stock of social capital by partially determining patterns of marriage (Sieciechowicz, 2010).

Physical Capital

Physical capital consists of assets that are created as a result of economic activity (Ellis, 2000). Buildings, tools and machines are typical examples of physical capital. In the Sieciechowicz Report (2010) the stocks of physical capital that are discussed are quite limited: handmade fish nets were widely used, cabins on a bay are noted, along with wooden teepees and houses. Presumably, trapping and hunting also relied heavily on small stocks of physical capital, such as trapping equipment, tools and rifles, as did the use of Lake St Joseph for transport, but these are taken for granted in the oral histories that serve as the principal source for the report. Nonetheless, it is reasonable to assume that physical capital was relatively less important to the livelihood of the Slate Falls people than their stocks of human, social and natural capital.

Financial Capital

Financial capital refers to the stocks of cash, savings and credit to which a household has access (Ellis, 2000). The integration of Slate Falls Nation into the market economy prior to 1934 was remarkable in that it was quite limited. Trapping was the main source of trade and, notwithstanding the annual CAN$4 treaty payments at the trading post of Osnaburgh and some income accruing from low-paid commercial fishing, the principal source of income. Small amounts of money were needed because of the limited exchange relationships that existed between the Slate Falls people and the Hudson's Bay Company. The lack of emphasis on the financial rewards accruing from participation in economic activities demonstrates the essentially subsistence livelihood strategy of the hunter-gatherers of Slate Falls Nation. It also demonstrates that financial capital was less important to the livelihood of the Slate Falls people than their stocks of human, social and natural capital.

LIVELIHOOD STRATEGIES AND OUTCOMES PRIOR TO 1934

Despite the fact that it remained peripheral to the aggregate livelihood platform of the Slate Falls people, in the early 1930s the fur trade, which had dominated the externally-oriented economy of the region for more than a century, remained central to the overall social and economic organization of the livelihoods of Slate Falls Nation. This meant that trapping was the principal determinant of the annual patterns of economic activity of Slate Falls Nation and the movements of its members across the land. Trapping of beaver, muskrat, otter, mink, lynx, fox and weasel was done during the late autumn and winter: groups of two to three 'core' families dispersed prior to freeze-up onto the lands they occupied, trapping through late spring on lands adjacent to the central and western part of Lake St Joseph. These social arrangements around livelihood strategies created strong partnerships between the men of 'core' family groups who shared trapping responsibilities as well as between the women of 'core' family groups who shared household care activities. Thus, the social dimensions of trapping reinforced the stocks of social and human capital of the livelihood platform. As already noted, trapping was the principal source of money – financial capital – for households and provided the resources needed to buy the tea, sugar, rice, lard and flour that were amongst the few food items that the peoples of Slate Falls Nation did not provide for themselves.

While hunting was a year-round activity, the primary period for the hunting of moose, bear, deer, caribou, ducks, geese and partridge on the lands abutting Lake St Joseph was late summer or spring. Hunted animals provided both high-protein food and non-food resources. Similarly, fishing was also a year-round activity for some, and a seasonal activity for others. Subsistence fishing of sturgeon, pickerel, jackfish, whitefish and suckers was very important in providing the key food staple for the Slate Falls people, while limited amounts of low-paid commercial fishing for cash to supplement incomes from trapping took place on the central and western part of the lake in the fall and spring. In the summer the gathering of eggs, berries, medicinal herbs and roots, teas and wild rice was an ongoing activity (Sieciechowicz, 2010).

For Slate Falls Nation in the early 1930s there was little opportunity for economic or other kinds of specialization to develop. While women did most of the gathering and snaring and there was some gendered specialization in fishing, beyond this there was little by way of a clear division of labour within, and between, the households of the community, and there was little by way of accumulated wealth. The autonomous, reciprocally-dependent extended groups of the Slate Falls people were, as a consequence, relatively egalitarian.

As is documented in the Sieciechowicz Report (2010) the livelihood strategy of Slate Falls Nation in the early 1930s was self-sufficiency. While some small income from trapping and fishing was used to purchase essential items that the community did not produce, by and large it was Lake St Joseph that provided food and other necessary resources throughout the year. The Slate Falls people trapped, fished, hunted, gathered, gardened and travelled across expansive tracts of territory around Lake St Joseph in a way that minimized their environmental footprint and fostered the sustainability of the environment, the economy and the community of Slate Falls Nation. Thus, as Charles Wesley noted, 'the whole lake is what they got their livelihood from' (Sieciechowicz, 2010, p. 64).

THE IMPACT OF THE RAT RAPIDS GENERATING STATION ON LIVELIHOOD PLATFORMS, STRATEGIES AND OUTCOMES

The construction of the Rat Rapids Generating Station significantly made the people of Slate Falls Nation vulnerable to disruptions in their livelihood strategies and outcomes because it diminished their livelihood platform. The immediate problem that the Slate Falls people faced was unanticipated changes to Lake St Joseph. The construction of the dam for the generating station at first raised water levels by between 6 and 10 feet, and in some areas the water breached the shoreline by 150–200 feet. The opening and closing of the dam also led to irregular water levels. Within the framework of the SLA, it could be said that the vulnerability context of the livelihoods of Slate Falls Nation underwent a shock. The ecosystem upon which Slate Falls Nation relied was transformed, to the detriment of many of the key animal and plant species that the community relied upon for their subsistence and their survival (Sieciechowicz, 2010).

The oral histories contained within the Sieciechowicz Report provide ample information on the impact of the flooding. Campsites, islands where people lived and grew vegetables for part of the year, places where people visited, including sacred sites and graves: all became submerged. Charles Wesley identified 41 places which were submerged or partially submerged. These were concentrated in the western two-thirds of the lake used by the Slate Falls people and many of them were not suitable for use in the aftermath of the flooding. Changes to the shoreline as the topography of Lake St Joseph changed, along with fluctuating water levels, prevented animals from living near the lake, resulting in the wipe-out of beaver and muskrat trapping close to the lake and the loss of moose and bear hunting. Handmade fishing nets were also lost as the water levels rose, and the presence of submerged trees under the water made fishing more hazardous. Finally, the ability to gather wild foods by the lake was made much more challenging by the dramatic environmental changes (Sieciechowicz, 2010).

Viewed from the perspective of the livelihood platform of the Slate Falls people, the construction of the Rat Rapids Generating Station and the subsequent increase in the water levels of Lake St Joseph was nothing short of a calamity. The principal source of their limited financial capital – trapping – was, for a period of time, made extremely difficult. Stocks of their physical capital were submerged in the flooding and thus lost. The natural capital upon which Slate Falls Nation relied rapidly transformed in a way that the community could not have foreseen and did not have the means to immediately comprehend. The transformation of Lake St Joseph rendered the localized knowledge and specific practical skill sets needed to secure subsistence on and around Lake St Joseph far less relevant – human capital was immediately devalued as the lake changed. For example, people no longer knew where to set their fishing nets because of the changing water levels or where to hunt for bears because of the loss of rapids that had been close to the lake and which had been a favoured fishing area for bears. At the same time, the stock of human capital of the Slate Falls people was an outcome of the community's stock of social capital; but that stock of social capital – its norms, values, precepts and understanding – was diminished because of a set of unforeseen circumstances that were outside the community's experience.

But there was more: movements across Lake St Joseph had historically solidified social networks within the community and thus contributed to the formation of stocks of social capital, which in turn were the basis by which stocks of human capital were formed. The rising and irregular water levels in Lake St Joseph disrupted both these social networks and the socialization that sustained the community's stock of social capital because the use of the lake as a means of travel and as a meeting place diminished.

When viewed within the framework of the SLA it can be seen that the transforming processes of culture, social institutions and relations which mediated the ability to transform a livelihood platform into a livelihood strategy were upended. Households of Slate Falls Nation were enmeshed with these processes but were unable to adequately navigate them. The human capabilities of the people were reduced in the wake of the transformation of the ecology in which they lived. The shock in the vulnerability context caused by the flooding of Lake St Joseph significantly reduced the livelihood platform of the Slate Falls people in the wake of the construction of the Rat Rapids Generating Station and the increase in the water levels that resulted from it. At the same time the transforming processes that had previously been the norm for households were overturned. The aggregate effect on the livelihood platform is illustrated in Figure 17.2, which provides an asset pentagon for Slate Falls Nation in the aftermath of the flooding.

It is clear from the evidence and from the oral histories of the flooding contained in the Sieciechowicz Report that it had a major impact on the food supplies available to the peoples of Slate Falls Nation and that those who chose to stay on Lake St Joseph rapidly went hungry. Claude Loon put it bluntly: after the flooding 'we were hungry' (Sieciechowicz, 2010, p. 105). A stable, adequate and risk-reducing standard of living was lost; the sustainable livelihoods of the Slate Falls people were rendered unsustainable. In order for the peoples of Slate Falls Nation to cope with their enhanced vulnerability there was, over the course of a very difficult

Social capital

Financial capital   Human capital

Physical capital   Natural capital

Key:
Prior to 1934   ▬▬▬▬
After the flooding   ▬ ▬ ▬ ▬▪

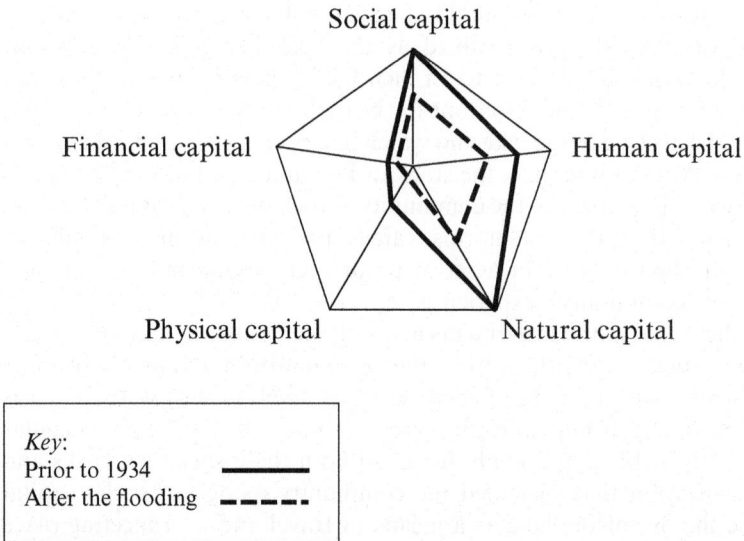

Source: Author's derivation based upon Ellis (2000, p. 49) and Sieciechowicz (2010).

Figure 17.2   A Slate Falls Nation Asset Pentagon after the flooding

year, a withdrawal from Lake St Joseph after 1935 as people moved north-westward and inland towards Slate Falls and Fry Lake, within the territo-ries of Slate Falls Nation. For example, John Cook and Isaac Loon shifted their livelihood activities from around Osnaburgh to the area north-west of Lake St Joseph immediately after the flooding. Similarly, Sam Carpenter gave a list of people who left the Lake St Joseph region because of the flooding. A people that had been reliant upon the lake for generations were, in effect, dispossessed of it as they were forced by declining food availability to relocate to lands with which they were much less familiar.

This move brought with it new risks to the livelihood strategies and outcomes of the peoples of Slate Falls Nation. To begin with, while the Slate Falls people moved inland and north-westwards, they did so within their pre-existing territories. The result was a greater concentration of subsistence activities in a smaller land area, which significantly raised pres-sures on land and other resources in a way that was less compatible with the hunter-gatherer livelihood strategies of Slate Falls Nation. Trapping continued, but became less viable as trap lines compressed and the returns to trapping in a more heavily-used area declined. Trapping also became less sustainable because of the increase in the intensity of it. According to Charles Wesley, after the shift in the location of livelihood activities there were 'many people over here hunting', rendering it less viable than had previously been the case. Prior to the flooding, fishing had been year-round for some; after the flooding, it became seasonal. The gathering of wild rice decreased because the flooding submerged paddies and it took time to redevelop plots in new locations to grow garden vegetables. Robert Wesley summed up the impact of the far tighter resource constraints facing the Slate Falls people when he noted that, in the aftermath of the construction, the arrival of his first child meant his remaining land was no longer capable of supporting his family; they had to move (Sieciechowicz, 2010, p. 93).

Finally, with the decline in trapping there was far less economic advantage to be got from travel to Osnaburgh in the summer to trade furs, while the loss of animals and wild foods by the lake meant that hunting and gathering on the trip to Osnaburgh became less feasible. So the peoples of Slate Falls Nation began to travel less, and this, in turn, had implications for the operation of society and the economy.

While it is apparent that the construction of the Rat Rapids Generating Station had major implications for the economy of Slate Falls Nation, it is the decrease in human capabilities arising out of the immediate need to cope with enhanced vulnerability that had the most long-term impact. Lake St Joseph was a source of social capital; social networks and stocks of social and human capital lost their intensity as the transformation in the lake reduced the ability of the Slate Falls people to use it. Simply put, the lack of knowledge about coping with dams precluded the use of the practical knowledge upon which the peoples of Slate Falls Nation relied. The 'situated practice' – which was a function of the social relations within the community and which was so central to the livelihoods of Slate Falls Nation – was degraded and social isolation rose (Sieciechowicz, 2010).

According to Gordon Carpenter it took the Slate Falls people three to five years to adapt to the new circumstances in which they found themselves (Sieciechowicz, 2010); and some components of the community's previous livelihood strategy, such as the trapping of beaver or the gathering of wild rice around Lake St Joseph, never recovered from the impact of the flooding. As Slate Falls Nation adapted to the very different circumstances in which it found itself, the terms and conditions of hunter-gathering in Northern Ontario changed markedly. In 1948, the Ministry of Natural Resources required that trap lines be registered; as Dinah Loon put it, 'white men came with boundaries' (Sieciechowicz, 2010, p. 66) in an apparent attempt to convert trap lines into private property. When placed in the context of substantial reductions in trapping because of the construction of the generating station and the need for practical knowledge on trapping in new areas to be developed and disseminated within the community, the impact of the registration of trapping was to effectively remove access to the fur trade as a source of income for the Slate Falls Nation.

Over a period of 15 years, the Slate Falls Nation fishery trade gradually recovered from the impact of the flooding to the extent that, in the 1940s, a commercial fishery was established on Lake St Joseph to supply the mining industry. This, along with ongoing treaty payments, became the principal source of financial capital for the peoples of Slate Falls Nation for several years to follow.

The construction of the generating station led to a wholesale reconfiguration of the livelihoods of the Slate Falls people. The need to adapt to the new circumstances had profound implications for the social organization. The decline of trapping, the establishment of commercial fishing, changing arrangements around obtaining treaty payments and the ongoing operation of the residential school system led to the Slate Falls people becoming increasingly settled. It could be argued that the flooding of Lake St Joseph led directly to the hunter-gatherer peoples of Slate Falls Nation being slowly transformed into a sedentary settled society. The process of social dislocation which began for the indigenous populations of Northern Ontario in the 1750s, following contact with Europeans, can be said to have assumed a new form in the 1940s and 1950s. This new form has implications for the present day, given that the Slate Falls people remain unable to pursue an autonomous, self-sufficient, reciprocally dependent sustainable livelihood that produces a stable, adequate and risk-reducing standard of living.

STRENGTHS OF THE SLA

Clearly, and as starkly demonstrated in this lengthy example, the SLA asked complex questions, not only about patterns of productive and reproductive work but also about social relations and how they change over time, and territoriality and the natural world. Moreover, its recognition of diversity – something that had been integral to agrarian political economy analysis from the end of the nineteenth century – was long overdue. Rural labour markets are often critical to the ability of individuals, households and communities to construct a livelihood over a period of time, in particular by allowing people to compensate for inadequate stocks of certain assets. Thus, the recognition that rural people both farm and undertake rural waged labour was very important.

Those multilateral and bilateral agencies, academic and research institutions, and international NGOs which became strong advocates of the SLA did so largely because of a perception of its having three particular

strengths. First, the SLA was seen to be *people-centred.* As clearly demonstrated in the example of Slate Falls Nation, the priority of research, policy
and advocacy was to support the grass-roots livelihood strategies of people
in a way that enhanced sustainability over time, and this criterion was to
be the basis upon which interventions were assessed. The second strength
of the SLA was that it was *holistic.* The approach was predicated upon the
idea that the ability of people to construct a livelihood strategy could be
enabled or constrained by a variety of interlocking factors that could not
be addressed in isolation, but rather had to be approached in an integrated
fashion. Thus, the SLA focused on understanding the multiple economic
and social relationships that influenced people and affected their livelihood
strategies, as is clear from the Slate Falls Nation example. To that end, SLA
advocates employed both quantitative and qualitative evidence when seeking to understand livelihood strategies. This was done while explicitly recognizing that livelihood strategies could have multiple dimensions in which
people sought to construct a standard of living, and, as a consequence,
analysis would have to be non-sectoral. Moreover, livelihood strategies
were affected by a diversity of actors from within local communities, civil
society, the private sector and local, regional and national government.
Thus, in this context, people sought to achieve a diversity of livelihood
outcomes, which were determined not by the state or by civil society but by
people themselves. The third strength of the SLA was its *dynamism.* It was
predicated upon the idea that livelihood strategies adapt to iterative chains
of events and cause-and-effect relationships, and are, as such, complex. As
evidenced by the example of Slate Falls Nation, the SLA did not see people
as passive recipients but rather as active agents of change.

The SLA analysed the livelihood strategies of people, households and
communities within an institutional setting in which civil society organizations and local governments operated under constraints imposed as a consequence of the national policy framework. In so doing, the SLA clearly
operated in a terrain that was staked out by a broad set of constituents in
international development. As such, it allowed those who used it to try to
understand how people may or may not affect the policy-making process,
as well as how the policy-making process actually affected people.

WEAKNESSES OF THE SLA

Despite having a hegemonic position within the field of rural development
studies for a period, latterly the SLA came to be criticized from several
perspectives. The first criticism related to its lack of attention to questions
of wider power dynamics beyond the community. Broader, more global

processes can strongly restrict the response capacities of local actors. Local political and economic actors may be subordinately linked to larger, more powerful political and economic actors and this can affect flows of goods, services and money both into and out of communities. Both factors can strongly impinge upon the range of responses that local social networks can undertake and the agency that individuals and households can express. Consequently, livelihood options may be severely constrained or even imposed from beyond the community, especially when outsiders explicitly limit local livelihood options because of concerns around their normative suitability; the production of the plants that produce the opioids that fuel the global illicit drug trade is a case in point.

The second criticism related to aspiration, which was seen as being modest, if not very limited, with regard to the design of a framework to facilitate poverty analysis. By focusing on the ways in which poor people could make better use of available assets to improve their living standards, the SLA was promoting a simplistic poverty alleviation strategy whereby the poor should help themselves (O'Laughlin, 2004). Moreover, the emphasis was clearly one that focused upon the development of coping mechanisms to deal with existing livelihood constraints, rather than understanding household adaptation strategies. At the same time, the structural constraints on adaptation were resolutely ignored; the macro-economic environment within which overarching policy frameworks are developed, in particular core fiscal and monetary policy approaches, were removed from the domain of analysis. The third criticism follows from this and relates to an apparent unwillingness on the part of the SLA to engage with fundamental economic issues. Whereas prior approaches to rural development stressed the importance of analysing social arrangements governing production and reproduction among people, the SLA stressed the importance of individuals undertaking multiple activities to minimize risk. Thus, it clearly falls within the maximizing logic of orthodox neoclassical economic theory, albeit a neoclassicism that was infused with a dose of the new institutional economics that resulted in Joseph Stiglitz winning the Nobel Prize in 2001. The SLA failed to ask the core questions of agrarian political economy, as laid out by Henry Bernstein (2010):

> Who owns what?
> Who does what?
> Who gets what?
> What do they do with it?

Indeed, that charge of implicit neoclassicism leads to the fourth, and perhaps most important, point of criticism which relates to the SLA position that everyone has assets and all assets are essentially equal. This point sidesteps a few critical issues: first, why do some have particular assets and others do not? Second, why are some assets of relatively greater importance to certain groups and of relatively lesser importance to other groups? Third, are there causal relationships between those who have larger quantities of relatively more important assets and those who have lesser quantities of relatively more important assets? These questions make it clear that the position that all assets are equal needs to be demonstrated rather than assumed, as proponents of the SLA do.

The fifth and final criticism of the SLA was that it did not investigate how social groupings relate to each other. In particular, in its failure to differentiate among – or prioritize – assets the SLA approach failed to identify and focus on the relations of social inequality that are found within and among households, and on relations of class and class divisions within communities and beyond (Veltmeyer, 2007). Such relations, in their totality, structurally underpin poverty processes and must be understood, if the creation of poverty and its persistence are to be understood. This final failing should not come as a surprise because, with its focus on people, households and community, politically the most the SLA could make claims for would be redistributive action.

This all combines to make it clear that the solution to the poverty problematic requires abandoning or moving beyond the SLA, which, by design if not intent, falls short of prescribing structural change: collective action by the poor, yes, but not action against the structure of power that sustains and reproduces their poverty.

THE DECLINE OF THE SLA

If one were to identify a pivotal point that facilitated the decline of the SLA's 'moment' as a hegemonic approach within rural development studies, it would be the publication of the World Bank's (2007) *World Development Report 2008: Agriculture for Development*. The WDR 2008 was explicitly supportive of the SLA, and investigated how rural livelihoods could be constructed to build a 'pathway out of poverty'. However, in trying to understand those pathways, the report in fact critically undermined the SLA. The WDR 2008 identified three pathways out of rural poverty:

1. Commercially-oriented entrepreneurial smallholder farming, in which 50 per cent of all farm production is sold in markets and 75 per cent of total household income is derived from farming.
2. Rural non-farm enterprise development, and in particular rural

non-farm waged labour, with more than 75 per cent of total household income from waged or non-farm self-employment.
3.   Outmigration, with more than 75 per cent of total household income coming from transfers or other non-labour sources.

What is remarkable about these three pathways is that they are all predicated upon some kind of specialization, and not on the diversity that is integral to the SLA. And so, the World Bank was implicitly arguing that diversity was in fact a constraint to poverty alleviation. However, if this was the case, why would the Bank be supportive of the SLA? It is quite contradictory. Moreover, of the three pathways, only the first would see farmers continuing to be farmers. This raises a question as to where these commercial entrepreneurial farmers are to be found. The implicit answer in the WDR 2008 is from subsistence-oriented farmers, who sell less than 50 per cent of their farm output in markets and who derive at least 75 per cent of total household income from farming, or from the aforementioned commercially-oriented smallholder farmers that are already operating in the countryside. Thus, despite its adoption of the SLA, the WDR 2008 conceives of farmers as a heterogeneous group that is differentiated by economic factors – principally natural, physical and financial. In other words: not all assets are equal. The economic factors which underpin the potential success of commercially-oriented entrepreneurial smallholder farmers lie in their capacity to generate consistent agricultural surpluses that they can reinvest in the expansion of their business, in both scale and scope and, in so doing, enhance their productivity efficiency over time. Yet the WDR 2008 did not discuss how the development of, what is, in essence, capitalist modes of farming would shape processes of agrarian change and poverty reduction, other than by having farmers cease farming. Nor did it consider how the development of capitalist modes of farming in developing countries takes place within the context of the larger capitalist world food system. Thus, the WDR 2008 offers a very limited understanding of peasant households, agrarian change and structural transformation, and their intra- and extra-household power dynamics. In supporting the SLA, the WDR 2008 in fact showed how the SLA reifies the local and, in so doing, critically ignores contestations of agrarian power taking place beyond the local. Most fundamentally, globalization has generated, and continues to generate, real-world macro challenges for peasant farmers that the micro-complexity of livelihoods frameworks have been unable to address, and which have resulted in the SLA falling into disuse. Indeed, it is these macro challenges which have thrown up La Via Campesina,[4] and its explicit recognition that the only sustainable pathway out of poverty for small-scale farmers is political mobilization against the character of the capitalist world food system (Akram-Lodhi, 2015).

CONCLUSION

My former colleague, Bridget O'Laughlin has, without doubt, put it best when she wrote that livelihoods research 'presents itself as a method without a theory. It frames no questions' (2004, p. 387). Although its focus on individual agency facilitates empirical research, such research is not theoretically situated. In consequence, there is a generalized failure to investigate structural constraints to individual agency, let alone to the possibilities of collective action and political responses. The result is an approach that stresses individual maximization within a set of binding constraints that give rise to a set of choices that, through research, policy and advocacy, could be reformulated to improve outcomes. It is thus a thoroughly neoclassical agenda that has only a limited ability to contribute to our understanding of the structural basis of inequality and conflict that is found in much of the countryside in the developing world.

NOTES

1. This is a significantly revised version of Akram-Lodhi (2010).
2. The Washington Consensus is a term first coined by John Williamson in 1989 to refer to a set of ten broadly free-market economic policy prescriptions, supported by prominent economists and international organizations, such as the IMF, the World Bank, the EU and the US.
3. As explained in *Report on Slate Falls Nations' Land Use and Occupancy* (Sieciechowicz 2010; hereafter, the Sieciechowicz Report) the Big Lake people consisted of two social groups, of which one was the Slate Falls people. As Charles Wesley put it, 'People who lived in that lake, belonged to that lake' (Sieciechowicz, 2010, p. 20). The Slate Falls Nation was only recognized as an independent band in 1985 by Canada's Department of Indian Affairs. Throughout this chapter 'Slate Falls people' is used interchangeably with 'Slate Falls Nation'.
4. A group of farmers' representatives – women and men – from four continents founded La Via Campesina in 1993 in Mons, Belgium. At that time, agricultural policies and agribusiness were becoming globalized and small farmers needed to develop and struggle for a common vision. Small-scale farmers' organizations also wanted to have their voice heard and to participate directly in the decisions that were affecting their lives. It is now recognized as a main actor in food and agricultural debates. It is heard by institutions such as the FAO and the UN Human Rights Council, and is broadly recognized among other social movements from local to global level.

REFERENCES

Akram-Lodhi, A.H. (2010), 'The sustainable livelihoods approach', in Veltmeyer, H. (ed.) *Critical Development Studies: Tools for Change*, Halifax and Winnipeg: Fernwood Press.
Akram-Lodhi, A.H. (2015), 'Accelerating towards food sovereignty', *Third World Quarterly*, vol. **36** (3), pp. 563–83.

Bernstein, H. (2010), *Class Dynamics of Agrarian Change*, Halifax and Winnipeg: Fernwood Press.

Bernstein, H., Crow, B. and Johnston, H. (1992), *Rural Livelihoods: Crises and Responses*, Oxford: Oxford University Press.

Chambers, R. (1983), *Rural Development: Putting the Last First*, London: Longman.

Chambers, R. and Conway, G. (1992), 'Sustainable rural livelihoods: practical concepts for the 21st century', *Discussion Paper*, Issue 296, Sussex: Institute of Development Studies.

Ellis, F. (2000), *Rural Livelihoods and Diversity in Developing Countries*, Oxford: Oxford University Press.

Moser, C. (1998) 'The asset vulnerability framework: reassessing urban poverty reduction strategies', *World Development*, vol. **26** (1), pp. 1–19.

O'Laughlin, B. (2004), 'Book review', *Development and Change*, vol. **35** (2), pp. 385–403.

Scoones, I. (2015), *Sustainable Livelihoods and Rural Development*, Halifax and Winnipeg: Fernwood Press.

Sieciechowicz, K. (2010) *Report on Slate Falls Nations' Land Utilization and Occupancy.* Available from A. Haroon Akram-Lodhi.

Veltmeyer, H. (2007), *On the Move: The Politics of Social Change in Latin America*, Peterborough, ON: Broadview Press.

World Bank (2007), *World Development Report 2008: Agriculture for Development*, Oxford: Oxford University Press.

18. Development and inequality: a critical analysis
Ray Kiely

INTRODUCTION

Is the world becoming less (or more) unequal, and, if so, what role has development played in reducing (or increasing) inequality? How do we account for global inequality? What development strategies are more or less egalitarian than others? How does inequality relate to poverty? Does inequality actually matter? How does inequality manifest itself and what are the mechanisms which sustain it? What, in fact, is inequality and how can we measure it? These are significant questions and this chapter cannot provide detailed answers to all of them. What it tries to do is provide some suggestive answers to some of them, and it does this by looking at the question of the relationship between development and inequality in terms of 'emergence', 'debates' and 'strategies', and then, in a more detailed discussion, draws on these debates to critically survey some recent trends in the relationship between development and inequality. This relationship covers a number of related but distinct issues: first, the 'emergence' of the discourse of development after 1945; second, different theoretical explanations of global inequality in the context of post-war development; and, third, the effect of concrete development processes and strategies that emerged in this period. This chapter examines these in separate but relatively brief sections, and in doing so shows how they are linked together. It then uses this discussion to reflect on a fourth issue, namely whether or not the world is becoming more or less unequal in the current era. This has been described as an era of neoliberalism, while others suggest it is an era where a new South has emerged which is changing a highly unequal world, and indeed it might be both these things. This fourth section discusses these issues in some depth, challenging both the neoliberal and (to some extent) the rising South arguments. The conclusion then summarises the argument and briefly analyses the recent rise of interest in inequality.

THE 'EMERGENCE' OF THE DEVELOPMENT DISCOURSE AFTER 1945

Some writers (Sachs, 1992) date the emergence of the development discourse to Harry Truman's inaugural presidential address in 1949. He argued:

> [W]e must embark on a bold new program for making the benefits of our scientific advances and industrial progress available for the improvement and growth of underdeveloped areas. More than half the people of the world are living in conditions approaching misery. Their food is inadequate. They are victims of disease. Their economic life is primitive and stagnant. Their poverty is a handicap and a threat both to them and to more prosperous areas. For the first time in history, humanity possesses the knowledge and the skill to relieve the suffering of these people . . . The material resources which we can afford to use for the assistance of other peoples are limited. But our imponderable resources in technical knowledge are constantly growing and are inexhaustible. I believe that we should make available to peace-loving peoples the benefits of our store of technical knowledge in order to help them realize their aspirations for a better life . . . Our aim should be to help the free peoples of the world, through their own efforts, to produce more food, more clothing, more materials for housing, and more mechanical power to lighten their burdens . . . It must be a worldwide effort for the achievement of peace, plenty, and freedom. (Sachs, 1992, p. 8)

The argument that development was invented in this period is without doubt an exaggeration. Locke's ([1869] 2014) seventeenth-century argument for 'improvement' was essentially an argument about development, and classical political economy from the eighteenth century concerned itself with the wealth of nations (Smith, [1776] 2014), while Marx ([1867] 1976) focused in part on the development of the productive forces. What was new after 1945 was the recognition that the world was divided into technologically advanced, or developed countries, and technologically backward, or 'undeveloped' countries. The US and the USSR were both committed (albeit selectively) to the end of colonialism and the promotion of state sovereignty, but equally they recognised that this sovereignty existed in a highly unequal world, and the solution to such inequality was 'development'.

Seen in this way, post-war development was an attempt to reduce inequality, and the solution was in the main to focus on technological fixes which would increase productivity and output, and thereby 'free the peoples of the world' (the meaning of which of course sharply differed across Cold War lines). Critics have suggested that this construction or invention itself reflected a further inequality, based on culture and knowledge, in which the rich world claimed to speak for the needs of the poorer world (Sachs, 1992; Escobar, 1995), and in doing so conflated difference with backwardness. In this respect the invention of post-war development constituted a new form of colonialism, based on cultural imperialism. This debate is not the main focus of this chapter but some brief comments are in order. First, while knowledge claims can be, and undoubtedly are, also claims to power, it is less clear that this point could be applied to all forms of development, as though the discourse of development were homogeneous. At times, 'post-development' critics present the discourse of development as so homogeneous that it is difficult, or impossible, to escape its homogenising logic. Second, and following on from this point, even if the discourse is a Western invention, it is quite something else to then reduce agents in what came to be called the Third World to passive recipients of this discourse, as though agency in the developing world did not, or does not, matter. Reducing 'Third World agency' in this way itself carries all kinds of assumptions every bit as Eurocentric as those that post-development theory claims to be challenging.

For our purposes, however, the main point is that post-war development emerged in the context of economic and political inequality, and the recognition that something needed to be done about this. What precisely should be done depended, in part, on how one explained how the division between the 'developed' and 'undeveloped' world emerged in the first place, and this is considered in the next section.

EXPLAINING INTERNATIONAL INEQUALITY: THE DEVELOPMENT DEBATE AFTER 1945

The first section explained the context in which the debate over the causes of global inequality emerged. Though there were considerable variations and nuances in the debate, we can identify two basic positions: modernisation and dependency theories. The former was the mainstream theory of development, which essentially argued that developing societies – the Third World – were backward and undeveloped, and therefore in need of development. This position was articulated most famously by Walt Rostow (1960), who suggested that all nation states pass through similar stages of development. So, poorer societies in the 1960s were at a similar stage of development to, say, Britain in the 1780s. The task of development was to hasten the transition to development in the poorer societies, which could be facilitated by poorer countries embracing Western investment, technology and values such as entrepreneurship and meritocracy. The question of whether or not meritocracy was an accurate description of Western societies was not one asked by modernisation theory, though of course it was central to the concerns of anti-racist movements in the US at the time. But for our purpose, the crucial argument of modernisation theory was that contact with the West was, on the whole, favourable to the development of the Third World.

Critics, however, had a very different explanation for inequality. One of the legacies of colonialism was that Third World countries specialised in producing primary products, and this led to an excessive dependence on the world price movements of the one or two goods that accounted for most of their foreign exchange earnings. This was in contrast to the developed countries, which were far more industrialised and diversified (Truman's point), and so were not excessively reliant on the price movements of a handful of products. Raul Prebisch (1959) and Hans Singer (1950) thus argued that primary producers faced certain disadvantages which meant that there was a tendency for the terms of trade to decline for primary goods as against industrial goods. What this meant in barter terms is that in a ten-year period, primary producers would have to exchange increasing amounts of cocoa in order to buy a similar number of tractors. Both Prebisch and Singer suggested that this tendency occurred because there was a low income elasticity of demand for primary products; in other words, as average incomes rise, so consumers spend a disproportionate amount of their income on primary products. Furthermore, while the prices of manufactured goods may fall, they are less likely to fall as quickly as those of primary goods as there are many primary goods producers but comparatively few producers of industrial goods. This account of inequality focused on hierarchies in the world economy, and on how colonial powers enforced specialisation in lower value primary production in the colonies.

While Prebisch and Singer believed that this problem could be overcome by industrialisation (see next section), dependency theory challenged this view, suggesting that industrialisation remained dependent on the West. The mechanisms that sustained dependence included reliance on foreign capital, foreign technology and foreign markets. Furthermore, the industrialisation that was said to be occurring in the developing world was highly exploitative and reliant on cheap labour. None of this was leading to convergence with the developed world; instead it was simply promoting new forms of subordination, hierarchy and dependence in the world economy. Some theories of dependency related this to a crude zero-sum game which suggested that the rich world was rich only because it had underdeveloped the poor world, implying that protectionist import substitution industrialisation (ISI) policies did not go far enough, and that de-linking from the Western dominated world economy was the only effective way forward for the Third World (Frank, 1969). In this account, poorer societies were not so much undeveloped as *underdeveloped*. While the mechanisms that sustained underdevelopment were not always made clear, it was suggested that the rich world became rich through a process of surplus extraction from the poorer countries. Again, the precise mechanisms of such surplus extraction were also not entirely clear, but the argument tended to focus on surpluses being extracted through unequal trade (or plunder) and foreign investment in which more money left a poor country than was actually invested in it in the first place (see Frank, 1969). These practices reflected dependence which is described as 'a conditioning situation in which the economies of one group of countries are conditioned by the development and expansion of others' (Dos Santos, 1970, p. 231). Dependency thus reflected and exacerbated inequality.

DEVELOPMENT PROCESSES, STRATEGIES AND INEQUALITY

For the period from around 1950 to 1982, the main development strategy in the developing world was ISI. As we have seen, this involved protectionist policies designed to replace the import of at least some manufactured goods with their domestic production. To develop domestic industrial production (either by national or foreign capital, provided the latter is invested in industry in the country concerned) it was envisaged that the state would protect industry through subsidies, tariffs and even import controls. This was very common in places like Tanzania, Ghana, Brazil, Argentina and India, but also in countries which combined import substitution with export promotion, such as South Korea and Taiwan. As we have seen, the rationale for this policy was to reduce dependence on the export of primary commodities and the import of some manufactured goods, but also to develop industry which usually involves higher productivity (compared to agriculture and services) and more intensive linkages throughout the economy. Both modernisation and structuralist economics supported the need for industrialisation as part of a modernising process in the developing world.

In terms of inequality, the most famous argument was put forward by Kuznets (1955), who argued that development was associated with an initial increase in inequality within countries, which was later followed by a decline in inequality. The reasons for this are associated with the consequences of a structural transformation, in which national economies move from focusing on agriculture to industry. In the process, there is a period in which development absorbs an influx of supply of labour moving from the countryside to the city, which leads to growing inequality between town and country, but also to urban inequality because of the growing supply of cheap labour (see also Lewis, 1954). Inequality will then later decrease as labour supplies are absorbed, per capita incomes reach a certain level, and welfare states ensure safety nets for those who might remain marginalised.

This essentially linear approach is problematic and I return to the 'Kuznets curve' in the conclusion. We might however immediately note that in the context of the 1950s, very different patterns of inequality existed across the developing world. East Asian take-off was immediately accompanied by lower rates of inequality, reflecting land reform (in South Korea and Taiwan) and investment in education, while in Latin America inequality was much more acute and appeared to conform to the predictions made by Kuznets (though this was not the case in the period from the 1980s). Inequality was also particularly acute in apartheid South Africa, which, of course, showed the importance of political factors in determining levels of inequality.

This laid the basis for a critique from the left which argued that ISI was not challenging particular social and political contexts, and would therefore not alleviate inequality. Also, it might replace the dependence on the import of certain industrial goods (such as cars) with dependence on the technology needed to make these goods. ISI was thus seen as a flawed strategy by many on the left. But on the right, there emerged a critique which suggested that in protecting industries from competition, ISI was, in effect, encouraging inefficient, uncompetitive sectors and what was needed instead was a more open policy in which economics competed in the world economy, and thus promoted market-led development. This critique became increasingly influential in the context of the 1982 debt crisis and laid the basis for the turn to neoliberalism, which is considered in the next section.

INEQUALITY AND DEVELOPMENT: THE CURRENT DEBATE

The most important issue then is how these debates manifest themselves in what we might call the neoliberal era, which began in the 1980s, and continues, albeit in modified form, to this day (Ostry et al., 2016). It is also of course the subject of considerable challenge, and some have tried to identify a BRIC model of state capitalism, or a Beijing Consensus as an alternative to neoliberalism (Ramo, 2004; Beeson, 2009; *The Economist*, 2012). This is not the place for a full analysis of these issues (see Kiely, 2015), but we will look at the broad contentions (and sometimes shared assumptions) of both the neoliberal and China/rising South positions, and then outline a sceptical response to these arguments.

The Optimistic Positions: Neoliberalism and/or China/Rising South

This position argues that, through 'neoliberal development', global inequality has been reduced in recent years, or if it has not been, then this does not actually matter and what does matter – poverty reduction – has taken place. The main evidence used by the optimists is that the number, or proportion, of people living in absolute poverty has declined since the 1980s, and that parts of the Global South have risen due to adopting market-friendly policies. So, for example, based on a poverty benchmark of living on less than US$1.25 a day, the proportion of the world's people living in extreme poverty fell from 43 per cent in 1990 to 22.4 per cent in 2008 (UNDP, 2013, p. 12). More recent estimates, based on poverty counts of people living on less than US$1.44 or US$1.78, suggest that the numbers are 449 million or 745 million, both of which represent significant downward trends over the last thirty years (Edward and Sumner, 2015, p. 33).

In terms of inequality, there also appears to be some good news. From 1820 to 1950, the share of Africa, Asia and Latin America in world GDP fell from 63.1 per cent to 27 per cent (Maddison, 2003; Nayyar, 2009). After 1950, however, there was a small upward trend in global GDP share for the South, from 27 per cent in 1950 to 28.5 per cent in early 1973. But by 2001, the share had increased to 42.5 per cent (Maddison, 2003; Nayyar, 2009), and to as much as 47.9 per cent by 2010, according to World Bank data (Akyuz, 2012). Thus, in the neoliberal era inequality between countries appears to have declined. The neoliberal argument is that the reason for this decline is that high rates of economic growth have occurred, caused by policies of trade and investment liberalisation – in other words, by the decision of countries of the South to embrace the opportunities afforded by globalisation. Poverty is thus a *residual* problem, a result of insufficient globalisation, reflecting poor policy choices by some states in the South. Good policies are those that encourage competition and specialisation, rather than protection, which means tariff and subsidy reduction, the removal of import controls and an openness to foreign investment. It may also mean financial liberalisation, the freer movement of money into (and out of) countries, but there is some disagreement over the extent to which this should occur (a point that also applies to the free movement of labour). The basic argument however is that trade liberalisation has encouraged specialisation in those sectors in which countries have a comparative advantage, and so they have stopped producing the high cost, inefficient goods that were associated with ISI. Furthermore, investment liberalisation will encourage investment by transnational companies, and thus lead to a shift of investment from capital rich to capital poor areas. There has indeed been a surge in foreign capital investment, including to the South, since the early 1990s. For much of this period around two-thirds of foreign direct investment (FDI) went to developed countries and one-third to developing (and transition) economies, but, by 2015, developing and transition economies accounted for 55 per cent of global FDI inflows (UNCTAD, 2015). The so-called BRIC (Brazil, Russia, India and China) countries were central to this change, with (in 2013) China the second largest recipient (and Hong Kong China fourth), Russia third, Brazil fifth and India fourteenth (UNCTAD, 2014). Furthermore, the BRICS (to include South Africa) have also emerged as major foreign investors themselves, and in 2013 outward FDI flows from developing countries stood at 32.2 per cent of the total outflows (of US$1.41 trillion), in contrast to 1998 when the proportion (of a much lower figure) was just 7 per cent (UNCTAD, 2014). Optimists thus contend that industrialisation can occur through open investment policies which allow foreign (or national) companies to take advantage of low labour costs, and this promotes properly competitive industrialisation rather than the high-cost, white elephant approach associated with ISI. Critics who point to the cheap labour associated with industrialisation do not offer a viable alternative, and anyway this should be seen as a necessary stage that developing societies must pass through. In the long run, competitive industrialisation will lead to full employment, which in turn will lead to upgrading to a more developed kind of manufacturing, as occurred in the case of the earlier developers (Bhagwati, 2004). Though this argument does not follow the rigid stages associated with modernisation theory, the broad contention – that embracing 'the West' and/or 'globalisation' – is similar.

An alternative optimistic position is that the rise of China, and to some extent other BRIC countries, has impacted favourably on the South as a whole as 'the world's economic centre of gravity has moved towards the east and south, from OECD members to emerging economies ... This realignment of the world economy ... represents a structural change of historical significance' (OECD, 2010, p. 15). Although the OECD itself would largely put this down to the liberalisation policies adopted by these countries, it might be argued instead that state capitalist policies, above all in China, have helped to promote an alternative to neoliberalism, but one that is indeed reducing inequality in the international order. Thus, while one may be sceptical of the claims made by advocates of neoliberal globalisation, one could still argue that the success of China represents an opportunity for reduced inequality and the rise of the South. Thus, for example, prices for all non-oil primary commodity prices rose sharply in the period before 2008, and while there was a decline in 2009, significant year-on-year price increases started again in 2010 (UNCTAD, 2012) leading some to identify the continuation of a commodity super-cycle, in which the South as a whole benefits from high Chinese demand, both in terms of volume and price (Kaplinksy and Farooki, 2010).

At the very least, then, neoliberal globalisation has brought about a reduction in poverty in the international order, and on some measures inequality has also been reduced. This is the argument made by neoliberal optimists.

The Sceptical Position

The sceptical position does not necessarily reject the neoliberal position outright. Some versions might, at least, accept that there has been some reduction in poverty in recent years and, on some measures, inequality has also been reduced. However, sceptics suggest that this is not as great as the optimistic position suggests, and they go on to argue that such reductions as there have been are not caused by neoliberal policies.

There are some grounds for questioning the view that absolute poverty has fallen. This poverty headcount is based on the value of a US dollar in the US, which is then adjusted to take account of local purchasing power in particular national economies. Purchasing power parity (PPP) is measured through a system of international price comparisons (in 1985, 1993, 2005 and 2011) which are then adjusted to take account of annual changes to particular economies. With different methodologies used for different comparisons, poverty decline might simply reflect these shifts rather than any reality on the ground. The idea of PPP is to make comparisons across regional variations in prices based on comparable prices of certain commodities. However, what comprises this basket is fraught with difficulty. In the 2005 International Price Comparison, various African countries had to price a 2003 or 2004 bottle of Bordeaux, a particular front-loading washing machine and a Peugeot 407 with air conditioning (Deaton and Aten, 2014). These commodities are useless in terms of measuring poverty in France, let alone in African countries. While the 2011 comparison appears to be less methodologically problematic, we should at least recognise that there are serious issues in the measurement of absolute poverty, and that some headline figures of significant reduction in the past simply reflected changing methodologies and different price comparisons.

Perhaps more important is the argument that poverty reduction has taken place in certain countries because of neoliberal policies. The argument here is that poverty reduction has occurred because of trade and investment liberalisation, and that other countries can enjoy high growth and poverty reduction if they follow the model supposedly set by these countries (Dollar and Kraay, 2001; World Bank, 2002). This argument has also been applied to explain the rise of the BRICS (O'Neill, 2013). There are, however, serious problems with these arguments, and, in particular, the evidence does not support the argument that greater openness is sufficient to promote growth and poverty reduction (Wade, 2003; Kiely, 2007, 2015). For example, it is true that both China and India have lowered tariff rates significantly in recent years, but they are no more open than some of the poorest developing countries that (until the 2000s) experienced little growth. Thus, average tariff rates in India declined from 80 per cent at the start of the 1990s to 40 per cent at the end of the decade, while China's declined from 42.4 per cent to 31.2 per cent in the same period, but the latter figures were still higher than the average for developing countries (Rodrik, 2001). Indeed, in 1997 (a crucial benchmark year in the 2002 World Bank report), allegedly high globalisers had higher average tariffs (35 per cent) than low globalisers (20 per cent) (Sumner, 2004).

Moreover, the picture in terms of inequality is hardly a promising one, and the increased share of the developing world in world GDP is accounted for by one region, namely Asia (an argument that might be compatible with the rising China position). Thus, measured in PPP dollars, the global share of GDP in Africa was 3.8 per cent in 1950 and 3.4 per cent in 2008, while Latin America's share increased from 7.8 per cent to 7.9 per cent over the same period (Maddison, 2003; Nayyar, 2013). In contrast, Asia's share increased from 15.4 per cent to 38 per cent (Maddison, 2003; Nayyar, 2013). World Bank 2007 data, which uses constant market prices, rather than those adjusted for PPP, present a slightly different picture. The story is still one of an upward trend from the 1970s onwards, but at lower levels. The share stood at 15.4 per cent in 1970, 17.7 per cent in 1980, following the lost decade of the 1980s, 17.5 per cent in 1990 (despite continued growth shares in East Asia), and 19.1 per cent in 2000. By 2005, the figure was 21.5 per cent (World Bank, 2007).

The story is complicated even further by the fact that population growth was higher in the developing world. When *per capita* GDP is factored in, we see a different picture with the rise effectively wiped out and the share standing at 4.7 per cent in 1970, 4.9 per cent in 1980, and 4.9 per cent in 2005 (World Bank, 2007). Indeed, based on market exchange rates, while the ratio of per capita GDP in Asia to that of the developed world shifted from 1:20 in 1970 to 1:11 in 2010, in Latin America it remained broadly the same (1:5) while in Africa it shifted from 1:12 to as much as 1:24 over the same period (Nayyar, 2013). Thus, once population is factored in, the inexorable rise of the South appears to be somewhat limited. Indeed, the 2010 OECD report on 'Global Shift' actually concedes the following point:

... the convergence observed in the 2000s was not statistically significant. This suggests that any improvement is tentative, and the situation could quite easily be reversed if, for instance, the strong growth performance of the largest convergers (above all India and China) fails. Nonetheless, the 'change of gear' in the 2000s was important in psychological terms, helping to shake off the development pessimism of the 1990s. (OECD, 2010, p. 37)

Furthermore, there is another issue, which goes to the heart of the debate over globalisation, contemporary development and inequality. Following the 2011 international price comparison, one could argue that the benchmark figures (above) are too low and if we shift to US$2 then the figure is 0.963 billion, while US$2.50 gives us a figure of 1.45 billion. Most disturbing of all, US$10 a day gives us a figure of 4.7 billion (Edward and Sumner, 2015, p. 33). A US$10 a day measurement might seem high, but in response to this objection, a number of points may be made. First, even if there is a downward trend, this does not establish causality in terms of 'globalisation friendly policies', for reasons already discussed, and downward trends existed in periods before neoliberal globalisation. Second, US$2.50 is a very low benchmark, not least as US$2.50 in the US (a US and PPP measurement) is not a feasible figure for lifting an American citizen out of absolute poverty. Third, and related to this point, even a slight shift in income for people living in poverty could translate to a massive downward measurement in poverty numbers, a point reinforced by the methodological issues addressed above. Fourth, this point also applies to those living just above the US$2.50 line but below the US$10 line, so that even if there are 'only' 1.5 billion people living in absolute poverty, there are 3 billion more people close to, or at risk of falling back into absolute poverty, which is precisely why the US$10 benchmark remains important. Fifth, almost all of those living below US$2.50 and (to a slightly lesser extent) the US$10 measure live in the Global South. This is hardly then a story of (neoliberal) development reducing inequality, and points 2 through to 5 hardly conform to the rising South thesis.

One possible response to this is the neoliberal argument that inequality per se does not matter, and what matters is the fact that people are lifted out of poverty. In other words, poverty is a residual phenomenon that can be conquered by more neoliberal development, and inequality is just a side-show. However, there is a stark contrast between the 1945–90 period, and the period since 1990, based on where the poor live. In the former period, they lived mainly in the least developed countries, but post-1990, this is no longer the case. Using World Bank data, Kanbur and Sumner (2012) estimate that between 71 per cent and 76 per cent of the world's poor live in middle-income countries (850–950 million people), while between 24 per cent and 29 per cent (350 million people) live in low-income countries, mainly in sub-Saharan Africa. China and India (both middle-income countries) accounted for half of the world's poor in 2007–8, compared to around 66 per cent in 1990. However, this is not the whole story as there is a significant concentration of the world's poor in three other middle-income countries, namely Pakistan, Nigeria and Indonesia (Kanbur and Sumner, 2012).

One might argue that this simply reflects the fact that some low-income countries moved up to middle-income countries in the period from 1990 to 2007–8. However, a close look at the data presents a darker picture, showing that the benefits of economic growth do not automatically trickle down to the poor, and thus that inequality matters and has an enormous impact on poverty. Whereas in the past poverty was largely concentrated in low-income countries where almost everyone was poor, and therefore the residual account of poverty might have been more plausible (though there may still have been relational causes operating at a global level), the geography of global poverty today suggests that inequality is more significant. In China, inequality has risen rapidly and the Gini coefficient measuring distribution within countries has risen from 0.28 in the early 1980s to 0.48 in 2008 (Nolan, 2012). Moreover, while incomes might have risen, the financial burden of health care and education has risen even more sharply for some, leading to less than impressive social development indicators (Reddy, 2007). From 1980 to 2010, life expectancy rose from 67.8 to 73.5, but this is actually around 50 per cent slower than other countries with similar life expectancy levels in 1980, even though these latter countries experienced much slower growth rates (ibid., p. 53). More widely, there was a clear trend of increased inequality within countries in the 1980s and 1990s. Based on household income in 104 countries, inequality increased in 73 of these countries in this period and fell in only 24, with the rest remaining broadly the same (UNCTAD, 2012). This was also true in most of the developed world as well (UNCTAD, 2012).

While the picture in the 2000s saw greater differentiation, with some countries in the South experiencing falling inequality, this was partly the result of the rise of 'left populist' regimes in Latin America as well as some contingent benefits derived from high commodity prices, which have since been reversed (Kiely, 2016), something discussed further below. These points apply to both the neoliberal and rising South optimistic positions.

What then of the foreign investment boom, which has undoubtedly taken place since the early 1990s? First, we must recognise that, although levels have increased, in many cases this has simply been because of a shift in ownership from the (national) state to the (foreign) private sector, rather than genuinely new, 'greenfield' investment. This can be seen if we examine investment/GDP ratios since the neoliberal era began in the early

1980s. Investment/GDP ratios for sub-Saharan Africa fell from a peak of around 23 per cent in the early 1980s, to around 15 per cent in 1985, but by 2000 they were only up to around 17 per cent; for the five biggest Latin American economies (Argentina, Brazil, Chile, Colombia and Mexico), the investment/GDP ratio peaked at close to 25 per cent in 1981, fell to 16 per cent by 1984, and by the time of the FDI boom in 1989 it stood at 19 per cent. However, by 2000, it had only increased to 20 per cent (Kozul-Wright and Rayment, 2004). The case of Brazil – one of the so-called leaders of the 'rising South' phenomenon – is instructive. Essentially, for much of the globalisation era, Brazil has developed on the basis of cheap imports, short-term foreign capital flows (and high interest rates to attract it), foreign loans and mass privatisations. While the 2000s saw a partial retreat from neoliberalism, development was essentially fuelled by a primary commodity boom, based on expanding demand in China. Thus, while in 1980 productivity levels were similar to that of South Korea, by 2011 these were on average three times lower than that of South Korea (Palma, 2012). When commodity prices began to fall from 2013 onwards, Brazil's economy fell back into recession, followed by political and social crisis. In effect, the pre-neoliberal era of ISI was replaced by one of 'production substitution', disguised by mobile capital inflows and high commodity prices (Saad-Filho, 2010), something common to both the neoliberal era and the increased 'turn to China' in the 2000s.

This is far from unique, both in terms of dependence on capital flows and the decline of manufacturing. It now appears that we are moving towards a new era for much of the South, which will see a significant reduction of capital flows. While, in the period before the financial crisis and from 2009 onwards, net private inflows to emerging markets exceeded outflows (with a positive 'surplus' of US$417 billion in 2010), this situation was in effect reversed as net capital outflows exceeded inflows by US$98 billion in 2013 and by as much as US$299 billion in 2014 (IIF, 2015). This may well signal the start of a third wave of the 2008 financial crisis, the first being the sub-prime crash of 2007–8, followed by the Euro crisis of 2010 onwards and now possibly an emerging markets crisis from 2015–16. In terms of the decline of manufacturing, the share of manufacturing value added in GDP in Latin America and the Caribbean stood at 19 per cent in 1990 and again in 2000 but fell to 16 per cent by 2013, while in sub-Saharan Africa the corresponding figures were 15 per cent in 1990, 13 per cent in 2000 and 11 per cent by 2013 (Rodrik, 2015). Rodrik has called this phenomenon 'premature industrialisation'. Indeed, with the fall in primary commodity prices in recent years, the Prebisch-Singer thesis concerning the dangers of excessive dependence on primary goods is pertinent once again. Thus, the IMF commodity price index, which measures the prices of all commodities, shows a sharp fall in prices from a post-crisis peak of 210 in the first quarter of 2011 down to a figure of less than 125 in January 2015 (IMF, 2015).

Moreover, even the rise of manufacturing has its limits, and here we need to examine the *type* of manufacturing that is most common in the developing world. There has been some growth in both manufacturing exports and manufacturing value added from the South in recent years, but as well as being mainly concentrated in East Asia, the former has grown more rapidly than the latter (Nayyar, 2013). This suggests that developed countries (and parts of East Asia) still tend to dominate in high-value sectors, based on high barriers to entry, high start-up and running costs, and the requirement for significant skill levels. In the developing world, where there are large amounts of surplus labour, and where barriers to entry, skills and wages are low, lower value production is more dominant. While this gives such countries considerable competitive advantage in terms of low start-up and labour costs, the fact that those barriers to entry are low means that competition is particularly intense and largely determined by cost price, which also means low wages. Thus, the clothing industry, where developing countries have achieved considerable increases in world export shares in recent years, has a very low degree of market concentration. In contrast, more capital intensive or high-tech sectors have very high degrees of market concentration, and are mainly located in the developed world (UNCTAD, 2002). In effect the Prebisch-Singer thesis is now applied not only to primary goods as against manufactured goods, but also to different kinds of industrial goods (Maizels et al., 1998; Zheng, 2002). Intense competition within sectors, where barriers to entry are low, leads to competition between developing countries, all trying to increase their exports in low-value manufacturing. Seen in this way, China's growth is less an opportunity and more a problem for other developing countries. This is because it has either led to over-dependence on primary commodities, which provide comparatively few linkages to the rest of the economy (in contrast to manufacturing) or it has intensified competition among manufacturing producers and thus served to drive prices down and keep wages low. Furthermore, as we have seen, the primary commodities boom is now over, with negative consequences for the developing world as a whole. These problems are also reinforced by the discourse of competitiveness, which encourages countries to compete through lower costs, including lower tax rates. This has not led to convergence on tax rates and it is this very divergence which encourages multinational companies to declare profits in low-tax countries, or indeed in tax havens. This has the effect of undermining the prospects for developing those public goods in all countries, but especially in developing countries, desperate to invest in education, skills and infrastructure. A recent estimate suggests that as much as US$12 trillion has been siphoned out of emerging markets in recent years (see Stewart, 2016). It is further estimated that China accounts for US$1.2 trillion of this, which again hardly fits the analysis of China's rise benefiting the South as a whole. This analysis suggests then that tax avoidance has implications for inequality within countries, but also for inequality between countries, in that it undermines the prospects for upgrading in developing countries.

For global inequality to be substantially eroded, there needs to be far more diversity in production, and a shift towards scale economies, technological sophistication, and skills and infrastructure development – neither low-value manufacturing nor primary commodity production can provide this, and neither are they likely to do so in the future. There are thus indeed structured inequalities in the global economy, and these are particularly acute for would-be late developers. Contrast this picture with that of the US, a power said to be in decline. Using the Forbes Global 2000 as a benchmark, which is based on the assets, market value, profit and sales of the top 2,000 corporations, Starrs (2013, 2014) examines the national distribution of profit across 25 economic sectors. He found that, even after the financial crisis, the US was leader in 18 of the 25 sectors and, while the share of the BRIC countries increased, this was largely accounted for by the rise of China. Moreover, China's rise is largely due to the dominance of its own companies in its own domestic market, and not because of the rise of Chinese global companies (Huawei is a notable exception). Thus, in 2011 China emerged as the world's largest PC market, but the Chinese profit share in this sector was just 2 per cent, compared to 72 per cent for US companies (Starrs, 2014).

In the most innovative sectors such as nanotechnology, the European Union, Japan and the US remain the world's leaders. In 2005, they filed 84 per cent of triadic patents, compared to just 2.6 per cent for the BRIC countries (see Kiely, 2015). By 2010, the US and Japan generated 60 per cent of triadic patents,[1] compared to 1.79 per cent for China (Starrs, 2014). In terms of Research and Development (R&D) spending as a proportion of GDP, in 2013 the US figure was 2.806 per cent compared to China's 2.019 per cent and an OECD average of 2.398 per cent (OECD, 2015). The European Commission carried out surveys of R&D spending in 2007 and 2011, and found that while the US share declined from 38.4 per cent to 34.9 per cent, Japan's share increased from 18.4 per cent to 21.9 per cent (Starrs, 2014). In fact, the only BRIC country with significant R&D spending in 2011 was China, with a share of just 2.7 per cent (Starrs, 2014).

CONCLUSION

The post-war development discourse emerged in the context of growing inequality between countries, which had sharpened in particular in the period from 1820 onwards. The idea of development was to reduce inequality (and poverty), initially through developmentalist strategies such as import-substitution industrialisation. This strategy was challenged by dependency theory on the left, which argued that it led to new forms of dependence and did not necessarily erode inequality; and neoliberalism on the right, which suggested that ISI was not conducive to freedom and efficiency, and in any case inequality did not matter. The current era has seen the rise of two distinct, but at times overlapping, optimistic positions. The first of these, neoliberalism, argues that inequality might have been reduced because of market friendly policies and even if it has not, poverty has been reduced and this is what matters. The second position, which we have called a rising China, rising South position, argues that inequality has been reduced due to the rise of countries like China which present opportunities for the South, and even a possible alternative to the neoliberal Washington and post-Washington Consensus.

This chapter has argued that, in fact, there are good reasons for questioning both these optimistic positions and that inequality remains a key issue in development today. This is because (in contrast to Kuznets' expectations) inequality has increased within many developing countries and, depending on which measures are used, and especially when population is factored into measurement, in many respects inequality between countries remains acute. Even if some limited progress has been made, the neoliberal position that this has been caused by market friendly policies is not convincing. While this in itself does not necessarily undermine the rising China position, recent developments in the South suggest that its supposed rise has been greatly exaggerated and, indeed, that we might well be witnessing a new crisis in the South, which is likely to lead to an exacerbation, rather than an alleviation, of inequality. This argument portrays a very different picture from that generated by various linear understandings of development and inequality, from modernisation theory, to Kuznets, through to neoliberalism and even the rising China/rising South thesis.

Indeed, the significance of inequality is something increasingly recognised by mainstream official accounts, as well as by highly considered scholarly works (WEF, 2014; OECD, 2015) and a best-selling academic book (Piketty, 2014). Much of this recognition of the importance of inequality reflects two things: first, its dysfunctionality, even when viewed in narrowly economistic terms, so that at least some of the causes of the 2008 financial crisis (the impact of which continues to this day) can be linked to the way that debt was used to sustain demand in conditions of stagnant wages in the developed world (and indeed how the super-rich devoured new financial instruments which, given their high risk, in the end led to crisis); second, in the context of far slower rates of growth in the post-2008 world, inequality is bound to be back on the agenda as the 'pie' is growing more slowly. However, when Oxfam (2016) reports that in 2015, the wealth of 62 individuals is equal to the wealth of 3.6 billion people, and that in 2010 that first figure was 388 individuals, we realise how far we have to go.

NOTE

1. These are patents registered at national patent offices and thus can be used as a kind of rough proxy for significant patents in terms of innovation, as opposed to relatively basic ones.

REFERENCES

Akyuz, Yilmaz (2012), *The Staggering Rise of the South?*, Geneva: South Centre Research Paper no.44, pp. 1–54.

Beeson, Mark (2009), 'Trading places? China, the United States and the evolution of the international political economy', *Review of International Political Economy*, vol. **16** (4), pp. 729–41.

Bhagwati, Jagdish (2004), *In Defence of Globalization*, Oxford: Oxford University Press.

Deaton, Angus and Bettina Aten (2014), 'Trying to understand the PPPs in ICP 2011: why are the results so different?' Available at: https://www.princeton.edu/~deaton/downloads/Deaton_Aten_Trying_to_understand_ICP_2011_V5.pdf (accessed 5 November 2015).

Dollar, David and Art Kraay (2001), 'Trade, growth and poverty', Washington, DC: World Bank Policy Research Working Papers, pp. 1–46.

Dos Santos, Theotonio (1970), 'The structure of dependence', *American Economic Review*, vol. **60**, May, pp. 231–36.

Edward, Paul and Andrew Sumner (2015), 'New estimates of global poverty and inequality: how much difference do price data really make?' Available at: http://www.cgdev.org/sites/default/files/CGD-Working-Paper-403-Edward-Sumner-New-Estimates-Global-Poverty.pdf (accessed 5 November 2015).

Escobar, Arturo (1995), *Encountering Development*, Princeton: Princeton University Press.

Frank, André Gunder (1969), *Capitalism and Underdevelopment in Latin America*, New York: Monthly Review Press.

IIF (2015, 14 January), *Capital Flows to Emerging Markets*, Washington: IIF, pp. 1–36.

IMF (2015) *Commodity Market Monthly*, February. Available at: http://www.imf.org/external/np/res/commod/pdf/monthly/020115.pdf (accessed 5 March 2015).

Kanbur, Ravi and Andrew Sumner (2012), 'Poor countries or poor people?', *Journal of International Development*, vol. **24** (6), pp. 686–95.

Kaplinsky, Raphael and Mamood Farooki (2010), *The Impact of China on Global Commodity Prices: The Global Reshaping of the Resource Sector*, London: Routledge.

Kiely, Ray (2007), 'Poverty reduction through liberalization, or intensified uneven development?: neo-liberalism and the myth of global convergence', *Review of International Studies*, vol. **33** (4), pp. 415–34.

Kiely, Ray (2015), *The BRICs, US 'Decline' and Global Transformations*, Basingstoke: Palgrave.

Kiely, Ray (2016), *The Rise and Fall of Emerging Powers*, Basingstoke: Palgrave Pivot.

Kozul-Wright, Richard and Paul Rayment (2004), 'Globalization reloaded: an UNCTAD perspective', UNCTAD Discussion Papers no. 167, pp. 1–50.

Kuznets, Simon (1955), 'Economic growth and income inequality', *American Economic Review*, vol. **45** (1), pp. 1–28.

Lewis, W. Arthur (1954), 'Economic development with unlimited supplies of labour', *The Manchester School*, vol. **22** (2), pp. 139–91.

Locke, John ([1869] 2014), *Two Treatises of Government*, Indianapolis: Liberty Fund.

Maddison, Angus (2003), *The World Economy: Historical Statistics*, Paris: OECD.

Maizels, Alfred, Theodosios Palaskas and Trevor Crowe (1998), 'The Prebisch-Singer hypothesis revisited', in David Sapsford and John-ren Chen (eds), *Development Economics and Policy*, Basingstoke: Palgrave Macmillan, pp. 45–70.

Marx, Karl ([1867] 1976), *Capital vol. 1*, Harmondsworth: Penguin.

Nayyar, Deepak (2009), *Developing Countries in the World Economy: The Future in the Past?*, Helsinki: United Nations University World Institute for Development Economics Research, Annual Lecture 12, pp. 1–46.

Nayyar, Deepak (2013), *Catch Up*, Oxford: Oxford University Press.

Nolan, Peter (2012), *China Buying the World?*, Cambridge: Polity.

OECD (2010), *Perspectives on Global Development, 2010, Shifting Wealth*, Paris: OECD Development Centre.

OECD (2015), *In it Together: Why Less Inequality Benefits All*, Paris: OECD.

O'Neill, Jim (2013), *The Growth Map*, London: Portfolio Penguin.

Ostry, Jonathan, Prakash Loungani and Davide Furceri (2016), 'Neoliberalism: Oversold?', *Finance and Development*, June, pp. 38–41.

Oxfam (2016), 'An economy for the 1%', Oxfam Briefing Paper 210. Available at: https://www.oxfam.org/sites/www.oxfam.org/files/file_attachments/bp210-economy-one-percent-tax-havens-180116-en_0.pdf (accessed 31 January 2016).

Palma, Gabriel (2012), 'Is Brazil's recent growth acceleration the world's most overrated boom?', Cambridge: Cambridge Working Papers in Economics no. 1248, pp. 1–70.

Piketty, Thomas (2014), *Capital in the Twenty First Century*, Cambridge, MA: Harvard University Press.

Prebisch, Raul (1959), 'Commercial policy in the underdeveloped countries', *American Economic Review*, vol. **44**, pp. 251–73.

Ramo, Joshua (2004), *The Beijing Consensus: Notes on the New Physics of Chinese Power*, London: Foreign Policy Centre.

Reddy, Sanjay (2007), 'Death in China', *New Left Review*, vol. **45** (May–June), pp. 49–65.

Rodrik, Dani (2001), *The Global Governance of Trade as if Development Really Mattered*, Geneva: United Nations Development Programme.

Rodrik, Dani (2015), 'Premature deindustrialization', Cambridge, MA: Harvard University, unpublished paper.

Rostow, Walt (1960), *The Stage of Economic Growth*, Cambridge: Cambridge University Press.

Saad-Filho, Alfredo (2010), 'Neoliberalism, democracy and development policy in Brazil', *Development and Society*, vol. **39** (1), pp. 1–28.

Sachs, Wolfgang (ed.) (1992), *The Development Dictionary*, London: Zed Books.

Singer, Hans (1950), 'The distribution of gains from trade between investing and borrowing countries', *American Economic Review*, vol. **40**, pp. 473–85.

Smith, Adam ([1776] 2014), *The Wealth of Nations*, [no location]: Shine Classics.

Starrs, Sean (2013), 'American economic power hasn't declined – it globalized! Summoning the data and taking globalization seriously', *International Studies Quarterly*, vol. **57** (4), pp. 817–30.

Starrs, Sean (2014), 'The chimera of global convergence', *New Left Review*, vol. **87** (May–June), pp. 81–96.

Stewart, Heather (2016), 'Offshore finance: more than $12 trillion siphoned out of emerging countries'. Available at: https://www.theguardian.com/business/2016/may/08/offshore-fin ance-emerging-countries-russia-david-cameron-summit (accessed 9 June 2016).

Sumner, Andrew (2004), 'Epistemology and "evidence" in development studies: a review of Dollar and Kraay', *Third World Quarterly*, vol. **25** (6), pp. 1160–74.
The Economist (2012), 'The rise of state capitalism', 21 January.
UNCTAD (2002), *Trade and Development Report 2002*, Geneva: UNCTAD.
UNCTAD (2012), *Trade and Development Report 2012*, Geneva: UNCTAD.
UNCTAD (2014), *World Investment Report 2014*, Geneva: UNCTAD.
UNCTAD (2015), *World Investment Report 2015*, Geneva: UNCTAD.
UNDP (2013), *Human Development Report 2013*, New York: UNDP.
Wade, Robert (2003), 'The disturbing rise in poverty and inequality: is it all a "big lie"?', in David Held and Mathias Koenig-Archibugi (eds) (2003), *Taming Globalization*, Cambridge: Polity, pp. 18–46.
WEF (2014), *Global Risks 2014*, Geneva: World Economic Forum.
World Bank (2002), *Globalization, Growth and Poverty*, Oxford: Oxford University Press.
World Bank (2007), *World Development Indicators 2007*, Washington, DC: World Bank.
Zheng, Zhihai (2002), 'China's terms of trade in world manufactures, 1993–2000', UNCTAD Discussion Paper no. 161, pp. 1–61.

19. Water and a fluid international development agenda
G. Honor Fagan

INTRODUCTION

Access to, and the socio-ecological management of, water resources is a vital component of any international development framework that seeks to eradicate poverty and address global socio-economic inequities. The shifting approaches taken to the question of water over the past 30 years neatly reflects the changes, continuities and challenges in the evolution of development policy itself. The negotiation around the Sustainable Development Goals (SDGs) has shown the limitations and contradictions of the international development agenda, and none has shown those limitations more so than the water goals. Perhaps this is because the efforts made around water resourcing and distribution are being made in the context of an unfettered top-down political economy of water. We are in an era of the global 'water grab' (Transnational Institute (TNI), 2013) with ten major firms controlling water in over 100 countries (Salleh, 2016, p. 958). It is increasingly unlikely that even these most compromised water goals will be delivered (Salleh, 2016), based as they are on a public-private partnership model. This may best express the failure of global international development policy itself to deliver on meeting basic needs, given ongoing legitimation of what remains a non-transformative economic growth model.

WHY WATER RESOURCING PERTAINS TO OUR GLOBAL FUTURE

Water as a resource is critical to individual survival, and so its social organisation is inherently political. It has been argued that the prosperity or decline of civilisations throughout history has borne a direct relationship to their ability to manage water supply, and the social organisation and distribution of access to water defines the political systems of those societies (Wittfogel, 1957). Social power and the forms it takes in our hydro-social landscapes has featured in much recent socio-political research (for example Strang, 2005; Swyngedouw, 2015; Obertreis et al., 2016). Therefore, it will come as no surprise to learn that economic criteria and consumerist charged reasoning drive water resource development decisions at most local, regional, national, and international levels. These decisions are proving immune to sustainability criteria or to a logic of just distribution, despite an increased sustainability and crisis rhetoric. As we go hurtling into our 'anthropocene' future (labelled as such because of the extensive impact of human activity on the earth's ecosystems), the salvation of our water systems for all is by no means secure. Degradation of the biodiversity of our freshwater ecosystems is more significant than that in any other ecosystem. In fact, our freshwater systems are under extreme pressure from the paradox of increased production, consumption, and wastage, being defined as economic development, rather than ecological and social destruction. It is clear that there is a politics of water, and a political economy of water that has organised water as a resource, which appears to have led us to startling water resourcing material realities. The quality and quantity of fresh clean water is such that we have reached a material crisis point of scarcity on a global scale.

While about 71 per cent of the earth's surface is covered by water, 97.5 per cent of that is saline water, largely held in the oceans. For the most part, reference to water crisis and scarcity is usually taken to refer to freshwater resources only (United States Geological Survey (USGS), 2016). Only 2.5 per cent of earth's water is fresh and is located in rivers and lakes, icecaps and glaciers, in the air as water vapour and in the ground as soil moisture and in aquifers. It naturally circulates and continuously changes form between liquid, vapour and ice, through a process described by scientists as the hydrologic cycle. Rivers and lakes are the primary source of the freshwater that most people use but they make up just 0.026 per cent of total freshwater (USGS, 2016). Problems in relation to people's access and use of this 0.026 per cent of freshwater, its quality arising from pollutants, and its quantity given population increases, drive the discussion on scarcity.

The capacity of freshwater ecosystems to provide clean and reliable sources of water is declining in an accelerated fashion all over the globe and responsible water resource management is in short supply. Every day, two million tons of human waste is disposed of in watercourses, and in developing countries vast quantities of industrial and agricultural waste are dumped untreated into waters. Ninety per cent of wastewater flows untreated into rivers, lakes and coastal fishing waters in developing countries, polluting the usable water supply (World Water Development Report (WWDR), 2017). These facts indicate a rapidly worsening crisis in our hydrologic cycle, such that even a rapid turn of economic production towards sustainable growth, or green growth, may simply be a shift in defence of lost causes.

From a sustainability perspective, it is obvious that the earth's environment is a finite resource wherein water scarcity, water pollution and water mismanagement constitute a threat to vast numbers of its population. The complicated and fluid hydrological landscape is riven with problems, sometimes scarcity or pollution triggers a political crisis, sometimes mismanagement. This is not just a problem of the developing world – water resourcing is in crisis throughout the globe. In the European regions, some 120 million people do not have access to safe drinking water. Water quality remains a persistent problem, with agrochemicals in particular having had a detrimental impact on water resources throughout the region (WWDR, 2012, p. 9). Globally, 750 million people (one in nine) around the world lack access to safe drinking water, and approximately 2.5 billion (one in three) do not have access to basic or improved sanitation (WWDR, 2012). Most of the world's poor are deeply water insecure and face intolerable water-related risks, which in turn create and contribute to their ongoing poverty.

The continuing failure to safeguard, and sustainably and equitably manage and govern, water resources is most likely to lead to an environmentally driven socio-economic crisis. The World Economic Forum (WEF) in its *Global Risks 2015* report (WEF, 2015) identified the water crisis as the number one global risk based on impact to society (as a measure of devastation), and the eighth global risk based on likelihood of occurring within ten years (WEF, 2016).

Climate change is set to exacerbate the water management crises. The World Meteorological Organization has indicated that climate change, as evidenced in the record-breaking heat that made 2016 the hottest year ever recorded, is pushing the world into 'truly uncharted territory'. While the hydrological landscape is a complex one, it is a fact that water is the primary medium through which climate change affects the earth's ecosystem and people. While it is impossible to definitively predict how intensive the water problems will be, UNESCO predict that, by 2025, 1.8 billion people will be living in countries or regions with absolute water scarcity, and two-thirds of the world population could be living under water stress conditions (WWDR, 2012). This is due not only to climate change but also to water demand increasing significantly over the coming decades. In addition to the demand of the agricultural sector, the World Water Assessment Programme (WWAP) expects large increases in water demand, for industry and energy production (WWAP, 2015). Changing consumption patterns, including shifting diets towards highly water-intensive foods such as meat will no doubt worsen the situation (Bosire et al., 2017).

Water as a resource is vital to our future, and the mode through which we organise access to it, and protect it, shapes our society. At the level of principle, we have seen some progress in this regard. If we use access to water as a measure of the value we place on human life and human security, the United Nations General Assembly in July 2010, cognisant of the rapidly changing socio-economic and ecological dimensions of water security and of the extreme human suffering caused by water poverty, recognised 'the right to safe and clean drinking water and sanitation as a human right that is essential for the full enjoyment of life and all human rights' (United Nations, 2010, p. 1).

How water resources are provided for all, how its quality is ensured, and how that is reconciled with economic development are central to a sustainable development agenda. The three goals of sustainable develop-ment of water to be resolved are as challenging in our future as they have been in our past. The progressive social project of our water future will be characterised by creating the dynamics of water as a human right, ensuring equity of access, establishing the infrastructure for fair distribution glo-bally, and pursuing implementable sustainable practices that protect water quality. However, there is very little about the principles and practice of capitalist economic development that supports any of these dynamics – and much that contradicts them.

WATER PRESSURE ON NATIONAL POLITICS

It is not surprising, then, that the politics of water is contested in national contexts. Water 'costs' and the material problems of water resourcing create a political context in which the multiple dynamics of the environ-mental crisis, economic production as usual, and social distribution are played out. The politics of an unsustainable future is under debate and reflected in liberal democratic representative parliaments in national juris-dictions. Many national political fracas provide evidence of the structural ecological crisis of water pressure emerging. For example, we can cite recent water-related disputes in the US and in Ireland (in the European jurisdiction) where we see two very different positions playing out.

In the US, the new right politics emerging is contributing to a worsen-ing of the water quality there, since this regime from a pro-capitalist perspective is determined to exacerbate and fuel its crisis by reconstructing national policies that favour polluters. For example, on 21 February 2017 President Trump basically recreated the conditions for the fouling of US freshwater water supplies, when he ordered his administration to rescind an environmental rule on regulating waterways nationwide, on the basis of his concerns over business and industry's objections to it. He signed a directive compelling the US Army Corps of Engineers and the Environmental Protection Agency to reconsider the 2015 'Waters of US' rule, calling it 'one of the worst examples of federal regulations' (cited in Daniels, 2017). Indeed, he has promised to take steps to abolish the Environmental Protection Agency (EPA) itself. Myron Bell, who headed up Trump's transition team, described the environmental movement as 'the greatest threat to freedom and prosperity in the modern world'. Meanwhile, Trump's nomination of Scott Pruitt to lead the EPA, a businessman who had previously sued the agency 13 times, is the ultimate example of the appointment of the poacher to the role of gamekeeper (Mosbergen, 2017).

In Ireland, the new left politics, which encompass 'right to water' campaigns, have driven a challenge to European regulations on water, and to the wedding of these regulations to neoliberal pro-privatisation policy at national policy level. The Irish government led by Fine Gael, a centre-right political party, under pressure to sort out the national water situation after years of neglect, made decisions that led to the setting up of an Irish Water Company in 2013, and the introduction of household levies on water. Although this was presented by the government as a requirement of European neoliberal inspired sustainable water legislation, the decision has played a destabilising role in post-collapse Irish national politics over the past four years, much as Trump's reversal of pro-sustainable regulations will likely prove destabilising to his. After a long drawn-out successful campaign by parties to the left and social movements, resistance to the laying of the meters and to the paying of bills resulted in a defeat for the Irish government. The year 2016 brought with it the suspension of water charges by the new, minority, Fine Gael-led government.

In March 2017, the Irish government was once again on the point of defeat on the issue of water, this time in relation to charges for wasting water specifically with the political parties clashing on how to handle the charges. As the government returned to crisis, the 'Right to Water Campaign' was activated once again and brought protesters on to the streets, in what some called the 'final push' against the levies, and against the validity and legitimacy of the decision to establish the company Irish Water (Holland, 2017).

That there is a political division on water policy today in many countries, including the two Western ones mentioned above, signifies that the political ground has shifted. There is a move away from a modernist trust in a rational objective scientific programme that will deliver 'development' and 'progress' on water at national level even in so-called rich and scientifically advanced countries. Water distribution, costs and protection are now recognised as a political question and this is the case whether referring to the socio-economic organisation of water resourcing in the US, Europe or sub-Saharan Africa, to which we now turn.

A CRITICAL EXPLORATION OF INTERNATIONAL DEVELOPMENT FRAMEWORKS AND WATER

Despite economic growth, development theory and practice are unlikely to deliver on meeting basic needs globally. Critiques of development approaches have identified an 'impasse' in development theory (Escobar, 1995; Munck and O'Hearn, 1999; Ziai, 2007; Chambers, 2012), which, in so far as it operated within dominant structuralist and modernist discourses, could not provide 'sufficient tools for transformation' (Fagan, 1999) as we moved into the new millennium. Yet development practices, development agencies and interventions continue. Delivering drinking water and sanitation to households is so integral to international development policy that, in sub-Saharan Africa, its delivery is equated with delivering development itself. Likewise, the power-laden relations of development aid and international development policy are worked out in the lives of poor communities through forms of governance of their water resources. Access to water resources has been on the agenda of international policy makers for many decades. A critical exploration of the history of water interventions over the past 30 years, as driven from an international development perspective, provides a clear picture of the possibilities and limitations of the overall trajectory of international development.

While there is much discussion on water scarcity and water insecurity globally, and much politics around that discussion, in the international development context the crisis in water resources has, more usefully, been described as one of equity of access, benefits and entitlements to water resources. Defining and quantifying inequalities in access to this resource has been a key component of international development research. Additionally, international development discourse has, more recently, advocated a pro-poor approach to water and development. Thus, the focus in international development has been on the promotion of access to water as a human right, on pro-poor policy making regarding water resourcing and on water as a key enabler of social development.

International development has focused on water poverty specifically, and has highlighted the shocking differences between access in 'first world' countries and access in the 'developing' countries. Geographically, 40 per cent of 750 million without access live in sub-Saharan Africa. The differences in access to water between rural and urban areas in sub-Saharan

Africa has also been a key focus – 82 per cent of those who lack access to improved water live in rural areas (JMP, 2015). Gender inequality is also a major issue, with women and girls expending a lot more time and energy in collecting water compared to men and boys (JMP, 2015). In Africa, 90 per cent of work gathering water and wood, for household use and for food preparation, is done by women, which significantly decreases the time available for economic activities or education. There are also inequalities in the area of health since the lack of access to safe drinking water, combined with inadequate sanitation and poor hygiene, is responsible for a rise in poverty and water-related diseases, mainly diarrhoea. Diarrhoea kills an estimated 842,000 people every year globally, or approximately 2,300 people per day (JMP, 2015). Hundreds of millions of people have no access to soap and water to wash their hands, preventing them engaging in a basic act that would empower them to block the spread of disease. The collection of these key social statistics and the articulation of their impact in terms of equity of access to an essential ingredient of life have been central to international development policies and debates. Due to this focus, the social, economic and health burden placed on people and countries by inadequate access to water resources is now considered to be a significant global humanitarian crisis – one which needs to be resolved by the global community, through agreement with national governments. However, despite this, as we have seen in the introduction to this chapter, insufficient progress has been made on delivering water as a human right, on ensuring equity of access, on establishing the infrastructure for fair distribution globally, and on implementing sustainable practices that protect water quality.

UN WATER DECADES

Three decades of intervention do not add up to three decades of progress. Many facets of development policies, particularly some of those espoused by Western leadership, relied heavily on a philosophy of developmentalism, which is, as described by Pieterse, 'universalist and ahistorical, teleological and ethnocentric' (1991, p. 5). Developmentalism, as opposed to the dynamics of structural inequalities and environmental sustainability, has been central to Western approaches to resolving water issues. In fact, much of development thinking pushed ahead without any systematic consideration of the sources, effects and practices of structural inequality. Structural inequality does not form the basis of many of the key interventions in water, rather what seems to direct action is a developmentalist paradigm of linear progress, which sees nature – including water resources – as something to be tamed and harvested for the good of development. Developmentalism is dominant when the Promethean myth drives Western science and philosophy – in development discourse this is pervasive in the approach taken in what has come to be termed the two UN decades of water. The politics behind development policies, up until the 1980s, varied from those attempting to achieve social and economic transformation through redistribution, to those attempting to ameliorate the worst excesses of capitalism in order to protect capitalism itself and ensure its further development. There was quite a lot of the latter and very little of the former where 'developmentalism' prevailed as the inspiration.

The 1977 United Nations Water Conference at Mar del Plata set up an International Drinking Water Decade, 1981–1990. Its aim was to make access to clean drinking water available across the world, with the focus on safe water and sanitation for everybody by 1990. It was hoped that where there were deficiencies or lack of commitment at national government level, these could be bypassed by the creation of an effective organisation within countries to carry out a water and waste programme, with appropriate training and financing, and the development of advanced technologies to solve the water problems. Subsequently, in December 2003, the United Nations General Assembly proclaimed a second decade, the years 2005–2015, as the International Decade for Action 'Water for Life'. Its primary goal was to promote efforts to fulfil international commitments made on water and water-related issues in the United Nations Millennium Development Goals (MDGs) by 2015, with the ultimate aim of achieving universal access to water.

The development project has always indicated a one-way path towards modernity that all countries must travel. The diffusion of capital and modern values into what were deemed backward or traditional areas was seen as the key to development. The path to universal access to water was guided by a range of science and enlightenment values. As a recent influential text, *Science and Innovation for Development*, puts it, the sequence is quite clear:

> The goal of international development is to reduce poverty and to help poor people build a better life for themselves . . . Science can make a valuable contribution to this goal . . . Scientific knowledge and technology can be applied to specific technical challenges, like achieving the Millennium Development Goals (MDGs). (Conway and Waage, 2010, p. 7)

Except of course the challenge is not just 'technical', but is one of structural and embedded inequalities that goes to the heart of the uneven development of capitalism and a globalisation that has created great wealth only by generating great inequality between, and within, countries (see Arrighi et al., 2003). Ignoring the colonial heritage – or rather bypassing it, with technological fixes provided by Northern science and with loans from the World Bank – has marked interventions in these decades (Ferguson, 2006). The 'hydraulic mission' of the modern era aligns closely with a logic of developmentalism, which portrays water as a purely technical issue beyond politics.

The International Decade for Clean Water and Sanitation (1980s) came after the Second Development Decade (1970s) and there is little doubt that it sought to implement the ideology and practice of developmentalism in the field of water and sanitation (Munck, 2015). It was launched in a mood of great confidence, with a commitment to the 'eminently achievable' goal of 'safe water and sanitation for all by 1990'. At the time only one person in five in the developing world had access to clean water. The rhetoric was inspiring, the formula for delivery of the goal, however, was less so, given that it was based on international loans and structural adjustment policies. Jolly (2003) outlines the percentage increase in delivery of water in developing countries over the period. He identifies an increase in delivery from 67 per cent to 75 per cent in urban populations and from 14 per cent to 29 per cent in rural populations. This left basic water needs unmet for 25 per cent of urban populations and 71 per cent of rural populations. The years 1990–2000 saw a greater increase – to 95 per cent of urban populations, but only 66 per cent of rural populations benefiting (see Table 19.1).

Nonetheless, between 1990 and 2000 the rate of change slowed down. In Africa, Asia, Latin America and the Caribbean, where most of the 'developing countries' are located, urban water coverage dropped from 92 per cent to 91 per cent given urban population growth. Rural water coverage went up from 63 per cent to 69 per cent, and total water coverage increased from 73 per cent to 78 per cent in the same time frame, leaving 22 per cent of the population without coverage (JMP, 2000, p. 9). This, combined with an insubstantial sanitation coverage change from 44 per cent in 1990 to 53 per cent in 2000 (ibid.), left the aim – of the delivery of water and sanitation for all – in serious deficit.

Table 19.1   Percentage increase in delivery of water and of population benefited in developing countries

	1970–80	%	1980–90	%	1990–2000	%
Urban	66	67	108	75	35	95
Rural	217	14	109	29	24	66
Total	100	29	130	43	29	79

Source: Jolly (2003), p. 34.

Even in the course of implementation of the water delivery programme, serious problems had been identified, most of them associated with the formula for development aid applied and its alignment with structural adjustment policies. Much of the improvement in terms of increased access was achieved simply through the repair of existing facilities rather than by the provision of state investment in infrastructure in developing countries. By 1990 the global slowdown had already led to 'structural conditionality' for international loans. So, although some small-scale initiatives on the ground were able to succeed, strict cost recovery in the operation and maintenance of water facilities overwhelmed the developmentalist mission.

The failure of affluent states, their advanced technologies, and international organisations to deliver the most basic development water needs to the poorest populations discredited international development policy in general. The intellectual and moral legitimacy of international development's alignment with the capitalist promise of trade and assistance going to 'developing' countries to eliminate poverty, already deeply suspect from a post-colonial perspective, was in question at the end of the last millennium. Yet the 2000 verdict of the World Health Organization (WHO) was that 'The 1980s were not a lost decade for water; it had been declared a water decade. During that time, more people had gotten access to water than ever before . . . The challenge is to remobilise the commitment to global action on water' (JMP, 2000).

In conclusion, we could look at the international development policies on water through the 1980s and 1990s as being steeped in developmentalism. Without sufficient impact on the material realities of poor people's access to water, without the delivery of that universal access, and without achieving its objectives, these 20 years of international development policy can be seen largely as a period of promotion of a modernist discourse of power in the guise of a programme for social change.

THE WATER MILLENNIUM DEVELOPMENT GOALS

By 2000, UN policy makers, charged with promoting globalising economic policies, became cognisant of the growing criticism of those policies that the benefits of globalisation were accruing to the few as opposed to the many. At the United Nations Millennium Summit in September 2000, the largest-ever gathering of world leaders adopted the Millennium Declaration (United Nations, 2000). From the Declaration emerged the Millennium Development Goals (MDGs), an integrated set of time-bound targets for extending the benefits of globalisation to the world's poorest citizens. Among them was Target 10 – to cut in half the proportion of people without sustainable access to safe drinking water. This target was far more modest than the one set in 1980, and indeed was more modest that those set in many of the other MDGs (Hemson, 2015). In South Africa, at the Johannesburg World Summit for Sustainable Development, in 2002, this target was expanded to include basic sanitation, and water as a resource was recognised as a critical factor for meeting all the MDGs. Why was the target so undemanding, why was sanitation missing from the 2000 Declaration and why the retreat from universal coverage? According to Hemson, when those who were responsible for planning to eliminate water poverty were faced with the development challenge of the millennium 'the sights were lowered rather than raised, additional capital spending was cautious, and debate tended to limit, rather than endorse, commitments' (ibid., p. 216). Perhaps this was a moment in which there was some reflection on those past failures, and an acknowledgement that without changing the underlying rules of the game of international development, further rhetoric could only be hypocritical.

Nonetheless, given the magnitude of the water and sanitation needs, in December 2003 the United Nations General Assembly proclaimed 2005–2015 the International Decade for Action 'Water for Life'. The decade officially started on World Water Day, 22 March 2005. The UN emphasis was on furthering cooperation at all levels, so that the water-related goals of the Millennium Declaration, the Johannesburg Plan of Implementation of the World Summit for Sustainable Development, and Agenda 21 could be achieved. The decade was to focus on action-oriented activities and policies that would ensure the long-term sustainable management of water resources, in terms of both quantity and quality, and would include measures to improve sanitation. This was to be achieved by sustained commitment, and cooperation and investment on the part of all stakeholders from 2005 to 2015, rather than on generous development assistance.

Once again there were some achievements in terms of access and equity of access. The MDG target of halving the proportion of the population without sustainable access to safe drinking water by 2015, was met in 2010, five years ahead of schedule, although it is not clear that this had much to do with the specific UN policies. Rather, it was seen to result from specific countries like China making their own national interventions. Despite meeting this target, it was the case that, in 2012, 748 million people still relied on unimproved drinking water sources. It was clear that a full water and development agenda needed to be so much greater than that expressed in the MDGs. In areas directly targeted by the UN, such as sub-Saharan Africa, only a handful of countries had halved the proportion of people without access to safe drinking water by 2015 (JMP, 2015). Thirty-two per cent of the region's population did not have access to an improved drinking water source, with that figure being higher for rural areas (44 per cent) (JMP, 2015). But even these statistics, collected in order to assure development organisations that targets were being met (although they do report failures as well as successes) should be treated with some caution. Thomas Pogge (2010) goes so far as to describe them as merely 'cosmetic'.

If we bypass meta statistics and national figures and investigate water poverty at a community level we get a different picture. In such a study in Uganda in 2011 it became clear to us the ways in which the national and regional figures – the collection of which is to prove improvements at the meta level – can cloak water poverty and provide a cosmetically adjusted picture of success in meeting water goals (Fagan et al., 2015). The study found that the national statistics were not fully reflective of what was happening on the ground (nor should they necessarily be). Ugandan national statistics on access to an improved water source showed an increase from 39 per cent in 1990 to 68 per cent in 2010 (JMP, 2012). In 2011, it was estimated that in rural areas 20 per cent of hand pumps had broken down and 17 per cent of improved water sources were not functioning (Ministry of Water and Environment (MWE), 2011; Rural Water Supply Network (RWSN), 2012). The national average in terms of use of unprotected sources for rural communities was reported at 30 per cent (Uganda National Bureau of Statistics (UBOS), 2010, p. 121). The community we considered had experienced water interventions from a number of development agencies to the degree that all the surveyed households were within a 1 km radius of an improved water source. Thus, by definition, they were included in the number of people reported to have access to water and whose water was managed through Integrated Water Resource Management (IWRM) fashioned governance structures. At the time of the survey in 2011, these 'improved' sources comprised of ten boreholes, 24 shallow wells, and one protected spring, each managed by a Water User Committee. And so, WHO and UNICEF reports take this to indicate that this community now has access to clean water – as in it was within a 1 km radius of an 'improved' water source. However, the reality was that the community only had access if the improved water source was functioning and if the householders were (1) in an economic position to afford jerrycans, (2) were able to carry them and (3) had time to queue for two hours a day. At the time of our presence in that community, only one of the ten boreholes was functioning, and of the 24 local shallow wells only seven were functioning (Fagan et al., 2015, p. 4). These figures bring the number of dysfunctional 'improved' water sources well above the 20 per cent reported rural average. Consequently, 40 per cent of those surveyed said they used unprotected sources as their main supply, a figure that correlates to pre-2000 development country access to water in rural communities.

This local level research would indicate that singular water interventions that seek to 'override as opposed to reverse' the realities of poor people's lives (Cornwall, 2008) are unsustainable and ineffective. To quote Metha and Movik (2015), the meta policy 'remains disconnected from the everyday experiences of poor and marginalised women and men' and approaches fall short of addressing emergent challenges of 'liquid dynamics' (p. 31). Even if evaluated within their own logic, evidence of the failure of the MDGs approach after another decade of international development policy on water was overwhelming. As Gourisankar Ghosh put it 'the emphasis in the MDGs on focusing on the indicators rather than the process and direction of development has led to hasty, often top-down approaches that ultimately fail because they do not take people's actual needs into consideration' (2012, p. 17). The approach used to analyse issues such as access to 'improved water resources' was flawed and thus the statistics become meaningless. Those with access to 'improved water sources' were considered to have access whether or not these 'improved water sources' were in fact working. Criticism of the design of the MDGs programme became so pervasive that perhaps what is most memorable about them is Peggy Antrobus's 2009 re-forming of the acronym of MDG as 'Most Distracting Gimmick' (cited in Salleh, 2016, p. 953).

By 2015 it was clear that the MDG framework was too limited to address inequalities, sustainability and human rights and the synergies between water and development and other global concerns. Its particular focus on poverty, understood as meeting basic needs, dominated the process of achieving the MDGs. This narrow conception of development dominated a policy decade, and more radical or global understandings of inequalities, which had some sway internationally before the introduction of the MDGs, received much less attention. The MDG framework did not address the full water and development agenda, nor fully recognise its synergies with other areas and concerns. Emphasis on 'sustainability' was not included and human rights and inequalities were largely ignored. Subsequently, member states agreed that human rights, equality and sustainability should form the core of the future development agenda and be recognised as critical for true development.

Managing water resources, and all aspects of the water cycle, sustainably and equitably, was beginning to be seen more clearly as fundamental to the future of both people and the environment in the new millennium. The interdependence between water and other development foci such as food, land, energy, health, biodiversity and climate change, poorly

articulated in the MDGs, clearly inspired the shift to a post-2015 development agenda of 'securing sustainable water for all'. While it could be
argued that some progress has been made on access through the MDGs
and other measures, there has been little or no progress on water quality.
Eighty per cent of wastewater is discharged into the natural environment
without any form of treatment. Pollution resulting from agricultural and
economic production remains largely unmonitored and water quality
continues to decline. Natural water-related disasters such as floods and
droughts continue to occur, and the frequency and intensity are magnified
by climate change. By the end of the first decade of the millennium the
question of access – always an issue for the poor – had become replaced by
the question of 'access to what' for both the poor and the affluent. Global
environmental and ecological problems were set to inform any future
frameworks for international development policies, and development was
about to go 'more global' (Scholte and Söderbaum, 2017).

THE SUSTAINABLE DEVELOPMENT GOALS – A TRANSFORMATIVE AGENDA?

The UN development targets for 2030, the Sustainable Development
Goals (SDGs) (adopted in September 2015), were formulated in terms of
'ending poverty', 'transforming all lives' and 'protecting the planet'. In
short, they are called sustainable development goals because the intention,
at least at a rhetorical level, is to embrace the principles of the sustainable
development model. This model, at its best, brings together the overall
objective of development policy – which is to meet basic needs of everyone
– with ecological sustainability policies. Transformation of water resourcing underpins the model and is fundamental (as opposed to cross-cutting)
to the achievement of the overall objective of sustainable development.
Goal 6 of the 17 SDGs is to 'ensure availability and sustainable management of water and sanitation for all' (see Table 19.2). Among its targets
are to support the protection of water resources from over-exploitation
and pollution, while meeting water and sanitation needs, and protecting
communities from water-related disasters.

While these targets recognise the fundamental importance of water
management and resourcing, and both its soft and hard infrastructures for
achieving overall sustainable development, it remains at the level of principle, given that the quantitative aspects of the targets are aspirational only.
Unparalleled transformation over a short time frame would be required to
achieve even the first of these targets, given the depth and breadth of the
challenges of water resourcing, water use and water distribution on a globe

*Table 19.2   Goal 6: ensure availability and sustainable management of
water and sanitation for all*

Goals and targets (from the 2030 Agenda)		Indicators	
6.1	By 2030, achieve universal and equitable access to safe and affordable drinking water for all	6.1.1	Proportion of population using safely managed drinking water services
6.2	By 2030, achieve access to adequate and equitable sanitation and hygiene for all and end open defecation, paying special attention to the needs of women and girls and those in vulnerable situations	6.2.1	Proportion of population using safely managed sanitation services, including a hand-washing facility with soap and water
6.3	By 2030, improve water quality by reducing pollution, eliminating dumping and minimizing release of hazardous chemicals and materials, halving the proportion of untreated wastewater and substantially increasing recycling and safe reuse globally	6.3.1	Proportion of wastewater safely treated
		6.3.2	Proportion of bodies of water with good ambient water quality
6.4	By 2030, substantially increase water-use efficiency across all sectors and ensure sustainable withdrawals and supply of freshwater to address water scarcity and substantially reduce the number of people suffering from water scarcity	6.4.1	Change in water-use efficiency over time
		6.4.2	Level of water stress: freshwater withdrawal as a proportion of available freshwater resources
6.5	By 2030, implement integrated water resources management at all levels, including through transboundary cooperation as appropriate	6.5.1	Degree of integrated water resources management implementation (0–100)
		6.5.2	Proportion of transboundary basin area with an operational arrangement for water cooperation
6.6	By 2020, protect and restore water-related ecosystems, including mountains, forests, wetlands, rivers, aquifers and lakes	6.6.1	Change in the extent of water-related ecosystems over time
6.a	By 2030, expand international cooperation and capacity-building support to developing countries in water- and sanitation-related activities and programmes,	6.a.1	Amount of water- and sanitation-related official development assistance that is part of a government-coordinated spending plan

Table 19.2   (continued)

Goals and targets (from the 2030 Agenda)		Indicators	
	including water harvesting, desalination, water efficiency, wastewater treatment, recycling and reuse technologies		
6.b	Support and strengthen the participation of local communities in improving water and sanitation management	6.b.1	Proportion of local administrative units with established and operational policies and procedures for participation of local communities in water and sanitation management

Source: United Nations Water (2016), Report of the Inter-Agency and Expert Group on Sustainable Development Goal Indicators, 9–10 (E/CN.3/2017/2).

facing climate change. Despite political support for universal access, it was still the case in 2014 that less than one-quarter of 94 countries reported reaching universal access targets for sanitation and fewer than one-third of countries had achieved universal access for drinking-water (JMP, 2012). Furthermore, less than one-quarter of countries reported that they had national sanitation plans that are being fully implemented, funded and regularly reviewed. In terms of global governance, the discrepancy between establishing targets and providing adequate funding and monitoring of targets at national level has never loomed so large.

The sustainable development model is not new, and it has failed in the past where the requirements of economic development have repeatedly overridden the social sustainability agenda. Thirty years of development policy have failed in providing universal access to water precisely because of reliance on market-led models of growth, since 'growth neither leads to reduced environmental impacts nor substantially reduces poverty' (Lorek and Spangenberg, 2014, p. 42). Neoliberal approaches, as in structural adjustment policies and economic liberalisation, did not deliver sustainable development; indeed, quite the contrary. In terms of water provision, it took the pressure off governments to provide water to its citizens in any way other than through public-private partnerships. Water infrastructure was not an area that attracted private investment in its infrastructure because of the capital density of investment in it, and the unlikely investment returns from poor people. And so, there was very little investment in sustainable water infrastructure, meaning that these policies only produced further inequalities, as only those with sufficient income were provided with public water. The political pro-poor commitment was simply not there in public water provision to deliver sustainable development.

Does the post-2015 SDG moment present more of the same? Is it a *déjà vu* agenda as Muchhala and Sengupta (2014) ask – a neoliberal privatisation agenda? Is the implementation of the SDGs 'underpinned, in practice, by a new global development paradigm' as Charles Gore (2015) asks? Securing water as part of the common good and to safeguard it against privatisation is not one of the goals, and in no place is there reference to 'free' water or water rights; rather it mentions equitable access to 'affordable' drinking water, thus enshrining the notion of payment for water. The indicator for achieving Goal 6.1 is the proportion of the population using safely managed drinking water services, not equitably distributed or affordable water services. This, in itself, indicates that market mechanisms are taken to be the backbone of sustainable consumption in achieving the water goals. So, citizenship in a water future, even at this level, can be reduced to one in which you only have a right to it if you can pay for it.

The achievement of sustainable development has been severely curtailed by actions and policies that emphasise economic growth over social and environmental goals. Twenty-five years on from the Brundtland Report (Brundtland Commission, 1987) sustainable development is simply not in train. Current trends are actually taking us in the opposite direction. Have the SDGs reconciled these contrary forces, or have they balanced them towards a pro-poor policy as one would hope? Gupta and Vegelin (2016) perform a textual analysis of the SDGs to decipher if there is, what they term, 'an inclusive' development approach favouring the poor's ecological concerns, or whether the text leaves this open to the degree that the ecological and development concerns of the rich can be prioritised. They ask whether economic development is emphasised more than other forms of social and ecological development. In their analysis, they are clear that the SDG document features the marginalised and is pro-poor in its approach, with 11 out of the 17 goals directly relating to improving their welfare. Nonetheless, they conclude that it:

> ... confirms our fear that there is a risk that the SDGs will go the way of the sustainable development discourse and make trade-offs in favour of growth over social and ecological issues. Business-as-usual growth is justified as necessary for reducing social inequalities and for addressing ecological issues instead of making clear commitments to redefine the development process. (Gupta and Vegelin, 2016, p. 440)

The WHO has very recently produced a *UN-Water Global Analysis and Assessment of Sanitation and Drinking-Water (GLAAS)* report on financing progress towards the universal targets of the SDGs (WHO, 2017, p. ix). It notes that 'more than 80 per cent of countries report insufficient financing to meet national water, sanitation and hygiene (WASH) targets, let alone the higher levels of service that are the focus of the SDGs'. It reports financial unsustainability as the estimated capital investment needed to reach the SDGs is three times higher than current investment levels. Aid commitments for water and sanitation have declined since 2012: global aid commitments decreased from US$10.4 billion to US$8.2 billion, and aid commitments to sub-Saharan Africa decreased from US$3.8 billion to US$1.7 billion from 2012 to 2015 (ibid.). Additionally, few countries indicate that they are able to consistently apply financing measures to target resources to poor populations (WHO, 2017, p. x). This would appear to answer the earlier question as to whether the SDG era will introduce transformative change. The *GLAAS* report now, as early as 2017, articulates the SDGs as aspirational only, given what it refers to as 'national realities'.

CONCLUSION

Currently, in 'developing' countries hyper-competition for water resources has been increasing due to the combination of population growth and increased requirements of both agriculture and industry. Water withdrawals are increasing given that they are shared between agricultural (70 per cent), domestic (10 per cent) and industrial (20 per cent) usage, and all three are in a 'developing' phase. Water commodification, and 'water grabbing' has spiralled, as has water pollution. So, while a global crisis has been declared, the international development policies, focusing as they do on poorer countries rather than on the problems of water scarcity in the Western world, see water as a key enabler of social development. Yet, after decades of policy promising the establishment of universal access, 750 million people (one in nine) around the world lack access to safe drinking water, and approximately 2.5 billion (one in three) (JMP, 2017) do not have access to basic or improved sanitation.

What we learn from the exploration of international development policy on water, specifically the policies associated with the two water decades and the current SDGs, is that – while fluid – they do not embrace a transformative agenda. Rather, at a rhetorical level they have been aligned with modernist scientific developmentalism or neoliberalism. While the most recent international water policies are aligned with a sustainable development agenda, they are still enmeshed in the dominant paradigm of global economic development's reliance on private interests. In terms of impact, they have not delivered on universal access, indeed this goal of universal access was withdrawn in the early years of the millennium. Perhaps the SDGs' most important contribution may be that their global aspirational nature, rather than their practical application, opens up a discursive space, marked by the undercurrent of a transformative global futures agenda. However, a new post-development water paradigm better suited to ecological sustainability, resource redistribution and the eradication of poverty has yet to be born. This new paradigm seems to lie in the cross-currents of the human rights, solidarity and social justice movements rather than within the trajectory of international development policy which, given both its past and recent history, is now irretrievably linked to the multiple crises of global capitalism.

REFERENCES

Arrighi, G., B. Silver and B. Brewer (2003), 'Industrial convergence, globalization and the resistance of the North-South divide', *Studies in International Comparative Development*, vol. **38** (1), pp. 3–31.
Bosire, C.K., M. Lannerstad, J. de Leeuw, M.S. Krol, Joseph O. Ogutu, P.A. Ochungo and A.Y. Hoekstra (2017), 'Urban consumption of meat and milk and its green and blue water footprints – Patterns in the 1980s and 2000s for Nairobi, Kenya', *Science of the Total Environment*, vol. **579**, pp. 786–796.
Brundtland Commission (1987), *Report of the World Commission on Environment and Development: Our Common Future*, Oxford: Oxford University Press.
Chambers, R. (2012), *Revolutions in Development Inquiry*, New York and London: Earthscan from Routledge.
Conway, G. and J. Waage (2010), *Science and Innovation for Development*, London: UK CDS.
Cornwall, A. (2008), 'Unpacking participation; models, meanings and practices', *Community Development Journal*, vol. **43**, pp. 269–289.
Daniels, J. (2017), 'Trump executive order seeks to roll back controversial Obama water rules', *CNBC News*, accessed 3 May 2017 at: http://www.cnbc.com/2017/02/28/trump-executive-order-seeks-to-roll-back-controversial-obama-water-rule.html.
Escobar, A. (1995), *Encountering Development: The Making and Unmaking of the Third World*, Princeton, NJ: Princeton University Press.
Fagan, G.H. (1999), 'Cultural politics and (post) development paradigm(s)', in R. Munck and D. O'Hearn (eds), *Critical Development Theory: Contributions to a New Paradigm*, London: Zed Press, pp. 178–196.
Fagan, G.H., S. Linnane, K. Mc Guigan and A. Rugamayo (2015), *Water is Life – Progress to Secure Water Provision in Rural Uganda*, Rugby, UK: Practical Action Publishing.
Ferguson, J. (2006), *Global Shadows, Africa in the Neoliberal World Order*, Durham, NC and London: Duke University Press.
Ghosh, G. (2012), 'Some for all rather than more for some: a myth or a reality?', *IDS Bulletin Special Issue: 'Some for All': Politics and Pathways in Water and Sanitation*, vol. **43** (2), pp. 10–12.
Gore, C. (2015), 'The post-2015 moment – Towards sustainable development goals and a new global development paradigm', *Journal of International Development*, vol. **27**, pp. 717–732.
Gupta, J. and C. Vegelin (2016), 'Sustainable development goals and inclusive development', *International Environmental Agreements*, vol. **16**, pp. 433–448.

Hemson, D. (2015), 'Beyond the MGDS: can the water crisis for the poor finally be resolved?', in R. Munck, N. Asingwire, G.H. Fagan and C. Kabonesa (eds), *Water and Development: Good Governance after Neoliberalism*, London: CROP and Zed Press, pp. 213–246.

Holland, K. (2017), 'Thousands attend anti-water charges protest in Dublin', *Irish Times*, 8 April 2017, accessed 5 May 2017 at: http://www.irishtimes.com/news/politics/thousands-attend-anti-water-charges-protest-in-dublin-1.3042399.

JMP (2000), *Global Water Supply and Sanitation Assessment 2000 report*, Geneva: WHO/UNICEF Joint Monitoring Programme for Water Supply and Sanitation.

JMP (2012), *Progress on Drinking Water and Sanitation – 2012 Update*, Geneva: WHO/UNICEF Joint Monitoring Programme for Water Supply and Sanitation.

JMP (2015), *Progress on Sanitation and Drinking Water – 2015 Update*, Geneva: WHO/UNICEF Joint Monitoring Programme for Water Supply and Sanitation.

JMP (2017) *Progress on Drinking Water, Sanitation and Hygiene – 2017 Update and SDG Baseline*, Geneva: WHO/UNICEF Joint Monitoring Programme for Water Supply and Sanitation.

Jolly, R. (2003), *Evaluating and Monitoring the Access to Water Supply and Sanitation*. Report of the Third World Water Forum, Kyoto: WSSC.

Lorek, S. and J.H. Spangenberg (2014), 'Sustainable consumption within a sustainable economy: beyond green growth and green economies', *Journal of Cleaner Production*, vol. **63**, pp. 33–44.

Metha, L. and S. Movik (2015), 'Liquid dynamics: challenges of sustainability in the water domain', in R. Munck, N. Asingwire, G.H. Fagan and C. Kabonesa, *Water and Development: Good Governance after Neoliberalism*, London: CROP and Zed Press, pp. 30–60.

Ministry of Water and Environment (MWE) (2011), *Water and Environment Sector Performance Report, 2011*, Kampala: Government of Uganda.

Mosbergen, D. (2017) 'Scott Pruitt has sued the Environmental Protection Agency 13 times. Now he wants to lead it', *Huffington Post*, accessed March 2017 at: http://www.huffington post.com/entry/scott-pruitt-environmental-protection-agency_us_5878ad15e4b0b3c7 a7b0c29c.

Muchhala, B. and M. Sengupta (2014), 'A déjà vu agenda or a development agenda?', *Economic and Political Weekly*, vol. **49** (46), pp. 28–30.

Munck, R. (2015), 'Water, development and good governance', in R. Munck, N. Asingwire, G.H. Fagan and C. Kabonesa (eds), *Water and Development: Good Governance after Neoliberalism*, London: CROP and Zed Press, pp. 11–30.

Munck, R. and D. O'Hearn (1999), *Critical Development Theory: Contributions to a New Paradigm*, London: Zed Press.

Obertreis, J., T. Moss, P. Mollinga and C. Bichsel (2016), 'Water, infrastructure and political rule: introduction to the Special Issue', *Water Alternatives*, vol. **9** (2), pp. 168–181.

Pieterse, J.N. (1991), 'Dilemmas of development discourse: the crisis of developmentalism and the comparative method', *Development and Change*, vol. **22** (1), pp. 5–29.

Pogge, T. (2010), *Politics as Usual: What Lies Behind the Pro-Poor Rhetoric*, Cambridge, UK and Malden, MA: Polity Press.

Rural Water Supply Network (RWSN) (2012), *Sustainable Groundwater Development: Use, Protect and Enhance*, St Gallen: Rural Water Supply Network.

Salleh, A. (2016), 'Climate, water, and livelihood skills: a post-development reading of the SDGs', *Globalizations*, vol. **13** (6), pp. 952–959.

Scholte, J. and F. Söderbaum (2017), 'A changing global development agenda?', *Forum for Development Studies*, vol. **44** (1), pp. 1–12.

Strang, V. (2005), 'Common senses: Water, sensory experience and the generation of meaning', *Journal of Material Culture*, vol. **10** (1), pp. 92–120.

Swyngedouw, E. (2015), *Liquid Power: Contested Hydro-Modernities in 20th Century Spain*, Cambridge, MA: The MIT Press.

Transnational Institute (TNI) (2013), *The Global Land Grab – A Primer*, accessed on 3 May 2017 at: www.tni.org.

Uganda National Bureau of Statistics (UBOS) (2010), *Uganda National Household Survey, 2009/2010: Socio-economic Module*, Entebbe: UBOS.

United Nations (2000), UN Millennium Declaration. Resolution adopted by the General Assembly at its fifty-fifth session, A/RES/55/2.

United Nations (2010), The Human Right to Water and Sanitation. Resolution adopted by the General Assembly, United Nations General Assembly Document A/RES/64/292. New York: United Nations.

United States Geological Survey (USGS) (2016), *Earth's Water Distribution*, accessed 2 May 2017 at: https://water.usgs.gov/edu/earthwherewater.html.

WHO (2017), *UN-Water Global Analysis and Assessment of Sanitation and Drinking-Water (GLAAS) Water Financing Universal Water, Sanitation and Hygiene Under the Sustainable Development Goals*.

Wittfogel, K. (1957), *Oriental Despotism: A Comparative Study of Total Power*, New York: Random House.

World Economic Forum (2015), *Global Risks 2015. 10th Edition*, Geneva: World Economic Forum.

World Economic Forum (2016), *Global Risks 2016. 11th Edition*, Geneva: World Economic Forum.

World Water Assessment Programme (WWAP) (2015), *The United Nations World Water Development Report 2015: Water for a Sustainable World*, Paris: United Nations Educational, Scientific and Cultural Organization (UNESCO).

World Water Development Report 4 (2012), *Managing Water Under Uncertainty and Risk*. Paris: UNESCO.

World Water Development Report (2017), *Waste Water – The Untapped Resource*. Paris: UNESCO.

Ziai, A. (2007), *Exploring Post-development: Theory and Practice, Problems and Perspectives*, London and New York: Routledge.

20. Gender equality and the discursive landscape of non-governmental action in development: the inevitable failure of international NGOs to represent the interests of women?

Fenella Porter

INTRODUCTION

The discursive landscape of non-governmental action in development is a landscape of norms and assumptions of knowledge and legitimacy (Ferguson, 1994; Crush, 1995). In the context of non-governmental action to address gender inequality in development, it is the conceptual space in which international NGOs, and other actors, engage with both the system of development governance, and with the lives and interests of the women they claim to represent.[1] In the current context of development, governmental (or disciplining) norms are dominated by: the norms of effectiveness and 'value for money' (further accentuated by commercial funding mechanisms such as 'payment-by-results' (PBR) that are now embedded in many major funding relationships); the need for high-profile expertise (encouraged by the increasing popularisation of development and the competition between NGOs for funding); and the continuing dominance of managerialist technologies in the management of development (building on, and extending, the goal-based measurement regimes of the UN Millennium Development Goals (MDGs)).

The interests of women are represented by being inserted into the development system often via international NGOs operating successfully at the highest levels of policy-making (Elias, 2013). At this level, the discursive landscape of development is as a global project, based on the MDG/SDG (Sustainable Development Goals)[2] agenda. This has had a specific impact on the meaning of gender equality, in which the interests of women are aligned with 'instrumentalised ideas of economic and political participation reduced to buzzwords that garland policy discourses' (Cornwall and Rivas, 2015), rather than with more politicised ideas of empowerment and women's rights. This chapter will build on these ideas, and seek to develop them through an analysis of international development NGOs, not only as complex players representing the interests of women in an externally shaped project, but also as actors in, and shapers of, the discursive landscape of non-governmental action. It will consider what this means for the representation of women's interests in development.

Rather than focusing on development as a project, the chapter identifies how a set of UK-based international development organisations (with all their internal complexities) understand and address gender equality in their *practice*, and the implications this has for the discursive landscape in which they operate.

The chapter combines analysis of the literature on development NGOs and development aid and gender, with empirical illustrations of how policy and practice on gender equality in four large UK-based international development NGOs has been influenced by the discursive landscape in which they operate. Critical examination of the discursive landscape of non-governmental action is particularly relevant at this time, as development policy-making and practice is shifting in response to the increasing influence and power of other (non-governmental) actors such as private foundations, large consultancy companies, businesses and corporate retail organisations, who are having a significant impact on the development landscape (Richey and Ponte, 2014), and particularly on the way in which women's interests and issues are represented (Elias, 2013; Koffman and Gill, 2013; Wallace and Porter, 2013).

The analysis of the role played by international development NGOs in the discursive landscape takes an 'actor oriented approach' as articulated by Norman Long (1990), and developed and applied by scholars such as Brock et al. (2004). By building on the actor-oriented approach, it is possible to gain greater insight into how the structures of power and discipline are negotiated by non-governmental actors. In the context of recent shifts in the landscape larger international NGOs are actively locating themselves alongside other actors, as outlined above, and moving ever closer to the discourse of efficiency, effectiveness and value for money in their own practice. This shift towards market-oriented norms appears to eclipse understandings of women's empowerment and social justice in many contexts and to lay bare the limits of current NGO action on gender equality (Elias, 2013; Cornwall and Rivas, 2015; Kabeer, 2015).

A BRIEF NOTE ON METHODOLOGY

The analysis of the discursive landscape of non-governmental action contained in this chapter is based on both theoretical engagement, and a long-term and embedded study of UK-based international development

NGOs. The research has involved examination and discussion of NGO literature from the 1990s to the present, alongside formal interviews, group discussions, and observations, carried out in four large UK-based international NGOs through a number of research and consultancy projects over a ten-year period. It also draws on a study into the impact of public-private partnerships on NGO programmes addressing women's health carried out in 2013–14.[3]

The research approach is qualitative and uses an ethnographic methodology. This involves participant observation (Bryman, 2008; Mosse, 2011; Eyben and Turquet, 2013), and reflection, reflecting the role of the author as a 'committed participant and critical observer' (Eyben, 2013, p. 80). This embedded approach also serves to reflect feminist ideas of positionality in knowledge, in which the meaning of the data is a reflection of knowledge and understanding gained from recognising the positionality and reflexivity of the researcher (Fonow and Cook, 1991).

The research took place over a ten-year period, 2005–15. It involved over 40 formal (documented) interviews and focus group discussions (FGDs) as well as the development of ideas through seminars and lectures at Birkbeck (University of London) and workshops held through the Development Studies Association Gender, Policy and Practice study group over the five years, 2010–15.[4]

USING GOVERNMENTALITY TO UNDERSTAND THE DISCURSIVE LANDSCAPE

Dominant ideas about the way the world looks, and how it needs to be changed, are assembled within a hierarchical 'development machine'/or industry, which is implicated in networks of power that shape the way that actors work and behave (Ferguson, 1994). It is easy to get an impression of a simple domination of one knowledge over another, but discourse is both 'an instrument and an effect of power; a hindrance, and a point of resistance' (Foucault, cited in Crush, 1995, p. 20). The interactions between different actors and knowledges serve either to reinforce existing relations of power (Mercer, 2002), or to subvert them (Wallace et al., 2006). Development can, perhaps, most usefully be understood as a series of situated knowledges, in which we can 'decipher exactly how deeply development (and the discourses that claim to reject it) are implicated within one another' (Crush, 1995, p. 20).

Both the discourse of development, and the discourse that challenges it, are tied up with each other, and operate together within a system of governmentality (Sending and Neumann, 2006). With an understanding of a system of governmentality in development, it is possible to see how the struggles over meaning and over discourse are all necessary parts of the same whole. This recognises that discourse and discursive power *grow and evolve* with new influences and new narratives (Sending and Neumann, 2006, p. 658; Mosse, 2013). It can be seen that power in development (and therefore whose voice is heard) cannot be understood just as a question of structures, but also as one of how people and organisations react to, support or resist agendas in different ways. International development NGOs play an important part in the overall governmentality of development – not just as co-opted players, but in their own right, having a part to play in the way development is understood and (ultimately) governed, as well as how interests are understood and negotiated within the discursive landscape of non-governmental action.

DISCURSIVE LANDSCAPE OF GENDER AND DEVELOPMENT

The current discursive landscape of gender and development can be seen to have evolved from two competing discourses of the 1990s: human rights and human development (Kabeer, 2015). The discourse of human rights was built up in the international conferences of the 1990s, where feminists played an active part and where debates included issues around the language of gender and rights, particularly on issues of sexual rights. The new development paradigm of human development was also being developed during the 1990s, but without the participation of feminists. The United Nations Millennium Declaration of 2000 sometimes referred to as 'the world's biggest promise', (ibid., p. 383) included commitments to women's empowerment and gender equality, but was 'couched in broad, open-ended and somewhat instrumental terms' (ibid.). The process of translating the Millennium Declaration into the MDGs saw the 'evaporation of the language of rights and its replacement by a narrow interpretation of capabilities' (ibid., p. 384), which were easier to monitor, achieve and measure, and which reflect the 'strong influence of results-based management thinking' (ibid., p. 382).

Despite ongoing critical engagement by feminists with the MDGs (particularly around the annual Commission on the Status of Women (CSW) sessions) there have been continuing 'struggles for interpretive power', particularly over the 'politics of the body' (ibid., p. 386). For example, although many countries have officially 'achieved' the goals of MDG 3A, some are in the bottom decile of the 2012 Gender Gap Index, indicating that targets on girls' education can be achieved without much change in the broader context of women's lives (ibid., p.389). The OECD Development Centre Report (Ferrant et al., 2015) re-states 'Beijing's message that discriminatory social norms restrict women's empowerment throughout their life course'. These have not been addressed, and therefore gender inequality continues to shape the lives of women everywhere. Despite the more open engagement with the process, and the success in ensuring a stand-alone goal for gender equality, the SDGs continue to be based on even more goals and targets. The tension between rights and development continues to be played out in the geopolitics of gender justice, but now with more focus on a market-driven agenda (Kabeer, 2015, pp. 391–2).

Cornwall and Rivas (2015) argue strongly that the way the current discursive landscape of SDGs has embraced the rights agenda has resulted in the terms 'gender equality' and 'women's empowerment' being 'eviscerated of conceptual and political bite [which] compromises their use as the primary frame through which to demand rights and justice' (ibid., p. 396). They see the UN-led agenda of women's empowerment as 'frames that have led feminist activists into a cul-de-sac and away from a broader-based alliance of social change activists' (ibid., p. 397). The individualism that lies at the heart of neoliberal agendas of development means that the collective struggles of women have been marginalised and de-legitimised. By tracing the trajectory of gender equality through the MDGs, Cornwall and Rivas uncover how 'gender equality' has become denuded of its power to transform: 'Cecilia Sardenberg and colleagues were told emphatically "we wanted *gender,* not feminism", the extent of the de-politicisation of "gender" becomes amply evident' (ibid., p. 404). The women's empowerment agenda has similarly seen gender consciousness-raising and feminist activism turned into an agenda of 'smart economics' and women's entrepreneurialism (ibid., p. 406).

Private sector influence can be seen through the 'plethora of corporate actors whose arrival in the development marketplace has had such a significant impact in recent years' (ibid., p. 399). This, in turn, has led to the representation of gender inequality as a problem to be solved by 'investing in women', 'unleashing women's potential' or 'lifting' women from poverty. An example of this was the Women Deliver conference held in Copenhagen in May 2016, where corporate influence came together with high-profile NGOs to promote these ideas. But this representation of gender inequality denies the institutional context of discrimination that surrounds individual women and their lives (ibid., p. 400), and the 'relational dimensions' so crucial to feminist conceptualisations of gender inequality (ibid., p. 406).[5]

If large UK-based international development NGOs locate their organisational discourse within the dominant managerial, neoliberal and market-led discursive landscape, its effect on individual actors can be understood to 'discipline dissent' (Montesinos Coleman and Tucker, 2011), and thereby reinforce the dominant discourse, and close off the space within the organisations for voices promoting women's rights and empowerment.

In the following section, interviews and observations of practices within NGOs show how the dominant discursive norms and practices on gender equality have been incorporated within these organisations. They also show how NGOs power to shape the discursive landscape has moved them further away from the reality of the lives of the women they try to represent, disciplining the political understanding of women's rights and empowerment.

GOVERNMENTALITY IN DEVELOPMENT PRACTICE AND THE SPACE FOR NON-GOVERNMENTAL ACTION

Based on embedded experience, interviews and observations, this section provides a short set of illustrations of how UK-based NGOs have engaged with the current norms of development governmentality set out at the beginning of this chapter: funding-led norms of effectiveness, the need for high-profile narratives of 'expertise', and the continued dominance of managerialist technologies. It specifically looks at these norms in terms of their effect on understandings of gender equality in both the policies and practices of the organisations.

The discursive landscape of non-governmental action is the space in which actors represent their overall 'narrative' of development (Mosse, 2005), and establish relationships of influence and power around agenda-setting norms and interests (Ferguson, 1994; Tvedt, 2002), as well as engage with the communities in which they work (Brock et al., 2004). The extensive literature on NGO partnerships reveals much about power in these relationships, with governments, funders and communities, and how they can understand and represent the interests of people on whose behalf they work. It shows both how NGOs are profoundly affected by these relationships, but also how they themselves are able to affect partnerships (for example Tvedt, 2002; Groves and Hinton, 2004; Van Rooy, 2004; Wallace et al., 2006; Bebbington et al., 2008; Pinkney, 2009; Banks and Hulme, 2012; Wallace and Porter, 2013; Banks et al., 2015). The literature shows that it is through the development of an understanding of NGOs in terms of their discursive landscape, that it is possible to see clearly how different NGOs negotiate this landscape, and how this negotiation affects their representation of women's interests within the development system.

The discursive landscape of non-governmental action is increasingly influenced by market-led assumptions of development, and the partnership space is also occupied by other non-governmental actors, for example private philanthropic foundations and corporate players (such as accountancy or consultancy companies). Many large international NGOs have been disciplined by the strength of these norms and practices, as the current movement towards funding mechanisms such as 'Payment by Results' (PbR) shows.

However, as an understanding of governmentality, and the literature on NGO partnerships over the last 20 years reveals, the dominant ideology has not just been imposed upon them, but has been accepted, and acted upon, by international NGOs. This has served to reshape the discursive landscape, perpetuating and strengthening further market-led norms and practices. This is not to say that there are no dissenting NGO voices, but those that express dissent, and try to represent more complex and challenging interests in development, find that the space in which to do so is increasingly squeezed and difficult to occupy.[6]

FUNDING-LED NORMS OF EFFECTIVENESS (IMPACT)

Many UK-based international NGOs now receive high levels of funding from the UK Department for International Development (DFID) (Wallace and Porter, 2013), often above the cap that previously existed on levels of state funding (NGO B1, NGO C1). It may not ever have been the case that an NGO was truly financially independent of the state, but the important point is that it was part of accepted NGO practice to adhere to the ideal of independence to uphold the principles of 'non-governmental' (Wallace and Porter, 2013). The removal of the funding cap means that the larger international NGOs can bid for contracts which are worth millions of pounds, thus increasing their financial turnover significantly. In an interview with a senior manager of a UK-based international NGO, lifting the cap on greater DFID funding was justified because there is a greater level of 'synergy' between the NGOs' own priorities and those of the DFID (NGO B1). This position was reiterated by senior respondents from two other large international NGOs, where their close relationships with the DFID, as well as with large private philanthropic and corporate organisations, were justified along similar lines (NGO A1, A2, NGO C1).

It seems that synergy and the potential for growth are now seen to be more desirable in NGO relationships than preserving independence.

Funding relationships embed highly disciplined norms of value for money and efficiency, and (increasingly) the need for increased 'scale' in development work. This is shown clearly in PbR funding agreements, but also exists in other high-value funding contracts, with clear consequences for understandings of gender. Interviews conducted with representatives of NGOs working on issues of women's health in development indicated that the norms of 'scale' and 'value for money' were hugely influential and had been fully incorporated into NGO practice and discourse. This has directly shaped their work on women's health and empowerment, and their relationships with partner women's organisations (NGO B4–8, NGO A3–5). Consequently, women's health has increasingly been reduced to issues around reproductive and maternal healthcare, often focusing on large-scale technical responses which can provide ample quantitative evidence of 'value for money' and 'impact at scale'. This has squeezed out many of the more complex women's health issues, such as those affecting adolescent girls not in school, sex workers, older women, and the health and safety of women at work (Gideon and Porter, 2014, 2015). This narrowing of focus has come about even though people interviewed within NGOs recognise that these discourses *do not reflect all we know about women's health* (NGO C1, C2; emphasis added).

In their funding relationships, large UK-based international NGOs are increasingly locating themselves discursively closer to the interests of funding organisations, and the model of development promoted by large funders, including state, foundations and consultancy organisations. This is a considerable move away from the position of relative independence and representation of the interests of communities that many UK-based international development NGOs held previously. The discursive landscape has therefore shifted to value growth, scale and 'synergy' with funders, over independence and a closer understanding of women's lives.

HIGH-PROFILE NARRATIVES OF 'EXPERTISE'

Between international NGOs operating in the UK, there is now also a heightened sense of competition, and, within them, a need to develop delineated areas of organisational expertise. Several UK-based NGOs have developed a focus on gender equality, or women's and girls' rights. Many NGOs claim this 'expertise', and present an overarching vision on gender equality along the same lines as described by Mosse (2005):

... our vision of gender justice for all: of a renewed world in which women and men live alongside one another in mutually empowering relationships; a world in which both women and men are empowered to pursue their human rights and fundamental freedoms; a world in which both women and men are valued as equal and active participants in the social, political and economic wellbeing of their households, communities and societies. (Christian Aid, 2014)

In this case, a world without gender inequality is a powerful and easily understood concept. It is a far neater fit into a system that values clear and positive messaging (Elias, 2013; Koffman and Gill, 2013) than would be a reflection of the complex lived realities that have been expressed over many years by women themselves and their organisations (Wallace and Porter, 2013). This creation of a shared 'narrative' of development has established a new type of dependency between international NGOs, the DFID and other (often private sector) funders, built on not just financial agreements, but also on political and *discursive* agreements.

Respondents interviewed from a number of departments within the NGOs studied (including programme finance, policy and corporate partnerships) argued that this new level of cooperation between their organisations and funders gives them increased power and influence in policy-making arenas, and that this enables them to bring about positive changes (for example, in the negotiations for a gender-specific goal in the SDGs, NGO B2). This is undoubtedly the case, but some of the same respondents also acknowledged that this is not a space in which other actors such as local women's organisations, social movements or trade unions have a voice (NGO A1, A2, NGO B2, B3). The interests of women are therefore often expressed by large UK-based international NGOs, with clear, positive, but simplified, narratives of gender equality.

In locating themselves as 'experts' representing women's interests in the discursive landscape of non-governmental action, UK-based international NGOs are also exerting increasing levels of control over Southern women's organisations and the voices of the women themselves. Some activists working with these organisations see this control as 'taking up the space' in which women's interests can be articulated:

There are major implications for the work that is done with women, and the relationships that are built with partner organisations. Supporting women's organisations in the global South, and facilitating their voices and accessing the voices of women themselves is becoming increasingly rare; narratives of gender are changing away from an analysis of why women are marginalised and often poor to a focus on 'quick wins' for women and girls. The moves are away from targeting the structural causes of their inequality.

'Building democracy doesn't make good photos ... and so doesn't get funded.' (Saranel Benjamin, cited in DSA-GADPP, 2015)

DOMINANCE OF MANAGERIALIST TECHNOLOGIES

Long-term observation of UK-based international NGOs shows that there is an extremely strong donor-led conformity in the landscape of development practice, and we see an increasing dominance of rational management over other ideas of management that emphasise membership and shared interests (Mowles, 2010; Lewis, 2013). The technologies that reflect the ideology of rational management have been embedded via the targets and measurement culture, analysed by Fukuda-Parr et al. (2014) with a reliance on the 'power of numbers', associated with the MDGs. With reference to Human Rights, Engle Merry (2011) analyses how:

> the reliance on simplified numerical representations of complex phenomena began in strategies of national governance and economic analysis and has recently migrated to the regulation of nongovernmental organisations and human rights ... the deployment of statistical measures tends to replace political debate with technical expertise. The growing reliance on indicators provides an example of the dissemination of the corporate form of thinking and governance into broader social spheres. (p. 83)

The need to define and measure development work has led to a focus on 'finding the right indicators' and ensuring results meet the targets that are set (Fukuda-Parr et al., 2014). Buss (2015) shows that the current 'measurement obsession' impacts on how gender equality work is understood and carried out. The analysis by Cornwall and Rivas (2015) shows that the understanding of gender at the international level has been fundamentally affected by the target-based culture of the MDGs, often creating behaviours whereby the measurement of gender equality obfuscates a focus on more fundamental inequalities and discrimination, and the much longer and more complex process of empowerment.

This culture of goals and targets also restricts the way that NGOs can engage with partner organisations in communities, and represent their complex (and sometimes conflicting) interests. Girei's (2015) article draws on research in Uganda, to understand: '. . . how development management orthodoxy narrows the possibility for NGOs to engage in transformative practice and in social change agendas, while it wittingly or unwittingly supports the expansion of the political and cultural hegemony of Western donors' (p. 1).

When considering issues of gender equality in the practice of international development NGOs, many respondents are aware of the difficulty of 'proving' women's empowerment, and making a quantitatively demonstrable link with improved outcomes for women (NGO X1).

For these respondents, the search for the 'perfect indicator' of women's empowerment has silenced their own understanding of the impossibility of 'proving' empowerment, or of establishing any simplistic causal link between women's empowerment and a particular NGO intervention (NGO A2–5). This target-driven way of working is also passed on to partners, often via the disciplining technology of 'capacity building'. This is often designed to enable those partners to absorb and process increasing amounts of funding, rather than to create processes to listen to partner organisations, and work with them to respond to the lived realities of the communities they work with. Thus, the *way* that many international UK-based NGOs engage with partners is reinforcing dominant norms and ideologies via uniform management approaches.[7]

And so it is possible to see the relationship between the disciplining norms that are currently dominant in the development system and the NGO interaction with the discursive landscape of non-governmental action in their work on gender equality. An understanding of governmentality shows that it is not just a question of imposing one set of norms or ideologies on another set within that discursive landscape. Power *circulates* (Foucault, 1980, p. 100), and international development NGOs participate in this system as more complex actors in their own right.

RE-ESTABLISHING A SPACE FOR NON-GOVERNMENTAL ACTION ON GENDER

The 'actor-oriented' approach to development (Long, 1990) built an understanding of development that did not rely on structural models, but rather saw the behaviour of people and their organisations as integral, and central to their relationship with the structures that surround their lives:

> All forms of external intervention necessarily enter the existing life-worlds of the individuals and social groups affected, and in this way are mediated and transformed by these same actors and structures . . . The different patterns of social organization that emerge result from the interactions, negotiations, and social struggles that take place between the several kinds of actor. (pp. 6–7)

Long (1990) saw development intervention as a negotiated terrain. This has been a hugely influential perspective within development, particularly at the level of development practice, illustrated by the participatory approaches developed by Robert Chambers (see Chambers, 2005). However, it was not without its critics, some of whom saw the approach as static, and others who saw the idea of negotiated terrain as being a far more complex arena which needed more careful analysis, both of the actors and of the landscape in which they operate (Mosse and Lewis, 2006, pp. 9–11). It is with this in mind that this chapter extends and develops this approach.

According to Brock et al. (2004), actors interact with knowledge and policy spaces, engaging with power structures and relationships that are visible (where conflicts are clearly identified and debated), hidden (where the construction of the boundaries of the debates and the manoeuvrings take place in 'backroom' spaces) and invisible (associated with limited and limiting self-beliefs that exclude some actors from the policy-making space, particularly those who are constrained by gender, class, caste, etc.). These power relationships also operate discursively through assumptions of knowledge and legitimacy (Gaventa, 2004). The knowledge possessed and perpetuated by actors is similarly complex, with some forms of knowledge privileged and carried across the spaces in which policy is negotiated, often communicated by individual actors, occupying more than one location within the landscape. Other forms might be found at local level, but are excluded from the policy spaces at national or international levels (ibid.). This analysis reflects a dynamism and complexity of power relations (also visible in ethnographic work by scholars such as Mosse, 2005, 2013; Gardner and Lewis, 1996; Crewe and Harrison, 1998; Lewis and Mosse, 2006) and creates a more complex understanding of a discursive landscape, in which the representation of interests can be moulded according to how norms and assumptions of knowledge are used by individual actors.

It is clear that many working within UK-based NGOs value their relationships with communities, and see their role as being a bridge between the knowledge of the lives of poor and marginalised people and the policy spaces of development. This is particularly clearly expressed by people working with overseas programmes and partner organisations.

> 'The programmes need to lead the work on gender, not the other way around.' (NGO A3).
> 'How much is [NGO B] learning from its partners on gender? What is the main driver of this process?' (NGO B FGD5).

These relationships are also drawn upon by people working in other parts of these NGOs, notably advocacy and communications departments, where there were many who expressed their commitment to gender in terms of wanting to reflect the realities of women's lives (NGO A6–8, NGO B9–12). This reflects much of the knowledge about the centrality of partnerships with communities and community organisations which exists within the sector (Groves and Hinton, 2004; Chambers, 2005), and is often reproduced in reports and evaluations (see, for example, Beardon and Otero, 2013). O'Connell (2012, p. iv) has argued in a *Comic Relief* review that work in communities with organisations managed, and led by, women brings significant value by creating an understanding of the complex realities of women's lives, and opening out spaces for women to speak and represent themselves and their own interests.[8]

By moving closer to the donor-led and market-oriented norms of development, underpinned by managerialist technologies, many people working within UK-based international NGOs fear that they are squeezing out the space for this kind of community- and partner-based knowledge and learning.

> [There is an] impact of people coming from outside of the organisation, from the private sector, but also the public sector, and this has introduced the language of corporate policies, performance and targets. All this moves [NGO B] away from the lives of poor people, including the [work on] gender. (NGO B FGD 3)

In the discursive landscape of non-governmental action that currently operates in development, international UK-based NGOs can, and do, privilege knowledge and action that is acceptable and recognisable at the international level. For example, when considering how to represent gender equality in advocacy strategies, there are frequently discussions about whether these should be framed in terms of 'women's rights' (NGO A6–8, NGO B9–12, NGO C2, C3), as there is a fear that this will alienate key allies in the field, particularly potential funders, who see women's rights as too political. Also, in taking up the cause of women's health, international NGOs often frame knowledge and understanding of gender inequality in instrumentalist terms (Gideon and Porter, 2014, 2015). Arguably, this can secure access for UK-based international development NGOs to high-level policy spaces, but in doing so a more challenging discourse of rights and empowerment is avoided. As Kabeer (2015) argues, the process leading up to the MDGs helped to shape gender politics in a way that excluded the gains of women's rights activists, and helped to shape the narrower understanding of gender equality that is dominant in the current landscape.

In moving towards closer engagement with the dominant system of governmentality of development, international NGOs are themselves reinforcing the existing discursive landscape of non-governmental action. This also has the effect of further excluding and de-legitimising narratives from outside the organisation that might express other more challenging, or more complex, ideas, such as those expressed by feminist, anti-capitalist or Trade Union organisations, as well as excluding those more challenging voices from within the NGOs themselves. This inevitably undermines the dynamism that enables different actors to challenge the structures that shape the knowledge and policy spaces.

Kabeer and Sulaiman (2015) analysed how NGOs in Bangladesh have become increasingly homogenised, many turning away from an early commitment to social mobilisation at the community level. These authors show the impact of one NGO using a 'radical capability approach', and argue that this reflects a more challenging relationship with the development mainstream, based on social mobilisation and strengthening collective capacities, and a more effective response to changing the structures of poverty and exclusion. Their article concludes that this approach is under threat from lack of funding:

> The social mobilization model is very much on the wane. Development aid to NGOs has become heavily skewed towards the promotion of financially sustainable service provision and there are no promising alternative sources of finance to keep such an organization alive. (Ibid., p. 64)

As can be seen, the space for resistance – and for working cooperatively with feminist allies and partners within the current discursive landscape of non-governmental action – is heavily constrained by dominant norms and assumptions contained within the system of governmentality in development. These are pressures felt keenly by many people who have informed this research, and their disquiet chimes with others in the NGO sector who work in the area of gender:

> Many people within development NGOs are trying to work together and 'do the right thing', and personal relationships are still hugely important, but it is becoming increasingly difficult as organisations are forced to compete against each other – as well as against corporate actors who are also bidding for development contracts now. (DSA-GADPP, 2015)

The governmental system continues to discipline the space for non-governmental action *through* the development practice of NGOs. The UK-based international NGOs studied here have shaped their representation of the communities that they work with in line with the current discursive landscape of development. They have responded to the disciplinary norms in the current development context by adapting the understanding of gender equality to what fits easily within the landscape, and this has effectively squeezed out the space for challenge and dissent amongst individual actors within (and outside) the organisation, and ultimately led to the failure of these NGOs to accurately represent the interests of women.

The international development NGOs have aligned themselves with the dominant narratives on gender equality, which are reinforced not just internally in their own work but also in their relationships with partner organisations. However, this situation could be reversed. NGOs are far from monolithic, and many people working on gender within international development NGOs can see very clearly how their work is being distorted by the dominant narratives, as outlined above. The NGOs themselves could also challenge the dominant narratives and technologies by recognising these dissenting voices within the discursive landscape of non-governmental action in development, which is a negotiated space in which actors continually interact with policy and knowledge spaces. Organisations which continue to hold narratives of partnership could re-focus on their relationships with the women's organisations they work with and insist on these as the basis for their knowledge and action.[9] It is then possible to see a space for dissent and challenge to the dominant elements of the development system: funding imperatives, the demand for expertise, and managerialist technologies. At this stage, however, this kind of challenge can only be seen as another 'road not taken', as suggested by Kabeer and Sulaiman (2015, p. 64): 'It throws light on the possibilities for social change that may have been forgone in the shift away from a radical engagement with the power structures in favour of market-mediated approaches.'

CONCLUSION

This chapter has shown how the discursive landscape of non-governmental action on gender equality both shapes and is shaped by the organisations which enter into, and influence, it. The analysis has focused on funding-led norms of effectiveness, the need for high-profile narratives of 'expertise', and the continued dominance of managerialist technologies. The research has shown how international NGO actors in development respond to, and negotiate, this space, operating according to current norms and assumptions in the dominant discursive landscape. The discursive landscape governs whose voices are heard, and which interests are represented in development, and how these are 'framed'. Increasingly, organisations representing the interests of women are becoming more distant from the complex realities of poor women's lives, and more contained by a system that insists on knowledge and action that can be represented simplistically and schematically. The result of this is often an instrumentalisation of gender equality which, while it might make space for gender at the international level, in fact results in a much narrower discourse, from which more politicised notions of women's rights and empowerment are excluded.

I argue that a rethinking of this discursive landscape in terms of an actor-oriented approach could create a more complex and dynamic space, with a role for challenging and resistant voices within the discursive landscape of non-governmental action. As we reach a point where the dominant discourse of development seems to be closed to radical ideas of equality and social justice, it is even more urgent to understand the power structures of development in a more nuanced way, and to seize the opportunities these might provide, as well as recognise the constraints they represent. We need to understand how all development actors – individuals working within development NGOs, as well as civil society, social movements, community groups, campaigns, private sector bodies, state, organisations – are engaging with, *and shaping*, the discursive landscape of non-governmental action in development, rather than being seen as merely cogs in the wheel of the development machine, or excluded altogether. International NGOs must also take responsibility for their role in the development system – both discursively and politically. All actors within the landscape of non-governmental action need to examine how they are representing women, and whether their representation of women's interests is challenging the institutional structures that maintain gender inequality, or whether they are in fact reinforcing the embedded inequalities that ultimately constrain women's ability to influence the institutions that govern their lives.

CODING

NGO A1–A8	Interviews carried out between January and July 2012
NGO B1–21	Interviews carried out between August and December 2013
NGO B FGDs x 7	Interviews carried out between October and December 2013
NGO C1–3	Interviews carried out between January and July 2012
NGO D1–2, X1	Interviews carried out between January and July 2012

NOTES

1. In some ways this idea builds on similar theoretical principles used by feminist analysis of global governance, for example Rai and Waylen (2008).
2. The Sustainable Development Goals are the successor to the Millennium Development Goals. They are officially known as *Transforming our World: The 2030 Agenda for Sustainable Development* and consist of 17 'Global Goals'.
3. See Gideon and Porter (2014, 2015). This research took place over a period of 15 months,

with 20 main respondents from seven different UK-based NGOs, as well as global health governance experts and representatives from transnational women's health networks.

4. For reasons of confidentiality none of the international NGOs or participants involved can be identified. As an analysis based on an individual set of engagements with NGOs, this research necessarily reflects the author's individual positionality and therefore cannot be seen to be comprehensive. The intention here is to record these insights, and use theoretical frameworks to open out the ideas for further discussion and reflection, by both practitioners and academics.

5. Further discussions of gender in these discourses have been undertaken by scholars such as Elias (2013), Koffman and Gill (2013) and Switzer (2013).

6. For example, the closure of One World Action in 2011 can be understood to be at least partly related to a lack of financial and discursive support for their more challenging narrative on women's rights.

7. This is extensively documented by contributions to the volume *Aid, NGOs and the Realities of Women's Lives: A Perfect Storm* (Wallace and Porter, 2013).

8. This is also emphasised in Wallace and Porter (2016), as well as in other contributions to the Gender and Development Network *Feminist Development Alternatives* pack.

9. This is the approach taken by some international women's NGOs, such as Womankind Worldwide (www.womankind.org.uk) and the Association for Women's Rights in Development (AWID) (Arutyunova and Clark, 2013).

REFERENCES

Arutyunova, Angelika and Cindy Clark (2013), *Watering the Leaves, Starving the Roots: The Status of Financing for Women's Rights Organising and Gender Equality*, Toronto: AWID.

Banks, N. and D. Hulme (2012), The role of NGOs and civil society in development and poverty reduction. Brooks World Poverty Institute Working Paper 171, University of Manchester.

Banks, N., D. Hulme and M. Edwards (2015), 'NGOs, states and donors revisited: still too close for comfort?', *World Development*, vol. **66**, pp. 707–18.

Beardon, Hannah and Eva Otero (2013), *Women's Right to Be Heard: An Evaluation of Oxfam GB's 'Raising Her Voice' Portfolio*, Seville: Letimotiv Social.

Bebbington, Anthony J., Samuel Hickey and Diana C. Mitlin (2008), *Can NGOs Make a Difference? The Challenge of Development Alternatives*, London: Zed Books.

Brock, K., R. McGee and J. Gaventa (eds) (2004), *Knowledge, Actors and Spaces in Poverty Reduction in Uganda and Nigeria*, Kampala: Fountain Publishers.

Bryman, A. (2008), *Social Research Methods* (3rd edition), Oxford: Oxford University Press.

Buss, Doris (2015), 'Measurement imperatives and gender politics: an introduction', *Social Politics: International Studies in Gender, State & Society*, vol. **22** (3), pp. 381–9. Available at: https://doi.org/10.1093/sp/jxv030.

Chambers, Robert (2005), *Ideas for Development*, London and Washington, DC: Earthscan.

Christian Aid (2014), 'Gender Justice for All: Achieving Just and Equitable Power Relations between Women and Men'. Available at: http://www.christianaid.org.uk/programme-pol icy-practice/sites/default/files/2017-02/Christian-Aid-Gender-Justice-Strategy-Feb2017. pdf.

Cornwall, Andrea and Althea-Maria Rivas (2015), 'From "gender equality" and "women's empowerment" to global justice: reclaiming a transformative agenda for gender and development', *Third World Quarterly*, vol. **36** (2), pp. 396–415.

Crewe, E. and E. Harrison (1998), *Whose Development? An Ethnography of Aid*, London and New York: Zed Books.

Crush, Jonathan (ed.) (1995), *Power of Development*, London and New York: Routledge.

DSA-GADPP (2015), 'Is there still space for gender equality in the current gender narratives of development? How are narratives shifting and can we use these to rethink gender work?'

Available at: http://www.devstud.org.uk/studygroups/gender_policy_and_development-33. html.

Elias, J. (2013), 'Davos woman to the rescue of global capitalism: postfeminist politics and competitiveness promotion at the World Economic Forum', *International Political Sociology*, vol. **7**, pp. 152–69.

Engle Merry, Sally (2011), 'Measuring the world: indicators, human rights, and global governance: with CA comment by John M. Conley', *Current Anthropology*, vol. **52** (S3), Corporate Lives: New Perspectives on the Social Life of the Corporate Form: edited by Damani J. Partridge, Marina Welker and Rebecca Hardin (Supplement to April 2011), pp. S83–S95.

Eyben, R. (2013), 'Struggles in Paris: the DAC and the purposes of development aid', *European Journal of Development Research*, vol. **25**, pp. 78–91.

Eyben, R. and L. Turquet (eds) (2013), *Feminists in Development Organisations: Change from the Margins*, Rugby: Practical Action Publishing.

Ferguson, J. with L. Lohmann (1994), 'The anti-politics machine: "development" and bureaucratic power in Lesotho', *The Ecologist*, vol. **24** (5), pp. 176–81.

Ferrant, Gaëlle, Keiko Nowacka and Annelise Thim (2015), 'Living up to Beijing's vision of gender equality: social norms and transformative change', OECD Development Centre, March.

Fonow, M. M. and J. A. Cook (1991), *Beyond Methodology: Feminist Scholarship as Lived Research*, Bloomington: Indiana University Press.

Foucault, Michel (1980), *Power/Knowledge: Selected Interviews and Other Writings 1972–1977*, edited by Colin Gordon, Hertfordshire: Harvester Press.

Fukuda-Parr, Sakiko, Alicia Ely Yamin and Joshua Greenstein (2014), 'The power of numbers: a critical review of Millennium Development Goal targets for human development and human rights', *Journal of Human Development and Capabilities: A Multi-Disciplinary Journal for People-Centered Development*, vol. **15** (2–3), pp. 105–17.

Gardner, Katy and David Lewis (1996), *Anthropology, Development and the Post-Modern Challenge*, London and Sterling VA: Pluto Press.

Gaventa, J. (2004), 'From policy to power: revisiting actors, knowledge and spaces', in K. Brock et al. (eds) *Knowledge, Actors and Spaces in Poverty Reduction in Uganda and Nigeria*, Kampala: Fountain Publishers, pp. 274–301.

Gideon, J. and F. Porter (2014), Unpacking women's health in public-private partnerships: A return to instrumentalism in development policy and practice? UN-WIDER Working Paper 2014/009, World Institute for Development Economics Research, Helsinki.

Gideon, J. and F. Porter (2015), 'Unpacking "women's health" in the context of PPPs: a return to instrumentalism in development policy and practice?', *Global Social Policy*, vol. **16** (1), pp. 68–85.

Girei, E. (2015), 'NGOs, management and development: harnessing counter-hegemonic possibilities', *Organization Studies*, online, pp. 1–20.

Groves, L. and R. Hinton (eds) (2004), *Inclusive Aid: Changing Power and Relationships in International Development*, London and Sterling, VA: Earthscan.

Kabeer, Naila (2015), Tracking the gender politics of the Millennium Development Goals: struggles for interpretive power in the international development agenda, *Third World Quarterly*, vol. **36** (2), pp. 377–95.

Kabeer, Naila and Munshi Sulaiman (2015), Assessing the impact of social mobilization: Nijera Kori and the construction of collective capabilities in rural Bangladesh, *Journal of Human Development and Capabilities*, vol. **16** (1), pp. 47–68.

Koffman, O. and R. Gill (2013), '"The revolution will be led by a 12-year-old girl": girl power and global biopolitics', *Feminist Review*, **104**, pp. 84–102.

Lewis, David (2013), 'Reconnecting development policy, people and history', in T. Wallace and F. Porter (eds) *Aid, NGOs and the Realities of Women's Lives: A Perfect Storm*, Rugby, Warwickshire: Practical Action Publishing, pp. 115–27.

Lewis, David and David Mosse (2006), *Development Brokers and Translators: The Ethnography of Aid and Agencies*, Bloomfield, CT: Kumarian Press.

Long, Norman (1990), 'From paradigm lost to paradigm regained? The case for an actor-oriented sociology of development', *European Review of Latin American and Caribbean Studies*, vol. **47**, pp. 3–24.

Mercer, Claire (2002), 'The discourse of Maendeleo and the politics of women's participation on Mount Kilimanjaro', *Development and Change*, vol. **33**, pp. 101–27.

Montesinos Coleman, Lara and Karen Tucker (2011), 'Between discipline and dissent: situated resistance and global order', *Globalizations*, vol. **8** (4), pp. 397–410.

Mosse, D. (2005), *Cultivating Development: An Ethnography of Aid Policy and Practice*, London and New York: Pluto Press.

Mosse, D. (ed.) (2011), *Adventures in Aidland*, New York: Berghahn Books.

Mosse, D. (2013), 'The Anthropology of International Development', *Annual Review of Anthropology*, vol. **42**, pp. 227–46.

Mosse, D. and D. Lewis (2006), 'Theoretical approaches to brokerage and translation in development', in D. Lewis and D. Mosse (eds) *Development Brokers and Translators: The Ethnography of Aid and Agencies*, Bloomfield, CT: Kumarian Press, pp. 1–26.

Mowles, C. (2010), 'Post-foundational development management: power, politics and complexity', *Public Administration and Development*, vol. **30** (2), pp. 149–58.

NGO A1–A8, Interviews carried out between January and July 2012.

NGO B1–21, Interviews carried out between August and December 2013.

NGO B FGDs x 7, Interviews carried out between October and December 2013.

NGO C1–3, Interviews carried out between January and July 2012.

NGO D1–2, X1, Interviews carried out between January and July 2012.

O'Connell, H. (2012), 'What added-value do organisations that are led and managed by women and girls bring to work addressing the rights, needs and priorities of women and girls?', London: Comic Relief.

Pinkney, Robert (2009), *NGOs, Africa and the Global Order*, London: Palgrave Macmillan.

Rai, S. and G. Waylen (eds) (2008) *Global Governance: Feminist Perspectives*, Basingstoke: Palgrave Macmillan.

Richey, Lisa Ann and Stefano Ponte (2014), 'New actors and alliances in development', *Third World Quarterly*, vol. **35** (1), pp. 1–21.

Sending, O. J. and I. B. Neumann (2006), 'Governance to governmentality: analysing NGOs, states, and power', *International Studies Quarterly*, vol. **50** (3), pp. 651–72.

Switzer, J. (2013), '(Post)Feminist development fables: *The Girl Effect* and the production of sexual subjects', *Feminist Theory*, vol. **14** (3), pp. 345–60.

Tvedt, T. (2002), 'Development NGOs: actors in a global civil society or in a new international social system', *Voluntas: International Journal of Voluntary and Nonprofit Organizations*, vol. **13** (4), pp. 363–75.

Van Rooy, Alison (2004), *The Global Legitimacy Game*, Palgrave Macmillan: Basingstoke.

Wallace, Tina with Lisa Borstein and Jennifer Chapman (2006), *The Aid Chain: Coercion and Commitment in Development NGOs*, Rugby, Warwickshire: Practical Action Publishing.

Wallace, Tina and Fenella Porter, with Mark Ralph-Bowman (eds) (2013), *Aid, NGOs and the Realities of Women's Lives: A Perfect Storm*, Rugby, Warwickshire: Practical Action Publishing.

Wallace, Tina and Fenella Porter (2016), 'Feminist alternatives to the development paradigm', in *Feminist Development Alternatives Pack*, Gender and Development Network. Available at: http://gadnetwork.org/gadn-news/2016/6/21/feminist-development-alternatives-pack-now-live (accessed 29 June 2016).

21. Development and poverty in the twenty-first century: a challenge for research and social transformation

Alberto D. Cimadamore

INTRODUCTION

The notion of development has been traditionally linked to the historical process of social transformation that encompasses the production, consumption and distribution of public and private resources, goods and services. Economic growth and alleviation of extreme poverty were at the centre of a strategy that aimed to modernize and integrate national economies, according to the patterns set by international regimes and institutions that had emerged in the post-World War II era.

However, in recent decades, the dimension of sustainability has been added due to the fact that negative consequences (e.g. poverty, inequality, global environmental change, etc.) of the current model of development have impacted on the ability of present and future generations to meet their own needs and to fulfil expectations of a good life for all.

The persistence of extreme poverty after decades of high economic growth and the increase in inequality both at domestic and international levels, undermines the legitimacy of governance structures in a way that makes urgent the search for solutions. Consequently, the twenty-first century began with an ambitious plan to eradicate poverty that was expressed in the Millennium Declaration, and operationalized in a more modest way in the Millennium Development Goals (MDGs).

In 2015, the even more ambitious Sustainable Development Goals (SDGs) replaced the MDGs. These were developed within the context of the 2030 Agenda for Sustainable Development, a plan with a transformative potential not seen before in the history of international development. A set of integrated goals, linking eradication of poverty and the promotion of inclusive and sustainable economic growth with full and productive employment and decent work for all, constitutes substantial progress vis-à-vis the past. All of these in the context of the proposed implementation of a model of development marked by sustainable consumption, production and management of natural resources. If we add the fact that the other key elements of the plan contained in the 17 SDGs and 169 targets are seen as

414

an indivisible ensemble, we then can argue that this is a transformational agenda for positive social change.

There are some doubts about the possibility of its realization and its capacity to achieve structural transformation to eradicate poverty. The first one relates to the fact that the MDGs process was not successfully completed even though it was far less ambitious than the SDGs. Another, and perhaps most important, relates to the unprecedented concentration of wealth and power at both national and international levels, which logically and practically plays in favour of the status quo. Agenda 2030 will likely have difficulties in overcoming the vested interests of rich and powerful elites in its efforts to go beyond the modest SDG targets 1.1[1] and 10.1[2] to achieve the indivisible set of goals and targets that constitute the core of the new international development model.

The elites' bias towards the status quo on international development issues and their influence on political outcomes are more perceptible in Northern countries which have been the main beneficiaries of the post-WWII development model. Although the effects of these outcomes are relatively less visible in the international organizations' (IOs') decision-making processes, it could be hypothesized that the most transformative aspects of Agenda 2030 (for instance, the required changes in the pattern of production of consumption to achieve sustainability) will be relatively less supported than those goals and targets dealing with the legitimization of the current development model (for instance, extreme poverty eradication) they contributed to consolidate.

Despite all the criticisms and challenges, the traditional notion of development has endured the twentieth century and was substantially improved in the twenty-first century by the transformational flavour of the 2030 Agenda for Sustainable Development (United Nations, 2015). However, the forces towards the status quo are as powerful as ever, thanks to the unprecedented concentration of wealth (and therefore, political influence). These forces could push the development strategy towards the less transformational SDG goals and targets (that is, target 1.1) as an attempt to provide an analgesic to the suffering poverty creates within the current development model. In this line of thinking, poverty eradication is seen as a desirable objective to address due to the increasing visibility of the suffering and death caused by poverty worldwide. Success in this area would distract attention from other urgent targets of the integrated and indivisible Agenda 2030 (e.g. climate and environmental change, the creation of sustainable patterns of production and consumption, full decent employment for all, and so on).

Both conservative and transformational forces and agents agree in principle on the urgent need to eradicate extreme poverty as soon as possible and to substantially reduce multidimensional poverty. This consensus although relevant, may not apply (at least, not with the same strength) to other goals and targets, particularly those with more potential to deal with the underlying structures that cause poverty. The integral realization of Agenda 2030 has the potential to produce a transformation of the development model, while addressing some of the causes of persistent poverty. However, focusing solely on the alleviation of extreme poverty, without dealing with its systemic causes, might legitimize the new agenda and governance institutions but will most likely fail to create a sustainable future for all.

Science and research need to accommodate to the requirements of this transitional stage towards sustainability in order to produce meaningful contributions to change a status quo which structurally reproduces poverty. Traditional disciplinary knowledge needs to be articulated and channelled through renewed transdisciplinary methodologies that concentrate on problems and solutions, while working beyond traditional disciplinary boundaries. At the same time, this new kind of science needs to deal with normativity in a way traditional science cannot, due to preferences and influences (i.e. Positivism) that are at the core of dominant epistemologies. Sustainability science appears to be particularly suited to produce the type of knowledge required for the kind of social transformation proposed by Agenda 2030. This chapter will now go on to present a proposal to move forward in the construction and implementation of an integrated science framework that could transform poverty and development research to address the development and global challenges of the twenty-first century.

DEVELOPMENT'S RISE, OBITUARY AND REVIVAL

Development has been described as a set of practices necessary for the reproduction of society that requires the general transformation and destruction of the natural environment and of social relations (Rist, 2014). This destructive potential, along with the widespread poverty and inequality that characterize contemporary global society, constitute strong incentives to promote a complete re-evaluation of the notion of development as well as of the theory of international development that guides research and practice. The serious life-threatening consequences of maintaining current patterns of development create the political incentive for such an exercise, as well as for feeding with scientific-based knowledge the process of implementation of Agenda 2030 for sustainable development, which has the declared ambition of transforming our world (United Nations, 2015).

Revisiting development in this way implies, to some extent, questioning the Western imaginary and its core assumption: economic growth and progress (as they have been normally understood by states and international organizations, from the Industrial Revolution to the end of the twentieth century) are processes that not only can, but also should, continue indefinitely. This assumption has been questioned by the empirical evidence showing the negative impact on human life and the environment of the huge transformations caused by the Western pattern of development, with capitalism as the predominant mode of production and consumption.

Nevertheless, it was one of the pillars of the 'Long Peace' that followed the end of WWII and was marked by the absence of major wars between the great powers of the period (Gaddis, 1987). This period could therefore be regarded as the 'age of development'. The idea that poverty and basic human needs could be eliminated by economic growth and social progress was especially attractive in a world that experienced, at the same time, an increase of military capabilities of destruction never before seen in the history of humankind. The liberal view of international relations supported both theoretically and ideologically the premise that socio-economic development and growing global interdependence based on shared interests tend to reduce, or even eliminate, conflict.

The assumption that accelerated economic growth and an equitable distribution of resources would substantially reduce or even eliminate the causes of conflicts both at national and international levels was disputed by mainstream theories of international relations such as Realism and Neo-Realism (that have Hans Morgenthau and Kenneth Waltz as their most visible exponents). The priority given to the autonomy of the political sphere by mainstream Realists led them to concentrate on national interests, balance of power and rationality not contaminated with legal or moral obligations to the weakest member of any system. In fact, the maintenance of order based on different power capabilities is essential for the functioning of a system, particularly one characterized by anarchy (as defined by Neo-Realism) as the international one is today.

Nevertheless, the material and institutional forces operating at a global level reinforced a liberal discourse, aiming to understand and solve the structural international conflict of the post-war period, with a specific idea of development as articulated by the Bretton Woods system.[3] The contradictions between these different views and ideas were not resolved, but evolved to more sophisticated versions that feed the debate on the political economy of international relations.

Some of the arguments have influenced the present as strands of a liberal discourse that was refurbished, based on the same conviction that accelerated economic growth, accompanied by a more equitable distribution of incomes, would substantially reduce structural conflicts (North-South, developed-underdeveloped world, and so on). This view identifies poverty as the main development problem that topped the list of priorities from the Millennium Declaration onwards.

International organizations embraced the fight against poverty as a way of legitimizing the world order by eliminating the most visible feature of underdevelopment, namely extreme poverty. The fact that most abject forms of poverty remain despite critical discourses and palliative measures calls into question the ability of international orders, institutions and governments to deal with a problem that has led to more suffering and deaths than all of the major wars of the past century.

The focus on the reduction of poverty has been a central strand of the international development strategy and action for many decades. It was perhaps best represented by Robert McNamara, then President of the World Bank, who when addressing that institution's Board of Governors in 1979 argued that 'the liberation of the 800 million individuals in the developing world who are trapped in absolute poverty' is an essential and ultimate objective of development (Krasner, 1985, p. 19). This idea was, in different ways, incorporated into the discourse and practice of IOs that were promoting the expansion and globalization of the economies in a way that shaped Southern nations' policies in their journey through post-war history (Sachs, 2010).

The effective development trajectory of Southern countries, the sequence of economic crises that took place after the 1970s, and the visible levels of poverty increased the scepticism about the effectiveness of the hegemonic model of development to deal with the question of global welfare. Post-development thought became more visible and the idea of development was compared to 'a star whose light can still be perceived even though it has been dead for a long-time, and forever' (Rist, 2014, p. 256). Therefore, the last decades of the twentieth century were considered the right time to write its 'obituary' (Sachs, 2010). The question of whether this epoch is coming to an end still remains an active concern for the critical perspective. But perhaps the time to write its obituary will have to be postponed due to the revival of what could be considered a revisited notion of development that started with the Millennium Declaration[4] and then adopted a more comprehensive shape with Agenda 2030. A renewed discourse on a notion of development that prioritizes extreme poverty eradication grew to the extent that two UN Decades on poverty eradication preceded the international commitment on global targets that aimed first to reduce it and later to eradicate it. And four decades after McNamara denounced that millions of human beings were living in a condition 'below any rational definition of human decency' (McNamara, quoted in Krasner, 1985, p. 19), the trap of poverty still holds around 900 million human beings captive (World Bank, 2017, p. xv).

This reality has challenged the idea of development that prevailed and permeated the international post-WWII discourse and has created fertile intellectual geographies for the expansion of critical voices.[5] Post-development exponents argue, for instance, that this current of thought – in its most succinct formulation – 'was meant to convey the sense of an era in which development would no longer be a central organizing principle of social life' (Escobar, 2012, p. xiii). This school of thought was also the object of criticisms that converged on three main points: (1) the focus on discourse put poverty and capitalism as real problems in a subordinated place; (2) it presented an 'essentialized view of development' that missed noticeable variances; (3) it 'romanticized local traditions and movements, overlooking that the local is also embedded in power relations' (ibid., pp. xiii–xiv).

The alleged subordinated place poverty had in post-development thought contrasted with the place it had in the official development discourse. A revival of a discourse on development, centred on poverty, took a particular shape in the 1990s with the first UN Decade for Poverty Eradication initiated in 1997 (United Nations, 1997) and then more clearly in the next decade with the Millennium Declaration and the MDGs.

The notion of development that emerged in the post-WWII period evolved and, despite all criticisms, endured until the present. However, it is a widespread perception that revision and changes need to be made to both the idea and practice of development. Placing in perspective the transformative proposal embodied by Agenda 2030, we can see it as one of a variety of conceivable practical ways of evaluating and addressing the need for social change. An advantage of this specific way is that there is an explicit agenda and plan that operationalized the idea and its role in the international agenda.

In any case, the process that culminated in Agenda 2030 was apparently influenced by a more comprehensive notion of development that spins around poverty and environmental related problems that were identified as the greatest challenges of our time (United Nations, 2015). In other words, the indivisible and integrated set of 17 SDGs and 169 targets constitutes a comprehensive revision of both the idea and practice of development.

POVERTY ERADICATION AND DEVELOPMENT: DISCOURSES AND PRACTICES

A growing consensus on the need to eradicate extreme poverty as the first objective of development efforts at a global scale was consolidated by the end of the twentieth century. The United Nations General Assembly showed the existing international consensus when it decided in 1997 that:

> the objective of the first United Nations Decade for the Eradication of Poverty is to achieve the goal of eradicating absolute poverty and reducing overall poverty substantially in the world, through decisive national actions and international cooperation in implementing fully and effectively all agreements, commitments and recommendations of major United Nations conferences and summits organized since 1990 as they relate to poverty eradication. (United Nations General Assembly, 1997)

Three years later, the Millennium Declaration builds on the previous declaration stating in its Article 11 that the international community:

> will spare no effort to free our fellow men, women and children from the abject and dehumanizing conditions of extreme poverty, to which more than a billion of them are currently subjected. We are committed to making the right to development a reality for everyone and to freeing the entire human race from want. (United Nations General Assembly, 2000, Millennium Declaration, Article 11)

This document also set the basis for the creation of an environment – at the national and global levels alike – 'conducive to development and to the elimination of poverty' (United Nations General Assembly, 2000).

The discourse adopted a more precise shape when the MDGs emerged with a set of specific targets that represented an international commitment made by the international community. The MDGs clearly expressed that the eradication of extreme poverty and hunger was set at the top of a list of eight goals and priorities. The MDG targets were more precise and showed the limits of these commitments, expressing clearly that extreme poverty eradication would not be achieved before 2015. Instead, the very modest objectives to halve, between 1990 and 2015, the proportion of people whose income is less than US$1.25 a day (target 1.A) and the proportion of people who suffer from hunger (target 1.C) became the core of a strategy that set measurable targets whose progress could be tracked. It also placed the aim for poverty reduction and eradication within the context of the achievement of full and productive employment and decent work for all, including women and young people (target 1.B). This proved even more difficult to achieve in reality. However, the goals, taken together, expressed an evolution of the discourse into an incipient and modest strategy to eradicate poverty, within a context marked by diffuse responsibilities and loose accountability.[6]

Criticism of the MDGs came not only from academia (Cimadamore et al., 2016b) but also from within the UN system when a High-Level Panel evaluated that the MDGs 'fell short by not integrating the economic, social, and environmental aspects of sustainable development as envisaged in the Millennium Declaration, and by not addressing the need to promote sustainable patterns of consumption and production' (United Nations, 2013b, p. 1).

Nevertheless, there was a triumphalism in the MDGs' official discourse which heralded that the MDG target had been met, and that 700 million fewer people lived in conditions of extreme poverty in 2010 than in 1990 (United Nations, 2013a, p. 6). At the same time and in the same document, it was signalled that 1.2 billion people still lived in extreme poverty, indicating how far short the process had fallen of the aspirations made explicit in previous UN Declarations. The discourse that expressed that '(t)he Millennium Development Goals (MDGs) have been the most successful global anti-poverty push in history' was a far more attractive message for the establishment and mainstream media than the number of extreme poor reported in the same document (Ban Ki-moon, Secretary-General, United Nations, Foreword to *The Millennium Development Goals Report, 2013*, United Nations, 2013a, p. 3).

Twelve years after the Millennium Declaration and the launch of the MDGs, a new impetus to the global development framework was received with the announcement made by the UN Secretary-General of the creation of a High-Level Panel (HLP). The Panel was co-chaired by President Susilo Bambang Yudhoyono of Indonesia, President Ellen Johnson Sirleaf of Liberia and Prime Minister David Cameron of the United Kingdom to advise on the new development framework beyond 2015; that is, after the expiration of the MDGs. The Panel also included representatives from civil society, the private sector and governments. This was under a mandate that emerged from the 2010 MDG Summit, where UN Member States called for open, inclusive consultations to advance the development framework beyond 2015.

The work of the Panel drew on the established discourse on development and the experience of previous years in the implementation of the MDGs. The fact that it operated in coordination with the working group that had to design the SDGs made its results quite influential in terms of shaping the strategy that emerged in 2015. The creation of a new global partnership to eradicate poverty and transform economies through sustainable development was a central aspiration of the HLP, which considered it to be its 'responsibility' as representative of the international community 'to end extreme poverty in all its forms in the context of sustainable development and to have in place the building blocks of sustained prosperity for all' (United Nations, 2013b, p. 6).

The SDGs were born out of this process with an even more ambitious set of goals and targets than their predecessor, the MDGs. The goal of eradicating extreme poverty was expressed plainly in the text of target 1.1, marking a difference with MDG target 1.A which aimed to halve the proportion of people with incomes less than $1.25 a day (now $1.90). By contrast, SDG 1 includes in its target the reduction of multidimensional poverty according to the many national definitions. This redefined target takes on board criticisms about the minimal and insufficient approach on basic needs condensed in arbitrary numbers like US$1/US$1.25/US$1.90 and opens the way for meaningful debate between scientists and decision-makers on defining, measuring and monitoring global poverty.

The 2030 Agenda for Sustainable Development contains a plan of action which recognizes that eradicating poverty in all its forms and dimensions 'is the greatest global challenge and an indispensable requirement for sustainable development' (United Nations, 2015, Preamble). The 17 SDGs and 169 targets set the level of ambition of a universal, integrated and indivisible agenda that includes highly relevant issues that affect all forms of life on the planet. Most relevant for the theme of this chapter is the fact that poverty eradication (in all its forms and dimensions) is confirmed at the top of an indivisible agenda that demands from politics and science new approaches to deal with the level of complexity it entails.

One of the solutions that Agenda 2030 appears to offer to the intractable poverty that was not dealt with by previous initiatives is the implementation of 'nationally appropriate social protection systems and measures for all, including floors' to achieve by 2030 a substantial coverage of the poor and the vulnerable (target 1.3).

SOCIAL PROTECTION AND FLOORS: ANALGESIC FOR DEVELOPMENT'S STRUCTURAL PROBLEMS

Social protection has been defined as a 'set of public and private policies and programmes aimed at preventing, reducing and eliminating economic and social vulnerabilities to poverty and deprivation' (UNICEF Evaluation Office, 2015, p. 6). This idea of protection included in the new development agenda aims to ameliorate the suffering of the poorest and most vulnerable members of our societies by means of social transfers, for example, cash or in-kind transfers; programmes to ensure economic and social access to services (health, education, etc.); social support and care services; and legislation and policies to ensure equity and non-discrimination.

In the recent past, scientific and professional large-scale evaluations provided a set of broad conclusions about cash transfer-based social protection programming that seem to signal a viable road towards the eradication, or at least the alleviation, of extreme poverty under certain favourable conditions. It is quite clear that these transfers allow for the meeting of immediate needs but, further to that, they also provide modest investment in long-term solutions to poverty and to improve household welfare in a modest but concrete way. For instance, evaluations conducted by UNICEF show that when children are swiftly removed from the labour market, strong positive effects have been registered in the area of improved dietary diversity, nutrition, education (enrolment rates, attendance, learning and performance both in primary and secondary levels), health (access to healthcare and vaccinations, declining adolescent pregnancy rates), capital and labour investment in the core economic activity of the household (in agriculture among the Africa-centred evaluations), diversification of production, and increase of consumption and savings and debt reduction (UNICEF Evaluation Office, 2015).

These findings have contributed, during the past decades, to the emergence of a consensus, strongly supported by international organizations that place social protection as a development priority. According to leading institutions in this field:

> well-designed and implemented social protection systems can powerfully shape countries, enhance human capital and productivity, eradicate poverty, reduce inequalities and contribute to building social peace. They are an essential part of National Development Strategies to achieve inclusive growth and sustainable development with equitable social outcomes. (ILO-WBG, 2016, p. 1)

This assessment refers to universal social protection, understood as an integrated set of policies designed to ensure income security and support to all people across the life cycle – paying particular attention to the poor and the vulnerable. For both the International Labour Organization (ILO) and the World Bank (WB) this kind of support involves adequate levels of cash transfers for all who need it; benefits/support for people of working age in cases of maternity, disability, work injury and unemployment; and pensions for all older persons. This protection can be provided through social insurance, tax-funded social benefits, social assistance services, public works programmes and other schemes guaranteeing basic income security. Such 'well-designed and implemented social protection systems can be the foundation for sustained social and economic development' (ibid., p. 1).

Current WB President Jim Yong Kim summarized the role leading institutions attribute to social protection within the new development agenda as well as the challenge ahead (World Bank, 2016):

> Social protection is a means to reduce poverty, achieve greater gender equity, reduce economic inequalities, and to promote good jobs. While many developing countries are already achieving universal schemes designed to ensure

that nobody is left behind, only one in five poor people in the lowest-income countries is covered by any form of social protection today. It is profoundly significant that we have come together collectively to help countries close these coverage gaps.[7]

Universal or semi-universal social protection programmes exist in around 30 countries and over 100 others are scaling up social protection to reach population groups targeted by Agenda 2030. This push towards the universality of protection has been formally endorsed by the African Union, ASEAN, the European Commission, the G20, the OECD and the United Nations (ILO-WBG, 2016, p. 2). Consequently, the international organizations' shared objective is to increase the number of countries that can provide universal social protection and their mission is to support countries to design and implement universal and sustainable social protection systems (ibid., p. 3). This push towards the universalization of social protection as an effective way to reach SDG1 and alleviate the situation of vulnerable segments of society is also well aligned with the WB's twin goals of ending extreme poverty and boosting shared prosperity in the world by 2030. It is also at the core of the ILO's mandate to promote Social Protection Floors (Recommendation No. 202, adopted in 2012 by 185 states), understood as nationally-defined sets of basic social security guarantees which secure protection aimed at preventing or alleviating poverty, vulnerability and social exclusion (International Labour Organization, 2012).

The attractiveness of the analgesic effect is also based on its financial feasibility. The ILO estimates that a complete social protection floor package for all vulnerable groups, from children and mothers to older persons, would cost between 1 and 5 per cent of GDP in many middle-income economies. SDG 1.3 calls for nationally appropriate social protection systems and measures for all by 2030. This is something that could be achieved in those countries where the poor are now most concentrated: the middle-income countries (MICs). Today, two-thirds of the poor are living in MICs, while a decade ago most poor people lived in low-income countries (LICs) (Braathen et al., 2016, p. 2).

The world is still a long way from providing the basic protection that social security could offer to the most vulnerable and poorest segments of our society. It is estimated that currently only 27 per cent of the world population has access to comprehensive social security systems, which means that the rest of the population is either partially covered or not covered at all (International Labour Organization, 2014, p. xxi).

Social protection is increasingly recognized[8] as a critical strategy for poverty reduction and inclusive growth alongside other interventions which have proved effective. Cash transfer programmes (conditional or not) have shown a broad range of social and positive impacts in different social contexts, including enhancing the economic and productive capacity of poor families as well as that of the communities and economies in which they live. (Universal Social Protection Brief, 2016, pp. 1–2)

Latin America is a region which has pioneered the utilization of conditional cash transfer (CCT) programmes as a tool. They became the flagship intervention that reached 21 countries and provided benefits to more than 130 million people (around 21 per cent of the regional population), at a cost of only 0.39 per cent of the regional GDP. Both economic growth and social interventions help explain a slight decrease in income inequality, the first ever recorded since data has been available. However, despite these improvements, structural poverty and income inequality continue to be determining features of Latin American society. Studies carried out during the present decade estimate that the poverty headcount index in selected Latin American countries would be 13 per cent higher, on average, had CCTs not been implemented. In many instances, 'CCTs have become the backbone of social assistance, replacing previous ineffective transfers and working in synergy with complementary programmes focusing on key areas of human capital development such as child nutrition and early childhood development'[9] (Stampini and Tornarolli, 2012, pp. 2–3).

Social protection has proved to be effective as an analgesic. It helps to momentarily deal with the pain; but if the causes of the pain are not addressed, it will recur, in the absence of an appropriate treatment. The concentration on social protection alone carries the risk of relying on the analgesic effect rather than dealing with the structural causes of poverty and inequality. Such concentration needs to be avoided if the transformational advantages of Agenda 2030 are to be realized.

IOs have been central actors in the maintenance of the post-WWII economic and social order that produced, and reproduced, poverty in a time when there are enough resources to eradicate its most extreme forms. Global poverty is a highly complex phenomenon caused by factors at different levels of analysis, from local to national, and from regional to international and global. A report published in 2015 on existing consensus in academic research shows that although all of those interviewed for the report were aware of this complexity, they generally find convincing causal explanations principally (but not exclusively) at international level. Due to the greater focus of the interview on the global economic order, responses tended to address that level more than others, displaying the highest degree of consensus about the causes of global poverty and its current persistence in the international institutional economic order, especially as it has been advanced by the International Monetary

Fund (IMF), the WB and the World Trade Organization (WTO). The overwhelming majority of interviewees remarked on the negative impacts of the global order, which keeps in place arrangements that have been advantageous to developed countries but are detrimental to developing countries where poverty is widespread[10] (Cimadamore and Lange, 2015, p. 7).

While the international discourse signals the commitment of IOs to the achievement of the SDGs and its targets, there are inertial forces operating at different levels of analysis, particularly at the international and national (state) levels where the preference for the status quo could prevent the achievement of the most transformational aspect of Agenda 2030, while still favouring the achievement of SDG1. Without those structural transformations, the preference for economic growth will not be enough to achieve even the most modest SDGs and targets. There is evidence that the growth we have experienced so far produces and reproduces poverty. It was also observed that economic expansion promoted by international organizations 'benefits the poor less under structural adjustment' while more critical views insist that the IMF's new Poverty Reduction Strategy (PRS) is acting as a barrier to policies benefiting the world's poorest people (Easterly, 2003, p. 362). The negative effect on the development of agencies that are charged with promoting it through poverty reduction measures is evident, even from internal reviews. After five years of the implementation of the PRS Initiative by the WB and the IMF,[11] a review carried out by the World Bank Operations Evaluation Department (2004) found that:

- There was no mechanism or guidance to adapt the Initiative's processes and requirements to different country conditions;
- Countries focused more on completing documents, which give them access to resources, than on improving domestic processes that eventually would lead to poverty reduction;
- There were no intermediate indicators for what the principles were expected to achieve, which made it difficult to assess progress;
- The PRS process underscored the need for more analytical work about how development policies and programs could best lead to poverty reduction;
- Most PRSPs had not considered the full range of policy actions required for growth and poverty reduction. They focused largely on public expenditure – not paying enough attention to infrastructure, rural development, and other areas with poverty reduction potential. Analysis needed to address the sources of growth, the quality of strategies in other social sectors, and the integration of macro frameworks with structural and social reforms. (World Bank Operations Evaluation Department, 2004, pp. viii and ix)

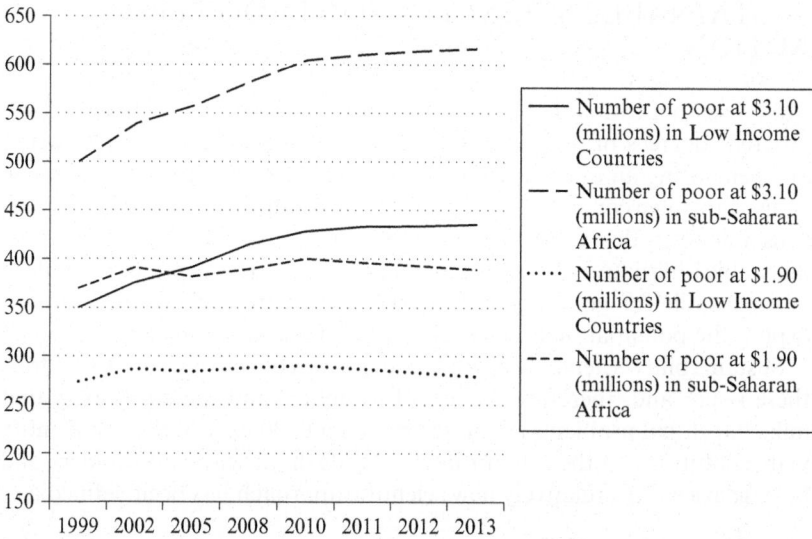

Note: Low-income economies are defined as those with a GNI per capita, calculated using the World Bank Atlas method, of $1,025 or less in 2015. https://datahelpdesk.worldbank.org/knowledgebase/articles/906519-world-bank-country-and-lending-groups.

Source: World Bank, Poverty and Equity Database updated on 18 October 2016. http://databank.worldbank.org/data/reports.aspx?source=poverty-and-equity-database#.

Figure 21.1   Number of poor in low-income and sub-Saharan countries, 1999–2013

Discourses have a clearer meaning when evaluated against the data observed. The results of economic and development policies carried out during the most intense international campaign to eradicate poverty can be seen in Figure 21.1, which shows how the number of poor people evolved according to most recent statistics produced by the WB.

Absolute numbers matter more in times when the objective is zeroing poverty or leaving 'no one behind'. They show that many are going to be left behind if there are no substantial changes in the way poverty has been addressed so far.

SUSTAINABLE SCIENCE: KNOWLEDGE FOR ACTION

Most research available on poverty and sustainable development shows different degrees of difficulty in addressing complexity in the real world and generating an operational nexus between science and policy that can be used to solve concrete social problems. Description frequently replaces causal analysis that could facilitate political and social action by proposing viable alternatives to solve concrete problems. Descriptions are indeed indispensable for good science; but when they are just that they do not exploit the potential that science has as an instrument for social change.

Sustainability science is being created as a collective effort to address these issues and, therefore, be a tool to understand the complexity that links the global problems addressed by Agenda 2030, as well as to identify viable solutions to them in an interactive fashion with stakeholders and beneficiaries. This relatively new scientific approach has been defined as:

> an emerging field of research dealing with the interactions between natural and social systems, and with how those interactions affect the challenge of sustainability: meeting the needs of present and future generations while substantially reducing poverty and conserving the planet's life support systems. (Kates, 2011)

Sustainability science does not fit easily with established criteria of the quality of science due to its constituent features: normativity, inclusion of non-scientists, sense of urgency, and cooperation of natural and social scientists (Ziegler and Ott, 2011). Normal scientists do not feel comfortable with at least its first three features. However, it is clear at this point of the history of science that normativity is present in the notions, concepts, theories and ideologies that social scientists deal with on a daily basis. Dealing with poverty and development means accepting concepts that have been normatively defined and interpreted in many different ways. When we include non-scientists and stakeholders in defining social problems, the question of normativity becomes unavoidable and needs to be dealt with using existing methodological resources such as those provided by transdisciplinary research.

Grounded on needs, practices and urgencies, sustainability science has been growing explosively since the late 1980s. It operates largely as a collaborative network, a giant cluster of co-authorship of more than 2,000 located in different regions of the world with a considerable range of contributing disciplines: social sciences (34 per cent of the total output in terms of number of publications); biology (23 per cent); and chemical, mechanical and civil engineering (22 per cent). The mapping of the field established the case for the existence of a unified scientific practice of sustainability science and bodes well for its future success at facing some of humanity's greatest scientific and societal challenges (Bettencourt and Jasleen, 2011, p. 11).

Sustainability science is best suited as an approach to move beyond traditional descriptions of poverty by dealing with causes and solutions (Kates and Dasgupta, 2007). This is why research on poverty and development is so appropriate in the context of Agenda 2030. These are challenges of a magnitude rivalled only by those of climate and environmental change and peace and security (ibid.). All of them interact in different ways in different parts of the world and are included in Agenda 2030.

The search for a useful nexus between science and research has been a long-standing issue in science organizations (like UNESCO, ICSU, ISSC) for quite a while. Transdisciplinary research (TDR) provided instruments to build a bridge. Sustainability science can be considered a specific case of TDR (Cimadamore et al., 2016a). Key figures in the field proposed the use of it as a tool to understand the reasons for sub-Saharan poverty, with a view to finding solutions. For them, understanding African exceptional features and contributing to poverty reduction in a geography where poverty is actually increasing in absolute numbers, is one of the grand challenges of sustainability science (Kates and Dasgupta, 2007, p. 16747).

Similar challenges are facing us all over the world. We need to be properly equipped to deal with them, both scientifically and practically.

FINAL REMARKS

Social protection seems to be the most viable strategy for relevant international actors to use to achieve, at least partially, SDG1 target 1.1 to eradicate extreme poverty for all people everywhere, by 2030. While its achievement would be laudable, particularly considering the poor track record of the international community to date, it is actually a moral and political imperative as contemporary societies have more than enough economic resources to have achieved that modest target many years ago.

However, monitoring and independent evaluation of progress towards the achievement of the SDGs needs to pay special attention to the integrity and indivisibility of the entire development agenda, of which target 1.1 is but one component. Irrespective of the importance of that one component, the overall integral perspective must be maintained in order to preserve the transformative potential of the development agenda to create a more just and sustainable world. Formidable political obstacles will have to be overcome. The unprecedented concentration of wealth and power acts in favour of the status quo and against transformational efforts to address the structural causes of poverty and unsustainability that may impact on the vested interests of the rich and powerful.

The achievement of the SDGs would see the post-war development model changed radically in a way that would be conducive to creating sustainable societies around the globe that leave no one behind. To achieve this, it is necessary to learn from recent history (the MDGs) and from the conclusions of critical studies which argue that 'without understanding, and addressing, the systems and paradigms that produce and perpetuate both poverty and unsustainability, even the best-intentioned Sustainable Development Goals are likely to have only superficial effects, and there is the risk that they might achieve nothing more than replicating the shortcomings associated with the Millennium Development Goals' (Cimadamore et al., 2016b, p. 17).

NOTES

1. By 2030, eradicate extreme poverty for all people everywhere, currently measured as people living on less than US$1.25 a day (later increased to US$1.90).
2. By 2030, progressively achieve and sustain income growth of the bottom 40 per cent of the population at a rate higher than the national average.
3. The World Bank (WB) and the International Monetary Fund (IMF) were set up in Bretton Woods (New Hampshire, USA) in 1944, with the purpose of contributing to the rebuilding of the post-war economic system. Plans for the creation of an international trade organization were also tabled but were not enacted until the World Trade Organization (WTO) was set in motion on 1 January 1995. The WTO replaced the General Agreement on Tariffs and Trade (GATT) that had commenced in 1948, some years after the other two institutions.
4. United Nations Millennium Declaration. Resolution adopted by the General Assembly on 8 September 2000, A/55/L.2.
5. The concept of 'development' has been the subject of these and other criticisms and controversies during the past 50 years and needs – at least – to be taken into consideration when evaluating the new agenda (Boserup, 1970; Furtado, 1990; Rahnema, 1997; Sounders, 2002; Escobar, 2012; Cimadamore et al., 2016a).
6. For a critical approach to the MDGs see Cimadamore et al. (2016b).
7. World Bank press release 21 September 2016: 'World Bank, ILO announce new push for universal social protection'. Available at: http://www.worldbank.org/en/news/press-release/2016/09/21/world-bank-ilo-announce-new-push-for-universal-social-protection (accessed 2 February 2017).
8. Rigorous impact evaluations of cash transfer programmes in seven countries in sub-Saharan Africa were developed under the Transfer Project/From Protection to Production (PtoP) initiative, led by the Food and Agriculture Organization of the United Nations (FAO) and the United Nations Children's Fund (UNICEF), in partnership with national governments and research organizations (Universal Social Protection Brief, 2016, p. 1).
9. This study is based on data from 43 household surveys from 13 countries over the period 2000–11.
10. Several respondents pointed out that the features of this global order are not solely responsible for poverty and it is more a question of the relative effects of international versus domestic factors, which cannot be assessed abstractly but only concretely in particular

cases. Nonetheless, there was an agreement that the 'global order generally puts limits on possibilities in developing countries, which can be quite severe' (Stampini and Tornarolli, 2012, p. 7) (http://academicsstand.org/activities/institutional-reform/gpcr01/).

11. 'Poverty Reduction Strategies (PRS) are central to IMF-supported economic and financial programs in low-income countries. PRS documents assess poverty challenges, describe how macroeconomic, structural, and social policies and programs can promote growth and reduce poverty, and outline external financing needs and the associated sources of financing. They are prepared by governments in low-income countries generally through a participatory process involving domestic stakeholders and external development partners' (IMF factsheet 'Poverty Reduction Strategy in IMF-supported Programs' (September 2016). Available at: https://www.imf.org/en/About/Factsheets/Sheets/2016/08/01/16/32/Poverty-Reduction-Strategy-in-IMF-supported-Programs (accessed 3 February 2017)).

REFERENCES

Bettencourt, L.M. and Jasleen, K. (2011), 'The Structure and Evolution of Sustainability Science', SFI Working Paper 2011-02-004, New Mexico: Santa Fe Institute.

Boserup, E. (1970), *Women's Role in Economic Development*, New York: St Martin's Press.

Braathen, E., J. May and G. Wright (2016), 'Introduction: poverty and politics in middle income countries', in *Poverty and Inequality in Middle Income Countries: Policy Achievements, Political Obstacles*, London: Zed Books.

Cimadamore, A. and L. Lange (2015), *The Global Poverty Consensus Report*. Available at: http://academicsstand.org/activities/institutional-reform/gpcr01/ ASAP & CROP (accessed 26 January 2017).

Cimadamore, A., G.T. Lie, F.G. Ottemöller and M.B. Mittelmark (2016a), 'Development and sustainability science: transdisciplinary knowledge for positive social change', in A. Cimadamore, M. Mittelmark, G.T. Lie and F.G. Ottemöller (eds), *Development and Sustainability: The Challenge of Social Change*, London: Zed Books.

Cimadamore, A., G. Koehler and T. Pogge (2016b), 'Poverty and the Millennium Development Goals: a critical look forward', in A. Cimadamore, G. Koehler and T. Pogge (eds), *Poverty and the Millennium Development Goals: A Critical Look Forward*, London: Zed Books.

Easterly, W. (2003), 'IMF and World Bank Structural Adjustment Programs and poverty', in Michael P. Dooley and Jeffrey A. Frankel (eds), *Managing Currency Crises in Emerging Markets*, Chicago, IL: University of Chicago Press.

Escobar, A. (2012), *Encountering Development: The Making and Unmaking of the Third World*, Princeton, NJ: Princeton University Press.

Furtado, C. (1990) *Economic Development of Latin America: Historical Background and Contemporary Problems*, Cambridge: Cambridge University Press.

Gaddis, John Lewis (1987), *The Long Peace: Inquiries into the History of the Cold War*, New York: Oxford University Press.

ILO-WBG (2016), *A Shared Mission for Universal Social Protection: Concept Note*. Available at: http://socialprotection-humanrights.org/ilo-and-world-bank-call-for-universal-social-protection/ (accessed 31 October 2016).

International Labour Organization (2012), *Social Protection Floors Recommendation No. 202 Concerning National Floors of Social Protection*. Presented at 101st ILC session, Geneva, 14 June.

International Labour Organization (2014), *World Social Protection Report 2014/15: Building Economic Recovery, Inclusive Development and Social Justice*, International Labour Office. Geneva: ILO.

Kates, R. (2011), 'What kind of a science is sustainability science?', *Proceedings of the National Academy of Sciences*, vol. **108** (49), p. 19449. Available at: http://sustainability.pnas.org/page/about (accessed 24 January 2017).

Kates, R. and P. Dasgupta (2007), 'African poverty: a grand challenge for sustainability science', *Proceedings of the National Academy of Sciences*, vol. **104** (43), pp. 16747–16750. Available at: http://www.pnas.org/content/104/43/16747.full (accessed 24 January 2017).

Krasner, S. (1985), *Structural Conflict: The Third World Against Global Liberalism*, Berkeley, CA: University of California Press.

Rahnema, M. (1997), 'Introduction' to *The Post-Development Reader*, London: Zed Books.

Rist, G. (2014), *The History of Development: From Western Origins to Global Faith*, London: Zed Books.

Sachs, W. (2010), 'Introduction', in W. Sachs (ed.), *The Development Dictionary: A Guide to Knowledge as Power*, London: Zed Books.

Sounders, K. (2002), 'Towards a deconstructive post-development criticism', in K. Sounders (ed.), *Feminist Post-Development Thought: Rethinking Modernity, Post-Colonialism and Representation*, London: Zed Books.

Stampini, M. and L. Tornarolli (2012), *The Growth of Conditional Cash Transfers in Latin America and the Caribbean: Did they Go too Far?* IDB-Policy Brief-#185, Washington, DC: Inter-American Development Bank.

UNICEF Evaluation Office (2015), *Cash Transfer as a Social Protection Intervention: Evidence from UNICEF Evaluations 2010–2014*, New York: United Nations Children's Fund.

United Nations (1997), *First United Nations Decade for the Eradication of Poverty*. Resolution A/RES/51/178 adopted by the General Assembly on 11 February 1997. Available at: http://www.un.org/documents/ga/res/51/ares51-178.htm (accessed 27 January 2017).

United Nations (2013a), *The Millennium Development Goals Report 2013*, New York: United Nations. Available at: http://www.un.org/en/development/desa/publications/mdgs-report-2013.html (accessed 30 January 2017).

United Nations (2013b), *A New Global Partnership: Eradicate Poverty and Transform Economies Through Sustainable Development. The Report of the High-Level Panel of Eminent Persons on the Post-2015 Development Agenda*, New York: United Nations. Available at: https://www.un.org/sg/en/management/beyond2015.shtml (accessed 30 January 2017).

United Nations (2015), *Transforming our World: The 2030 Agenda for Sustainable Development* A/RES/70/1. Available at: https://sustainabledevelopment.un.org/post2015/transformingourworld (accessed 23 January 2017).

United Nations General Assembly (1997), *First United Nations Decade for the Eradication of Poverty* A/RES/51/178. Available at: http://www.un.org/documents/ga/res/51/ares51-178.htm (accessed 30 January 2017).

United Nations General Assembly (2000), *United Nations Millennium Declaration* A/RES/55/2. Available at: http://www.un.org/millennium/declaration/ares552e.htm (accessed 30 January 2017).

Universal Social Protection Brief (2016), *Economic and Productive Impacts of National Cash Transfers Programmes in Sub-Saharan Africa*. Available at: http://www.social-protection.org/gimi/gess/NewYork.action?id=34 (accessed 28 October 2016).

World Bank (2016), *World Bank, ILO Announce New Push for Universal Social Protection* [press release 21 September]. Available at: http://www.worldbank.org/en/news/press-release/2016/09/21/world-bank-ilo-announce-new-push-for-universal-social-protection (accessed 2 February 2017).

World Bank (2017), *Monitoring Global Poverty: Report of the Commission on Global Poverty*, Washington, DC: World Bank.

World Bank Operations Evaluation Department (2004), *The Poverty Reduction Strategy Initiative: An Independent Evaluation of the World Bank's Support Through 2003*, Washington, DC: The World Bank.

Ziegler, R. and K. Ott (2011), 'The quality of sustainability science: a philosophical perspective', *Sustainability: Science, Practice, & Policy*, vol. **7** (1). Available at: https://sspp.proquest.com/the-quality-of-sustainability-science-a-philosophical-perspective-32d0fc1b7573#.xsnqq87fv (accessed 30 January 2017).

22. From the ghost of development to Buen Vivir (living well): building utopias

Alberto Acosta

First they ignore you, then they laugh at you, then they fight you, then you win.
Mahatma Gandhi

INTRODUCTION

With its postulation of harmony with Nature and harmony among individuals and communities, as a proposal laden with experiences – and as long as it is unobstructed by prejudice and assumed to be always under construction – Buen Vivir (literally living well, but also meaning good coexistence) allows alternative visions of life to be formulated.[1] In this chapter, we will start by laying bare the limitations of the concept of development. Then we will provide a quick read on the recent origins, meaning, scope and mobilizing potential of Buen Vivir.

Let us begin, therefore, with an appetizer. Buen Vivir, in the form of visions and living practices in diverse corners of the planet, offers multiple options to reconsider the logic of production, movement, distribution and consumption of goods and services, as well as the structures, social experiences and dominant politics that are typical of capitalist civilization.

By questioning such civilization – which suffocates life and everything to do with it, as the Ecuadorian philosopher Bolívar Echeverría (2010) affirmed – Buen Vivir acquires the potential to construct alternatives from an enormous multiplicity of experiences, taking those focal points that constitute its fundamental basis as reference points: above all harmonious relations with Nature and community. This task will require opening up all possible dialogues and exchanges, without falling into the trap of useless romanticism or vulgar and impossible copies, nor into dogmatic positions that block the discussion and construction of alternatives.

Thus, not forgetting or manipulating its ancestral origins and its community potentiality, Buen Vivir can act as a platform to discuss, agree and even respond to the devastating effects of climate change and the increasing marginalization and social violence in the world. This opportunity arises in the midst of a multifaceted crisis – social, economic, ecological, political, and even a crisis of civilization – that is battering the planet. Humanity can, and must, learn from those human groups which have learnt how to live in harmonious communities and alongside Nature, those which have accumulated a long life memory.

But we must first ask ourselves why it is necessary to definitively dismiss the idea of development.

DEVELOPMENT, AN UNATTAINABLE GHOST

Let us cast our minds back. Since the mid-twentieth century a ghost has traversed the world . . . that ghost is development. And even though most people certainly don't believe in ghosts, they have, at least at some time, believed in 'development', they have been influenced by 'development', they have pursued 'development', they have worked for 'development', they have lived off 'development' . . . and it is most likely that they continue to do so today.

Without denying the validity of a long-standing process by which human beings have attempted to satisfy their needs in the best way, which could be understood as the search for development, we argue that the global mandate for development was institutionalized on 20 January 1949. The then President of the United States, Harry Truman, in the inaugural speech of his second term of office before Congress, defined the greater part of the world as '*underdeveloped areas*'. In 'point four' of his address he affirmed that:

> . . . we must embark on a bold new program for making the benefits of our scientific advances and industrial progress available for the improvement and growth of underdeveloped areas. More than half the people of the world are living in conditions approaching misery. Their food is inadequate. They are victims of disease. Their economic life is primitive and stagnant. Their poverty is a handicap and a threat both to them and to more prosperous areas. For the first time in history, humanity possesses the knowledge and skill to relieve the suffering of these people. (Truman, 1949)

In a few words, Truman set down a powerful ideological mandate:

> Our aim should be to help the free peoples of the world, through their own efforts, to produce more food, more clothing, more materials for housing, and more mechanical power to lighten their burdens. It must be a worldwide effort for the achievement of peace, plenty, and freedom. With the cooperation of business, private capital, agriculture, and labor in this country, this program can greatly increase the industrial activity in other nations and can raise substantially their standards of living.

> The old imperialism – exploitation for foreign profit – has no place in our plans. What we envisage is a program of development based on the concepts of democratic fair-dealing. (Truman, 1949)

In conclusion, the head of state of the world's most powerful country – conscious that especially the United States and other industrialized nations were 'at the top of the evolutionary social ladder' (Sachs, [1992] 1996) – announced that all societies would have to walk the same path (which would serve as the basis for Walt Whitman Rostow's Stages theory) and aspire to a single goal, 'development'. And, incidentally, set down the conceptual bases for another form of imperialism, 'development'.

The metaphor of development, appropriated from the natural world, acquired a rare vigour. It transformed into a goal to be achieved by all humanity. It became, and this is fundamental, a global mandate that involved the spread of the North American model of society, heir to many European values. Although Truman was assuredly not fully aware of what he was talking about, or of its transcendence, this would, to say the least, be an historic proposal. To better understand why this conclusion has been reached, it is worth remembering, as does Koldo Unceta (2014, p. 411), that:

> ... when Adam Smith wrote *The Wealth of Nations*, the debate on development that is today ongoing was in some way 'inaugurated'. Prior to that, other thinkers – from Kautilya in ancient India, to Aristotle in Classical Greece, or Saint Augustine in medieval Europe – had theorized about the chances, or lack thereof, of certain actions or decisions when it came to achieving greater prosperity for citizens, countries, and kingdoms, and for their inhabitants. However, it would not be until the eighteenth century when, at the hands of enlightened thinking, a rational and universal perspective on these issues would begin to clear a path.
>
> With it, a development of knowledge would prevail that was increasingly emancipated from religion, as would a global understanding that was capable of going beyond the particular views influenced by local beliefs.[2]

Thus, after the Second World War, when the Cold War was getting under way, and during the rise of the nuclear threat and terror, the debate on 'development' established (and consolidated!) a structure of dichotomous domination: developed-underdeveloped, rich-poor, advanced-backward, civilized-savage. Even from critical positions that duality was accepted as indisputable, central-peripheral.

From this visualization, the world was arranged in order to attain 'development'. Plans, programmes, projects, theories, development manuals and methodologies flourished, as did specialist banks to finance development, development aid, development training and education, communication for development and so on.

Revolving around 'development', at the height of the Cold War, was the confrontation between capitalism and communism. The 'Third World' was invented and its members were used as pawns in the chess of international geopolitics. Both sides, the left and the right, establishing diverse specificities and differences, took on the challenge of achieving 'development'. Across the length and breadth of the planet, communities and societies were – and continue to be – reordered to conform to 'development'. This became the common fate of humanity, a non-negotiable obligation.

At no point, in the name of 'development', did the central or developed countries, the benchmarks for the underdeveloped countries, renounce the various interventions and operations that interfered in the internal affairs of the peripheral or poor countries. Those same development aid policies were a sort of continuance of the previous policies applied to their former colonies. Thus, for example, in recent times we have noted recurring economic interventions by the IMF and the World Bank, and even military actions to drive the 'development' of backward countries, thereby protecting them from the influence of any of the rival powers. There has been no lack of interventions that have supposedly sought to safeguard or introduce democracy, as a political basis for the longed-for development.

Meanwhile, the poor countries, in an act of generalized subordination and submission, accepted this state of affairs as long as they were considered to be developing countries or on course for development. In the exclusive circles of diplomacy and international institutions it is not common to speak of underdeveloped countries, and less common to accept that they are poor or peripheral countries, even in the quest for 'development'. We know very well that it often considered a process of 'development of underdevelopment', as was noted with extreme lucidity by André Gunder Frank (1970, 1979), the German economist and sociologist and one of the greatest thinkers on dependency theory.

In this way, and almost without need of an inventory, the countries that were deemed backward accepted the application of a set of policies, instruments and indicators in order to break out of their 'backwardness' and achieve that desired condition of 'development'. That's how things have been over the course of recent decades, where almost all the countries in the world considered to be undeveloped have tried to follow the path mapped out. How many have achieved it? Very few, and that is if we even accept that what was achieved was, indeed, 'development'.

On the way, when problems began to undermine our faith in 'development' and the grand theory of development began to leak on all sides, we sought alternatives to development. We affixed descriptions or adjectives to development to differentiate it from what made us uncomfortable, but we continued on the development trail: economic development, social development, local development, global development, rural development, sustainable development, eco-development, ethno-development, development on a human scale, endogenous development, development with gender equality, co-development, transformative development . . . at the end of the day, development. 'Development', like any belief that was never questioned, was simply redefined by its most high profile characteristics.

It is worth pointing out that Latin America played an important role in generating controversial revisions to conventional development, such as structuralism or the different emphasis of the dependency theory, before arriving at other more recent positions. Its critiques were convincing; however, its proposals did not prosper.

These unorthodox positions and critiques have great importance, but also suffer from several limitations. On the one hand, the proposals did not seriously question the conceptual centre of the idea of conventional development – understood as a linear progression – and in particular expressed in terms of economic growth. And when they did question it they failed in shaking off the bonds of anthropocentrism (Acosta, 2016).

On the other hand, each of these questionings generated a wave of disconnected revisions. In some cases, they generated a peak in the critiques and even in the proposals, but, soon after, these efforts languished and the conventional ideas reclaimed centre stage.

Later, and this is what interests us most in this chapter, it was realized that the issue is not simply accepting one or other path towards development. The paths towards development are not the big problem. The difficulty stems from the concept itself. Development, as a global and unifying proposal is utterly unaware, or in denial, of the dreams and struggles of the peoples deemed to be underdeveloped. This denial – which on some occasions was even brutal – was often a product of direct or indirect action by the nations considered to be developed; let us remember, by way of example, the destructive activities of colonization or those of the IMF policies themselves.

We now know that development, insofar as it means reproducing the lifestyles of the central countries, turns out to be unrepeatable on a global scale. Moreover, that consumerist and predatory way of life is putting the global ecological balance at risk and increasingly marginalizes masses of human beings from the (supposed) advantages of the much sought-after development. Despite undeniable technological advances, not even hunger has been eradicated from the planet. Note that this is not a matter of lack of food production. Food exists. According to the Food and Agriculture Organization of the United Nations (FAO), in a world where obesity and hunger live side by side, each year more than 1.3 billion tonnes of perfectly edible food, that could feed 3 billion people, are wasted: 670 million in the

Global North and 630 million in the Global South, including the poorest countries on the planet.[3] Seventy per cent of cereals traded in the world are determined by speculative logic. Food for cars is produced, whether it be called agrofuel or biofuel. The orientation towards profit and a lack of infrastructure, a result of bad public policy, means that in India a third of food goes bad before it reaches the consumer.

An increasing amount of land mass is dedicated to an agriculture that is based on monoculture, which leads to a rapid loss of biodiversity. Genetically modified organisms (GMOs) and their technologies do their own thing. Since the beginning of the twentieth century this combination of activities has led to the loss of 75 per cent of the genetic diversity of plants. Currently, according to data from the German Ministry of Agriculture, 30 per cent of seeds are in danger of extinction. While 75 per cent of the world's food comes from 12 species of plants and five species of animals, just three species – rice, corn and wheat – contribute about 60 per cent of the calories and proteins obtained by humans from plants. Barely 4 per cent of the 250,000 or 300,000 species of known plants is used by human beings. According to Maristella Svampa (Brand, 2016), in Argentina 22 million of the 33 million hectares available for agriculture were converted into transgenic soybean crops. And in this scenario, when hunger assails more than a billion people in the world, we see how the large transnational food conglomerates such as Monsanto – now merged with Bayer – continue to concentrate their power through control of seeds. Water is another resource at risk, presenting enormous inequality in its distribution and its increasingly unjustifiable use.

In this context, it has been established that the world is undergoing generalized 'bad development', and that includes those countries considered developed. José María Tortosa (2011) points out that:

> The functioning of the contemporary world system is 'bad development' . . . The reason is easy to understand: it is a system based on an efficiency that tries to maximize results, reduce costs and achieve an incessant accumulation of capital . . . If 'anything goes', the problem is not who is playing or why, the problem is the rules of the game itself. In other words, the world system has been badly developed as a result of its own logic and it is to this logic that we must look.

Now, as multiple simultaneous crises swamp the planet, we discover that the development ghost has provoked and continues to provoke disastrous consequences. It is possible for development to have no content, but it can justify the means and even the failures. We have accepted the rules of 'anything goes'.[4] All is tolerated in the name of eschewing underdevelopment and in the name of progress. All is sanctified in the name of such a lofty and promising goal: we have to at least look like our superiors and to achieve this, '*any sacrifice goes*'.

Therefore, we accept environmental and social devastation in exchange for achieving 'development'. In the name of development, to give an example, the grievous social and ecological destruction caused by mega-mining is accepted, even though it strengthens the system of extractivist accumulation, inherited from colonial days. And it is one of the direct causes of underdevelopment.

We even reject our historical and cultural roots to modernize ourselves by emulating advanced – that is to say modern – countries. By doing this we reject the search for what could be taken to be self-modernization. The economy, seen from the point of view of capital accumulation, dominates the scene. Imported science and technology lay down the rules for the organization of societies. Along one path lies commercialization at any cost; we accept that everything is up for grabs. Therefore, the rich have determined that for the poor to escape from poverty (that is, for the poor to be like the rich) the poor must now pay to imitate them: buying their knowledge, and marginalizing and rejecting their own knowledge and ancestral practices.

In summary, the path followed since the post-war years and up to the present day has been complex. The results have not been satisfactory. In terms of global impact, as the great Peruvian thinker Aníbal Quijano (2000, p. 89) noted, 'development' became:

> ... a term of random biography ... Since the Second World War it has changed identity and name many times, a tug of war between a constant economistic reductionism and the insistent calls of all the other dimensions of social existence. That is, between very different power interests. And it has been greeted very unevenly from one time to another in our changing history. At the beginning it was without doubt one of the most mobilizing propositions of the second half of the century that is now approaching its end. Its promises swept along all sectors of society and somehow ignited one of the most bemusing and vibrant debates in history, but they slipped out of sight over an increasingly elusive horizon and their standard bearers and followers were caged by disillusionment.

Wolfgang Sachs, in 1996, was already conclusive in that respect:

> The last forty years can be called the development era. That era is reaching its end. The time has come to write its obituary.
>
> Like a majestic lighthouse that guides the sailors towards the coast, 'development' was the idea that guided the emerging nations on their journey through post-war history. Independently of whether they were democracies or dictatorships, having been liberated from their colonial subjugation, the Southern countries declared development to be their primary aspiration. Four decades

later, governments and citizens still have their eyes fixed on that light, twinkling now as far away as ever: every effort and every sacrifice is justified to achieve that goal, but the light continues to fade into the darkness.
    . . . the idea of development rises like a ruin in the intellectual landscape . . . deception and disillusionment, failures and crimes have been permanent companions of development and all tell the same tale: it didn't work. Moreover, the historical conditions that catapulted the idea to prominence have disappeared: development has become antiquated. But above all, the hopes and desires that gave wings to the idea are now spent: development has come to be obsolete. ([1992] 1996, p. 1)

When the futility of continuing to chase the *development ghost* is evident, the search for alternatives to development emerges forcefully. That is to say, ways of organizing life outside development, getting beyond development. This compels us to reject the conceptual kernel of the idea of conventional development – understood to be the realization of the concept of progress that was imposed several centuries ago. To go beyond capitalism and its logic of social and environmental devastation is an indispensable step.

In this way, we probe the complex terrain of post-development and post-capitalism. Let us accept that for the majority of inhabitants of the planet, capitalism does not represent a promise or a dream to be fulfilled, it is a nightmare made reality.

As Wolfgang Sachs himself indicated, it has taken time to begin to bid 'farewell to the defunct idea in order to clear our minds for new discoveries'. In any event, even when 'the idea of development is already a ruin in our intellectual landscape . . . its shadow . . . still obscures our vision . . .' ([1992] 1996, p. 101). Despite the failure of the fundamental ideas of development, there are still those who believe that it is possible to '*return to development*' through a critical revision of what development means as a proposition with colonial origins.

If indeed the idea of development is in crisis in *our intellectual landscape*, we must necessarily also question the concept of progress that emerged forcefully 500 years ago in Europe. The fundamental elements of the dominant view imposed by development are nourished by the values imposed by the progress of civilization in Europe. It was, and is, an extremely expansionist and influential process that is also destructive.[5]

Simply put, even though we know that development is outmoded, its influence will weigh upon us for quite some time. Let us accept, and this is no consolation, that we may escape development (and capitalism) while dragging many of its imperfections with us and that this will be a long and tortuous journey, with advances and setbacks, the duration and robustness of which will depend on the political clarity and action to take on the challenge. And we know that within the model of capitalism itself alternatives are emerging to overcome it. Besides, at its core there are indeed many experiences and practices of Buen Vivir that could transform into the germ of another civilization.

The question that arises forcefully is whether it will be possible to escape from the grim embrace of the ghost of development and from that Leviathan *par excellence* we call progress?

BUEN VIVIR, UTOPIA MADE REALITY

To appreciate the contributions of Buen Vivir, one must understand that it reflects diverse ways of life present in various communities in various parts of the planet, as well as those practices of resistance to the alienation and marginalization provoked by capitalist modernity and its consequences. These visions emerge from ancestral cultures, or more clearly from 'indigeneity', in the terms of Aníbal Quijano (2014b).

It is not a utopia yet to be built. Its values, experiences and civilizing practices as alternatives to capitalism make Buen Vivir an attainable and attained utopia. And insofar as it can be converted into a tool that expands the criticism of current civilization and offers concrete proposals for action, it could contribute to 'a great transformation', in the terms proposed by Karl Polanyi (1992).

It is true that these life lessons exist largely in communities that have not been totally absorbed by capitalist modernity or that have stayed on the periphery. However, even in indigenous communities that have 'succumbed' to modernity, there are distinctive elements that could be recognized as Buen Vivir. Even in other spaces, not directly linked to the indigenous world, harmonious community life options are built between their members and Nature. Gradually, because of the debates that are taking place, useful bridges are being built for a joint reflection on what, for example, degrowth in the Global North and post-development in the Global South would represent, of which Buen Vivir is one of the most proactive exponents.

Let us consider that Buen Vivir, or good coexistence, does not encapsulate any fully formed or indisputable proposal, does not stem from academic reflections or from partisan proposals. Nor does it attempt to become a single global mandate as happened with the concept of 'development' in the mid-twentieth century. Therefore, when speaking about Buen Vivir we think in plural terms, that is of good coexistence (Albó, 2009), and not of a single Buen Vivir, homogeneous and impossible to construct. This good coexistence (or Buen Vivir, as it will be presented in the remainder of the text, but always thinking in plural terms) can open the door to pathways that, on the one hand, must be imagined in order to be built, but that, on the other hand, are already a reality. This is the great potential of these visions and experiences.

From the start, we need to be aware that broadly speaking the indigenous worlds have been victims of colonial conquest as a process of exploitation and repression, something that has carried forward to the present day. The colonial and capitalist influence is present in these worlds under multiple guises, impeding any romantic approximation to its realities. Growing segments of the indigenous population have been absorbed by the capitalist logic and many indigenous people are even primary actors in the processes of capitalist accumulation. Equally there are indigenous groups, in extremely precarious situations, trapped in the mythical dream of development and progress which – objectively speaking – they will never attain. Moreover, as the migration processes from the countryside to the city intensify, so does the uprooting of the urban indigenous peoples, people who gradually become distanced from their traditional extended communities, but who even so, in certain cases, are somehow bearers of elements of Buen Vivir.

Buen Vivir is therefore a task of (re)construction that depends on dismantling the universal goal of all societies: progress and its offshoot, development, as well as its multiple synonyms. But it does not only dismantle them; Buen Vivir – in a plural sense – proposes different visions, richer in content and, incidentally, more complex. Therefore, Buen Vivir presents an opportunity to build new ways of life as a community and to imagine other worlds, without being the sum total of either isolated practices nor of the good wishes of those who wish to interpret Buen Vivir in their own way.

It is worth noting that in the constitutions of Bolivia and Ecuador this proposal gained strength, in the Constitution of the Republic of Ecuador in 2008 and the Constitution of the Plurinational State of Bolivia in 2009. Regrettably, in practice, the governments of these countries took their inspiration from the logic of economic development, very distant from that of Buen Vivir. Not just that but in these countries Buen Vivir, drained of its conceptual content, was transformed into a power mechanism to consolidate authoritarian regimes.

Their expressions refer us back to Buen Vivir (Ecuador) or Vivir Bien (Bolivia),[6] originating from indigenous languages of South America, traditionally marginalized, but not vanished, such as *sumak kawsay* (in kichwa), *suma qamaña* (in aymara), *ñande reko* or *tekó porã* (in guaraní), *pénker pujústin* (shuar), *shiir waras* (ashuar) *inter alia*. There are similar notions in other indigenous peoples, for example among the Mapuche of Chile: *kyme mogen*, the Kuna of Panama: *balu wala*, the Miskito in

Nicaragua: *laman laka*, and also in the Mayan tradition of Guatemala and in the Chiapa of Mexico.

It is worth highlighting that such standpoints and proposals – similar in many regards, but not necessarily in all regards – are also present in various other areas, with different names and characteristics. They concern values, experiences and, above all, practices that existed in different periods and in different regions of Mother Earth. It is worth highlighting the *ubuntu* (sense of community: a person is a person only through other people and other living beings) in Africa[7] or *Swaraj* (radical ecological democracy) in India.[8]

These proposals gained exceptional political momentum at the beginning of this millennium, when they entered the national debate – particularly in Bolivia and Ecuador – at a time of general crisis in the nation-state, which was oligarchic and had colonial roots. In these two countries, there was a time of intense revolt during the era of neoliberalism, thanks especially to the growing organizational strength of the indigenous movements, in an alliance with other popular forces.

This emergence of the indigenous movements is noteworthy, as vigorous political standard bearers of their own *Weltanschauung*. It explains the emergence and positioning of the paradigmatic ideas of Buen Vivir, typical of an indigenous world that had not managed to erase the processes of conquest and colonization, still present during the Republican era. In this context, the questioning and the ecological alternatives also began to be consolidated, many of them attuned to the vision of harmony with Nature that characterizes Buen Vivir. In one way or another, all these anti-establishment visions have deep roots and are of great contemporary interest.

This Buen Vivir proposal is based on a principle of historical continuity that needs the past and the present of the indigenous peoples and nationalities. It is nourished by the knowledge and experiences of the indigenous communities, and from their diverse ways of producing knowledge. It is fostered by their distinct ways of seeing life and by their relationship with *Pacha Mama*, Mother Earth. It accepts as a cohesive central concept the relationality and complementarity between all living beings (human or otherwise). It is forged from the principles of interculturality. It exists through socially responsible and reciprocal economic practices. Above all, as it is immersed in the search for, and construction of, alternatives by the popular and marginalized sectors, it will have to be re(constructed) from the bottom up and with Mother Earth, on a base of a democratic and community logic.

What is most notable and profound about these alternative ideas is that they emerge from traditionally marginalized groups, excluded, exploited and even decimated. They are proposals that have been invisible for a long time, that now invite us to uproot various concepts that were accepted as indisputable. In summary, they constitute post-development visions that go beyond the formerly valuable contributions of the unorthodox and *dependentista* Latin American trends that focused on 'alternative development'. It is now increasingly necessary to generate 'alternatives to development'. This is what Buen Vivir is about.

BUEN VIVIR: ITS CENTRAL CONCEPTS

The concept of 'development' does not exist in any indigenous wisdoms and it is often rejected. That concept of a linear life-process that establishes a previous and subsequent state: underdevelopment and development, a dichotomy by which people and countries should act to attain well-being, as it is usually interpreted in the Western world. Neither do concepts of wealth and poverty exist as determined by the accumulation or lack of material goods. That is, dignified life for the community has to be assured today and is not a promise for tomorrow. There is no need for growth for all members of the community to live with dignity, as long as – as a starting point – an adequate distribution of income and redistribution of wealth is assured for all members of a community.

Buen Vivir must be accepted as something dynamic, under permanent construction and reproduction. It is not a static or backward-looking concept. As a holistic proposal, one must understand the multiple elements that condition the human actions that promote Buen Vivir: knowledge, ethical and spiritual codes of conduct in relation to the environment, human values, a vision of the future, *inter alia*. Buen Vivir, ultimately, constitutes a central category of what could be understood to be the life philosophy of indigenous societies.[9]

From that perspective, conventional development (even progress) has been seen as a cultural imposition inherited from Western, hence colonial, knowledge. That is why many reactions against colonialism involve a distancing from developmentalism. Therefore, Buen Vivir requires a process of decolonization (this should even be 'depatriarchalization'[10]). A process of intellectual, political, social, economic and above all cultural decolonization is necessary to achieve this.

One of the key challenges is encapsulated in how we take control of knowledge and technology. Machines must be prevented from controlling human beings, as Ivan Illich recommended.[11] Technologies, especially those that save work and physical effort, should generate conditions that liberate human beings from capital-accumulating work. This has to be encouraged, liberating scientific knowledge[12] and motivating a respectful dialogue with ancestral wisdom, while the structures of production and consumption are transformed, as part of establishing other types of societies that exclude exploitation of human beings and nature.

As it has emerged from non-capitalist community roots, Buen Vivir is proposing a world view different from that of the West. It also breaks with the anthropocentric logic of capitalism that is so dominant in Western civilization. In fact, it also questions the diverse socialisms that have existed to date. Let us not forget that capitalists and 'socialists' of every hue dispute which system best ensures development and progress, with economic growth among its principal tools. From this reading, Buen Vivir proposes a transformation with a civilizing effect, as it is not an anthropocentric proposal. To achieve it one would have to move towards a biocentric view, although in reality this would mean a system of harmonious relations with no central core. This points us towards community practices, not just individualistic ones; proposals based on plurality and diversity, not one-dimensional or monocultural.

This does not mean that we first leave capitalism behind to then immediately press ahead with Buen Vivir. In fact, many life lessons of Buen Vivir have survived from colonial times until today. What is interesting to acknowledge is that now, as part of a profound emancipatory process, these proposals have emerged to construct elements that allow us to overcome, from within, capitalist civilization itself. Within the body of that 'old society', the forces that will overcome it are being incubated.

Buen Vivir is a proposal that will have an impact in the present; it is not extending a simple invitation to go back in time and re-encounter an idyllic world, inexistent for others. Nor can it transform itself into a sort of religion with a catechism, manuals, ministries or even political commissars.

Buen Vivir does not deny the existence of conflicts, but it does not exacerbate them by promoting an organized society based on the permanent and inequitable accumulation of material goods, driven by an interminable competition between people who, en route, destructively expropriate from nature. Human beings cannot be seen as a threat or as subjects to be beaten and defeated. And Nature cannot be accepted as only a mass of objects to be exploited. Starting from this double verification, one must launch the search for answers in diverse spheres of strategic action.

In summary, Buen Vivir is a civilizing proposal that reconfigures the prospect of a move beyond capitalism, the dominant civilization. However, it is necessary to accept that the indigenous vision is not the only inspiration that motivates Buen Vivir. Reflections on this (re)construction of civilizing alternatives can also be based on other philosophical principles that could change with the times, as long as these approaches overcome the dominant anthropocentric visions and accept that a dignified life is for all living beings or for none.

ELEMENTS TO CONSIDER BUEN VIVIR IN A BROADER CONTEXT

To begin with, let us acknowledge the global unviability of the dominant lifestyle, based on premises of anthropocentric exclusion and exploitation. On a global scale the idea of growth, based on inexhaustible natural resources and a market that absorbs everything produced, has not led, nor will it lead, to achieving dignified living standards for all inhabitants of the planet. Quite the opposite.

We know very well that economic growth does not guarantee 'development' and nor does it ensure happiness. We also know that the 'developed' countries are showing increasing signs of what is, in reality, *maldevelopment*. Apart from being mainly responsible for the acute environmental problems – such as those stemming from climate change, among other critical issues – the rifts that separate the rich from the poor in these countries are getting ever wider.

Even when there is growth, this ends up widening the cracks in society: the wealth of the few is almost always based on the exploitation of the majority (a process that is ever-accelerating). Sometimes, even when poverty levels fall – laudable without a doubt – it does not affect the structures of capitalist accumulation. The concentration of wealth grows and the levels of inequality increase.

The complex and painful consequences of this reality – both nationally and internationally – are plain to see; for example, the increasing migration from the Southern countries to the United States and Europe, caused by multiple factors. Let us not fool ourselves: inequity, inequality and injustice, provoked by the increasing and boundless demands of capitalism, trigger more and more violence that ends up expelling populations from their territories – because of mega-mining, for example.

The demands of accumulation, which require a growing economy, are based on the exploitation of labour, oligopolistic and monopolistic practices to control markets, increased financing of the economy, and, especially, the destruction of Nature. It is enough to see the brutal destruction – to varying degrees – caused by the expansion of activities typical of capitalist modernity: industrialization, urbanization and extractivism[13] which rapidly go beyond natural limits.

The gauntlet has been thrown down. The maelstrom of economic growth must be stopped in its tracks, and even pushed back, especially in the Global North.[14] A finite world cannot tolerate permanent economic growth. To follow this path would lead us to an ever more unsustainable environmental situation, a socially more explosive situation. This sort of religion of economic growth, especially in the Global North, will have to be overcome at the hands of post-extractivism in the Global South.[15]

Degrowth, in short, does not just involve physically slowing the 'economic metabolism': the economy must be subordinated to the mandates of the Earth and the demands of humanity, which is Nature itself. This requires a socio-environmental rationality that deconstructs the current logic of production, distribution, circulation and consumption. One has to uncouple from the perversity of global capitalism and, above all, speculation.[16]

We must abandon the search for profits obtained by exploiting human beings and Nature. We require life options other than the utilitarianism and anthropocentricism of modernity. This alternative ethical perspective accepts intrinsic values in the environment: all beings have the same ontological value, even when they have no human use.

Therefore, a larger question arises: how to build an economic structure that is independent from use and exchange value? And, above all, to do this without excluding useful human values, so we can put together policies that move us beyond anthropocentrism.

In summary, to achieve this we need to overcome the fetish for economic growth, decommercialize Nature and common goods, introduce interrelated and community criteria to value goods and services, decentralize and deconcentrate production, change the patterns of consumption, and especially redistribute wealth and power. These are some bases on which to collectively build another civilization.

The need now arises to consolidate transdisciplinarity, advancing beyond interdisciplinarity and multidisciplinarity. The range of the various readings of reality needs to be widened. We must aspire to the most complete and global knowledge possible, maintaining a dialogue with diverse human wisdom, considering the world both as a question and an aspiration. Above all, we require a post-economy that goes beyond the current 'economic science', as well as social sciences willing to learn from each other and to research together, accepting and studying the world as a diverse unit. It will mean a post-economy that must be subordinated to human demands and those of Nature, assuming a subordinate position among the social sciences, from which it can be nourished and which it must support, not dominate, as occurs frequently today.

It does not mean 'living better' (better than others, in an indefinite and unsustainable way), it means building alternatives to Mal Vivir (literally bad living, but also meaning poor coexistence) that, although it exists across the entire planet, does not affect all equally. With the globalization of capital and its multiple forms of accumulation, most of the world's population is anything but materially comfortable and they observe how this evolution is affecting their safety, freedom and identity more and more. As in the Middle Ages, today most of the population is structurally marginalized from progress. Very many people do not participate in the profits of technology, they are either excluded or merely receive the scraps. In many cases they do not even have the 'privilege' of being exploited while they dream of reaching standards of living that are unrepeatable on a global scale.

This is a complex question: the spread of certain patterns of consumption, in a pirouette of absolute perversity, seeps into the collective imagination, even into broad groups without the financial wherewithal to access this consumption, keeping them as prisoners of the permanent desire to attain it. Remember that the media – private and even public and state – promote consumerism and individualism, in a maelstrom of information where everything dissolves into a *programmed banality*. And similar to medieval inquisitorial practices the media marginalize what they should not, based on the logic of power, by denying space for its diffusion.[17]

In this context, not only do institutions appear which control information but they convert the individuals themselves (simple consumers) into the authors of their own alienation. Very many people produce while thinking about consuming, but at the same time they live with the permanent lack of satisfaction of their needs, exacerbated by the demands of accumulation. Therefore, production and consumption create a vicious circle without a future, irrationally exhausting natural resources, contaminating the countryside and the cities, straining social inequities. In addition, several technological advances have accelerated this perverse circle of increasing production and unsatisfied appetites.

Without denying the importance of many technological advances, not all of humanity benefits from such achievements. The technique moreover is not neutral. Frequently it is developed according to the demands of capital accumulation. We human beings have seen ourselves become simple tools for machines, when the relationship should be inverse. From this perspective, to create another type of technique one has to transform the conditions of social production.

The search for these new ways of life involves revitalizing the political discussion, which has been obfuscated by the economistic vision of available means and ends. When the economy is deified, and in particular the market, many non-economic instruments are abandoned, instruments that would be indispensable for improving living conditions. For example, believing that the global environmental problems will be resolved by market measures is a mistake that could cost us dearly; it has been demonstrated that standards and regulations (still insufficient) are more effective than the 'laws' of the capitalist economy of supply and demand.

But that is not all. We cannot continue commercializing Nature, a process that promotes its unchecked exploitation; quite the opposite, it has to be de-commercialized; we have to re-engage with it, ensuring its capacity for regeneration, based on respect, responsibility and reciprocity.[18] In fact, the resolution of these problems demands a multidisciplinary approach as we live in a situation of multiple complexities that cannot be explained by mono-causal accounts.

When these proposals are considered from the Buen Vivir perspective, as long as they are actively accepted by the societies especially at the community level, they can be forcefully transmitted in debates held in diverse regions of the world and could even be a trigger for using proposals to confront the increasing alignment of a great majority of the planet's inhabitants. In other words, the discussion on Buen Vivir should go beyond the Andean and Amazonian realities, and be taken to those constituencies in diverse parts of the planet where similar options are experienced or constructed.

If indeed it is extremely difficult to take on the challenge of constructing Buen Vivir in societies that are immersed in the maelstrom of capitalism – above all in the big cities – we are convinced that there are many options to begin construction of this utopia in other parts of the planet, and even in industrialized countries and the cities themselves.

The starting point is not in the states, in the governments and less still in the market, for as long as it is an all-embracing body. The state has to be profoundly rethought, perhaps going down the road of plurinationality, as indigenous movements would argue.[19]

An authentic democratization of power requires the social control and participation of the bases of rural and urban society, of the neighbourhoods and the communities. The social movements and new political parties play a central role, profoundly attuned to, and rooted in, the respective society. That society, founded on a flat power structure, demands democracy and direct action as well as self-management – not new forms of top-down leadership, and still less individual leaders, autocrats and visionaries. Resolution of day-to-day problems and demands form favourable ground for transformative grass-roots political action.

But in this collective search for multiple alternatives, above all in the community spaces, the current global challenges cannot be ignored. For example, one would have to tackle the current international economic situation – intolerable in social, ecological and even economic terms.

Without going into this subject in too much depth, due to lack of space, it is broadly accepted that the speculative structure of the international financial market has to be dismantled, where ill-gotten capital absconds to tax havens, as do monies linked to wars and terrorism. Equally questionable is the existence of diverse financial institutions which serve as tools of political pressure, so that a large state or an authority controlled by a few powerful states can impose conditions (typically unsustainable) on weaker countries; that has happened and still happens with external debt, which has been transformed into a tool of political domination.[20]

It is equally necessary to encourage routes to world peace. That involves promoting massive disarmament, using these resources to meet the most pressing needs of humanity and thereby deactivating many violent processes. But one has to go further. If humans do not re-establish peace with Mother Earth, there will be no peace for humans on Earth: therefore, a harmonious re-engagement with Nature is required, as proposed by the essential logic of Buen Vivir. The door to this approach will open if the rights of Nature are crystallized.[21]

Therefore, Buen Vivir calls for the construction of a life of self-sufficiency and self-management among human beings living in community, ensuring the self-regenerating power of Nature. That is certainly a great challenge for humanity. This will promote what is local and autochtonous, renewed local spaces, national and regional decision-making, and from there global democratic spaces will be constructed, creating new territorial and conceptual maps.

BUEN VIVIR AND THE RECOVERY OF UTOPIAS

To try to solve this riddle will not be easy. For a start, we must re-encounter the 'utopian dimension', as the Peruvian, Alberto Flores Galindo, proposed in the 1980s. This involves strengthening those conceptual approaches and assessments of community life, such as relationality and reciprocity. Equally the basic values of democracy will have to be consolidated: liberty, equality, solidarity and equity, as well as political, religious, sexual and cultural tolerance. And this, as was noted earlier, involves a political-cultural re-engagement with Nature.

In summary, Buen Vivir opens the way to building an emancipatory project. A project that, by taking many stories of struggle, of resistance and proposals for change, by taking nourishment from experiences that are, above all, local and adding them to those contributions springing forth from different latitudes, it positions itself as a starting point for democratically constructing sustainable societies in all spheres. Thus, subjects such as the construction of a new economy or the rights of Nature or making human rights a full and valid reality, are outlined also as questions that interest humanity and as such must be discussed and tackled.

There is no simple recipe for constructing a different society. However, not having a predetermined path is not a problem. Quite the opposite. It frees us from dogmatic views, although it does demand greater clarity from us in terms of the destination we wish to reach, accepting the transition towards another civilization as a part of Buen Vivir itself. Not only does the destination count, but also the path or paths to achieve human life with dignity, guaranteeing a present and a future for all human beings and non-humans, thereby ensuring the survival of humanity on the planet.

Calling again on the thoughts of Flores Galindo: construct a different society, 'there is no recipe. There is no trail blazed, no alternative defined. It has to be constructed' (1993).

NOTES

1. The list of texts dealing with this subject is ever increasing. We mention, among many other contributions, the texts of the author of these lines. It is worth noting therefore that a large part of the reflections of this article form part of a process of permanent learning and criticism that the author has carried out over many years.

2. To track the origins of this debate on development one has to go back to the works of Adam Smith, Karl Marx or especially Friedrich List (1789–1846), who, with his book *Das nationale System der Politischen Ökonomie* (1841), can be considered a pioneer in this field of development. More recently we have the contribution of Joseph Schumpeter (1912), with his book *The Theory of Economic Development*; he maintained, let us remember, that development is an economic fact, rather than a social one. The list of authors who tackled this topic after 1949 is long and diverse in focus and contributions: Arthur Lewis, Gunnar Myrdal ([1957] 1959), Walt Whitman Rostow, Nicholas Kaldor, among many others. Of course, one would also have to include dependentistas and structuralists, highlighting Raúl Prebisch, Celso Furtado, Aníbal Quijano, Ruy Mauro Marini, Agustín Cueva, André Gunder Frank, Samir Amin, Theotonio dos Santos, among others, to complete a long list of people who have participated in one of the richest and most intense debates in the history of humanity. A recommended book on this subject is that by Jürgen Schuldt (2012).

3. Cited by Jürgen Schuldt (2013). This Peruvian economist is another of the most prominent researchers on the subject of development and its criticism.

4. In the form of combat known as '*Anything Goes*' the fighters may use any martial art or contact sport, as the rules allow any technique and type of fighting.

5. From 1492, when Spain invaded Abya Yala (America) with a strategy of domination for exploitation, Europe imposed its imagination to legitimize the superiority of the European, the 'civilized', and the inferiority of the other, the 'primitive'. At this point the coloniality of power, the coloniality of knowledge and the coloniality of the being emerged. These colonialities remain valid until today. And it has in the idea of race, consolidated then, the most effective instrument of social domination in the last 500 years. It is not a memento of the past. Coloniality explains the current organization of

the world in its entirety, in that fundamental point in the agenda of modernity. Among the critics of coloniality we highlight Aníbal Quijano, Arturo Escobar, Boaventura de Sousa Santos, José de Souza Santos, Enrique Dussel, Edgardo Lander, Enrique Leff, Alejandro Moreano, *inter alia*. Above all we recommend from among these various authors the contributions of Aníbal Quijano, whose most outstanding works are mostly contained in *Cuestiones y Horizontes – Antología Esencial – De la dependencia histórica-estructural a la colonialidad/decolonialidad del poder*, Buenos Aires: CLACSO (2014a).

6. The list of texts that tackle this subject is ever longer. It is worth noting the contributions of Fernando Huanacuni Mamani (2010), Atawallpa Oviedo Freire (2011), Josef Estermann (2014), Omar Felipe Giraldo (2014), Eduardo Gudynas (2016), Pablo Solón (2016), *inter alia*; one could even retrieve the approaches to the common good of humanity by Francois Houtart (2011).

7. A brief approximation to the subject is available in the book by Giacomo D'Alisa et al. (2015).

8. Can be consulted in Ashish Kothari et al. (2015).

9. Normally in the indigenous world there are few written texts. As they are oral cultures this is understandable. A text that contributed, in Ecuador, to spreading these ideas was that by Carlos Viteri Gualinga (2000), 'Visión indígena del desarrollo en la Amazonía', Quito (mimeo). Someone who has worked on the origin of Buen Vivir, above all in Ecuador, is David Cortéz.

10. It must be recognized that in many indigenous communities, patriarchal and *machista* characteristics are deeply rooted.

11. See the compilation of the main texts by Ivan Illich (2015). This author is regaining renewed strength in the framework of the debates on degrowth and in the search for profoundly transformative alternatives.

12. On this subject one may consult, for example, the book by several authors, Varios autores (2015) *Flok Society – Buen Conocer, Modelos sostenibles y políticas públicas para una economía del conocimiento común y abierto en Ecuador*, Quito: Instituto de Altos Estudios Nacionales.

13. A recommended study on extractive activities is offered by Eduardo Gudynas (2015).

14. Texts on this issue are increasingly numerous. It is interesting to note the contribution by various authors in the book by D'Alisa et al. (2015).

15. Alberto Acosta and Ulrich Brand (2017).

16. See the proposals summarized by Alberto Acosta and John Cajas-Guijarro (2015).

17. It should be pointed out that despite the existing limitations, via social networks other forms of freer communication are beginning to emerge.

18. Here it is worth highlighting the valuable reflections of Vandana Shiva (1996) in this respect in the *Diccionario del desarrollo – Una guía del conocimiento como poder*, edited by Wolfgang Sachs in the 1990s (see 1996 edition, Peru: PRATEC).

19. Discussions on plurinationality and the contributions of the indigenous world in this sense are extremely broad in Bolivia and to a lesser degree in Ecuador. From a very long list, one can recommend German texts by Isabella Radhuber (2013), as well as contributions by Aníbal Quijano and Raúl Prada Alcoreza (2010, 2014), *inter alia*.

20. The proposal to form an International Tribunal for Arbitration of Sovereign Debt by Oscar Ugarteche and Alberto Acosta (2007). The convincing elements of this initiative have already been debated and approved in the core of the United Nations, although with the expected rejection by the great powers that benefit from these inequitable structures in the international financial sector.

21. An important contribution to this discussion is the book by Eduardo Gudynas, *Los Derechos de la Naturaleza – Respuestas y aportes desde la ecología política* (2016).

REFERENCES

Acosta, Alberto (2016), 'Las dependencias del extractivismo – Aporte para un debate incompleto', Magazine *Aktuel Marx Intervenciones* No. 20, *Nuestra América y la Naturaleza (colonial) del capital: La depredación de los territorios/cuerpos como sociometabolismo de la acumulación*, Santiago de Chile: LOM Ediciones.

Acosta, Alberto and Brand, Ulrich (2017), *Salidas del laberinto capitalista – Decrecimiento y Postextractivismo*, Quito: Fundación Rosa Luxemburg.

Acosta, Alberto and Cajas-Guijarro, John (2015), 'Instituciones transformadoras para la economía global – Pensando caminos para dejar atrás el capitalismo', in various authors *La osadía de lo nuevo – Alternativas de política económica*. Grupo de Trabajo Permanente de la Fundación Rosa Luxemburg. Quito: Abya Yala.

Albo, Xavier (2009), 'Suma Quamaña= el buen vivir', in *Revista Obets*, vol. **4**, pp. 25–40.

Brand, Ulrich (2016), *Lateinamerikas Linke – Ende des progressiven Zyklus*, Hamburg: VSA Verlag.

D'Alisa, Giacomo, Demaria, Federico and Kallis, Giorgis (eds) (2015), *Decrecimiento. Vocabulario para una nueva era*, Barcelona: Icaria.

Echeverría, Bolívar (2010), *Modernidad y blanquitud*, Mexico: Ediciones ERA.

Estermann, Josef (2014), 'Ecosofía andina: Un paradigma alternativo de convivencia cósmica y de vida plena', in various authors *Bifurcación del Buen Vivir y el sumak kawsay*, Quito: Ediciones SUMAK.

Flores Galindo, Alberto (1993) (s/f), *Reencontremos la dimensión utópica*, Lima, Peru: Instituto de Apoyo Agrario and El Caballo Rojo.

Frank, André Gunder (1970), *Capitalismo y subdesarrollo en América Latina*, Buenos Aires: Editorial Siglo XXI.

Frank, André Gunder (1979), *Lumpenburguesía y lumpendesarrollo*, Barcelona: Laia.

Giraldo, Omar Felipe (2014), *Utopías en la era de la supervivencia – Una interpretación del Buen Vivir*, Mexico: Editorial ITACA.

Gudynas, Eduardo (2015), *Extractivismos – Ecología, economía y política de un modo de entender desarrollo y la Naturaleza*, La Paz: CLAES|CEDIB.

Gudynas, Eduardo (2016), *Los Derechos de la Naturaleza – Respuestas y aportes desde la ecología política*, Quito: Abya Yala.

Houtart, François (2011), 'El concepto del sumak kawsay (Buen Vivir) y su correspondencia con el bien común de la humanidad', *Magazine – Ecuador Debate* No. 84, Quito: CAAP.

Huanacuni Mamani, Fernando (2010), *Vivir Bien/Buen Vivir Filosofía, políticas, estrategias y experiencias regionales*, Convenio Andrés Bello, Instituto Internacional de Investigación y La Paz: Coordinadora Andina de Organizaciones Indígenas (CAOI).

Illich, Ivan (2015), *Obras Reunidas*, Mexico: Fondo de Cultura Económica.

Kothari, Ashish, Demaria, Federico and Acosta, Alberto (2015), 'Buen Vivir, Degrowth and Ecological Swaraj: Alternatives to sustainable development and the Green Economy', in *Development*, vol. **57** (3), Inequalities (pp. 362–75). Available at: http://www.palgrave-journals.com/development/journal/v57/n3-4/full/dev201524a.html.

List, Friedrich ([1841] 1955), *Das nationale System der Politischen Ökonomie* (1841), reprinted (in Spanish) in *Sistema nacional de economía política* (1955), Madrid: Aguilar.

Myrdal, Gunnar ([1957] 1959), *Economic Theory and Underdeveloped Regions*. Spanish version *La teoría económica y los países subdesarrollados*, Mexico: Fondo de Cultura Económica, 1959.

Oviedo Freire, Atawallpa (2011), *Qué es el sumakawsay: Más allá del socialismo y capitalismo*, Quito: Ediciones Sumak.

Polanyi, Karl (1992), *La gran transformación: Los orígenes políticos y económicos de nuestro tiempo*, Mexico: Fondo de Cultura Económica.

Prada Alcoreza, Raúl (2010), 'Umbrales y horizontes de la descolonización', in various authors *El Estado – Campo de Lucha*, La Paz: CLACSO Ediciones, Muela del Diablo Editores.

Prada Alroreza, Raúl (2014), *Cartografías histórico-políticas: Extractivismo, dependencia y colonialidad*, La Paz: Dinámicas moleculares.
Quijano, Aníbal (2000), 'El fantasma desarrollo en América Latina', in Alberto Acosta (compiler), *El Desarrollo en la globalización – El reto de América Latina*, Quito: Nueva Sociedad e ILDIS.
Quijano, Aníbal (2014a), *Cuestiones y Horizontes – Antología Esencial – De la dependencia histórica-estructural a la colonialidad/decolonialidad del poder*, Buenos Aires: CLACSO.
Quijano, Aníbal (ed.) (2014b), *Descolonialidad y bien vivir – Un nuevo debate en América Latina*, Lima: Cátedra América Latina y la Colonialidad del Poder, Universidad Ricardo Palma.
Radhuber, Isabella (2013), *Der plurinationale Staat in Bolivien: Die Rolle der Ressourcen- und Budgetpolitik*, Münster: Westfälisches Dampfboot. (Also available in Spanish: *Recursos naturales y finanzas públicas. La base material del Estado plurinacional de Bolivia*, La Paz: Plural Editores.)
Sachs, Wolfgang (ed.) ([1992] 1996), *Diccionario del desarrollo – Una guía del conocimiento como poder*, Peru: PRATEC. (First edition in English 1992.)
Schuldt, Jürgen (2012), *Desarrollo a escala humana y de la Naturaleza*, Lima: Universidad del Pacífico.
Schuldt, Jürgen (2013), *Civilización del desperdicio – Psicoeconomía del consumidor*, Lima: Universidad del Pacífico.
Schumpeter, Joseph (1912), *The Theory of Economic Development*, Cambridge, MA: Harvard University Press.
Shiva, Vandana (1996), 'Recursos', in Wolfgang Sachs (ed.) *Diccionario del desarrollo – Una guía del conocimiento como poder*, Lima, Peru: PRATEC.
Solón, Pablo (2016), *¿Es posible el Buen Vivir?: Reflexiones a Quema Ropa sobre Alternativas Sistémicas*, La Paz: Fundacion Solón.
Tortosa, José María (2011), *Mal desarrollo y mal vivir – Pobreza y violencia escala mundial*, in Alberto Acosta and Esperanza Martínez (eds), *Serie Sobre Debate Constituyente*, Quito: Abya-Yala.
Truman, Harry S. (1949), 'Inaugural Address', 20 January 1949. Published online by Gerhard Peters and John T. Woolley, in *The American Presidency Project*. Available at: http://www.presidency.ucsb.edu/ws/?pid=13282.
Ugarteche, Oscar and Acosta, Alberto (2007), 'Global economy issues and the International Board of Arbitration for Sovereign Debt (IBASD)', in *El Norte – Finnish Journal of Latin American Studies*, **2** (December). Available at: http://www.elnorte.fi/archive/2007-2/2007_2_elnorte_ugarteche.pdf.
Unceta, Koldo (2014), 'Desarrollo, postcrecimiento y Buen Vivir – Debates e interrogantes', in Alberto Acosta and Esperanza Martínez (eds), *Serie Sobre Debate Constituyente*, Quito: Abya-Yala.
Varios autores (2015), *Flok Society – Buen Conocer, Modelos sostenibles y políticas públicas para una economia del conocimiento común y abierto en Ecuador*, Quito: Instituto de Altos Estudios Nacionales.
Viteri Gualinga, Carlos (2000), 'Visión indígena del desarrollo en la Amazonía', Quito, (mimeo).

Index